Smart Machines in Education

Smart Machines in Education

The Coming Revolution in Educational Technology

Edited by

Kenneth D. Forbus and Paul J. Feltovich

AAAI PRESS / THE MIT PRESS
Menlo Park, California   Cambridge, Massachusetts   London, England

Copublished and distributed by The MIT Press, Massachusetts Institute of Technology, Cambridge, Massachusetts, and London, England.

Library of Congress Cataloging-in-Publication Data

Smart machines in education : the coming revolution in educational technology / edited by Kenneth D. Forbus and Paul J. Feltovich.
    p. cm.
  Includes bibliographical references and index.
  ISBN 0-262-56141-7 (pbk. : alk. paper)
1. Intelligent tutoring systems. 2. Artificial intelligence—Educational applications. 3. Computer-assisted instruction. 4. Instructional systems—Design. I. Forbus, Kenneth D. II. Feltovich, Paul J., 1947–

LB1028.73.S53 2001
371.33′4–dc21   2001041247

Printed on acid-free paper in Canada.

10 9 8 7 6 5 4 3 2 1

Contents

Smart Machines in Education

The Coming Revolution in Educational Technology

Kenneth D. Forbus and Paul J. Feltovich

Two hallmarks of our species are our ability to make tools and our need to spend many years learning what we need to know to make our way in the world. Consequently, it is not so surprising that we use our tool-making abilities to help make learning more effective. The impact of computers in education is only now beginning to be felt on a large scale, due to the widespread availability of computer technology that would seem a science-fiction dream to most people for almost all of the twentieth century. The promises of multimedia, simulation, computer-mediated communication and communities, and internet-based support for individual and distance learning all have the potential for revolutionary improvements in learning. Educational systems in this country and others are now struggling to achieve this revolution, learning how to best use these new technologies in their circumstances. It is not easy, and experimentation and refinements will continue for years to come.

However, we see an even larger revolution coming. This next revolution will be based on the widespread use of artificial intelligence in educational technology, guided by the growing body of research on human cognition and learning provided by cognitive science. This revolution is only possible given the context of the current one, since the broad-scale availability of powerful computers is a prerequisite. The other driver of this revolution has been scientific progress. This progress comes from two sources. Progress in artificial intelligence has led to a deeper understanding of how to represent knowledge, how to reason, and how to describe "how to" knowledge itself, i.e., *procedural knowledge.* Progress in cognitive science has led to a deeper understanding of how people think, solve problems, and learn. There is a powerful synergy here. Cognitive scientists often use artificial intelligence techniques to create simulation models of cognitive processes and behaviors. Artificial intelligence scientists use results from cognitive science to guide their explorations, and to create software with more human-like abilities. When applied to education, this synergy can lead to combinations of software and activities that can help more students achieve better learning.

This book provides a snapshot of some of the products of this synergy. We believe that these ideas and systems, and others like them, will ultimately provide a new revolution in educational technology. Some of the systems described in these chapters are already regularly used in classrooms, and spreading widely. A few are still laboratory efforts. In some cases careful evaluations have documented significant improvements in learning, in others it is too early to tell. What we have strived for is to focus on some landmark efforts that we believe will serve as the foundations for the revolution to come.

The first three chapters highlight how AI can be used as an ingredient in a stew of other technologies, in other words, as a component technology in educational systems. The chapter by Suthers and his colleagues on Belvedere illustrates how knowledge representation techniques can, when combined with a computer-mediated collaborative environment, help students formulate and discuss arguments. The work of Schank and his colleagues shows how his models of memory and learning can be combined with multimedia to provide compelling learning experiences for students. The work described by Bransford and his colleagues illustrates how simple AI problem solving techniques can help students in learning mathematics. Their work on "Betty's Brain," while preliminary, illustrates how students can learn by teaching a "virtual student" whose subsequent misconceptions force students to reflect on their own knowledge.

The next two chapters highlight progress in *intelligent tutoring systems*, an important approach for using AI in educational technology. The survey by Woolf and her colleagues provides a broad discussion of the kinds of capabilities that are used in intelligent tutoring systems, illustrated with examples of systems created and fielded by their group. Koedinger's chapter documents what is perhaps the most spectacular success to date in intelligent tutoring systems, their Pump Algebra Tutor, and the role that careful cognitive analysis and design played in it. The Pump tutor has been shown through careful evaluation to produce significant increases in student learning across several school systems.

The next four chapters focus on how specific AI technologies can be used to create new kinds of educational software. Mostow and his colleagues report on using speech recognition technology in tutors that help students learn to read. Their discussion of the trials and tribulations in experimenting with and evaluating technology in school settings is fascinating reading. Forbus's chapter describes how his group is using qualitative physics to create software for science and engineering education that can produce conceptual explanations as well as numerical results. Their articulate virtual laboratory for thermodynamics is being used in a growing number of classrooms. Lester and his colleagues show how AI can be used to automatically generate and choreograph animated explanations, based on the system's understanding of the domain and the pedagogic goals. Their pedagogical agents provide one of the most engaging technologies described here. de Koning and Bredeweg describe how model-based diagnosis techniques, originally developed for engineering tasks, can be adapted to diagnosing student misconceptions. They use techniques from qualitative physics to automatically produce an analysis of the kinds of knowledge and operations needed to answer a question, and this analysis is then used to determine what combinations of missing and/or incorrect knowledge and skills could explain the student's behavior. One thread that runs through these chapters is that AI techniques can fundamentally alter the economics of creating educational software. Instead of laboriously plotting out example-specific explanations, follow-up questions, and animations by hand, software that understands the domains and tasks can automatically figure out what to do and construct such responses dynamically, based on student inputs.

The final three chapters address broader issues in using smart machines in education. Feltovich and his colleagues illustrate the kind of insights that cognitive analyses can provide for education in their analysis of misconceptions and the stability of systems of concepts. For example, their concept of *knowledge shields*, strategies that students use to avoid correcting misconceptions, is an example of a phenomenon that must be addressed in future tutoring systems. Bouillion and Gomez discuss the assumed values and practices associated with artifacts such as educational software, their *cultural entailments* and how those entailments affect their use. Understanding how to make such entailments explicit is important in understanding how to adapt technologies to new contexts of use. Bellman provides a unique perspective, that of a research program manager, on the technical, sociological, and political issues involved developing and deploying new educational technologies in schools. These observations are based on her experience creating and running DARPA's Computer-Aided Education and Training Initiative (CATIE). While the setting of CATIE was schools serving the families of US military personnel stationed abroad, the difficulties observed and lessons learned are broadly applicable and of interest to everyone involved in using technology to improve education.

Chapter One

Representational and Advisory Guidance for Students Learning Scientific Inquiry

Dan Suthers, John Connelly, Alan Lesgold, Massimo Paolucci,
Eva Erdosne Toth, Joe Toth, and Arlene Weiner

Scientific knowledge is dynamic in two senses: it changes and increases extremely rapidly, and it is thrust from the lab into the wider world and public forum almost as rapidly. This implies increasing demands on secondary school science education. Besides knowing key facts, concepts, and procedures, it is important for today's students to understand the process by which the claims of science are generated, evaluated, and revised—an interplay between theoretical and empirical work (Dunbar and Klahr 1989). The educational goals behind the work reported in this chapter are to improve students' understanding of this process and to facilitate students' acquisition of critical inquiry skills, while also meeting conventional subject matter learning objectives.

In addition to the need to change what is taught, there are grounds to change how it is taught. Research shows that students learn better when they actively pursue understanding rather than passively receiving knowledge (Brown and Campione 1994, Chi et al. 1989, Craik and Lockhart 1972, Greeno et al. 1996, Resnick and Chi 1988, Perkins et al. 1985, Webb and Palincsar 1996). Accordingly, the classroom teacher is now being urged to become a "guide on the side" rather than the "sage on the stage." Similarly, new roles have been recommended for artificial intelligence applications to education, replacing computer-directed learning with software that supports the learning processes of students engaged in collaborative critical inquiry (Chan and Baskin 1988, Koschmann 1996, O'Neill and Gomez 1994, Roschelle 1994, Scardamalia and Bereiter 1994).

This chapter describes an educational software package, known as

BELVEDERE, that supports students in collaboratively solving ill-structured problems in science and other areas (such as public policy) as they develop critical inquiry skills. BELVEDERE exemplifies two ways in which artificial intelligence can contribute to student-centered approaches to learning: by informing the design of representational systems that constrain and guide the learners' activities, and by responding dynamically to descriptions that learners construct in these representational systems.

We begin with an overview of the BELVEDERE software environment and its use, followed by a discussion of the design history of BELVEDERE's diagrammatic interface. This leads to conclusions concerning the role of external representations in learning applications. Then, the design of BELVEDERE's automated advice on-demand facility is detailed. Discussion of two advisory systems illustrates how useful functionality can be obtained with minimal knowledge engineering, and incrementally extended as the tradeoffs and limitations are better understood. The chapter concludes with a discussion of several approaches to machine intelligence in educational applications, including the approaches exemplified by BELVEDERE.

BELVEDERE: Software for Collaborative Inquiry

The BELVEDERE software is a networked system that provides learners with shared workspaces for coordinating and recording their collaboration in scientific inquiry. The versions described in this chapter, BELVEDERE 2.0 and 2.1, are complete redesigns and reimplementations of BELVEDERE 1.0, previously reported in Suthers and Weiner (1995) and Suthers et al. (1995).

Software Interface

BELVEDERE supports the creation and editing of evidence maps. *Evidence maps* are graphs, similar to concept maps (Novak 1990), in which *nodes* represent component statements (primarily empirical observations or hypotheses) of a scientific debate or investigation; and *links* represent the relations between the elements, i.e., consistency or inconsistency. The software also includes artificial intelligence advisors, a chat facility for unstructured discussions, and facilities for integrated use with Web browsers.

The diagramming window is shown in figure 1. The default palette (the horizontal row of icons) makes salient the most crucial distinctions we want learners to acquire in order to conduct scientific inquiry. Left to right, the icons are *data* for empirical statements, *hypothesis* for theoretical statements, and *unspecified* for others statements about which learners disagree or are uncertain; then there are links representing *for* and *against* evidential relations. The rightmost icon invokes the automated advisors. Learners use the palette by clicking

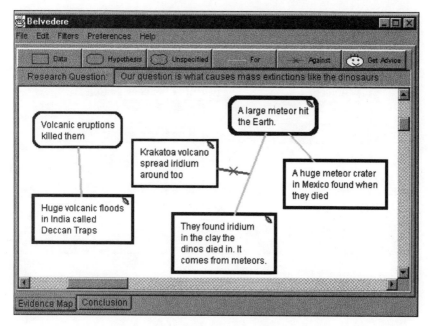

Figure 1. BELVEDERE *evidence mapping software.*

on an icon, typing some text (in the case of statements) and optionally setting other attributes, and then clicking in the diagram to place the statement or create the link. The palette is configurable; other categories and relations can be added, such as *principle* for lawlike statements, and a link for conjunction, enabling expression of evidential relations involving groups of statements. Extensions underway in BELVEDERE 3.0 include alternate views on the workspace (e.g., evidence *tables*), as well as alternate workspace types (e.g., concept maps and causal loop diagrams).

Other features, briefly noted, include the following. Users can set different belief levels for the statements and relations and display these as line thickness. Java applets have been embedded in the Web-based curricular materials, enabling learners with a click of a button to send references to these pages into the workspace. (The small link icons in the upper right corners of objects in figure 1 indicate the presence of URLs linking back to these pages.) References to external objects can also be sent from other applications directly into the BELVEDERE workspace. For example, Koedinger, Suthers, and Forbus (1999) enabled one of Forbus's Active Illustration simulations (Forbus 1997) to send summaries of simulation runs as data objects into BELVEDERE. The feasibility of embedding other kinds of documents in BELVEDERE (such as MS Word™ and Excel™ documents) and subsequently reinvoking these applications on

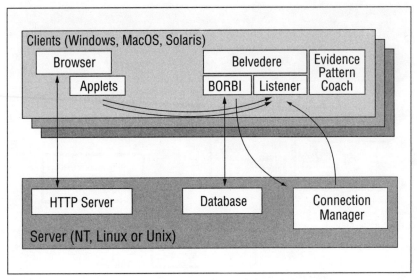

Figure 2. BELVEDERE 2.1 architecture (JDBC).

the documents from within BELVEDERE has been demonstrated. Thus BELVEDERE can be used as a conceptual organizer for use of various tools during an inquiry.

Software Implementation

The BELVEDERE client application is written in Java and is available for MacOS™, Windows '95™, NT™, and Solaris™. It is deployed within a client-server architecture that is designed to provide intelligent collaborative functionality on a variety of desktop platforms. We summarize the architecture here. See Suthers and Jones (1997) for a detailed discussion.

The architecture for BELVEDERE 2.1 is shown in figure 2. The client applications record all modifications to diagrams in a server database via the BELVEDERE *Object Request Broker Interface* (BORBI, figure 2).[1] In BELVEDERE 2.1, BORBI forwards user changes to a connection manager, a small Java process on the server that keeps track of the client applications using any given workspace and informs other clients (via their listener sockets) of the changes to their workspace. This results in automatic "what you see is what I see" update of the displays. The client application includes an evidence-pattern coach that provides advice on demand.[2] BELVEDERE can also operate in stand-alone mode, in which case a local file directory replaces the database server in a manner transparent to the user, and the networked collaborative functionality is not available.

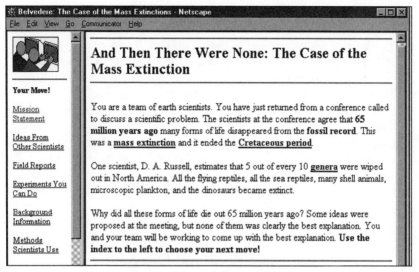

Figure 3. Science challenge problem.

We developed *science challenge* curricular materials for BELVEDERE as part of a comprehensive classroom implementation package, described briefly in the next section. Applets embedded in these Web-based materials facilitate easy transfer of references to on-line articles into BELVEDERE applications through their listeners, as shown in figure 2.

Classroom Implementation

BELVEDERE 1.0 was initially used by students aged 12-15 working alone or in pairs in our lab, as well as by students working in small groups in a tenth grade biology classroom (Suthers and Weiner 1995). Subsequently, BELVEDERE 2.0 and 2.1 were used by ninth and tenth grade science classes in Department of Defense Dependents Schools (DoDDS) overseas. At this writing, use in DoDDS continues, and is expanding to DoD schools in the United States.

Recognizing that no software, however well designed, will improve education if it is not well integrated into the classroom environment, we developed an integrated instructional framework for implementing BELVEDERE-supported collaborative inquiry in the classroom. The approach includes student activity plans worked out in collaboration with teachers. Students work in teams to investigate *science challenge problems,*[3] designed with attention to National Science Education Standards, to match and enrich the curriculum. A science challenge problem presents a phenomenon to be explained, along with indices to relevant resources (e.g., figure 3). The teams plan their investigation, perform hands-on experiments, analyze their results, and report their conclusions to others. Investigatory roles are rotated among hands-on experiments, tabletop data analyses, and computer-based activities of various sorts. The latter include literature review and use of simulations and analytic tools as well as BELVEDERE. The classroom activity plans provide teachers with specific guidance on how to manage these activities with different levels of computer resources. Teachers and students are also provided with assessment instruments designed as an integral part of the curriculum. Assessment rubrics are given to the students at the beginning of their project as criteria to guide their activities. The rubrics guide peer review, and help the teacher assess nontraditional learning objectives such as the integration of multiple sources of information and critical thinking about potentially conflicting evidence. See Suthers, Toth, and Weiner (1997) for further information on this integrated instructional framework, and Toth, Suthers, and Lesgold (in press) for evaluations undertaken in the classroom context.

Representations and Discourse

In our view, BELVEDERE's representations serve as stimuli, coordinators, and guides for various learning interactions between agents, including the automated advisors as well as learners. In essence, the representations help provide a loose *semantic coupling* among the activities of the human and machine agents, but by no means control or capture the full meaning of their interactions. In this section we describe how the evolution of BELVEDERE's interface from BELVEDERE 1.0 to BELVEDERE 2.1 reflects this view.

Our goal in constructing BELVEDERE 1.0 was to help students understand the larger process of science. Although science education reform was emphasizing hands on experimentation, we wanted students to understand that the practice of science is not just a collection of isolated experiments, but also involves a process of collective argumentation over time. Inspired by Toulmin, Rieke, and Janik (1984), our goal was to help students be able to engage in sophisticated scientific arguments, including various argument moves by which one can support or attack a claim, the grounds on which the claim is based, or the warrant by which one reasons from the grounds to the claim. BELVEDERE 1.0 was designed under the assumptions that a visual representation language (augmented with automated advice giving) can help students learn these nuances of scientific argumentation, provided that

1. The language is capable of capturing all of these nuances.
2. Students express their arguments in the language.

Guided by assumption 1, BELVEDERE 1.0 was provided with a rich palette of statement types (theory, hypothesis, law, claim, data) and relationships (supports, explains, predicts, conflicts, undercuts, warrants, causes, chronology, conjunction). Assumption 2 was motivated by the intention that the representations provide a semantic common ground for various learning activities involving students and software coaching agents. We reasoned that it would be possible to construct an artificial intelligence agent that participated in and coached argumentive discourse, provided that learners' attempts at scientific argumentation were fully expressed in a representational medium with mutually shared semantics.

Locus of Discourse

As indicated by assumption 2, we expected students to express all of their significant argumentation using the primitives in the palette. However, whenever more than one student was present, we found that much relevant argumentation was *external*, arguing *from* the representations rather than arguing *in* the representations. Faced with a decision concerning some manipulation of the representations, students would begin to discuss substantial issues until they reached tentative agreement concerning how to change the representation. In the process, statements and relations we would have liked students to represent were not represented in the diagrams.

Our initial frustration soon gave way to an understanding that this is an opportunity: proper design of manipulable representations can guide students into useful learning interactions. Thus, we downplayed the originally intended roles of the representations (1) as a medium *through* which communication takes place, (2) as a complete record of the argumentation process, and (3) as a medium for expressing formal models—in favor of their role as (4) a stimulus and guide for the discourse of collaborative learning. The following discussion summarizes subsequent observations and further work that took place under this new view.

Discussion of Ontological Choices Posed by the Medium

BELVEDERE requires all knowledge units (statements and relations) to be categorized at the time of creation. We often observed that learners who were using BELVEDERE initiated discussion of the appropriate categorical primitive for a given knowledge unit when they were about to represent that unit (Suthers 1995). Although this is not surprising, it is a potentially powerful guide to learning, provided that discussion focuses on the underlying concepts rather than the interface widget to select. For example, consider the following interaction in which students were working with a version of BELVEDERE that required all statements to be categorized as either *data* or *claim*. (The example is from a videotape of students in a tenth grade science class.)

S1: So data, right? This would be data.
S2: I think so.
S1: Or a claim. I don't know if it would be claim or data.

S2: Claim. They have no real hard evidence. Go ahead, claim. I mean who cares? Who cares what they say? Claim.

The choice forced by the tool led to a peer-coaching interaction on a distinction that was critically important for how they subsequently handled the statement. The last comment of S2 shows that the relevant epistemological concepts were being discussed, not merely which toolbar icon to press or which representational shape to use.

Yet it is not always useful to confront learners with choices, even if they may become important at some point in the development of expertise. For example, in other interactions with a version of BELVEDERE that provided more categories, we sometimes observed students becoming confused:

S1: "So what would that be..."
S2: "Uhh..."
S1: "An **ob**—"
S2: "A **claim**?"
S2: consults sheet of paper in front of her; [pause] "How about a **law**? Scientific color?"
S1: "Do you want to say a **warran**— uhh, no."
S2?: "Wait, what's a **warrant**? I just read that; why some things..."
S1: "[sigh] Oh dear."
S2: "Kind of like a **law**, like ..." [pause]

Unlike the first example, in which one student coached another on the essential difference between data and claims, the students in this example jump from one term to another apparently without grasping their meanings. It was not necessary for these students to be struggling with all of these concepts at the outset of their learning experience.

Refinements for Ontological Clarity

Based on these observations, we simplified BELVEDERE's representational framework to focus on the most essential distinction needed concerning the epistemological source of statements: empirical (data) versus hypothetical (hypothesis). Further simplifications were motivated by observations concerning the use of relations (links). The original set of argumentation relations included evidential, logical, causal, and rhetorical relations as well as the various classifications of statements exemplified above. Sometimes more than one applied. We felt that the ontologically mixed set of relation categories confused students about what they were trying to achieve with the diagrams, and did not help them focus on learning key distinctions. In order to encourage greater clarity, we decided to focus on evidential reasoning, and specifically on the most essential relational distinction for evidence based inquiry: whether two statements are consistent or inconsistent. Other complexities of scientific argumentation would be introduced once this foundation was solidly understood.

Eliminating Artifactual Distinctions

Furthermore, we eliminated directionality from BELVEDERE's link representations of relations. At one time there were at least three versions of the consistency relation: *predicts* and *explains* (both drawn from hypotheses to data), and *supports* (drawn from data to hypotheses). Early versions of our evidence pattern coach (to be described later) attempted to reason about and even enforce these semantics. However, we found that users' use of these relations (as expressed in their links) was inconsistent and sometimes differed from the intended semantics, consistent with other research on hypermedia link categories (Marshall and Rogers 1992, Shipman and McCall 1994). When the users' semantics differed from the coach's semantics, confusion or frustration resulted. For example, one subject drew a complex map of a hypothesis with seven *supports* links leading from the hypothesis to data items. The coach, failing to see any support paths from data to the hypothesis, highlighted the hypothesis and indicated that it lacked empirical evidence.

The use of *predicts*, *explains*, and *supports* links was misguided not only because different agents had different semantics for them, but also because the links were *surface* level discourse relations that did not encourage learners to think in terms of the more fundamental consistency relationships. Whether a hypothesis predicts or explains a datum is an artifact of the chronology of the datum with respect to statement of the hypothesis. Whether one uses *supports* or one of the other two links is an artifact of the focus of the discourse process by which the diagram is being constructed (argumentation about hypotheses versus explanation of data). Hence we eliminated these in favor of a single nondirectional relation that expresses the more fundamental notion of evidential consistency.

Discussion Guided by Salience and Task

Consideration of ways in which subjects interacted with the representations led us to appreciate subtle ways in which external representations may guide discourse. For example, figure 4 outlines a diagram state in which three statements were clustered near each other, with no links drawn between the statements. One student pointed to two statements simultaneously with two fingers of one hand, and drew them together as she gestured towards the third statement, saying "Like, I think that these two things, right here, um, together sort of support that" (from a videotape of an early laboratory study of BELVEDERE).

This event was originally taken merely as an example of how external representations facilitate the expression of complex ideas (Clark and Brennan 1991). However, this observation applies to any external representation. Reconsideration of this example led to the hypotheses that several features of the representational system in use made the student's utterance more likely. First,

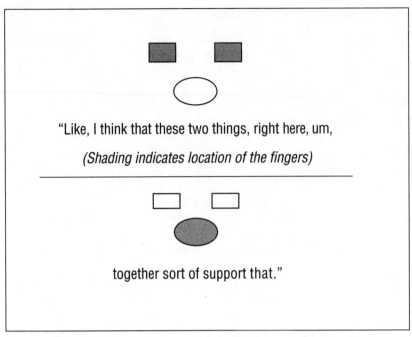

Figure 4. Gesturing to express a relationship between adjacent units.

elaboration on these particular statements is more likely because they (instead of others) are expressed as objects of perception in the representation. Second, this event is more likely to occur in a representational environment that provides a primitive for connecting statements with a support relation than in one that does not—the students perceive their task as one of linking things together. Third, it may have been easier to recognize the relationships among the three statements because they happened to be spatially nearby each other (Larkin and Simon 1987). In this example, proximity was determined by the users rather than intrinsic to the representational toolkit. However, we might design software to place potentially related knowledge units near each other.

Roles of External Representations in Learning Interactions

The foregoing experiences led to a reconceptualization of the role of external representations in learning, particularly in collaborative learning situations. Specifically, facilities for constructing visually inspectable and manipulable external representations of learners' emerging knowledge provide cognitive, social, and evaluative support as summarized in figure 5. The figure can be read as an expression of how external representations provide a loose "semantic coupling" between different kinds of learning interactions.

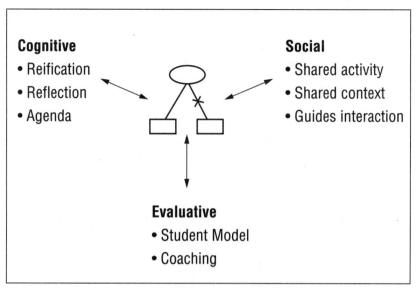

Figure 5. Learning interactions guided by external representations.

Cognitive Support

Concrete representations of abstractions such as evidential arguments can *help learners "see," internalize, and keep track of abstractions* while working on complex issues, serve as *a record of what the learners have done,* and *provide an agenda of further work* (Smolensky et al. 1987; Streitz, Hannemann, and Thuring 1989). The kind of external representation used to depict a problem may determine the ease with which the problem is solved (McGuiness 1986, Larkin and Simon 1987, Kotovsky and Simon 1990, Zhang 1997), just as appropriate design of (internal) representations for machine intelligences facilitates problem solving (Amarel 1968) and learning (Utgoff 1986). The constraints built into representations may make the problem very difficult to solve (e.g., the nine-dots problem; Hayes 1989) or may enhance problem solving (Stenning and Oberlander 1995, Klahr and Robinson 1981).

Social Support

The interaction of the cognitive processes of several agents is different than the reasoning of a single agent (Okada and Simon 1997, Perkins 1993, Salomon 1993, Schoen 1992, Walker 1993), and so may be affected by external representations in different ways. Shared learner-constructed representations such as diagrams provide *shared objects of perception that coordinate distributed work,* serving as referential objects and status reminders. We often observe learners using gestures on the display to indicate prior statements and relationships. In some group configurations we have seen learners work independently, then use gesturing on the display to re-coordinate their collaboration when one learner finds relevant information (Suthers and Weiner 1995). Different representations will serve this function different ways according to their representational biases.

Also, the mere presence of representations in a shared context with collaborating agents may change each individual's cognitive processes. One person can ignore discrepancies between thought and external representations, but an individual working in a group must constantly refer back to the shared external representation while coordinating activities with others. Thus it is conceivable that external representations have a greater effect on individual cognition in a social context than they do when working alone.[4]

Evaluative Support

Shared learner-constructed representations such as diagrams provide mentors (including the teacher, peers, and the computer) with *a basis for assessing learners' understanding* of scientific inquiry, as well as of subject matter knowledge. The use of concept maps (Novak 1990) as an assessment tool is an area of active investigation (O'Neil and Klein 1997; Ruiz-Primo, Shavelson, and Schultz 1997). We are currently developing similar techniques for evidence maps. Assessment based on external representations can also support computer coaching of the inquiry process, as described in the remainder of this chapter.

Design of Computer Advisors

Ideally, we would like to have an advisor that understands the students' text as well as the domain under discussion, and provides advice based on a deep understanding of the domain of inquiry. Although much of the technology is available, a large investment in system development and knowledge engineering is required. It is unclear which portion of this effort results in worthwhile learning gains. Instead, we have adopted the strategy of investigating how much useful advice we can get out of minimal semantic annotations before we move on to more complex approaches. In this manner we hope to better understand the cost/benefit tradeoff between knowledge engineering and added functionality.

In this section we discuss two methods of advice generation that we have implemented (Paolucci, Suthers, and Weiner 1996; Toth, Suthers, and Weiner 1997). First, *evidence pattern* advice strategies make suggestions from the standpoint of scientific argumentation, based solely on the syntactic structure of students' evidence maps. The strategies help the learners understand principles of inquiry, such as: hypotheses are meant to explain data, and are not accepted merely by being stated; multiple lines of evidence converging on a hypothesis are better than one consistent datum; hypotheses should try to explain all of the data; one should seek disconfirming evidence as well as confirming evidence; discriminating evidence is needed when two hypotheses have identical support; etc.

Second, *expert-path* advice strategies perform comparisons between the learners' diagrams and an evidence map provided by a subject matter expert. This advisor can challenge or corroborate relationships postulated by the students, or confront learners with new information (found in the expert's diagram) that challenges learners in some way. We first briefly describe the design constraints under which we operated, and then the basic algorithms behind our advice giving methods.

Pedagogical Constraints on Advice

We believe that the most important kind of advice is that which stimulates and scaffolds constructive activity on the part of the students. Our design of the advisors to be discussed was guided in part by the following constraints.

Maintain the Student-Initiated Character of Belvedere's Environment.

BELVEDERE encourages reflection by allowing students to see their evidential argumentation as an object. They can point to different parts of it and focus on areas that need attention. They can engage in a process of construction and revision, reciprocally explaining and confronting each other. An advisor that is not aware of these discourse processes should not intervene excessively or prematurely. Students should feel free to discard an advisor's suggestions when they believe them to be irrelevant or inappropriate. Also, students should be free to introduce information that is not known to the system. The advisors should still be able to provide feedback.

Anderson and colleagues have substantial empirical evidence in favor of immediate feedback in tutoring systems for individual learning in domains such as Lisp programming, geometry, and algebra (Anderson et al. 1995, Corbett and Anderson 1990, McKendree 1990). We take a less tightly coupled approach to feedback for two reasons. First, we are dealing with ill-structured problems in which it is not always possible to identify the correctness of a learner's construction. Second, we want students to develop skills of self and peer critiquing in a collaborative learning context. A computer advisor that intervened in an authoritative manner would discourage students' initiative in evaluating their own work (Nathan 1998).

Address Parts of the Task that are Critical to the Desired Cognitive Skill.

Research on confirmation bias and hypothesis driven search suggests that students are inclined to construct an argument for a favored theory, sometimes overlooking or discounting discrepant data (Klayman and Ha 1987, Chinn and Brewer 1993). Also, they may not consider alternate explanations of the data they are using. An advisor should address these problems. For example, it should offer information that the student may not have sought, including information that is discrepant with the student's theory.

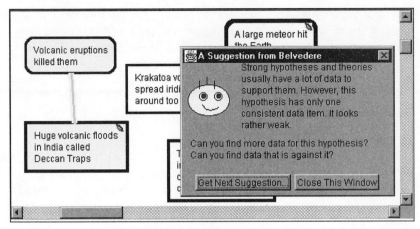

Figure 6. Example evidence pattern advice.

Be Applicable to Problems Constructed by Outside Experts and Teachers.

The advisor should be able to give useful advice based on a knowledge base that an expert or a knowledgeable teacher could easily construct. BELVEDERE has been used for topics as different as evolution, mountain formation, mass extinctions, AIDS, and social psychology. It is not feasible to develop, for each topic, a representation of the knowledge needed to deal with the argumentation in which students could potentially engage. We were instead interested in a general approach in which either no knowledge engineering is required or a teacher can construct the knowledge base.

Hence a *minimalist* AI approach was taken, in which we implemented an advisor that can provide reasonable advice with no domain specific knowledge engineering. Advice was provided only on request. Identification of specific needs and consideration of the cost of meeting these needs then motivated extensions to this advisor.

Evidence Pattern Strategies

The first approach we implemented gives advice in response to situations that can be defined on a purely syntactic basis, using only the structural and categorical features of the students' argument graphs (i.e., the students' text is not interpreted). Principles of scientific inquiry are instantiated as patterns to be matched to the diagram and textual advice to be given if there is a match. Example advice is shown in figure 6, and example advice patterns from our BELVEDERE 2.0 implementation are given in figure 7. This Lisp implementation used representation and retrieval facilities from the Loom knowledge representation system (Bates and MacGregor 1987). When the solid-lined portions of figure 7 are present and the dashed portions are missing, the corresponding

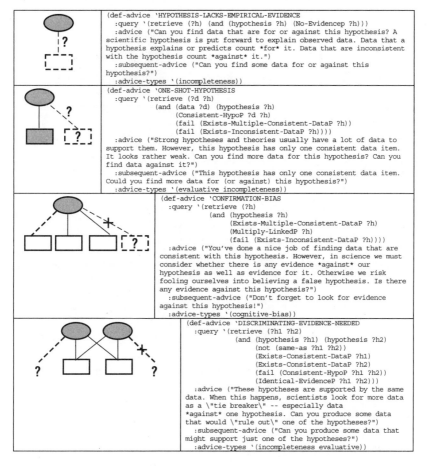

```
(def-advice 'HYPOTHESIS-LACKS-EMPIRICAL-EVIDENCE
   :query '(retrieve (?h) (and (hypothesis ?h) (No-Evidencep ?h)))
   :advice ("Can you find data that are for or against this hypothesis? A
scientific hypothesis is put forward to explain observed data. Data that a
hypothesis explains or predicts count *for* it. Data that are inconsistent
with the hypothesis count *against* it.")
   :subsequent-advice ("Can you find some data for or against this
hypothesis?")
   :advice-types '(incompleteness))
```

```
(def-advice 'ONE-SHOT-HYPOTHESIS
   :query '(retrieve (?d ?h)
               (and (data ?d) (hypothesis ?h)
               (Consistent-HypoP ?d ?h)
               (fail (Exists-Multiple-Consistent-DataP ?h))
               (fail (Exists-Inconsistent-DataP ?h))))
   :advice ("Strong hypotheses and theories usually have a lot of data to
support them. However, this hypothesis has only one consistent data item.
It looks rather weak. Can you find more data for this hypothesis? Can you
find data against it?")
   :subsequent-advice ("This hypothesis has only one consistent data item.
Could you find more data for (or against) this hypothesis?")
   :advice-types '(evaluative incompleteness))
```

```
(def-advice 'CONFIRMATION-BIAS
   :query '(retrieve (?h)
               (and (hypothesis ?h)
               (Exists-Multiple-Consistent-DataP ?h)
               (Multiply-LinkedP ?h)
               (fail (Exists-Inconsistent-DataP ?h))))
   :advice ("You've done a nice job of finding data that are
consistent with this hypothesis. However, in science we must
consider whether there is any evidence *against* our
hypothesis as well as evidence for it. Otherwise we risk
fooling ourselves into believing a false hypothesis. Is there
any evidence against this hypothesis?")
   :subsequent-advice ("Don't forget to look for evidence
against this hypothesis!")
   :advice-types '(cognitive-bias))
```

```
(def-advice 'DISCRIMINATING-EVIDENCE-NEEDED
   :query '(retrieve (?h1 ?h2)
               (and (hypothesis ?h1) (hypothesis ?h2)
               (not (same-as ?h1 ?h2))
               (Exists-Consistent-DataP ?h1)
               (Exists-Consistent-DataP ?h2)
               (fail (Consistent-HypoP ?h1 ?h2))
               (Identical-EvidenceP ?h1 ?h2)))
   :advice ("These hypotheses are supported by the same
data. When this happens, scientists look for more data
as a \"tie breaker\" -- especially data
*against* one hypothesis. Can you produce some data
that would \"rule out\" one of the hypotheses?")
   :subsequent-advice ("Can you produce some data that
might support just one of the hypotheses?")
   :advice-types '(incompleteness evaluative))
```

Figure 7. Evidence pattern advice.

advice can be given. Objects that bind to variables in the patterns (the shaded boxes in figure 7) are highlighted in yellow during presentation of advice to indicate the target(s) of definite references such as "this hypothesis." For example, figure 6 shows BELVEDERE 2.1's version of the "one-shot hypothesis" advice of figure 7.

Some advice patterns not shown in figure 7 include the following:

Alternate hypothesis: When only one hypothesis is stated, asks whether there is another hypothesis that provides an alternate explanation for the data (pointing out that it is important to consider alternatives so as not to be misled).

Attend to discrepant evidence: Motivated by research showing that people sometimes ignore discrepant evidence, this counterpart to the confirmation bias advice detects hypotheses that have consistent and inconsistent data, and asks whether all the data are equally credible.

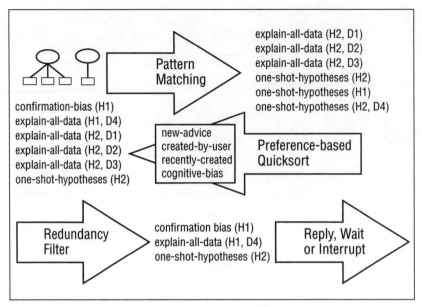

Figure 8. Advice selection.

Contradicting links: When both a *for* and *against* link have been drawn between the same two statements, asks if this was intended.

Data supports conflicting hypotheses: Asks if this configuration makes sense; if so, suggests a search for discriminating data.

Explain all the data: Matching to a hypothesis that has explained some of the data but has no relation to other data, points out the importance of attempting to explain all the data and asks whether the hypothesis is consistent or inconsistent with the as of yet unrelated datum.

Many objects and no links: After acknowledging that it's OK to be gathering data and hypotheses, suggests that the user begin to consider the relationships between them.

Nothing in diagram: Suggests that a theory or hypothesis be formulated when none is present in the evidence map. Provides basic instructions on use of the toolbar icons.

Advice Selection

Typically, several advice patterns will match an evidence map, sometimes with multiple matches per pattern. This is more than a student can be expected to absorb and respond to at one time. It is necessary to be selective in a context sensitive manner. For example, figure 8 (top) shows an evidence map with 6 matches, called *advice activation records* (AARs), to three advice patterns.

Selection is performed by a preference-based quick-sort algorithm, following a mechanism used by Suthers (1993) for selecting between alternate expla-

Preference Name	Prefers AARs ...
New-Advice	... that have not been given before (based on a bounded history of prior communications).
Expert-Path	... that were created by the expert-path advisor (described in next section).
Created-by-User	... that bind variables to objects created by the user to be advised.
Interrupting-Advice	... that are marked as worth an interruption (interrupting advisor only).
Cognitive-Bias	... for advice types that address problematic cognitive biases.
Incompleteness	... for advice types concerned with ways the user can engage in constructive activity.
Incoherence	... for advice types that address semantically incoherent diagram configurations.
Many-Siblings	... for advice patterns that have many instantiations (AARs).
Recently-Created	... that bind variables to objects recently created (by anyone).
Evaluative-Advice	... for advice types that address, in part, the evaluation of hypotheses based on the data (this preference is high priority in the "late" strategy).
Getting-Started	... for advice useful to someone learning to use the evidence mapping tool (this preference is high priority in the "early" strategy).

Table 1. Prioritized preferences.

nations. Preferences (table 1) take into account factors such as prior advice that has been given, how recently the object of advice was constructed and by whom, and various categorical attributes of the applicable advice. Given an ordered pair of AARs, a preference will return >, <, or = indicating whether it prefers one over the other. For example, given two AARs, the first of which binds a variable to an object created by the current user and the second of which does not, Created-by-user will return >. The sort algorithm is given a prioritized list of preferences, as exemplified in figure 8 (middle). Our variation of the quicksort algorithm first partitions the set of AARs into equivalence classes under the first (highest priority) preference on the list. The equivalence classes are ordered with respect to each other. It then calls itself recursively on each equivalence class with the remaining list of preferences. When the list of preferences becomes empty on a recursive call involving a nontrivial set of AARs, the AARs are ordered randomly for variety. Finally, the sequence of equivalence classes that is returned by the recursive sorts is concatenated to yield the prioritized list of AARs.

There are three advice selection strategies for early, mid, and late phases of an evidence map. The phases are defined in terms of the complexity of the diagram: The user is *getting started* if there is no data, no hypothesis, or only one evidential relation. The user is *late* in the process if there are at least two hypotheses and the number of data items and evidential relations is at least 4 each and greater than the number of hypotheses. Otherwise the strategy shown in table 1 is used. Strategies are expressed as different priority orderings of the preferences. For example, following the ordering of figure 8, the preference *new-advice* is applied first to partition the AARs into those that have been given before and those that have not. Then *created-by-user* partitions each of these into ordered subpartitions, and so on down the list. In the example of figure 8, the *late* strategy applies, although for simplicity of presentation only four of the preferences are shown in the figure. Suppose all of the AARs are new (have not been presented); that one user created all of the objects; and that object D4 was created most recently. Preferences *new-advice* and *created-by-user* have no effect: all AARs go into one equivalence class. Preference *cognitive-bias* creates two equivalence classes: the confirmation-bias AAR, and all the rest. Finally, *recently-created* is applied to each of these equivalence classes, resulting in the reordering of AARs according to recency.

After sorting, a *redundancy filter* is applied that removes all but one of multiple instantiations of a given advice pattern, retaining the highest priority instantiation. This provides the final prioritized list of advice, as exemplified in figure 8 (bottom). The advice-on-demand version of the advisor then sends the first AAR on the list to the requesting client application. If further advice is requested before the diagram changes, subsequent advice instances on the sorted list are used without reanalysis.

We have been experimenting with an intrusive advisor that differs from the on-demand advisor in the final step of figure 8. This advisor recomputes the list of advice after every user action. It then examines the top N (usually we set $N = 1$) AARs on the advice list, and determines whether the advice merits an interruption, based on two considerations. First, only certain categories of advice are deemed to be sufficiently important to merit an interruption. Second, each AAR is given a delay factor to allow the user sufficient time (measured by counting modifications to the diagram) to anticipate and address the issue that would be raised by the advice. For example, one would not want the advisor to interrupt with the advice, "Your hypothesis lacks empirical evidence," every time one creates a hypothesis. It takes two steps to create a data object and link it to the hypothesis. Hence this advice pattern is given a delay of 2, meaning that AARs for this advice pattern are filtered until they recur three times, allowing for the creation of the hypothesis, the data, and the link.

Evaluations of the Evidence Pattern Advisor

The evidence pattern advisor provides advice about abstracted patterns of relationships among statements, but has nothing to say about the contents of these statements. Its strengths are in its potential for pointing out principles of scientific inquiry in the context of students' own evidential reasoning and its generality and applicability to new topics with no additional knowledge engineering.

Empirical evaluation of this advisor took two forms: it was made available in DoD dependent school (DoDDS) classrooms in Germany and Italy; and laboratory studies of expert advisors were conducted. At this writing, John Connelley is undertaking a controlled comparison of intrusive and nonintrusive strategies.

Although distance prevented detailed classroom observations, data available to us from DoDDS in the form of limited personal observations, third party observations, videotapes, and computer logs indicate that (1) the on-demand advisor was almost never invoked, although the advice icon was readily available on the toolbar; (2) there were situations where students did not know what to do next, situations in which the advisor would have helped if it were invoked; and (3) the advice and its relevance to the students' activities were sometimes ignored as if not understood. Items 1 and 2 indicate that in spite of our reluctance to interfere with students' deliberations, unsolicited advice is sometimes needed. In response to this need, we have implemented and begun laboratory experimentation with the intrusive version of the advisor described previously.

We have two explanations for the third observation. First, the wording may require some simplification and shortening. The current strategy is to give a general principle and interpret this in terms of the diagram, for example:

> *Principle:* "... in science we must consider whether there is any evidence *against* our hypothesis as well as evidence for it. Otherwise we risk fooling ourselves into believing a false hypothesis.

> *Specific advice:* Is there any evidence against this hypothesis?"

Students may become confused by the more abstract justification and never read or process the specific suggestion, or the advice may simply be too long. Second, a modality mismatch may also be a factor: students are working with diagrams, but the advice is textual. We would like to modify the advice presentation to temporarily display the suggested additional structure directly in the students' diagram, perhaps using dashed lines as was done the left column of figure 7.

In the laboratory studies (Katz and Suthers 1998) we used the chat facility to enable subject matter experts—geologists[5]—to coach pairs of students working on the Mass Extinctions issue. The geologist for a given session could only see what the computer advisor sees, namely the users' changes to the diagram. However, we allowed students to ask the geologist questions in natural language. Categorization of the geologists' communications for four sessions showed that most advice giving was concerned with domain specific knowledge rather than the general principles applied by the evidence pattern advisor, although there were some clear examples of the latter as well. Many communications either (1) introduced relevant information or suggested that students search for new relevant information, or (2) commented on the correctness of evidential relations that the students drew. These results confirmed what we knew all along: that the evidence pattern advisor would be too limited. However they also helped guide the next direction taken in our incremental approach: the addition of simple techniques with low knowledge engineering costs that would yet enable the machine to (1) introduce or suggest new information and (2) evaluate students' evidential relations.

Expert-Path Advice Strategies

The expert-path advisor was designed to offer specific information that the student may not discover on her own. It makes the assumption that a correspondence can be found between statements in a student's evidence map and those in a pre-stored expert's evidence map. The path advisor searches the latter *expert graph* to find paths between units that students have linked in their evidence maps, and selects other units found along those paths that are brought to the students' attention. Our claim is that this enables us to point out information that is relevant at a given point in the inquiry process without needing to pay the cost of a more complete semantic model of that information, such as would be necessary in traditional knowledge-based educational software. The only costs incurred are in the construction of the expert graph consisting of semantic units that are also available to the student, and the additional mechanisms needed to identify the correspondence between statements in the student and expert diagrams.

Constructing and Using Expert "Snippets"

A teacher or domain expert first authors HTML-based reference pages to be used by the students. Each page consists of one or more semantic units, which we call *snippets*. A snippet is a short text describing a hypothesis or an empirical finding, such as a field observation or the results of an experiment. *Reference buttons*—the icons in the HTML page on the right of figure 9—are then attached to each snippet. These buttons invoke Java code that presents a dialog by which users can send statements containing references to the snippets into BELVEDERE. An example dialog is shown in the left of figure 9. The dialog requires users to summarize snippets in their own words.

The lower box in figure 9 shows the data statement that would be created by this dialog. As shown, the user's wording is displayed in the diagram. The link icon in the upper right corner of the data shape indicates that it has a URL reference to a source page. One can reload this page in the web browser by clicking on the link icon.

After authoring the snippet-annotated reference pages, teachers or domain experts can then construct an expert evidence map in BELVEDERE by using the

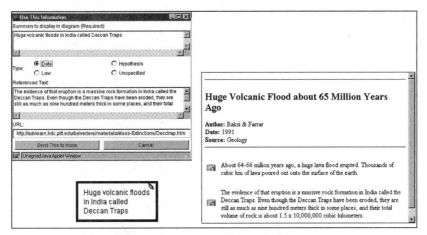

Figure 9. Generating a reference to a snippet.

buttons to send in references and connecting them with links. This map is converted and stored as an *expert graph.*

Then, during student sessions, students can use the reference buttons to send references to snippets into their diagrams, where they may express evidential relationships between the snippets. (Thus, reference buttons are the mechanism by which we obtain a correspondence between statements in users' evidence maps and those in an expert graph.) The expert-path advisor will then compare consistency relations in the student's evidence map with paths of consistency relations between the same statements in the expert graph. Mismatches in the polarity of these paths and/or the presence of extra information on the expert's paths are be used to provide advice, as described below. Advice on the expert's path provides a consistency check on the way students are using evidence.

Computing Expert-Path Advice

The BELVEDERE 2.0 expert-path advisor was implemented in Lisp (along with one version of the evidence pattern advisor). One server-based advisor process serves multiple clients. Expert diagrams are read from the Postgres server into a Loom knowledge base and instantiated as Loom objects. During a session the expert diagram is read-only and not visible to the students. Each time a change occurs in a student diagram, the expert advisor notes the change, and the Loom knowledge base is updated with the new information.

As students construct an evidence map, they may include references to expert snippets. The expert-path advisor is utilized only when a student assigns a relationship between two of these references with a *for, against,* or *and* link. The expert-path advisor has no advice on statements that did not reference snippets, but can work with diagrams containing such statements. The evi-

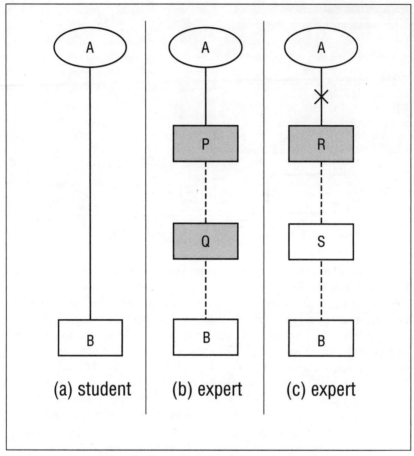

Figure 10. Comparison of student to expert graph.

dence-pattern advisor can respond to such nonsnippets.

After an initial experimental implementation using a marker-passing algorithm in BELVEDERE 1.0 (Paolucci, Suthers, and Weiner 1996), the expert advisor was implemented with an A* best-first heuristic search (Nilsson 1980) in BELVEDERE 2.0 (Toth, Suthers, and Weiner 1997). The search finds an optimal path from the start node to the goal node in the expert diagram according to the following cost heuristics. (The start and goal statements in the student diagram must be snippets and must also exist in the expert diagram.)

1. Shorter paths are given lower costs, based on the heuristic that more direct relationships are less likely to lead to obscurely related information. This heuristic takes precedence over the following two.

2. If the student has indicated a *for* link, all paths in the expert diagram that

contain a single *against* link will be assigned lower costs than paths with only *for* links. Likewise, if a student has indicated an *against* link, all paths in the expert diagram that contain only *for* links will be assigned lower costs than paths with *against* links. This addresses the confirmation bias by seeking information that might contradict the student's link.

3. Paths with more than one *against* link are given higher costs than other paths. Experience showed that the meaning of such paths is unclear to users.

Once a lowest-cost path is found between the start and the goal statements, advice is generated as follows:

1. When the expert diagram has a direct link between the start and the goal, simple feedback is generated based on a comparison to the student's link:

   • If a student has indicated a *for* link between the start and goal, and the expert diagram has an *against* link between them, return an AAR (advice activation record) that would ask the student to reconsider the link.

   • If a student has indicated an *against* link between the start and goal and the expert diagram has a *for* link between the start and goal, return an AAR that would ask the student to reconsider the link.

   • If the links agree, return an AAR that would indicate agreement.

2. When a nontrivial path is found between the start and the goal (figure 10), the advisor can confront the student with information that may contradict or corroborate the student's link as follows:

   • If the student has connected two snippets with a *for* link (e.g., figure 10a), and the lowest cost path in the expert evidence map has an *against* link in it, identify the statement connected by the *against* link that is internal to the path (e.g., node *R* of figure 10c), and return an AAR that would bring this statement to the attention of the student.

   • If the student has connected two snippets with an *against* link, and the lowest cost path in the expert evidence map consists entirely of *for* links, return an AAR that would bring the student's attention to statements in that path (e.g., if figure 10a were an inconsistency link, communicate nodes *P* and *Q* of figure 10b).

   • If the student's path is of the same polarity as the expert's path, return an AAR that would agree with the student's link, but elaborate on it by presenting an internal node (e.g., *P* and *Q* of figure 10b in response to figure 10a).

Our implementation presents the selected snippet in a pop-up dialog. A better approach might be to show users the web page containing the source information, or, for students requiring more scaffolding, to temporarily display the relevant portion of the expert graph. Presentation could also be sensitive to whether or not the student has viewed the source web page.

All of the above strategies are advice *generators*; it remains for the preference mechanism discussed previously to decide when the generated advice is actually worth giving. One preference was added to promote expert path advice over others, because this advice is more specific to the situation at hand than

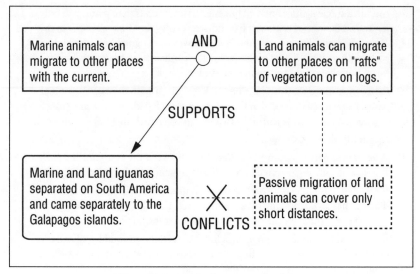

Figure 11. Example of expert-path advisor.

the evidence-pattern advice. This arbitration scheme can easily be extended to manage additional sources of advice.

Formative Experiments

Although the expert-path advisor has not been deployed in classrooms, formative evaluation took place during development. We conducted two experiments with BELVEDERE 1.0's version of the expert-path advisor (Paolucci, Suthers, and Weiner 1996). In the first experiment we were interested in testing consistency relations that we expected to be difficult or that required some inferential power. We used a subset of a knowledge base used in some of the studies with students, this subset being composed of nineteen nodes, fourteen consistent and inconsistent relations, and two and-links. (The problem concerns the origin of Galapagos marine iguanas.) Three of the present authors made judgments of consistency between pairs of statements corresponding to the nodes. Then we compared our judgments with the advisor's judgments. In all the relations about which all three authors agreed, the advisor made the same judgment. The only disagreements were on relations about which the authors disagreed. These cases were all characterized by the lack of a connecting path between the tested nodes. Either the search process was blocked by an inconsistency link, or a critical link was missing in an intermediate step of the search.

In the second experiment, we were concerned with the advice that would be given in a real interaction with students. We constructed a consistency graph of ninety statements and seventy-three relations from the materials used in one of the sessions with students and performed path analyses on each link from two student sessions. The performance was similar to the previous experiment. We always agreed with the system's judgment, and the intermediate steps were sequences of coherent proofs. On most of the links the advisor agreed with the students (these were among our best students). In one case only, the advisor gave a different judgment: see the support link in figure 11. (This study was performed with the earlier representational toolkit that differentiated *supports*, *explains*, and *predicts*.) The path the advisor constructed starts at the *and* node, crosses the upper right and lower right nodes (the latter is not displayed in the students' graph), and ends at the lower left node. The advisor recognizes that this path (dashed lines) crosses an inconsistency link, and so conflicts with the students' support link. If the students would ask the advisor for a critique of their arguments, the advisor would highlight the link and display the node on the lower right (the only information on the path that they have not seen), confronting them with the conditions for land animals' migration that they overlooked.[6]

Although we have selected an appropriate level of representation, the snippet, to allow the student to access domain-relevant material, we have also considered the pedagogical value of both a finer and a coarser grain size. A finer grain would reduce ambiguity and increase the accuracy of feedback. On the other hand, a coarser grain (i.e., at the level of a normal paragraph, or of a typical Web document), would enable quicker authoring of the Web-based materials described earlier. The model of advising with a larger grain size would be a "for your information" advisor, which would function like a research librarian forwarding new information to those likely to be interested in it. It would still be possible to specify *for* and *against* relations in a general sense, just as a paper can give evidence for or against a particular view. However, coarse-grained representation has obvious limitations. For example, it is important for students to learn that one can often extract evidence for a view from a paper that is generally unfavorable to that view. Indeed, scientific papers are obliged to take note of divergent views and limitations.

Comparison of Advisors and Future Directions

Table 2 summarizes a comparison between the two advisors. The evidence-pattern advisor can make suggestions to stimulate students' thinking with no knowledge engineering required on the part of the teacher or domain expert. However, the advice is very general. It could better address confirmation bias by confronting students with discrepant information they may be ignoring. The expert-path advisor can provide students with assistance in identifying relevant information which they may not have considered (perhaps due to confirmation bias), and which may challenge their thinking. The pattern-

	Evidence Pattern Advisor	Expert Path Advisor
Knowledge Required	Principles of scientific inquiry (author once for many domains) Pattern matching	Expert evidence map (author for each area of inquiry) Search for and compare paths
Inference Required Advantages	Expresses general principles in terms of student's constructions	Can point out relevant information
	Very general; widely applicable without additional knowledge engineering	No special training needed for authoring
Functional Limitations	Cannot point out relevant information due to lack of model of domain.	Shallow domain model does not support advice on causal or temporal reasoning

Table 2. Comparison of BELVEDERE's advice strategies.

based advisor cannot provide this assistance, because it requires a model of evidential relationships between the units of information being manipulated by students. With the expert-path advisor, we have shown this assistance can be provided without deep modeling of or reasoning about the domain.

An attractive option is to combine the two advisors. Patterns could be matched to both student and expert diagrams to identify principled ways in which students might engage in additional constructive inquiry, along with information that is relevant to that inquiry. For example, if the pattern matches the expert's graph but one pattern component is missing in the student's graph, the advisor could then present this information as indicated by the missing component's role in the pattern.

In both advisors, the knowledge engineering demands on educators who prepare materials for students are very low. Clearly, a minimal semantic approach has limitations. For example, the advisor cannot help the student in the construction of an argument, find a counter argument that attacks her theory, or engage the student in a scientific discussion of causal or mathematical models underlying the theories. It cannot infer the goals of the student, in particular which theory she is trying to build or support. However, continued investigations of the utility of advice obtained from these minimal semantic annotations will provide insight into the cost-benefit tradeoff between knowledge engineering and educational gains, and point the way toward further artificial intelligence approaches that may be worth pursuing.

Alternative Approaches to AI and Education

We have discussed our changing view of the role of representations in supporting learning interactions, and our adoption of an incremental approach to the design of minimal automated advisors that can yet usefully contribute to these learning interactions. In this work, those of us who are trained in Artificial Intelligence have found new ways to apply the methods and sensitivities of our field to education. The chapter concludes with a summary of these alternative approaches.

Strong AI and Education

The phrase *artificial intelligence and education* (AIED) most immediately brings to mind the endeavor to build smart machines that teach. Ideally, under this vision, such machines would know a great deal about a particular subject matter, being able to both articulate concepts and principles and engage in expert level problem solving behavior (Clancey and Letsinger 1984; Reiser, Anderson, and Farrell 1985). They would also know about pedagogy, being able to track the progress of individual students and choose the best feedback strategies and trajectory through a curriculum for a particular student (Van Lehn 1988a). This vision of AIED might be termed *strong AIED*.

Strong[7] approaches to AIED have been behind work resulting in major contributions to artificial intelligence, and (less often) education. For example, Clancey's efforts to transform a rule-based expert system, MYCIN, into a teaching machine, drawing upon the clinical knowledge supposedly embodied in MYCIN, led to fundamental insights into the limitations of rule-based systems for supporting explanation and the need for causal, conceptual, and strategic knowledge structures (Clancey 1983, 1986). Early work on instructional simulations on the SOPHIE and STEAMER projects have led a long and fruitful research program in automated qualitative reasoning (De Kleer and Brown 1984, Forbus 1984a), resulting in software with new pedagogical capabilities (Forbus 1997, Forbus and Whalley 1988).

Some criticize strong AIED approaches to computer-supported learning, questioning whether computers can know enough about the student (Self 1988), the domain, or teaching; or questioning whether observed learning gains are actually due to the artificial intelligence elements, or to contextual factors (Nathan 1998). Skepticism concerning the potential of strong approaches is warranted. However, in our opinion some such efforts are worthwhile for the synergistic interaction of AI and education that benefits further understanding in both fields, provided other approaches that promise to yield more immediate benefits are pursued as well.

Minimalist AI and Education

Contributions are also being made by others who take an approach we will characterize as *minimalist AIED* (Nathan 1998, Schank and Cleary 1995). The advisors discussed in this chapter are an example of minimalist AIED. Instead of attempting to build relatively complete knowledge representations, reasoning capabilities and/or pedagogical agent functionality, this alternative approach provides machines with minimal abilities to respond to the semantics of student activities and constructions, tests the educational value of these abilities, and adds functionality as needed to address deficiencies in the utility of the system. An incremental approach interleaved with evaluation keeps the work focused on technologies with educational relevance. It also provides a viable research strategy, ensuring that we evaluate the capabilities and limitations of each representational and inferential device unencumbered by the simultaneous complexities of an attempted complete pedagogical agent.

The feedback provided by a minimalist approach may be characterized as *state-based* rather than *knowledge-based* (Nathan 1998): the software helps students recognize important features of their problem solving state. A minimalist approach is consistent with instructional approaches in which students are expected to take greater responsibility for management of their learning, including self-assessment.

Residual AI and Education

The design history of BELVEDERE's representational tools suggests to us that the relevance of AI for education goes beyond attempts to build reasoning machines, even of the minimalist sort. Artificial intelligence offers concepts and techniques that can be applied to the design of software that would not itself be considered an artificial intelligence at any level, yet which constitutes a contribution of AI to education, and potentially even a source and test-bed of AI ideas. This kind of application can be seen most clearly in the design of representational systems. An artificial intelligence sensitivity to the expressive and heuristic utility of formal representations for automated reasoning can be applied to the analysis and design of external representations for both human reasoning and machine reasoning (Larkin and Simon 1987, Stenning and Oberlander 1995). External representations for learning and problem solving can differ in their expressiveness and in their heuristic bias—the perceptual salience of different kinds of information. Such differences can be exploited to design interactive learning environments that guide individual and group learning activities. The AI in software systems built under this approach is residual, influencing the design but being a run-time factor only for human rather than artificial agents. Examples of work in this category include Kaput (1995), Koedinger (1991), Reusser (1993), and Suthers (1999, 2001).

Acknowledgments

We thank Violetta Cavalli-Sforza for conceiving and programming the predecessor to BELVEDERE, and for contributions to the design of BELVEDERE 1.0; Johanna Moore for contributions to BELVEDERE 1.0; Dan Jones and Kim Harrigal for work on the BELVEDERE 2.x server and clients; Sandy Katz for empirical studies that informed the design of the expert-path advisor; Cynthia Liefeld for her assistance on empirical studies; Micki Chi for discussions concerning the role of representations in learning, and the editors of this book for suggested improvements to the presentation. Work on BELVEDERE was funded by DoDEA's Presidential Technology Initiative (1997-1998); DARPA's Computer Aided Education and Training Initiative (1995-1997); and the NSF Applications of Advanced Technology program (1992-1995). This work was completed while all authors were at the Learning Research and Development Center of the University of Pittsburgh.

Notes

1. The database is Postgres in BELVEDERE 2.0 and 2.1's UNIX servers; and MSQL in BELVEDERE 2.1's NT™ server. BORBI was CGI-based in BELVEDERE 2.0 and is JDBC-based in BELVEDERE 2.1.

2. In BELVEDERE 2.0, the advisors ran as a server-based process. The evidence pattern advisor was partially ported to Java for a client-based advisor in BELVEDERE 2.1.

3. See http//lilt.ics.hawaii.edu/belvedere/materials/

4. Micki Chi, personal communication to the first author.

5. Jack Donahue, and graduate students John Dembosky and Brian Peer.

6. However, Ellen Censky has evidence that land iguanas migrated between Caribbean islands two hundred miles apart on trees downed during a hurricane in 1995.

7. "Strong AIED" versus "minimalist AIED" is not identical to "strong methods" versus "weak methods," although there is a relationship. Strong methods are domain specific procedures that are justified by, if not compiled from, a great deal of domain knowledge. Weak methods are domain independent, may require encoding of significant domain knowledge to be applied, and may engage in a great deal of inferencing. Strong AIED makes significant use of at least one of these two. Minimalist AI techniques minimize both knowledge and inferencing.

Chapter Two

Motivation and Failure in Educational Simulation Design

Roger Schank and Adam Neaman

Experts cannot tell you much of how they do what they do and even if they could, telling this information to novices would not turn them into experts. Given these constraints, how can we help novices to develop expertise? Learning by doing is the answer. Of course, learning by doing is open to many different interpretations. We are going to talk about learning by doing in the context of educational simulations. We take as a given the premise that people only learn by doing. Although many consider this claim to be controversial, we will take it as a given for the purposes of this essay (Dewey, 1916, Schank 1999) and focus instead on its implications for designing learning experiences. We will make a number of claims about the design of learning by doing (LBD) environments and then substantiate these claims with both research and examples of software we have built at The Institute for the Learning Sciences (ILS) over the past ten years.

Claim 1: Students should be put in personally-meaningful and responsible roles in which they are required to perform either real-world tasks or simulations of them. This doesn't mean that kindergartners need to be engaged in nothing but pre-professional pursuits. It means that when kindergartners study history, they should *do* history in the ways that people who use history do so, be they historians, journalists, technology forecasters, sociologists, or just people trying to make sense of a novel or the day's newspaper.

Often, people see this first claim as a suggestion that all education have a pre-professional focus. We are making no such claim. We believe that giving students meaningful roles and goals when learning will help them to develop knowledge that is more useful in many contexts, ranging from the purest intellectual inquiry to the most pragmatic earning of a paycheck.

Claim 2: Well-designed LBD environments don't simply throw students into "sink or swim" situations, they are carefully designed experiences that provide a variety of supports for learning. Some of these supports are credible plot contrivances that have been built into the simulated or real experiences in which students are placed; others are external to those tasks, functioning more like contextual help in a software package. Although the "sink or swim" teaching strategy has many merits, throwing people into a new domain and just saying "go" is usually not the optimal strategy for helping them learn. We certainly don't want to put flight students in real airplanes and just send them off to start flying. Safety is obviously a serious concern, but there's a larger issue than just safety here. It's generally inefficient to throw students into learning-by-doing experiences without providing them with a variety of supports that will engage them and help them to explain their mistakes faster.

Claim 3: The opportunity to make mistakes and experience failures is essential to learning. Any well-designed LBD environment is carefully designed to bring students to the specific set of mistakes or failures from which they will learn the most. Learning from real-world experience often provides learners with valuable failure experiences. On the other hand, it is also quite possible for a novice to work at a real world job for a long time without ever encountering the difficult situations that separate the experts from the novices. For example, an expert customer service representative at a complaints desk probably knows how to handle a violent client whereas a novice does not. Violent customers at the complaints desk may be rare but the ability to handle them appropriately is a highly desirable skill in a customer service representative.

In a simulation, we can make certain that novices are quickly exposed to rare but important experiences. Of course, we can also expose them to the more routine experiences and failures they might have if they simply learned through real on-the-job experiences. In short, with simulations, we can bring students to the most useful failure experiences quickly because we can rig the simulation so that all the worst things that can go wrong do. In this way, we compress the amount of time it takes to develop real expertise.

Claim 4: One of the most important learning supports we can provide to a novice in an LBD environment is the ability to ask questions of experts right when they experience failures. The answers to these questions should provide novices with support for explaining and overcoming their recent failures as well as for figuring out how to avoid similar failures in the future. If you care about what you are doing and you find yourself failing, it is very likely that you will find it engaging to hear from experts.

Experts' knowledge is often in the form of "war stories." Typically, these stories are examples of failures that an expert has either experienced, witnessed, or cleverly avoided. They are often rich in memorable details and they tend to capture the subtleties and complexities of expertise that would get lost if that knowledge were reduced to rules.

The fact that the stories are told just in time, when students are dealing with similar failures and have questions about them, is important for several reasons. One reason is that students are likely to recall knowledge in the contexts in which that knowledge was acquired (Tulving and Thompson 1973; Godden and Baddeley 1975; Schank 1982, 1999). A second reason for telling stories just-in-time is that necessity is the mother of *attention*. Stories should be told only when students want or need to hear them because it is only then that they will pay attention and learn from them.

Claim 5: In order for any learning environment to work well, it must engage students by appealing to their goals and interests. Certainly, you can force students sit through endless hours of school doing things that don't interest them. This may even help them to pass standardized tests. From a learning perspective however, there's a serious problem with this strategy. Insofar as the work students are given is irrelevant to their interests and goals, they will be more likely to forget what they have learned once the tests are over. Furthermore, what they do remember will probably not be all that useful outside of the context of standardized tests. Instead of developing some qualitative understanding of how a historical event occurred or why a car skids on ice, they will learn a bunch of historical facts or a bunch of physics equations without understanding how to apply them in the world.

To briefly recap our claims:

- Experts cannot really tell you how they do what they do
- "Telling" students doesn't work as a teaching strategy
- Learning by doing is the solution to these problems
- Good learning by doing environments provide students with opportunities to experience the right failures quickly; and just-in time support for explaining failures in the form of experts who tell stories
- Motivation is critical in the design of learning environments because it determines the quality of the attention that students will give to what they are learning.

Before we begin to talk about the educational software we've built based on these beliefs, we want to discuss our first two claims.

Experts Cannot Tell You How They Do What They Do

The most important skills an education can provide are not easily articulated. Specifically, we want to teach social skills, analytical skills, and communication skills. No one seems to be able to articulate what comprises these skills. Certainly we can describe what we do at some crude level of analysis but, when we're trying to teach someone else a skill, we often fail to describe the things we do in any way that would enable our pupils to do what we are trying to teach. When we talk about experts being unable to articulate their knowledge, we're not simply talking about a lack of vocabulary, we're talking about experts' inability to gain conscious access to how they do what they do.

One of the skills that defines someone as an expert is the ability to single out the important features of a problem. Often, this is described in terms of "encoding deep structure" (Bédard and Chi 1992; Chi, Feltovich, and Glaser 1981; Reimann and Chi 1989). Experts can often look at complex problems and quickly single out where to focus their attention. While they can sometimes give post-hoc explanations of why they ignored certain solutions and focused on others, it isn't clear that any of this reasoning is going on in their conscious minds. Many studies have found that experts' abilities are heavily founded on tacit knowledge (Schon 1983; Brown, Collins, and Duguid 1989; Wilson, et al. 1993). While some of these studies discuss efforts to make tacit knowledge more explicit, the emphasis is on the "more." It just isn't clear that experts have conscious access to most of their reasoning processes.

Consider leadership, a skill we might want to teach that comprises many other skills. One leadership skill we might want to teach is the ability to select good followers. For instance, some of the best business managers are skilled at interviewing job candidates. What skills enable a manager to accurately determine whether someone will make a compatible work team member? It isn't the ability to administer a Myers-Briggs test.

A large consulting firm recently formalized their interviewing process so that it is now governed by a set of rigid rules. The result, according to several managers, is that the firm is filling up with people who could be characterized as "psychopaths with otherwise good credentials." The problem with having a rigid set of rules for performing inverviews is that managers who are skilled at interviewing typically make hiring and team formation decisions in about five minutes of conversation. They say things like "I liked the candidate," "he'll fill out the team well," and "he's pretty smart." They can tell you some of the details they noticed that may have informed their decision, but they basically have little idea how they make these rapid assessments. Nonetheless, they can make them with confidence and, in the case of managers who are skilled interviewers, with far-better-than-average accuracy (by definition).

To take another example, consider the socialization process that kids experience in school. Children learn much of how they will navigate the social world from their experiences in school. Teachers can explicitly teach children to say please and thank you and a myriad of other formal behaviors that are indeed a part of our natural socialization. However, teachers cannot explicitly teach kids most of the interesting skills required for getting along with other kids. They can neither articulate nor explicitly teach kids how to be empathetic, how to negotiate roles for themselves in the community, or how to get a date, all critical skills for navigating through life. Schools cannot teach these things not only because they are not possible to articulate in language but because, for the most part, even experts at skills like getting dates don't really understand how they do so.

At this point, many readers may be saying "Sure, we can't articulate what we know in social domains, but surely we can articulate our knowledge of mathematics or physics." Again, we would argue that this is not really the case. People can articulate how they solve textbook mathematics and physics problems and they can articulate what principles they applied when solving a particular problem. Most people cannot articulate *how* they figured out which principles to apply. If we go into more sophisticated work in these domains, involving the solution of complex novel problems or the development of theorems and proofs, even experts can only articulate some of the principles on which their theories or solutions are founded. They cannot necessarily tell you how they knew which principles to apply or what approaches to consider. Scientists, mathematicians, and engineers cannot explain the difficult and interesting aspects of physics, mathematics, and engineering they use in any way that would make either a computer or a human able to do similar work.

In fairness, some real and interesting research inroads are being made into gaining qualitative understandings of the ways engineers solve basic problems in a variety of physics-based disciplines (Forbus 1994, Forbus and Whalley 1994). Basic engineering lends itself particularly well to qualitative explanations of expert performance because the artifacts produced in engineering lend themselves to being described with rules and equations. Unfortunately, the implications of this research for education are greatly limited by the fact that most of the skills we want to teach do not lend themselves so easily to either rule-based or mathematical characterizations.

Telling Won't Work

Lecture-based education tends to be based on the wrong material because the nature of lectures limits their content. Expertise lies in experiences and one's reflections on those experiences. For the most part, sitting in lectures is the antithesis of having effective learning experiences. It is possible for a lecture to help students understand their experiences but that only works if the lecture is delivered as a support to reflection, responding to specific and meaningful challenges that students are currently facing. In those cases, lectures become answers to questions and stimuli for further reflection and inquiry.

A majority of school-based education is lecture-based. For the most part, this kind of teaching does not focus on engaging in or even examining the practices of experts. For instance, schools break education into disciplines that have little or nothing to do with the way work is done outside of academia. How many nonacademics "do" history the way it is taught in schools? Or English? Or biology? The material that schools try to teach doesn't look like the material that experts deal with (e.g., White and Frederiksen 1990). It doesn't even look like the materials of expert academics (Wiley and Voss 1996).

Course content in schools is usually carved up in ways that don't make sense outside of academia and it is usually focused exclusively on knowledge that can be explicitly taught in lectures. In other words, much of what is being taught in schools has little or nothing to do with the knowledge that comprises real expertise in a variety of domains. As Scardamalia and Bereiter (1994) wrote,

"Schooling deals with only the visible parts of knowledge: formal knowledge and demonstrable skills. Informal or tacit knowledge—both the kind that students bring in with them and the kind that they will need in order to function expertly—is generally ignored in school curricula. The result, frequently, is inert knowledge, unconnected to the knowledge that actually informs thought and behavior."

Their claim is that students are learning things in school that they cannot apply in any useful context. The medium is inseparable from the message. What students are taught is determined by the methods that are used for teaching. The information that can be represented in lectures will not capture a lot of the knowledge that experts have developed. This means that students are memorizing all sorts of equations and names and dates without having any idea how to use them.

Returning briefly to the leadership example, we can tell a student that our abilities to successfully lead teams at work involve a laundry list of things we do and skills we have. We state team goals clearly, we give praise where it is due, we're not afraid to criticize people, et cetera and so on. Some of this may even be useful to a student. However, no matter how long a list we generate, memorization of this list will never turn another person into a good leader. Knowing and even understanding a list of terms for requisite skills does not make someone able to actually perform those skills. In one study of physics students, Bransford, et al. (1989) wrote that one of the problems with teaching students skills outside of the contexts in which they will use those skills is that they tend to learn to think "about the model" rather than to think "in terms of the model." Most students who have only learned physics in lectures can pass their exams and spout physics equations but they can't use physics to explain or predict events in the world. The way to overcome this problem, ensuring that students' learning is applicable in the real world, is to have students' learning take the form of practice either in the real world or at least in approximations of it. Learning through practice in realistic contexts goes a long way toward solving the problem of developing knowledge that will transfer from educational experiences to real-world practice.

Learning in Authentic Contexts Supports Useful Future Recall

Developing knowledge that will transfer to appropriate novel situations is one of the core problems in all of education. Since educators obviously cannot put students in every possible situation they might face in the world, they must find ways to teach students skills that will transfer from the contexts in which those skills were learned to analogous novel contexts in which students may later find themselves. The ability to transfer knowledge in this way turns out to be difficult (Gick and Holyoak 1980, Gick and Holyoak 1983, Detterman 1993). The more distant the analogy between the two situations (i.e., the "farther" the transfer), the less likely it is to happen.

Knowledge transfer is a huge subject on which many tomes have been written (e.g., Detterman and Sternberg 1993, Hirschfeld and Gelman 1994). For the purposes of this chapter we simply want to characterize our strategies for tackling the problem. Transfer is about having useful remindings. In other words, it is about recalling analogous prior memories that can be effectively applied to novel situations. One way to help students to have useful remindings is to have them learn skills in similar contexts to the ones in which those skills will ultimately be used. This is because knowledge tends to be recalled in the contexts in which it was learned.[1] A problem we solved in the swimming pool may well come to mind the next time we are swimming. This is particularly so if the goals of the problem we solved are related to the context in which we solved them. For instance, a swimming problem we had while in the pool is much more likely to come to mind the next time we are in a pool than a software engineering problem we also solved in a pool. This is because pools are relevant to the goals of our swimming problem where they are not relevant to the goals of our software engineering problem. The design implications of this for education are that educational experiences should provide students with the opportunity to learn in contexts that are both similar to the contexts in which those skills will ultimately be used and relevant to the goals normally achieved in those contexts.

Goal Based Scenarios, A Learn By Doing Approach to Education

Consider three of the educational design problems we have already identified:

- Much of what experts know is known only tacitly
- Telling is an ineffective teaching strategy
- Knowledge is retained longer and recalled in more useful situations when it is learned in authentic contexts

There is an obvious, if not simple, solution to the issue of tacit knowledge and the shortcomings of teaching by telling. Well-designed learn-by-doing experiences will help students to develop the tacit knowledge of experts because learning-by-doing is how all experts developed that tacit knowledge themselves. Furthermore, learning-by-doing, if it is done in appropriate contexts is much more likely to support students' ability to recall what they have learned at times when doing so is useful.

Fundamentally, most people believe in learning by doing. After all, no one would consider a doctor to be well-qualified if she had only learned medicine from books. The question then remains, what should a learn-by-doing environment look like? In order to answer this, we want to start by describing some educational simulations we've developed which we call goal-based scenarios (GBS's). We'll start with *Return of the Wolf*,[2] a GBS designed to teach wildlife ecology to high school students.

Return of the Wolf ("Wolf" for short), is a prototype of a simulation designed to teach high school students about wildlife ecology. In Wolf, a learner is placed in the role of "rookie biologist" at a fictional national park. The simulation begins with a park ranger explaining that a pack of wolves was re-introduced into the park three years ago but that the park's wolf population appears to be declining. She then charges you with the responsibility of identifying the cause of the decline. In order to guide the park's efforts to save the wolves, you will have to determine which of five possible explanations accounts for the decline in population and provide evidence in support of your determination. Are the wolves:

Leaving the park?

Starving?

Not reproducing at a normal rate?

Dying from disease?

Being killed by humans?

At this point, you have been given a mission. Presumably it is one that would be motivating to the many high school students who like the idea of working with and helping animals.[3] In addition, you have been given a role and some details about the context in which you will work. The role provides you with more responsibility than you would normally be given as a high school student, requiring you to be the expert in making an important decision that will impact the fate of a national park's wolf population. The role also suggests some of the things you'll be doing. The context, a national park with a wolf population, is potentially motivating for students who are interested in wolves, even if only at the level of wanting to look at them. In test runs, many students were even excited to just be able to watch interesting video footage of wolves.

In order to achieve your mission, you must not only identify the cause of the problem, but also support your diagnosis with data. To gather this data, you need to do research and perform tests. The main interface lists the specific tasks you can perform in order to gather your data. You can perform field tests, review reference materials, and consult with experts. In addition, you have access to a research and field test notebook as well as a form for submitting your final report. The selection and execution of the tests, the collection of relevant expert stories and advice, and the reasoning involved in using the data to make a final recommendation are the tasks that comprise the primary "doing" part of Wolf.

Figure 1. Scenes from a video in Return of the Wolf,
simulating the capture of a wolf for examination.

Jumping into the action of the simulation, imagine that you were unsure of where to begin. In that case, you might want some advice from an expert. Fortunately, experts are readily available through the ASK system. The ASK system is a component of the simulation that provides students with the ability to ask context-relevant questions. In Wolf, it looks like a set of four buttons with questions on them, running down the right side of the screen. Which questions appear on the buttons constantly changes in order to remain relevant to the activities in which you are currently engaged. At the beginning of the simulation the questions are very general, speaking mostly to how you might get started. Examples include: "How would you research a declining wolf population?" and "What are the major reasons that wolves die?" You might want to ask the latter of these if you had a hunch that the wolves are dying off prematurely. If you did so, you would see a video of Doug Smith, a real Wolf Project Coordinator from Yellowstone National Park. To summarize his more lengthy explanation, he would tell you that wolves generally die for three reasons: starvation, disease, or being killed by other animals.

Perhaps you find Smith's mention of disease an interesting avenue to explore. It certainly has ravaged many human populations. When you're won-

Figure 2. A captured wolf, ready for examination and blood tests.
Note the expert answering a student's question on the right side of the screen.

dering about whether disease is killing off the wolves, you might want to capture a wolf and examine it. If you choose to capture a wolf, you watch video taken from inside a helicopter as it takes off and locates a wolf. The wolf is then captured with a net and your helicopter lands (see figure 1). A wolf is now lying in front of you, identified as Wolf #6, a two-year-old male, omega-status wolf (see figure 2). At this point, you can perform several types of examinations: you can weigh the wolf, test its blood and visually inspect its body. As always, the ASK system is providing you with the opportunity to ask directly relevant questions as well. Inspection of various body parts such as teeth, body, and paws, suggest that the wolf is healthy. Though a bit thin, the wolf does not appear to be starving. Blood tests reveal that he is clear of several diseases but does have a tapeworm. All of this data now appears in the field test section of your notebook.

Going to the ASK system to find out about tapeworm, you would learn that tapeworms are parasitic creatures that attach to host animals' stomach walls or intestines and consume the nutrients that the host animals eat. Since that sounds somewhat gruesome, you might argue in your report that disease is killing the wolves. To support your claim with evidence, you could include in your report the positive test for tapeworm that appeared in your field test note-

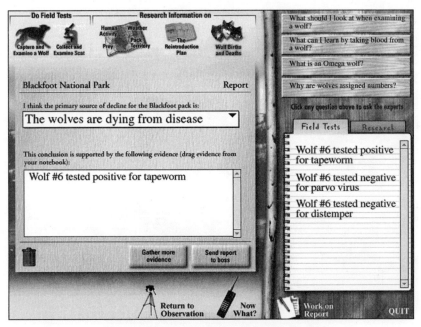

*Figure 3. A student fills out a report prematurely,
indicating that the wolves are dying from disease.*

book (see figure 3). Submitting this report would result in criticism from your
boss, the ranger. She would tell you that tapeworm doesn't usually kill wolves
and that you need to go back and do a lot more investigation. At this point, you
could return to the simulation and continue working. Perhaps now you would
be motivated to ask more questions about tapeworms or disease. Maybe you'd
want to examine other wolves, or pursue other avenues of investigation such as
researching wolf births and deaths in the park.

Although we've just given you a very brief picture of what an experience in
the simulation might look like, the complete simulation is quite complex. It's
not an egg-hunt in which you have to find the magic single clue that provides
the simple answer to the whole simulation. The actual conclusion that you
need to reach in Wolf is that: humans are bringing domestic dogs into the park;
the dogs are spreading parvo virus to the wolves; while parvo virus won't kill
adult wolves, the adults spread the disease to their puppies for whom it is fatal.
To reach this explanation, you would almost certainly have to review tables of
wolf births and deaths, test many wolves for diseases, look at maps and charts
of human presence in the park, and talk to locals. Along the way, it is very likely
that you would explore a number of other possible explanations. For instance,
at one point, a rancher with a gun talks to you menacingly about his intention
to shoot any wolf he finds near his sheep. This might lead you to explore the

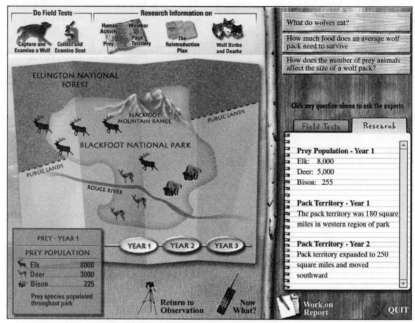

Figure 4. A map of prey which enables students
to compare prey populations over three years.

Notes about the map appear in the research section of the student's notebook on the right of
the screen.

possibility that ranchers were killing all the wolves. To give another example of
a hypothesis that you might explore, some of the maps of weather and prey
(see figure 4) could be interpreted as support for the hypothesis that the wolves
are starving. Each of these possible hypotheses represents another opportunity
for exploration and expectation failures. The system is filled with the twists,
turns and red herrings of a good mystery. At the same time, it is scientifically
realistic in the sense that the "red herrings" in the system are those that a
novice or even expert scientist might actually encounter solving a similar problem in the real world.

A Note about the Distinction Between Skills and Beliefs

We now want to talk in more detail about what learning looks like in Wolf. In
the following section we will discuss learning as a process of belief change. This
sounds somewhat antithetical to our initial position that skill development
and the acquisition of tacit knowledge are the interesting parts of learning. In
fact, it is not. To clarify this, we want to elaborate our position on the relationships between skill development and belief change. When we talk about Wolf
and goal-based scenarios in general, we often talk about developing skills by
modifying existing beliefs. We are drawing a careful distinction here between

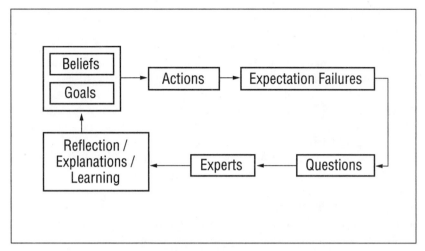

Figure 5. Learning cycle.

beliefs and skills. By skills, we mean the ability to perform certain tasks. Skills however, are founded on beliefs. We mean this in the sense that a skilled person has beliefs that enable her to make distinctions about what is and is not worth attending to when working in a domain. In this sense, beliefs are a critical component of skills, especially cognitive skills. For the purposes of this article, when we talk about skill development then, we will be focusing on the alteration of beliefs that affect performance in cognitive skills. For the most part, the beliefs we will discuss are tacit. They are not easily articulated and generally don't fall neatly into the category of propositional knowledge.

How Wolf fits into Our Learning Theory

In it's simplest form, the example of a student using Wolf that we described is an example of the learning cycle illustrated in figure 5.

Novices' beliefs and goals lead them to take the actions that they believe will achieve their goals. Novices, by definition, usually take actions that fail to achieve their goals when they take action at all. When a novice uses her beliefs to choose actions in the pursuit of her goals, and the actions she selects fail to achieve those goals, her expectations fail. If she cares about the goals she is pursuing, she will have questions about where she went wrong. Experts' stories about their own experiences with failures and successes will often be the best answers to those questions. Listening to what experts have to say will help our novice to reflect on her mistakes, explain them, and figure out how to avoid them in the future. This reflection and explanation process completes the cycle illustrated above because the results of reflection and explanation are changes in beliefs and goals.

The learning process starts with students' existing goals and beliefs. They bring these to every learning experience. High school students often come to Wolf with very general pre-existing goals like "helping animals," and "gaining responsibility for making adult decisions." The software appeals to these goals, adding the additional specific goal of helping the wolf population at the park. The student also brings a vast range of beliefs with her when she approaches the software. These probably include biases about reasons for animal mortality as well as whatever beliefs are involved in making a majority of students suspect that worms living in an animal's intestines will probably be fatal. It also includes other beliefs about medicine, health, and wildlife. The software augments the student's pre-existing beliefs by providing her with beliefs about the state of the simulated world in which she is working (i.e., the wolves are dying, they were introduced to the park three years ago, one has tapeworm, etc.). In addition to these various beliefs, the student comes to the simulation with the beliefs on which her diagnostic and investigative skills are founded. In short, the student comes to the simulation with pre-existing beliefs, skills, and goals. Her goals and beliefs are then augmented by the mission she is given and the state of the world presented in the simulation.

A person's decisions about how to act are guided by her beliefs and goals. In the hypothetical example we described, several things may have motivated the student to investigate disease in the wolf population. She may simply have suspected that the population decline was the result of disease. Perhaps she was less motivated by beliefs about animal mortality than she was by a personal goal since many students simply find it exciting to examine a wolf up-close. In this latter case, discovering the tapeworm may simply have been an incidental result of the student's general interest in examining a wolf and testing its blood. Whatever motivated her actions, it was the result of some combination of her goals and beliefs. The results of her actions added to her beliefs about the simulated world so that she now believes that one wolf does not have parvo or distemper but does have tapeworm. This is a very simple example of a student's actions having consequences that changed or augmented her beliefs.

In contrast to the simple example above, deep changes in beliefs usually involve altering or eradicating a person's strongly-held beliefs. These changes typically result from a person's discovery that her existing beliefs were wrong or inadequate (Schank 1982) and having undesirable consequences. A much more interesting belief change occurred in our Wolf example when the student's beliefs motivated her to act in a way that resulted in a failure. She used a single test result to not only form the hypothesis that the wolves were dying from tapeworm but also to confirm it. Quick to over-generalize, she assumed that her new hypothesis was correct without looking for any additional confirming or disconfirming evidence. The consequences of this mistake were a reprimand from her boss and an explanation of the nature of her error. At this point, the student knows that her existing beliefs have failed her in the pursuit of one of her goals. She has just experienced an expectation failure.

Expectation failures usually raise questions in people's minds. The expectation failure that resulted when the student's report was criticized would be likely to make her question her assumptions about tapeworm. More importantly, it would be likely to make her question the beliefs she had about hypothesis confirmation in scientific reasoning. We're not claiming that our hypothetical student will have such a well-articulated recognition of her misconceptions. Instead, she will have questions like "Where did I go wrong?" and "How can I avoid making this mistake again?" With these questions in our student's mind, we have a real opportunity for learning. Now the student is thinking about a specific expectation failure that she has experienced and wants explained.

Each question that a student has is an ideal opportunity for teaching. With questions in her mind about her expectation failures, our hypothetical student is ready to listen to an expert in an effort to learn from her mistakes. This brings us to the ASK *system* which is an integral part of any GBS. ASK systems are video repositories of experts' advice and war stories. The advice and stories are organized around a task so that they are easy for people to access as they work on that task.[4] In the case of Wolf, the ASK system is organized around the task of investigating changes in wolf populations. This organization enables students to get to the most relevant questions just when they want to ask them. The right side of the main interface in Wolf shown in figures 2, 3, and 4 includes a list of questions that students can ask of real experts who have been captured on video in the system. This list is constantly changing to reflect the specific task in which the student is currently engaged. For instance, as mentioned earlier, at the beginning of the simulation, the system lists questions about where to start. To give another example, When a student has captured a wolf and is taking blood from it, the system presents questions like "What can blood tests tell you about a wolf's health?" If you were to ask this question, an expert would explain how blood tests can identify dietary problems and diseases. ASK systems are incorporated into GBS's in order to seize the opportunity every time a student has a question.

ASK Systems support the kind of reflective process that occurs in a Socratic dialogue. They have a dialectic quality to them in which questions lead to answers and answers tend to lead to more questions. When you ask a question in an ASK system and get an answer, it usually provides you with the ability to then ask follow-up questions about the answer you received. In Wolf, if you asked the question about what blood tests can tell you about wolves' health then, after hearing the answer, you would have a list of available follow-up questions such as "What kinds of diseases kill wolves?" and "What can I tell about a wolf's diet from a blood test?" Each of these would also have follow-up questions. "How much do wolves eat?" and so on. Ideally, this goes on ad infinitum; in reality, a well-developed ASK system will typically let students go three or four levels deep before the system runs out of follow-up questions. In general, this limitation is not a problem because students tend to want to return to the action before they've gone this deep. There is more to say about ASK systems in general, but we first want to go into further detail about the pedagogical strengths of Wolf and other GBS's.

We have just described what the learning process looks like in the context of a student using Wolf. In the rest of this chapter, we will discuss the design considerations that went into constructing Wolf so that it would best support that learning process. We will start by talking about integrating failure into learning environments. We will then discuss the supports needed to help students explain their failures. The remainder of the chapter will then discuss motivation in learning environment design, including ways to keep failure from being discouraging and the cognitive significance of motivation in guiding student explanations.

Giving Students Access to Failures

Failure is critical to learning (Schank 1982, 1999). Experts are thus people who have failed many times. There is a wonderful Michael Jordan commercial for Nike. He is on screen shooting baskets and talking about all of his failures:

> I've missed more than 9,000 shots in my career. I've lost more than 300 games.
> Twenty-six times I've been trusted to take the game-winning shot—and missed.
> I've failed over and over and over again in my life.

He finishes this litany by saying "And that is why I succeed." The lesson is, if you want to be the best, you have to fail over and over again. It's old wisdom that is often overlooked. Nevertheless, it does appear manifest in many different practices. These days, venture capitalists specifically look for companies that are run by CEO's who have had failure experiences and recovered from them. They know that a person who has recovered from failure is a lot more knowledgeable and skilled than one who has never failed at all. GBS design is founded on the same belief.

We're not claiming that a person should or would prefer to go to a doctor whose patients are dying in record numbers. Obviously, one reason that experts are hired is that they make many fewer mistakes than novices. The point here is that, in order to reach the point of expertise, people first have to make and explain many mistakes. Simulations enable novices to make these mistakes in environments where the results won't be catastrophic.

GBS's develop students' expertise by providing them with quick access to failures. When the designers of Wolf began the design process, they started by asking experts about the kinds of mistakes that novices make. They asked wolf experts what mistakes novices make when dealing with issues of wildlife ecology and they asked high school science teachers what mistakes their students make in scientific reasoning. The designers knew that these mistakes were flags for parts of the domain where students had something to learn.

Working from their interviews with wolf experts and science teachers, the designers of Wolf developed a simulation that quickly brings students to the activities in wildlife ecology where novices would normally make mistakes. For instance, knowing that novices in scientific reasoning would be apt to form conclusions prematurely, they filled Wolf with small amounts of evidence in support of false conclusions. An expert would recognize the evidence as inconclusive and would investigate further in the simulation. A novice however, might see some single and insufficient piece of evidence, consider it conclusive, and submit a report based on the little information she had gathered. She would then experience an expectation failure, learning that her assessment of the evidence had been faulty.

Expectation failures signal the beginning of most learning experiences. They are a natural indication to people that there is some gap in their understanding of the world. When our expectations fail in the pursuit of a goal, we usually know that we've encountered a situation that needs explaining. Typically, this leads us to ask questions which are a starting point for forming explanations and thus learning.

The fact that expectation failures motivate most of our questions and explanations has important implications for the way we learn. Expectation failures and our explanations of them are central features of the way our memories are organized. In *Dynamic Memory,* Schank (1982) argued that we are case-based reasoners.[5] In other words, we figure out how to cope with novel experiences in the world by searching our memories for analogous prior cases or experiences. Failure is a central organizing theme in this search. When our expectations fail or when we anticipate a failure to achieve a goal, we have a strong tendency to recall analogous prior failures in the pursuit of analogous or identical prior goals (Schank 1982, Gick and McGarry 1992, Read and Cesa 1991, Van Lehn 1988b, 1991). We can use these memories to help us explain our current situation. We can also use them to overcome and/or avoid future failures.

The reasons why a goal and expectation failure-based organization for memory is useful are simple. When we are faced with a potential failure to achieve a goal in a novel situation, we would like to think of ways to avoid or overcome that failure. What better place to look than our memories of similar failures we've handled in the past?

Memories of similar failures are a way to learn from our pasts. They remind us of strategies to avoid and ways to recognize when things are going wrong. They can also help us to identify successful strategies we've used in the past to achieve similar goals. Seen in this light, experts are people who have experienced and explained many expectation failures in a particular domain; they can refer to these explanations when faced with new problems in that domain. Turning novices into experts then is a process involving giving students many opportunities to experience the right expectation failures and giving them the supports to help explain and overcome those failures.

One question that is often raised when we talk about the importance of failure to learning is, given our beliefs, why wouldn't it be better to simply use the trial by fire method for teaching and let students learn "on-the-job?" Putting aside the obvious physical, economic, and emotional dangers of serious on-the-job failures, there is a cognitive motivation for teaching some skills with simulations. While practical, real-world experience is almost always critical for developing expertise, there are many times when practice in the real world is not the most efficient way to start learning. Practicing real tasks does not necessarily quickly provide novices with many expectation failures. To give a simple example, a cashier needs to know how to handle voids, price checks, irate customers, and a host of other exceptions to the regular routine of ringing up products. A novice cashier however, could easily work at a cash register for a long time without ever having to deal with any of these situations. Common sense might get her through a number of days before she made a serious mistake. All of that time would be time spent not learning. An overly-realistic learn-by-doing environment such as real on-the-job training, may not give novices quick enough access to failure experiences. In contrast, if a simulation is well designed, it will bring students to the right failure experiences more quickly and provide them with more support for explaining those experiences just when they need that support.

Motivating Student Failure

Creating opportunities for students to fail in simulations involves more than providing them with the ability to make bad choices. We need to provide them with the influences that normally motivate people to make those choices. In simulations, we can rig things so that students find themselves in the contexts that normally motivate particular failures. For instance, let's imagine we were building a simulation to teach managers to investigate the causes of an employee's poor performance before deciding to reprimand the employee. In the simulation, we would want to create an opportunity for a manager to prematurely reprimand an employee. In a relaxed environment, this would be difficult; a manager would be less likely to make this mistake because she would feel that she had the time to investigate. On the other hand, when time is tight, deadlines are being missed and budgets are running over, a manager might no longer be willing to take the time out to investigate an employee's problem. In our simulation, we can rig things so that the employee's poor performance coincides with an extremely hectic time at the office. This "crunch" time would create the kind of pressure that often makes managers less careful with people. It's crunch time and an employee's performance looks like it is going to result in a missed deadline. Now our novice manager might start yelling at the employee without first looking for the root cause of the problem.

We have already stated that people's actions are dictated by their beliefs and their goals. Their beliefs however can be broken into two categories: beliefs about the nature of the world and beliefs about the state of the world. Beliefs about the nature of the world are our beliefs about how the world works. They are our expectations about causality and correlation in the world. For instance, we may believe that a gray sky means impending rain. If we believe that the state of the world includes a sky that is gray, our beliefs about the nature of the world will result in the expectation that rain will soon fall. These expectations may, in turn, lead us to take actions like going home to get an umbrella or canceling a picnic.

The two types of beliefs we have just described can be seen as two kinds of pressures that work in tandem to motivate us to act in particular ways. Students bring beliefs about the *nature of the world* to every educational experience. By simulating *states of the world* that typically motivate novices to fail (e.g., tight deadlines), we can lead them to act on their misconceptions and fail. When they fail, we have an opportunity to show them the inadequacies of their novice beliefs about the nature of the world and help them to develop more useful beliefs.

It is critical to stress that we are not advocating designing educational environments to deceive students into making mistakes. We are advocating identifying the pressures that motivate novices to fail in the real world, and then incorporating as many of those pressures as is credibly possible into learning environments. We refer to the influence of these pressures in a simulation as "dramatic tension." Consider another example. In Yes, another GBS built at the ILS, the student is learning negotiation skills by playing the role of an agent for an opera singer. The student's mission is to negotiate a good contract for the singer with one of the opera company's lawyers. One of the primary lessons in the GBS is that negotiators should avoid committing themselves to numbers too early in a negotiation. In Yes, the opera company's lawyer is very aggressive, continually reiterating, "Let's just get down to the numbers." Learning to handle this situation is important because it is a situation that most negotiators in the real world will face at one time or another. It is fraught with peril because it is both easy to annoy the lawyer by being evasive and easy to damage the negotiation process by committing to hard numbers too early. The interesting parts of designing failure into Yes were first figuring out what pressures exist in normal negotiations that would motivate someone to make the mistake of committing too early to numbers and then figuring out how to simulate those pressures in a credible manner in the GBS.

In the Yes example we just described, motivating the failure was reasonably straightforward. We presented students with a negotiation partner who only wants to talk about money thus forcing them to struggle with the conflicts between talking about money too soon and keeping their partner satisfied. There are many examples however, where dramatic tension in the simulation cannot be so easily copied from life. One group of students built a prototype of a GBS to teach kids how to be better babysitters. One of the lessons they wanted to teach is that watching television instead of attending to your wards is a dangerous thing to do. The problem is that babysitters in the real world are motivated to watch television because they find themselves with hours to kill in a strange house. They are also motivated to watch TV because their favorite shows are on. All of this may be difficult to simulate. The computer-based babysitting GBS isn't going to require students to sit idly for hours, isn't likely to be able to offer to show new episodes of students' favorite TV shows, and isn't necessarily going to keep students in contexts where they don't have access to the personal belongings that interest them. Here, creating dramatic tension was more difficult. We are left with the question of how we can create a credible, realistic way to motivate novice babysitters in a simulation to ignore their wards. Design challenges similar to this one arise frequently and each requires a creative solution. To give some other examples, how would you motivate a heart patient in a computer simulation to eat fatty foods and smoke? How would you motivate a politician to take bribes in an ethics simulation?

One of the best ways to discover what motivates novices to make mistakes is to talk to experts about both their own learning experiences and their experiences with novices. Once you have generated a catalog of possible motivations for a particular failure in the real world, you have to evaluate which of them can be credibly simulated. Sometimes it is impossible to motivate a failure in a simulation, given the current state of simulation technology. In these cases, it may be necessary to teach the skill through real practice in the world. Sometimes you can avoid this limitation by putting students in an advisory role, overseeing the work of a simulated novice who makes mistakes and looks to the user for advice. For instance, in a recent simulation designed at Cognitive Arts, the corporate spin-off of our lab, we taught employees about corporate ethics. We didn't try to tempt them to take bribes, which is hard to do in a simulation, but instead had them manage other people who were being tempted to take bribes. The students, faced with an advisory mission, are asked to make a credible case for why various forms of corrupt behavior are a bad idea. This forces the students to consider the consequences of corrupt behavior and also puts them in the challenging position of being a manager who has to cope with corrupt staff members.

How to Support The Explanation of Failures

In order for students to learn from their failures, we have to help them to explain where they went wrong. Just motivating a novice to fail in the pursuit of a goal she cares about will not turn her into an expert. There are many personally-meaningful goals that we never pursue because we cannot see how to do anything but fail in their pursuit. We might really want to win the lottery but not see any way to learn from our past losses. In this case, giving up is a good strategy. For many people however, failures to succeed in all sorts of tasks seem no more opportunities for skill development than does losing the lottery. Consider a bad manager in an organization. This person may genuinely want to stop running over-budget on every project but may not see a way to do so. In order to turn these failures into learning experiences, we need to provide novices with supports for explaining failures.

Novices Want to Hear Experts' Advice

Novices tend to have questions either when they fear failing or when they actually fail in the pursuit of a personally-meaningful goal. These times are "teachable moments," when students are ready to listen to explanatory stories and form their own explanations. Faced with your own failure to perform some personally-meaningful task, you are very likely to want relevant advice from an expert, so long as that expert can keep to the point and communicate clearly with you. This is just common sense.

Expert Advice Should Often Be in the Form of Stories

While prescriptive advice can be helpful, it is often not the best way to help students to understand their mistakes or remember lessons from them. Stories are more memorable because they are rich with contextual information that we can use to index them in our memories. Thus, a story about a negotiation between a lawyer and an opera singer's agent in which the lawyer is overly focused on numbers can be associated in our memories not only with negotiation strategies but also with our memories of aggressive people, opera singers, failed negotiations, and various negotiation-related plans and goals, among other things. In contrast, lessons about negotiation learned outside of the context of a particular negotiation tend to be more difficult to recall because they are less richly indexed; fewer cues in the world are apt to bring them to mind.[6]

Explanations Should be Supported Just in Time

A common educational error is to provide students with explanations about the world for which they currently have neither a simulated nor a real need. Typically, this is done in the name of "doing their homework," preparing them for some unspecified future time when they will need what they have learned. There are many problems with this strategy. First of all, we have already argued that the context for learning may determine the context of recall. By definition, the "doing-your-homework-first" kind of teaching is always done out of context in the sense that the material is being taught without students being in a situation in which they currently need to use the knowledge they are supposed to learn. Beyond the memory organization problems this causes, it also creates a motivational problem since it is often hard to stay motivated to learn something when you cannot see how it will be useful. (We will talk more about motivation later in this chapter.) Third, learning skills before they can be put to use is dangerous because there is no real check on whether you have learned them well.

Larry Birnbaum, a faculty member at our institute, often talks about a business context parallel to the problem of not having checks on what you have learned. In the last couple of decades, many businesses have realized that failure is the right time to learn. These businesses engage in what is known as "just in time" (JIT) production. The idea is quite simple: businesses should produce only what they need, minimizing the stockpiling of inventory. While JIT production offers many benefits to businesses in terms of overhead for storage and liquidity of assets, one of the most interesting benefits of the JIT strategy is that it helps businesses to learn from their mistakes.

When a company employs JIT production, they only produce their products in quantities for which there is immediate demand. For instance, where a traditional automotive muffler company would produce mufflers day in and day out, stockpiling them in anticipation of future orders from car manufacturers, a JIT manufacturer would only produce mufflers for which an order had already been placed. This means that the JIT manufacturer's mufflers will be used almost as soon as they are produced. It also means that flaws in an order of mufflers they produce are likely to come to light as soon as possible. From a learning perspective, this is ideal. It means that the people who produced the flawed mufflers are much more likely to remember how the production of the defective order varied from previous orders. This gives the company the greatest likelihood of being able to identify and then repair flaws in their production process.

In contrast to companies using JIT production, a company that stockpiles inventory might have no idea how their oldest inventory differed in production from more recent production runs. The machines that had turned out bad products might have been repaired. The workers who produced them might have been replaced. Any number of other variables in the process could have changed, leaving the company unable to identify the causes of their failed production run and thus leaving them vulnerable to similar failures in the future.

The old model of business is like the traditional model of education. Many teachers simply think of teaching as a process of packaging up knowledge and pouring it into kids' heads (Strauss and Shilony 1994). The hope is that sometime in the future, they might need that knowledge. Rather than give students the opportunity to fail, most traditional teachers simply tell them as much information as possible regardless of whether there is any immediate need for that information. This means that students are unable to see where their beliefs will fail them. We know that students don't simply know how to do things when they are told how to do them. They start by misunderstanding. If they don't have the opportunity to use what they are learning, they are free to develop more and more distorted understandings of what they are learning. With each new bit of flawed knowledge they acquire, the problem gets exponentially worse. They build more and more misunderstandings on their misconceptions. Just-in-time learning solves this. When a student learns something incorrectly or develops an insufficiently rich understanding of a problem she is facing to enable her to solve it, her failure to solve her problem is an immediate and effective mechanism for identifying gaps and misconceptions in what she has learned.

Making Failure Motivating

Failure is critical to learning but it does have the potential to be difficult and even painful. Certainly, fear of failure is one of the most profound impediments to learning. It paralyzes people so that they are afraid to try anything new. We're not claiming that it isn't a good thing when fear of failure prevents us from trying to see what happens when we jump off a cliff. The problem is that people's fears about failure are not limited to failures with catastrophic consequences. People are afraid to take new jobs, try new physical activities, speak new languages and so on all because of the possibility that they might fail, almost regardless of the severity of the consequences.

Not surprisingly, many people object to our claims that failure is critical for learning. They argue that students' motivation will be ruined by the experience of failure. In contradiction to their claim is the fact that trial and error represents much, if not most, of human learning. In all fairness, people often do find failure discouraging. This presents us with two challenges. The global challenge is to help students develop a view of the world in which modest failures are not so repugnant when they provide opportunities for learning. The more local challenge is for us to find ways to prevent people who already have some fear of failure from giving up when they experience minor failures while learning in our simulations. For this chapter, we'll focus on the smaller challenge.

The first way to minimize the discouragement that any failure can cause is to lessen the humiliation of failure. Public humiliation is one of the most common sources of pain that people fear. Computer simulations lessen the threat of public humiliation to learners. They enable students who are overly-concerned about public humiliation to fail privately. When they screw up, they aren't being watched by a room full of peers who might ridicule them. The only one looking is a computer.

A second way to minimize discouragement from failures is to make it clear to students that the consequences of their failures will be limited. Many people worry that failing in an unfamiliar domain might have unforeseen catastrophic consequences. For example, many new computer users are afraid to get started using a computer because they worry that they might somehow permanently damage the mysterious, expensive, and incomprehensible box in front of them. Done right, simulations solve this. While failures in simulations may have significant simulated consequences, students still know that they are just simulated consequences. A well-designed simulation will enable students to experience simulated failures that have a strong but tolerable emotional impact on them. It will not allow them to make real catastrophic mistakes and it will not forcibly expose them to public humiliation for their simulated mistakes.

Lessening the trauma of failure is not enough to keep students using our software. In order to prevent students from being discouraged by experiences of failure in our simulations we need to provide them with motivations that either outweigh the unpleasant aspects of those failures or distract students from them. Think of a child who falls and scrapes her knee twenty or thirty times before she's learned to skate. Unless she is tragically frail or doesn't care about skating, a scraped knee and the threat of future scraped knees don't keep her from getting back up and trying again. She is willing to scrape quite a few knees because she considers it to be a small price to pay for being able to roller skate.

Strangely, motivation is mostly overlooked in the literature on education. It is nonetheless critical for both cognitive and humanitarian reasons. The relationship between motivation and cognition is complex, involving the ways our memories and our goals affect the ways we understand events taking place in the world around us. The humanitarian reasons are more straightforward so we'll start with those.

On a humanitarian level, we've already talked about ways to mitigate the pains associated with failure in learning. We see another serious humanitarian concern with regard to motivation in education. Simply put, school is often painfully boring. How many kids come to school each day to sit and count the hours until each school day ends? "School" isn't much more fun for adults. Most corporate training is modeled after the dullest types of school education. In both contexts, students are typically expected to spend most of their time sitting silently as the passive recipients of lectures. In both contexts, the relationship between the content of the lectures and the goals of the students is rarely clear to the students (if such a relationship even exists). The boredom that inevitably accompanies this kind of education simply isn't necessary. Worse, it's destructive. Boring education is creating children and adults who hate learning. It's also focusing workers on the drudgery that is so often a large part of their jobs.

Of course, there is dull content in most things we learn. Before we can design a house, we need to learn a lot of relatively dull facts about building materials. When people pick this knowledge up as they need it however, the learning process is relatively painless. A bunch of facts about the dietary needs of wolves can be incredibly dull unless they help someone to solve an interesting problem related to wolves. Many dull facts become interesting if learned in a context that brings their utility to light. Some facts remain dull in and of themselves, but are less painful to memorize when it is in the service of a motivating goal.

Creating the right motivations in an educational experience will help students to look past the pain of their failures to see ways that those failures are helping them to achieve their goals. The links between goals and motivation are so tight that it is sometimes hard to distinguish between the two. There may be goals that aren't accompanied by motivation however, there is no motivation that is not accompanied by goals. Motivation always has an end in mind, no matter how vaguely defined that end or the means to it may be. We may be motivated to accomplish simple goals like avoiding physical pain or highly complex goals like developing a better ability to communicate with a lover. Aside from unadulterated interest, motivation is really anything that enables us to expend effort or tolerate discomfort in the belief that we are working towards some higher goal. What is interesting about this in the context of this chapter is the fact that the goals that motivate us will determine both whether we learn and what we learn.

Motivation and Cognition

Many people who design education don't understand motivation or its importance to education. These people mostly fall into two categories: the "borrowed interest" people and the "eat-your-spinach" people. The borrowed interest people argue that things like chemistry can be made motivating by incorporating nonchemistry-related motivations into lessons. They use the same old chemistry problems found in textbooks but they dress them up with irrelevant contextual motivations like superheroes, lecturers in clown suits, or equivalents to them. The "eat-your-spinach" people argue that you simply must learn chemistry and feel either that this alone means you should enjoy it or else feel that enjoyment and interest are simply irrelevant. In this section, we will argue that both the borrowed interest people and the eat-your-spinach people are wrong because students' motivations affect what they learn.

The reasons that you are motivated to do something or learn something will directly affect the way you interpret new experiences and store them in memory. We want to talk about three ways that motivation affects cognition. First, insofar as motivation and goals are tightly linked, motivation will affect what you learn because what you learn and how your memories are organized are both determined by the goals you have when you are learning. We'll call this the indexing issue. Second, motivation affects the degree to which you pay attention when you are participating in a learning activity. Third, motivation determines whether you participate in a learning activity at all. We'll call these last two the attention and participation issues.

The Indexing Issue

If explanation is fundamental to most learning then what we learn is determined greatly by the way we reason about our expectation failures. Goals are an important part of reasoning since they greatly influence what we attend to when figuring out how to respond to a new experience. They influence the ways in which we mentally encode (and thus later recall) the problems or situations that we face (Schank 1982, Barsalou 1991, Ross 1996, Trzebinski and Richards 1986). This is well illustrated by the "Yes" GBS discussed earlier.

"Yes" was designed to teach people how to negotiate. One of the most important things to teach in negotiation is that the goal of a good negotiator is to collaboratively construct a solution that is mutually acceptable to all involved parties. Good negotiators are not trying to defeat the other involved parties in an argument. The difference between these two goals (collaboration and argumentation) is completely determinative of the strategies that a negotiator will take and is usually determinative of the ultimate outcome of the negotiations.

With the goal of winning an argument, a negotiator faced with an agreement she doesn't like will recall argumentation strategies in an effort to defeat her opponent. For instance, she may spend much less time looking at the needs and desires of her opponent, tending to recall threat strategies and other intimidation tactics. In contrast, a negotiator with the goal of collaboratively constructing a solution is more likely to be reminded of strategies for collaboration and compromise. This negotiator would be apt to recall prior memories of consensus building during negotiations. She might think of strategies for acknowledging concessions made by other parties and might give more attention to their needs, looking for win-win situations. Her goals will determine the remindings she has and her remindings will determine the tactics she uses. In short, a person's goals play a large part in determining her actions because they play a large part in determining which memories are activated when she is pursuing her goals (Seifert, et al. 1986).

Of course, what we've just described are memory recall and reasoning processes; we haven't said anything about learning. Recall that in Yes, the student is playing the role of an opera singer's agent, negotiating with a lawyer who represents an opera company. Let's imagine that our student thought up and pursued a clever strategy that backed the opera company's lawyer into a corner and acted on it. She might expect the lawyer to realize that making concessions was his best option. When the lawyer instead turned vicious, she might be surprised, and she would probably want to figure out what went wrong. Here, her goals would affect her learning on two levels. First, the goals she was pursuing when she experienced the surprise, such as her goal to defeat the lawyer, would be an index point into memory for that surprise. That way, the next time she is negotiating with lawyers or pursuing similar goals, she can recall the particular mistake she made and try avoid making it again. Second, the goals she had as a learner will affect the explanations she forms for what went wrong.

If a negotiator thinks of negotiation as war and has warlike goals, then she may explain her failures and expectation failures in warlike terms, worrying that she didn't set up a solid enough defensive strategy or wasn't aggressive enough. If, instead, she thinks of negotiation as collaboration, she may explain failed negotiations by evaluating whether she adequately explored the needs of the party with whom she was negotiating. This explanation is a product of her goals and the parts of her memory that were used to form the explanation. When she has formed the new explanation, she will store it in her memory, indexed according to these goals and according to the memories on which the explanation was based. What she learns from her failures is thus directly affected by the particular goals she perceives herself to be failing.

Preventing Students from Trying to "Game" the System

The effects of people's goals on what they learn should be a serious concern for any educational software designer. Too often, students approach educational software the way they approach most standardized multiple choice tests. They work in the software with an eye towards beating the system or completing the test in the software. They do this instead of focusing on what the software might actually be intended to teach. This is mostly the result of bad software design, but it is motivated by technological limitations as well.

It doesn't look like we're close to having AI technology that will enable computers to give intelligent critiques of free-form student work in nontechnical domains. In the mean time, educational software that teaches skills in domains that aren't well simulated with mathematics and rules will be forced into having some underlying multiple choice characteristics. Without the multiple choice structure, current software just isn't smart enough to comment on students' work. When we teach wildlife ecology in Wolf, we can't simply let students make any diagnosis they want. We have to constrain their options to some degree in order to ensure that our system will have intelligent things to say when students make mistakes. In general, this need for constraints on students' actions poses a serious challenge for education designers who want to teach something other than airplane piloting or Newtonian mechanics (i.e. content in nonmathematical or nonrule-based domains). They have to find ways to prevent constrained sets of choices from feeling like multiple choice tests. Otherwise, students will start to reason about their learning activities in terms of multiple choice strategies. Rather than learning real-world skills like hypothesis evaluation, they will develop standardized test-taking skills like searching for keywords and eliminating two choices before randomly picking among the other three.

Needless to say, students' gaming the system is a problem that long pre-dates educational software. John Bruer summarized research on traditional word problems done at Vanderbilt:

> Children hate word problems, don't understand their purpose and see them as just another weird school task. (Cognition and Technology Group 1992). However, being clever they approach theses tasks appropriately. The trick is to figure out which mathematics operation to apply to the quantities stated in a problem to the

get the correct answer. Children use a superficial but adequate strategy: they look for a key word that reveals which operation to use. (Bruer 1993).

Whenever students are being taught something out of context, there is a danger that they will try to find a way to circumvent the hard lesson in favor of a quick solution. First of all, it's always efficient to look for quick solutions. Second, students' interest in finishing an activity quickly is highly correlated with their interest in what it is they are doing. Bored students want to get through simulations as fast as possible. In the process, they lose the fiction of the simulation and begin to think like simulation gamers rather than thinking like someone who is trying to successfully perform the target task. When this happens, their goals change. The explanations they begin to form for their mistakes stop being relevant to the target task and instead relate solely to getting through the simulation quickly.

In order to prevent students from losing the fiction of a simulation and losing their focus on its mission, education designers need to present them with realistic, motivating contexts for learning. This is because students are less likely to try to game a learning system if they are excited about and engaged in the activities they are doing. For instance, if a student is really excited about building rockets, she is much less likely to try to game a chemistry learning activity if the chemistry work is integral to her mission to design fuel for the rocket she is designing.

An important, and often-overlooked aspect of creating motivating contexts for learning is the need to provide students with sufficiently complex problems that they will both perceive the problems as interesting and be unlikely to be able to make lucky guesses in order to solve them. Problem complexity is thus one solution to the multiple choice problem. Perhaps more important however, is the need to present students with realistic choices. If the alternatives to expert performance in a simulation (i.e. action options that are bad choices to select) seem false, students will stop believing in the simulation and begin thinking in terms of how to beat it. To avoid this and keep students thinking in terms of the problems presented in the simulation, designers need to provide credible choices that anticipate a realistic range of actions that novices might take. In order to do this, they must observe experts and novices performing the tasks that the simulation is intended to teach. It is the most common action choices of both experts and novices that should be available as options for students in any simulation.

Typically, when we design software, we start by designing an "expert path," identifying the actions that an expert would take to perform the target task. We then examine the expert path for points in which experts and novices diverge in their actions. From these points of divergence, we identify the choices that result in novices' failures. Each choice that, in real practice, results in many novices failing represents a point in the simulation where we should give students the same choice. An important part of the solution to the gaming problem then is to keep students engaged in the fiction of the simulation by providing them with a range of choices that matches the range of choices they would be likely to consider. We do this through observation of real task performance and through discussion with experts and novices.

Motivation, Attention and Participation

Fundamentally, the solution to the gaming problem in schools and software lies in designing educational experiences that foster interest and require that students have understanding as a primary goal. This is a dangerous claim to make because lots of "educational reformers" use the concept of "understanding as a goal" to simply mean better test performance or trivially wider applicability of lessons learned. What we mean when we use the term is that students need to have as a goal, the desire to master or at least successfully execute some useful task that is, at some level, of personal interest.

Whether or not your learning environment is motivating (i.e. appealing to students' goals), will greatly affect the degree to which your students' pay attention to what they are learning or even participate in learning activities at all. If educational activities are not motivating, students will do their best to avoid participating in them. The educational disadvantages of that are self-evident. If however, students are forced to participate in activities that are not motivating then, as we discussed in the section above, they will do their best to focus their attention anywhere but on the material they are supposedly being taught. Pointing back to our discussion of the importance of expectation failures in learning, the less attention a student pays to what she is doing, the less likely it is that what she is doing will stimulate her to have relevant expectations. Without these expectations, she cannot have the expectation failures necessary for learning.

We previously discussed the ways in which students try to game the system when they are forced into activities for which interest has not been generated. "Gaming" is about minimizing the effort expended to solve whatever challenges you face at the expense of understanding the challenges or their solutions deeply. This means that even when an unmotivated student does experience an expectation failure, discovering, for instance, that she needs to test her scientific hypotheses more carefully, she is likely to respond by taking the expedient route, either forming no explanation or else forming the simplest one possible. The result is poorly-formed and poorly-indexed explanations of the material to be learned. It is knowledge that is likely to neither be recalled at useful times nor useful when recalled at all.

The degree to which we pay attention to experiences we are having is greatly determinative of what we remember (Langer 1989). For instance, experiences that have resulted in strong emotional responses tend to hold our attentions. This results in lasting memories of those experiences. In contrast to the consequences of emotionally evocative experiences, we simply do not attend to things about which we do not care. We are constantly filtering out or ignoring experiences and perceptions that don't interest us. If educational experiences do not captivate students' interest, they are mostly ignored and little or no learning takes place.

Everything we've said about motivation points back to a need to appeal to students' goals. It is important to note however that we are not claiming that educators cannot help students to develop new goals. Quite the contrary, helping students to define and develop new goals is an important function of education. The development of new goals however, must be founded on students' existing goals. A student who is interested in rocket ships can easily become interested in some aspects of chemistry if they will help her to design her own rocket ship. Some of the same chemistry might be interesting to an art enthusiast if it were learned in the service of helping her to design new glazes or paints. Seen in the service of some higher personal goal, student interest is easily developed in a myriad of disciplines.

Goals focus our attention, determining the ways we interpret new experiences and encode them in our memories. They also determine which of our remindings we select as useful when dealing with new experiences. The goals we have when we are learning determine what we learn. They determine whether the knowledge we acquire will be useful. The wrong goals may mean that something a person learns will not be indexed in her memory in useful ways, making it difficult or impossible to recall when it is needed. In short, students' goals must be a driving force in the design of learning environments because they will determine both what students learn and how effectively they do so.

GBS's In Use

In this chapter, we have tried to describe some of the key principles on which the design of all educational simulations should be founded. To illustrate the scope and power of these principles, we would like to briefly describe the range of skills taught in our simulations and the ways our simulations are currently being used to substantially improve education and training.

We have been building GBSs for more than eight years at the ILS. Using our proprietary authoring tools, students, faculty, and staff members have been able to construct hundreds of prototype systems. Though we have been selective about which projects we develop to completion, we have developed roughly twenty complete GBS's at The ILS. We have developed perhaps another twenty to twenty-five reasonably rich prototype systems as well. Some examples of completed systems include:

Sickle Cell Counselor, one of our first systems, designed to teach high school-age or younger children about sickle cell anemia. In it, you play a counselor who must run various tests and then use the results to advise various couples about the risks of their children being born with sickle cell anemia.

French Revolution, a system designed to teach college students French history. In it, students go back in history to try to persuade the various factions in the French revolution not to have a war.

Yes (discussed above), a system designed to teach professionals how to negotiate. In it, students negotiate on behalf of various characters including an opera singer who is being considered for a role in a major opera.

Fire Commander, a system designed to teach grade school students about fires and fire prevention. In it, students command a fire team as it works to rescue people and put out a fire in a burning house.

Nutrition Clinician, a system designed to teach medical students about nutrition. In it, students see patients with various health problems and make nutritional recommendations for them.

Is it a Rembrandt, a system designed to teach undergraduates about the Rembrandt School of painting. In it, students must authenticate various paintings by examining them, running tests on them, and talking to various connoisseurs, professors, and curators.

Crisis in Krasnovia (discussed above), a system designed to teach high school students about modern political history and give them insight into the recent Balkan Crises. In it, students must advise a simulated U.S. president on how to handle a crisis in a fictional country called Krasnovia that is analogous to the crisis in the Balkans.

Several of these systems have been used to replace a day or two of undergraduate classes at Northwestern University. In addition, Sickle Cell Counselor was deployed in several museums. Students have expressed great enthusiasm for virtually every ILS system we've deployed. To give one example, the following paragraph comes from a study of Sickle Cell Counselor done by its authors:

> Officials at the museum told us that visitors spend, on average, 1.5 minutes at a display. It was unclear therefore whether museum goers would spend the requisite time using the system or make use of the variety of videos. ... If we consider all 1,416 transcripts, the average time using the system is 5 min. 33 sec. If we consider only the 1,126 transcripts that remain after excluding the people who quickly walk away, the average time using the system is 7 min. (Bell, et al. 1993, p. 367).

Of course, enthusiasm is at most half the battle. After answering the question "Do they use it?" we have to answer the question "Do they learn from it?" Ironically, the majority of the people who have been willing to pay to answer this question have been corporate rather than academic clients. To get a sense of whether students learn more from GBS's, we have to turn to work done at Cognitive Arts, a corporate spin-off of The ILS.[7] Cognitive Arts has built and deployed roughly 180 GBS's since it was founded roughly six years ago. Our client list includes corporations such as GE Capital, IBM, First Union, Deloitte Consulting, Eaton, Hewlett Packard and Merrill Lynch. In addition, we have built systems in partnership with Columbia and Harvard University. The systems we develop with them are delivered on CD-ROM and via the Web. Some are also delivered as live, human-run simulations. GBS's have taught people everything from how to run a cash register to how to run a business. We have designed systems to teach not only so-called "hard" procedural skills but also "soft" skills such as management coaching, interviewing, and delivering great call center customer service.

Similar to our findings with software developed at The ILS, studies we have run with Cognitive Arts' clients again find that students find GBS's more engaging and enjoyable than traditional training. In addition, these studies show that GBS's often shorten training times and almost always improve student performance substantially over traditional training. In one study with a Fortune 500 financial services corporation, for instance, new customer service representatives (CSR's) who used our GBS's shortened their call handling times by 6 seconds per call in comparison to expert CSR's. They did this with no loss in customer service quality and performed at a level close to that of expert CSRs. In comparison to novice CSR's who had taken traditional training, the difference is even more drastic. The average call time of GBS-trained novice CSR's was 29 seconds shorter than the average call time for a novice CSR who was traditionally-trained. Across roughly 50 million calls per year, even a six second reduction in each call represents a huge savings to our client. Needless to say, having new employees who can perform with the skill of highly-experienced employees also represents a substantial cost savings and improvement in training.

To give another example, a different population of employees at the same corporation described above went through a compliance training GBS we developed. These students performed significantly better than people who had been through a general orientation on compliance and read a standard booklet on compliance policy. Specifically, the GBS-trained students were significantly better at recognizing potential compliance violations and significantly less likely to miss violations. In addition, students who went through the GBS consistently reported that they found it engaging and enjoyable, a claim we cannot make of the more traditional training that was previously used.[8] In short, we have consistently found that students using GBS's develop more effective skills more efficiently than they do in traditional training and enjoy the learning process more as well.

Conclusion

If you take only two things away from this chapter, we hope that they will be strengthened beliefs about the importance of motivation and the importance of failure in educational experiences. We have focused on the design of software but our claims are every bit as relevant to the classroom. Education is a process of developing expertise and expertise is acquired through the experience and explanation of many interesting failures. Motivating students is critical to this process for, without motivation, students will neither risk failure, nor expend the effort to thoughtfully explain their failures.

In order to develop the best educational experiences for students, we must spend time with experts and novices, figuring out what mistakes novices make and what motivates these mistakes. We must then design engaging learning experiences that both provide students with access to these motivations and mistakes and provide them with expert supports to explain their mistakes.

Notes

1. This is a recurring theme in research in anchored instruction (Bransford, et al. 1990, Bransford and Stein 1993, Cognition and Technology Group at Vanderbilt University 1992) and Situated Cognition (Brown, et al. 1989).

2. This GBS was designed by Tanneke Dillingh, Robert Schnieders, and Todd Carter with assistance from Marko Krema and a number of faculty members at The Institute for the Learning Sciences.

3. It is worth noting that wolves were selected because many high school students seem to find them particularly interesting animals.

4. For more discussion of the theoretical underpinnings of ASK systems, see Bareiss and Osgood (1993).

5. A vast array of subsequent research supports this claim. Kolodner (1993), for instance, cites Lancaster and Kolodner (1987); Kopeikina, Bandau, and Lemmon (1988); and Klein and Calderwood (1988) among many others.

6. The complexities of the relationship between memory and stories is beyond the scope of this chapter. For a more detailed exploration, see Schank (1982, 1992).

7. Formerly known as The Learning Sciences Corporation, Cognitive Arts is the for-profit spin-off of The Institute for the Learning Sciences. At Cognitive Arts, we use the Institute's technologies to develop GBSs for corporations and, more recently, for universities as well.

8. The results of all of these studies are unpublished because they are competitive data. They were communicated to me in January and February, 2000 through informal conversations with Ray Bareiss, an executive vice president and senior design architect who has been with Cognitive Arts since its inception.

Chapter Three

Technology Support for Complex Problem Solving

From SAD Environments to AI

*Gautam Biswas, Daniel Schwartz, John Bransford,
and the Teachable Agents Group at Vanderbilt*

For the past decade, the Cognition and Technology Group at Vanderbilt (CT-GV) has been studying how technology can help students learn to approach the challenges involved in solving complex problems and learning about new topics. Work centered around our video-based *Jasper Woodbury Problem Solving Series* represents one example; a book written by our group summarizes this work (CTGV, 1997). A summary of work that goes beyond the Jasper series appears in CTGV (1998).

We note in the Jasper book (CTGV, 1997) that our work began with simple, interactive videodisc technology, plus software for accessing relevant video segments on a "just-in-time" basis. We needed the interactivity because Jasper adventures are twenty-minute video stories that end with complex challenges for students to solve. All the data relevant to the challenges (plus lots of irrelevant data that students have to sort through) have been embedded in the story line. An overview of the Jasper Series is illustrated in figure 1; a brief description of one of the Jasper adventures, *Rescue at Boone's Meadow* (RBM), appears in figure 2.

After viewing a Jasper adventure, students usually work in groups to solve the challenge. (A CD-ROM that accompanies the Jasper book illustrates this process; see CTGV, 1997.) To succeed, students need access to the data embedded in the Jasper story. Even if they cannot remember the details about required data, they can usually remember where in the story the data had been provided. The software lets them return to the relevant part almost instantly. For example, in the RBM adventure, students may return to the flying field scene to review how

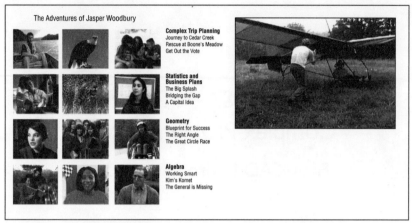

Figure 1. (left) The twelve adventures of Jasper Woodbury.
Figure 2. (right) Overview of the Jasper adventure, Rescue at Boone's Meadow.

much fuel an ultralight contained; go to the restaurant scene to find a conversation that explained how large the landing field was in Boone's Meadow; access Dr. Ramirez's office to review how far it was from one city to the next, and so forth. An example of the visually organized, random-access environment for RBM is illustrated in figure 3.

The software environments developed for each of the twelve Jasper adventures are very simple for students and teachers to use and extremely helpful as a support for student learning. From the perspective of AI, however, the software is trivial. Our approach to research has been to start with stone-age design (SAD) environments, and add sophistication and complexity only as necessary to achieve our instructional goals. Our SAD approach has allowed us to work closely with hundreds of teachers and students and, in this process, identify and test situations where increased technology support can further facilitate learning. In this chapter we especially emphasize situations where AI insights and techniques have become extremely helpful.

We will describe two examples where principles from AI have allowed us to improve student learning. One involves creating an AdventurePlayer program, plus offshoots of that program, to accompany the Jasper series (Crews et al. 1997). A second involves the use of AI techniques to create "teachable agents" whom students explicitly teach to perform a variety of complex activities. (The emphasis on teachable agents is different from an emphasis on learning agents that learn on their own without explicit teaching and without assessments of the adequacy of the agents' new knowledge. In other words, our teachable agents do not have machine learning algorithms embedded into their reasoning processes.) Our work on teachable agents is quite new, so the ideas and data we present are still preliminary. We hope

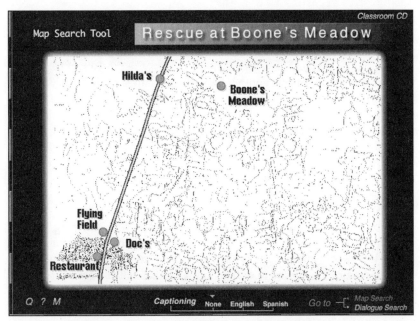

*Figure 3. Map controller software for randomly accessing
video scenes from* Rescue at Boone's Meadow.

that our discussion of this project will help connect us with others who can
provide insights about ways that we can strengthen and accelerate our current work.

An Example of Moving from SAD to AI

As noted above, our approach to research and development has been to begin
with very simple uses of technology (SAD) and work in classroom settings to
identify instances where increased technological sophistication could have a
significant impact on student (and often teacher) learning. One example
comes from our work on transfer. Our early data on Jasper showed that after
students solved a Jasper challenge, they were better able to solve similar, complex challenges (e.g., CTGV, 1997, chapter 4; Van Haneghan et al. 1992). However, their abilities to transfer were still relatively brittle and inflexible (CTGV,
1997, chapters 4 and 5). One reason is that teachers sometimes had difficulty
managing the learning of all the students in the classroom, so their degree of
initial learning was not sufficient to support transfer (e.g., see Bransford,
Brown, and Cocking 1999 for an overview of the transfer literature). Another
reason was that research on transfer shows that learning can be "welded" to a

particular concrete context and that transfer can suffer unless it is facilitated by opportunities to see concepts applied in multiple contexts rather than only one (e.g., Bransford et al. 1999; Gick and Holyoak 1980, 1983).

Our original plan had been for teachers to always use at least two Jasper adventures that build on one another. For example, after students solved RBM (which involves concepts of distance, rate and time in the context of trip planning), teachers could present *Journey to Cedar Creek* (which involves distance, rate and time in the context of a boat trip). However, teachers often did not desire, or have the time, to ask their students to solve two adventures that related to the same topic. Instead, many wanted to move to Jasper adventures that focused on other topics like introductory statistics, geometry and algebra. As a consequence, we faced the challenge of designing a series of adventures that could be used flexibly yet also overcome impediments to transfer.

We found that we could increase the flexibility of students' learning by having them solve a series of "what-if" problems after solving a Jasper adventure (CTGV, 1997). For example, the challenge of RBM is to find the fastest way for Emily to rescue an eagle and to explain how long that will take (most students' solutions make use of an ultralight that is shown in the adventure). After students solve the initial challenge they complete what-if problems that ask questions such as: What if the speed of the ultralight was x rather than y, how would that have affected the rescue? What if the fuel capacity was a rather than b, how would that affect your current plan to rescue the eagle? Flexibility and the ability to transfer also increase when students solve analog problems like Lindbergh's flight from New York to Paris. (His planning for the trip is very similar to the planning required to rescue the eagle in RBM.)

We used videodisc technology to deliver the what-if scenarios and analog problems. A limitation of this approach was that we could only present a limited set of "canned" problems. In addition, our computer environment did not allow us to present feedback to students about their planning and thinking—this had to be left to the teacher. When one is teaching 20 to 30 students, providing "just-in-time" feedback is an extremely difficult task. In addition, we found that students liked to explore their own what-if scenarios and even create scenarios for others. This was not possible with the "canned" problems that we had used.

Efforts to develop a more flexible, feedback–rich environment brought us to our first attempt to use some of the techniques made possible through AI. The result was AdventurePlayer, developed initially by Thad Crews and Gautam Biswas in consultation with the Jasper group. It allows students to work either alone or in groups to attempt to solve a Jasper problem and what-if analogs, and to see the effects of their efforts via a simulation (figure 4). For example, if they have not accounted for fuel needs, the plane has to land prematurely or it crashes. Students can then go back and revise their planning. If they get terribly stuck, they have access to a coach. AdventurePlayer is designed both to fa-

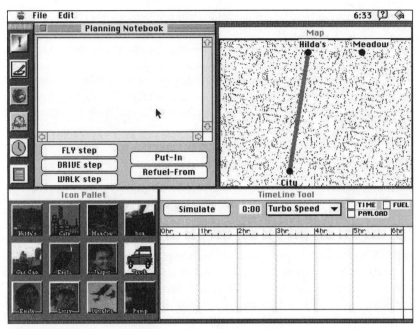

Figure 4. AdventurePlayer interface.

cilitate initial learning of each Jasper adventure and to promote flexible transfer with "what-if" scenarios.

AdventurePlayer combines features of intelligent tutoring systems (ITS)
(Wenger 1987) and cognitive tools (Lajoie and Derry 1993). The system provides an intelligent simulation environment that enables students to test partial
(and complete) solutions to problems and receive feedback. Unlike traditional
ITS (e.g., Anderson et al. 1990) the focus is not on student modeling (i.e., discovering the students' misunderstandings) or how their errors should be corrected.
The feedback mechanisms borrow from the cognitive tools framework in which
the emphasis is on highlighting important aspects of the domain and the problem solving techniques. In AdventurePlayer the feedback is designed to make
explicit the consequences of errors and incompleteness in defining and execut-
ing solution steps. For example, if a student fails to check the payload on the ultralight, and the total weight is too great, the ultralight fails to take off. Similarly,
if the student specifies an excessive flying time from the city to Boone's Meadow,
the ultralight flies past its destination. We have tried to stage the feedback so
students can readily map explicit failures onto the relevant parameters of their
plans. Ideally, this helps students learn to identify, reflect upon, and correct
their own errors. However, if students continually experience difficulty, they also have access to the coach (we say more about this below).

AI techniques and representation mechanisms also underlie a suite of AdventurePlayer tools that assist students in their problem solving efforts. For example, the environment includes an information pallet that enables students to access information about people, locations, vehicles, and distances that are part of the video adventure. There is a planning notebook that students use to sequence their solution steps while considering the resources they need to make their solution steps work. There is also a timeline tool to help students organize their solution steps, and to assign start and completion times for each of the steps.

The planning notebook and timeline tool present important representational structures that we hope students will appropriate as their own. They also serve as scaffolds by simplifying the planning and calculation tasks that may otherwise overwhelm students in their problem solving. Our pedagogical strategy is to offer scaffolds that permit students to freely explore the problem space and experience complex problem solving without excessive floundering. We gradually remove the scaffolds as students move on to solve analogous "what if" problems and other related adventures.

Overall, the intelligent simulation and its suite of tools provide students with an exploratory environment for guided discovery learning. Such environments have been criticized because they can frustrate students who cannot recover from errors during problem solving or who get stuck at a plateau of performance. This is why we have also implemented a coaching system (cf. Burton and Brown 1979) that observes student problem solving, and intervenes to make suggestions at specific points in the problem solving process. The coaching system is useful because the task of generating working plans in the RBM domain is complex for middle school students, and in many cases they generate incomplete plans (Van Haneghan et al. 1992). The trip planning coach helps move students to the next level; for example, by assisting them in generating an optimal solution to the trip-planning problem once they have a feasible plan to rescue the eagle. The reasoning engine of the coach employs a generic algorithm that combines hierarchical planning and best first search. A small set of predefined heuristics guide the search process. After a student generates a complete solution, the coach intervenes to ask if the student could find a better solution. If the student says no, the coach compares the optimal solution to the student's solution, and based on the differences, makes a number of suggestions to the student directing him or her toward a more optimal solution. Details of the coach and the AdventurePlayer system appear in Crews et al. (1997).

Data show that the use of the Jasper AdventurePlayer software greatly facilitates students' abilities to solve RBM (Crews et al. 1997). For example, we know from early studies on Jasper that students working alone can have difficulty solving the challenges (e.g., CTGV 1997, chapter 4; Van Haneghan et al. 1992). Their performance levels are higher when teachers guide the learning process and when they can work collaboratively in groups (see CTGV, 1997). However,

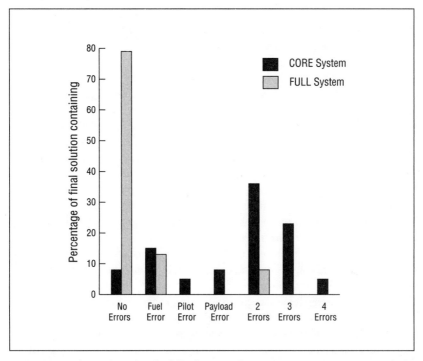

Figure 5. Student gains using the full AdventurePlayer system versus a core system that only includes the planning tool and the information pallet.

teachers often have difficulty managing the complexity of helping each student learn to solve each adventure. AdventurePlayer is very effective in managing this complexity.

In one study we tested AdventurePlayer by asking sixth grade students, who had no prior experience solving Jasper problems, to solve the problem by themselves. From previous studies (e.g., Van Haneghan et al. 1992, CTGV, 1997), we knew that even students who scored very high on standardized tests of mathematical skills and understanding were not prepared to deal with Jasper-like problems; instead, they were used to dealing with simple one- and two-step word problems. So we wanted to see if AdventurePlayer could help the students succeed. Overall, students performed much better in the AdventurePlayer environment than when solving a Jasper adventure on their own.

In our study, we also varied the support provided by AdventurePlayer by turning off some of its key features and comparing students' learning in these situations with ones where all the features were operable. Figure 5 shows that the full system led to fewer errors in sixth-grade students' final RBM solutions compared to a partial system called the CORE system. The CORE system simply provided students with the map interface, information pallet, and planning tool, but not the simulation environment, timeline tool, and coach. Additional data showed that seventy-nine percent of the students who used the complete simulation environment generated a complete plan compared to only eight percent of the students who used the CORE system.

In more recent work (Katzlberger 1998), the AdventurePlayer design has been generalized using a generic object-oriented architecture for problem solving with visual interfaces that retain the pedagogic characteristics of the original AdventurePlayer system. The environment uses Java internet foundation classes (Netscape) making it accessible remotely via the Web. Domain experts can build problem-solving environments as subclasses of the abstract simulation class. The simulation contains and displays actors implemented as "agents" that perform roles based on properties assigned to them. Class libraries provide support for implementing many different kinds of actors.

This framework has been extended by introducing agents that add additional "intelligence" to the environment and to the interaction between the student and the environment (cf., Lester et al. chapter 8). Agents come in various forms. Some are assistants that help users retrieve relevant data and remind them of salient features about the domain. Others watch user actions to keep track of their preferences and their progress in problem solving tasks. Still others act as coaches to help students who make repeated errors or generate suboptimal solutions with their problem solving steps. Agents have been designed to take on characteristics of some of the actors in the Jasper adventures (Balac, Katzlberger, and Leelawong 1998). As a result, students encounter multiple interaction styles and a variety of opportunities for learning.

One of the major goals of recasting AdventurePlayer in an object-oriented architecture has been to support a reconceptualization of the Jasper series—a reconceptualization that emphasizes the importance of invention and modeling in order to "work smart" in particular environments. As an illustration, note that the Jasper Adventure *Rescue at Boone's Meadow* (RBM) asks students to solve a single problem—rescuing the eagle (see figure 2). The what-if analogs to this adventure change the parameters of the problem, but it's still the same problem. The Lindbergh analog adds another problem, but it is still a single problem involving flight time and fuel from New York to Paris.

Problem-solving in the Jasper series is reconceptualized when one moves from attempts to solve one or two complex problems to attempts that prepare one for a large class of recurring problems. This is done by inventing tools that allow one to "work smart." For example, a "working smart" extension for RBM involves Emily (the heroine who saves the Eagle) setting up a rescue and delivery service where she flies into various areas in her region depending on the needs specified by customers. She and her employees need to be able to tell the customer—as quickly as possible—the type of plane needed (depending on payload constraints), the flying time for the trip (depending on the speed of the plane), the fuel charges (which vary by plane size), and so on. To calculate these anew for each problem is cumbersome. Students learn to work smart by inventing tools like graphs, charts, and spreadsheets that help them solve these problems at a glance. Examples of smart tools, and of the learning processes and motivation involved in creating, testing and using them, are discussed in Bransford, Zech, et al. (2000).

The new object-oriented architecture of the Smart environment makes it easy for students to transport tools, like rate-time-distance graphs, from one working smart environment to another. This helps students see both the generality and possible limitations of their representational tools as they move to new environments. For example, a spreadsheet is more likely to be generally useful than a particular graph or chart, but students may still prefer the latter, once they tailor it to a specific set of constraints in a new environment (see Bransford, Zech, et al. 2000).

The object-oriented architecture has also facilitated the development of an AdventureMaker environment. AdventureMaker lets students create their own simulated problems for other students to solve. A current version of the environment provides students with a map background on which they can construct locations, paths for travel between locations, and a number of vehicles. The system allows students to create a variety of challenge problems that include RBM-type planning problems, overtake and catch up problems, and even versions of the traveling salesman problem. Students responding to the challenge have to import tools they created in other problem solving environments, tailor them for the particular problems, and then find the best solution as quickly as possible. We find that this is highly motivating for students, and that prior experience with the Jasper series affects the quality of the problems they construct (see CTGV, 1997). One of our hypotheses about why Adventure-Maker activities are so motivating to students is that it puts them in the position of creating programs that others can learn from (see also Kafai et al. 1998). This fits the general idea of "learning by teaching," which is discussed below.

Creating Designs That Give Students More Responsibility by Asking Them to Teach

Over time, our work in classrooms helped us see that some types of activities were consistently motivating to students and helped them appreciate feedback and opportunities for revision. These involved cases where students were preparing to present their ideas to outside audiences (e.g., adults), preparing to teach others to solve problems that they had learned to solve previously (e.g., college students; see CTGV 2000; Bransford, Brophy, and Williams 2000), and creating new problems to present to other students (see the preceding discussion of AdventureMaker). These observations led us to consider the value of using AI-techniques to create intelligent social agents (teachable agents) for whom students could take the responsibility of teaching.

We differentiate teachable agents from other agent technologies such as agents that coach people as they learn new skills and knowledge, or agents that search the web for a user and gradually learn preferences to tailor more efficient searches. Our agents currently have no automated learning algorithms built into their learning processes. For us, teachable agents are social agents who need explicit instruction to do well. Students provide this instruction to the agent as knowledge structures or procedures that can be directly executed by the agent in response to given queries and problems. For example, an agent may need to be taught how to deal with trip planning problems like the "working smart" version of RBM, or an agent may need to learn how to monitor the quality of rivers to discover evidence of possible pollution. We situate our agents in particular task environments that provide a focus for teaching and assessment that is more domain targeted than simply asking students to "teach this agent to do something—anything." The agents do poorly or well in these task environments depending on how well they are taught.

A number of factors motivated us to explore the idea of creating "teachable" agents whose behavior would depend on the quality of the teaching provided by students. One is that the challenge of teaching others appears to create a sense of responsibility that is highly motivating to individuals of all ages. In a study that interviewed sixth graders about the highlights of their year as fifth graders, doing projects that helped the community and tutoring younger students received the highest praise from the students (CTGV, 1997). In "reverse mentoring" studies headed by Kay Burgess, inner-city students who had solved a Jasper adventure were highly motivated to help adults and college students solve an adventure for the first time (see Bransford, Brophy, and Williams 2000). In work with teachers, we consistently find that the opportunity to teach their peers is highly motivating and develops a strong learning community among the teachers (CTGV, in press).

The motivation to teach others also carries over to virtual environments. In the newest release from the Little Planet Literacy Series that the Learning Technology Center at Vanderbilt helped create (CTGV, 1998), students are highly motivated to write letters to a character named Maria to help her learn to read (see *The Dougout Collection* Sunburst, 2000). In early versions of our SMART Challenge series (Barron, et al. 1995; Vye, et al. 1998), students eagerly wrote e-mails to virtual students who asked for help in solving the Jasper Adventure that they were working on. In video games, students are consistently motivated to affect the fate of agents as they attempt various adventures. However, the fate of these agents usually depends on physical and mystical powers. We want to change the paradigm so that their fate hinges on the development of useful knowledge, attitudes and skills.

A second reason for exploring the idea of teachable agents stems from the

Task	Preparation for Teaching	Preparation for Testing
Students Initial Framing of the Preparation Task		
Consider larger context of studies	100%	0%
Must memorize details	0%	50%
Spontaneously Questioned Purpose of Experiment (percent of challenged experiments)	92%	33%
Spontaneously Mentioned Flaw in an Experiment	83%	17%
Spontaneously Mentioned Alternative Experiment	50%	0%
Successfully Graphed Experiments Afterwards (successful graphs)	89%	56%

Table 1. Comparative effects of preparing to teach versus preparing to take a test on students' emphasis during study and final understanding.

strongly shared intuition that attempts to teach others is an especially powerful way to learn. There is research literature on learning by teaching. Research on mentoring has shown that tutors learn as much or more than tutees (Webb 1983), and that lessons in which students tutor each other are beneficial (King 1998) especially if well-scaffolded (e.g., reciprocal teaching; Palinscar and Brown 1984). Nevertheless, the research on learning by teaching does not consistently show a benefit for teaching over and above learning for oneself (Bargh and Schul 1980; Willis and Crowder 1974; Cohen, et al. 1982). We believe that some of this has to do with a lack of a research base about where to look for the benefits of teaching. It seems unlikely that the unique payoff of teaching would appear in memory tests, although memory tests are typically used. It seems more likely that the payoff would be in the structure of people's knowledge and their readiness to learn from further instruction and feedback (Bransford and Schwartz 1999). In addition, there are many aspects of learning by teaching that have not been explored.

We identify at least three phases of teaching that might be expected to enhance learning: planning to teach, explaining and demonstrating during teaching, and interpreting the questions and feedback that come from students during and after teaching. Research has concentrated on the effects of planning to teach. For example, Bargh and Schul (1980) found that people who prepared to teach someone else to take a quiz on a passage learned the passage better than people who prepared to take the quiz themselves. Chi, deLeeuw, Chiu, and LaVancher (1994) showed benefits of explanation, even when there was no audience. For example, directions to "self-explain" while reading a passage on the heart improved comprehension relative to students who simply studied without directions to self-explain.

In our initial studies on preparing to teach, we are finding benefits that suggest preparing to teach can spontaneously affect the way students learn and self-explain. In a recent study, we videotaped twelve students separately as they studied a psychology article that described a series of experiments on memory. Half of the students heard they were studying in preparation for a class test, and the other half heard they would have to teach their class about the article. They had up to thirty minutes to prepare.

The teaching students spent twice as much time studying the article. More interesting is the way they prepared and what they learned. Table 1 presents some of the important contrasts. Students who prepared to teach spent a substantial amount of time trying to understand "the why" of the studies, whereas the students who prepared for the test tried to memorize the results of the studies. As a consequence, the latter were less successful at reconstructing the studies, their results, and their rationale (see table 1).

Written reflections collected by X. D. Lin and J. D. Bransford also show benefits of learning by teaching. They asked different groups of graduate students in a class on cognition, culture, and technology to teach the undergraduates in the class about some articles on stereotypes that included empirical tests of various theories. Some of the graduate students worked individually to prepare to teach, and others worked in small groups.

After their teaching experiences, the graduate students were asked to discuss any benefits of being asked to teach the material to the undergraduates (compared to simply studying the materials in preparation for a test). All the graduate students were convinced that preparing to teach, plus actually doing the teaching, resulted in levels of learning that exceeded what they would have experienced if they had only studied for a test.

Planning to Teach: Some students focused on the fact that the responsibility of teaching forced them to make sure they understood the materials:

> The article that described the three theories was very hard for me to read.... I had to be sure that I understood this article.... After my clear understanding of how the theories work I was then able to prepare a comprehensive and compact presentation.... In short, I cannot prepare a presentation on something I do not understand.

Other students focused on the increased importance of a clear conceptual organization:

To teach something in a specified amount of time means that you need to be able to differentiate what is important from what is less important and identify component parts and relationships. In other words, it's necessary to conceptualize the framework of ideas that are presented in the article. When I read an article with the mind set of discussing it, I am not so diligent about understanding the hierarchy of the ideas presented. If I'm teaching something, I have to categorize and prioritize the ideas. This insures I present the important ideas in a coherent manner.

It seems clear that the planning that takes place depends on knowledge of one's audience and the constraints of the teaching opportunities. For example, the graduate students in the Lin and Bransford course had a good idea of their audience (the undergraduates in their course) and the time constraints on their presentations, and these seemed to affect their thinking. Similarly the data illustrated in table 1 involved graduate students planning to teach other graduate students. The students relied on their knowledge of their audience to prepare for the types of questions they might receive. But it is worth noting that all students envisioned giving a lecture rather than teaching in some other, more interactive manner. Moreover, students in primary and secondary school may not readily anticipate the demands of teaching, or their expectations, may be unduly constrained by the experiences that they have had in classrooms (e.g., prior experiences with lectures). This suggests that it is worthwhile to explore different ways to set the preparation "stage" for students rather than simply ask students to prepare to teach.

Learning During the Act of Teaching

We noted earlier that the advantages of learning by teaching involve more than just planning to teach. For example, there would appear to be additional advantages from the actual act of teaching—especially from the opportunity to get feedback from one's students' about what they do and do not understand. In a review of the literature on self-explaining and explaining to other people (as might occur during a collaboration), Ploetzner, Dillenbourg, Preier, and Traum (1999) conclude that feedback from a collaborator is a significant component of other-explanation, yet its effects on learning have not been investigated.

The graduate students in the Lin and Bransford study at Vanderbilt University spontaneously noted some of the things they learned by actually attempting to teach their subject matter. The following quote comes from a graduate student who collaborated with three colleagues in order to prepare to teach the undergraduates. The student discusses the preparation process and then writes about his group's actual attempts to teach.

> We had a list of ideas and feelings that we wanted the class to experience with us. When it came time to present, however, I realized how difficult it was to explain the emotions of our small group discussion to a large group who were not all that familiar with the article. Our presentations became more a dissemination of facts

instead of a sharing of emotion, as I had hoped (and planned) that it would. I think the undergraduates got our basic points and left having a better understanding of stereotypes and our charge to open up to each other, but I don't feel that they had the same experience with the message that I had. I feel my experience was more intense and more memorable because my small group took the article down to its bare issues and discussed how those made us feel and think about stereotypes.

The student's comments suggested that the goal of planning in order to teach helped his group learn effectively. In addition, the act of teaching helped him experience the differences between merely "transmitting" information and helping people experience the effects of their own stereotypes.

Despite the benefits, it seems clear that not all teaching experiences will create significantly new learning on the part of the teacher. Most teachers are familiar with pupils who make them think and learn and with pupils who do not. This is one reason why the idea of creating AI-based teachable agents can be so valuable; it allows us to provide students with teachable agent pupils that optimize their chances of learning, for example by ensuring the teachable agent asks questions most relevant to the domain and the student's level of development. And, unlike peer tutoring, the teachable agent is not hurt if its teacher is really quite bad.

The idea of teachable agents has its precursors in activities such as teaching the "turtle" to do things in LOGO (Papert 1980). This is a very motivating task environment; we have worked with a large number of middle school students in this context and know how motivating it can be (e.g., Littlefield et al. 1988). However, it is also clear from the literature on Logo that it can be very difficult to demonstrate clear advantages of these kinds of activities unless one structures them around particular types of goals and feedback structures (see Klahr and Carver 1988; Mayer 1988). Our approach to teachable agents differs from LOGO in the sense that we situate our agents in particular, anchored task environments, which require specific sets of knowledge, skills and attitudes in order for the agents to succeed. An example of a teachable agent is discussed below.

Meeting a Teachable Agent in Its Native Context

An example of a teachable agent is Billy Bashinall, high school student (figure 6). He and friend Sally have been monitoring a local river to test for water quality. Billy is ready to hand in the report, which says that the river is in excellent shape. Sally is not so sure that their findings are accurate. She worries that the river is polluted and will eventually kill the fish and other aquatic life. Billy's response is, "Lighten up Sally. This is only a school assignment. Besides, five pages is always good enough for a C in Mr. Hogan's class." Billy's negative atti-

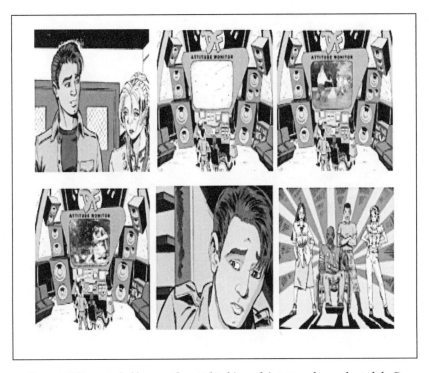

Figure 6. Billy, a teachable agent, learns that his work is not good enough, and the D-Force challenges students to teach Billy.

tude comes to the attention of the D-Force—a group dedicated to helping students avoid the mistakes that they made as students. Billy needs their help.

Billy is transported to D-Force headquarters, where he is shown videos of students monitoring a river by collecting macroinvertebrates, calculating a water quality index, measuring dissolved oxygen and so forth. Billy is asked to explain what is happening. His answers reveal that he understands some things (e.g., macroinvertebrates can provide an index of the health of the river). However, he seriously misunderstands other things like how and why some types of macroinvertebrates need considerable oxygen and are more sensitive indicators of water quality than other macroinvertebrates that need less oxygen. Consequently, he does not understand why the formula for water quality weights some macroinvertebrates more than others. And he does not understand how the amount of dissolved oxygen in the water is related to water quality and pollution.

The episode ends with Billy realizing that he needs help, and the D-Force asking people to help teach Billy. This becomes the task of the students in the classroom. By adjusting Billy's attitude and helping him learn important skills and concepts, students learn by being teachers. By seeing how Billy performs

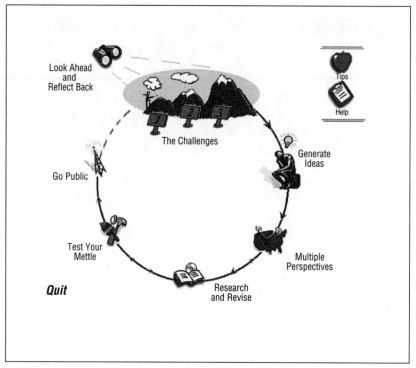

Figure 7. The STAR.legacy interface that organizes complex inquiry activities.

following their teaching, students can assess the quality of their teaching. After a series of iterative teaching-assessment cycles, students eventually learn about rivers as ecosystems and see that Billy has learned, too.

Initial SAD Studies Using Teachable Agents

As was true with our work on Jasper, our research on teachable agents began with a SAD approach. In particular, we began with a pre-scripted agent in order to test our ideas in fifth-grade classrooms. Over time, we are replacing our scripted agents with ones that have intelligence.

In a recent set of experiments led by Nancy Vye, fifth grade students began their inquiry by meeting "Billy Bashinall," the character introduced earlier (figure 6). Students saw him attempt to perform in a particular environment that required knowledge of ecosystems and water quality. They did research in order to teach Billy, and they observed the effects of this teaching on his behavior. The Billy Bashinall environment was a scripted environment in the sense that we pre-specified everything beforehand.

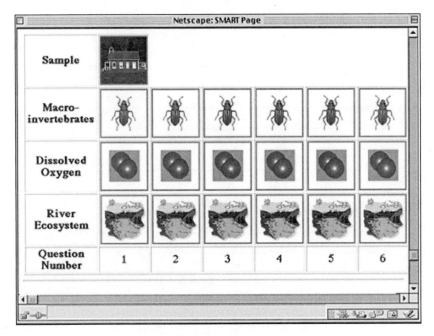

Figure 8. Formative assessment interface.

We used a software program called STAR.Legacy to organize students' inquiry into water quality monitoring (Schwartz et al. 1999). STAR.Legacy is a multimedia shell that helps teachers, students, and instructional designers manage complex inquiry activities. The interface shown in figure 7 organizes different stages of inquiry: students click on the icons to access relevant multimedia content. Students begin with a Challenge that, in this case, asks students to help Billy learn about macroinvertebrates and why they are used to check water quality.

Using the Legacy framework, students then generate their own ideas on the topic of macroinvertebrates (generate ideas) and hear some ideas from experts (multiple perspectives). In the course of discussing these ideas, students generate many questions about macroinvertebrates, which set the course for their research (research and revise). Students also have the opportunity to access specially-designed computer tools to help them learn; for example, they use a simulation in which they learn how to sample and sort macroinvertebrates to check water quality.

After studying macroinvertebrates, students take an assessment in *Test Your Mettle*. Figure 8 shows the software interface that organizes the assessment questions (the software was developed by Jay Pfaffman). By clicking on a square, students are brought to a question from the D-Force that Billy has

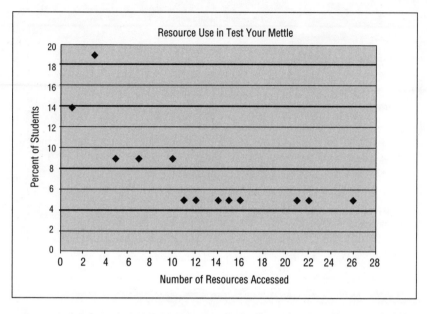

Figure 9. Students consulted resources numerous times in preparation for teaching Billy.

already tried to answer. Students give "advice" to Billy on how he should have answered the question. For example, one of the questions on macroinvertebrates begins, "The D-Force asked Billy to explain how scientists use macroinvertebrates to check water quality." Students then see Billy's response to the question, in this case, "Scientists count the total number of macroinvertebrates that are found in their sample." Students are asked to teach Billy by either telling him that his answer is correct or by choosing a better answer for him from a set of alternatives that we provide. If the students select correct advice, the relevant square in the grid turns green. If they are wrong, the square turns red. The teacher (and class) can look at the accuracy of the students' advice to Billy to get an assessment of class understanding. Although the students believe they are assessing and remediating Billy's understanding in *Test Your Mettle,* they are actually completing assessment activities relevant to their own understanding.

One of the goals of the assessment environment is to help students self-assess whether they are ready to advise Billy, and if they are not, to learn to consult resources. Before advising Billy, students have the option to see online resources such as relevant readings or animations By structuring the environment so students may learn during an assessment, we encourage students to be reflective about whether they understand well enough to teach Billy. The system's backend database tracks student use of resources. Among other things, this feature provides a measure of student motivation to teach Billy; if students are motivated to give Billy good advice, we assume that they will consult resources when they are uncertain or want to verify their advice. Figure 9 suggests that students are highly intent on teaching Billy well. All students from the class represented in the figure spontaneously consulted resources at least once before advising, and most consulted multiple resources. As noted by a fifth grader, "It feels good to help somebody out even though they are computer animated."

In *Test Your Mettle*, students give advice on all aspects of water quality monitoring, even aspects that they have not yet studied. They give advice on issues related to macroinvertebrates and also on dissolved oxygen and river ecosystems. In this way, the assessment is formative and students can use it to self-assess what they have learned or have yet to learn. Once students have completed their teaching in *Test Your Mettle*, we give them class-level feedback on their performance. The feedback shows average performance for the class on each water quality topic.

Having "taught" Billy in *Test Your Mettle*, students watch (in *Go Public*) a cartoon vignette in which Billy answers questions from the D-Force. Billy's behavior is scripted and it is not closely contingent on what the students actually taught Billy in *Test Your Mettle*. Instead, it is contingent only at a general level. For example, if the class as a whole does relatively well in *Test Your Mettle*, the subsequent vignette shows Billy successfully answering the set of questions that were the focus of attention in that particular legacy cycle. If the class did very poorly, the "go public" video shows the D-Force asking the students to try again.

We created a different vignette for each challenge in the legacy cycle. The vignette for challenge one on macroinvertebrates shows Billy doing a good job answering questions about macroinvertebrates, but the D-Force makes it clear that he still does a poor job with questions about dissolved oxygen and ecosystems— topics that students had not yet studied and that we can reasonably assume students will not know much about. At the end of challenge 2, which focuses on learning about dissolved oxygen, students see an epilogue in which Billy is now able to answer questions about dissolved oxygen (and macroinvertebrates), but is still unprepared to answer questions about ecosystems. In this way, we create the idea that student performance in *Test Your Mettle* changes Billy's ability to answer queries from the D-Force.

One important goal of our research is to study whether asking students to teach an agent is effective in helping them learn. Our findings show that over time, students improve their performance on the assessment. And, these improvements occur in a predictable time course. After each challenge, students improve most on the topic related to that challenge.

Bringing Agents to Life with AI

As noted earlier, the long-term goal of our work is to use insights from AI to "bring Billy to Life." Our major focus is not to make Billy learn on his own through inductive, machine learning methods. Billy is a teachable agent not a learning agent. Our goal is to create an environment that allows students to learn both by preparing to teach agents, and by observing how the agents behave once the teaching is completed (if there are problems, students can revise their teaching). We are building teachable agents that can respond to different forms of teaching (complete and incomplete) in flexible and informative ways so that students may learn.

A simple example of this approach comes from *Betty's Brain*, which we developed for instruction in the life sciences. (Betty is a second member of the Bashinall family.) Betty, as an agent, is able to execute and portray inferences implicit in a semantic network. Students and teachers can ask Betty questions as a way to assess the quality of her knowledge. To develop her semantic network, students teach Betty by drawing concept maps and taxonomic trees. In their drawings, students define entities that are of interest in pollution studies (e.g., sunlight, carbon dioxide, dissolved oxygen, algae, fish, etc.). And, they define the relations between these entities (e.g., produce, breathe, and so on). Figure 10 illustrates a concept map that was created by a student early in his learning. In contains misconceptions that are quite typical for middle school students. After students create their concept map, it serves as Betty's semantic network and permits her to draw inferences. In this way, students can get feedback on the quality of what they believe and have taught. Given the map in figure 10, the agent offers many mistaken answers that the student then has to explore and correct.

One of our tasks is to make sure that the effort of teaching an agent does not incur the overhead of learning to program. For example, students do not need to teach Betty how to draw inferences with a concept map. She already knows how to do that. Moreover, the "programming" the students perform occurs in the form of manipulating representational tools, like concept maps, which students need to learn in the course of their normal studies. (Novak 1998) Similar to asking students to develop their AdventurePlayer plans with the timeline tool, we scaffold student acquisition of useful tools and concepts by asking them to teach using "smart tools," in this case, networks that help organize complex declarative knowledge.

Figure 11 shows an interface that students can use to build Betty's network. To teach Betty, students can select from a list of entities relevant to a river ecosystem using a pull down menu. They can also create new entities not available in the menu. Students must also construct relations among the entities they select or create. Students can use relation names from a pull down menu or create relation names of their own. When they create new relation names,

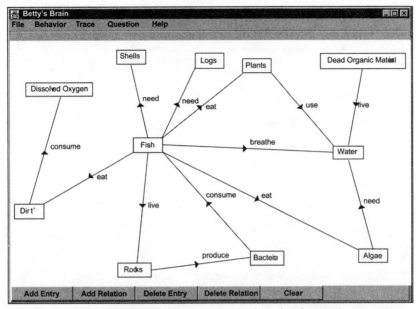

Figure 10. A representative, student concept map (early in their learning) given to Betty.

they are prompted to categorize them into one of four classes that enable Betty to draw inferences. One type of relation is qualitative causal, where an increase or decrease in one entity can cause an increase or decrease in the other; for example, fish breathe (decrease) dissolved oxygen. For Betty's future inferences, this implies an increase in the fish population results in a decrease in dissolved oxygen. All causal links are defined as an increase (+) or decrease (-) relation between two quantities. For example, if quantity A has a produce relation with quantity B, then an increase (decrease) in A causes an increase (decrease) in B. On the other hand, if quantity A has a consume relation with quantity B, an increase (decrease) in A will cause a decrease (increase) in B. A qualitative amount relation, defined as a large, normal, or small change, may further qualify the qualitative relations. (If the amount is not specified, a default value of a normal change is assumed.) This way, an increase in quantity A may cause a large increase in quantity B. This framework allows the inference mechanism of Betty's Brain to implement a simple qualitative arithmetic scheme for propagating amount values through a chain of causal relations in a concept map (see Leelawong et al. 2001 for details). Work done in the qualitative reasoning community (e.g., deKleer and Brown 1984, Forbus 1984a, and Kuipers 1986) define more sophisticated qualitative reasoning mechanisms for dynamic systems that reason simultaneously with amounts and rate of change.

A second type of relation is dependency where one entity needs another without implying quantitative changes; for example, plants need sunlight but

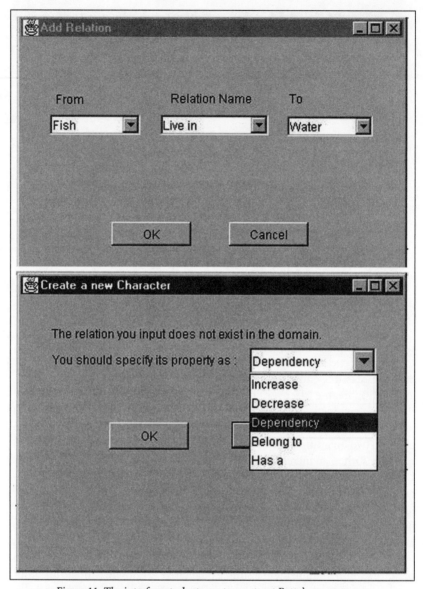

Figure 11. The interface students use to construct Betty's concept map.

do not use it up. A third relationship is belongs-to where one entity belongs to another entity; for example, fish belong to the class of living objects. Finally, the has-a relationship allows students to define entity attributes; for example, water has dissolved oxygen.

After students teach Betty's Brain by building her concept map, they can

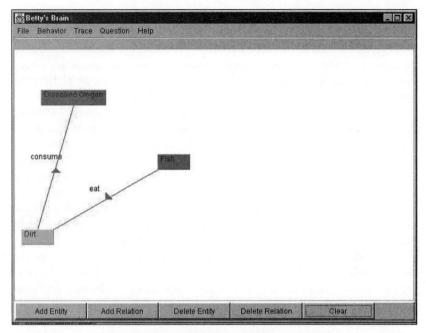

Figure 12. Betty portrays how she inferred that an increase in fish increases the amount of dissolved oxygen.

"test her mettle" by asking questions composed from a pull-down menu. For example, a student can ask, "How does an increase in fish change dissolved oxygen?" In full-discourse mode, Betty uses an exhaustive forward chaining algorithm (a brute force, depth-first search) to find all possible paths connecting the entities in the query. If there are multiple paths with conflicting solutions, the system weights the paths to arrive at a conclusion. To present her conclusion, Betty can explain her answer in stylized natural language, or she can highlight the relevant portion of her concept map. For the concept map in figure 10, there is only one path and Betty replies, "I think an increase in fish increases dissolved oxygen," and she shows her inference path as in figure 12. If there were more than one path, Betty would offer a single answer, but show that there is more than one chain of inference.

In more detail, students and teachers can ask Betty three kinds of questions:

1. What happens to quantity *B* when the amount of quantity *A* increases (decreases)?

2. What is the effect of an increase(decrease) in quantity *A?*

3. What quantities can cause an increase(decrease) in quantity *A?*

For query types 1 and 2, the mechanism does an exhaustive search over the entire concept map, identifying all possible forward paths from quantity A. A single step in the forward search process involves identifying a forward causal link from the current (source) concept, and applying the qualitative reasoning mechanism to compute the resultant value for the destination concept. When multiple paths exist between two entities, the reasoning mechanism applies qualitative rules of the form, a large increase and a small decrease imply a normal increase, and a normal decrease and small increase, imply a small decrease. Situations, such as a normal increase and a normal decrease lead to an ambiguous situation, and Betty responds by saying that she is unable to tell whether the result is an increase or a decrease. For query type 3, the reasoning mechanism employs an exhaustive backward search instead of a forward search.

In addition to the concept map provided by the student, the Betty system can include an age-appropriate network created by the instructor (using the same interface tools) that can also draw inferences. If needed, these inferences can be used to help students rectify their concept maps. Betty's Brain is similar to AdventurePlayer in that it can operate with and without this type of domain model. The students can simply create and test their own concept maps, just like they can create their own simulations in AdventureMaker. When there is a domain model available, the Betty system, also like AdventurePlayer, can compare the discrepancies between Betty's inferences based on the map provided by a student and the domain model's inferences to determine possible points for instruction. However, unlike AdventurePlayer, the Betty system produces indirect coaching based on discrepancies. We say "indirect" because we make the feedback come through Betty to maintain the student's sense of responsibility. For example, Betty can ask, "I know I figured that an increase in fish would increase the dissolved oxygen, but I remember my teacher said the opposite. Where have we gone wrong?" The system can gradually increase the directness of the feedback depending on student difficulties. For example, Betty can ask, "Are you sure that fish eat dirt?" because the teacher's domain model does not include a dirt entity. At an even greater level of support, Betty can say she asked a teacher or friend who handed her a concept map. She can show the student the map that is the subset of the domain model deemed most relevant to the question.

After students assess and revise Betty's Brain, they ask her to go public. This can take a variety of forms. For example, each student in a class may create a separate Betty. When ready, the students submit their Betty to the teacher's website. (Betty has Java genes. She is implemented as a platform-independent Java applet.) The teacher can then ask the same question of all the Betty's, and students can see the different responses. This serves as an excellent context for classroom discussion as students try to resolve which answers are correct and why. A similar form is that students generate questions for one another that they know their own Betty can answer. A third form of going public involves collaborative problem solving. Under this model, students join their Betty's into team Betty. (The Betty system supports the automatic merging of databases and the redrawing of the subsequent concept map.) Team Betty then tries to answer questions. In the best of cases, team Betty can answer questions that none of the Betty's could resolve in isolation. In other cases, team Betty contradicts herself, because the students had conflicting concept maps. Our hope is that it will be highly motivating for teams of students who build a team Betty, and it will provide an excellent context for developing classroom discussions about knowledge organization.

One of the exciting possibilities with teachable agents is that they can help students reflect on the dispositions of effective learners. The students can explore how different attitudes affect an agent's ability to learn and reason. For example, students can adjust Betty's "attention" parameter that determines how well she "encodes" the relations she is taught. If her attention is poor, she may put an entity into the wrong relationship or leave it out all together. Of course, the goal is not to teach children that good attention is all that is needed for learning. Therefore, we plan to include a complex of different disposition parameters that students can adjust, balance, and discuss. For example, Betty can be stubborn and refuse to do homework so she forgets some relationships over time.

Students can adjust disposition parameters that affect her reasoning. Although students do not program the search algorithms, they can indirectly change them via Betty's disposition. For example, if they receive a lazy Betty and do not adjust her "thoroughness" parameter, Betty only searches one level or stops after finding one solution. Betty can be too wordy and report every step of every inference chain she tries, right or wrong. Betty can be a little too loose in her reasoning and chain across nodes that have no actual relationship. Students get a chance to explore and change disposition parameters as they work with Betty. Ideally, this activity can help students reflect upon and discuss the appropriateness of their own dispositions for learning.

Summary

Our goal in this chapter was to describe some examples where AI techniques have helped to improve learning in classroom environments. We noted that our research strategy has been to begin with SAD applications of technology. This has allowed us to identify situations where increased technological sophistication could have a significant impact on student (and often teacher) learning. We discussed two examples of moving from stone-age designs to designs enriched through AI.

One example involved creating the AdventurePlayer program to accompany the Jasper Series (Crews et al. 1997). Students can work on the program either individually or in groups. Tests of the program (Crews et al. 1997) show that it facilitates initial learning and leads to more flexible transfer. Teachers who have taught Jasper with and without the aid of AdventurePlayer have noted how helpful the program was for managing the complexity of the learning environments that Jasper adventures entail.

We also noted that we have created object-oriented variations on AdventurePlayer that allow students to create tools for "working smart," plus create simulations for other students. The "smart tools" application supports the reformulation of Jasper from a series where students only solve a single complex problem, to one where they must learn to work smart in order to solve large classes of frequently recurring problems (Bransford, Zech et al. 2000). The AdventureMaker applications allow students to create new adventures of their own.

A second example of moving from SAD to the use of AI techniques centered around the concept of "teachable agents" whom students explicitly teach to perform a variety of complex activities. Our focus on teachable agents is part of a larger effort to explore the potential benefits of learning by teaching. There is a great deal of intuitive support for the benefits of learning by teaching—both motivationally and conceptually. By contrast, the research literature on the topic is extremely modest. Our research is helping us understand the conditions under which learning by teaching can have powerful effects. We find benefits of planning to teach, as well as benefits of actually trying to teach and getting feedback from students. But we noted that even these categories are very general and need to be explored more carefully. For example, how one plans to teach is affected by knowledge of (1) who will be taught; (2) under what conditions (e.g., time constraints), and (3) the range of possible teaching strategies that might be used (e.g., lecture versus alternatives).

We also argued that people learn during the act of teaching (and when reflecting on their teaching), and that what a teacher learns will depend on the quality of his or her students (e.g., the kinds of questions they ask). And we wanted to ensure that students are not harmed by inexperienced or underprepared teachers. Therefore, we are creating virtual "teachable agents" who are not hurt by poor teaching, and who provide the kinds of questions and feedback that best enable their teachers to learn from them.

Our effort to design teachable agents follows the tradition of viewing computers as not only tools and tutors, but also as tutees (Taylor 1980). Attempts to program the Logo turtle represents an excellent example of the computer as tutees approach (e.g., Papert 1980). However, unlike Logo, we situate our teachable agents in particular environments that require specific sets of attitudes, skills, and knowledge to function effectively. This allows us to focus on the acquisition of conceptual knowledge that is important for areas such as science, mathematics and history.

Our work on teachable agents has followed our strategy of beginning with SAD approaches and adding complexity as needed. Our initial SAD designs involved agents whose behaviors were all prespecified. This work has allowed us to learn a great deal about student motivation and learning, and about ways to provide feedback to students that facilitate this process. Subsequent work is allowing our agents to be much more flexible by using agent-based AI techniques.

Our work on teachable agents is quite new, so the ideas and data we presented were preliminary. Nevertheless, students' reactions to the "faux" agents have been highly promising, and the AI-based agents are making the learning situations even more exciting. One of our ultimate goals is to change the nature of video games from environments that primarily emphasize weapons and fighting abilities to ones that highlight important sets of knowledge, skills, and attitudes. Combing our teachable agent software with the AdventurePlayer type simulation environments will allow students to design agents for particular challenge environments, and then evaluate and cheer for the superior problem-solving performance of their agents in these environments. As the environments become more complex, the knowledge students will need to teach will become increasingly sophisticated and flexible. In this way, students can develop an appreciation for the "big ideas" that organize thinking in different domains.

Acknowledgements

This chapter was made possible by the Teachable Agents grant—NSF REC-9873520T, and by a grant for The Challenge Zone—NSF ESI-9618248. The opinions expressed in the chapter do not necessarily reflect those of the granting agency. Members of the Teachable Agents Group at Vanderbilt who contributed to this chapter are Gautam Biswas, John Bransford, Sean Brophy, Thomas Katzlberger, Xiaodong Lin, Taylor Martin, Jay Pfaffman, Daniel Schwartz, Nancy Vye, and Yingbin Wang.

Chapter Four

Growth and Maturity of Intelligent Tutoring Systems

A Status Report

Beverly Park Woolf, Joseph Beck,
Christopher Eliot, and Mia Stern

This research is concerned with improving the ability of software tutors to enhance the quality of individual human-computer interaction and to extend the range of students who can be reached. We address long-term questions, such as how tutors can facilitate learning and how this learning can be measured. Several case studies are presented, along with remaining hurdles on the way toward achieving stronger learning outcomes. Research has led to the development of several effective teaching systems, achieved by modeling learning at the cognitive level and then using artificial intelligence (AI) techniques, such as planning, machine learning, cognitive modeling and dialog management, to adapt curriculum topics and hints based on greater knowledge of the domain and student learning.

However, available cognitive models are not adequate for building all the types of learning systems wanted. Cognitive models have contributed some pedagogical and subject-matter theories, instructional design and enhanced instructional delivery to the field. On the other hand, many issues remain, beginning with understanding learning at a deep level, understanding educational methods and social organization and adequately representing alternative learning styles such as collaborative learning, scaffolding, mentoring and partnering. The lack of AI development tools, e.g., shells and frameworks, similar to those used to build expert systems, also limits development in this field.

Cognitive studies of instruction have shown that learners must remain active and motivated (Fletcher 1995, 1996; Regian and Shute 1993; Seidel and

Perez 1994; Shute and Regian 1993). Learners must want to learn and be involved, active and challenged to reason about the material presented. Flashy graphics and simulations are not enough; the experience must be authentic and relevant to the learner's work (Woolf and Hall 1995, Woolf 1992). Simple presentations of text, graphics or multimedia often result in systems that encourage passive learning and provide little, if any, adaptability to different learning needs. Students do not learn by pressing buttons and flipping pages, even if the pages contain images, sound or video. Interactive exercises are required that involve students in the material.

AI-based systems overcome such drawbacks through sophisticated feedback, customized curriculum and focused methods for remediating errors. Adaptive systems are based upon explicit representations of tutoring, student knowledge and pedagogy, rules of inference about possible ways to teach content knowledge and dynamic generation of customized paths through the knowledge in response to student behavior. They might reason about stored knowledge and customize curriculum, feedback, help, and error detection.

Intelligent tutors have many benefits for education. By adapting the curriculum to each student, learning could be customized to different learners. This allows self-directed learning. In the ideal case, this is similar to one-on-one tutoring and is in sharp contrast to the current condition of an entire class of twenty-five students progressing at the same pace. One-on-one tutoring by human tutors has been shown to increase the average student's performance to around the ninety-eighth percentile of students in a standard classroom (Bloom 1984). Formal evaluations have shown that intelligent tutors can produce the same improvement that results from one-on-one human tutoring and can effectively reduce by one-third to one-half the time required for learning (Regian 1997).

AI applications can also make asynchronous learning effective. Current web-based material has proliferated beyond any individual's ability to evaluate or fully utilize. AI techniques will enable students to learn about selected material at their own rate before it is taught or as a supplement to course activities. Such systems might become routine supporting group collaboration of students-at-a-distance, exploration of hypothetical worlds, and the making and testing of hypotheses. Learning need not be constrained to place and time.

The remainder of this chapter is organized as follows. First, we describe a variety of abilities tutors can demonstrate (generative, student modeling, expert modeling, instructional modeling, mixed initiative and self-improving) and then present four tutors that exhibit some of these abilities. These tutors are described in some detail with special attention to their artificial intelligence components. Next we discuss evaluation of tutoring systems and finally examine remaining research issues.

Abilities of Tutors

Intelligent tutors have certain abilities that set them apart from earlier examples of computer-aided instruction (CAI) (Fletcher 1988, Lesgold et al. 1990, Regian and Shute 1993, Fletcher and Rockway 1986, Seidel et al. 1988, Shute and Psotka 1995). Some of these abilities are defined in table 1, adapted from Regian (1997). No universal agreement exists on which abilities are needed or present in intelligent tutors. However, the most sophisticated tutoring systems include, to some degrees, a large variety of these abilities.

Current published data suggest that, in general, the more effective instructional systems are the more powerful with regard to these abilities (Fletcher 1996, 1995). However, this is probably not universally true. It is likely that the relative importance of these abilities is a function of the nature of the knowledge or skills being taught and the quality of pedagogy applied in the teaching context (Regian and Shute 1993). Researchers are now collecting data to quantify the independent contributions of each ability (Regian 1997). The goal is to quantify the effectiveness of each ability under varying pedagogical implementations for teaching various types of knowledge and skills (Regian and Shute 1993; Seidel and Perez 1994; Shute and Regian 1993).

However, the efficiencies of certain instructional strategies may be dependent upon context, including the skills of the student. For example, students with *less* prior domain knowledge need *more* guidance than students with *more* prior domain knowledge, and the level of guidance required to support students with less domain knowledge is frustrating and counterproductive for students with *more* prior knowledge (Regian 1997). Student modeling (ability 2) tracks student performance, models student knowledge and infers student learning, and instructional modeling (ability 4) allows tutoring systems to appropriately modify the level of guidance provided to each student. In one very effective, highly interactive tutor that taught college statistics, the combination of student modeling and instructional modeling produced an additional 10 percent boost in student outcome performance as compared to traditional computer aided systems (Shute 1995; Shute and Psotka 1995). Research such as this, which serves to quantify the relative instructional impact of specific abilities and to provide specific pedagogical details, supports a new approach to the implementation of instruction, termed "instructional engineering" (Fletcher 1995, 1996).

Every intelligent tutor will incorporate one or more of the abilities listed in table 1. The case studies below discuss the use of these abilities in working tutoring systems.

Generative. Generates appropriate instructional material, including problems, hints and help based on student performance. This ability is to be distinguished from storing multiple canned responses and then selecting one for each student.

Student Modeling. Assesses the current state of a student's knowledge and does something instructionally useful based on the assessment. The system identifies presumed student knowledge and makes inferences about his or her grasp of skills. Frequently, a system will use a student model to represent how the student has organized and incorporated new knowledge. The student model might display its changing view of the student's strengths and weaknesses as well as aspects of his or her currently (mis)understood knowledge.

Expert Modeling. Models expert performance and does something instructionally useful based on knowledge of the domain. Current systems vary in the type of knowledge they teach, e.g., velocity and acceleration, as well as processes within whole systems, e.g., emergency shut-down procedure in a boiler system [Woolf et al., 1986], or a hydraulic process involved in folding a helicopter's blades [Towne et al., 1990]. Some teach formal logic and formal knowledge, e.g., ALGEBRALAND [Foss, 1987] and the Geometry Tutor [Anderson et al., 1985]. Building an *expert* model requires specification of the relative difficulty of topics, identification of the strategies and tactics used for tailoring instruction to an individual student, and a corpus of analogies, examples and error diagnosis techniques for teaching in the domain. Without the aid of shells, e.g., expert systems shells and authoring systems, which currently do not exist, this task is time consuming. Even with such software tools, each new domain requires identification of curriculum topics, prerequisite topics, causal and temporal relations between topics, and the relative difficulty of learning each topic.

Instructional Modeling. Changes pedagogical strategies based on the changing state of the student model, prescriptions of an expert model, or both. Tutoring style might also vary across domain types. Explanation, guided discovery learning, coaching, coaxing or critiquing might be preferable depending on the domain. Tutoring style also varies *within* a tutorial domain. For example, guided discovery learning might be replaced with opportunistic one-on-one tutoring once the student requests a specific activity or shows the need for remediation. How and why human teachers change teaching style is an open research question.

Mixed-initiative. Human-computer communication in which the student or system controls the conversation or asks a question. Such control is now assumed in responsive human instructional situations. The ability to initiate interactions with the student as well as to interpret and respond usefully to student-initiated comments is required. Natural language dialog is sometimes taken as the focus of this ability. *Error diagnosis*, or system's ability to diagnose mistakes, plausible misconceptions, overgeneralizations and missing information, is often a goal of this ability. A diagnostic tutor compares student behavior with that of an expert before reasoning about how to elicit better learning performance.

Self-Improving. The capacity to monitor, evaluate and improve its own teaching performance as a function of experience. Machine learning, or some other technique which changes behavior over time, is required.

Table 1. Abilities of intelligent tutoring systems.

Case Studies

Tutors can provide a variety of interaction modes to address a variety of knowledge types. For example, for problem solving domains, such as physics or mathematics, a tutor might encode "correct" knowledge and then track the student's actions for explicitly right or wrong answers (see Cardiac and Mathematics Tutors in this section). On the other hand, some inquiry-based activities might provide an environment for exploration and ask a student to generate hypotheses and analyze data. Such tutors (see Engineering Tutors or Adaptive Courses, in this section) will not necessarily check for correct answers. Intelligent technology plays a role in both types of teaching.

Early tutors, that dealt with correctable knowledge, were often *omniscient* or *despotic* in nature; incorrect student actions were quickly identified, based on reference to an error knowledge base, and remediated. However, immediate help has several disadvantages: it may compete for short-term memory with newly learned material and students might also become dependent on it (Schooler and Anderson 1990). Explicitly correctable knowledge can also be handled in an empathetic manner in which tutors implicitly elicit information about student goals and plans. Such systems require less knowledge about the domain and more information about the student and teaching rules. They coach rather than tutor and reason about several forms of behavior before taking action. In their most sophisticated form they might reason based on knowledge about how people solve problems or make inferences in the domain. Theoretical focus has shifted from exclusive diagnosis and remediation to identifying and supporting students in managing their own cognitive processes.

In this section, four tutors are described which use several of the abilities to achieve rich interactivity with the student. These tutors are summarized, along with the intelligent abilities that give them their power, in table 2.

The Cardiac Tutor

The Cardiac Tutor helped students learn an established medical procedure through directed practice within an intelligent simulation (Eliot and Woolf 1994). It incorporated substantial domain knowledge about cardiac resuscitation and was designed for training medical personnel in the skills of advanced cardiac life support (ACLS) (Eliot and Woolf 1995). The system evaluated student performance according to procedures established by the American Heart Association (AHA 1987) and provided extensive feedback to the student.

A formative evaluation based on physician-administered final examinations with two classes of fourth-year medical students, suggested that working with the Cardiac Tutor was equivalent to being trained by an emergency room doctor, "running codes" and testing the student's knowledge of procedures on a

Ability	Example System	Description of Intelligent Ability
	Cardiac Tutor	Generates new cardiac arrythmias based on student learning needs. Biases the simulation (alters the probabilities of traversal among topics) to increase the probability of reaching states with good learning opportunities.
Generative	Mathematics Tutor	Generates new mathematics problem based on subskills needed by student. Uses a machine learning mechanism to adjust problem difficulty. And constructs problems that require a predicted amount of solving time.
	Adaptive Courses	When a subtopic is displayed to the student, the actual content is dynamically generated based on the student model. Additionally, quizzes are dynamically constructed based on the student model.
	Cardiac Tutor	Tracks student's knowledge and reasons about which therapy should be studied next. Each student action is recorded as states connected to the knowledge base, so the student can request additional information about past actions.
Student Modeling	Mathematics Tutor	Tracks known and unknown mathematics skills and predicts both the time for solving problems and the type of hint that works best for the individual student.
	Adaptive Courses	Tracks student "ability" on each topic. The student model is built on the student's quiz performance and on how well he studies the material. The system judges how well a topic has been "learned," and this judgement is used to determine which new topics are ready to be learned.
	Cardiac Tutor	Simulation corresponds closely with the medical procedures both in terms of level of detail and structure. Nodes represent states of cardiac arrest and arcs represent the probabilities of moving to a new physiological state following a treatment event.
Expert Modeling	Mathematics Tutor	Represents topics such as "subtract fractions" and "multiply whole numbers" in a topic network. The tutor generates new problems, hints and help based on student learning need.
	Engineering Tutors	An internal representation of rules dynamically generates an animation of the moving mechanism required to build the part designed by the student.
	Adaptive Courses	The system stores topics in a simple semantic network, with link types indicating the relationship between topics and re-topics. Generates new slides based on student's readiness to learn.
Self-Improving	Mathematics Tutor	The tutor learns how to generate problems in order to reduce student problem solving time. A machine learning agent enables the tutor to better generalize what it teaches.

Table 2. Cases studies and intelligent abilities.

mannequin for an equal amount of time (Eliot and Woolf 1996a; Eliot et al. 1996). This implies that an emergency room doctor would not be called away from clinical duties to train students, at least for the procedural part of the training.

A primary contribution of the Cardiac Tutor was use of an adaptive simulation to improve student learning. Technologies were integrated, including simulation, tutoring and plan recognition, in novel ways. The algorithm that identified procedural steps, for example, performed plan recognition in a multi-agent and real-time environment using knowledge-based methods for generating common sense plan interpretation in unexpected situations. Representation of expert action, represented as protocols listing a series of procedures, closely resembled the form in which domain experts express their knowledge. Consequently, when new ACLS protocols were adopted by the medical community the system was easily modified.

The Cardiac Tutor addressed several issues of reasoning about a user's knowledge and skills within a real-time system. The training context (i.e., choice of topics) was changed based on a tight interaction between user modeling techniques and simulation management. The tutoring process was enhanced by providing appropriate new patient cases when the user model was accurate, without creating serious problems when it was not. The impact of tutoring decisions on the student was considered carefully. The student model was constructed using fallible heuristics, so inferences from that model were restricted to ensure that inaccuracies did not create serious problems for the student. Adaptivity built into the Cardiac Tutor was designed to reduce the consequences of incorrect assumptions. These abilities will be more fully explained below.

An Example of the Cardiac Tutor

One problem in treating a patient with a cardiac problem is that the heart sometimes spontaneously changes state and goes into one of several abnormal rhythms or arrhythmias. Proper training for ACLS requires that the medical leader apply specific procedures for each new rhythm. Approximately two years of closely supervised clinical experience in an emergency room, ambulance, or similar medical facility is often required. The cost of this training is high, because medical instructors must constantly supervise medical students to ensure that patient care is not compromised.

Figures 1–3 show screen images from the Cardiac Tutor, a simulation of a patient experiencing a series of arrhythmias. Figure 1 shows that the intravenous line has been installed and the patient is being intubated. The icons on the chest and mouth indicate that compressions are in progress and ventilation is not being used. A pacemaker was installed (shown in figure 2). The student tried a sequence of drugs, specifically epinephrine and atropine and following the second dose of atropine, the ECG converted to ventricular fibrillation.

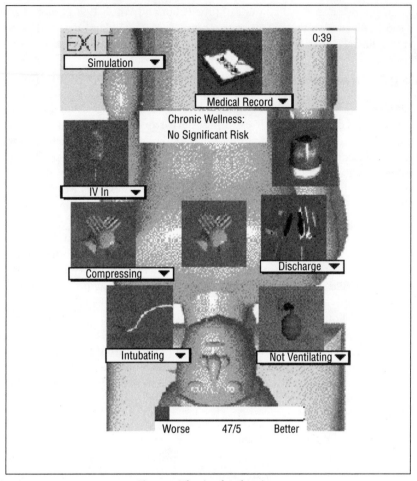

Figure 1. The simulated patient.
Reprinted with permission from The Gale Group.

The protocol for ventricular fibrillation requires immediate electrical therapy, repeated at increasing strength up to three times or until conversion to another rhythm is seen. Electrical therapy begins by charging the defibrillator to the desired setting, i.e. 200, 300, or 360 joules. When the unit is ready, the student must press the "stand clear" icon to ensure that caregivers are not injured. Once the "stand clear" command has been processed, the student may apply the countershock by pressing the "defibrillate" icon. Synchronized cardioversion may also be selected or the procedure aborted using the "dump charge" command. All of these simulated actions were monitored by the tutor and evaluated in comparison with medical protocols.

During the retrospective feedback, or post resuscitation conference, every

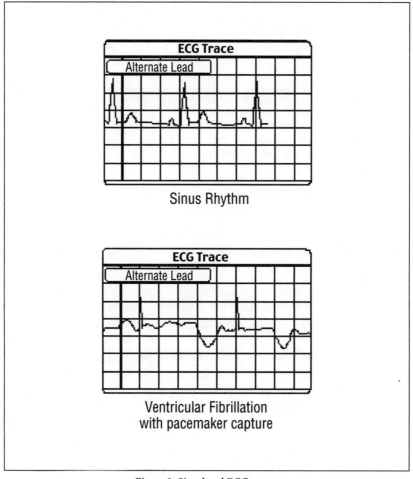

Figure 2. Simulated ECG traces.
Reprinted with permission from The Gale Group.

student action was reviewed, and a history a performance shown, listing correct and incorrect actions taken by the student (see figure 3). Each action in the history and performance review was connected to the original simulation state and knowledge base, so the student could request additional information about his past actions.

Each state transition to a new rhythm was associated with a different probability as shown in figure 4. The nodes represented states of cardiac arrest or arrhythmias, and the arcs represented probabilities of moving to a new physiological state following a specified treatment event or other significant occurrence during the simulation. The left side of figure 4 represents the normal

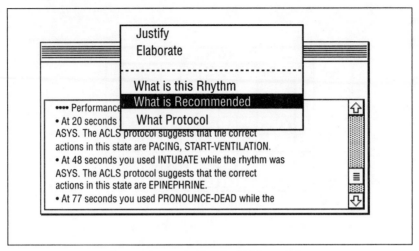

Figure 3. Requesting help in the hints window.
Reprinted with permission from The Gale Group.

traversal of the system from one arrhythmia (VFIB) to alternative possible arrhythmias (VTACH, ASYS, and BRADY). The tutor altered the path of traversal to
increase the probability that a specific learning opportunity would be available
to the student. In other words, if the student needed to practice a bradycardia
rhythm (BRADY), the transverse probability listed on the arc for BRADY, which
was 10 percent, would be modified to 65 percent (right side of figure 4). Bias-
ing the simulation to reach states with good learning opportunities is a novel
way to implement goal directed behavior.

Traditional simulations used for training are not truly adaptive to the learning needs of the student. At most, simulations allow users to select among fixed
simulation scenarios or to insert isolated events (such as a component failure)
(Self 1988). On the other hand, the Cardiac Tutor analyzed the simulation
model at every choice point to determine if any goal state could be reached. It
altered the simulation model dynamically to increase the learning value of the
time spent interacting with the student, without eliminating the probabilistic
nature inherent in the domain.

Multi-Agent Systems

Expert behavior, i.e. a series of correct procedures performed in response to a
specific rhythm, was represented as a protocol (figure 5, third line from the
bottom). Domain actions within the protocol recognition algorithm were augmented with planning knowledge to enable the system to make a common
sense interpretation of the protocols in situations resulting from student mistakes or unexpected events initiated by the simulation (Eliot and Woolf
1996b). The system ensured that every domain recommendation was possible

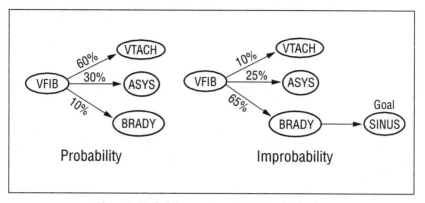

Figure 4. Underlying representation of arrhythmias.

in the current situation and conformed to some interpretation of the student's actions applied to the protocols.

The system employed planning technology as a knowledge-based critic to determine teaching goal states. The goals in this directed graph corresponded with arrhythmias, different heart rhythms that the student should practice. However, the Cardiac Tutor reasoned about several issues: which arrhythmia to present; interrelations among goals; several goal states in the simulation which might satisfy a single tutoring goal; and the fact that all tutoring goals need to be satisfied eventually. The tutor also reasoned about which tutoring goals might fail, e.g., the student could not reach a rhythm that needs practice.

The tutor moved to a new goal state by searching forward from the current state whenever the simulation reached a branch point. Normally, the simulation would choose a direction randomly based upon the domain specific probabilities of the outcome. Before making this random selection, however, the tutor searched several states forward to determine if a high priority simulation state was easily accessible. When a goal, or high priority state, was accessible, the tutor considered altering the base probabilities of the chosen point. The choice was then made randomly based on "improbability," see figure 4.

The Plan Recognition Mechanism

The Cardiac Tutor was based on integrating a simulation, tutoring and plan recognition mechanism. Figure 5 shows a time varying trace of the integrated simulation, planner, plan recognition system, and student-model reflecting the actions of the student, the system and their effects on each other. The next to bottom line, *simulation*, represents clinical reality, in this case, the independent succession of rhythms of the heart during a cardiac arrest. Sometimes the heart spontaneously changed state and went into one of several abnormal rhythms or arrhythmias. The student was expected to respond to the state changes correctly, *expert model.* However, the student's response, *user actions,*

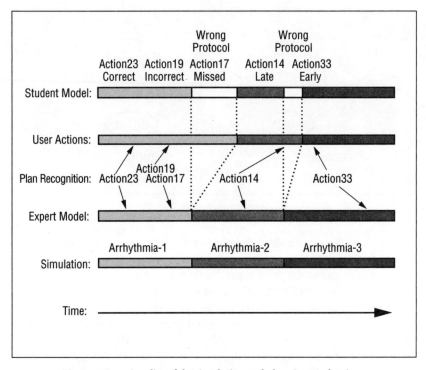

Figure 5. Functionality of the simulation and planning mechanisms.

was frequently inconsistent with the behavior of the expert model. During such inconsistencies, a *plan recognition* phase predicted what an expert would do and compared this with the student's actions.

The relation among tutor, plan recognition mechanism and simulation was cyclic: the plan recognition module monitored the student interacting with the simulation (user actions in figure 5) and produced information that was interpreted by the tutoring module to define goal states. The adaptive simulation responded to the current set of goals so the student spent more time working in problem solving situations with high learning value for the individual. As the student learned, the system continued to update its model thereby keeping the curriculum focused on the student's most important learning needs.

Student learning needs were determined by evaluating past student behavior. Observed deviation from standard medical practice was interpreted as a need to better understand the relevant procedure. Student performance measures were combined with knowledge about the difficulty of each procedure to estimate which topics currently provided the maximum potential for learning, or maximum expected learning value. The maximum expected learning value combined the probability that the student would, in fact, learn, the importance of the topic and the quantity of expected learning. The goal of these combined heuristics was to maximize the student's improvement in performance per unit of time spent in the learning environment. Once learning goals were identified as required, the tutor probabilistically increased the priority of simulation states in which those medical topics had to be applied. We assumed that this would result in increased time on task and hence improved learning.

The student model was built passively by comparing student actions with expert protocols (similar to plans or scripts) representing expert behavior (figure 5 top line). Medical interventions by the student were mediated by the computer and compared to protocols representing expert behavior. The computer offered automated tutorial help in addition to recording, restoring, critiquing and grading student performance. It customized the simulation to suit different previous levels of achievement and might, for example, require one student to work on a two or three rhythms for an hour, while another student experienced a dozen rhythms and contexts during that same hour. Good or improved performance was noted with positive feedback; incorrect behavior was categorized and commented upon.

The Student as Agent

The plan recognition system modeled an expert's behavior in the domain for comparison with the student's actions. The student performed actions in the simulation that were evaluated by the tutor to assess consistency with the expert's actions, encoded as a planning formalism.

The tutoring system reasoned about the student, both as an agent within the simulation and as a student learning a task. The student was responsible for directing simulated agents and most commands were simulated as orders for assistants to perform medical tasks. In other words, the student might initiate electrical therapy by first asking an agent to charge the defibrillator and then pressing the "stand clear" button. The student was represented within the simulation as he directly operated the simulated defibrillator and shouted orders for another agent to perform some action by selecting a menu command. Each order was simulated as realistically as possible, including an appropriate real-time delay as the task was performed.

The domain of cardiac arrest and the protocol of required procedures necessitated complex representations and reasoning mechanisms. Many abilities had to be generalized for multiple instances: multiple agents, (e.g., including doctors, nurses and EMTS), multiple roles (e.g., airways or medications manger), multiple actions (e.g., start iv, intubate, defibrillate) and multiple orders, (e.g., action performed out of order due to parallel activity).

The Protocol Interpreter

The system reasoned about the student's ability by comparing student actions with a model of expert behavior. Representation of expert behavior as a series

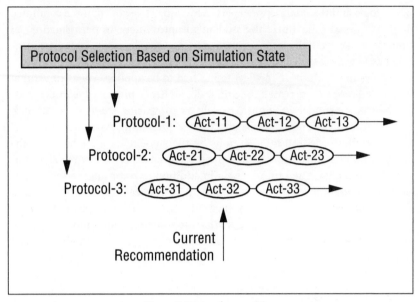

Figure 6. Protocol recognition.

of actions, see figure 5, third line from the bottom, encoded a leader's correct procedures in relation to the simulated arrhythmias, see figure 4 and figure 5, second line from the bottom. The team leader was expected to perform a limited set of actions and to direct the actions of other members of the resuscitation team. The system varied the number of assistants available in each scenario, thus affecting the possible number of parallel activities. Actions were assigned to a specific agent both for evaluating student performance and while updating the simulation. An action was considered valid if an available agent was ready to perform it. We assumed that simulated agents could remember a sequence of actions and perform them in order.

Figure 6 shows a simplified version of the protocol interpreter. The correct protocol had to be selected initially by analyzing the state of the simulation. In this example, protocol-3 was selected so protocol-1 and protocol-2 remained inactive. If the simulation had been in some other state initially then protocol-1 or protocol-2 could have been selected.

Encoding knowledge in this domain required a more sophisticated representation than depicted in figure 6. Some actions were optional in some situations. For instance, if act-32 was optional then the current recommendation would be the set including actions: $R = [Act-32, Act-33]$. If the student's actions were always correct, updating the protocol pointer was comparatively straightforward. However, incorrect student actions were allowed to affect the state of the simulation, possibly resulting in movement to a state where currently recommended actions were impossible or meaningless (Broverman, 1991). The protocol interpreter required additional planning knowledge to detect and correct such problems.

The knowledge base allowed preconditions and post-conditions to be specified for protocol actions. When the protocol interpreter detected an incorrect student action it notified the student, then examined the preconditions of actions in the current set of recommendations and then skipped impossible actions by moving the pointer forward.

Feedback during the simulation was considered carefully. Providing descriptive information during a simulation was found by the students to be quite intrusive. Only a small number of mistakes were considered important enough to force termination of the simulation for immediate feedback. For other mistakes, the tutor would beep and record information for presentation during retrospective feedback. This allowed students to continue working with the simulation despite imperfect performance. The simulation history was saved, so that mistaken actions could be reviewed in context by the student during retrospective feedback, see figure 3.

Actions and Synchronization

Actions of agents were not simple. The role assigned to each action was part of the static knowledge about actions. The assignment of roles to agents was automatically defined at the beginning of each simulation depending upon how many helper agents were available. The number of helpers and their role assignments did not change during a simulation. The simulated team leader was controlled by the student and assigned the single role of leader. The other roles were distributed among the available helper agents as equally as possible.

In sum, the Cardiac Tutor utilized mechanisms for goal selection, plan formation, and plan instantiation within situated contexts. It included an accurate descriptive model of the emergency room environment and general patient status, combined with a causal model of cardiac function and related physiologic systems. The tutor consisted of a simulation, representing the problem-solving environment; a student model, to guide the learning process; a bias mechanism, making the simulation adaptive; and a plan recognition system, for constructing the student model.

Multiple agent and planning technology enabled the Cardiac Tutor, unlike typical teaching systems, to go beyond simple classification of student actions as correct or incorrect by specifying how an incorrect user action related to the expert action. For example, student actions could be classified as too early or too late. In addition, matching student action against that of an expert enabled the system to recognize an action that was correct, but used an incorrect parameter value. This was labeled partially correct. Dynamic construction of the student model involved monitoring student actions during the simulation and evaluating these actions in comparison with an expert model encoded as a multi-agent plan.

Mathematics Tutor

A second tutor applied machine learning to the problem of generating new problems, hints and help. AnimalWatch learned how to predict some characteristics of student problem solving such as number of mistakes made or time spent on each problem. It used this model to automatically compute an optimal teaching policy, such as reducing mistakes made or time spent on each problem.

AnimalWatch was a National Science Foundation funded arithmetic tutor designed for fourth through sixth grade elementary school students. The top-level goal was to increase girls' confidence in their ability to do mathematics (Beal et al. 1998b). The hypothesis was that the abilities that make an intelligent tutor powerful, e.g., curriculum sequencing, personalized help and intelligent problem selection, also serve to bolster a student's interest and enjoyment of mathematics. In contrast to most educational software which is designed primarily with the male user in mind, AnimalWatch was tailored to girls' interests and needs (Arroyo et al. 1999, 2000). It engaged girls' interest in math by blending mathematics with environmental biology, the science that is of highest interest to female students. An environmental biology storyline, in which math problems were embedded, unfolded as the narrative progressed. Students selected an endangered species, such as the right whale or the giant panda, which included an initial story context and joined an environmental team to monitor the behavior of the species. For example, in the case of the Giant Panda, problems involved research at the library about the panda's habitat, reading about the birth of a new panda at the San Diego Zoo, estimating the expenses associated with a trip to China, and analyzing the rate of decline of the panda population over time, etc.

AnimalWatch helped girls sustain their belief in their ability to learn difficult mathematics concepts (Arroyo et al. 2000, Beal et al. 2000). After working with AnimalWatch, both boys and girls showed significant increases in math self-concept, as indicated by responses on a questionnaire originally developed by Eccles et al. (1993), with girls in some cases matching boys' responses. In addition, AnimalWatch improved girls' attitudes towards their desire to study mathematics (Beal et al. 1998a, 1998b; Hart et al. 1999). Several evaluation strategies were employed. First, performance data (accuracy of problem solving; number and type of errors; hints and instruction selected after errors; effectiveness of hints; latency to solve and problem difficulty level achieved) were automatically collected for subsequent analysis, and showed that the system was effective for both boys and girls (Beal et al., 2000). Second, pre- and post-test questionnaires to assess math self concept, math value and math liking have showed, based on standard instruments developed by Eccles et al. (1993), benefits to students' math attitudes of working with AnimalWatch. The results of several other evaluation studies indicate that AnimalWatch provided effec-

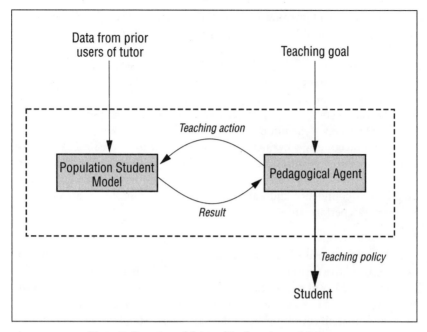

Figure 7: Overview of the machine learning architecture.

tive individualized math instruction and had a positive impact on students' belief in the value of learning mathematics.

Sophisticated machine learning algorithms reasoned about students' knowledge and provided customized examples and hints tailored for each student (Beck and Woolf, 2000; Beck et al. 1999, 2000). The goal of the machine learning component was to automatically compute an optimal teaching policy, such as reducing the amount of mistakes made or time spent on each problem by using a "two-phase" learning algorithm, see figure 7. The architecture used two learning agents. One learning agent was responsible for modeling how a student interacted with the tutor (the population student model, or PSM), and the other was responsible for constructing a teaching policy (the pedagogical agent, or PA). The student's interaction with the tutor was modeled in the population student model. "Classical" tutors use cognitive modeling to understand how a novice or expert solves problems in the domain. In AnimalWatch, the PSM was trained to understand student behavior by observing hundreds of students using a prototype of the tutor and was therefore capable of predicting an individual student's reaction to a variety of teaching actions, such as presentation of specific problem type.

The second learning agent, the pedagogical agent (PA) was responsible for constructing a teaching policy that met a configurable teaching goal. The PA was a reinforcement learning agent and used the PSM to simulate the environment of working with hundreds of students. The reward for the PA was whatever high-level learning goal an instructor specified, such as reducing time spent on problems. Casting the problem in this way permitted instructors to ignore low-level issues, such as specific teaching rules, e.g., which analogy worked best on which problem. The PSM and PA worked together to permit the tutor to learn a good teaching policy directly from observing students using a simplified version of the tutor.

The architecture was evaluated by comparing it to a "classical" tutor that taught via heuristics without the aid of machine learning agent. The metrics used to assess student performance included subjective measures, (e.g., mathematics self-confidence and enjoyment) as well as objective measures (e.g., mathematics performance).

Motivation

Use of machine learning was motivated in part to produce more flexible tutors. In other words, to expand the population of students reached by tutors and to expand the quality of responses for an individual student. For example, if a tutor were designed to teach algebra to ninth graders, it might be programmed to assume that all incoming students had a fairly standard set of skills and would acquire new knowledge about the domain in a fairly standard way. Such assumptions would probably not even be valid for all ninth graders, and it is unlikely they would apply for an eight year old math superstar learning algebra at a young age, or for a thirty year old community college student who has tried to learn algebra in the past and failed. The latter two students are likely to learn very differently. In particular, the community college student probably has some experience with algebra, and may have some misremembered rules. Such misconceptions from prior exposure can be a major stumbling block to reteaching the material (Stern et al. 1996). It is not feasible to construct a separate tutor for every new population of students. Thus some means of constructing more adaptable tutors are needed.

Another obstacle to the acceptance of tutors in many training situations is the high cost of development and lack of flexibility once deployed. Cost and flexibility are two very similar problems: the actual difficulty is the high cost per student taught. If some means could be found of either decreasing development cost, or broadening the range of uses of a finished tutor, intelligent tutors would be more cost efficient. In addition to problems of cost, institutional acceptance is another factor blocking tutor deployment (Bloom 1996). Few organizations are willing to accept teaching software that cannot be modified.

Research Objectives

AnimalWatch addressed difficulties in tutor construction and especially the large amount of time required to build tutors. Currently, a large part of the effort of building tutors is spent on encoding a human teaching knowledge (Quafafou et al. 1995).

The machine learning agent in AnimalWatch was able to change the tutor's *model of how to teach*, rather than simply changing the tutor's explicit *teaching* in a specific instance. This fundamentally differs from traditional tutor adaptation. A "classical" tutor has encoded rules that enable it to use a student model based on student performance to adjust its teaching. Thus, an individual student may be treated differently from another student, but all such similar students, for the life of the tutor, will be treated with the generation of exactly the same problem, hints or help. Machine learning, on the other hand, enables the tutor itself to change and thus, over time its treatment of this typical student will be different.

Machine learning alters how a tutor reasons and makes inferences about the student. This permits it to reason "outside" of the variables that make up its student model. For example, a tutor could realize that one student who has the multiplication tables memorized can solve multiplication problems with small numbers much more quickly than expected and somewhat more quickly than expected on multiplication problems with large numbers. From this, it could adjust its mechanism for estimating how a student will perform on a problem and indirectly influence its teaching. This form of adaptation is not applicable to an entire population of students, but only to the student currently using the tutor. However, the tutor does not understand why the student is working more quickly. Thus, another student who, for some other reason, produced the same overt behavior would be categorized with the fast multiplier.

By allowing the tutor's modeling to be more flexible, the tutor is usable on a wider range of students. Also it improves the tutor's adaptivity with a particular student. In the ideal case, machine learning techniques will adjust the system's modeling techniques on-line as the student interacts with the tutor. This modeling is more challenging than off-line machine learning, which is done before students begin using the tutor (generally with data previously gathered). Students generally do not use a tutor for a long period of time; 20 hours of instruction is current state of the art (Koedinger and MacLaren 1997) which severely limits the number of training instances available to the machine learning agent.

Interacting with the Mathematics Tutor

The expert model in AnimalWatch was arranged as a topic network where nodes represented skills to be taught. The links between nodes frequently represented a prerequisite relationship. For instance, the ability to add is a prerequisite to learning how to multiply. Figure 8 shows a portion of the topic network from AnimalWatch.

Throughout this discussion topics are major components of the curriculum about which a student may be asked a question, while skill refers to any cur-

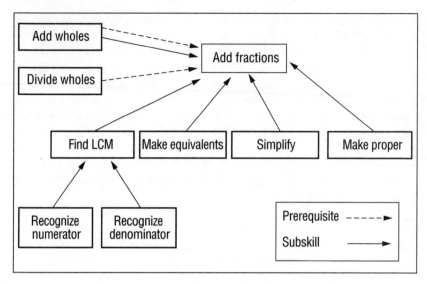

Figure 8. A portion of the AnimalWatch topic network.

riculum element (including topics). For example, borrowing (as in subtraction) was not tested separately and so was a skill but not a topic. Whole number subtraction was tested and can be considered both a skill and a topic. When we use the term "topic," we refer to the type of problem on which the student was currently working.

Subskills are steps within a topic the student performs in order to accomplish a task. For example, adding fractions has the subskills of finding a common denominator, converting the fractions to equivalent form with a new numerator, adding the numerators, simplifying the result, and making the result proper. Note that "add wholes" was both a prerequisite and a subskill for "add fractions." For a given problem, not all of these were required. Table 3 shows the subskills required for some sample problems.

AnimalWatch provided an environment for students to practice mathematics and receive immediate feedback about their work. The tutor generated the topic on which the student worked. Figure 9 shows an example of a problem for addition of whole numbers and figure 10 is an example of a topic generated from the "prefractions" area of the curriculum. Generating the topic on which the student worked was one way the tutor adapted the curriculum to the learning needs of the student. Students moved through the curriculum only if their performance for each topic was acceptable. Thus problems generated by the tutor were an indication of mathematics proficiency, as described below.

AnimalWatch adjusted the difficulty of each problem presented. For example, addition of fraction problems can widely vary in their degree of difficulty.

Subskill	Problem 1	Problem 2 1/3 + 1/4	Problem 3 2/3 + 5/8
Find LCM	No	Yes	Yes
Equivalent fractions	No	Yes	Yes
Add numerators	Yes	Yes	Yes
Make proper	No	No	Yes

Table 3. Three sample add-fractions problems.

Figure 9. A typical addition problem with a simple text hint.

This process is illustrated in table 3. The more subskills required, the harder the problem. Similarly, larger numbers also increased the tutor's rating of the problem's difficulty: it is harder to find the least common multiple of 13 and 21 than it is to find the least common multiple of 2 and 3. AnimalWatch also selected from a variety of hints, some requiring manipulation of small rods on the screen (see figure 11) and others describing procedural rules. The tutor recorded information about the difficulty of problems presented and abilities of hints, such as the amount of text they contain, whether they were interactive, and how much information they provided. Figures 9, 11, and 12 demonstrate hints that provide varying amounts of information. The hint in figure 9

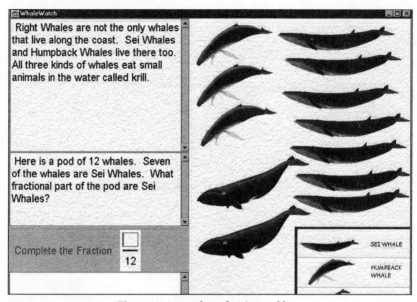

Figure 10. A sample prefraction problem.

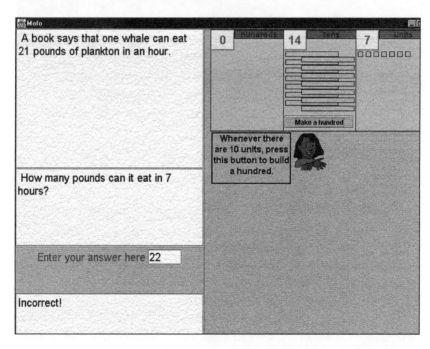

Figure 11. An example of an interactive hint.

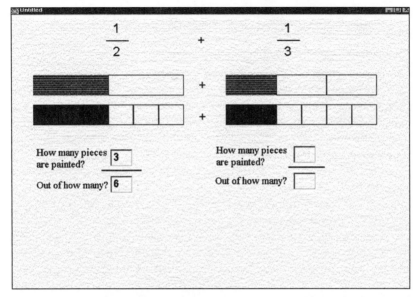

Figure 12. A highly concrete hint.

is brief and text based, while the hint in figure 11 is interactive. If the student continued to make mistakes, more and more specific hints were provided until he answered the question correctly.

A database of the student's current state of knowledge, or student model, tracked the student's level of ability for each skill being taught. It noted how long the student took to generate a response, both after the initial problem presentation and (in the event of an incorrect response), the delay in responding after a hint was presented. It also measured the student's level of cognitive development (Arroyo et al. 1999) according to Piaget's theory of intellectual development (Piaget 1954). This measure correlated with the student's math performance and was used to further customize the tutor's teaching (Arroyo et al., 2000).

Knowledge about the Student and the Tutor

The tutor tracked a variety of information about the student's behavior in the student model. A primary task of this model was to track the student's level of ability for each skill. In addition to "snap shots" of the student's current performance, the tutor also kept track of trend information. A history of the student's proficiency in each topic was maintained; this allowed the tutor to determine if the student was making progress or not. The student model also contained the average amount of time the student required to solve each problem.

The tutor recorded information about problems presented to the student. When a student was shown a problem, the tutor noted the topic of the problem and the operands. The tutor used a set of heuristics to assess the difficulty of the problem based on the topic and operands. For example, a numerical difficulty rating was based on how many subskills the student must apply and the complexity of applying each such operation (Beck et al. 1997).

The Machine Learning Agent

A layered machine learning architecture (figure 7) was used to allow each learning component to be considered and optimized independently and separately from the design of the rest of the tutor. One layer of learning (PSM) was concerned with describing student behavior in different contexts. The other layer (PA) determined how to map this description of the student's behavior onto a correct teaching action.

The first objective was to construct a model of how students behaved while using the tutor. This model predicted how a student would act in a certain situation, given that the tutor had previously taken certain teaching actions. By experimenting with this model, the pedagogical agent determined which actions taken in which context resulted in this (simulated) student achieving the desired objective. This objective was customizable and provided the basis for the reinforcement learning (RL) agent's reward signal. If the RL agent took actions that resulted in the student achieving desirable states, the reward was high. Figure 7 provides an overview of this process.

Thus, the RL agent provided a model of how students behaved and a desired teaching goal, such as reducing the amount of time an individual student spends solving problems. The agent took as input a set of abilities that describe the current teaching situation (how the student was doing, prior help given, etc.) and output a recommended teaching action. This teaching policy was used by the tutor to direct its teaching decisions, including which problem to generate and what type of hints to show.

The tutor observed whether the student's response was correct and how much time it took her to generate this response, a relatively simple set of goals. It did not attempt to create a general simulated learner for all conditions, or even a general learner for this particular domain. Rather, it built a simulation for how a learner responded (at a directly observable, not cognitive process, level) in a specific domain to specific teaching actions. This restriction made the problem tractable.

In order to gather enough information to make predictions, data about the entire population of users was gathered. When AnimalWatch was deployed with hundreds of students, logs from each user were saved and then merged. This allowed a much larger training set than if the tutor were restricted to data from a single user. This PSM made predictions about "an average student with a proficiency of x who has made y mistakes so far on the problem."

Architecture of AnimalWatch

The learning algorithm for the PSM took as input a state and determined the student's likely behavior. Ideal characteristics of this algorithm were robustness to noise, low computational cost, and being capable of learning from little data. Even though the PSM was first trained off-line, where training data were plentiful, there might also be an on-line learning component that attempts to reason about an individual student while she uses the tutor. In this situation, training data are scarce.

The PA optimized its decisions to maximize the expected future reward it received. Since the tutor was designed to increase confidence in mathematics, students might be frustrated by spending a lot of time (or making many mistakes) on a problem.

AnimalWatch integrated both the PSM and PA into the tutor. The PSM was responsible for predicting the student's action in a given context. This prediction was used by the PA to predict the effect of its proposed teaching action. The PA then directed the tutor about which teaching decision to use.

Evaluation of AnimalWatch

The performance of the PSM and PA in isolation was evaluated before testing the combined system on actual students. To evaluate the PSM, the data were split into training and a test set. The PSM was constructed with the training set and its predictions were evaluated on the test set (this can be extended to cross-validation techniques). Each prediction of the PSM (e.g. likelihood of correct answer and time to generate response) can be verified in this manner.

To measure effectiveness, a variety of performance metrics were used. Pre- and post-test scores used a standard test for mathematics confidence (Eccles et al. 1993) and were used to measure the tutor's impact on girls' self-confidence in mathematics. Data concerning student's qualitative assessment of using AnimalWatch was also gathered. Finally, actual performance data of students using the tutor was evaluated.

A critical issue was what it meant for this architecture to "work." It was possible for the PSM and PA to work flawlessly together and produce no improvement in any of the above metrics. The difficulty was that the system tried to optimize an externally defined learning goal.

To determine if the PSM was sufficiently accurate, we compared its predictions to how the students in the training data set actually performed. Figure 13 shows its accuracy for predicting how long students required to generate a response, the PSM's predictions correlated at 0.629 with actual performance. Training on half the data set and testing on the other half dropped this correlation to 0.619, which was still very strong for predicting as noisy a variable as time.

It was necessary to validate whether the pedagogical agent had learned anything useful from its training. The PA could not be validated in as simple a manner as the PSM. It was difficult/impossible to split the data into training and test sets, since the PA made active decisions. The actual data may not follow the path the PA would have chosen. The PA's experience occurred in the context of a simulated student using a simulation of a tutor. To determine if the pedagog-

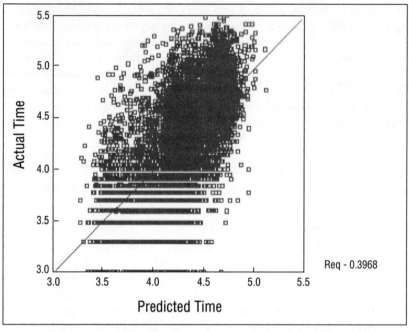

Figure 13. AnimalWatch's accuracy in predicting student response time.

ical agent would interact correctly with the PSM, we constructed a simulation. This simulation contained all the typical steps in a tutoring session. First, the PA selected a topic and a problem. The PSM was then invoked to see if the student would make a mistake or answer correctly. In the event of an incorrect answer, the PA was responsible for finding the hint that appeared best. From the PA's standpoint, this was identical to interacting with an actual student.

Figure 14 shows the improvement of the PA's performance at minimizing the amount of time students spent per problem. The *x*-axis is the number of trials (in thousands) the agent has spent learning. The *y*-axis is the exponential-average of the amount of time the simulated student required to solve a problem. Performance started at around forty seconds per problem, and eventually reduced to around sixteen seconds per problem.

To test whether this architecture would work with actual students using an actual tutor, we evaluated the system in a controlled experiment. The first version of AnimalWatch used a fairly weak teaching model with some basic heuristics, and was tested in two local elementary schools. This data was used to train the PSM and PA. The AnimalWatch tutor was then taken to a different school for testing. The students at this school were broken into two groups. One group, the control ($n = 39$), were taught with a set of teaching heuristics. The second, experimental ($n = 58$), group was taught using just the machine

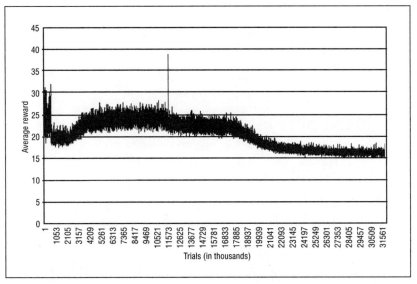

Figure 14. The pedagogical agents learned to reduce time spent by students on problems.

learning (ML) architecture. The ML architecture had the goal of minimizing the amount of time a student spends on a problem.

Students using the ML version of the tutor averaged 27.7 seconds to solve a problem, while students using the classic version of AnimalWatch averaged 39.7 seconds. This difference was significant at $P < 0.001$ (two-tailed t-test). Just as important, the difference was meaningful: reducing average times by thirty percent was a large reduction. Thus, the agent made noticeable progress in its goal of reducing the amount of time students spent per problem. We are not arguing this was necessarily the best pedagogical goal, just what we asked the agent to do.

Further evidence of the ML agent's ability to adapt instruction can be seen in table 4. Students in the experimental group, i.e. those who used the machine learning version of the tutor designed to minimize the amount of time per problem, solved whole number ($P < 0.001$) and fraction problems ($P = 0.02$) significantly faster than students in the control group. Particularly impressive was that experimental group students were faster at solving fraction problems in spite of having a significantly lower Piaget score. Students in the control group, that is students who were taught using a set of heuristics, who got to fraction problems averaged a Piaget score of 7.9. However, students in the experimental group averaged 7.3; this difference was significant at $P < 0.001$. In other words, even students with a weaker cognitive development, as shown by their lower Piaget score, were able to succeed at whole and prefraction problems in order to be allowed to move into fraction problems. Thus, in spite of

Problem Type		Control	Experimental
Whole Numbers	Percentage of Problems	73.6%	60.0%
	Time	43.4 sec	28.1 sec
Prefractions	Percentage of problems	19.3%	27.3%
	Time	22.7 sec	21.7 sec
Fractions	Percentage of Problems	7.2%	12.7%
	Time	44.5 sec	38.5 sec

Table 4. Summary of performance by math topic area.

being less restricted about which students saw fraction (i.e. difficult) problems, the experimental group still solved such problems more quickly. For whole number problems, students in the experimental group made 0.28 mistakes per problem, which is significantly fewer mistakes ($P < 0.001$) than the control group (0.44 mistakes per problem). However, for fraction problems both groups made an equivalent number of mistakes (0.39 in the experimental versus 0.40 in the control).

In sum, this research has contributed to the field of intelligent tutoring systems in the automatic construction of a teaching policy. Learning techniques were used to increase a tutor's flexibility, determine how to teach and allow the teaching policy to change over time for a changing student population. No prebuilt set of teaching rules offers this degree of adaptability. Another contribution was exploring how to combine data from a single user with data previously gathered from a population of users. For the field of student or user modeling, this was a powerful idea. This application of reinforcement learning allows an agent to view the student as the "environment" and the tutor as the actor. Finally, the potential to customize teaching goals allows a software tutor to be used in a wider variety of conditions.

Engineering Tutors

The next two tutors provided open design environments to support independent student exploration and implicitly elicited information about student knowledge and goals. These tutors coached rather than taught and required less knowledge about correct answers and more information about the domain. The Engineering Tutors coached about "design for manufacturing"

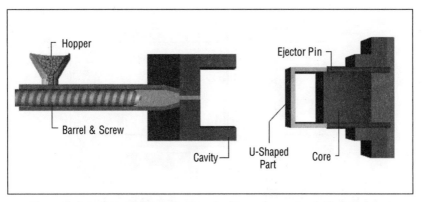

Figure 15. Injection molding tooling required to produce a simple U-shaped part.
Reprinted with permission from The Gale Group.

(DFM) and provided students with a realistic understanding of complex processes through interaction with three-dimensional animations (Woolf et al. 1996, 1997). Students designed parts and then the tutor simulated fabrication of the dies used in the manufacturing process. This provided immediate feedback about manufacturing costs, three-dimensional visualizations to supply intuition behind complex geometric problems and environments within which a student could experiment. Individual tutors addressed topics such as injection molding, stamping, forging, die casting, and finite element analysis. Some of these tutors contained an expert system based on visual components of the solution, as explained below.

The *injection molding tutor* enabled students to construct and examine molded polymer part designs. It showed an animation of an injection molding machine along with a simple open/shut mold, see figure 15. The student then created new designs, using either an "L-bracket" (see figures 16a and 16b) or a box as the base, as in figure 15. The student selected features to add to the base from a restricted set, shown in the pallet right side of figure 16a and b, including ribs, "thru" holes and bosses. As an example, shown in figure 16a, a student placed a "thru" hole on the short end of the L-bracket. The tutor provided an animated three dimensional view of the tooling needed to manufacture the part (see figure 16b), critiqued the design and provided alternatives to save money. The tutor stored an animation of a manufacturing die needed to produce every option a student might take. After the student created a part, the appropriate animated solution was selected from the visualization library and displayed (figure 16b).

The *Stamping Tutor* helped students understand the relationship between sheet metal part design and the required stamping stations. The tutor identified design issues and showed how they impacted the number of stations required. Design issues included dissimilar abilities, closely spaced abilities, nar-

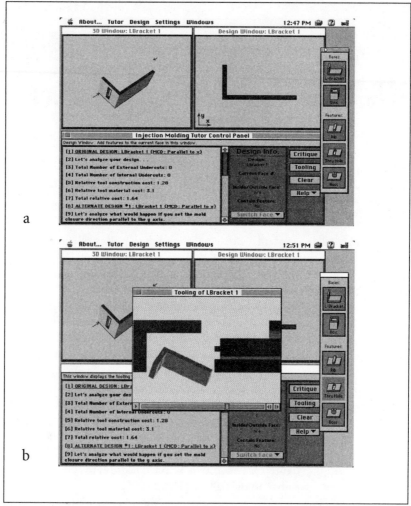

Figure 16. The student created new designs using an "L-bracket."
a. The student created a part by placing a "thru" hole in an L-bracket.
b. The tutor showed an animation of the die needed to manufacture the part.

row cutouts, projections and bends. For example, a student might design a new part by dragging a feature (hole, rib, emboss or extruded hole) onto the blank metal strip (figure 17, bottom left). Using a knowledge-based representation of stamping rules, the tutor dynamically generated a manufacturing solution, including the proper number of moving stamping stations required to build the part designed by the student (figure 17, top), and included a critique of the design (figure 17, bottom right). Similarly, when explaining how to bend a metal part, the tutor generated both an animated tooling solution (see figure

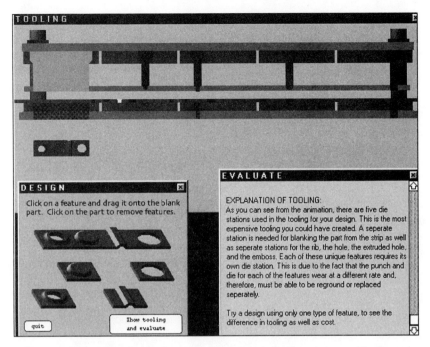

Figure 17. The student designed a stamped part by moving features onto a blank metal part (bottom left). The tutor's solution is generated (top).

18, bottom) and the plan view (shown on the top). These animated toolings were not stored or canned. The tutor selected graphic objects (film strips) stored in a simple network along with simple rules of design and manufacturing. Based on the decision of the expert system, certain stamping stations were selected to illustrate the manufacturing process and new film loops animating additional stamping stations were added to the evolving animation. The tutor also suggested design alternatives and critiqued the student's design, explaining why certain feature combinations or geometry would result in an inefficient design. Since the animation and critique were presented in real time, in response to a student design, the probability was increased that the feedback would address a specific learning opportunity.

Formative evaluation of these Engineering Tutors showed that they were as effective as several lectures and homework assignments within a traditional classroom setting (see table 5) (Poli et al. 1999, Woolf et al. 1997). The evaluation involved both introductory freshmen and junior engineering majors who used the tutors as a normal part of the course. The Injection Modeling Tutor was tested with 125 freshman divided into two groups. The first group (table 5, software first) used the software first and then took an evaluation test. The other group (table 5, lecture first) attended traditional lectures, worked on prob-

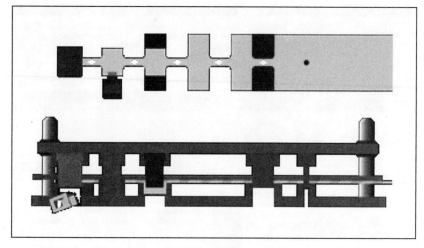

Figure 18. The tooling stations (bottom) and plan view (top) were generated by adding film strips based on expert systems analysis.

lems both at home and in class and then took the evaluation test. Both groups eventually received the lecture and were allowed to use the software (table 5, both). The scores indicate that the software alone can teach the relevant concepts of injection molding for manufacturing. Students who did not attend lectures and only used the tutors understood the relationship between part geometry and tool complexity and were as knowledgeable about the manufacturing process as those who had the advantage of being exposed to a human manufacturing expert during lectures.

The Injection Molding Tutor was also evaluated with forty-two junior engineering majors, twenty-nine of whom (see table 5, "previous exposure") had previously been exposed, via lectures and homework assignments two years earlier, to the processes and concepts of design for manufacturing. The other thirteen students (table 5, "no previous") included foreign students and transfer students, who had never heard of injection molding and had never been exposed to design for injection molding concepts. After using the tutor for about forty-five minutes, a quantitative evaluation test was administered. The average score achieved by students who two years earlier had been exposed to injection molding was eighty percent. The average score achieved by student with no previous exposure was seventy-nine percent. However, this latter group included two students who received exceptionally low scores and obviously had not clearly read the problem. If these two scores are dropped, the average score of this latter group becomes eighty-five percent. Again, the software seems to be able to replace several lectures and homework assignments, even among engineering majors.

	Average Score
Freshmen	
Software first	80
Lecture first	81
Both	85
Juniors	
Previous exposure to injection molding	80
No previous exposure to injection molding	79
Forging	72

Table 5. Evaluation of learning.

Junior engineering majors were also evaluated on their understanding of forging concepts for manufacturing after using the Forging Tutor (not described here). These student received no classroom lectures and were not given reading or homework problems dealing with the subject of forging. The overall average of all students was seventy-two percent. This subject is more complicated than injection molding and so the lower scores were expected. However, the results indicate that the concepts of design for forging, that is knowledge of the combinations of geometry and material selection for manufacturing, can be achieved without the need for standard classroom lectures and assignments.

Adaptive Courses

The final tutor customized an existing set of video-taped courses ("traditional" MANIC) for an individual student, using an overlay student model that recorded student ability and preferences. Traditional multimedia asynchronous networked individualized courseware (MANIC) delivered audio and HTML versions of lecture slides over the world wide web and began to take advantage of the increased interactivity and flexibility provided by the web as compared to usual lectures. Web-based courses can be considerably more interactive than existing computer-based courses, allowing students to take more control over their learning. For example, in traditional MANIC, students had several options for viewing course material (see figure 19, left). They controlled the speed, direction, and linearity of both the slides and audio playback. They played the audio from the beginning of the course to the end, or could stop and start the audio and slides, or "randomly" traverse the material using the table of contents provided as a guide. A more detailed description of the traditional MANIC can be found in Stern et al. (1997a, 1997b).

However, this traditional version of MANIC did not take advantage of all the benefits of web-based delivery. Students still felt they were in a lecture hall and thus took a passive role in their learning. iMANIC was designed to give students

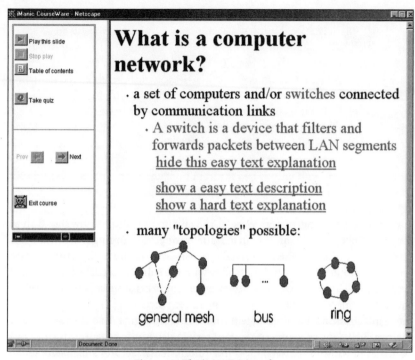

Figure 19. The iMANIC interface.

a more active role in their learning. Although the audio and slides for iMANIC were still taken from existing video-taped courses, the tutor's courses were not simple direct translations of those courses. By examining which slides were seen and which quizzes taken, the student model in the tutor determined a student's learning, as explained below, and guides the student through the material, dynamically generating course content and constructing interactive and adaptive quizzes at the appropriate level of difficulty. Course content was generated by using adaptive hypertext techniques including adaptive navigation support and adaptive content.

iMANIC provided an interface similar to the traditional MANIC, using slides and audio. Students traversed the course using either the "next" and "previous" buttons to linearly proceed through a topic or they used the table of contents to randomly jump to another point in the course. However, since the topic structure was not linear, adaptive navigation support was supplied; when a student reached the end of one topic, guidance was available to choose the next topic. Additionally, iMANIC provided *stretchtext*, which allowed the student to see more detailed information about the content by clicking on the text to get more information associated with that text.

Domain Organization

Lectures, and therefore video-tapes from lectures, are linear from start to finish. However, the on-line version of a course need not be. iMANIC stored topics in a simple semantic network, with links indicating the relationship between a topic and its pretopics (connected topics preceding the topic in the semantic net). Links represented prerequisite, corequisite, and related topics, similar to the link types used by *Intelligent Guide* (Carr and Goldstein 1977).

Each topic was divided into subtopics. These subtopics allowed the tutor to reason at a finer level about the student's knowledge. When a topic was displayed, a set of material, consisting of a linear ordering of pieces of text or graphics called content objects was presented to each student. As the topic was presented, it was broken into pages, or "slides," containing these content objects.

In addition to the topic structure, there were also keywords, or concepts, that were part of the domain. These concepts appeared throughout the content objects which taught a topic. As the tutor presented the topics, and a concept word appeared, it dynamically chose additional material for that concept, for example, extra explanations, graphics and definitions. Each piece of additional content had a level of difficulty assigned by a domain expert, indicating the level of knowledge needed to understand that information.

The tutor also reasoned about where to put page breaks, based on how much additional content was being shown. When displaying a slide, only one screen's worth of material was presented at a time, to prevent making the student scroll. However, before the slides were to be displayed, the tutor did not know how much supplementary information it would choose to show (see the adaptive content section that follows for how the tutor makes these decisions). Therefore, as the tutor presented a topic, it dynamically decided where to put page breaks after deciding how much supplementary material to provide.

Motivation for Sequencing Curriculum

In nonlinear domains, users might find themselves "lost in hyperspace" (Brusilovsky et al. 1996). An intelligent guide can be useful in avoiding this problem. To this end, iMANIC selected relevant topics on the basis of the current student model (Anderson 1990; Anderson and Reiser 1985) and helped sequence the curriculum topics based on a two part process. It was assumed that a student was "ready to learn" a topic only if he performed sufficiently well on its pretopics. The problem thus decomposed into determining (1) how well the student had performed on topics in the course, called the "learned" score; and (2) how to combine the ratings for all the pretopics, as well as the rating for the current topic, called the "ready" score.

Traditional intelligent tutoring systems determined how well a topic was learned by examining quizzes and tests. In open environments like the web, additional information is needed because students are free to explore without being required to take tests. For example, items used to determine how well a topic is learned include the student's access pattern for viewing the course material, e.g., time spent studying a topic and whether topics are reviewed multiple times.

Learned Score

Three factors were important in grading a student's knowledge of a topic: how well the student performed on quizzes, how well the topic was studied, and how much the topic was reviewed. These three pieces of evidence were combined to determine how well a topic was "learned."

Quizzes were a good source of information about a student's knowledge and were considered important for the student model. Because quizzes provided such concrete evidence of a student's knowledge, students were required to take quizzes on all topics in the domain. Quizzes were dynamically constructed from a question database and covered the topics most recently completed, as well as topics that should be reviewed. Each question had a level of difficulty as determined by the course instructor (Anderson and Reiser 1985, Boyle and Encarnacion 1994, Brusilovsky and Pesin 1994, Brusilovsky et al. 1996) indicating the level of mastery a student should have to answer the question correctly. This level of difficulty was used to update the student model after the student answered the questions posed. Clearly, correctly answering a harder question demonstrated a higher ability than correctly answering an easier one. Similarly, failing at a harder question was not as damaging as failing at an easier one.

Students using iMANIC spent most of the time reading and listening to course material. Therefore, some judgement was made about the comprehension a student gained through these activities.[1] The problem of determining if a student understood the material became one of judging how sufficiently each content object in the topic was studied. The premise was that students who did not spend enough time studying were not learning the material well and students spending too much time were having difficulty understanding the material. In order to assess the time spent on a content object, the tutor plotted the amount of time spent studying the object using a normal curve, with the mean and standard deviation determined by the course instructor before the course was presented. Once the content objects were plotted for a student and the new scores obtained, they were averaged over all content objects in the topic. This became the studied score for the topic.

This measure was flawed in at least two ways. First, it used time, which is an inherently inexact measure in assessing educational effort. If the student left the room for five minutes, the tutor did not detect this. Second, differences in individual learners needed to be considered. Spending a certain amount of time studying material did not imply comprehension. For example, some people read slower than others but comprehend just as well. The tutor needed a way to learn the optimal time for each student as he or she used the course. Future research involves improving the metrics for measuring how well material has been studied and understood.

Additionally, a student often studied a topic multiple times. The reviewed score on a topic recorded how many times the student returned to visit the same topic again. In general, if he reviewed frequently, then perhaps he did not retain information sufficiently and thus did not learn the material. Of course frequent reviewing might reflect individual differences, which were not taken into account.

The three scores on a topic, (i.e., quizzed, studied and reviewed) were combined into a single score to determine how well a topic was learned. A weighted average of the three individual scores was used, giving the most weight to quizzes.

Selecting the next topic. Once each topic's "learned" score was calculated, a "ready" score for other topics was determined. This score determined which topic the student should study next, based on how well the pretopics were learned. Rules that adjusted the pretopics' learned scores took into consideration the link types between a topic and its pretopics in the semantic network. Each link type had a threshold, indicating the minimum score for mastery of the pretopic. The weights were adjusted based on how close the learned score was to the threshold. Scaling rules were used to give more weight to different kinds of relationships. Once the weights of links were determined, the ranking on the topic was computed by averaging the adjusted link weights of the pretopics of the topic in question.

When the student linearly progressed through a topic and came to the end of that topic, he had the option of letting iMANIC choose the next topic. Topics which were not sufficiently learned had a higher priority over new topics to study. Thus among topics to be repeated, the one with the lowest "learned" value was chosen as the next topic to study.

If no topics needed to be repeated, the tutor's goal became guiding the student forward through the curriculum. To fulfill this goal, the "next" topics from the current topic were evaluated to see if they were "ready." If one or more topics have "ready" values, the one with the highest value was chosen to be taught. If no such next topic existed, then the semantic net was recursively searched backwards from these next topics, looking for a previous topic with the highest "ready" value. This policy ensured that topics that could help the student move on to new topics would be taught next and, thus, momentum through the curriculum preserved.

Adaptive Content

The goal of adaptive content in iMANIC was to provide a presentation that was not too hard nor too easy, while taking into account a student's learning style preferences. For example, one student might have preferred pictures to textual explanations, while another preferred definitions at first but examples later on.

A two-pass method was used to determine which supplemental information should be given to each student. The first determined which content objects from the concepts were at the correct level of difficulty, taking into consideration how much a student knew about the concept. The second determined student preference and took into consideration how the student preferred to learn.

The tutor analyzed how well the student knew the concept when deciding which supplemental content objects were at the correct level of difficulty. To do this, the tutor examined how well the concept had been learned. Each concept had a mastery value for each level of difficulty. The tutor simply determined the highest level of difficulty the student had mastered. A level of difficulty is said to be mastered if its mastery value is greater than a threshold, in this case 0.85 (on a 0 to 1 scale). The tutor then chose those content objects that were at the same level of difficulty as the student's highest mastered level of difficulty.

Both quizzes and time spent studying an object were used to update the mastery values for a concept. When a quiz was taken or a content object seen, the mastery value for each level of difficulty of the concept was updated, based on regression equations designed by a domain expert. To create these equations, the expert was given prior values of a level of difficulty mastery value and asked what the next values should be under the various circumstances. For example, if the student's level 0 mastery value was x, and a level 2 object had been seen, what should the student's new level 0 mastery be? For each such circumstance, the expert provided 5 pre- and post-action pairs. We then used polynomial regression to fit a curve to those points.

A machine learning algorithm was used to decide which additional objects to present to the student. The tutor chose objects that matched the student's preferences as he demonstrated on previous pages, from among those objects at the correct level of difficulty. Each content object had a set of features, including instructional type (e.g., definition, explanation, example), media type (e.g., picture, text), place in concept (e.g., beginning, end), and wanted (e.g., yes, no). The tutor deduced which features the student liked to see and which he did not, by analyzing which objects the student had elected to view or hide in previous browsing activities. Those objects comprised the naïve Bayes classifier's example space. When a concept was to be presented, the tutor examined the content objects at the right level of difficulty and used the Naïve Bayes Classifier to predict if the object would be wanted or not. If the classifier returned a "yes" answer, the object was shown; otherwise, it was not. It should be noted that if an object was shown, the student was given the option to hide the object. Similarly, hidden objects had an option that allowed them to be shown.

iMANIC Architecture

The architecture consisted of four main parts: the client, the web server, the port server, and the student model servers (see figure 20). The client consisted

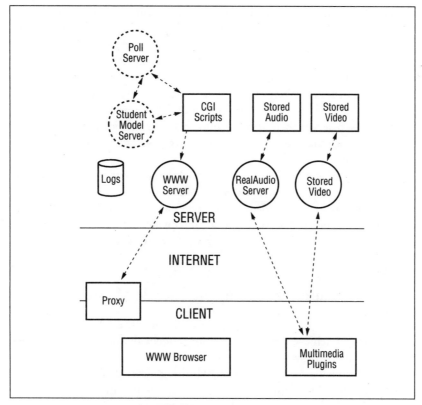

Figure 20. The iMANIC architecture.

of a web browser (Netscape Navigator was the preferred browser) and a control applet that allowed the student to traverse the course material. The applet contained buttons such as "next page" and "glossary." Also, the RealAudio plugin was embedded in the applet.

The web server used common gateway interface (CGI) scripts to interact with the port server and with the student model servers. The port server controlled the creation of the student model servers; one server was created for each student using the system. When a student first logged on to the system, the port server was contacted in order to get a port for this student. This was the port the student used each time he logged in. The port server spawned a student model server on that designated port. These servers ran continuously until a long period of interactivity, at which point they terminated. By running continuously, the student model server maintained state. This architecture was chosen so that the tutor did not have to rebuild state each time the student performed an action.

The main communicati on link in the architecture was between the web server and a student model server. The web server used "cookies" to maintain state with a given client and thus knew which student model server to contact for each interaction. Cookies stored the student's name, the server's internet protocol address and the port on which the student's server was listening.

Once the web server contacted a student model server, it simply waited for the student model server to send back a reply, which was in the form of HTML code. The web server then sent the information received from the student model server directly to the web browser. Thus the web server contained no intelligence at all.

Student model servers were the elements of the system that performed all of the "reasoning" and dynamic construction of course content. Each time the student made an action, his student model server was connected both to log that action and to generate the content as a consequence of the action. The HTML seen by the student was generated dynamically by his student model server.

Evaluation of Intelligent Tutoring Systems

Formal evaluation of student performance with intelligent tutors has shown that tutors can achieve performance improvement that approaches the improvement afforded by one-on-one human tutoring compared to classroom teaching (Bloom 1984). Several success stories indicate that computer tutors effectively reduce by one-third to one-half the time required for learning. In the past ten years a series of careful, comprehensive reviews of automated instruction have been conducted (Fletcher and Rockway 1986; Fletcher 1988, 1995, 1996; Fletcher and Orlansky 1986; Fletcher et al. 1990; Johnston and Fletcher 1995; Lesgold et al. 1990, 1992; Seidel and Park 1995; Shute 1995; Shute and Psotka 1995; Wiggs and Seidel 1987). In these studies, traditional CAI effectively raised average student performance from fifty percent to sixty-five percent, reflecting a fifteen percent improvement on the median of the Gaussian curve which typically results when evaluating student performance. Traditional computer instruction commonly achieves an improvement in teaching effectiveness in this range and it is now considered to be routinely obtainable, although it is not universally obtained. However, the addition of AI technology, such as described in this chapter, based on three studies (not from this chapter) raised average student performance from fifty percent to eighty-four percent, reflecting a thirty-four percent increase in performance due to the tutors (Fletcher 1995; Regian and Shute 1992, 1993, 1994; Regian 1997). Given the small sample of tutor studies, the tutor results are suggestive rather than authoritative. All things considered, it is safe to say that CAI works quite well in a variety of settings and for lots of different instructional domains. It is also safe to say that tutors work well, may be considerably more effective than CAI, and could be enormously more effective.

Automated instruction also supports students to achieve a given performance level in a shorter period of time. Thus it is useful in reducing the time required to achieve some desired level of performance (Regian 1997). In these studies, students were required to reach predetermined instructional objectives, and allowed to spend more or less time doing so. Traditional computer aided instruction resulted in an average instructional time reduction of twenty-nine percent compared to lectures. These results are commonly reported and routinely obtainable. Tutoring systems, using AI techniques, based on three studies, resulted in an average instructional time reduction of fifty-five percent (Regian 1997). Again, given the small sample of tutor studies, the tutor results are suggestive. It is safe to say that traditional computer based instructional systems can reduce the time required to reach instructional objectives, in a variety of settings and for lots of different instructional domains. Tutoring systems can also reduce instructional time, and probably more so than traditional computer-based instructional systems.

In one special case, students working with an Air Force electronics troubleshooting tutor for only twenty hours gained proficiency equivalent to that of trainees with 40 months (almost four years) of on-the-job experience (Lesgold et al. 1992). In another example, students using the LISP tutor at Carnegie Mellon University (Anderson 1990, Anderson and Reiser 1985) completed programming exercises in thirty percent less time than those receiving traditional classroom instruction and scored forty-three percent higher on the final exam.

Although limited but encouraging results have been shown for tutors, the fact remains that classroom tests often do not provide a measure of success for these systems because the material presented is not the same as that taught in a traditional classroom, and a system's content cannot easily be integrated into a traditional curriculum. For instance, both the original geometry and algebra tutors (Anderson et al. 1985, 1995) automated much of the symbol manipulation, e.g., addition and multiplication, in the domain and provided an environment for students to learn problem solving, whereas the original classroom curriculum focused on symbol manipulation. The systems, in part, redefined the curriculum content to focus on problem solving, and this made evaluation of learning outcomes difficult. Current versions of the algebra tutor, especially the Pump Algebra Tutor (PAT) were designed using content guidance from national standards and working closely with classroom teachers. They have achieved a one standard deviation effect in the classroom as well as improvement in the range of fifty to one hundred percent on the new standards assessment (see chapter 5). PAT is now the most widely used tutor in K–12 schools and was in over three hundred high school or one percent of the USA high school market in fall 2000.

Several aspects of evaluation remain major research issues. For example, if a system succeeds, which components should be assigned the credit, and how might the various models be fine-tuned to improve the next generation of systems? Portability between subject matter has been shown in only a few systems (Anderson et al. 1995); most systems are less effective when rebuilt in another domain, and generalizability has yet to be demonstrated.

Research Issues

One crucial issue of tutor research and development is the need for continuous refinement of system behavior based on computer-student performance. That is, results from one iteration are needed to inform and constrain development of the next version if we are to see improvement in the field: working tutors should foster clear refinement and evaluation of AI and cognitive theories and vice-versa. There is nothing so practical as a good theory. However, too little theory currently guides development of new tutors. Additionally the field has many research issues to address, as discussed below.

Cognitive Modeling

Cognitive modeling is now making rich contributions to progress in this field. It is applied to develop pedagogical and subject matter theories, design instruction and present instruction (Regian and Shute 1992, 1993). Expert models and student models have achieved the most direct benefit from cognitive modeling thus far, including substantial benefits from modeling subject matter experts. For instance, Anderson et al. (1990) attribute much of the success of their tutors to the cognitive task analysis of experts in LISP, geometry and algebra.

Instructional modeling, i.e. the actual presentation of instruction, is the area where cognitive modeling has thus far found the least fruitful application, mostly due to a historical accident. Working with classroom teachers and trainers needs to be more commonplace during research and development of these systems.

Communication Modeling

Developing systems that are sensitive to student idiosyncrasies and able to customize their language responses is still very difficult. Achieving flexible mixed dialog between human and machine, whether text- or visually-based, is a current goal in tutoring systems (Graesser et al. 1995, Freedman and Evans 1996, Freedman et al. 2000). One early success, e.g., SOPHIE (Brown et al. 1982), suggested this was achievable, yet advances in reasoning about language as well as statistical and semantic analysis were required before we could achieve natural dialogue. Human-human dialog succeeds despite ambiguity and digressions because both participants model the dialog, subject matter, and other speaker, and both actively change models and language when working towards success of the dialog. Studies show that even naïve human tutors, including nonexperts and fellow students, are successful in part because they use general tutoring strategies (Graesser and Person 1994). Several outstanding research projects have shown that portions of the dialog task are feasible. Suthers et al. (1992) showed that responsive explanations can be planned and generated dynamically, and Lester and Porter (1996) produced humanlike complex explanations. This suggests that continuing efforts be made to enhance the machine's ability to do its part to model the user and dialog context. Building responsive intelligent interfaces requires building mechanisms to support cooperative dialog and developing a deeper understanding from the viewpoint of the learner.

Choosing and organizing domain knowledge for the communication effort provides the next set of research issues. Control should account for the tutor's ability to switch strategies dynamically according to multiple constraints and to do so in a manner that is sensitive to abilities that human tutors use in tutorial interactions. Further work is required to research relevant topics, hints and help, especially when multiple perspectives of the topic are available.

Adequate Models

Other research issues center on development of adequate models of the student, the pedagogical context and the recognition of how to stimulate the student's own abilities and creativity. Although much is known about student motivation and cognitive development, it is mostly general knowledge about which activities engage particular students and how novice behavior is distinguished from expert behavior (Larkin et al. 1980, Chi et al. 1981). This field requires information at a finer grain size. Thus we need knowledge about particular student actions in specific contexts. If a student behaved in a certain way, in the last half hour, can we predict his or her behavior (time on a problem or success in completing the problem) on the next problem.

A separate issue concerns how relevant knowledge should be presented once it has been selected. Presentations, whether explanations or examples, should be customized for the learning needs of the user and should enable her to build on existing knowledge. A model of the *teacher* might include strategies for providing remediation for errors as well as a selection of examples, analogies, and strategies—including when to remediate, when to provide examples, etc. Teaching strategies of expert teachers are not well understood at the level of granularity needed. A *communication* model might include dialog and teaching strategies, e.g., which graphic to present, and/or how to phase, which would be couched within principles of good interface design.

Implementation Issues

Though some success has been seen in the development of intelligent tutors, one might ask why more systems have not been deployed. The answer is that deep design and implementation issues remain, beginning with the lack of AI development tools, e.g., shells and frameworks, similar to those used to build expert systems. Expert systems shells have sped up development of industrial-strength systems such as systems to evaluate a person's likelihood of repaying a house mortgage (McDonald et al. 1997), to schedule rail for a large railroad (Murphy et al. 1997), and to configure a passenger aircraft cabin (Kopisch and Gunter 1992). Though several AI tutoring shells have been built (Murray 1998, Van Marcke 1998, Major et al. 1997), none has wide usage or has shown the ability to scale up properly. Perhaps authoring tools for tutoring systems will become available as part of the growth of authoring tools for the Internet. Development tools would facilitate large-scale development; a simple tool, such as a simulation tied to an expert system or to a lock-step tutor, might be a practical way for designers to get started on a path of incremental design through feedback from the expert and student. A developer should be able to interact with a variety of tools, in much the same way that a computer artist develops an animation by using one package to model, another to animate, and yet another to add special effects or edit in music and voice. Each tool adds separate functionality and each interoperates smoothly with the others to produce the final product.

Another reason for slow development has been the inability to reduce cognitive task analysis to engineering practice. An excessive amount of time is still required to analyze each task to the depth required for building a tutor. The use of new knowledge representations should result in greater expressive power than that offered by first-generation expert system tools. For instance, qualitative representations might be used to represent domain knowledge (Forbus, chapter 7).

Social and cultural issues provide the final set of barriers to producing generalizable and pervasively deployed tutors. A transition towards student-active discovery or inquiry-based instruction has begun (Weaver 1989), and tutors such as described here would play a large role in such classrooms for supporting discovery and open-ended investigations. However, this instructional transition is slow and traditional didactic, lecture-based teaching remains the norm. Although one-on-one tutoring is in fact very old (Plato 1922, Gordon and Gordon 1990), its reintroduction through this technology represents a radical change for some educators. This research field can help revive an old tradition of tutoring that is largely inquiry-driven in nature. Since educational change works very slowly, the new technology will require curricular and infrastructure changes as computer-based systems are integrated into learning environments.

Discussion

Much success has been achieved, and yet more remains to be done to support the effective use of AI technology in education. Current instructional technology research has succeeded in exploring many domains and some nontraditional pedagogical strategies, such as partnering, mentoring and scaffolding. However, many of the rich and detailed tutoring methods used by talented teachers, such as mentoring and inquiry-based teaching and collaborative learning, still elude researchers, and the next generation of tutors will require development of accessible shells and test-beds to facilitate further experimentation and expansion.

Several predictions can be made about future development of intelligent teaching systems based on near-term goals and long-term opportunities. As the computer price-performance ratio continues to improve, a wide expansion of tutoring systems will continue to be seen in new teaching and training arenas. Initiatives incorporated within these systems, such as qualitative reasoning, machine learning, case-based reasoning, general purpose architectures and multimedia, will facilitate the study of human learning and teaching and will accelerate the power of tutors, their acceptance in the classroom and the willingness of developers to build them.

A paradigm shift has begun in some classrooms in which the educator is no longer the "sage on the stage" and has become the "guide on the side" assisting students in their navigation through remote libraries, museums, databases or institutional archives. The planet has come on-line and yet there is still more information than knowledge available in this global electronic network. Intelligent agents and explainers are needed to retrieve, construct, understand and modify conceptual models for individual learners. Agents will support intelligent retrieval, configure themselves to the learner based on current goals and provide a learning focus. The global information infrastructure enables easy access to information, and artificial intelligence is needed to play a central role in bringing this knowledge to a new level of realism and usefulness for students. The tutors described in this chapter provide merely the foundational technology for what might become powerful and globally sophisticated personal tutors.

Acknowledgements

This chapter is based upon work supported by the National Science Foundation under several grants. Any opinions, findings, and conclusions or recommendations expressed in this chapter are those of the authors and do not necessarily reflect the views of the National Science Foundation. Grant HRD-9714757 from the National Science Foundation to Carole Beal, Beverly Woolf, and Klaus Schultz at the University of Massachusetts, Amherst supported the mathematics tutor work. An NSF/ARPA, grant EEC-9410393 to the Engineering Academy of Southern New England, involving the University of Massachusetts, the University of Connecticut and the University of Rhode Island, a grant from NSF/DUE — 9813654, and a grant from the University of Massachusetts, College of Engineering supported the Engineering Tutor work.

Apple Computer Technology Reinvestment Award (CDA-9408607), NSF awards CDA-9502639 and NCR-9508274, and a University of Massachusetts graduate fellowship also funded this work.

Figures 1, 2, 3, and 15 in this chapter first appeared in Sigmund Tobias's and Dexter Fletcher's *Training and Retraining: A Handbook for Business, Industry, Government, and the Military,* published in 2000 by the Gale Group. They are reprinted herein with permission from the publisher.

Note

1. Previous work in Interbook (Brusilovsky and Schwarz 1997) also used information about pages read to update the student model.

Chapter Five

Cognitive Tutors as Modeling Tools and Instructional Models

Kenneth R. Koedinger

What gets measured, gets done.
If you don't measure results, you can't tell success from failure.
If you can't recognize failure, you can't correct it.
If you can't see success, you can't reward it.
If you can't see success, you can't learn from it.

   – *David Osborne and Ted Gaebler (Reinventing Government)*

Effective technologies for learning and doing mathematics should be based on sound cognitive theory, be empirically tested against alternatives, and be primarily addressed at mathematics as a modeling language. I illustrate these points in the context of an educational technology we call *cognitive tutors* (Anderson, Corbett, Koedinger, and Pelletier 1995). Cognitive tutors are based in computer science research on artificial intelligence techniques and cognitive psychology research on the nature of human learning and performance. Cognitive tutors have been created to help students learn in a variety of mathematics and computer programming domains and have been subject to laboratory and classroom evaluations that demonstrate the potential for dramatic learning gains from appropriate use of this technology.

   This chapter will focus primarily on a cognitive tutor for algebra originally called the Pump Algebra Tutor (PAT) (Koedinger, Anderson, Hadley, and Mark 1997; Koedinger and Sueker 1996). PAT is part of a complete algebra course that, in the 1998–1999 school year, had been disseminated by our university-based PACT Center[1] to thousands of students in some 70 schools across the country. This course, now called "Cognitive Tutor Algebra I," was designated by the US Department of Education as an exemplary mathematics curriculum in 1999. With the help of the Technology Transfer Office at Carnegie Mellon University, we formed a spin-off company "Carnegie Learning"[2] to market, support, and further develop cognitive tutors. In the 1999-2000 school year, Carnegie Learning had spread Cognitive Tutor Algebra I to over 150 schools. A few of these schools are high performing, resource rich suburban schools, but most of them are urban or rural schools, involve average teachers, and include a large number economically disadvantaged, minority or learning disabled students.

Before turning to a summary of cognitive tutors in general and Cognitive Tutor algebra in particular, I want to make three general comments about the role of empirical testing in the development of technology-enhanced learning innovations, the role of cognitive theory in guiding such development, and the role of mathematical modeling as an appropriate core focus for mathematics instruction.

Why Empirical Tests Against Alternatives?

Why is it important that we perform empirical tests of educational innovations in comparison with alternatives? If the intuitions and beliefs that guide the design of learning environments were fully informed and perfect, there would be no need for such experiments. Unfortunately, intuitions and beliefs about learning and instruction are limited and are not always accurate. One problem is that intuitions are based largely on conscious learning experiences, but a great fraction, perhaps the majority, of what we learn is at a level below our awareness. The grammar rules of our first natural language, English in my case, are an excellent example. We learn these rules, in the sense that they determine our behavior in language comprehension and production, well before we are consciously aware of them. To use an old twist of phrase, as early language learners we go from "not knowing we don't know" to "not knowing we know" without going through the intermediate states of conscious learning: "knowing we don't know" and "knowing we know." As we get older, of course, conscious learning processes play a greater role. However, it is a mistake to think conscious learning takes over. In fact, there is ample evidence from cognitive psychology research that our brains continue to engage in implicit learning processes (e.g., Berry and Dienes 1993, Dienes and Perner 1999).

Our intuitions about learning are biased by limited information—overly influenced by our memories of our conscious learning experiences. We are subject to what I call *expert blindspot*—as experts in a domain we are often poor judges of what is difficult and challenging for learners. Perhaps few would disagree about the importance of evaluating our educational innovations to better understand how they do or do not improve on current practice. Nevertheless, I think it is worth emphasizing the danger of being biased by expert blindspot and lured by our personal intuitions into assuming that our educational innovations and reforms will necessarily be for the better.

Why design systems based on cognitive theory? Not every experiment can be run comparing alternative features of instruction and their interactions. Thus, we need a way to guide the generation of new instructional designs. Such a guide should help us prune design ideas not likely to enhance learning and inspire new ideas that will. Cognitive theory also provides a way to accumulate reasons for past successes and failures to inform future practices.

Why address math as a modeling language? Although technology has mastered calculation of various kinds—arithmetic, graphic, symbolic, logical—humans are the only masters of translating problems into mathematics, building theories and producing communicative forms. Learning how to create mathematical models of problem situations is difficult but it is the key to mathematical success in our modern world.

An Example: Cognitive Tutors

Cognitive tutor technology is particularly suited (though certainly not exclusively) to facilitate these three goals: need for empirical testing, need for cognitive theory, and a focus on mathematics as a modeling language. Cognitive tutors are based on the ACT theory of learning and performance (Anderson and Lebiere 1998). ACT is a complex and broad "unified theory of cognition" (Newell 1990). I highlight just a few key features that are particularly relevant to learning mathematics. The theory distinguishes between tacit performance knowledge, so-called "procedural knowledge" and static verbalizable knowledge, so-called "declarative knowledge." According to ACT, performance knowledge can only be learned *by doing*, not by listening or watching. In other words, it is induced from constructive experiences—it cannot be directly placed in our heads. Such performance knowledge is represented in the notation of if-then production rules that associate internal goals and/or external perceptual cues with new internal goals and/or external actions. Here are three examples of English versions of production rules:

IF   the goal is to prove two triangles congruent
and the triangles share a side

THEN   check for other corresponding sides or angles that may
congruent.

IF   the goal is to solve an equation in X

THEN   graph the left and right sides of the equation
and find the intersection point(s).

IF   the goal is to find the value of quantity Q
and Q divided by Num1 is Num2

THEN   find Q by multiplying Num1 and Num2.

It is important to note that the rules of mathematical thinking (which production rules are intended to represent) are *not* the same as the rules of mathematics (e.g., theorems, procedures, or algorithms) as they appear, for instance, in textbooks. Production rules represent people's tacit knowledge of when to chose particular mathematical rules as well as other tacit performance knowledge like plans and informal intuitions. Reading English versions of production rules like those above can be misleading because the rules are stated explicitly: however, production rules represent tacit or implicit knowledge. When we say people know a production rule we do not mean they can state it, as written above or otherwise, but only that it characterizes their behavior. In other words, a person is said to know a production when in the situation described by the if-part of the production, the person can perform the action described by the then-part.[3]

The particular if-then notation of production rules is not as important as the features of human knowledge that production rules represent and the implications of these features for instruction. Production rules are *modular,* and this means that we can diagnose specific student weaknesses and focus instructional activities on improving these. Production rules are *context specific,* and this means that mathematics instruction cannot be effective if it disconnects mathematics from its contexts of use. Students need true problem solving experiences to learn the if-part of productions, the conditions for appropriate use of mathematical rules, as well as some occasional small exercises (which are still over-emphasized in many curricula) to introduce or reinforce the then-parts of productions, the mathematical rules themselves. Production rules are of *limited generality.* In other words, cognitive research (e.g., Singley and Anderson 1989) has shown that the performance knowledge, though general (i.e., it applies in multiple contexts), tends to be fairly narrow in its applicability and tied to particular contexts of use and limited generalizations thereof (cf., Cheng and Holyoak 1985). Thus, we must gauge our expectations about how far student learning will transfer and construct curricula that both encourage general encodings of mathematical ideas and also provide multiple examples and activities that apply these ideas in a variety of well-chosen contexts.

In applying the ACT theory to instruction, we have focused on the idea that human one-to-one assistance or tutoring is extremely effective in facilitating learning. Bloom (1984) showed that an individual human tutor can improve student learning by two standard deviations over classroom instruction. In other words, the average tutored student performs better than 98 percent of students receiving classroom instruction. This result provides a sort of "gold standard" for comparing the effectiveness of educational technologies. The results of meta-analyses of hundreds of studies of traditional computer-aided instruction (CAI) suggest that CAI leads, on average, to a significant 0.3 to 0.5 standard deviation improvement over noncomputer-aided control classrooms (e.g., Kulik and Kulik 1991). There are too few studies of multimedia and simulations at this point to provide a generic figure, though some of these studies indicate little effect, for instance, of animations (e.g., Pane, Corbett, and John 1996) or of gamelike simulations (e.g., Miller, Lehman, and Koedinger 1999). In studies of our cognitive tutor technology we have shown cognitive tutors to yield about a one standard deviation effect (Anderson, Corbett, Koedinger, and Pelletier 1995; Koedinger, Anderson, Hadley, and Mark 1997).

To build a cognitive tutor, we create a cognitive model of student problem solving by writing production rules that characterize the variety of strategies and misconceptions students acquire. These productions are written in a modular fashion so that they can apply to a goal and context independent of what led to that goal. For simplicity of illustration, I provide an example from the domain of equation solving:

Strategy 1

IF   the goal is to solve $a(bx + c) = d$
THEN   rewrite this as $bx + c = d/a$

Strategy 2

IF   the goal is to solve $a(bx + c) = d$
THEN   rewrite this as $abx + ac = d$

Misconception

IF   the goal is to solve $a(bx + c) = d$
THEN   rewrite this as $abx + c = d$

The first two productions illustrate alternative strategies for the same problem-solving goal. By representing alternative strategies for the same goal, the cognitive tutor can follow different students down different problem solving paths of the students' own choosing. The third "buggy" production represents a common misconception (cf., Matz 1982). Buggy production rules allow the cognitive tutor to recognize such misconceptions and thus, provide appropriate assistance. The cognitive tutor makes use of the cognitive model to follow students through their individual approaches to a problem. It does so using a technique called "model tracing." Model tracing allows the cognitive tutor to provide students individualized assistance that is just-in-time and sensitive to the students' particular approach to a problem.

The cognitive model is also used to trace students' knowledge growth across problem-solving activities. The "knowledge tracing" technique is dynamically updating estimates of how well the student knows each production rule (Corbett and Anderson 1994). These estimates are used to select problem-solving activities and to adjust pacing to adapt to individual student needs.

Cognitive tutors have been subject to comparative evaluations in the lab and in classroom for more than twelve years (Anderson, Corbett, Koedinger, and Pelletier 1995). A cognitive tutor for writing programs in the Lisp computer language (Anderson, Conrad, and Corbett 1989) was compared to a control condition in which students solved the same programming problems without the aid of the cognitive tutor. Students in the experimental group completed the problems in *one-third the time* with better post-test performance than students in the control group. The LISP tutor allowed students to engage in productive problem solving search, but reduced unproductive floundering. Two different cognitive tutors for geometry proof design were used in classroom studies compared to control classes using a traditional geometry curriculum without the cognitive tutor. In both studies, students in the experimental classes scored *one standard deviation better* than students in control classes (Koedinger and Anderson 1993).

There were two important lessons from these studies. First, echoing results from experiments with LOGO (Lehrer, Randle, and Sancillo 1989; Klahr and Carver 1988), we demonstrated that careful curriculum integration and teacher preparation were critical to our effectiveness results (Koedinger and Anderson 1993). A second lesson came from a third party evaluator who studied changes in student motivation and classroom social processes as a consequence of the use of the Geometry Proof Tutor. Schofield, Evans-Rhodes, and Huber (1990) found the classroom evolved to be student centered with the teacher taking a greater facilitator role supporting students as-needed on the particular learning challenges each was experiencing. This point was repeated in a *Math Teacher* article by one of the participating teachers (Wertheimer 1990). In that article, Wertheimer emphasized that because the cognitive tutor was effectively engaging students he was more free to provide individualized assistance to students who most needed it.

The Pump Algebra Tutor (PAT)

When we began to develop the Pump Algebra Tutor, two past experiences led us to take a different "client-centered" approach to development (Koedinger et al. 1997). First, at the time of the geometry studies, the National Council of Teachers of Mathematics Standards (1989) were coming out and suggesting a deemphasis on proof in high school geometry. Second, we had experienced the importance and difficulty of integrating the technology with the classroom and paper-based curriculum (Koedinger and Anderson 1993). Thus, in the PAT project we designed the tutor and the curriculum hand-in-hand. A high school math teacher, Bill Hadley, and a curriculum supervisor, Diane Briars, had been working on a new algebra curriculum. Their goals were to make algebra accessible to more students, to help students make connections between algebra and the world outside of school, and to prepare students for the "world of work" as well as further academic study. We teamed up with Hadley and began evolving the curriculum and designing the tutor by sharing ideas from both research

Your friend has decided he is very interested in a career as a photographer. You look up Photographer in the Pennsylvania Career Guide and find out that there are three different paths to becoming a photographer.

High School Diploma: Start photographing right away and make $1,115 per month.

Technical School: Study for 18 months, pay $18,000, and make $1,925 per month.

College: Study for 4 years, pay $50,000, and make $2,754 per month.

Table 1. The first part of a two-day performance assessment
used in the Pump algebra curriculum.

and practice. This client-centered process we used and continue to use is a form of "participant design" (cf., Beyer and Holtzblatt 1998) whereby end-users, in this case teachers, fully participate on the design team.

Functional Models of Authentic Problem Situations

Table 1 shows the first part of a two-day performance assessment used in the Pump algebra curriculum. Students are asked to analyze the financial costs and benefits of three alternative educational paths to a photography career. Unlike traditional algebra story problems that ask for a particular numerical answer, activities in Pump algebra and PAT ask students to produce an analysis and models of that analysis in multiple mathematical representations including tables, graphs, equations, and words.

The assessment activity in table 1 illustrates a number of key features of the course that are typical of both the text curriculum and computer tutor. Students are expected to read realistic problem contexts and compare alternative plans. Students are asked to use algebra to make this analysis and, like most activities in the curriculum, they build tabular and graphical models of these alternatives as well as symbolic equations like $1115x = 1925(x - 18) - 18.000$. Students use these models to find break even points (e.g., how many months before technical school pays off), for instance, by finding points of intersection in a graph or by solving equations. In other words, the course emphasizes the use of multiple representations and strategies to provide students with both different perspectives on mathematical understanding and a variety of tools for problem solving. In the classroom component of the course, writing is emphasized and students are asked to make recommendations based on the mathematical models they create: "use this analysis to write a letter to your

Drane & Route Plumbing Co. charges $42
per hour plus $35 for the service call.

1. Create a variable for the number of hours the company works. Then, write an expression for the number of dollars you must pay them.	Symbolization Question
2. How much you would pay for a 3 hour service call?	Result-Unknown
3. What will the bill be for 4.5 hours?	Questions
4. Find the number of hours worked when you know the bill came out to $140.	Start-Unknown Question

Table 2. A problem from a popular algebra textbook.

friend explaining clearly the advantages and disadvantages of each option. You also want to make a recommendation to him as to what he should do!"

The beginning of the course starts with simpler situations than the photographer problem, but such activities usually include many of these features: reading a problem situation, constructing multiple representations, comparing alternatives, and writing an answer. A major goal is to aid students in developing successively more sophisticated models of quantitative relationships using multiple representations each with different costs and benefits (cf., Koedinger and Anderson 1998; Tabachneck, Koedinger, and Nathan 1994).

Learning to Model with Algebraic Symbols: The Inductive Support Strategy

To reach the goal of creating improved instructional supports to help students learn to be successful on assessments like the photographer career problem in table 1, we began to research issues of mathematical modeling and the underlying competencies required. In particular, we focused on studying what students know and do not know about symbolic modeling. Skills for symbolic modeling are important because they are not currently automated, they are the entry point to using today's powerful calculation tools (e.g., graphic and symbolic calculators, spreadsheets, programming), and they are particularly difficult skills for students to acquire. We began to experiment with different approaches to helping students learn to model with algebraic symbols (Koedinger and Anderson 1998).

Table 2 shows a problem from a popular algebra textbook (Forester 1984). Hadley had been using a similar problem format, but put a particular emphasis on problem contexts that would be more authentic to students and that contained real data. Forester intended this problem format to illustrate the nature of an algebraic variable as truly varying, in contrast to traditional algebra word problems (e.g., leave out questions 1–3 in table 2) in which there is an unknown constant, but no variable. As I began to observe and analyze student thinking on such problems, I formed the simple hypothesis that having students answer the concrete "result-unknown" questions 2 and 3 before answering the symbolization question 1 might facilitate student learning, particularly of the symbolization process.

This hypothesis followed from my prior cognitive science research on the importance of inductive experiences in the evolution of geometry knowledge (Koedinger and Anderson 1990). It also followed from observations of students who could successfully solve concrete result-unknown questions, like 2 and 3, but could not produce the corresponding algebraic sentence to answer question 1 (Koedinger and Anderson 1998). Such students already had effective performance knowledge (or production rules) for comprehending the English problem statement, for extracting the relevant quantities and quantitative relations, and for a producing a numerical answer. However, production rules for "writing algebra," that is, for taking a problem understanding and expressing it in algebraic symbols, were either weak or missing (cf., Heffernan and Koedinger 1997, 1998). One such production rule is illustrated below:

If the goal is express a quantity $Q1$ in algebraic symbols
   and $Q1$ is result of combining $Q2$ and $Q3$ with operator Op
   and the expression for $Q2$ is $Expr2$
   and the expression for $Q3$ is $Expr3$
Then set a goal to write: $Expr2\ Op\ Expr3$
   set a goal to check for correct order of operations

This production rule characterizes *tacit* performance knowledge for composing algebraic "embedded clauses" for a quantity, like $42h + 35$ for the total bill ($Q1$), from knowledge of simple clauses, like $42h$ for the hourly charge ($Q2$) and 35 for the service charge ($Q3$).

Why should learners solve result-unknown questions (questions 2 and 3 in table 2) before attempting to symbolize (question 1)?[4]

It is easier for students to step through the arithmetic operations in a problem with concrete numbers than to write the corresponding algebraic sentence. As they do so, declarative memory traces are stored that characterize the problem's quantitative structure (e.g., 42 times 3 is 126 and 126 plus 35 is 161). These traces are analogous to the structure of the algebraic sentence students need to produce (e.g., $42h$ and $42h + 35$). In attempting this more difficult step of symbolizing, students' brains perform analogical problem solving processes (Anderson and Lebiere 1998) that make use of these concrete traces to guide

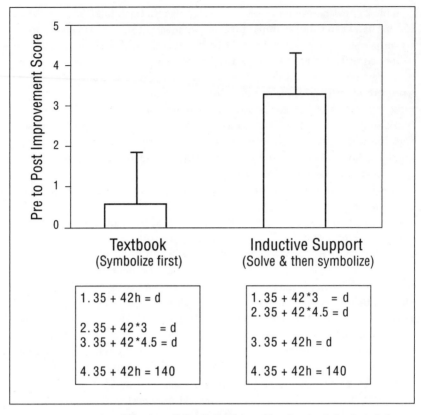

Figure 1. Improving algebraic modeling by bridging off students' existing knowledge.

the writing of an algebraic sentence. As a side effect of these processes the brain induces new production rules, like the one illustrated above, for writing algebraic sentences.

I call this learning strategy of making use of concrete modes of thinking (numeric instances in this case) to help induce abstract modes of thinking (writing algebraic sentences) the *inductive support strategy*.

We used an early version of PAT to implement an experimental learning study in which we compared a control "textbook" condition to an experimental "inductive support" condition. In the textbook condition students solved problems in the Forester textbook format. In the inductive support condition, students solved the same problems but with the questions rearranged so that the concrete result-unknowns (2 and 3) appeared before the symbolization question (1). Figure 1 shows the results of that study. Students in the inductive support group learned significantly more from pretest to posttest than students in the textbook group (Koedinger and Anderson 1998). This inductive support effect was successfully replicated by Gluck (1999), who also collected eye movement data that provides an interesting and more direct window into the changes in the thinking process that result from inductive support.

A crucial point to emphasize here is that students not only need to learn mathematical concepts, but they must also develop a mastery or fluency with mathematical modeling languages such as algebraic symbols, programming languages, statistics notation, and dynamic geometry tools. This experiment illustrates one effective way to assist students in developing mathematical language fluency. The inductive support strategy suggests that we create instructional activities that help students bridge from existing, more concrete modes of thinking (e.g., situations and numbers) and more familiar languages (e.g., English) to more abstract and powerful modes of thinking and languages (e.g., algebra and algebraic symbols). The inductive support strategy is a demonstrated realization of "progressive formalization" (Bransford, Brown, and Cocking 1999, p. 125).

Description of PAT: A Cognitive Tutor for Practical Algebra

As part of the development of PAT, Pittsburgh teachers wrote problem situations, like the Photography problem discussed above, intended to be personally or culturally relevant to students. Some problem situations are of potential general interest (e.g., the decline of the condor population), while others are somewhat more specific to Pittsburgh ninth graders (e.g., making money shoveling snow or declining population in Pittsburgh after the demise of the steel mills). These problems were added to PAT using an intelligent problem authoring system in which teachers type the problem description and enter an example solution (Ritter, Anderson, Cytrynowitz, and Medvedeva 1998). This authoring system has an incomplete and imperfect model for reading English text but can make reasonable guesses about how quantities and relations in the entered solution map to phrases in the text. The author can then correct or edit these guesses. The connections formed between elements of the problem and elements of the solution are the basis for the automated feedback and hints the tutor can provide as needed.

Students begin work on PAT problem situations by reading a description of the situation and a number of questions about it. They investigate the situation by representing it in tables, graphs, and symbols and by using these representations to answer the questions. Helping students understand and use multiple representations is a major focus of PAT (cf., Hall, Kilber, Wenger, and Truxaw 1989; Janvier 1987; Koedinger and Tabachneck 1994; Tabachneck, Koedinger, and Nathan 1994).

In figure 2, the PAT screen shows a student's partial solution for a problem. This problem appears in the later stages of the curriculum after students have

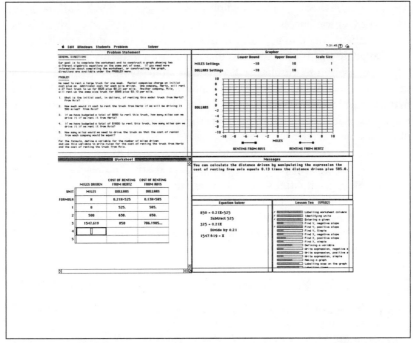

Figure 2. In PAT, students create tabular (lower-left), graphical (upper-right), and symbolic (lower-center) models of problem situations (upper-left) with as-needed assistance (middle-right) and dynamic assessment (lower-right) from the cognitive tutor.

acquired some expertise with constructing and using graphs and tables for single linear equations. The top-left corner of the tutor screen provides a description of the problem situation. This problem involves comparison of costs between two rental companies, Hertz and Avis, that charge different rates for renting large trucks. Students investigate the problem situation using multiple representations and computer-based tools, including a spreadsheet, grapher, and symbolic calculator (in figure 2 these are the worksheet, grapher, and equation solver windows, respectively).

Students construct the worksheet (lower-left of figure 2) by identifying the relevant quantities in the situation, labeling the quantities (at the top of the columns), identifying appropriate units (first row), answering the questions in the problem description (numbered rows), and entering algebraic expressions (in the "formula" row). The formula row is at the bottom of the table in early lessons to facilitate use of the inductive support strategy, but moves to the top in later lessons. Like a spreadsheet, in later lessons the formula automatically generates a dependent (y) variable value when a value of the independent variable (x) has been entered.

Students construct the graph of the problem situation (upper-right of figure 2) by labeling axes, setting appropriate bounds and scale, graphing the lines, and identifying the point of intersection. The equation solver (lower-center) can be used at any time to help fill in the spreadsheet or identify points of intersection in the graph. The student can use these representations to reason about real-world concerns, such as deciding when it becomes better to rent from one company rather than another.

The steps in table, graph, and equation construction and use emphasize multiple perspectives on quantities and their relationships through the description to these in multiple forms. Understanding of quantity emerges when students actively engage in making connections between, and practicing correct use of, these multiple representational forms (cf., Hall, Kilber, Wenger, and Truxaw 1989; Janvier 1987; Koedinger and Tabachneck 1994; Tabachneck, Koedinger, and Nathan 1994).PAT interface representations and problem structure encourage these connections, and PAT tutor component assists students, as needed, in appropriate use of these representations. By supporting students in thinking about quantity labels, PAT assists students in making connections to more concrete situational and verbal knowledge. By thinking about units, students are making connections to more abstract verbal knowledge. By thinking about numerical relationships, students make connections to arithmetic knowledge and, as we have shown in the inductive support studies (Koedinger and Anderson 1998; Gluck 1999), this thinking process facilitates the difficult developmental transition to fluent use of algebraic symbols. In addition to the aspects of PAT's worksheet noted above, students are also assisted in graph and equation construction and use. The problem-solving activities in the PAT curriculum are structured and ordered to engage students in increasingly sophisticated uses of and translations among a variety of representations. The goal is for students to achieve "representational fluency" through developmentally appropriate connections and sufficient practice.

At all times the tutor is monitoring student activities and providing feedback and assistance as needed. This provision of timely feedback is one way in which cognitive tutor's individualize instruction. Like good human tutors, PAT's tutorial interactions with students are brief and focused on individual students' particular learning needs as they arise in the context of problem solving. When a student is having trouble, PAT does not immediately provide correct answers or even detailed advice. Instead, PAT tries to maximize student opportunities to discover or reinforce appropriate concepts or skills on their own. PAT provides two kinds of assistance: just-in-time feedback on problem solving steps taken and on-demand hints on next steps needed.

Like human tutors, PAT's feedback on student errors avoids direct verbal statements like "wrong" and instead uses nonverbal cues. PAT cannot raise its eyebrows, but it does provide nonverbal feedback by "flagging" errors using a font highlight such as outline text or color. As Schofield et al. (1990), Wertheimer

(1990), and many of our current teachers have observed, students do not feel the same social stigma when making errors on the computer as they do when making errors in class. Commonly occurring slips or misconceptions are recognized by "buggy" production rules and specific advice can be provided that may explain what is wrong with the current step or hint toward an appropriate correct step. Examples of student errors that are recognized by PAT's buggy productions include leaving out the initial value (intercept) in a formula, leaving out parentheses or otherwise violating order of operations, confusing the dependent and independent variable in a table, graph or formula, and many others.

The provision of timely feedback is a critical feature of cognitive tutors that leads to substantial cognitive and motivational benefits. In a parametric study with the Lisp tutor, Corbett and Anderson (1991) compared levels of timing of feedback. Students receiving immediate feedback (after each problem-solving step) learned significantly faster than students receiving delayed feedback (at the end of the problem). In addition to cognitive benefits, there also appear to be motivational benefits of timely feedback. Much like the motivational attraction of video games, students know right away that they are making progress and get satisfaction from this success at a challenging task.

In addition to timely feedback, a second way PAT individualizes instruction is by providing context-sensitive hints. Using the model tracing mechanism described above, PAT is always following each student's particular approach to a problem. At any point in constructing a solution, a student can request a hint and PAT will provide one that is sensitive to what the student has done up to that point. The tutor chooses a hint message by using the production system to identify the set of possible next strategic decisions and ultimate external actions. It chooses among these based on the student's current focus of activity, what tool and interface objects the student has selected, the overall status of the student's solution, and internal knowledge of relative utility of alternative strategies. Successive levels of assistance are provided in order to maximize the students' opportunities to construct or generate knowledge on their own. This approach to learning through assisted performance bears close resemblance to cognitive apprenticeship (Collins, Brown, and Newman 1989) and procedural facilitation (Vygotsky 1978).

The "message" window in figure 2 shows the result of a student help request. At any stage in problem solving, the tutor can provide assistance on whatever interface element the student has selected (e.g., a cell in the worksheet, a point in the grapher, an equation in the equation solver). Based on the tutor's representation of alternative strategies and solution contingencies, the tutor may suggest an alternative selection in some situations. For instance, it will recommend that students complete a row in the worksheet (an x-y pair) before graphing the corresponding point in the grapher.

In the situation shown in figure 2, the student has selected the worksheet cell for question 4 in the column she labeled "MILES DRIVEN." Question 4 reads "If we have budgeted a total of $1000 to rent this truck, how many miles can we drive it if we rent it from Avis?" To process the hint request, the tutor's cognitive model is run to see what different production rule paths are potentially relevant at this point in the problem. Possibilities include the following:

1. In the grapher, graph one or the other of the lines corresponding to either of expressions in the FORMULA row of the worksheet.

2. In the worksheet, enter the given value $1,000 in the "COST OF RENTING FROM AVIS" column in row 4.

3. In the equation solver, enter an equation, like "$0.13x + 585 = 1000$," that can be solved to find the MILES DRIVEN.

4. In the worksheet, enter the value or an expression for computing the value (e.g., "$(1000 - 585) / .13$") of MILES DRIVEN in the selected cell.

In tracing student problem solving, the tutor is flexible and would follow the student no matter which of these paths she pursued. In this case, though, the student has requested a hint and the tutor must decide which of these paths to hint toward. This decision is constrained by both flow and pedagogical concerns. To preserve the flow, if possible, a path is chosen that is relevant to the window in which the student is working. Thus, path 1 is not chosen since it is relevant to the grapher not the worksheet. Also to preserve flow, if possible, a path is chosen that is relevant to the currently selected interface object, in this example, the cell in column 1, row 4. Thus, path 2 is not chosen since it is relevant to the cell in column 3, row 4. Besides flow concerns, hint selection is also driven by content-specific pedagogical concerns (see Shulman 1987 for discussions of the importance of pedagogical content knowledge). Both paths 3 and 4 are relevant to the student's selected cell. Path 3 is an equation solving strategy, which is the typical textbook approach to such problems. Path 4 recommends an informal "unwind" strategy and is chosen for pedagogical-content reasons described below. In general, the flow constraints on hint selection are implemented within the cognitive tutor architecture and apply in all tutors, whereas the pedagogical constraints are implemented in content-specific production rules and apply to specific situations within a tutor.

To the surprise of many teachers (Nathan, Koedinger, and Tabachneck 1997), students are able to solve problems like question 4 without an equation (Koedinger and MacLaren 1997). Students use informal strategies, like guess-and-test and unwind, that they can perform more effectively and efficiently than equation solving on such problems (Koedinger and Alibali 1999; Nhouyvanisvong 1999). Thus, for problems like question 4, PAT hints toward the informal unwind strategy because it better builds off students' prior verbal knowledge of informal strategies. PAT also includes problems, like question 5, that thwart the unwind strategy and thus motivate the need for and practice the use of equation solving. I now provide examples of hint sequences associated with questions 4 and 5.

Hints along a chosen path begin with general assistance, and the tutor provides incrementally more specific assistance only as demanded by the student. In this example, the initial hint focuses the student's attention on the fact that the usual given and goal variables are reversed and therefore the need to "unwind" the arithmetic procedure: "To find the distance driven, instead of the cost of renting from avis, unwind your calculation. Do the reverse of what you would normally do." If the student asks for more help, the tutor provides a more specific hint toward how to unwind:

> To find the distance driven, instead of the cost of renting from Avis, take the value you are given for the cost of renting from Avis, first subtract numbers that you would normally add and then divide by numbers you would normally multiply.

This hint provides a general strategy for how to unwind expressions like the one in this problem. If student requests it, the next and final hint provides the specific expression to which the unwind strategy should be applied: "To calculate the distance driven, try unwinding as a way of solving the expression 1000 equals 0.13 times the distance driven plus 585." Sometimes the final hint in a sequence can be quite specific, for instance, "Subtract 585 from 1000 and then divide by 0.13" or even "Type 3192.3." Such detailed hints are like the examples provided in textbooks illustrating a new idea. The difference is that, in PAT, these examples come in the process of problem solving when students are better able to understand and make use of the example. Also, in such cases PAT will give students later opportunities to perform this skill on their own.

In the case above, the last hint is still fairly general. In some contexts, like this one, teachers have asked to have the hint stay relatively vague so that they are aware and can intervene if a student gets really stuck. This case is also an example of how our basic cognitive research, in this case on students' invented informal strategies (Koedinger and MacLaren 1997; Nathan, Koedinger, and Tabachneck 1997), has influenced teacher practices and the content of our teacher professional development. The vocabulary and associated strategy of "unwinding" an arithmetic procedure to find an unknown is emphasized in our teacher professional development workshops. However, like students, teachers also learn by doing, and thus it helps to have this idea reinforced as teachers observe the tutor and interactions with students in the computer lab.

Although the hint messages recommend the unwind strategy for questions like 3 and 4, the students are free to choose whichever path they like. The equation solver window (lower-center in figure 2) illustrates how the equation solving strategy (path 3) can be performed to answer question 3. The student enters her own equation, "$850 = 0.21X + 525$" and solves it by indicating standard algebraic manipulations. As is the case for all tools in PAT, students can receive feedback and hints in the equation solver that are sensitive to their chosen strategy and current state of the solution. If the student were to ask for hints prior to the second step shown in figure 2, the successive hints would be the following:

- What can you do to both sides to get x by itself?
- To change $0.21x$ to x, divide by 0.21.
- Divide both sides by 0.21.

In contrast, a second student might have started differently, by dividing both sides of the equation by 0.21 rather than subtracting 525 from both sides. If requested, a hint on the next step in this case would follow through on this student's chosen path[5] and be different from the hint sequence shown above.

Question 5 asks the student to find the crossover point where the cost of one option (Hertz in this case) catches up with the cost of another (Avis). Alternative strategies for finding this point include equation solving or using the Grapher tool (upper right in figure 2) to graph the lines to find the intersection. In this case if requested, PAT hints toward equation solving: "Given that the expression for the cost of renting from hertz and the cost of renting from avis are equal, write an equation and solve it to find the distance driven." If needed, the student is further hinted toward setting up and solving the equation "$0.21x + 525 = 0.13x + 585$."

By keeping students engaged in successful problem solving, PAT's feedback and hint messages reduce student frustration and provide for a valuable sense of accomplishment. In addition to these functions of model tracing, PAT provides learning support through *knowledge tracing*. Results of knowledge tracing are shown to student and teacher in the Skillometer window (labeled "lesson ten" in the bottom right of figure 2). By monitoring a student's acquisition of problem solving skills through knowledge tracing, the tutor can identify individual areas of difficulty (Corbett, Anderson, and O'Brien 1995) and present problems targeting specific skills that the student has not yet mastered. For example, a student who was skilled in writing equations with positive slopes and intercepts, but had difficulty with negative slope equations would be assigned problems involving negative slopes. Knowledge tracing can also be used for "self-pacing," that is, the promotion of students through sections of the curriculum based on their mastery of the skills in that section.

The activities in PAT are organized hierarchically so that related problem situations that draw on a core set of skills are organized into "sections" and then sections that use the same set of notations, tools, and broader concepts are organized into "lessons." For instance, the PAT curriculum used in schools in the 1997–98 school year included twenty-two lessons, each of which contained about four sections on average, and each section contained about five required problems and about five additional problems. Initially, students explore common situations involving positive quantities, mostly whole numbers and some simple fractions and decimals, and represent these situations mathematically in tables, expressions and graphs. As the year progresses more complex situations are analyzed, involving negative quantities, and four-quadrant graphing is introduced. Similarly, as situations increase in complexity, more sophisticated equation solving and graphing techniques are introduced to enable students to better find solutions. Systems of linear equations and quadratics are developed through the introduction of situations in which they naturally occur, for example, modeling and comparing the price structures of two rival companies that make custom t-shirts. Modeling vertical motion and area situations provide contexts for introducing and using quadratic functions.

Unlike the short "two minute problems" of most math software and traditional classroom instruction (Schoenfeld 1989), the PAT curriculum includes mini-projects, like the one in figure 2, which may last twenty to thirty minutes. Shorter practice exercises (e.g., equation solving exercises) are also interspersed to zoom in on particularly difficult and important skills. Over the weeks of the course, students alternate between playing the larger game of mathematical problem solving and engaging in decontextualized practice of the more difficult component skills, much like: play tennis, practice backhand, play tennis, practice serve, play tennis.... The emphasis is on using project activities first to motivate the need for particular kinds of practice and then, after practice, put them back to use in context.

Classroom Context of PAT Use

The majority of schools using PAT also use the Pump curriculum and text materials. The typical procedure is to spend 2 days a week in the computer lab using PAT and 3 days a week in the regular classroom. In the classroom, learning is active, student-centered, and focused primarily on learning by doing. Teachers spend less time in whole-group lecture and more time in individual and cooperative problem solving and learning. Teachers are often playing a facilitator role, but also lead whole-group discussions to highlight student discoveries or to introduce new concepts or procedures that, ideally, respond to student needs that have emerged from prior activities.

In the classroom, students often work together in collaborative groups to solve problems similar to those presented by the tutor. Teams construct their solutions by making tables, expressions, equations, and graphs that they then use to answer questions and make interpretations and predictions. Teachers play a key role in helping students to make connections between the computer tools and paper and pencil techniques and to see how the general concepts and skills for representation construction and interpretation are the same on paper and on the computer. Literacy is stressed by requiring students to answer all questions in complete sentences, to write reports and to give presentations of their findings to their peers.

The Pump curriculum uses alternative forms of assessment including performance tasks, long term projects, student portfolios, and journal writing. From the first day all answers must be written in complete sentences to be accepted. At the end of each quarter students are given a performance assessment, like the excerpt shown in table 1. At the end of each semester teachers grade these assessments in a group scoring conference. In the span of an intense afternoon, teachers inspect student solutions, construct a scoring rubric, and double-grade all the student papers. Because all teachers score papers from every other teacher's class as well as their own, they come to have a better understanding of the objectives of the curriculum, what students know and do not know, and in what ways other teachers' students may differ.

Replicated Field Study Results

An important, sometimes hard-learned, lesson of classroom use of educational technology is that to be effective in improving student learning, educational technology must be closely integrated with curriculum goals and other learning resources such as texts and teacher practices. Research with intelligent tutors (Koedinger and Anderson 1993) and other educational technologies, like LOGO (Lehrer, Randle, and Sancilio 1989; Klahr and Carver 1988), has demonstrated the importance of curriculum integration and teacher support. We have emphasized these contextual factors throughout the development of PAT. The benefits of cognitive tutors, as with individualized just-in-time assistance in the context of rich problem solving activities, can be reduced or masked if the social context of classroom use is not addressed (Koedinger and Anderson 1993). However, if such factors are addressed, use of cognitive tutors in the classroom can have dramatic impact on student learning and achievement. We have demonstrated this impact in experimental field studies in city schools in Pittsburgh and Milwaukee, replicated over 3 different school years. The assessments used in these field studies targeted both (1) higher order conceptual achievement as measured by performance assessments of problem solving and representation use and (2) basic skills achievement as measured by standardized test items, for instance, from the math SAT. In comparison with traditional algebra classes at the same and similar schools, we have found that students using PAT and the Pump curriculum perform fifteen to twenty-five percent better than control classes on standardized test items and fifty to one hundred percent better on problem solving and representation use (Koedinger, Anderson, Hadley, and Mark 1997; Corbett, Koedinger, and Anderson 1999).

Following the observations of Schofield, Evans-Rhodes, and Huber (1990) and Wertheimer (1990), we have also observed the impact of the use of PAT on changes in classroom social and motivational processes (Corbett, Koedinger, and Anderson 1999). Visitors to our classrooms often comment on how engaged students are. PAT may enhance student motivation for a number of different reasons. First, authentic problem situations make mathematics more interesting, sensible, or relevant. Second, students on the average would rather be doing than listening, and the incremental achievement and feedback within PAT problems provide a video-gamelike appeal. Third, the safety net provided by the tutor reduces potential for frustration and provides assistance on errors without social stigma. Finally, the longer-term achievement of mastering the mathematics is empowering.

In the computer lab, teachers are glad to essentially have a teacher's aid for every student and thus be freed to be facilitators and provide more one-on-one instruction with individual students. This experience is eye opening for many teachers who may see new aspects of student thinking and feel the advantages of greater student-centered learning by doing.

Cognitive Tutors as Teacher Change Agents

How and why does the use of cognitive tutors facilitate the spread of effective teaching principles and practices and the institution of curriculum reform? Is there something special about cognitive tutors that makes such spread more likely than from alternative educational technologies like books, traditional CAI, simulations, or representational tools? Unlike other educational technologies, cognitive tutors have a running model of student thinking and of adaptive student-centered instruction. Thus, the system provides an active "living example" of research-based principles and practices. Much like teachers use textbooks to guide their teaching practices, teachers often borrow from cognitive tutor problems, representational tools, feedback and hint strategies and incorporate them in their teaching practices. However, there are crucial differences between the instructional model provided by textbooks and that provided by cognitive tutors. Whereas examples of instruction in textbooks are static and noninteractive, examples of instruction in cognitive tutors are dynamic and can be observed in live interaction with students.

By serving as a teacher's aid for each student in the classroom, cognitive tutors free teachers to observe individual student thinking more often and more closely and to reflect on their instructional practices in this context. Student responses in such close interactions provide teachers with immediate and detailed feedback on the effectiveness of the tutor's or their own practices. Teachers can thus adjust their practices accordingly (as well as give feedback, as they often do, on how to improve the cognitive tutor).

We had the opportunity to observe PAT-inspired changes in curricula and teacher practices over multiple semesters through a Department of Education, FIPSE project in which we adapted PAT for use in college-level developmental math courses (Koedinger and Sueker 1996). These PAT-inspired changes were accompanied by significant quantitative improvements in student learning. The general methodology we employed, a multi-semester "design experiment" (Brown 1992; Collins 1992), involved an iterative process of course design, qualitative and quantitative observation and evaluation, and course redesign.

PAT was initially used at the University of Pittsburgh in the fall semester of

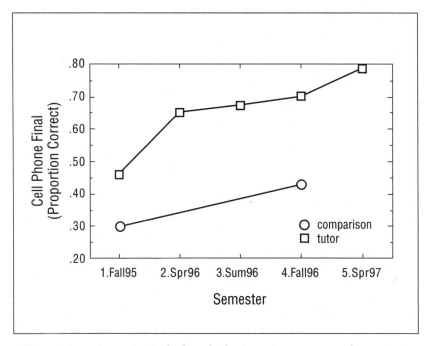

Figure 3. Increasing PAT*-inspired reforms lead to increasing scores across five semesters.*

1995 as an add-on to a traditional intermediate algebra course. As shown in the left of figure 3, this supplementary use led to significant improvement in students' problem solving abilities over a traditional course without PAT (45 percent versus 30 percent average correct as measured using a rubric scoring scheme of an assessment much like the one in table 1).

In the spring of 1996, University of Pittsburgh instructors used the PAT authoring tool to create new problems better adapted to the particular needs and interests of their students. More interestingly, changes were not limited to the software. Instructors began to use PAT problems in their regular classes and began to experiment with more student-centered learn by doing outside of the computer lab. The consequence of these new practices was an increase in end-of-course achievement beyond that found in the experimental classes in the fall (65 percent versus 45 percent).

Over the next two semesters, these practices evolved, and PAT use became better integrated with regular classroom instruction, resulting in further modest increases in student learning over past semesters (sixty-eight percent, seventy-one percent). In preparation for the Spring of 1997, the University of Pittsburgh, led by Lora Shapiro, made a decision to fully reform their intermediate algebra course to more generally target "quantitative literacy." Lecturing was deemphasized in favor of more "workshop" time in which students worked on projects in collaborative groups. The typical college level approach consisting of a lot of instructor-centered lecture time and a little student-centered recitation time, was replaced with a lot of student-centered work and a little whole-group reflection and targeted lectures. The consequence of these changes, in the first semester of their implementation, was another increase in end-of-course student performance (seventy-nine percent).

Conclusions

Effective technologies for learning and doing mathematics should be based on sound *cognitive theory,* be *empirically tested against alternatives,* and be primarily addressed at *mathematics as a modeling language.* I have argued for and illustrated these points in the context of cognitive tutors generally and in particular, the Pump Algebra Tutor. PAT is based on the ACT theory of cognition and a production rule model of student problem solving and mathematical modeling.

PAT has been subject to empirical tests both in the laboratory and in the field. In an early laboratory study with PAT, we contrasted a research-inspired "inductive support" strategy with an existing textbook strategy. This study demonstrated improved student learning, particularly of difficult symbolic modeling skills.

In field studies of the use of PAT and the Pump curriculum, we demonstrated that the combination of the two leads to dramatic increases in student learning on both standardized test items (fifteen to twenty-five percent better than control classes) and on new standards-oriented assessments of problem solving and representation use (fifty to one hundred percent better than control classes). The focus of PAT and the Pump curriculum is on developing student competence in creating mathematical models of problem situations rather than on answers to isolated questions. By developing mathematical modeling skills, students can construct a deeper understanding of problem situations such that multiple, unanticipated questions can be addressed and answered. Better mathematical understanding and learning result from such multi-representational approaches.

Cognitive tutors like PAT have the potential not only to dramatically increase student achievement, but also to serve a professional development function for teachers. Because of the underlying cognitive model and associated pedagogical strategies, cognitive tutors can provide a living example of effective instructional practices. Teachers working in the computer lab have more time to observe student performance on thought-revealing problems and to observe learn-by-doing instruction in action. In this way, cognitive tutors can carry research-based practices into the classroom and serve as change agents for professional development.

In addition to the Cognitive Tutor algebra course, our PACT Center has developed cognitive tutor courses for high school geometry (e.g., Aleven, Koedinger, and Cross 1999) and algebra II (e.g., Corbett, McLaughlin, and Scarpinatto 2000). These three courses are being marketed by our spin-off company, Carnegie Learning. Recently, Carnegie Learning has funded a three-year PACT Center project for research and development of cognitive tutor courses for middle school mathematics. Through the combined efforts of the PACT Center and Carnegie Learning, cognitive tutors are beginning to reshape the mathematics classroom, the way teachers teach, and what and how students learn.

Acknowledgements

This chapter reviews research that was supported by multiple sources. For support of research, development, and evaluation of the Algebra Cognitive Tutor, thanks to the National Science Foundation, the Department of Education's fund for the improvement of post-secondary education (FIPSE), the DARPA computer aided educational and training initiative, and the DoDEA presidential technology initiative. For support of related cognitive science research on early algebra, thanks to the McDonnell Foundation's Cognitive Studies for Educational Practice.

Notes

1. The Pittsburgh Advanced Cognitive Tutor (PACT) Center is codirected by Albert Corbett, Kenneth R. Koedinger, and John R. Anderson and is located in the Human-Computer Interaction Institute at Carnegie Mellon University. See http://act.psy. cmu.edu/ACT/ tutor/tutoring.html.

2. For more information on Carnegie Learning see the web site at http://carnegielearn-ing. com.

3. Because a number of different production rules can be applicable in any particular situation, a person may have a production rule yet we do not see evidence of it in that situation because some other competing production "fires" instead (cf. Anderson and Lebiere 1998).

4. The following explanation makes use of aspects of the ACT-R theory, in particular, the declarative and procedural memories and the analogical learning process that operates between them (Anderson and Lebiere 1998).

5. This hint would recommend to either distribute or to subtract 2500 (i.e., 525/.21) from both sides depending on the option settings in the equation solver, which would determine whether the second step is displayed as "$850/0.21 = (0.21x + 525)/0.21$" or "$4047.619 = x + 2500$."

Chapter Six

Evaluating Tutors that Listen

An Overview of Project LISTEN

Jack Mostow and Gregory Aist

This chapter is about a problem where even a partial solution would quickly pay back every dollar this nation has ever invested in artificial intelligence research. The problem is illiteracy. Its economic costs exceed $225 billion per year (Herrick 1990, University of California, San Diego 1991). Its human and social costs are incalculable. Individuals with low reading proficiency are much likelier to be unemployed, poor, or incarcerated (NCES 1993).

Difficulty in reading comprehension is surprisingly widespread (NCES 1992, OTA 1993). In its *1998 Reading Report Card for the Nation and the States*, the United States Department of Education's National Assessment of Educational Progress found that fully sixty-nine percent of the nation's fourth-graders read below desired proficiency; thirty-eight percent fell below even the basic level (Donahue et al. 1999).

Grades one to three emphasize "learning to read," in preparation for "reading to learn" in higher grades. Children who do not master reading by grade four are at risk of growing up illiterate, and of missing out on knowledge acquired from text. "Students' ability to read is essential to their educational progress. If students fall behind in reading proficiency, they may find it difficult to benefit from other aspects of the curriculum. In the future, poor readers may also find it difficult to participate effectively in a society requiring increasingly sophisticated job skills."[1]

One-on-one literacy tutoring has achieved some remarkable results (Wasik and Slavin 1993, Snow et al. 1998). However, human tutoring is expensive, not only in tutor time, but in tutor training. For example, training one teacher for the widely used Reading Recovery program (Clay 1993) takes a year and can cost $30,000 in tuition alone.

Automated tutoring holds out the promise of cost-effective individualized assistance. However, previous educational software for reading was limited by its inability to hear the student. Listening to the student is especially important when the student is learning to read aloud.

Project LISTEN was conceived in 1990 and founded in 1992 to address this limitation by combining state-of-the-art speech technology with expertise from other relevant fields. The list of fields continues to grow, and has turned out to include not only reading and education, but also intelligent tutoring, human-computer interaction, cognitive and motivational psychology, psycholinguistics, computational linguistics, artificial intelligence, machine learning, statistics, graphical design, typography, animation, and games.

The basic idea is simple: listen to children read aloud, and help them. In the course of translating this idea into reality, we have performed a series of evaluations of varying duration and formality. Different evaluations have different purposes. One purpose is to see if a proposed method (or theory, or idea) works at all. Another purpose is to understand a method better, by studying what happens when it is used. A third purpose is to improve on a method. A fourth purpose is to choose among competing methods. Other purposes may include persuading a particular audience, or establishing a monetary or other valuation.

We sketch the history of some of the main experiments we have performed in the course of developing the Reading Tutor. We describe the successive prototypes we developed, their goals, the criteria we used to evaluate them, and the principal outcomes and conclusions. The descriptions vary in level of detail. Many of these experiments are described in more detail in the cited publications. Other experiments, previously unpublished or not widely available, are described in more depth. Table 1 summarizes these experiments, with references to previous publications.

The purpose here is to give an overall sense of the path that Project LISTEN has taken to date, and some lessons learned along the way. We pay special attention to how tutors can evaluate—evaluate oral reading, evaluate student learning, even evaluate their own effectiveness.

We start by reviewing the experiments that preceded the Reading Tutor itself. The research described in this section was performed jointly with the authors of the cited publications, assisted by other members of the Project LISTEN team. Our first goal was to help children's reading comprehension by listening to them read aloud. We split this goal into two subgoals. First, what should a listening computer do? Second, how could it listen?

What Should a Reading Tutor Do?

To address the "what" goal, we started by studying the tutoring behavior of human experts, primarily Leslie Thyberg. Thyberg's extensive credentials includ-

Research Question	Experiment	Population	Results	Publications
How do reading experts help?	1992 case study of reading assistance by expert tutors.	A few grade 1-3 students	Corpus of mis-cues, expert responses	
What should a reading coach do?	1993 Wizard of Oz simulation of reading coach (WOZ). Iteratively test and refine usability by children.	Dozens of students	Specification of coaching behaviors	1993 video
Would coach help children read?	1993 compare same subject's reading level (on Spache test) with simulated coach's help versus without.	12 second graders	Read six months higher with help	AAAI 94
Can an automated coach listen?	1993 develop a prototype listener demo (Evelyn).	Developers	Followed reader Detected mistakes	AAAI 93 Eurospeech 93
How well does the coach listen?	1994 test on 514 sentences recorded in WOZ study: 5106 words read correctly, 82 serious errors.	15 second graders	96% if word correct Detect half of errors	AAAI 94 AAAI 94 video
Can children use automated coach?	1994 develop a prototype reading coach (Emily). Iteratively test and refine usability by children.	Dozens of children	Mostly easy to use Identified problems	AAAI 94 video UIST 95 video
Does coach help children read?	1994 compare same student's comprehension on story read with coach vs. similar story without help.	34 second graders	Comprehended 20% better with help	
How to scale to ex-tended use?	1995-96 redesign reading coach for extended use. Iteratively test and refine usability by children.	Dozens of children	1996 pilot version of Reading Tutor	UIST95 1996 video
How to add text?	1996 add mechanism to author and narrate new stories.	Us, students	United States patent	AAAI99
Do children who use the Reading Tutor improve?	1996-97 students used pilot Reading Tutor in a small room under individual supervision by a school aide; school administered Informal Reading Inventory.	6 bottom third graders	Averaged 2-year gain in 8 months from pre- to post-test	WPUI 97 1997 video
Can Tutor detect improvement?	1997 compare same student's first and last en-counter of the same word, averaged over hundreds of words.	Data from pilot study	16% better accuracy 35% shorter latency	AAAI 97
How to scale to independent use?	1997 develop child-usable login and story se-lection. Refine usability at clinic with 8:1 child-adult ratio.	62 children, grades K-5	Most children used Tutor without help	
How else to help?	1997 develop, test, and refine new Tutor interventions.	Clinic tests	Newer versions	ICSLP98, CAL ICO 1999
Do backchannels or Tu-tor prompts influence reader?	1997 if reader pauses, randomly backchannel or don't. If reader stays silent, pick a random prompt (of 4). Compare frequencies of what reader does next.	12,071 and 1,960 trials (clinic data)	Short coughs elicit speech just as often as longer prompts	ESCA 99 SC 2000
Does Tutor help stu-dents correct their mistakes?	1997 compare transitions from word misread to correct after Tutor gave help on that word vs. did not. Not randomized trials, so intepret with caution!	227,693 transitions (clinic data)	Word corrected 3x as often after Tutor helped on that word	AAAI AMLDP 1998
Does preemptive assistance help prevent mistakes?	1997 give help on one hard word but not another; what happens when student sees them next? Note: results only suggestive (significant at 90%).	3,469 trials (clinic data)	Helped word likelier accepted same day but *less* likely later?	
What is Tutor use in classrooms?	1997-98 live and "candid camera" video observations of Reading Tutor use in regular classroom conditions.	11 K-5 class-rooms	Identified factors affecting usage	AAAI IE 98 1998 video
Does Tutor help children learn?	1998 4-month comparison to 34 matched classmates in commercial software and baseline control groups.	17 students, grade 2, 4, 5	Tutor beat baseline compre-hension gain	In DeCloque & Holland, in press
Does Tutor help like human tutor?	1999-2000 8-month comparison to 84 matched students in human-tutored and baseline control groups.	60 students, grades 2-3	To be continued...	AIED 2001

Table 1. Summary of Project LISTEN Experiments, 1992–1999.

ed experience as a Master Reading Teacher at Falk School, a laboratory school associated with the Learning Research and Development Center (LRDC) at the University of Pittsburgh.

Who Says What in Oral Reading Tutoring?
Initial Data Collection in Magoo

The first prototype we built was a data collection program on a NeXT computer. We named this program "Magoo" (after the visually challenged cartoon character) because it could not see the student. Magoo simply displayed text on the computer screen, and digitally recorded children's individually assisted oral reading. A human reading expert provided assistance. The text consisted of passages at different grade levels, from George Spache's *Diagnostic Reading Scales* (Spache 1981). The child and tutor each wore Sennheiser noise-cancelling headset microphones, so that we could record the child's reading on one stereo channel, and the tutor's assistance on the other. The purpose of these sessions was dual—to collect children's oral reading as speech data, and to identify useful tutoring interventions to automate.

To bias the sessions in the direction of technical feasibility, we briefed the tutors beforehand on some limitations of current speech technology. In particular, we asked the tutors not to elicit unrestricted spontaneous dialogue, which we expected would be too difficult for automatic speech recognition to transcribe accurately. For example, a reading tutor might normally ask children to paraphrase passages in their own words. We asked the tutors to refrain from using this intervention.

Thus, the sessions provided a corpus of expert tutoring interventions. We analyzed this corpus to identify interventions that occurred most frequently, and that appeared feasible to automate.

What Should a Reading Tutor Do?
Wizard of Oz (WOZ) Experiments

Analysis of these protocols and discussion with Thyberg formed the basis for a series of "Wizard of Oz" (WOZ) experiments. In a Wizard of Oz simulation study, subjects interact with a system that appears automated, but is actually operated by a human "wizard." The purpose of these experiments was to specify and evaluate the tutorial interventions. The Wizard of Oz sessions took place in Pittsburgh-area public schools, with several dozen subjects. These experiments were designed and supervised by Steven Roth. The Wizard of Oz setup was designed, implemented, and operated by Matthew Kane. This arrangement benefited considerably from the implementer using his own system and seeing first-hand how children interacted with it.

WOZ used a NeXT computer with two monitors, as shown in figure 1. (This

One day Spotty left Bob and went off by himself. Bob called and whistled, but the dog did not come back to him. After a while Bob heard the dog barking a long way off. Bob walked toward the sound of the barking until he found the dog. Spotty thought he had caught a black and white kitten.

Figure 1. Wizard of Oz experimental setup.
From Mostow et al. 1993 (screenshot reconstructed).

configuration, suggested by LISTEN member Nancy Miller, simplified implementation by avoiding the complexity of a two-computer setup.) The child sat in front of one monitor, which displayed the text to read. The wizard sat in front of the other monitor, using keyboard and mouse to control the child's display. We tried to ensure that communication between child and wizard was restricted to channels available to the eventual tutor. Thus the child and wizard were positioned so as to prevent eye contact while using the WOZ system, and spoke via headset microphones. In addition, the child could request help by clicking a hand-held button. At first this button was connected to a flashlight to signal the wizard. Later the wire was connected into the mouse so as to generate an automated signal.

To start with, the interventions were specified informally in half a page of English instructions to the wizard on how to respond to children's reading mistakes. Over time, the interventions were iteratively refined and incrementally automated, based on children's use of the WOZ system, and on consultation with Steven Roth and Leslie Thyberg. For example, the "recue" intervention occurred after the child misread a word important to comprehending the sentence. In the sentence "Spotty thought he had caught a black and white kitten," a child misread "caught" as "count." The wizard then recued the misread word "caught" by rereading the words that led up to it ("Spotty thought he had–") and flashing the recued word "caught" so as to prompt the child to read it correctly. This intervention applied when the word occurred far enough into the sentence to recue, and was at least somewhat predictable from the context. Other interventions included prompting the child to reread the word or sentence, reading the word or sentence to the child, going on to the next sentence, or congratulating the child for correct reading.

At first the wizard performed the interventions by speaking to the child. As the set of spoken responses required was enumerated, live speech by the wizard was replaced with playback of prerecorded responses in a pleasant female voice.

WOZ now provided a menu of interventions from which to choose. The first

```
#:    TIME:     EVENT:     TEXT WORD:
At time 1179648, measured in samples (16,000 per second) of
the digitized oral reading, the coach displays "Spotty
thought he had caught a black and white kitten":
78>  1179648  NEXTSEN    Spotty#49
79>  1239040  OK         Spotty#49
After hesitating 4 seconds on "thought", the child pushes
the help button.
80>  1306624  SAYWORD 4  thought#50
81>  1314816  OK         thought#50
82>  1325056  OK         he#51
83>  1337344  OK         had#52
The child misreads "caught":
84>  1384448  MARK       caught#53
85>  1400832  OK         a#54
86>  1417216  OK         black#55
87>  1429504  OK         and#56
88>  1439744  OK         white#57
89>  1458176  OK         kitten#58
90>  1458176  START_EOS  .#58
91>  1458176  NUM_ERRS 1
The coach recues "caught":
92>  1458176  GOMARK     caught#53
93>  1458176  JUMPSTART  caught#53
94>  1458176  JUMPEND    caught#53
The child misreads it again...]
95>  1458176  MARK       caught#53
... so the coach speaks it:
96>  1458176  THISWORD   caught#53
97>  1458176  END_EOS
```

Figure 2. Annotated excerpt from a WOZ event file.

use of the menu of interventions required the human wizard to decide when to invoke each intervention, by using his own judgment to respond to children's reading according to our reading expert's written English instructions. As the conditions for invoking each intervention became clear enough to articulate, this manual invocation was replaced with automated rules. To illustrate the resulting interaction, figure 2 (Mostow et al. 1994b) shows an excerpt from a detailed log of timestamped events recorded by the WOZ system.

The rule conditions used three kinds of information. First, a child's click for help on a word generated a machine-detectable event (logged as SAYWORD).

Second, the wizard simulated a speech recognizer by following the child's reading in real-time, using designated keys on the console keyboard to tag each word as read correctly (OK) or misread (MARK). Third, events could be triggered by passage of time or by reaching the end of the sentence (START_EOS). For example, the "recue" intervention occurred when the following combination of conditions were satisfied:

- the student has reached the end of the sentence
- one content word (not on the system's list of function words) has been marked as misread
- the word is the third or later word of the sentence
- the word is predictable from the context (according to annotations supplied by the reading expert)

How Well Would Assistance Help Children Read? Within-Subject Evaluation of WOZ

We now evaluated WOZ to assess how well it helped children read. The purpose of this experiment was to see whether its assistance made any difference, and how to improve it. The subjects were twelve public school second graders identified by their teachers as having difficulties in reading. This within-subject experiment, detailed in Mostow, Roth, Hauptmann and Kane (1994), compared how well the same child read with WOZ's assistance, compared to reading without assistance from the same display. The experiment showed that children could read and comprehend material six months more advanced with WOZ's assistance than without. It also suggested that WOZ should read more to the child to help comprehension even more. This suggestion was motivated by seeing sentences where children managed to read all the words correctly, but so disfluently as to put their comprehension in doubt. Reading such sentences aloud to the student ought to assist their comprehension, based on previous findings (Curtis 1980) that children's listening comprehension surpassed their reading comprehension by a year or more. Curtis's study used the stories from Spache (1981)—the same stories used in WOZ.

A methodological lesson was that reading level was a time-consuming outcome variable to measure by listening to children read graded passages. The subjects in this experiment were second graders with reading difficulties, and they read slowly—typically only one word per second. The test protocol specified in Spache (1981) gave students successively harder passages to read until they exceeded a specified maximum number of oral reading miscues or wrong answers to comprehension questions. Moreover, we had to carry out this protocol not once but twice, in order to measure each student in both the assisted and unassisted conditions. Thus some subjects took over an hour to test.

How Should a Reading Tutor Listen?

Meanwhile, back at the laboratory we were working on the speech recognition issues. In fact even before formation of the Project LISTEN team in 1992, the first author had commenced preliminary attempts to adapt Carnegie Mellon's Sphinx-I recognizer to children's oral reading, albeit with slow progress. Those attempts explored off-line error detection in recorded oral reading.

Automated Tracking and Miscue Detection:
The Evelyn Prototype

We followed Raj Reddy's excellent advice to progress "from demo to demo," starting with the "low-hanging fruit"—that is, simplest capabilities first, so that we could test our approach as soon as possible in a running prototype. Thus our first goal for speech recognition was to build a proof-of-concept system to demonstrate the basic speech recognition capabilities required to tutor oral reading. To honor someone famous for reading, we named this prototype Evelyn, after Evelyn Wood (developer of a speed-reading method). (Evelyn also happens to be the name of the first author's mother, who in 1990 inspired Project LISTEN by answering "reading" when asked where intelligent tutoring could have the most impact.)

Evelyn (Mostow et al. 1993) was developed by Alex Hauptmann, using Carnegie Mellon's Sphinx-II Speech Recognition System (Huang et al. 1993). As figure 3 illustrates, Evelyn displayed a screenful of text, and listened to the reader read the entire text aloud. It attempted to track the reader's position in the text and detect mistakes. Afterwards, it responded without pretense of pedagogical correctness by highlighting each misread word, playing back the segment of oral reading aligned against the word, and saying "you should have said..." followed by the correct word. For example, Evelyn highlighted the word "birthday," played back the recording of the reader saying "elephant," and said "you should have said 'birthday.'" Evelyn used recorded human speech to speak canned phrases like "you should have said," and the Orator™ speech synthesizer to speak other words, such as "birthday."

How Well Does the Computer Listen?
Evaluation of Listening Accuracy

The basic idea for adapting speech recognition to listen to children read aloud was as follows. First, restrict the recognizer's vocabulary to the words in the known text. Second, bias it to expect those words in the same order as in the text. The resulting recognition system took oral reading as its speech input and then output the word sequence that provided the likeliest match to the student's oral reading. This scheme straightforwardly modeled some phenomena

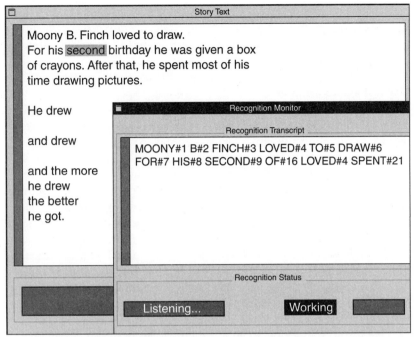

Figure 3. Evelyn prototype follows the reader, highlighting the word "second."

Smaller window shows speech recognizer output. Reader misread "birthday" as "elephant," recognized as "OF#16 LOVED#4 SPENT#21." (Screenshot reconstructed from 1993 video.)

of disfluent oral reading, such as regressions (rereading) and deletions. In addition, it approximated other phenomena, such as out-of-vocabulary words (and nonwords), false starts, and sounding out, by using text words (and sequences thereof) as "distractors" or "phonetic filler material" to approximate other sounds. For example, figure 3 shows that the recognizer assembled the word sequence OF LOVED SPENT to approximate the word "elephant," which the reader (somewhat whimsically) spoke instead of the correct text word "birthday." Thus Evelyn was able to detect that the word "birthday" was misread, even though the substitution "elephant" was not in its vocabulary. We evaluated Evelyn off-line on Magoo and WOZ data, enabling us to tune the speech recognizer's parameters to improve its accuracy (Hauptmann, Chase and Mostow 1993).

A number of simple ideas subsequently achieved improvements in recognition accuracy. We restricted the currently active text (and expected words) to one sentence at a time, rather than the entire page. We ignored mistakes on function words (such as "the," "a," and "and"), thereby reducing the false alarm rate with little effect on detection of miscues. We augmented the set of distractors for a given text word (say, "elephant") to include truncated versions of its phonemic pronunciations ("el-," "ele-," "eleph-," "elepha-"). (We subsequently omitted single-phone truncations like "elephan-" from the distractor set in order to reduce false alarms on dropped final consonants. This dialect phenomenon was common in our students' speech, and we did not want to treat it as a reading mistake.)

When evaluated off-line on WOZ data, the resulting recognizer accepted 96 percent of the correctly read text words, and detected about half the miscues flagged by the human wizard as serious enough to impair comprehension (Mostow et al. 1994). These results were achieved using acoustic models trained on adult female speakers. Alexander Hauptmann subsequently achieved further improvements by adaptive training of these acoustic models on a small (twelve-speaker) corpus of children's oral reading recorded by Maxine Eskenazi. Later we collected and transcribed larger corpora, either by hand (Eskenazi 1996, Eskenazi and Mostow 1997), or automatically from data captured by the Reading Tutor in the course of normal in-school use (Aist et al. 1998). The listening accuracy of the current Reading Tutor depends on a number of variables, such as the noise level of the environment, the quality of the noise-canceling headset microphone, and the positioning of the microphone with respect to the student's mouth.

There is still considerable room for improvement in speech recognition of children's oral reading. However, measures of recognition accuracy evaluate only the listening capability itself. How well must a computer listen in order to help children read better? In particular, had we reached a high enough level of recognizer accuracy to do any good? The time had come to address this question.

Automated Reading Assistance: The Emily Reading Coach

Once we had applied speech recognition to track oral reading and detect miscues, the next step was to complete the automation of the WOZ interventions by replacing human listening with automated listening. This step was easier said than done; although the WOZ experiments had worked out many of the usability issues, the imperfect accuracy and slower-than-realtime response of automated speech recognition required an extended cycle of user testing and design refinement. The user interface ran on a NeXT workstation, and the speech recognizer ran on a more powerful Unix workstation. The resulting system was named Emily (Mostow et al. 1994), after Emily Latella, a fictitious, auditorially challenged character created by the late Gilda Radner on the television show *Saturday Night Live.*

Emily was a reading coach, not a tutor: that is, it was designed as assistive

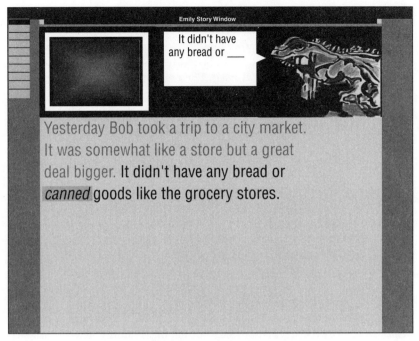

Figure 4. Emily reading coach recues the misread word "canned."
From Mostow et al. 1994 video (screenshot reconstructed).

software to help children read the text at hand, whether or not it helped them learn over time to read better. The design goals of this *shared reading* process were to let the child read whenever possible, provide assistance whenever necessary, maintain the flow of reading, and support comprehension.

The reading coach shown in figure 4 presented text one sentence at a time to read aloud, with the previous text grayed out. The coach tracked (rather imperfectly) the reader's position in the text by aligning the successive speech recognizer outputs against the text of the sentence. If the reader hesitated, the coach spoke the word at the current position, so as to maintain the flow of reading. If at any time the reader clicked on a word, the coach spoke the word, so as to help the child identify the word. The coach detected the end of the sentence by listening for the last two words of the text, or a prolonged silence.

The coach waited until it detected the end of the sentence to present any corrective feedback. It responded based on how many words the reader failed to read, not counting function words judged by our reading expert as unlikely to affect comprehension. If no words were missed—that is, if all the nonfunction words in the sentence were accepted as correct—the coach went on to the next sentence, based on the assumption that the reader had probably comprehended the sentence. If one or two words were missed, the coach prompted the child to reread the misread word(s), based on the assumption that correcting the word identification error(s) might improve comprehension. If the word was third or later in the sentence and annotated as predictable in context, the prompt consisted of recuing the word by rereading the words that led up to it and then highlighting the word itself. For example, if the student misread "canned" as "candy" in the sentence "It didn't have any bread or canned goods like the grocery stores," the reading coach would read aloud "It didn't have any bread or—" and then highlight the word "canned" to recue it. If a missed word was not recueable, the prompt consisted simply of highlighting the word and saying "please read this word." In either case, the coach would then listen for the child to read the one word, and respond by echoing the correct word. This response was intended to seem either confirmatory or corrective. The coach did not explicitly tell the student whether the word had been reread correctly or not, since speech recognition was not accurate enough to decide reliably. Finally, if more than two words were missed, or if hesitations and requests for help indicated difficulty in reading the sentence, the coach read the sentence aloud before going on. This response was based on the assumption that the student had probably not comprehended the sentence, but would likely do so if he or she heard the sentence read aloud.

The reading coach incorporated a number of additional features to support demonstrations, experimentation, and videotaping. Features included primarily for debugging and demonstration purposes included on-screen display of the speech recognizer output, visible tracking of reader position, and color-coding of words (pink if clicked, green if reread correctly, red if not, blue if misread but ignored). Most of these features were turned off in experiments to avoid distracting the student. For example, we turned off color-coding (which wasn't designed for children anyway) after one boy noticed that clicking on words turned them pink, and adopted the goal of turning all the words pink. To support comprehension experiments, a simple interface helped administer the comprehension test for each story by playing each prerecorded question and recording the student's answer. All of the spoken output of the reading coach—words, sentences, prompts, and comprehension questions—was prerecorded by a single professional narrator (Lee Ann Galasso). To support videotape analysis, a special window displayed experimental information useful to capture on videotape. This information, such as the subject ID and story number, helped us associate video segments with corresponding event logs and speech input.

The reading coach interacted automatically with the reader only within the context of reading a story. An adult human experimenter was needed to launch the reading coach and speech recognizer (on two different computers!), train the student, choose which story to read next, and operate a control panel to turn various features on and off. For example, in experiments that compared assisted versus unassisted reading, the experimenter selected "coach" or "independent" mode to present a given story with or without assistance. The Independent mode displayed a screenful of text in the same format as in coach mode, except all at once instead of one sentence at a time, and with no spoken or graphical assistance. Moreover, the stories were limited to a set of eighteen passages from Spache's *Diagnostic Reading Scales* (Spache 1981). Thus the reading coach was only a research prototype of a system that children could use on their own in classrooms. Nonetheless, it let us evaluate how helpful such use might be.

How Effective is Automated Assistance?
Within-Subject Evaluation of the Reading Coach.

To evaluate Emily's overall assistive effectiveness, in May 1994 we performed a within-subject controlled comparison similar to our evaluation of the woz system. This experiment was designed by Alex Hauptmann and conducted by undergraduate research assistant Morgan Hankins. The subjects were forty public school second graders at various levels of reading ability. To reduce the time required per subject, we used a more streamlined experimental design than we had for the woz study. Each subject read two similar stories displayed on the computer screen—one story with the assistance of the Emily reading coach, and the other story without. Both stories were taken from Spache's *Diagnostic Reading Scales*, level 3.5 (that is, month five of third grade). Both stories were displayed in the same format, except that the reading coach incrementally added one sentence at a time to the display, while the control condition displayed an entire screenful at a time. To reduce start-up effects, the subjects were first trained in each condition using a story at grade level 1.4. To avoid confounds, experiment design was counterbalanced by choice of story and order of condition—a precaution that proved essential, as we shall soon see.

The dependent measure consisted of the number of comprehension questions answered correctly out of Spache's eight comprehension probes for each story. To reduce variability between trials, we modified Spache's protocol somewhat. The comprehension questions were played in prerecorded form rather than read aloud by the experimenter. The subject's answers were recorded for later manual transcription and scoring. The subject could press a button to hear the question repeated, but the experimenter did not follow up partial answers to prompt for additional information. Some resulting scores are therefore slightly lower than would be obtained using Spache's exact protocol.

A few of the subjects were eliminated from the study, as follows. One subject was unable to read even the grade 1.4 material. One subject declined to complete the protocol. Two subjects read in only one of the two conditions, for reasons not recorded. Finally, two subjects had not taken the California Achievement Test because they were ESL (English as a second language) students. This left thirty-four subjects who had read under both conditions and had taken the California Achievement Test.

One important result was that the prototype automated coach was robust enough to perform the experiment. This result was far from a foregone conclusion, given the experimental nature of the software and the unpredictable nature of children's behavior.

As expected, we found many design improvements we needed to make. We sampled videotaped sessions with the reading coach to identify the most common problems, and then analyzed their causes by examining the detailed event logs recorded by Emily. We found three main causes of problems—recognizer error, time lag, and interface design.

Errors in speech recognition caused the reading coach to misidentify the reader's position in the sentence, and to make mistakes in classifying words as read correctly or incorrectly. The experiment exposed a design flaw in the commercial hardware we used to digitize the children's oral reading. The effect of this flaw (apparently inadequate shielding of the analog-to-digital converter) was to add an audible burst of noise to the speech signal approximately four times per second. This periodic noise (which we nicknamed "Red October" after the submarine movie *Hunt for Red October*) acted to degrade the accuracy of the speech recognizer. Consequently, the experiment measured the effectiveness of the coach when its speech recognition accuracy was degraded to an unknown extent by noise.

Time lag in speech recognition caused the reading coach to respond belatedly to the student's behavior. For example, if the child hesitated on a word long enough to trigger a response, sometimes the child had recovered and moved on further in the sentence by the time the reading coach supplied the word.

The interface design turned out to be mostly intuitive. Our goal was a "walk up and use" interface. Children were able to use the reading coach with five minutes of training or less. However, the reading coach failed to make sufficiently clear when the student was expected to reread a single word, versus continue reading the rest of the sentence; the prompts for these two cases looked confusingly similar. Moreover, a child who is prompted to reread a single word often spontaneously reads part or all of the sentence as well.

Despite these problems, comprehension averaged approximately twenty percent higher in the assisted condition than in the unassisted condition. To characterize which subjects were helped most by the reading coach, we plotted subjects' individual effects in comprehension versus an independent measure of their reading ability—namely, their scores on the California Achievement Test (CAT), administered by the school in May 1994, and expressed as a national percentile. Figure 5 shows, for each student, the difference between the number of comprehension questions answered correctly in the assisted and unassisted conditions, as a function of the student's CAT score. The assistive effect averaged much higher than twenty percent for the students whose CAT scores fell in the national bottom quartile, and who were therefore most at risk of growing up illiterate.

However, there were some difficulties with this measure. First, the effect size

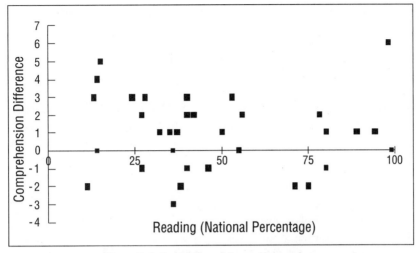

*Figure 5. Assistive effect of the reading coach on
the number of comprehension items correct (out of eight).*

varied somewhat, depending on which grader scored the answers. Evaluating
the correctness of a spoken free-form answer to a comprehension question is
subjective. Second, although Spache (1981) rates both stories at grade level 3.5,
our subjects' comprehension scores averaged substantially higher on one of the
stories than on the other, possibly due to the modifications to the test protocol.
This difference in apparent story difficulty strongly affected the results, and illustrates the importance of counterbalancing. For the "harder" story, comprehension was about 40 percent higher with assistance than without. For the
"easier" story, comprehension was about the same in both conditions. Third,
the small number of probes per story meant that the grain size of our comprehension measure was uncomfortably close to the effect size we were measuring: a twenty percent difference between comprehension scores on an eight-
item test amounts to a difference of barely one test item. In short, measuring
students' reading performance based on short-answer comprehension probes
turned out to be expensive, subjective, and imprecise—a lesson that we took to
heart in designing later evaluations.

Scaling Up to Extended Use:
From Reading Coach to Reading Tutor

We had now demonstrated that automated reading assistance by a reading
coach that listened could help children read and comprehend better than they
could on their own. The next question was whether such assistance could help

children learn to read better over time. To evaluate usability and assistive effectiveness, short user sessions had sufficed—seldom longer than an hour. We expected measurable improvement in reading skill to take much longer.

To afford long-term use, we had to move to a hardware platform that we could afford to leave in a school. The NeXT machine had served us well, but was no longer being manufactured. Running the recognizer on a separate machine was expensive and unwieldy. The reading coach was fairly robust, but the code had become unmanageable: fixing one bug introduced others. The reading coach was ripe for a complete redesign and new implementation. We wanted a platform that would be credible to schools to adopt—which narrowed the choices to Macintosh or IBM-compatible PC. We chose the PC. The Macintosh operating system of that time lacked the real-time preemptive multi-tasking we needed, and the Sphinx-II recognizer was already being ported to run on a PC.

To enable in-school use, we needed a system that children could use without us present. The reading coach was only easy to use *within a story*. Cumbersome procedures and technical expertise were required to launch the coach, register a student, and select a story.

Materials and Authoring

To enable long-term use, we had to scale up the set of narrated reading materials from an hour's worth to a year's worth, at multiple reading levels. The reading coach used a fixed set of eighteen passages from Spache (1981), narrated rather labor-intensively. Its successor would require a larger, open-ended set of text materials.

Accordingly, we developed (and patented) an authoring feature to let users type (or paste) in stories and narrate them in their own voices, using the speech recognizer to align the narration against the text, reject imperfect narrations, and find the start and end time of each word (Mostow and Aist 1999a). This information supported interventions such as recuing a word by replaying the recorded sentence up to but not including the word. At this stage, the authoring feature was restricted to our own in-house use, especially by Jennifer Gutwaks, then a Master's student in Human-Computer Interaction. This experience motivated usability refinements that paved the way for later use by children (Mostow and Aist 1999b).

In addition to the Spache passages used in the reading coach, the pilot Reading Tutor had dozens of stories at various reading levels. Some stories came from *Weekly Reader*, an illustrated weekly newspaper for children, published in separate editions for each grade level. These stories were adapted by Maxine Eskenazi to remove references to the illustrations that originally accompanied them, which we had neither the legal rights nor (at that time) the technical capability to display. Many stories came from various public domain children's literature. Stories were narrated by various Project LISTEN members.

Student-Tutor Interaction in the
1996 Pilot Version of the Reading Tutor

After considerable learning, design, engineering, development, materials acquisition, narration, user testing, and refinement, in October 1996 we finally had enough of the new system implemented to leave in a school. This system (after some additional refinement, described below) constituted the pilot version of the Reading Tutor. It ran on a single 64 megabyte, 90 megahertz Pentium™ computer.

The pilot version of the Reading Tutor (shown in figure 6) simplified the design of the reading coach. Like its predecessor, it displayed text incrementally, one sentence at a time, and spoke words the reader clicked on. A simple graphical persona simulated an animate listener by blinking now and then, and by gazing at the current word or mouse position.

The Reading Tutor provided more learner control than its predecessor. The *Back, Help,* and *Go* buttons let the learner return to the previous sentence, hear the current sentence, or advance to the next sentence (Mostow, Hauptmann, and Roth 1995; Mostow and Aist 1997b; Mostow and Aist 1997c). After corrective feedback, the student could click *Go* to go on, or try reading part or all of the sentence again, with the same kind of feedback as the first time. This flexibility was intended to accommodate individual differences. We expected that some children might want to read a sentence over and over again to perfect it, while others might be impatient to see what happened next in a story.

The pilot Reading Tutor operated in half-duplex—it had to stop listening whenever it spoke. The switching time was only about forty milliseconds. The fast switching time was a considerable improvement over the earlier WOZ system, which suffered from a similar limitation that caused it to truncate as much as 0.5 seconds from the beginning of student speech following system output. Nonetheless, this limitation precluded interventions that required speaking and listening at the same time. This limitation was eliminated in later versions when full-duplex sound card drivers became available.

The pilot Reading Tutor responded to a student's attempt to read the current sentence. The Reading Tutor responded when it detected the end of the sentence or a four-second silence. Its response depended on the number of words missed, not counting common function words. The Reading Tutor ignored mistakes on 36 common function words: *a, all, an, and, are, as, at, be, by, for, he, her, him, his, I, if, in, is, it, its, me, not, of, off, on, or, she, so, the, them, then, they, this, to, we, you.* Misreading these words does not usually affect comprehension.

The pilot Reading Tutor's limited range of responses embodied a simplified version of the reading coach's design, in order to reduce interface confusion, accommodate diverse student behaviors, and facilitate software implementation. If the speech recognition flagged no words as missed, the pilot Reading

Figure 6. November 1996 version of Reading Tutor used in pilot study.

Tutor went on to the next sentence. Otherwise the Tutor presented corrective feedback. If one word was flagged as missed, the Tutor highlighted the word in pink. If the missed word was the first or second word of the sentence, the Tutor read the word aloud. If the word came later in the sentence, the Tutor recued the word by reading the sentence aloud up to that point, thereby prompting the student to reread the word. If two or more words were flagged as missed, the Tutor highlighted the missed words in pink and read the entire sentence aloud. The Tutor then let the student try again.

One consequence of this design was that a child who got stuck on a word part way through the sentence would hear the entire sentence read aloud, rather than assistance or encouragement on the problem word. When the student got stuck in mid-sentence and hesitated for four seconds, the pilot Reading Tutor computed the number of missed words in the sentence. Such hesitations generally occurred only partway through the sentence, such as on the word "computer" or "thinks" in figure 6. Consequently, at least two (content) words of the sentence were missing from what the Reading Tutor had heard so far. The Reading Tutor then responded by reading the entire sentence. This response seemed excessive, and violated our cognitive and motivational goal of letting the student do as much as possible of the reading. We later extended the Reading Tutor to respond to hesitations in a less drastic manner. However, reading so much to the student may well have contributed to the pilot Reading Tutor's success.

Do Children Who Use the Reading Tutor Improve?
Pilot Evaluation of the Reading Tutor

We had a number of goals in evaluating the pilot Reading Tutor. Would it stay up long enough at a time to be usable? Would children be willing to continue using it once the novelty wore off? Would it help children learn to read?

To help address the last question, we asked Gayle Griffin, principal of Fort Pitt Elementary School, to select a small pilot group of test subjects. She chose the children most in need of help—the two lowest-reading students from each of the four grade-three classrooms. This decision reflected the fact that children who do not learn to read by grade four are at risk of growing up illiterate. The pilot group of eight children averaged nearly three years below grade level, according to a Burns & Roe Informal Reading Inventory administered in October-November 1996 by the school district reading diagnostician (Kelly Pasczkewicz). The principal allocated a small, relatively quiet room for the pilot test, and assigned a school aide (Lovelle Brooks) to escort each pilot subject to and from class to use the Reading Tutor.

The pilot Reading Tutor was a partial implementation of our new design. It embodied the minimal functionality required to support extended use. We had focussed on the core student-tutor interaction—reading a story. We deferred the "frame" activities of enrolling new students, launching the Tutor, logging in students, and choosing stories. We enrolled the pilot users ourselves by manually setting up the necessary directory for each one. Launching the pilot Reading Tutor remained unwieldy, because the speech recognizer still ran as a separately launched server process, albeit now on the same machine as the rest of the Reading Tutor. Launching took minutes to initialize the speech recognizer, so rather than launch it separately at the start of each student session, we left the Reading Tutor running all the time and added a simple login feature to the Reading Tutor. We used a generic file/directory picker to implement login and story selection. We trained the aide to help children put on the (Knowles VR) noise-canceling headset microphone, log in, and pick stories, but to refrain from intervening during stories except when the child remained stuck or asked her for help.

Based on initial pilot use, we made some additional modifications to the Reading Tutor, mostly to reduce dialogue breakdowns caused by speech recognizer errors. This problem arose when false alarms in recognition prevented the Tutor from accepting a correct reading, and hence from going on to the next sentence. Children could press the *go* button to go on, but often they did not. Instead, they reread the sentence—sometimes many times over. To address this problem, we modified the Tutor so that credit for reading a word correctly would persist across multiple attempts at a sentence. This "persistent credit" scheme dramatically reduced the average number of readings per sentence (Aist 1997a). We "froze" the pilot Reading Tutor code on November 7,

1996, and kept the same version for the rest of the pilot study, other than adding some stories about halfway through the school year, when the most voracious readers started running out of text. The pilot experiment concluded on June 12, 1997 at the end of the school year.

The results obtained with the pilot version were surprisingly good. Of the eight pre-tested pilot subjects, one transferred out of the school, and one was not available for post-testing due to behavior problems. The six remaining subjects were post-tested in June 1997 by the school's Title I Reading Specialist (Vinessa Turpin), using a MacMillan Informal Reading Inventory to measure accuracy, comprehension, and reading rate, as well as phonemic awareness, letter recognition, and letter-sound relationships. After using the Reading Tutor for under eight months, these subjects had advanced by an average of fully two years in instructional reading level. (Instructional reading level here was defined as the grade level of material that a student could read with at least 75 percent accuracy and 75 percent comprehension). For the pilot subjects, who had averaged virtually zero progress in reading since kindergarten, progressing by even eight months in eight months' time would have constituted a major improvement; progressing by two years was tremendous. Before using the Reading Tutor, these children had had "tremendous difficulties with traditional reading programs. They now could make meaning out of what they read. They now could have success in the classroom" (Gayle Griffin, Principal, Fort Pitt Elementary School, in videotaped interview, July 3, 1997).

Automated Detection of Oral Reading Improvement

The pre- and post-test results were exciting, but gave little insight into what was responsible for them. We wanted a more informative means of evaluation. We also wanted to address the problematic aspects of our earlier experiments with the reading coach. We decided to analyze improvements in fluency of the pilot subjects' assisted reading. In early grade levels, where the difficulty of reading is dominated by the task of decoding the words, fluency is highly correlated with comprehension (Deno 1985).

To estimate changes in fluency, we analyzed the six gigabytes of pilot study data captured by the pilot Reading Tutor. This quantity of data exceeded the size of the hard drive, so we configured the Reading Tutor to capture data directly onto removable one gigabyte (GB) JAZ™ disks, which we periodically replaced. This data included digitized oral reading by the children, time-aligned output of the speech recognizer, and timestamped event logs of interactions with the Reading Tutor. We estimated students' performance improvements from this data (10,498 utterances comprising 139,133 aligned words) as described in Mostow and Aist (1997b). To control for word difficulty, sentence memorization effects, and word recency effects, we compared a student's first and last encounter of each word, excluding sentences encountered before and words seen earlier on the same day. One measure of performance on a word is accuracy—whether the Tutor accepted the word as correctly read. A finer-grained measure is interword latency—the delay heard before an accepted word, starting from the end of the previous text word, and including any intervening speech such as false starts, sounding out, or self-corrections. On average over all eight pilot subjects, one hundred ten days elapsed from the first to last such encounter, with a sixteen percent relative increase in accuracy, and a thirty-five percent decrease in interword latency. Latency improvement was significant per-subject at ninety-five percent for seven subjects and at ninety percent for the other subject.

To illustrate, figure 7 shows two encounters by the same child of the word "help"—one in November 1996, and another in May 1997. For each encounter, the figure shows what the child actually says (a human transcript), what the pilot Reading Tutor hears (the speech recognizer output), and what the Tutor displayed (the correct text). Inter-word latency and sentence accuracy are estimated by aligning the recognizer output against the sentence text. Times are in centiseconds (hundredths of a second). Latencies preceding or following a misread word are italicized.

Individual latency values are too variable to rely on—not just because of imperfect speech recognition, but because a long repetition (such as restarting the sentence) yields an anomalously large latency (even tens of seconds) for the ensuing word. To alleviate variability, we aggregate over multiple observations.

As this evaluation illustrates, tutors that listen can exploit a much wider and more natural input channel from their students than the keyboard and mouse used in most educational software. They have the potential to realize a novel paradigm for analyzing student performance, in which evaluation is:

- *Ecologically valid*—done "in vivo" in the student's normal school or home setting, not just in a lab. The Reading Tutor recorded children at school, supervised only by a school aide in the pilot study. In subsequent experiments, children used the Reading Tutor under regular classroom conditions, supervised only by classroom teachers.

- *Authentic*—applied to normal activities relevant to student goals and interests, not just artificial test materials. The pilot Reading Tutor let students select stories to read, and they had definite preferences. Favorite topics included animals and food, but the most popular selection was "I Have a Dream"—in Martin Luther King's own voice.

- *Unobtrusive*—conducted "noninvasively" while the student is performing with assistance by the tutor, in contrast to conventional probes and pre- and post-tests. Evaluation of assisted reading performance was invisible to the student.

- *Automatic*—without human supervision, assistance, intervention, tran-

Child encounters the word "help"
(Fri Nov 08 10:43:07 1996):

Child says: *if the computer...takes your name...help it...take...s to you*

Tutor hears: IF THE COMPUTER THINKS YOU IF THE HELP IT
                   TO TO YOU

Correct text: If the computer thinks you <u>need</u> help, it <u>talks</u> to you.

Latency (csec):   43 39   1   60 41 226 7   1 242   1

*Child's actual accuracy = 64%, with 4 of 11 words missed ("thinks," "you,"
"need," "talks").*

*Tutor-estimated accuracy = 81%, with 2 of 4 mistakes detected, and no false
alarms.*

Same child encounters the word "help" several months later
(Mon May 12 09:33:27 1997):

Child says: *when some kids jump rope they help other people too*

Tutor hears: WHEN SOME KIDS JUMP ROPE THEY HELP
                   OTHER PEOPLE TOO

Correct text: When some kids jump rope, they help other people
                   too.

Latency (csec):   1   10   34   19   77   9   1   34   1

*Child's actual accuracy = 100%, with all 11 words read correctly and
accepted*

Tutor-estimated accuracy = 100%, with all 11 words read correctly

Figure 7. Example of improvement in accuracy and interword latency.
Latencies are in centiseconds.

scription, scoring, or interpretation. The output of the speech recognizer
was aligned mechanically against the text being read.

- *Fast*—word latencies can be computed in real-time on a PC.

- *Data-rich*—based on a large data sample. Word latencies were captured at
  the student's reading rate, giving on the order of ten data points for each
  minute of use.

- *Robust*—tolerant of inaccuracies in speech recognition. Latency is invariant to many recognizer errors.

- *Sensitive*—able to detect subtle, fine-grained, aggregated, or longitudinal effects. Latency is too noisy to rely on individual values, but detects subtle effects on subsets of words. For example, an improvement of ten centiseconds was statistically significant for an individual student.

Analysis of the captured data showed that each subject used the pilot Reading Tutor for approximately thirty to sixty sessions, averaging fourteen minutes each. This modest amount of interaction seems inadequate to account by itself for the children's dramatic gains in reading. For example, even though the pilot Reading Tutor gave no explicit instruction in decoding, the children's ability to decode unfamiliar words improved, according to pre- and post-tests and their teachers' observations. The pilot Reading Tutor did not sound out words, give rhyming hints, or otherwise provide clues to the graphophonemic code. We conjecture that the pilot Reading Tutor acted as a catalyst that helped the students gain more from their classroom instruction.

The natural character of the Tutor's spoken dialogue evidently contributed to its ability to remain compelling over time for students who had previously found reading an exercise in frustration. Interviews with the students and their teachers showed continued strong interest and motivation on the part of the children in using the pilot Reading Tutor right up through the last week of the school year, even after nearly eight months of use. The teachers attributed the children's changes in classroom attitude and reading performance to the Tutor, and reported that the children looked forward eagerly to their daily sessions with it. Teachers remarked on the children's increased confidence in reading.

What was responsible for this dramatic motivational effect? Motivation is complex, context-sensitive, and problematic to measure. However, it is instructive to point out some factors that could *not* be responsible for children's reported motivation to use the pilot Reading Tutor. The pilot Reading Tutor lacked the flashy graphics and sound effects of commercial software and video games. It did not even include pictures—just text, which (Malone 1981) found was the least interesting element of computer games. Moreover, reading was especially difficult and frustrating for the pilot subjects. We believe that the Reading Tutor's novel ability to listen is essential to its motivational power.

This was a small-group pilot experiment rather than a large controlled study. Although its outcome far surpassed expectations, the Reading Tutor was by no means the only possible factor responsible. Another factor was simply being selected for special attention, which can produce powerful improvements in reading. A related factor was individual supervision by the school aide. Children behave differently when watched. The pilot subjects probably interacted differently with the Reading Tutor with the aide present than they would have without the aide present. The aide's role in helping the children choose stories may have played an especially vital role. Many children prefer to

Figure 8. Summer 1997 Reading Clinic.

reread the same stories over and over. Encouraging the children to try new or harder stories may well have increased their opportunities to learn.

From One-on-One Supervision to Group Use: July 1997 Reading Clinic

The summer of 1997 saw expanded deployment of the Reading Tutor. The dramatic results of the eight-month pilot study had led the school principal to invite us to include the Reading Tutor as one of the activities in a month-long Reading Clinic for sixty-two children in grades K-5. The Reading Clinic was held at the school 8:30-11:30 AM Monday through Thursday for the month of July. Each clinic activity was held in a different room, with groups of children rotating from one room to another every 40 minutes. All the children were scheduled to use the Reading Tutor every day. The Reading Tutor room was run by Project LISTEN's Dan Barritt, a Master's student in Human-Computer Interaction, with occasional assistance from school personnel.

The successive clinic versions of the Reading Tutor ran under Windows NT 4.0 on eight 200 Mhz, 64MB Pentium Pro computers equipped with recordable CD drives for economical on-site collection of archival data. We placed these eight computers around the four walls of a classroom on three-foot by six-foot tables. Figure 8 shows the setup. The open area in the center was stocked with picture books for children who weren't using the Reading Tutor at the moment.

We had a number of research goals at the Reading Clinic. Scaling up from one Reading Tutor to eight Reading Tutors in a room exposed social effects emerging from simultaneous use by multiple children. Scaling out to a broader age range tested the Reading Tutor's well-suitedness to different ages and reading levels. Scaling down from one adult per Reading Tutor to one adult per eight Reading Tutors revealed effects of reduced supervision, and tested the mechanisms we introduced to reduce the need for adult assistance, such as "kid-friendly" menus for logging in and selecting stories. Our experience at the Reading Clinic guided iteration on the design of these mechanisms both during and after the clinic.

Our main priority was to address these immediate goals. However, the Reading Clinic also gave us an opportunity over a short period to record many hours of instrumented Reading Tutor use for later analysis. In one month we collected 14 gigabytes (GB) of Reading Tutor data from 62 children.

The Reading Clinic also provided an opportunity to let a few of the better readers try out the authoring feature. Children were enthusiastic about adding their own stories, and willingly spent hours doing so. However, this activity required considerable adult assistance. A leading reason was the children's poor spelling.

Richer Assistance

We had used the same (November 7, 1996) version of the Reading Tutor throughout the pilot study, but meanwhile we were continuing to implement and extend the rest of its designed capabilities. We replaced prototype-style *ad hoc* code with a conversational architecture to allow richer turn-taking behavior (Aist 1997b), including backchannelling (Aist and Mostow 1997b), deliberate interruption (Aist 1998), and an expanded repertoire of tutorial assistance, including preemptive hints to prevent mistakes before they occurred, and praise for good or improved performance (Aist and Mostow 1997a, Mostow and Aist 1999c). We incorporated a student model to track the student's accuracy both on each individual word, and averaged over the set of words containing a given letter-to-sound mapping, for example all words in which the letter "c" is pronounced "ess". Design iteration involved testing these capabilities in lab and classroom, and refining them accordingly.

The new interventions were an eclectic collection based on expert practice, published research, and technical feasibility. We were fortunate to have as a consultant Rollanda O'Connor, an expert on the effectiveness of different tutorial responses for special education children with phonological deficits. Some interventions were based on the research literature, such as sounding out a word or giving a rhyming hint. We added at least one intervention—spelling out a word ("C A T spells CAT")—just because it was easy to implement and might conceivably help. The Reading Tutor now included these interventions (Mostow and Aist 1999c):

Read the sentence to the student. To model appropriate expression, the Reading Tutor plays a recorded human reading of the sentence. To help the student follow along, the Reading Tutor highlights each word as it is spoken. If no recording is available, or to help the student read along out loud, the Reading Tutor reads the sentence one word at a time using the individual word recordings. If an individual word recording is not available, the Reading Tutor uses synthesized speech for that word. This intervention scaffolds students' comprehension of sentences they read too disfluently to understand (Curtis 1980), and provides corrective feedback for word identification errors that the Reading Tutor may not have detected.

Recue a word by speaking the words leading up to that word, and underlining the word. The intent of recuing a word is to put the student in the context where the word occurs, thereby giving syntactic and semantic cues to its identity. An empirical evaluation of different hints used by teachers found that recuing worked much more often in terms of eliciting the correct word than prompting students to sound out the word (Campbell 1988).

Play back the student's last recording for a word or sentence. The Reading Tutor cannot be sure that the student read correctly, so it provides this response only when the student clicks on "play back" in the *Help* balloon. Consequently this intervention is seldom used except for our own troubleshooting of microphone-related problems.

Read a word by playing a recording of that word. For homographs, the Reading Tutor speaks both pronunciations, e.g., "PREsent or preSENT."

Pronounce a word in context by playing the portion of the sentence narration corresponding to that word. This mechanism exploits the time-aligned narration to disambiguate homographs: [Mary bought Bob a] "PREsent."

Decompose a word into components (Olson and Wise 1992). The intent of such interventions is to emphasize the *alphabetic principle*—that is, the componential nature of the mapping from print to speech. Children who have not learned this principle may identify whole words based on particular distinguishing characteristics, such as the "ll" in "yellow" (Gough and Hillinger 1980, Gough et al. 1992)—a strategy that may work on small vocabularies, but breaks down on new words (e.g., "follow"), and fails to scale to large vocabulary (McGuinness 1997). The Reading Tutor models decomposition for the student rather than prompt the student to do it. One reason is pedagogical—to avoid frustrating students who are unable to decompose words themselves. But the main reason is technological—to avoid subdialogues introduced by asking the student to say anything other than the words themselves. Thus the Reading Tutor can:

Sound out a word ("head") by speaking each phoneme (/H/, /EH/, /D/) while highlighting the corresponding letter(s) ("h," "ea," "d").

Split a word into onset and rime (Goswami 1988). For example, for "dog," say and highlight "d" (/D/) and then "og" (/AW G/).

Syllabify a word ("dogtag") by saying each syllable (/D AW G/, /T AE G/) while highlighting ("dog," "tag").

Pronounce a grapheme in context. The Reading Tutor provides this "auto-phonics" assistance by picking out the letter-to-sound correspondence that the student model lists as most problematic, and supplying just that correspondence. For example, if the word is "dog," and the student has performed poorly on previous words where "g" is pronounced /G/, the Reading Tutor might highlight the "g," and say "G here makes the sound /G/."

Analogize to a graphophonemically similar word—one that has the same rime or onset as the word in question (Gaskins 1988, O'Connor and Jenkins 1994). Ideally, one might prefer a word that the child has read successfully in the past. To approximate this preference, the Reading Tutor chooses a hint word at least as short as the target word, on the assumption that the hint is at least as easy as the target. It displays the hint aligned below the target word so as to emphasize their orthographic commonality. The Reading Tutor can:

Give a rhyming hint for a word by supplying a hint whose rime sounds and is spelled the same as the target. As a hint for "wheat," the Reading Tutor might give the rhyme "beat" or "feat," but not "beet" or "feet." As the Reading Tutor says "rhymes with feat," it displays the word "feat" as a drop-down hint below the target word "wheat." By using precompiled tables, the Reading Tutor can match or exceed human speed at generating rhyming hints in real-time.

Give a hint that starts the same as the word. For example, as a hint for the word "dogs," say "starts like dog," displaying the word "dog" as a drop-down hint below the word "dogs."

Spell a word by saying each letter while displaying the letters in sequence. This intervention originally aimed at young readers who have not finished mastering the alphabet, careless readers who need to look more closely at how the word is spelled, and dyslexic readers who we thought might reverse letters. We later restricted spelling out to help-on-demand, so as to emphasize letter *sounds* rather than confusing young readers with letter *names* (McGuinness 1997).

More recent versions of the Reading Tutor have included various forms of semantic assistance for some words, such as displaying a picture, playing a sound effect, or providing textual assistance in the form of a synonym, antonym, or hypernym. However, these interventions came later.

We had only incomplete knowledge about which type of help to give for a word. The Reading Tutor computed which responses were feasible, based on the resources available. For example, the "rhyming hint" response is only feasible if the word has a rhyme. The Reading Tutor also computed felicity conditions based on research literature. For example, sounding out a word is only felicitous if the word is at most four phonemes long. The feasibility and felicity conditions reduced the set of applicable responses, but usually to more than one candidate. In the absence of further knowledge about how to choose which response to give, the Reading Tutor chose randomly among the remaining candidates.

Invisible Experiments to Evaluate Novel Features

Besides expanding the Reading Tutor's capabilities, we wanted to know whether the new features did any good. Conventional between-subject experiments, comparing variant Reading Tutors incorporating different subsets of the new features, would have been an impractical way to evaluate these features. Such experiments would have required many conditions to evaluate each feature and combination of features. Each condition would have required many subjects to compensate for intersubject variability. Each experiment would have required considerable time to detect measurable differences in student learning, and would have required considerable labor to design and administer.

Instead we took a different approach, which we dubbed the "invisible experiment." The idea was to evaluate alternative Reading Tutor actions by comparing their effect on tutorial dialogue in a given type of situation. For example, the situation might be "a new sentence was displayed seven seconds ago, and the user has been silent since then." The alternative actions might include reading the sentence, prompting the student, or just coughing. The outcome might be defined as whether the student speaks, clicks, or remains inactive. An invisible experiment compares alternative actions as follows. Each time the specified situation arises, the computer chooses randomly among its alternative actions. The computer records the machine-observable consequences of this choice on the ensuing dialogue. Subsequent analysis assesses the outcome of its chosen action. Over the course of many such randomized trials, each alternative is tried many times, and its outcomes are aggregated. Thus invisible experiments exploit three capabilities that are onerous or impossible for humans, but straightforward for computers—randomization, record-keeping, and aggregation. Although fine-grained randomized trials are not new in themselves, their use in the context of tutorial human-computer spoken dialogue appears to be novel. Singh et al. (1999) describe the use of a closely related reinforcement learning methodology to evaluate and improve nontutorial spoken dialogue systems.

The summer 1997 Reading Tutor incorporated multiple invisible experiments to evaluate various different features (Aist and Mostow 1997b). In particular, whenever the Reading Tutor displayed a new sentence and the student remained silent for a long time (seven seconds), it randomly chose among four different ways to prompt the student:

- Read the sentence aloud to the student.
- Make a short, soft coughing sound to gently indicate that the student is expected to do something.
- Explicitly prompt the student to read the sentence, e.g., "the computer expects you to start reading."
- Remind the student how to click for help, e.g., "you can click on a word for help."

We analyzed the 1,960 times in the summer 1997 data where a protracted silence caused the Reading Tutor to prompt a student. To prompt the student, the Reading Tutor either read the sentence aloud, or randomly played any of the recorded prompts. For natural variety, these prompts included multiple recordings of each type except for reading the sentence. Consequently, the Reading Tutor randomly chose 751 times to read the sentence, 627 times to cough, 290 times to ask the student to read, and 292 times to remind the student about clicking for help.

The invisible experiment just described examined only the first time the Reading Tutor had to prompt a student. If the Reading Tutor had to prompt the student a second time, it would simply read the sentence. If the Reading Tutor had to prompt the student yet a third time, it would sometimes suggest clicking *Go*. However, the Reading Tutor did not prompt indefinitely. If the student did nothing after several prompts, the Reading Tutor eventually entered a Pause mode, rather than continue to harangue a student who might very well have already gotten up and left.

The bar charts in figure 9 compare the outcome distributions of the different types of prompts in the ensuing tutorial dialogue. We defined outcomes in terms of the next student or tutor action. The first three types of prompts were about equally effective: the student spoke next over 80 percent of the time. After a prompt to click, the student spoke next only about 70 percent of the time, but clicked for help in more cases. This difference is not too surprising, though some researchers have reported that children using a computer program ignore instructions from a nearby adult (Halgren, Fernandes, and Thomas 1995). Prompting to click was followed more often by a tutor Pause than were the other types of prompts. We don't know why. Possibly some students found these suggestions confusing.

The main surprise here is the similar effectiveness of the different Tutor behaviors in eliciting student action. In particular, a short cough elicited student speech just about as often as reading the sentence or explicitly prompting the student to do so, but took much less time. We conclude that short, nonverbal, nonspecific prompts can elicit student response just as well as sentence-length, verbal, specific directives. However, this conclusion assumes that the student knows what to do when prompted to act. This dependency illustrates a limitation of invisible experiments. They compare the effects of a particular choice *in a system that may select the other choice(s) at other times*. We would expect coughing to be much less effective—perhaps just confusing—if the Reading Tutor did not sometimes spell out what it expected the student to do.

Invisible experiments offer several advantages in analyzing tutorial dialogue. First, they are *invisible*. Based solely on data collected unobtrusively during the normal interactive operation of a system, invisible experiments avoid observer effects introduced by other experimental methodologies. Invisible experiments can even be performed in the absence of the experimenters. This property is especially important because dialogue is a social process affected by who

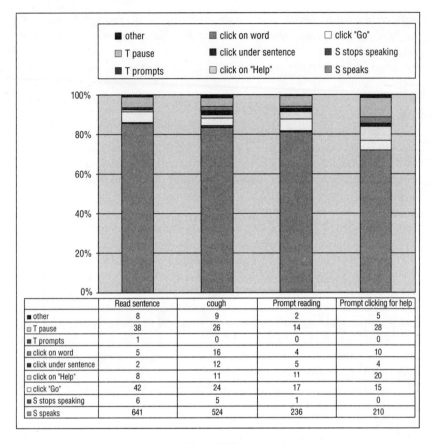

	Read sentence	cough	Prompt reading	Prompt clicking for help
■ other	8	9	2	5
▢ T pause	38	26	14	28
■ T prompts	1	0	0	0
▣ click on word	5	16	4	10
■ click under sentence	2	12	5	4
▢ click on "Help"	8	11	11	20
▢ click "Go"	42	24	17	15
▣ S stops speaking	6	5	1	0
▣ S speaks	641	524	236	210

Figure 9. Effect of different prompts.

is nearby. In particular, children tend to behave differently when they know an adult is watching them.

Invisible experiments can be *ecologically valid*—conducted with the natural users, tasks, and setting for a given system. For example, invisible experiments can analyze educational software used by children in a classroom.

Invisible experiments can be *objective*. In contrast to experiments that rely on human interventions or subjective evaluations, invisible experiments allow randomized choice among alternative behaviors, as well as automated evaluation of their consequences.

Invisible experiments can *handle variability* caused by differences between subjects or other contextual factors, because they are performed within-subject and within-context. Thus an invisible experiment can use data from a small number of subjects to compare alternative behaviors. In contrast, a conventional between-subject experiment compares alternative versions of a system by testing each version on a different set of subjects. The conventional experiment requires more subjects in order to ensure that experimental results are not due simply to subject variability.

Invisible experiments are *active*. Traditional methodologies for studying conversational behavior rely on passive observation of human-human dialogue or human-computer interaction. This "opportunistic" approach analyzes, after the fact, interesting phenomena that happen to arise. If the phenomena are rare, this approach is not very efficient. In contrast, invisible experiments explore the space of interactions more actively by systematically varying the behavior of the computer participant in order to discern its effects on the dialogue.

Invisible experiments are *inexpensive to implement*. Unlike conventional experiments that require assigning subjects to different experimental and control conditions, invisible experiments require no changes in the outside world, just to the system itself. In fact our initial generic implementation of invisible experiments in the context of the Reading Tutor allowed us to introduce an invisible experiment by inserting a one-line procedure call at the point in the code where the experimental choice is made. This procedure call specified a set of alternative actions to perform, the probability with which to take each action, and a set of (equiprobable) realizations of that action. This ease of implementation rendered invisible experiments so easy to set up that we did so as a standard practice when adding a new behavior to our system. The trivial cost of introducing an invisible experiment into a system in use freed us to focus on experimental design and analysis instead of implementation. In contrast, conventional experiments often take weeks of administrative effort to recruit subjects, assign them to different experimental conditions, train them for different conditions, and make sure each session runs under its assigned condition. With invisible experiments, the main limiting factor on experimentation shifts from administration to experimental design and analysis of results, especially for analysis that requires manual examination of data.

Invisible experiments are *economical to combine*. Suppose we want to compare m alternative behaviors $A = \{a_1, \ldots, a_m\}$ in one type of situation, and n alternatives $B = \{b_1, \ldots, b_n\}$ in another type of situation. We simply combine their invisible experiments in a single system, as follows. Whenever the first type of situation arises, the system chooses some behavior a_i to perform, selecting it at random from the set A. Likewise, whenever the second type of situation arises, the system chooses some behavior b_j at random from the set B. More generally, suppose there are k different types of situations, each with its own set of n alternative behaviors. Again, we simply combine their invisible experiments in a single system by selecting and recording a random alternative in each type of situation. As the different types of situations recur, the system will choose each alternative for that situation many times, recording their consequences. This data can be aggregated to compare the various alternatives for each type of situation. Along the way, the system will explore many combinations of choices, possibly enabling (with suitable analysis) the discovery of dependencies among different choices. In contrast, a conventional between-subject approach requires a separate system version and set of subjects for each evaluated combination of behaviors in the cross-product. The number of possible combinations is the exponential function n^k—typically far too many to evaluate each combination separately. Thus the ability to combine experiments economically is critical to analyzing complex interactive tutors with many features to evaluate.

It is important to reiterate a critical but subtle difference in the comparisons performed by invisible and conventional experiments. A conventional experiment typically evaluates each behavior *in a separate system that never chooses a different behavior*. In contrast, an invisible experiment evaluates each behavior in the same system, which includes alternative behaviors. This fact may affect user responses to a given behavior. For example, we compared alternative prompting behaviors for responding to a prolonged user silence. One behavior is to make a short coughing sound. Other prompts include explicit spoken directives. Our invisible experiment evaluated each behavior *in a system that sometimes chooses another behavior*. In particular, we evaluated the effectiveness of coughing *in a system that sometimes prompts the user more explicitly on what to do*. In this context, coughing proved just as effective as explicit prompts at eliciting spoken input. However, we would expect coughing to be much less effective in a system that never gave explicit prompts. A cough signals the student to do something, but does not specify what. A student is likelier to know what to do if he or she has received explicit prompts in the past. This example illustrates how the evaluation of a behavior in an invisible experiment may be affected by the alternatives, and must therefore be interpreted accordingly.

We next describe some data analysis that did *not* take full advantage of invisible experiments, and suffered accordingly. However, this analysis addressed some important technical issues, yielded some suggestive results, and motivated a follow-on invisible experiment that revealed some methodological difficulties in the design and analysis of invisible experiments.

Do Interventions Help?
Evaluating Local Effects of Tutorial Assistance

Our invisible experiments to evaluate alternative prompts looked only at *whether* students spoke, but not at *what* they said. To evaluate tutorial feedback, we wanted to see whether it had any measurable effect on reading performance. Eventually we wanted to learn which interventions work better for

Time	Student	Tutor
t_1	Encounters word	
	...	May or may not intervene on word
t_2	Encounters same word	

Figure 10. Does tutorial intervention change student performance on word from t_1 to t_2?

which students on which words in which contexts. As a first cut at this question, we asked whether students read words any better with assistance than without. A plausible null hypothesis was that students who used the Reading Tutor improved simply because they were reading aloud, with the Reading Tutor playing the purely motivational role of an attentive automated audience.

Method

To explore whether the Reading Tutor's specific assistance made a difference (Aist and Mostow 1998), we evaluated them based solely on the student's reading before and after each tutorial intervention. Figure 10 depicts the basic idea in simplified form: how does the student's performance on a given word change from one encounter to the next? The actual multimodal dialogue between student and Reading Tutor is more complex. For example, the Reading Tutor may take multiple turns between the student's successive attempts at a particular word. Also, student and Tutor speech frequently overlap. To illustrate, figure 11 shows a short but real example of a student's dialogue with the Reading Tutor. Here the student is a nine-year-old boy reading a *Weekly Reader* story (minus illustrations) about cheetahs.

To assess the effect of Reading Tutor assistance, we compared local performance improvement with versus without assistance. We defined local improvement in terms of successive attempts to read the same sentence. For a given student utterance, each word is labeled with the outcome "correct," "misread," or "omitted," based on the output of the speech recognizer—which isn't always what the student actually said.

Time	Student	Tutor
Tue Jul 15 09:24:47.093		displays: Years ago there were more than one hundred thousand of them in parts of Africa and Asia
Tue Jul 15 09:24:47.218– Tue Jul 15 09:24:48.125		says: 'thousand' – *"preemptive assistance" on a word the student is considered likeliest to misread*
Tue Jul 15 09:24:50.015– Tue Jul 15 09:24:53.203	says 'thousands \<breath\>…'	recognizes: THOUSAND
Tue Jul 15 09:24:52.640	clicks on 'Years'	
Tue Jul 15 09:24:52.750– Tue Jul 15 09:24:53.531		says 'Years'
Tue Jul 15 09:24:54.390– Tue Jul 15 09:24:58.515	says 'Years ago they were'	recognizes: YEARS AGO ASIA WERE

Figure 11. Real example of student-tutor dialog.

For example, the first utterance in figure 11 is "thousands \<breath\>," recognized as THOUSAND. Consequently the word "thousand" is labeled with the outcome "correct," even though the student actually said "thousands." The rest of the words in the sentence are labeled "omitted."

The second utterance is "Years ago they were," recognized as YEARS AGO ASIA WERE. Here the words "years," "ago," and "were" are labeled "correct." The word "there" (read as "they") is labeled "misread" because it was recognized as

ASIA. Why? The word "they" is outside the speech recognizer's active vocabulary because it does not appear in the current sentence. Consequently the recognizer uses the word ASIA (which shares the long /EY/ sound) to approximate the spoken word "they." As this example illustrates, the speech recognizer uses text words both to represent themselves and to approximate other spoken sounds. In aligning the recognizer output YEARS AGO ASIA WERE against the text "Years ago there were," the Reading Tutor marks ASIA as a substitution for "there." It classifies "there" as misread, and the rest of the words in the sentence as omitted. If the Reading Tutor instead aligned ASIA as a match for "Asia," it would classify "there" as omitted. This alignment would imply that the student skipped from the word "ago" to the last word of the sentence. Although this alternate alignment is clearly unlikely, other examples are less clear-cut.

We defined word *transitions* from one outcome to another. Two successive student utterances define a transition for each word from its outcome in the first utterance to its outcome in the second utterance. In the example above, the word "Years" has a transition from "omitted" in the utterance "thousands <breath>…" to "correct" in the utterance "Years ago they were." To define transitions into and out of the sentence, we introduced additional outcomes "new sentence" and "other event." Thus the word "years" also has a transition from "new sentence" to "omitted." For this study we looked only at transitions within sentences, not between sentences.

We distinguished "assisted" from "unassisted" transitions for a given word according to whether the Reading Tutor provided any assistance *on that word* during the transition. Thus the word "Years" has an unassisted transition from "new sentence" to "omitted" in the first utterance, followed by an assisted transition from "omitted" to "correct" in the second utterance. An unassisted transition need not imply that the Reading Tutor accepted the word as correct. For example, if the student missed two words, the summer 1997 Reading Tutor intervened on the first missed word and let the student read again, thereby generating an unassisted transition for the other missed word.

We defined "assistance on a word" as reading the word to the student in the course of an intervention, or giving a hint on how to read it, for example by sounding out the word. For example, suppose the Reading Tutor recues the word "were" by reading the words that lead up to it ("years ago there") and highlighting the word "were." This intervention would count as assistance both for the recued word "were" and for the words that lead up to it, but not for the rest of the words in the sentence.

To assess Reading Tutor assistance, we compared the frequencies of assisted versus unassisted transitions. For example, if the Reading Tutor's corrective feedback is effective, then transitions from "incorrect" to "correct" should be more frequent with assistance than without.

227,693	Transitions	...to new sentence		...to word correct		...to word misread		...to word omitted	
165,048	without word intervention		80,549		56,003		9,973		18,523
62,645	with word intervention		19,571		32,836		5,911		4,327
99,176	from new sentence								
72,845	without	40.41%	29,434	49.31%	35,918	5.66%	4,125	4.62%	3,368
26,331	with	29.01%	7,638	55.56%	14,630	9.82%	2,585	5.61%	1,478
87,945	from word correct								
59,787	without	63.28%	37,834	28.28%	16,910	3.11%	1,861	5.32%	3,182
28,158	with	36.59%	10,302	53.63%	15,100	6.03%	1,699	3.75%	1,057
15,715	from word misread								
10,637	without	48.12%	5,118	15.20%	1,617	31.58%	3,359	5.10%	543
5,078	with	26.68%	1,355	41.10%	2,087	29.93%	1,520	2.28%	116
22,762	from word omitted								
19,691	without	31.67%	6,237	7.88%	1,552	2.61%	514	57.83%	11,388
3,071	with	8.79%	270	33.18%	1,019	3.45%	106	54.58%	1,676
2,095	from other event								
2,088	without	92.24%	1,926	0.29%	6	5.46%	114	2.01%	42
7	with	85.71%	6	0.00%	0	14.29%	1	0.00%	0

Table 2. Comparison of word transitions with and without Reading Tutor assistance.
From summer 1997 clinic data.

Results

Did the Reading Tutor help students to correct errors? To assess the effect of the Reading Tutor's interventions, we analyzed the 227,693 word transitions from the summer 1997 reading clinic data. Each enumerated word transition describes two successive events involving a word: seeing a word in a new sentence, reading a word correctly, misreading a word, omitting a word, or going on to a new sentence. The "other" category may include starting a new story.

Table 2 categorizes word transitions based on whether the Reading Tutor did or did not intervene on that word between these two events. For the versions of the Reading Tutor used at the 1997 Summer Reading Clinic, "word intervention" included a rich set of responses to student mistakes or missed words (Aist and Mostow 1997a). Interventions included reading the word, reading the sentence, sounding out the word, breaking down the word into syllables, giving a rhyming hint, and providing a word that starts the same. Conversely, "without intervention" included cases where the Reading Tutor said nothing, backchanneled, (saying, e.g., "mm-hmm") helped with a different word, or went on to the next sentence.

Table 2 suggests a number of interesting observations. First, fewer than half the word transitions involve interventions on that word, according to our classification. For example, suppose the student reads a ten-word sentence, the

Reading Tutor gives feedback on one word, and the student rereads the sentence. This scenario yields only one transition with a word intervention, but nine without.

To assess the effects of word intervention compared to none, we must therefore compare transition frequencies rather than counts. For example, what happened after a word was misread? The next attempt was correct forty-one percent of the time with a word intervention—but only fifteen percent without. Likewise, attempts after omitted words succeeded thirty-three percent of the time with intervention, versus only 7.9 percent without.

Some transitions to missed words were more frequent with intervention, ostensibly due to sample bias or to going on less often. For example, 9.9 percent of assisted transitions from a new sentence led to misread words, compared to only 5.7 percent of unassisted transitions. Does this mean that preemptive assistance backfired? We had programmed the Reading Tutor to offer preemptive assistance on harder words. Therefore, a likelier explanation is that assisted transitions from a new sentence were more likely to be from difficult words than were unassisted transitions. The lesson? The cases under consideration must be equivalent when interpreting the results of invisible experiments.

Overall, the results seem to indicate that intervention on a misread or omitted word was indeed more effective than no intervention on that word. While the result itself merely confirms our strong suspicion, the methodology by which we obtained it is important. By analyzing (noisy) transcripts of students' oral reading automatically, we were able to obtain preliminary results on local effectiveness of the Reading Tutor's behavior.

Limitations

We now discuss several limitations of this experiment. One purpose is to make explicit some important caveats concerning the results. Another purpose is to motivate several follow-on directions.

Noisy labels: The word transitions were computed based on automated speech recognition. We were able to analyze much more data than would be feasible to transcribe by hand, but at the cost of imperfect accuracy. However, comparing aggregate transition rates helps to combat noise in the data. Even though speech recognition is unreliable on individual examples, comparing assisted to unassisted transitions should still reflect differences in student performance, assuming that recognizer errors are statistically independent of which transitions are assisted. This assumption seems reasonable given that the recognizer is functionally independent of Reading Tutor assistance.

Coarse-grained performance criterion: The labeling scheme used a qualitative performance criterion based solely on whether a text word is matched, substituted, or deleted in the output of the speech recognizer. A finer-grained, quantitative criterion might use word latency to estimate difficulty in reading the word. Also, many words are labeled "omitted" even though they are not part of the fragment of text the student was apparently attempting to read. A more sophisticated criterion might attempt to distinguish among three cases of deletion—skipping a word in the course of reading a fragment, getting stuck on the word following a fragment, and not attempting a word outside the fragment. However, these distinctions are tricky to turn into accurate algorithms, given how the speech recognizer works.

Local effects: Table 2 shows only immediate effects of intervention on reading a word in the context of the current sentence. These effects might plausibly be due entirely to memory recency, with no true learning or retention. We deferred analysis of how intervention affects subsequent encounters of the same or related words.

All-or-none relevance: Our simple criterion of assistance on a word ignores transfer to similar or nearby words. Consider our earlier example: "Years ago there were more than…." The initial "th-" makes the same sound in the words "there" and "than," so assistance on "there" might help the child decode the word "than." Similarly, assistance on the word "Africa" would likely help the child to decode the related word "African" if it occurred in the sentence—or in the next sentence. A finer-grained criterion of "assistance on a word" might attempt to include such transfer and recency effects based on some underlying model of cognitive processes in word identification (Firth 1972, Just and Carpenter 1987, Plaut 1996).

Undifferentiated assistance: The "word intervention" class lumps all interventions together. Other than distinguishing which words were being assisted, we treated all assistance the same. The Reading Tutor provides assistance preemptively (on the word "thousand," for example), when the student clicks for help (on the word "Years"), when the student hesitates (after "Years ago there were"), or as corrective feedback after completing the sentence. The Reading Tutor provides various different types of assistance, such as reading the word or sentence, recuing the word, decomposing words into phonemes or syllables, or presenting a rhyming or "starts like" hint. For this analysis, we did not distinguish interventions based on what triggered them or when they occurred, nor based on the type of intervention. We just asked whether assistance of any form affected student behavior. We deferred to future analysis a comparison of alternative interventions.

Multiple assistance: The Reading Tutor can take multiple turns between student utterances. Consequently, more than one intervention may take place before the student responds. If a word transition is assisted by multiple interventions, how should we allocate credit among them? We deferred this issue by considering only whether any of the Reading Tutor's actions between student turns were relevant to a given word, without distinguishing among alternative sequences of such actions.

Sample bias: Finally, decisions to intervene were not random. Consequently

Time	Student	Tutor
t_1	Word in new sentence	help/no help on word – trial starts
	...	
t_2	Word in later sentence	– trial ends

Figure 12. Does preemptive assistance affect later performance on word?.

the set of cases where the Reading Tutor intervened differed statistically from those where it did not. In particular, one would expect cases where the Reading Tutor intervened to involve poorer reading, on average. Thus the advantages found for assisted over unassisted transitions signify even stronger underlying effects than if the playing field were level.

Evaluation of Preemptive Assistance

To address some of the limitations discussed above, we designed an experiment to evaluate a particular class of intervention—"preemptive assistance." This intervention was motivated by discussions with Jay McClelland and other colleagues about a Hebbian theory of learning to read. In this theory, the brain reinforces student responses even when they are incorrect (Hebb 1949). Consequently, unlearning incorrect knowledge from corrective feedback is slow and difficult. Hebbian theory predicts that learning is more efficient if the learner can be guided to produce the correct response in the first place. Thus giving assistance on difficult words before the student has an opportunity to mislearn them should work better than letting the student try them first, and then giving corrective feedback on the mistakes.

Methodology

We performed an invisible experiment to evaluate whether preemptive assistance had any measurable effect. This experiment retained some limitations described above, including noisy labels, the same coarse-grained performance criterion, and the same all-or-none definition of relevant assistance. We still did not differentiate among different forms of assistance, but we confined our attention to preemptive interventions in newly displayed sentences. Instead of measuring local effects, we analyzed student performance in the next sentence where the word occurred. We treated multiple assistance on a word by designing our experiment to compare the effects of doing versus not doing a preemptive intervention, and assuming that subsequent interventions would be similar in both cases. Figure 12 shows our experimental design.

To "level the statistical playing field" between assisted and unassisted words, we randomized decisions about which words to assist. Instead of considering preemptive assistance only for the single hardest word in the sentence, the Reading Tutor heuristically selected the two hardest words, based on word length and the student's previous performance on any previous encounters of that word. If both of these words exceeded a difficulty threshold, the Reading Tutor then randomly chose one of the two words to give preemptive assistance on, and logged the other word as an unassisted control. Randomizing the decision of which word to assist served to eliminate sample bias between the preemptively assisted "experimental" word and the unassisted "control" word. This decision launched two statistically matched trials—an "experimental" trial for the assisted word, and a "control" trial for the unassisted word. To exclude immediate effects, the trial for each word did not end until the student next encountered that word in a subsequent sentence. The student's performance on that word constituted the outcome variable for the trial.

For example, suppose the new sentence is "This computer listens to you read aloud." The most difficult words are "computer" and "listens." Both words are hard enough that the student might misread them. The Reading Tutor randomly decides to give preemptive help on "listens," rather than on "computer." Out of various interventions that apply to the word "listens," the Reading Tutor randomly selects the "starts like" intervention. The Reading Tutor draws a box around "listens," displays the word "listen" underneath "listens," and says "Starts like 'listen.'" The student then makes zero or more attempts to read the sentence, possibly receiving other help from the Reading Tutor, and sooner or later moves on to another sentence. Time passes.... Eventually, the student encounters the word "listens" again, in a later sentence, possibly in a different story. Student performance on the word "listens" in the first attempt at this new sentence defines the outcome of the experimental trial for "listens." More time passes.... Eventually, the student encounters the word "computer" again. The student's performance on the word "computer" likewise defines the outcome of the "control" trial for the word "computer."

In this example, the experimental word happens to recur before the control word, but either word may recur first. Also, neither word is guaranteed to recur. Thus although the experimental and control trials are statistically matched, some of their outcomes are unpaired. Omitting unpaired outcomes

Time	Student	Tutor
t_1	Word in new sentence	help/no help on word – first trial starts
	...	
t_2	Word in later sentence	help/no help on word – second trial starts – first trial ends; is its outcome contaminated?

Figure 13. How one trial can contaminate another by giving additional help just before the first trial ends.

from the analysis would introduce statistical skew, because unpaired words are likelier to be rarer. To be statistically conservative we therefore treat all experiments as unpaired.

Results

An invisible experiment to evaluate preemptive assistance took place at the summer 1997 reading clinic. 5,324 trials were completed, that is, the reader encountered the same word again in a later sentence. Here a "later sentence" includes not just a different sentence, but the same sentence encountered on a different occasion, for example, in rereading the same story. We hypothesized that preemptive assistance would improve performance on the experimental word compared to the control word. To exclude repeated trials on the same word, we excluded 1,420 trials where the reader had already encountered the same word as the experimental or control word of a previous trial. As one might expect, the excluded trials involved shorter (presumably more frequent) words, averaging 4.14 letters versus 5.20 for the remaining 3,904 trials. (We used word length as a heuristic predictor of word difficulty.) However, the excluded trials turned out to exhibit the same qualitative characteristics reported below, though not as strongly.

We also excluded 435 trials "contaminated" by a *subsequent* trial just at the

Trial type	Variable	match	subst	del	endsent	Grand Total
helpon	Frequency of outcome	41.4%	2.3%	27.3%	29.0%	100.0%
	Average trial duration	0:03:37	0:05:31	0:03:06	0:03:29	0:03:29
	Average word length	4.46	5.48	5.04	5.36	4.90
	Count of outcome	457	25	302	321	1105
	Count of defined latency	270	15			285
	Average defined latency	37.4	79.1			39.6
nohelp	Frequency of outcome	39.1%	2.8%	29.6%	28.5%	100.0%
	Average trial duration	0:03:33	0:03:40	0:04:03	0:04:02	0:03:50
	Average word length	4.70	5.77	5.46	5.51	5.19
	Count of outcome	430	31	325	313	1099
	Count of defined latency	267	23			290
	Average defined latency	23.3	46.4			25.1

*Table 3. Invisible experiment to evaluate preemptive
assistance—trials that ended on the same day.*

point where the reader encountered the word again (figure 13). Preemptive assistance at this point would mask the true outcome of the original trial. However, we disqualified the trial only if the word received preemptive assistance in the new trial, not if it was merely selected as the unassisted control word. Selection of control words is invisible, and so should not affect outcomes.

Table 3 summarizes the 2,204 trials (1,105 experimental, 1,099 control) that ended on the same day that the preemptive assistance was given. Table 4 summarizes the other 1,265 trials (624 experimental, 641 control), which ended on a later day during the month-long clinic. Both tables show average trial durations in hh:mm:ss format. Trial duration is defined as the time from a randomized trial until its outcome. Same-day trials averaged under four minutes (00:03:40) long, so we would expect many of them to be influenced by memory recency effects. In contrast, multi-day trials averaged four days long, up to a maximum of 23 days.

Each table breaks down the experimental and control trials by the outcome of the reader's first utterance upon re-encountering the word. The Reading Tutor computed the outcome by matching the speech recognizer output against the text and classifying the word as correct ("match"), misread ("subst"), or omitted ("del"). The outcome "endsent" means that the reader proceeded to the next sentence without speaking. This outcome typically occurred when children clicked Go without reading the sentence aloud. Some children clicked Help to make the Reading Tutor read the sentence aloud. Some children read silently. In extreme cases, we sometimes saw children race through stories by clicking the Go button without even reading, whether out of boredom, to be

Trial type	Variable	match	subst	del	endsent	Grand Total
helpon	Frequency of outcome	35.7%	4.2%	40.7%	19.4%	100.0%
	Average trial duration	115:21:38	98:37:48	125:39:34	99:21:38	115:45:11
	Average word length	4.97	5.54	5.43	5.53	5.29
	Count of outcome	223	26	254	121	624
	Count of defined latency	154	17			171
	Average defined latency	44.9	42.9			44.7
nohelp	Frequency of outcome	40.6%	3.7%	38.4%	17.3%	100.0%
	Average trial duration	109:08:10	120:51:46	116:13:37	90:24:19	109:03:11
	Average word length	5.15	6.92	5.52	5.00	5.33
	Count of outcome	260	24	246	111	641
	Count of defined latency	176	17			193
	Average defined latency	28.8	109.3			35.8

Table 4. Invisible experiment to evaluate preemptive assistance—trials that ended on later days.

done with the story, or to rack up a longer list of "stories read" than their peers.

We expected that preemptive assistance would produce slightly higher performance on the reader's next encounter of the word. That is, we expected the Reading Tutor to be a bit likelier to accept the word at the next encounter if it had randomly provided preemptive assistance at the earlier encounter than if it had not. In fact, the same-day trials did have slightly more "match" outcomes and slightly fewer "del" outcomes for the experimental ("helpon") condition than for the control ("nohelp") condition, with negligible differences elsewhere. But the multi-day trials showed the opposite effect, with greater magnitude!

As a more sensitive measure of performance, we also computed interword latencies. This measure is defined only for a subset of outcomes; the number of defined latencies is shown in both tables. We expected latency of assisted words to decrease as a result of preemptive assistance. On the contrary, latency was *longer* for assisted than unassisted words. In the same-day trials, this difference was 60.5 percent: experimental trials averaged 37.4 ± 7.1 centiseconds (here 7.1 is the standard error), versus 23.3 ± 3.4 centiseconds for control trials. In the multi-trials, the difference was almost as dramatic, at 56.0 percent, with 44.9 ± 10.2 centiseconds in experimental trials, versus 28.8 ± 5.0 centiseconds in control trials.

These surprising results do not seem to be explained by differences in intrinsic word difficulty between the two conditions. To check this possibility, we computed average word length as a heuristic indicator of word difficulty. For both same- and multi-day trials, words in "match," "subst," and "del" outcomes were *shorter* (and presumably *easier*) on average for experimental than for control trials.

Discussion

We would expect students to do better on words the Reading Tutor had recently helped them with. It is therefore surprising to see evidence that suggests the opposite. Does preemptive assistance actually hamper word learning, on average? Perhaps preemptive assistance facilitates immediate word identification, but deprives the student of an important opportunity to practice identifying the word, thereby reducing performance at a later encounter. Or was something else going on? For example, our analysis examined only preemptive assistance. Perhaps the experimental trials included less on-demand assistance or corrective feedback. Or perhaps the longer latency was actually a sign of learning going on; studies of children learning mathematics (Siegler 1995) report long pauses at breakthrough points where children learn. Or this effect may merely be an artifact of student regression (rereading part of the sentence), which inflates interword latency as measured in Mostow and Aist (1997b); we are investigating better measures. And of course ordinary statistical variation is another possibility. Further work is required to understand the results.

A related challenge is to extend the invisible experiment methodology to perform subtler comparisons. As our colleague David Plaut pointed out, the experiment reported here does not hold constant the amount of exposure to the assisted word. We compared preemptive assistance against none; we did not attempt to compare preemptive versus corrective assistance. It is not obvious how to do so with an invisible experiment, because truly corrective assistance is conditioned on the student misreading the word, whereas preemptive assistance is conditioned only on the word being difficult. The Reading Tutor cannot a priori make an unbiased random choice between preemptive and corrective assistance for a given word, because it cannot know in advance whether the student will misread the word. Nor can the Reading Tutor make such a choice a posteriori, because by the time the student reads a word (whether correct or not), it is by definition too late for preemptive assistance.

This experiment is still a work in progress. The importance of the results is that automated invisible experiments can shed light on the effects of a conversational tutorial action. Low-cost, automated, within-subject invisible experiments can enable novel evaluations of computer conversational behaviors. The limiting factor is no longer setting up and administering the experiments, but analyzing the data they generate. We now have a backlog of data to analyze from other invisible experiments that we have already run.

It is embarrassing but important to acknowledge that a major obstacle to analyzing this data is its messy form. Such analysis is complicated by several factors.

Children's production data is intrinsically complex, as our psycholinguist colleague Brian MacWhinney pointed out to us. Children produce a diverse variety of phenomena, many of them unpredictable.

Dialogue in the Reading Tutor is richly multimodal. The Reading Tutor's spoken and graphical output overlaps in time with the student's input speech and mouse gestures. Such multimodal dialogue is hard to display understandably, let alone analyze.

The logged data is ill-structured. We used to think it was just us, but researchers at the CHI 99 special interest group on automated data collection for evaluating collaborative systems shared similar complaints about the data captured by other interactive systems as well (Drury, Fanderclai and Linton 1999). Reading Tutor logs are generated by hundreds if not thousands of "logprint" commands inserted throughout the code for diverse reasons, including software debugging and timing as well as invisible experiments and other research analysis. The use of a single logging procedure does provide some low-level uniformity in the log format. For example, every logged event includes certain standard parameters, such as an event number, a timestamp, and the name of the function that generated the event. However, this syntactic uniformity is at too low a level to suffice in itself for powerful analysis of tutorial dialogue. In fact, our analysis scripts typically rely on a small subset of log entry types. In particular, a generic logging procedure for invisible experiments records the randomized choice made in each trial. Similarly, the Reading Tutor's event-driven conversational architecture now records every architecture-level input or output event at a central point in the code, to improve uniformity and completeness.

The logged data is incomplete despite its copious detail. For example, analysis of the preemptive assistance experiment was hampered by the absence of a single uniform log entry for the generic event "give help on a word." Instead, an ad hoc script had to recover this implicit event by aggregating over the more specific events logged for each specific type of help, and for the Reading Tutor's spoken outputs. This script is sufficiently complex to doubt its correctness. Another example of incompleteness involves the logging procedure for invisible experiments. Although this procedure records the chosen alternative, it does not record the set of alternatives from which the choice was made. This omission is important when that set can vary. For instance, when the Reading Tutor gives a hint on a word, it chooses randomly from the set of applicable, felicitous hints for that word, such as giving a rhyming hint, speaking the word, or showing a picture. This set depends on what resources are available for that word, such as rhymes, recordings, and pictures. Therefore the set of possible types of hints varies from one word to another. Because the Reading Tutor did not record this set when it logged the type of hint it selected, analysis of the invisible experiment to compare different types of hints would be limited by sample skew: the "batting averages" for different types of hint would conflate their actual effectiveness with their range of applicability, which varied but was not recorded.

The content and meaning of the logs change over time. For example, a punctuation error in the enumerated type declaration of architectural events caused an off-by-one error in events logged in all versions of the Reading Tutor from when the error was introduced to when it was fixed. Thus an event name in logs from that epoch may actually denote the adjacent event in the enumeration. Analysis of those logs must compensate accordingly. Other changes of meaning are subtler. For example, as the Reading Tutor evolves, we have added more types of events to log—not just to reflect new interactive functionality, but to capture previously unlogged events, such as mouse clicks on certain program-defined buttons. Consequently, the *absence* of such an event in a portion of a log has a different meaning depending on when the log is from. In newer logs it means that the event did not occur, but in older logs it does not. These evolutions in log semantics complicate log analysis, because scripts that work for one epoch of logs may give incorrect results for another. One lesson is to analyze instead the simpler, more stable representations of data captured by the Reading Tutor for each user utterance. These representations include the digitally recorded speech, the word sequence hypothesized by the speech recognizer, and its alignment against the sentence being read. This data has supported useful analysis of students' oral reading, but omits the Reading Tutor's interventions. Another lesson is to enforce a stronger semantics on logged events. For example, the September 1999 Reading Tutor logs architecture-level events in a database using a uniform schema. The database explicitly records which event triggers which other events. This enriched representation helps us debug and analyze causal chains of Reading Tutor responses to reader behavior.

Bugs in invisible experiments tend to be invisible too. To debug the observable functionality of the Reading Tutor, we rely heavily on in-school testing by the target population. This approach is a much more realistic and extensive test than we can perform in our lab, and works well to expose bugs in the Reading Tutor's observable interactions with students. However, it does not reveal bugs in operations concealed from the user. Those bugs tend to stay hidden until we attempt to analyze the data from an invisible experiment, only to discover bugs such as those described above. Why? Computers lack the intrinsic common sense of human experimenters. A human who runs an experiment would presumably notice such anomalies as an extreme imbalance of subjects between conditions—or a program behavior specific to a particular experimental condition occurring in a classroom assigned to a different condition. However, if a programming bug causes such an anomaly, a computer will not notice it unless programmed to do so; it will simply execute the program as written, bug and all. Consequently, implementation and analysis of an automated experiment require careful measures to ensure fidelity to the study design.

Copious data does not suffice for meaningful evaluation. To be educationally meaningful, not only must the right data be captured from interaction with educational software, but the interaction itself must have the right form. Our experience has led us to be skeptical about the feasibility of interpreting such data meaningfully unless the analysis code is completed and tested before the data is collected. "After the fact" analysis suffers from incomplete instrumentation and messy comparisons of alternative conditions. We have concluded that for invisible experiments to succeed, data analysis must *precede* data collection. That is, unless the analysis scripts are developed and debugged on some pilot data first, data collection is all too likely to omit some essential data, or to capture it in a form that is awkward and error-prone to analyze. Unfortunately, in practice the development and debugging of analysis scripts has taken a back seat to preparing new interactive functionality in time to roll out and freeze a new version of the Reading Tutor at the start of the school year. So although in principle it might be possible to harvest additional invisible experiments by analyzing data captured by the Reading Tutor during the 1997-98 and 1998-99 school years, in practice the form of this data may render such analysis impractical and unreliable. It may be better simply to re-run the invisible experiments with better logging, than try to compensate for deficiencies of the already-recorded logs.

Machine-captured data is limited to an incomplete picture formed by the information available to the machine. Doreen Steg's observational studies of computer use in classrooms (Steg et al. 1982, 1994, 1998) cite examples such as a study of one computer program where the classroom teacher devoted extra lessons to topics addressed in the program. Her class's superior performance on those topics was due not to the program but to this instruction—which occurred outside the program and was known only thanks to human observers in the classroom. This example illustrates the value of multiple, redundant forms of data collection and analysis. Of course it would be exorbitantly expensive to station a human observer in every classroom where the Reading Tutor is used—and full-time observation would distort outcomes. Advantages of machine analysis include automated, objective processing of much more data than humans could record or analyze. Therefore we complement comprehensive, automated analysis with occasional human observations, as in the formative evaluation we now describe.

Formative Evaluation of Classroom Use

Results from deploying the Reading Tutor in a small room (1996-97) and in a computer laboratory (summer 1997) were encouraging. Ultimately, though, we wanted children to be able to use the Reading Tutor independently in a regular classroom setting. In fall 1997, we placed Reading Tutors in eight classrooms for a year-long formative evaluation—a kindergarten, a first grade, a second grade, all three third grades, and two fourth grades. This version is shown in figure 14. One of our main goals was to work with teachers to learn

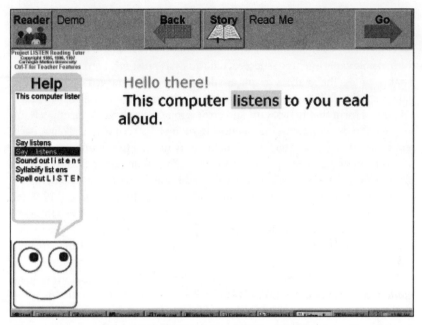

Figure 14. Fall 1997 version of the Reading Tutor.

how to make the Reading Tutor work effectively with minimal supervision in real classrooms as shown in figure 15.

Teacher training consisted primarily of a hands-on training session the week before school started. We started with a video about the 1996-97 pilot study and its results. We demonstrated the normal student operations of putting on the headset microphone, logging in, choosing stories, and reading them. Then we showed how to access the "teacher features" to add and edit students and stories, exit from the Reading Tutor, and relaunch. We helped the group coauthor and narrate its own short story. Then each teacher worked through the following exercise, guided by a 2-page handout supplemented by one-on-one assistance:

1. Start the Reading Tutor.

2. Add yourself as a Reader. (Turn Teacher Features on first, then off after you're done.)

3. Read the "Read Me" story. (Try to imitate how a struggling reader might read.)

In a group discussion, we explained that questions of educational implementation would be largely up to the teachers. Rather than dictate specific usage patterns ahead of time, we wanted to let the teachers explore how best to integrate the Reading Tutor into their classrooms.

The ongoing formative evaluation was interleaved with and guided contin-

*Figure 15. A third grader uses the Reading Tutor while the
teacher teaches the rest of the class (spring 1998).*

uing design refinement. Our evaluation methodology included classroom observation, occasional videotaping, frequent informal consultation with teachers, Problem Report forms for teachers to fill out, and year-end interviews and
questionnaires.

One experiment (Kominek et al. 1998) mounted a video camera on one of
the Reading Tutors to explore what information it might gain if it could see the
student. The video camera was connected to a VCR set to record certain hours
of use during the week. The hours of video collected without researchers present contributed to our understanding of the classroom context. For example,
analysis of this video showed that the classroom teacher approached the Reading Tutor only about once per hour of use, indicating that the students seldom
needed her assistance to operate the Reading Tutor. It is important to point out
that the video was recorded in a third grade class in December, when students
had used the Reading Tutor for three months and had a well-established rotation for using it. We would expect different results at the beginning of the year
or in a younger grade.

We now describe the main lessons we have learned so far about classroom use.

Usability

Overall, children in grades 2 and above were able to use the (1997–1998) Reading Tutor, but many younger children were not. The Reading Tutor received

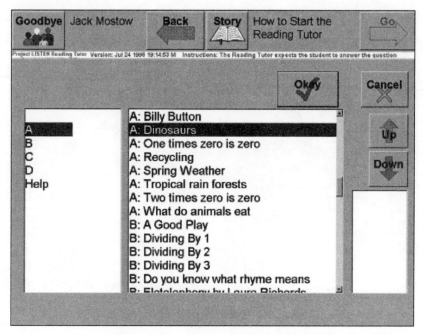

Figure 16. Story picker used in the 1997–1998 school year.
Click title to hear it; click "okay" to read that story.

little use in the kindergarten room where we placed it, so we removed it at mid-year to use elsewhere. The higher-functioning kindergartners were able to operate the Reading Tutor, but many children required more assistance than the teacher could provide. A similar but less severe pattern showed up in first grade. Interestingly, the apparent factor distinguishing children who could operate the Reading Tutor on their own was not reading level but metacognitive skills—for example, how aware children were of when they needed help. Some young children sat at the Reading Tutor for minutes at a time without doing anything or asking for help.

We had designed the "frame" operations surrounding reading a story (such as logging in, picking stories, etc.) to accommodate nonreaders (figure 16). The Reading Tutor gave spoken prompts on what to do. When a child clicked on a list item such as a reader name or story title, the Reading Tutor highlighted the list item and then read the item aloud. The child could then click *Okay* to accept that choice. Children often clicked on several titles to hear them before selecting one to read. However, (as our developmental psychologist colleague David Klahr pointed out) young children have difficulty with two-step plans—such as clicking on a story to hear its title, and then clicking *Okay*. Just-in-time prompts helped considerably, though young children sometimes re-

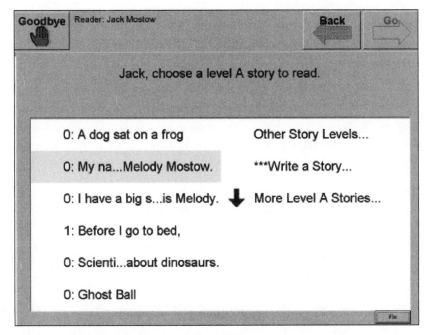

Figure 17. "One-click" story picker used in the fall of 1999.

Reading Tutor speaks the list; click item to pick it. Story title is preceded by number of times the reader has read that story before, as in "1: Before I go to bed."

spond unconditionally to conditional prompts such as, "click *Back* if you want to go back."

In 1998-99, we designed, implemented, tested, and refined the simplified "one-click pick" menu, shown in figure 17. This menu is designed to accommodate a wide spectrum of reading ability. To pick a story to read, students who can read the menu for themselves simply click on its title. Otherwise, the Reading Tutor gives spoken assistance. When it first displays the menu, it speaks the prompt shown above the menu. The Reading Tutor then successively highlights each item in the menu and reads it aloud to the student. If the student fails to select an item, the Reading Tutor reads the menu a second time. If the student doesn't respond within a few seconds, the Reading Tutor re-prompts the student. Finally, the Reading Tutor logs the student out, saying "ask your teacher for help on what to do next."

The "one-click" mechanism has proved easier than its two-step predecessor not only for children but for adults, and is employed throughout the Reading Tutor to select an item from a list. For example, the login menu consists of the readers' names, narrated by the readers themselves during the enrollment process. Each name is annotated with a reader-selected icon to further differentiate menu items and make it easier for nonreaders to recognize their names. As of fall 1999, the Reading Tutor is deployed only in grades two to four, but we look forward to testing its usability for younger children. Our experience at the summer 1999 reading clinic indicates that accommodating kindergartners will require changes to other aspects of the Reading Tutor, such as adding easier reading materials and modifying the Reading Tutor's basic assisted reading interaction to work more gracefully for pre-readers. Some very young children may even have trouble operating a standard mouse—very few, we hope, now that many children encounter computers at a young age. But if the mouse is a problem, possible solutions include children's mice or, more expensively, touchscreens.

One observation worth mentioning involves the wording of the initial prompt for menu selection. Because the prompt is spoken, there is a natural tendency to respond to it by speaking (Reeves and Nass 1996). It is therefore important to make explicit that the user should use the mouse. For example, "please click on a story to read" is a better prompt (at least for new users) than "what story do you want to read?"

Our experience confirms the well-known importance of user testing. Once a new feature is robust enough to work in our lab, the only reliable way to find out how well it works in practice is to have *children try it out at school.* Testing by children is indispensable because they stress software differently than adults do. Testing at school is essential because children behave differently there than in university labs, which are less familiar and more supervised. Moreover, although in-lab testing can be useful, the children available (such as children of faculty, or participants in university on-campus outreach activities) tend to be unrepresentative of children who use the Reading Tutor at school: they may be older, read better, or differ in motivation.

The summer reading clinics at Fort Pitt Elementary School have proven extremely useful for debugging and design iteration. Dozens of children used successive experimental versions of the Reading Tutor daily for a month, subjecting it to diverse student behaviors. Children arrived every twenty to forty minutes in shifts to use eight Reading Tutor stations in one classroom supervised by Project LISTEN personnel. Generally one LISTENer handled major problems, which arose many times daily due to the buggy nature of new code. This on-site support was essential for in-school testing of experimental versions of the Reading Tutor not yet reliable enough for normal classroom use. Typical workarounds included relaunching the Reading Tutor or hiding a bug-prone story. Meanwhile, a second LISTENer observed student use of the Reading Tutor and recorded subtler problems. Given reports of the most frequent and serious problems, other LISTENers diagnosed them based on the observed symptoms and the Reading Tutor logs, designed fixes in consultation with the rest of the team, and implemented them. This intensive cycle let us install a new version as soon as the next day. To reduce the time spent installing new versions on eight machines, we typically batched our changes into weekly updates. We found it useful to implement, test, and debug newer experimental versions on a laptop computer. The laptop let us take new versions to the school to test without installing them on the eight machines, and bring back the logged data without copying it.

Factors Affecting Amount of Use

In grades 2 and above, teachers reported extensive use, but the amount of use varied considerably among classrooms. Factors affecting the amount of use included competing with other priorities, scheduling Reading Tutor use, and handling technical problems.

Prior to the 1997-98 classroom test, we viewed the Reading Tutor as analogous to a human tutor. But a human tutor can call or fetch a child. The Reading Tutor cannot. Instead, the Reading Tutor is more like a museum exhibit—it must wait for a child to arrive, guided to it by external forces. But even that analogy is flawed, because unlike museum attendees, most schoolchildren are not free to choose where to go and what to do. When it comes to computer use in the classroom, the teacher acts as gatekeeper, setting and implementing policy for who will use it when—or if anyone will use it at all. Thus establishing and following a regular schedule proved critical to Reading Tutor use. Some teachers are reluctant to allow computer use during whole-group instruction. Teacher preference strongly affects both the amount of such instruction and the degree of reluctance. Thus Reading Tutor use was suspended for special-subject teachers, special programs, and student teachers learning classroom control.

Another overall lesson from our experience was to view with skepticism any assumption of the form "The teacher will...." Teachers are busy teaching. Even the most enthusiastic proponents of the 1997-98 Reading Tutor seldom touched it themselves after enrolling their students. That version provided a rudimentary form-filling interface for teachers to enroll their students in the Reading Tutor. This interface was fairly straightforward for experienced Windows™ users, but had some usability problems. For example, it required keyboard input for all fields, then checked for illegal values, and reported any errors for the user to fix. Using menu selection instead of keyboard input could have prevented such errors in the first place. At least one teacher had trouble finding time to enroll students, and instructed them to read as "Demo." To discourage this practice, we restricted the Demo account (which we wanted to retain for demo purposes) to a small subset of stories.

Another illustration of "the teacher will..." fallacy is the fact that, so far as we know, *no* teachers added stories in the 1997-98 school year, even though some children had authored stories in the July 1997 clinic. This outcome surprised us because we had demonstrated the authoring feature (Mostow and Aist 1999a) at the August 1997 teacher training session, and had encouraged teachers to enter stories authored (collectively or individually) by their students. However, the training exercise for the teachers had not included authoring. Moreover, the authoring feature was accessible only via the Teacher Features menu, activated in a deliberately obscure fashion by the Ctrl-T key combination.

Although most teachers apparently seldom touched the 1997-98 Reading Tutor themselves, teachers were key *indirect users* of the Reading Tutor. They influenced and guided students' interactions with the Reading Tutor in important ways, such as telling them to use the Reading Tutor when, for how long, and/or on what stories or reading levels. The teachers devised various mechanisms to provide such guidance without interrupting their teaching—for example, a schedule posted near the Reading Tutor to get students on the computer, a kitchen timer to keep track of session length, and an index card on top of the monitor to show which story to read that day. These mechanisms exercised a profound influence over how much the Reading Tutor got used, how much each student used it, and what they read.

The actual impact of these mechanisms on usage varied. Where teachers supported Reading Tutor use, students soon learned whose turn was when, and whom to get next. However, a common problem involved forgetting to start the schedule or rotation in the morning. Some teachers assigned a child to remember. Teachers told students how many stories to read, or how long to use the Reading Tutor per turn. To enforce time limits on Reading Tutor sessions, one teacher (soon imitated by others) placed a kitchen timer next to the Reading Tutor and told each student how long to set it for. However, students did not necessarily use the Reading Tutor for the same duration. In some cases, teachers assigned more time to students who needed it. In other cases, students adjusted the time left on the timer when the teacher wasn't looking—whether to get off sooner, or to stay on longer. Most teachers let students choose what to read. However, some students preferred to reread the same story rather than attempt a new story. One teacher responded to such a student by posting an index card on top of the Reading Tutor showing that student which story to read that day.

The 1997-98 Reading Tutor proved fairly robust in classrooms, often staying up for weeks at a time. (Launching the Reading Tutor takes a few minutes to initialize the speech recognizer and other components, so it is normally left up.) However, problems are inevitable: software crashes, dead microphone headsets, and unplugged cables all caused interruptions in Reading Tutor use. Also, the Reading Tutor slows down with extended use, probably due to memory leaks. Although many PC problems are fixed by rebooting, few teachers know how. Thus time to detect, report, diagnose, and fix problems has a major effect on the total amount of Reading Tutor use.

In an admittedly desperate attempt to reduce problem-fixing time, we added short tutorials (at first not even illustrated) to the Reading Tutor on how to fix some common problems, such as "How to Restart the Reading Tutor" and "If the Reading Tutor is Slow." At each login, the Reading Tutor randomly chose a tutorial to read to the child. We hoped that when a problem arose, some student in the room might have memorized the relevant tutorial and know what to do. (At such points the Reading Tutor is typically not in a state to give on-line help.) We don't know if this low-cost ploy ever succeeded, and we would be surprised if it did, since we would not expect text-only "tutorials" that lack an experiential practice component to be effective at teaching technical support skills.

We are exploring more effective forms of enabling children to do on-site technical support. In 1998-99 we redesigned the Reading Tutor to make all Teacher Features visible to students, including student enrollment, story authoring, and program exit. To improve usability for teachers who might not use the Reading Tutor very often, we sought to provide a visible target on the screen for these operations—rather than rely on teachers to remember to type Ctrl-T. For example, the login menu in the September 1999 Reading Tutor includes an "Add a Reader" item, and the story picker includes a "Write a Story" item. Access to each feature is separately and optionally password-protected. For example, based on teacher preferences, we let students enroll a new reader and write or edit their own stories, but require a password to exit the Reading Tutor, modify reader information, or alter the story menu. We redesigned enrollment by requiring keyboard input only to enter names. Thus students who could type in their names could enroll themselves. To obtain other enrollment information such as student age and birthday, the redesigned Reading Tutor uses the same "one-click pick" multiple choice mechanism used to log in and pick a story to read.

Our informal experiments with problem report forms and procedures led us to conclude that the only reliable way to find out about problems is to visit the room or ask the teacher in person. Teachers are too busy teaching to report system problems when they occur, and may not remember to report them later. Unless a problem is solved by someone or something in the classroom, it is likely to interrupt Reading Tutor usage for a prolonged time.

Where possible, we are automating certain maintenance tasks. For 1999, we have configured the PCs so that every night they automatically reboot, log in as "student" (an account with limited privileges), and relaunch the Reading Tutor. Rebooting Windows™ cures or prevents many or most software problems. The automated reboot mechanism solves most problems by the next morning even without human intervention, thereby limiting the amount of downtime. We therefore believe that this one change has improved overall availability of the Reading Tutor more than any other.

However, rebooting does not fix broken microphones, which turned out to be our principal hardware problem. A malfunctioning microphone is much subtler to detect than a broken headphone or speaker, because it is an input device rather than an output device where missing or bad audio is obvious. Therefore, we added explicit feedback about possible microphone problems.

To detect microphone problems promptly, the 1999 Reading Tutor tests the microphone every time a reader logs in. This test prompts the student to "Please read your name aloud to make sure I can hear you." If the input audio quality is impaired enough for the Reading Tutor to reject this narration, it plays back the rejected narration and says, "That is what I just heard. The microphone could be broken." If audio input is missing altogether, the Reading Tutor eventually times out and says, "I'm not able to hear your voice. The microphone may be broken or not plugged in correctly. Please tell your teacher."

We hope that if we detect microphone problems automatically and supply teachers with spare microphones, teachers will be able and willing to solve microphone problems promptly without outside assistance. By facilitating faster recovery, we hope to increase Reading Tutor usage. However, microphone breakage remains a problem with headset microphones, because they get handled so much. The models we have tried tend to survive at best a few weeks or months of classroom use. Also, although close-talking, noise-canceling microphones improve speech recognition of children's oral reading in noisy classrooms, their performance is degraded by some common child behaviors. Wearing the headset microphone too far away from the mouth weakens the speech signal relative to classroom noise. Wearing the microphone too close to the mouth causes clipping and breath noise. Fidgeting with the microphone generates loud crackling noises in the Reading Tutor's input signal.

We hope that commercial array microphones will soon provide enough directionality to filter classroom noise out of children's oral reading, which is often quiet and tentative. Mounting such microphones on the desk or monitor should eliminate not only breakage caused by frequent handling, but recognizer errors caused by improper microphone treatment. We will still need headphones to keep Reading Tutor audio output from disrupting the class, but headphones are easier to use, diagnose, and replace than microphones.

Balancing Learner and Tutor Control

A recurring issue in the Reading Tutor is how to balance learner and tutor control. We believe in learner control on philosophical and motivational grounds. However, some children abuse learner control (Yang and Moore 1995), in the sense of making choices that we believe are not conducive to learning. For example, although rereading a story is part of successful human tutoring (Wasik 1998) and can improve comprehension (Bowers 1993), children often reread stories over and over—far past the point where we think they could learn much. Even with Reading Tutor guidance on choosing levels and stories, some children persist in reading too-easy material. Reading is hard, so this tendency isn't surprising.

As this example shows, to some extent the evolution of the Reading Tutor reflects the ongoing discovery of student paths we think are ill-chosen, and our attempts to block or discourage their use.

For another example, we initially found that students often read under someone else's name, sometimes because the previous student had left without first logging out. This practice corrupted the data recorded by the Reading Tutor, affecting its student models and our own research. To reduce this phenomenon without jeopardizing usability, we made the Reading Tutor log out the student automatically after prolonged inactivity. We also instituted a light-weight password scheme. To log in, students now had to confirm their identity by correctly selecting their birth month. We used birth month rather than adding conventional passwords for teachers to enter and students to remember. Birthdates were already entered in the Reading Tutor for research purposes, and we expected that children would know their birthdays. We have since found that even by second grade, some children still don't know their birthdays—month and day, let alone year—but their teachers typically do from their class rosters.

A related problem in at least one classroom involved students reading as the pseudo-user "Demo," because their teacher had not gotten around to entering their names in the Reading Tutor. We did not want to eliminate the "Demo" user, because it was too useful for such purposes as troubleshooting and teacher training. Therefore we kept the "Demo" account, but we restricted it to a handful of stories in order to deter its abuse.

To combat abuse of the *Go* button, we modified how the Reading Tutor responded to *Go*. If the reader had gotten credit for at least half (or some other specified fraction) of the words in the sentence, it went on. If not, it prompted the student to try reading the sentence, or to click for help. This mid-year (December 1997) modification was ill-received by students who were used to unrestricted *Go*, especially because it was accompanied by a general performance slowdown that we did not track down till much later. When usage of the Reading Tutor dropped off precipitously, we restored the old behavior (by reducing the required fraction to zero). However, students who were not already accustomed to unfettered use of *Go* accepted the new behavior when we installed the Reading Tutor in additional rooms for the spring 1998 controlled study that we shall describe shortly. This experience illustrates the obvious point that user acceptance of software can be affected by experience with previous versions—a problem in design iteration.

One previously unsuspected path appeared at the July 1997 reading clinic, where children who used the Reading Tutor engaged in many social interactions. Some were cooperative, such as helping a nearby student operate the Reading Tutor or read a word. Others were competitive, such as racing through a story. In one utterance captured by the Reading Tutor, the student read the sentence, then said, "I beat you, though!" The 1997 clinic version of the Reading Tutor displayed separate menus of "Old" and "New" (previously read versus unread) stories. Some children treated the length of the "Old" menu as a score and competed to rack up long lists. Unfortunately, the easiest way was to click *Go* without reading. This episode taught us to be wary of displaying anything that children might treat as a score, because tactics to score high might not align with good educational choices. However, scores may serve as a useful motivational tool provided they reward good educational choices, such as reading new, challenging stories.

Summative Evaluation:
Spring 1998 Within-Classroom Controlled Study

In spring 1998, we conducted a controlled evaluation of the Reading Tutor. (Meanwhile the eight-classroom formative study continued in all but the kindergarten.) The purpose of the controlled study was to evaluate the effectiveness of the Reading Tutor compared to spending the same amount of time in other treatments.

Method

Word identification, word attack, and passage comprehension were independently pre-tested in January and post-tested in May-June, using the Woodcock Reading Mastery Test. Testing was supervised by Rollanda O'Connor of the University of Pittsburgh School of Education, and performed at the elementary school by her graduate students. The testers did not know which students received which treatment.

To avoid confounds due to teacher effects, we designed the study as a within-classroom comparison rather than compare between classrooms. We chose three classrooms (grades two, four, and five) that had not yet seen the Reading Tutor. (We did not include a grade 3 classroom, because all three third grades were already using the Reading Tutor.) We split each classroom into three statistically matched treatment groups based on the pre-test. Specifically, subjects were matched within each classroom based on the average of their nationally normed scores on the three administered subtests of the Woodcock Reading Mastery Test, namely Word Attack, Word Identification, and Passage Comprehension. The seventy-two pretested subjects included the entire classes except for absentees. Sixty-three of the seventy-two students were post-tested; the others had moved away or were unavailable due to prolonged absences. Each student was scheduled to receive his or her assigned treatment twenty to twenty-five minutes every day for four months.

The experimental treatment consisted of using the December 1997 version of the Reading Tutor. Subsequent analysis (by Regina Tassone and Adam Wierman) of the captured utterance data revealed that the Reading Tutor was actually used much less than planned—only one day in four in the grade two and four rooms, and barely one day in eight in the grade five room. Likewise, analysis (by Hua Lan and Cathy Huang) of the Reading Tutor logs showed that session length averaged twelve minutes—only half of the scheduled twenty to twenty-five minutes. Thus the results of the study are based on a much less intensive contrast among conditions than we had intended.

As one control condition, an alternate treatment consisted of using commercial reading software that provided spoken assistance but did not listen to the student. The purpose of this condition was to let us evaluate the Reading Tutor against a state-of-the-art (or at least state-of-the-software-market) alternative. A nonlistening version of the Reading Tutor might seem at first like a more obvious control condition, but would not have made much sense, because listening is integral to its design. The actual amount of commercial software use was not recorded.

The baseline control treatment consisted of normal classroom activity, including computer use other than the reading software used in the first two treatments. We included this control condition in order to compare the Reading Tutor against whatever instruction (including computer use) students would have received if the study had not been performed. However, in practice, teachers reported giving all three groups similar amounts of computer time on grounds of fairness. Thus each treatment actually included a similar proportion of conventional instruction and computer use, and differed primarily in the type of software used.

Results

To compare the effectiveness of the three treatments, we measured students' improvement, not simply their posttest performance. We computed individual gains as posttest minus pretest, using normed scores. We used two-tailed paired T-tests to compare gains in each skill (word attack, word identification, and passage comprehension) between each two treatments. Only one difference was significant ($p = 0.002$): the Reading Tutor group gained more in comprehension than their classmates in the conventional instruction group. Moreover, the nationally normed scores allow comparison to progress by children elsewhere. As figure 18 shows, the pretest scores for the students in this study averaged about two standard deviations below the national average. While the control group fell further below its national cohort in Passage Comprehension, the Reading Tutor group climbed. As school principal Gayle Griffin put it, the Reading Tutor was "closing the gap."

Discussion

The results of the controlled study surprised us because the Reading Tutor gave lots of help for word identification and word attack, but helped comprehension only by reading aloud to the student.[2] The December 1997 Reading Tutor presented no definitions, explanations, or paraphrases, and few pictures. Why did

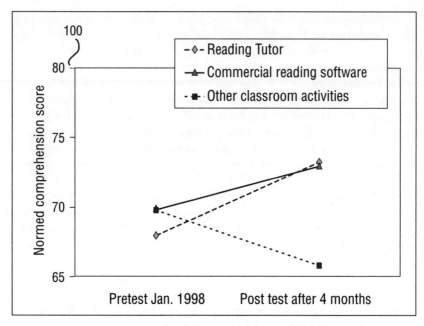

Figure 18. Results of the spring 1998 controlled study.

comprehension improve so much? Why didn't the Reading Tutor group significantly outgain the baseline control or alternate treatment groups in other reading skills? How can the Reading Tutor improve these skills more effectively?

For now, we have redesigned the Reading Tutor to address what we perceived as major limitations to its effectiveness. One problem was students' tendency to reread the same easy stories over and over. To expose students to dramatically more material, the fall 1999 Reading Tutor takes turns with the student picking what story to read next (Aist and Mostow 2000). Another limitation of previous versions was the lack of semantic assistance. The fall 1999 Reading Tutor dynamically inserts additional text to explain vocabulary that may be unfamiliar to the reader.

In the future, we hope that analysis of data captured by the Reading Tutor will let us assess students' progress in component skills of reading, and the Reading Tutor's own contribution to that progress. For example, the fall 1999 Reading Tutor assesses student understanding of vocabulary encountered in stories by administering automatically generated multiple-choice quizzes. To evaluate the effectiveness of the Reading Tutor's vocabulary assistance, we can compare the same student's performance on assisted versus unassisted words (Aist, AI-ED factoids paper 2001).

Follow-On Work:
1999-2000 Between-Classroom Controlled Study

As we improve the Reading Tutor, we will perform new studies to evaluate its effectiveness compared to alternatives. In September 1999, we launched a study to evaluate the fall 1999 Reading Tutor compared to current practice and to individual human tutoring. This study addresses several limitations of the Spring 1998 study. The new study will last for the entire 1999–2000 school year, not just four months. To generalize the results and to ensure that the subjects are uncontaminated by prior Reading Tutor use, this study is at a school that has not previously used the Reading Tutor. Although we are continuing other studies at the first school, the Reading Tutor is now sufficiently institutionalized there to preclude any study design that would take the Reading Tutor away from children and teachers who are used to it. The new study is starting with one hundred forty-four subjects, double the previous seventy-two subjects. The study focuses on the bottom-half readers in twelve second and third grade classrooms, rather than on three entire classes in grades two, four, and five. To compare better against current practice, the Reading Tutor group is in different classrooms than the control groups.

Conclusion

Using computers to listen to children read aloud has yielded exciting results to date. However, the Reading Tutor remains a work in progress. We have tried to give a sense of the path that Project LISTEN has followed to its current position—a path of questions asked, experiments performed, methods refined, and lessons learned. Our central goal has been to explore how an automated tutor that listens can help children learn to read. Experiments have ranged from short user tests to year-long field trials. Methods have included informal observation, Wizard of Oz studies, within- and between-subject comparisons, and randomized invisible experiments. Lessons learned have ranged from slippery statistical subtleties to nitty-gritty classroom realities.

Where Are We Now?

So how effective is an automated reading tutor that listens? We have addressed successive versions of this question for successive systems:

How well does the system help children read? To help shape this assistance, we developed and refined a Wizard of Oz system. To evaluate its assistive effectiveness, we conducted a within-subject comparison of 12 low-reading second graders' assisted vs. unassisted reading levels. The WOZ system's assistance enabled these subjects to read and comprehend material an average of six months above their independent reading level (Mostow et al. 1994). The Emily reading coach used speech recognition to automate this assistance. A within-subject study of 34 second graders showed that their comprehension averaged twenty percent higher with Emily's assistance than without.

How well does the system listen? We adapted the Sphinx-II speech recognizer to follow the reader and detect mistakes (Mostow et al. 1993). The Emily coach accepted over 96 percent of the words read correctly in a test set captured during the Wizard of Oz study, and detected about half of the miscues flagged by the human wizard as likely to cause miscomprehension (Mostow et al. 1994). Analysis of oral reading captured in the 1996-97 pilot study of the Reading Tutor showed that interword latency reflected individual students' subtle improvements in fluency over time (Mostow and Aist 1997b).

How well does the system help children learn? In a 1996-97 pilot test at an inner-city elementary school, six third-graders who started almost three years below grade level and used the (November 1996) Reading Tutor under individual supervision averaged two years' progress in under eight months. In a four-month controlled study in spring 1998, children who used the (December 1997) Reading Tutor under normal classroom conditions gained significantly more in reading comprehension than statistically matched classmates who spent the same time in regular activities. In fall 1999 we launched a year-long study of 144 second- and third-graders to evaluate the latest version of the Reading Tutor, compared to current practice and to human tutoring.

Work in Progress

The effectiveness of the Reading Tutor—as of any educational software—depends not only on its efficacy when used, but on how much it gets used. We are therefore studying variations in Reading Tutor usage within and among classrooms. We are identifying and addressing various factors that affect usage.

Start-up affects adoption. We modified the Reading Tutor to let children enroll themselves, or at least make it easier for teachers to enroll them. User training is another important issue. Although the Reading Tutor requires only a few minutes of training to use, the content of this training can greatly influence patterns of use. To make this training consistent, we worked with certified elementary teacher Mary Beth Sklar to develop an introductory tutorial for first-time users. The tutorial took the form of a story to read with the normal assistance of the Reading Tutor, which intervenes when the reader gets stuck. Many children were able to read this story. However, it proved too long and difficult for younger students, even with the Reading Tutor's assistance. An effective automated introduction will require further work. Also, teachers are often harder to train than students, both because they need to know more (such as how to fix problems), and because they may refuse to use software without human instruction.

Classroom management issues include creating and maintaining a regular schedule of usage. To provide schedule support, we added an on-line roster to show who has read. We modified the Reading Tutor to show how long the current reader has read.

Recovery from hardware and software problems is crucial. We have decided that problem severity matters less than obviousness of detection and ease of recovery. For example, a broken speaker is obvious, because there is no sound, but microphone breakage (our most vexing hardware problem) is not obvious, because it is not directly observable. We added a microphone test to detect this condition. Likewise, crashes are actually less problematic than degraded functionality or performance. It is obvious when a crash occurs: the Reading Tutor vanishes from the screen. It is also easy to recover from—just double-click on the program icon. To reduce software degradation caused by prolonged operation, we reboot the computer automatically every night.

Teacher acceptance is crucial. For example, some teachers may not let students use the Reading Tutor during whole-group instruction or special subjects. Widespread teacher adoption will require better understanding of how to fit the Reading Tutor into the social context of the classroom and school.

To improve the Reading Tutor, we must understand which students it helps, what skills it builds, and why. Initial evidence suggests that, as one might expect, lower-reading students benefit the most, in the sense of gaining more than students with similar pretest scores. In the 1994 within-subject study, the difference between assisted and unassisted performance in the Emily reading coach was largest for students in the bottom quartile on a national reading test. Likewise, in the 1998 within-classroom study, the difference in comprehension gains between the Reading Tutor and the control condition was largest among the children who pretested in the bottom half. However, although the Reading Tutor group gained significantly more in comprehension than the control group, the sample size was not large enough to make these aptitude-treatment interactions statistically significant. Besides increasing study duration and sample size, we are videotaping and analyzing protocols of students interacting with the Reading Tutor and human tutors in order to shed further light on these interactions.

To analyze how much the Reading Tutor builds different component skills of reading, we administered different subtests of the Woodcock Reading Mastery Test. The 1998 study tested Word Attack, Word Identification, and Passage Comprehension. In addition, we timed oral reading fluency. Now that we have added vocabulary assistance to the Reading Tutor, we are testing Word Comprehension as well.

To understand why the Reading Tutor has the effects that it does, we need much finer-grained instruments. For example, how can we exclude the hypothesis that the results are due to a Hawthorne effect? Perhaps children improved simply because of the extra attention that the Reading Tutor gave them, or because they liked reading to a computer, rather than because of anything more specific that the Reading Tutor did. Such an attention effect would of course be quite valuable, as long as it is reproducible on a larger scale. But it is important to know whether the Reading Tutor's interventions matter. We have begun to address this question by analyzing the effects of those interventions on the tutorial dialogue. For example, we found that students corrected errors much more often when the Reading Tutor intervened than when it did not (Aist and Mostow 1998). We are exploring invisible experiments as a way to control for Hawthorne effects in the comparison of different interventions. Where feasible, we especially favor within-subject experiments, because they control for individual differences, avoid subdividing the subject pool, and are easier both to administer and to conceal from subjects who might notice treatment differences between subjects. That is, if subjects are unaware of an experiment, then its outcome should reflect the intrinsic differences between the experimental and control conditions, rather than conflating the experimental condition with Hawthorne effects. However, teasing apart the effects of long sequences of interventions on many different words and skills is not easy. We will need more accurate listening in order to track improved performance. We will need better models of evolving skills in order to track student progress. We will need better experimental designs in order to track how different tutorial interventions affect student learning.

Future Work

How might future generations of the Reading Tutor (and its ilk) benefit from improved technology?

Speech recognition: Detecting more miscues with fewer false alarms could increase tutorial efficiency and reduce frustration. Accurate phonetic transcription of miscues could help pinpoint and remediate their underlying causes. Accurate voice dictation for children would open up new possibilities for assistance in writing. Spoken language understanding could help assess and assist student comprehension.

Additional sensory input: Proximity sensing could help distinguish silence from absence. Microphone arrays could reduce headset breakage and detect multiple users. Gaze tracking could help track student attention and position. Machine vision could make the Reading Tutor more sensitive to the student's emotions and social environment.

Miniaturization: Currently the Reading Tutor is limited to a few per classroom, partly for logistical reasons but also because of cost. As computer hardware becomes smaller and cheaper, incorporating Reading Tutor technology into inexpensive handheld devices would enable every student to have a portable Reading Tutor that he or she could use throughout the day.

Networking: With faster Internet connections, schools (and homes) could exchange student-narrated stories. Networked installation, upgrades, and support could reduce support costs and increase availability. Researchers could aggregate data from multiple Reading Tutors.

Data mining: Educational software has the potential to capture detailed, precise, fine-grained, longitudinal data of interactions with large numbers of students over long periods of time. Such data could open a powerful new window into student learning processes and how to support them better.

Automated experiments: Such data need not be limited to passive capture. Software can be instrumented to perform, record, monitor, and analyze (both within- and between-subject) experiments to compare alternative pedagogical strategies and tactics. For example, the Reading Tutor's within-subject "invisible experiments" compare tutorial alternatives such as different types of prompts, or whether to explain a new word or just let the student infer its meaning from context. These experiments take place in classrooms, without the expense and distortion of researchers' presence. Outcome variables need not be limited to gross assessments of effectiveness. Fine-grained analysis of educational alternatives could trace their effects on details of student performance. Such experiments could be aggregated over the Internet across multiple classrooms, schools, and communities.

Tutors that learn: Techniques from artificial intelligence, statistics, and machine learning could be used to automate the very design of such experiments, using the outcome of one experiment to help guide the design of the next, and using the results of experiments to continually improve the behavior of the educational software. This process could identify different categories of students in terms of what works best for each one. Such a system could acquire—and learn from—a million years' worth of individual interaction with students.

Acknowledgements

This chapter is based upon work supported in part by the National Science Foundation under Grant Nos. MDR-9154059, IRI-9505156, CDA-9616546, REC-9720348, and REC-9979894, by the Defense Advanced Research Projects Agency under Grant Nos. F33615-93-1-1330 and N00014-93-1-2005, and by the second author's National Science Foundation Graduate Fellowship and Harvey Fellowship. Any opinions, findings, conclusions, or recommendations expressed in this publication are those of the authors and do not necessarily reflect the views of the National Science Foundation or the official policies, either expressed or implied, of the sponsors or of the United States Government.

We thank current and previous members of Project LISTEN who have made substantive contributions: faculty Albert Corbett, Maxine Eskenazi, Alexander Hauptmann, Brian Junker, Rollanda O'Connor, Steven Roth, and Leslie Thyberg; professional staff Andrew Cuneo, Matthew Kane, Jim Kocher, Rebecca Kennedy, DeWitt Latimer IV, Shawn McBride, Nancy Miller, Brian Milnes,

Sharon Pegher, Mary Beth Sklar, Adam Swift, Debra Tobin, and Robert Weide; graduate students Jessica Abroms, Dan Barritt, Kate Bell, Peggy Chan, Lin Lawrence Chase, Audie Durand, Jennifer Gutwaks, Kristin Harty, Jeffrey Hill, Cathy Huang, Tzee-Ming Huang, Kerry Perlmutter Ishizaki, John Kominek, Hua Lan, Yue Pan, Stephen Reed, Peter Venable, and Calvin Yeung; and undergraduates Paige Angstadt, Scott Dworkis, Sreekar Gadde, Lee Ann Galasso Kane, Morgan Hankins, Andrew Kim, Kevin Liu, David Matsumoto, Brian Nagy, Cindy Neelan, David Sell, Herbert Stiel, Regina Tassone, Chetan Trikha, and Adam Wierman. Project LISTEN's distinguished Advisory Panel has included Robert Davis and James Flanagan (Rutgers), Fran Ferrara (first grade teacher), Elaine Fowler-Costas and Philip Gough (University of Texas), Louis Gomez (Northwestern University), Gayle Griffin (elementary principal), Mark Lepper (Stanford), Richard Olson (University of Colorado), Janet Schofield (University of Pittsburgh), and Herbert Simon (Carnegie Mellon). We apologize for any inadvertent omissions.

We thank the Carnegie Mellon Speech Group (especially Ravi Mosur) for the Sphinx-II speech recognizer. We are grateful for valuable advice from them and from many colleagues, especially Robert Kass, Charles Perfetti, and Larry Wasserman, and our LIS collaborators Julie Fiez, Jay McClelland, David Plaut, and Walter Schneider.

We thank educators and students for participating in and assisting our experiments in McKeesport at Centennial Elementary School (Joseph Fiori, Principal), in Wilkinsburg at Turner Elementary School, and in Pittsburgh at Colfax Elementary School (Patsy Nysewander, Principal), East Hills Elementary School (Richard Nicklos, Principal), Winchester Thurston School, and especially Fort Pitt Elementary School (Gayle Griffin, Principal). We also thank all the children who tried the Reading Tutor in our lab, and the parents or students who brought them.

We thank Richard Olson and Helen Datta at the University of Colorado for their data on oral reading miscues, and Weekly Reader Corporation and CTB Macmillan/McGraw-Hill for permission to use copyrighted reading materials from *Weekly Reader* and George Spache's Diagnostic Reading Scales, respectively.

Finally, we thank the editors for their helpful reviews, Debra Tobin and Sean McBride for help with several figures, and everyone (especially Raj Reddy) who has supported Project LISTEN over the years in so many ways. We are responsible for any errors or shortcomings that remain.

Notes

1. NCES 1998, http://nces.ed.gov/pubs98/condition98/c9816a01.html

2. See Scrase (1997) for suggestive evidence that reading aloud to children while they look at the text may help comprehension skills.

Chapter Seven

Articulate Software for Science and Engineering Education

Kenneth D. Forbus

Improving science and engineering education is a critical problem for technological societies, who, in addition to needing scientists, engineers, and technicians, need a scientifically literate population in order to make wise decisions. We believe a new kind of educational software, *articulate software*, can help solve this problem. Articulate software understands the domain being learned in humanlike ways, and can provide explanations and coaching to help learners master it. Articulate software is made possible by advances in artificial intelligence, particularly in qualitative physics, combined with the ongoing revolution in computer technology. This chapter explores the ideas underlying articulate software and describes two architectures for articulate software that we have developed:

- *Articulate virtual laboratories* (AVLs) help students learn by engaging them in conceptual design tasks. We illustrate this architecture with two examples: CyclePad, an AVL for engineering thermodynamics which is now routinely used at a number of universities worldwide, and FAVL, which is designed to help students understand feedback systems.
- *Active illustrations* provide an interactive simulation medium that enables students to experiment with physical phenomena, providing conceptual explanations as well as traditional simulator outputs. We illustrate this architecture with several examples, ranging from stand-alone simulation laboratories (e.g., evaporation laboratory, Mars Colony Ecosystem) to game-style simulations embedded in explanatory hypertexts (i.e., the principles of operations manual for a virtual space probe).

I describe the scientific and pedagogical principles underlying these architectures, and summarize some of the lessons learned by building and deploying them. I end with some suggestions for what is needed to bring these architectures into widespread use.

Qualitative Physics and Articulate Software

Creating new kinds of educational software has been one motivation for qualitative physics since its inception (cf. Forbus and Stevens 1981; Brown, Burton, and de Kleer 1982; Hollan, Hutchins, and Weitzman 1984). There are two reasons why qualitative physics is particularly appropriate for application to science and engineering education. The first is that *qualitative physics represents the right kinds of knowledge*. Much of what is taught in science in elementary, middle, and high school consists of causal theories of physical phenomena: What happens, when does it happen, what affects it, and what does it affect. Consider the water cycle, a key topic in middle-school science curricula. Understanding this cycle requires understanding the kinds of forms that water can be in (e.g., liquid water, water vapor, snow and ice), the sorts of places it can be (in bodies of liquid water, underground, in the air), and the processes that transform and move it from place to place (e.g., flows, evaporation, condensation, freezing, etc.). Traditional mathematical and computer modeling languages do not attempt to formalize such notions because they are designed for expert humans who already know such things. For example, the conceptual understanding that a simulation designer used to create a simulator typically resides at best in the program's documentation, and at worst only in the designer's mind. For many purposes this opacity is fine; however, the lack of tight coupling between concepts and their software embodiment makes it difficult for most educational software to explain its results.

On the other hand, uncovering how we think about physical entities and processes is one of the central scientific goals of qualitative physics. Progress in qualitative physics has led to new modeling languages that describe entities and processes in conceptual terms, embody natural notions of causality, and express knowledge about the modeling process itself (cf. Forbus 1984a, Weld and de Kleer 1990; Falkenhainer and Forbus 1991; Forbus 1996). These languages provide new capabilities for domain content providers of science education software. By embedding human-like models of entities and processes in software, the software's understanding can be used to provide explanations that are directly coupled to how specific results were derived. These explanations can delve into topics that traditional software cannot handle, for example, why a process was considered to occur or why a specific approximation makes sense. Figure 1 illustrates how qualitative physics encodes some sample everyday concepts.

The second reason that qualitative physics is particularly apt for science and engineering education is that *qualitative physics represents the right level of knowledge*. We believe that the tendency for engineering education to be highly mathematical at the expense of qualitative understanding is counterproductive. Rare is the instructor who does not lament that students memorize formulae without understanding basic principles. Indeed, cognitive scientists

What a student sees	What the software knows
"Evaporation of water from the cup"	`(evaporation PI2)`
"Temperature of the water depends on its heat."	`(qprop (temp water6)` `        (heat water6))`

"Heat flow occurs when two things are touching and their temperatures are unequal. Heat goes from the hotter one to the cooler one."	`(defprocess heat-flow`
	`  :participants`
	`    src a thermal-object`
	`    dst a thermal-object`
	`  :conditions`
	`    (> (T src) (T dst))`
	`  :consequences`
	`    (I+ (heat dst) (hf self))`
	`    (I- (heat src) (hf self))`

Figure 1. Qualitative reasoning provides formal languages for conceptual knowledge.

have extensively documented the existence of persistent misconceptions that survive college training in domains such as physics (cf. Gentner and Stevens 1983). We believe that a strong quantitative sense of the world is crucial for engineering. However, we believe that principles governing a domain (i.e., the laws, mechanisms, and causal relationships) need to be mastered at the qualitative level to provide the kind of deep, robust understanding that engineering education seeks to impart. Typically, expositions of such knowledge are centered around mathematical equations (particularly those which can be solved analytically), in the form of derivations that mimic the structure of proofs. While these equations are important, only a small subset of students gain the desired understanding from this method of presentation. An alternative is to focus more on teaching qualitative principles directly. Good textbooks attempt to do this by introducing ideas in qualitative terms before diving into quantitative details, but they rarely linger at the qualitative level. One reason for shortchanging qualitative understanding is the lack of a systematic formal vocabulary for qualitative knowledge, which makes this knowledge harder to articulate than quantitative knowledge. Qualitative physics provides such vocabularies, and we hope that as these ideas become more widespread, engineering educators will be able to use them to express aspects of their expertise that are currently described as "intuition" or "art."

Whether or not one believes that engineering education must be heavily mathematical, it is impossible to make such a claim about pre-college science education. Students learn calculus, at best, at the end of high school, and sometimes only encounter algebra at the start of high school. Making students memorize differential equations in the guise of teaching them science simply isn't an option. Even formal algebraic models are not feasible for elementary and middle school students. On the other hand, students are taught about the entities, relationships, and processes needed for a qualitative understanding of

Figure 2. Articulate software provides explanations.

phenomena. They learn what kinds of objects there are (e.g., bodies of water, clouds) and what parameters exist (e.g., temperatures, pressures, dew points). They learn partial information about relationships between parameters (e.g., "the rate of evaporation depends on the water temperature"). They learn when various relationships are relevant and what physical phenomena they are tied to (e.g., that boiling in the open air occurs at a constant temperature). In other words, the qualitative mathematics developed in qualitative physics provides exactly the right level of language for expressing relationships between continuous properties for precollege science students.

Properties of articulate software. What these two claims suggest is that qualitative physics can provide the ability to create much smarter educational software: software whose models of the world have much in common with people's mental models. Such software can use this understanding to explain, coach, and scaffold students in a variety of ways (figure 2). We call such software *articulate software.* Articulate software should have the following properties:

- It should be *fluent.* The software should have some understanding of the subject being taught, and be able to communicate both its results and reasoning processes to students in comprehensible forms.

- It should be *supportive*. It should include a mentoring component consisting of coaches and tutors that scaffold students appropriately, taking care of routine and unenlightening subtasks and helping students learn how to approach and solve problems.

- It should be *generative*. Students and instructors should be able to pose new questions and problems, rather than just selecting from a small pre-stored set of choices.

- It should be *customizable*. Instructors should be able to modify, update, and extend the libraries of phenomena, designs, and domain theories used by the software, without needing sophisticated programming skills. This simplifies maintenance and provides scalability.

There are potentially many types of articulate software. The rest of this chapter describes two architectures for articulate software that we have developed. These architectures provide students with experiences that would often be too expensive, time-consuming, or dangerous to deal with in the physical world. *Articulate virtual laboratories* provide students with design experiences, highly motivating settings for learning principles. *Active illustrations* provide students with simulations that can be used to explore phenomena. The next two sections examine each architecture in turn.

Articulate Virtual Laboratories

Design activities provide powerful motivation and meaningful contexts for learning fundamental physical principles. In designing a household refrigerator, for instance, students quickly discover that water makes a poor working fluid because its saturation curve requires very low operating pressures to achieve vaporization at typical operating conditions. Design requires that students use knowledge in an integrated fashion rather than memorizing isolated facts. Getting students to think in design terms leads naturally to building a strong interest in understanding complex, real-world relationships: The question "Why did they design it that way?" can be asked of any artifact in the world around us. Design environments that provide appropriate scaffolding for students, so that they can focus on particular areas of interest, could prove invaluable for instruction in basic science as well as engineering, and could better motivate interest in science learning.

The articulate virtual laboratory architecture my colleagues and I have developed addresses this need. Like existing virtual laboratories (e.g., electronics workbench, interactive physics) it includes a software environment for creating and analyzing designs without the expense (and sometimes danger) of creating physical artifacts. Unlike existing virtual laboratories, it provides explanation facilities and coaching, to help guide the student.

We have constructed two articulate virtual laboratories to date: CyclePad

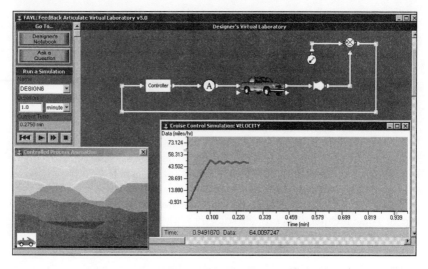

Figure 3. FAVL *helps students learn principles of feedback.*

(Forbus and Whalley 1994; Forbus et al. 1999) helps engineering students learn engineering thermodynamics by supporting students in designing and analyzing thermodynamic cycles. The feedback articulate virtual laboratory (FAVL) (Forbus 1984b; Ma 1998, 1999) helps high school students learn the principles of feedback by designing controllers (see figure 3). Since CyclePad is already in routine use, I will focus my discussion on it.

CyclePad: An AVL for Engineering Thermodynamics

CyclePad (Forbus and Whalley 1994; Forbus et al. 1999) is an articulate virtual laboratory for engineering thermodynamics. The analysis and design of thermodynamic cycles is a major task that drives engineering thermodynamics (cf. Whalley 1992). A thermodynamic cycle is a system within which a working fluid (or fluids) undergoes a series of transformations in order to process energy. Every power plant, engine, refrigerator, and heat pump is a thermodynamic cycle. Thermodynamic cycles play much the same role for engineering thermodynamics as electronic circuits do for electrical engineering: A small library of parts (in this case, compressors, turbines, pumps, heat exchangers, and so forth) are combined into networks, thus allowing a potentially unlimited set of designs for any given problem. (Practically, cycles range from four components, in the simplest cases, to networks consisting of dozens of components.) One source of the complexity of cycle analysis stems from the complex nature

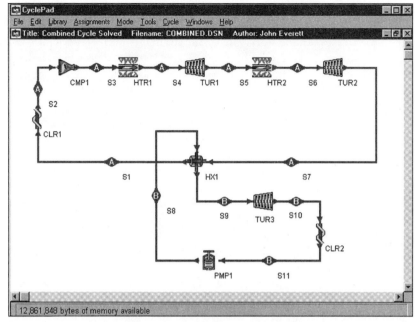

Figure 4. Example of a CyclePad design.

of liquids and gases: Subtle interactions between their properties must be harnessed in order to improve designs. Cycle analysis addresses questions such as the overall efficiency of a system, how much heat or work is consumed or produced, and what operating parameters (e.g., temperatures and pressures) are required of its components. As in many engineering design problems, an important activity in designing cycles is performing sensitivity analyses, to understand how choices for properties of the components and operating points of a cycle affect its global properties.

To illustrate, consider the power generation cycle shown in figure 4. Air from the atmosphere (S2) is compressed, which raises its pressure and causes its temperature to rise. More heat is added in the combustion chamber by injecting fuel and igniting it. Energy is extracted by expanding the gas through turbine 1, and the gas is reheated and then passed through turbine 2 to extract yet more energy. One consequence of the second law of thermodynamics is that a cycle must reject some heat as waste. A clever feature of this cycle is that it recycles some of this heat, using it to drive another cycle. This occurs via the heat exchanger, which heats the working fluid in the second cycle. I will return to the subcycle shortly. In the main cycle, the waste gases are exhausted back to the atmosphere after going through the heat exchanger. This return to the atmosphere is represented by a cooler, which enables us to take into account the heat lost in this transaction. Returning to the heat exchanger, the heat transferred from the gas cycle is sufficient to vaporize the working fluid (in this case water) in the lower cycle into superheated steam, which is passed through turbine 3 to extract yet more work. Finally, the steam is condensed back into water, exhausting more heat to the atmosphere, and is pumped back into the heat exchanger to complete the cycle. A thermodynamics expert would recognize this as a combined cycle, where a Brayton gas cycle with reheat drives a Rankine vapor cycle.

In thermodynamics education for engineers, cycle analysis and design generally appear towards the end of their first semester, or in a second course, since understanding cycles requires a broad and deep understanding of the fundamentals of thermodynamics. However, even the most introductory engineering thermodynamics textbooks tend to devote several chapters to cycle analysis, and in more advanced books the fraction devoted to cycles rises sharply. Indeed, some textbooks focus exclusively on cycle analysis (e.g., Haywood 1985). Aside from their intrinsic interest, the design of thermodynamic cycles provides a highly motivating context for students to learn fundamental principles deeply.

There are several reasons why thermodynamics is especially suitable for virtual laboratories. First, physical laboratories involving even simple thermodynamic cycles can be expensive and dangerous, due to the need for high temperatures and pressures, along with dangerous chemicals (e.g., fuels, ammonia). Second, many of the most interesting systems, such as jet engines and power plants, are far too expensive and time-consuming to build as student projects. Third, creating working physical artifacts requires what is known as detailed design, where many concrete choices are made, in addition to conceptual design, where the basic properties of a system are figured out. It is conceptual design that provides the most pedagogical value in teaching fundamental principles. For example, designing a working jet engine requires selecting an appropriate curvature for the turbine blades and worrying about shape and weight tradeoffs for every component. Designing a working power plant that uses water as its working fluid requires designing draining, cleaning, and lubrication systems. These topics are important for advanced engineering courses specializing in those areas, but are irrelevant and distracting when trying to help students master the fundamentals of the domain.

Using CyclePad: An Example

When students start up CyclePad, they find a palette of component types (e.g., turbine, compressor, pump, heater, cooler, heat exchanger, throttle, splitter, mixer) that can be used in their design. Components are connected together by *stuffs*, which represent the properties of the working fluid at that point in the system.

An important aside: There are actually two perspectives one can take on thermodynamic cycles: steady-flow versus closed cycles. In steady flow analyses one treats the fluid flowing through the system as essentially varying with location rather than time. Typical applications of steady-flow analyses include power plants and jet engines. In closed cycle analyses one follows a volume of fluid through a set of changes imposed by physical processes, regardless of their physical location. Typical applications of closed cycle analyses include automobile and diesel engines. Closed-cycle problems are also heavily used early in thermodynamics courses to focus students on the particular properties of substances and processes. While the laws of thermodynamics are the same for both perspectives, how the laws are applied varies as a consequence of the ontological choices each perspective makes. CyclePad supports both perspectives, but I only discuss steady-flow systems here for simplicity.

Once students put together the structure of the cycle, they continue to use CyclePad to analyze the system. The student enters assumptions such as the choice of working fluid and the values of specific numerical parameters. In addition to numerical assumptions, *modeling assumptions* can be made about components. For example, a turbine can be assumed to be adiabatic (i.e., no heat is lost from it to its surroundings), isothermal (i.e., no temperature change across it), or isentropic (i.e., constant entropy). Such modeling assumptions can introduce new constraints that may help carry an analysis further. They can also introduce new parameters (e.g., the efficiency of the turbine if it isn't isentropic) whose values the student must appropriately constrain.

CyclePad accepts information incrementally, deriving from each student assumption as many consequences as it can. *Meters* associated with each component and stuff are available to describe its properties (see figure 5). Like physical meters, these meters display numerical parameters of the entity they represent in a compact tabular form. Unlike physical meters, they also display the modeling assumptions the student has made so far, and what other assumptions might yet be made. At any point questions can be asked, by clicking on an element of a meter display to obtain the set of questions (or commands) that make sense for it. The questions and answers are displayed in English. They include links back into the explanation system, thus providing an incrementally generated hypertext (see figure 6). This hypertext is important for several reasons. First, it helps students understand the indirect consequences of their assumptions. Second, the nature of the domain is such that students often make inconsistent modeling assumptions.[1] CyclePad detects and flags such contradictions, and the hypertext system enables the student to explore the subset of assumptions responsible and decide which to retract.

In addition to the hypertext system, CyclePad incorporates several other tools and capabilities that help students understand their design. CyclePad will automatically create a T-S (temperature-entropy) diagram on request, a graphic commonly used by engineers to understand the global properties

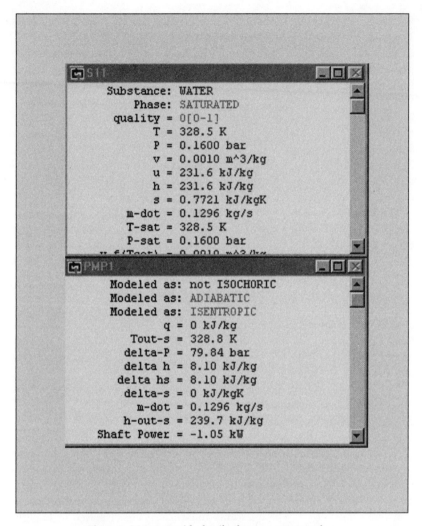

Figure 5. Meters provide details about parameter values.

of a cycle. CyclePad includes an optional economic analysis model, so that designs can be evaluated on the basis of their cost of construction and operation. CyclePad can carry out sensitivity analyses, enabling students to explore how changes in one parameter affect another. Reflecting on graphs of such sensitivity analyses is useful in understanding the properties of their design and how modifications might affect it. For instance, students might discover that to obtain the desired thermal efficiency with their current design the operating temperature would have to be raised so high that the materials to build it would be too costly.

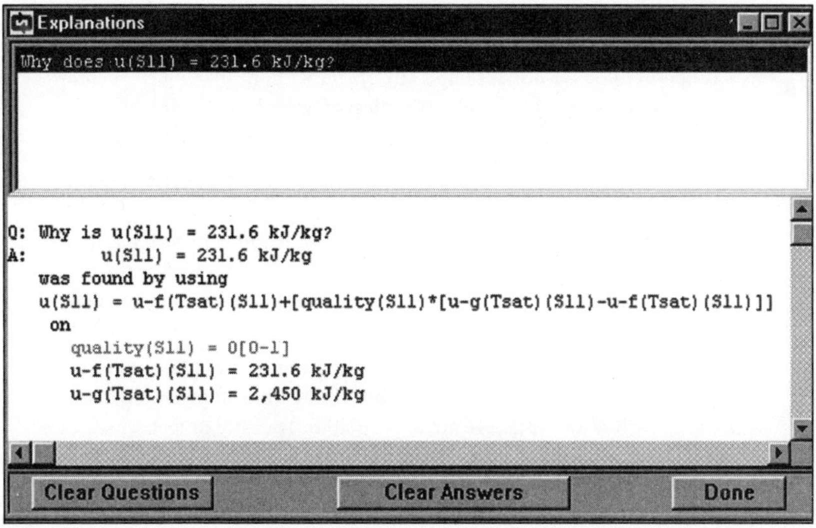

Figure 6. CyclePad's hypertext explanation system.

CyclePad includes two kinds of coaching. The *on-board coach* provides rapid feedback for some commonly encountered problems. For example, it recognizes the most common type of contradiction (i.e., requirements that push a state point outside the bounds of the property tables) and provides visualizations of the progress of the analysis (i.e., how much has been pinned down about particular aspects of the cycle so far). It can make suggestions about reasonable ranges for parameter values, based on its understanding of the teleology of the cycle. The *email coach* provides additional assistance with analysis and design. The most novel facility in the email coach is the ability to make suggestions about how to improve a student's design, based on analogies with a library of expert-authored cases. The coach provides step-by-step instructions illustrating how this suggestion can be applied to the student's design. It does not, however, evaluate whether or not this suggestion is a real improvement—that evaluation provides a valuable learning opportunity for the students.

How CyclePad Helps Students

The design of CyclePad was driven by addressing the needs of instructors in teaching engineering thermodynamics. A variety of common problems arise when teaching students how to design and analyze thermodynamic cycles:

1. Students tend to get bogged down in the mechanics of solving equations and carrying out routine calculations. They avoid exploring multiple design al-

ternatives and avoid carrying out trade-off studies (e.g., seeing how overall cycle efficiency varies as a function of turbine efficiency versus how it varies as a function of boiler outlet temperature). Yet without making such comparative studies, many opportunities for learning are lost.

2. Students often have trouble thinking about what modeling assumptions they need to make, such as assuming that a heater operates isobarically (i.e., no pressure drop across it), leading them to get stuck when analyzing a design.

3. Students typically don't challenge their choices of parameters to see if their design is physically possible (e.g., that their design does not violate the laws of thermodynamics by requiring a pump to produce rather than consume work).

4. Students typically have no basis for relating the values they calculate to the physical world and their everyday experience. The units of thermodynamic quantities, such as kilowatts, are not as accessible as pounds or feet. This lack of intuition about, for instance, whether 10,000 kilowatts is enough to light a room or a city causes students to treat thermodynamics problems as abstractions divorced from practical application.

These considerations drove the design of CyclePad. Here are how the features shown is the previous section address these problems:

1. CyclePad handles routine calculations, including equation solving and property-table interpolation. By facilitating sensitivity analyses, CyclePad encourages students to develop their intuitions through trade-off studies.

2. CyclePad's interface makes modeling assumptions explicit and highly salient. It helps them keep track of the consequences of their modeling assumptions.

3. CyclePad detects physically impossible designs, using a combination of qualitative constraints and numerical reasoning. It alerts students about such problems, and supports their investigations and resolution of them through its generated hypertext system.

4. CyclePad includes benchmarks that help ground parameter values in real-world examples, and a web-based design library whose entries are accessed based on analogies with the student's design.

How CyclePad Works

CyclePad uses a combination of artificial intelligence techniques to provide the abilities outlined in the previous section. These are described in detail elsewhere (Forbus et al. 1999), here I summarize them to highlight how they contribute to scaffolding student learning.

CyclePad's Knowledge Base

The domain knowledge in CyclePad is represented using techniques from qualitative physics (Forbus 1984a) and compositional modeling (Falkenhainer and Forbus 1991). The knowledge required to support design and analysis

```
(defEntity (Abstract-hx ?self ?in          (defEntity (Heater ?self ?in ?out)
                        ?out)               (abstract-Hx ?self ?in ?out)
   (thermodynamic-stuff ?in)               (?self instance-of heater)
   (thermodynamic-stuff ?out)              (heat-flow (heat-source ?self)
   (total-fluid-flow ?in ?out)                        (heat-source ?self)
   (== (mass-flow ?in)                                ?in ?out)
       (mass-flow ?out))                   ((heat-flows-in :cycle)
   (parameter (mass-flow ?self))              has-member (Q ?self))
   (parameter (Q ?self))                   (> (Q ?self) 0.0))
   (parameter (spec-Q ?self))
   (heat-source (heat-source ?self))     (defEquation Hx-law
   ((parts :cycle) has-member ?self)       ((Abstract-HX ?hx ?in ?out))
(?self part-names (in out))                (:= (spec-h ?out)
(?self IN ?in) (?in IN-OF ?self)               (+ (spec-h ?in) (spec-Q ?hx))))
?self out ?out) (?out out-of ?self))
                                         (defEquation spec-Q-definition
(defAssumptionClass                        ((Abstract-Hx ?hx ?in ?out))
   ((abstract-HX ?hx ?in ?out))            (:= (spec-Q ?hx)
     (isobaric ?hx)                            (/ (Q ?hx) (mass-flow ?hx))))
     (:not (isobaric ?hx)))
```

Figure 7. Samples from CyclePad's knowledge base.

goes far beyond just a set of equations, as the examples in figure 7 illustrate. CyclePad's domain theory includes the following.

Physical and conceptual entities: These include components such as compressors, turbines, pumps, and heat exchangers; physical processes such as compression, combustion, and expansion, and the representations of the properties of the working fluid between them. CyclePad's knowledge base currently contains over 29 entity definitions.

Structural knowledge: What kinds of relationships can hold between components, process occurrences, and the descriptions of working fluids that connect them. CyclePad's knowledge base currently contains 34 structural facts.

Qualitative knowledge: This includes the kinds of physical processes that can occur inside components, or in the sequence of operations in an open cycle. Physical processes constrain the parameters of the situation. For instance, the temperature of the working fluid coming into a heater cannot be higher than the temperature of the working fluid when it leaves. CyclePad's knowledge base currently contains definitions of five fundamental physical processes.

Quantitative knowledge: This includes equations that define relationships between the parameters of the constituents of a cycle, numerical constants (i.e., molecular weights), and tables of property values for substances (e.g., saturation and superheat tables). CyclePad also automatically derives equations for global properties. For example, equations for net work and heat flows into and out of the cycle are derived every time the structure of the cycle changes. CyclePad's knowledge base currently contains 167 equations, and saturation tables and superheat tables for 10 substances.

Modeling assumptions: Modeling assumptions describe what simplifications can be made about a component or process during an analysis. For instance, the pressure drop across a boiler is typically ignored in conceptual design because it is negligible for the purpose of the analysis. Rather than stipulating a particular pressure drop, it is simpler to assume that the heater used to model a boiler is isobaric (i.e., has no pressure drop). CyclePad's knowledge base currently contains 10 types of modeling assumptions.

Assumption classes: Assumption classes help structure reasoning by organizing modeling assumptions into sets. When an assumption class holds, one assumption from it must be included in the model of the cycle for the model to be complete. CyclePad's knowledge base currently contains 14 assumption classes.

Economic model: Economic tradeoffs are key issues in design. CyclePad incorporates standard engineering cost estimating functions that extrapolate capital costs for a cycle based on the size of the components, generally estimated by mass-flow. CyclePad contains information about several different materials, including stainless steel, nickel alloy, titanium, and molybdenum. Each material has limits on the temperatures (high and low, the latter for cryogenic applications) that it can endure. A special material, Unobtainium, with extraordinary properties (including price) is useful for suspending the economic constraints on a particular device or subset of devices. CyclePad also estimates the resulting weight of the cycle as a function of the materials employed, which may be a critical constraint, for example, in the design of an aircraft engine.

CyclePad's knowledge base is powerful enough to handle a wide variety of analyses found in introductory and advanced thermodynamics textbooks.

CyclePad's Analysis Methods

A student's activities with CyclePad shift between creating and/or editing the structure of the cycle and analyzing the properties of the cycle by supplying assumptions about its constituents. CyclePad interactively and incrementally derives the consequences of each student assumption. This work is performed via antecedent constraint propagation, with the derivations being recorded in a logic-based truth maintenance system (LTMS) (Forbus and de Kleer 1993). At any point the student can ask for explanations of derived values, the indirect consequences of particular assumptions, what equations might be relevant to deriving a particular value, and other similar queries. These explanation facilities exploit the dependency network created in the LTMS.

Explanations in CyclePad are represented by *structured explanations,* an abstraction layer between the reasoning system and the interface. The reason for this layer is that the reasoning system needs to be optimized for performance, while the interface needs to be optimized for clarity, and these goals are often incompatible. The structured explanation layer provides summarization, hiding aspects of how the reasoning system works that are irrelevant to the student. It also provides reification, making explicit dependencies that would otherwise be implicit, such as the various methods that could be used to derive a desired parameter.

Automating the tedious calculations involved in using thermodynamic equations and providing clear explanations of how the student's assumptions were used provides substantial scaffolding. Students can focus on thinking about the thermodynamic consequences of their assumptions, rather than using their calculators to solve routine equations. The LTMS also provides a useful mechanism for detecting and recovering from contradictory assumptions. For instance, if the parameters supplied by the student imply that physical laws are violated (i.e., that a turbine consumes work rather than generates it), this fact along with the subset of assumptions responsible is brought to the student's attention for correction.

CyclePad provides other analysis tools in addition to constraint propagation. It automates the process of performing sensitivity analyses, which involve seeing how a change in one parameter affects another parameter (e.g., how the boiler pressure affects the thermal efficiency of the cycle), using the dependency network in the LTMS to identify relevant parameters and automatically derive the necessary equations (see figure 8). Such analyses are viewed as important by instructors for gaining a deeper appreciation of the domain. CyclePad provides visualization tools that make apparent how parts of the cycle contribute to its overall performance. Graphical information about the bounds of available property tables, and in some cases automatically generated T-S (temperature versus entropy) diagrams, are also available. An on-line help system that describes the program's operation and knowledge is included.

Building student intuitions about the meaning of the properties of thermodynamics and helping them achieve a quantitative "feel" for the subject is an important pedagogical problem. Students initially know so little about thermodynamics and cycles that they can have problems spotting problems in their designs. For example, experienced designers will note that low quality (i.e., too much liquid in the mixture) in the working fluid exiting a heat engine's turbine is likely to cause damage to the turbine blades. Consequently, they will attempt to adjust the system's parameters to increase the exit quality, or failing that, make a structural alteration to the cycle. To spot problems like this and understand how to fix them requires knowledge of how function relates to structure. For example, low exit quality is only a problem if the cycle is intended as a heat engine. In a cryogenic cycle, turbines can be used to cool the working fluid sufficiently to cause precipitation, because a resisted expansion results in a greater drop in the working fluid temperature than a throttled expansion. Thus in the case of a cryogenic cycle we might be aiming for low quality. Giving advice

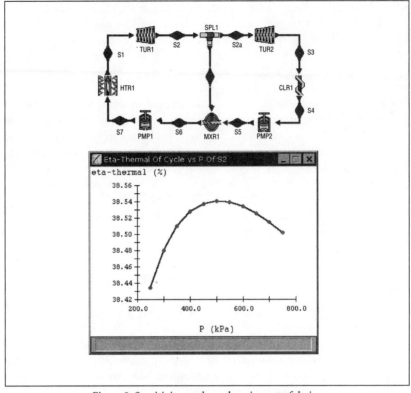

*Figure 8. Sensitivity analyses show impact of design
decisions, revealing underlying principles.*
Here the effect of feedwater pressure on thermal
efficiency in a regeneration cycle is being explored.

about cycle parameters, therefore, requires understanding the intended purpose of the system and the functional roles each component plays in achieving that purpose.

CyclePad incorporates Everett's Carnot teleological recognition system (Everett 1999) to understand the intended function of the cycle, in order to provide advice about values of cycle parameters. Different components can play different functional roles. For example, a mixer may act as a simple way to join flows, as a heat-exchanger, or as a jet-ejector, in which a high-velocity jet of fluid entrains and compresses another inlet stream. Understanding the intended function of a system requires assigning functional roles to each component and recognizing any larger-scale plans that the configuration of roles represent, such as regeneration. Carnot uses evidential rules and Bayesian inference to suggest plausible functional roles for each component in a student's cycle. The

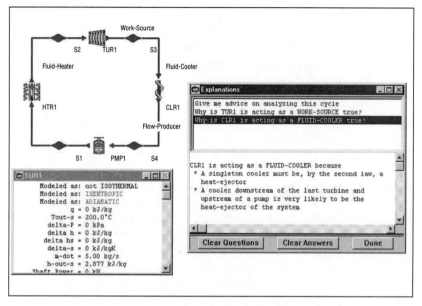

Figure 9. CyclePad uses evidential reasoning to infer student intent.

evidential rules provide evidence either for or against a particular role. This evidence is used to update the prior probability of each role for each component. The evidential reasoning is included in CyclePad's explanation system, so that students can find out why (and with what certainty) a particular role is believed and can also get an explanation of why other potential roles were rejected (see figure 9).

CyclePad combines Carnot's teleological inferences with *norms* to generate advice for adjusting parameters. A norm is a range for a component's parameter that is appropriate based on the component's functional role. For example, the temperature of the steam leaving a Rankine cycle boiler typically falls in the range of 300–600° C. Lower temperatures result in inadequate efficiency whereas higher temperatures require uneconomically expensive materials in the downstream components. In contrast, the range of temperatures for the refrigerant leaving the coils of a refrigerator (which are modeled as a heater) is quite different, typically in the range of 5–15° C. Inferring the role a component is playing is therefore essential to providing relevant advice to the student. Our knowledge base currently contains eighteen norms, between two and six per component depending on the number of potential roles for that component.

When the Analysis Coach is invoked, Carnot infers the teleology of the cycle. The functional roles assigned to each component are used to retrieve applicable norms, which are checked against known parameter values. Any violations or suggestions are noted using CyclePad's explanation system, providing explanatory text associated with each norm. In addition to being used to provide on-board advice, Carnot's teleological representations also play an important role in our case-based design coach, described below. The insight is that similarity in intended function and qualitative properties are better predictors of a case's relevance than the specific numerical values involved in it.

CyclePad's Coaching

CyclePad's on-board coaching facilities are supplemented by an email-based coaching system. We turned to email because CyclePad is used by students in a variety of institutions spread across the planet. Since CyclePad is distributed via the web, there is some likelihood that students have network access. Students can use an email system built into the software to send their current design and a query about it to our coach, which runs on a server at Northwestern. The coach is implemented as part of a *RoboTA Agent Colony* (Forbus and Kuenhe 1998), a software architecture designed for providing distributed learner support. Email to a RoboTA is handled by a post office agent, which ascertains which member of the colony is best able to handle it. The *CyclePad guru* is the agent designated for CyclePad-related messages. The kinds of messages supported by the CyclePad guru are:

1. *Turning in an assignment.* We are experimenting with a system that enables instructors to create assignments, including evaluation rubrics, that enable students to submit their solutions via email. The idea is to make it easier for instructors to collect student work and have the mechanical aspects of their evaluations applied automatically.

2. *Asking for help with a contradiction.* The coach provides some general feedback in response to this case.

3. *Asking for help in completing an analysis.* The coach provides advice based on an expert model of how to analyze cycles, pointing out the kinds of assumptions that might be appropriate to make given the student's progress.

4. *Asking for help in improving a design.* The coach provides suggestions for improving the design, based on a case library of design transformations.

Design coaching is the most novel feature of the CyclePad guru. We have two goals in giving design advice. First, we want to nudge students in useful directions, rather than solving problems for them. Consequently, the guru provides plausible specific suggestions, but does not attempt to validate those suggestions in the students' context. Understanding why a suggestion will or will not work in a particular circumstance is an important learning experience that we want students to have. Second, we want to motivate students to dig more deeply into the nature of thermodynamics-ideally, to immerse themselves in the culture of engineering thermodynamics by studying real-world systems and how they are connected to the assignments they are grappling with. Consequently, the guru uses case-based coaching to generate design advice, motivating students to explore the case deeply by showing exactly

From: robota@godzilla.cs.nwu.edu
Date: Mon, 20 Sep 99 00:49:47 -0600
To: forbus@nwu.edu
Subject: The CyclePad Guru's response to your message: Need help improving my Rankine cycle

You asked for help with your design.
I have 2 suggestions.
==
Suggestion #1
Your problem reminds me of a method: increasing boiler temperature in a Rankine cycle.
Increasing the boiler temperature increases the efficiency of the cycle.
You can find out more about this at <URL>.
Here is how you might apply this to your design:
1. Increase T(S2).
==
Suggestion #2
Your problem reminds me of a method: reheat in a Rankine cycle. Reheat adds another heater and
another turbine. The second heater, a reheater, heats up the working fluid at the turbine
outlet, and the second turbine extracts yet more work from that. This increases efficiency
because more heat is being added when the steam is still at a reasonably high temperature.
You can find out more about this at <URL>.
Here is how you might do this with your design:
1. Disconnect the outlet of TUR1 from the inlet of CLR1.
2. Create a new heater, which we'll call HTR2.
3. Connect the outlet of TUR1 to the inlet of HTR2. Let's refer to the properties of the working
fluid there as S5.
4. Create a new turbine, which we'll call TUR2.
5. Connect the outlet of HTR2 to the inlet of TUR2. Let's refer to the properties of the working
fluid there as S6.
6. Connect the outlet of TUR2 to the inlet of CLR1. Let's refer to the properties of the working
fluid there as S7.
You might find the following assumptions relevant or useful:
1. Assume that the working fluid at S5 is saturated.
2. Assume quality(S5) = 1.0000[0-1]
3. Assume that HTR2 is a reheater.
4. Assume that HTR2 works isobarically.
5. Assume that HTR2 is made of molybdenum.
6. Assume that HTR2 burns natural-gas.
7. Assume that TUR2 works isentropically.
8. Assume that TUR2 is made of molybdenum.
9. Assume that the working fluid at S7 is saturated.
10. Assume quality(S7) = 1.0000[0-1]

Figure 10. Design advice from the CyclePad guru.

how that case might be relevant to the improvement they are trying to make.

A sample of design advice from the guru is illustrated in figure 10. The guru has access to a library of cases, each describing a particular change to a design and what it is intended to accomplish. These changes can be either tuning the parameters of the cycle (i.e., increasing the operating temperature of a boiler to increase efficiency) or a structural change in the cycle (i.e., adding reheat to a cycle to enable more work to be extracted). Cases are authored by domain experts, using CyclePad and an HTML editor. Notice that a URL is supplied as part of the advice. These web pages describe the general principles involved in the library case, illustrated through a concrete example. The concrete example used in the case is generated by the domain expert, using CyclePad. The domain expert describes a transformation that implements the principle by making the appropriate changes to this design. A *case compiler* uses this information to compute a description of the transformation that can be used in analogical reasoning. Consequently, domain experts only need to be able to use CyclePad plus an HTML editor in order to add cases to the design library.

Given a student's design, the guru uses a cognitive simulation of similarity-based retrieval, MAC/FAC (Forbus, Gentner, and Law 1995) to retrieve relevant cases. Concrete advice as to how to apply the idea of the case to the student's design is generated by a cognitive simulation of analogical matching, SME (Falkenhainer, Forbus, and Gentner 1989; Forbus, Ferguson, and Gentner 1994). The use of cognitively motivated analogical processing software has two advantages over the typical state of the art in case-based reasoning (CBR) systems. First, most CBR systems require hand-indexing of new cases by experts familiar with both the domain and the retrieval system. By using MAC/FAC, we exploit human-like similarity computations to automatically retrieve cases without indexing. Second, most CBR systems use simple lists of features as their representation medium. By contrast, CyclePad designs are (internally) full predicate calculus descriptions, encoding relational structure such as the steps required to achieve a design modification. These richer relational structures lead to analogical inferences by SME, that are turned into step-by-step instructions on how to apply the case to the student's design.

Using a distributed coaching system has its disadvantages. It requires students to have access to email. It involves a delay in responding to a student's request, which may not be as effective as providing an immediate response. This is an inevitable limitation of email as a transport mechanism. Prior requests do not affect the answer returned, that is, one cannot enter into a correspondence with this coach. Creating a software coach capable of natural language conversations with students and maintaining an ongoing model of them and their progress would be an excellent research project, but is extremely difficult. On the other hand, by putting complex coaching facilities on a server at our site, we can make improvements in coaching strategy without asking users to reinstall our software. The potential value of a distributed coach becomes especially apparent when considering the issue of extending and maintaining a case library. A large, rich case library with lots of associated media (e.g., pictures of the real physical systems corresponding to the CyclePad design) is probably best treated as a network resource, rather than installed on each student machine. We are forming an editorial board for the web-based design library, to ensure quality control, and encouraging submissions from CyclePad experts worldwide, much in the manner of the Eureka community-maintained database of tips (Bell et al. 1996).

Discussion

CyclePad has been distributed for free via the Web since September 1997 and has been used in classrooms scattered all over the world. As of September 1999, we had over 2,500 distinct downloads from 63 countries. While some downloaders never use the software or do not find it to their liking, we know from surveys and email feedback that a number of instructors have adopted it successfully and use it in their courses in a variety of ways. Although the project is now over, we will continue to distribute CyclePad and run the CyclePad guru server, and will make CyclePad's source code publicly available through an open-source license.

CyclePad provides strong evidence for the utility of articulate virtual laboratories. It has been adopted by instructors in a variety of educational institutions for both introductory and advanced courses. Some institutions use it with traditional textbooks, while others are developing new curricula around it. In universities where we have direct collaborators, we have seen various benefits of CyclePad. For example, advanced thermodynamics students at the U.S. Naval Academy were able to tackle more complex term projects than they were able to previously, resulting in some cases in publishable technical papers (eg. Wu and Burke 1998; Wu and Dieguez 1998).

In engineering technology curricula, that is, curricula aimed at producing technicians rather than engineers, students often learn calculus later than thermodynamics. This makes the analysis-heavy approach of standard thermodynamics courses even less useful for this population. CyclePad provides a "simulated hands-on" experience for such students, helping them build solid, accurate intuitions about thermodynamics (Baher 1998). For example, at University of Arkansas, Little Rock, students use CyclePad in laboratory exercises to experiment with systems that would be too expensive or dangerous to physically build.

The design approach of articulate virtual laboratories fits quite naturally into many advanced thermodynamics courses. Regrettably, in the United States this has not been true of introductory courses. Traditional thermodynamics courses, like many current engineering courses, are analysis-centered, lavishing classroom time on mathematical derivations of thermodynamic principles at the expense of helping students understand the principles themselves and their implications. Many courses still spend time teaching students how to do complex analyses, including table interpolations, with just a simple calculator, even though as practicing engineers they will have more sophisticated computer support. This necessarily reduces the time available for understanding the principles of thermodynamics and time available for learning design skills. This has been a significant barrier in introducing CyclePad in introductory courses. Indeed, using CyclePad in such courses can lead to drops in student performance, since students are being tested on mechanical calculation skills that in practice are automated. This problem is analogous to the introduction of calculators into mathematics education. The introduction of intelligent systems that handle more of the analytic load of engineering tasks suggests rethinking what we should be teaching and how it can be taught. For example, in pilot studies we have experimented with exercises where students use CyclePad to do simple design and optimization tasks, weighing their written reports as to the "how" and "why" of their work as much as the specific answers they provided. A positive trend is the recent interest by ABET, the U.S. engineering education standards organization, on infusing design tasks throughout engineering curricula.

The articulate virtual laboratory architecture CyclePad embodies can, we believe, be fruitfully applied to many other engineering domains. The nature of the analysis tools will vary from domain to domain. AVLs for electronics or chemical engineering might end up looking very much like CyclePad, whereas AVLs for mechanism design or computer programming might be able to utilize similar structured explanation systems and distributed coaching, but with very different analysis and design methods. AVLs could make spreading design work through the engineering curriculum much more practical, for instance by providing support for portfolio assessment.

We also believe that with appropriately simplified domains, articulate virtual laboratories could also be used in science teaching. Design activities are commonly used in constructivist learning systems and curricula because they are so motivating (cf. Papert 1980; Lehrer 1998). The National Science Education Standards have identified design activities as a means of motivating learning of scientific content and process as well as a vehicle for understanding the technological world for K-12 education (National Research Council, 1996). Experience with physical systems is often an important aspect of learning through design, but AVLs could provide valuable complementary activities, and make rich design activities possible in domains for which it is now impossible. For example, CREANIMATE (Edelson 1992) used the idea of modifying animals as a motivation for students to watch videos that showed how animals behave. While this video-driven case-based approach has its attractions, an AVL for such a domain would provide much richer explanations and more freedom for students to explore animal behavior and biomechanics.

Active Illustrations

The power of illustrative examples is well-known in education. Traditional media offer high authenticity but low interactivity. Textbook illustrations and posters can provide thought-provoking pictures, tables, charts, and other depictions of complex information. Movies and video can provide gripping dynamical displays. But none of these media provide interaction. Students intrigued by a picture of a steam engine in a textbook (or a movie of a steam engine) cannot vary the load or change the working fluid to see what will happen. They cannot ask for more details about explanations that they don't understand. They cannot satisfy their curiosity about how efficiency varies with operating temperatures by testing the engine over ranges of values. The *active illustrations* architecture uses AI techniques to provide such interactive capabilities. An active illustration can be thought of as a hands-on museum exhibit, consisting of a virtual artifact or system, and (ideally) a guide who is knowledgeable about the exhibit and enthusiastically helps satisfy your curiosity about it. Active illustrations support student explorations, by allowing students to change parameters and relationships to see what happens. They are articulate, in that students can ask why some outcome occurred or some value holds, and receive understandable explanations that ultimately ground out in fundamental physical principles and laws.

Example: The Evaporation Laboratory

Suppose a student is interested in how evaporation works. Since evaporation happens in everyday circumstances that are neither dangerous nor expensive to set up, it can easily be experimented with. The student begins to set up different jars of water, varying in width and amount of water, and measures their initial level. The student places these jars on the window ledge in the classroom, and looks for something else to do while waiting for the outcome of the experiment. Seeing an unused computer, the student starts up an active illustration on evaporation, to try to gain some insights in minutes instead of days.

The student's interaction with the simulation laboratory starts with setting up a scenario. The student selects, from an on-screen catalog, a cup to use in an experiment. The cups are all the same shape and size, but they are made from a variety of materials, ranging from styrofoam to tin to titanium and even diamond. The student chooses a styrofoam cup, since such cups are common. From another catalog, the student selects an environment to place the cup in. Since it is hot outside, the student selects Chicago in the summer, and sets the simulator to run for four hours of virtual time. A few moments later, the simulation is finished. The student notices, by requesting a plot of how the level of water in the cup changes over time, that there is a slow but measurable decline. Using the explanation system, the student finds the following summary of the behavior:

Between 0.0 and 14,400.0 seconds:
    evaporation from cup occurs
    flow of heat from Atmosphere to water in cup occurs
    there is water in liquid form in cup
    water in cup touches the atmosphere

The student follows up by using the hypertext facilities of the explanation system:

In styrofoam cup in Chicago,
mass of water in cup can be affected by:
   water loss via evaporation from cup
In styrofoam cup in Chicago,
water loss via evaporation from cup can be affected by:
   vapor pressure of atmosphere
   saturation pressure of atmosphere
   surface area of water in cup
   temperature of water in cup

At this point the student conjectures that higher temperature should lead to more evaporation. To confirm this conjecture, the student runs a second simulation, using a diamond cup this time to increase the flow of heat from the atmosphere. (This is obviously not an experiment that is easily carried out in the physical world.) Qualitatively the behavior is the same, but the higher thermal conductivity of diamond means that the temperature of the diamond cup will quickly become close to the ambient temperature, and indeed leads to increased evaporation (figure 11).

The student might continue their explorations by deciding to see what happens with the same cup on the top of a mountain, where it would be very cold, or in the tropics, where the temperature could be adjusted to be the same as on the desert, but with a much higher relative humidity. These explorations can be accomplished in minutes, with reports produced for further comparison and reflection.

How Active Illustrations Work

The principle component of active illustrations for dynamical systems are *self-explanatory simulators* (Forbus and Falkenhainer 1990; Iwasaki and Low 1992; Amador, Finkelstein, and Weld 1993). A self-explanatory simulator combines qualitative and numerical representations to provide both accurate quantitative descriptions of behavior and conceptual explanations of it. The conceptual explanations are in terms of what physical processes are occurring in the system being simulated, and the causal relationships that govern its behavior. As the evaporation laboratory example showed, a self-explanatory simulator can describe at every point in the simulation exactly what is happening in the system being simulated and why. These explanations can in theory range from qualitative, causal explanations suitable for novices to sets of ordinary differential equations suitable for an expert audience. (We have focused on the former so far since many of our simulators have been designed for middle-school students.)

Traditional simulators can be difficult to build and tune, so it might at first seem that self-explanatory simulators must necessarily be more complex. This is not the case. In fact, self-explanatory simulators can be constructed auto-

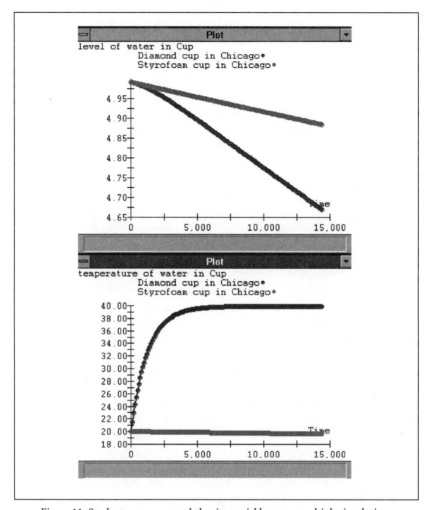

Figure 11. Students can compare behaviors quickly across multiple simulations.

matically, using AI techniques whose general form and operation are inspired by watching human simulation authors work. A person writing a simulator must first decide exactly what phenomena need to be simulated—what should be included and what should be left out. For example, in simulating global warming, including the thermal effects of the oceans is important, whereas the gasses produced by cigarette smoking is not. Once the phenomena to include have been decided, appropriate mathematical models must be found or derived. From these mathematical models simulation code is written, either from scratch or by assembling predefined modules. In the ideal case, the conceptual understanding process that the simulation author went through is well-docu-

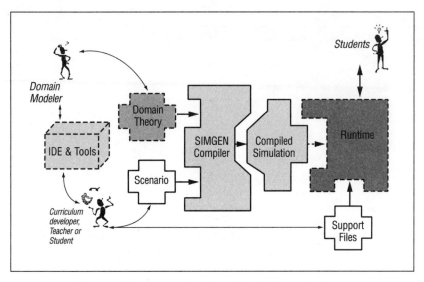

Figure 12. The process of creating self-explanatory simulators.

mented somewhere, perhaps even in material accessible to the simulation users. In reality, such documentation is rare, and often produced by reconstruction rather than during construction. This can lead to problems, as when the simulated behavior clearly is not consistent with the explanations about how it is generated.

A compiler for self-explanatory simulators operates in much the same way (Forbus and Falkenhainer 1995). The overall development process is illustrated in figure 12, and the details of the compilation process are illustrated in figure 13. It relies on a *domain theory* that describes relevant physical phenomena in general terms. Given a specific system to write a simulator for, the compiler starts by figuring out which general descriptions from the domain theory need to be used to understand the system (e.g., in the evaporation laboratory, heat flow to and from the atmosphere through the cup needs to be considered as well as evaporation of water from the cup). The compiler starts by creating a conceptual, qualitative description of the system, identifying what physical processes and parameters are relevant. This conceptual understanding is then used to retrieve mathematical models from its domain theory, in the form of equations or code fragments, that are assembled into a quantitative model of the system. The compiler then translates this quantitative model into efficient simulation code. Writing simulation code can be complicated, since changes in the phenomena occurring can lead to significant changes in the mathematical model. For instance, the set of equations that hold when simulating water heating on the stove is very different from the appropriate mathematical model needed to simulate that water boiling. The qualitative model provides the

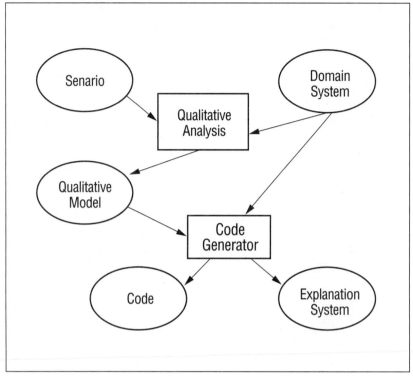

Figure 13. Automatic compilation process for Self-explanatory simulators.

necessary framework for detecting such potential situations, and for writing code to handle them properly.

The rich explanatory power of self-explanatory simulators comes from exploiting the fact that the simulation compiler itself has a conceptual understanding of what is being simulated. In addition to producing traditional simulation code, the compiler also produces a compact *structured explanation system* (Forbus and Falkenhainer 1995) that embeds its conceptual understanding of the system into the simulator it builds. Thus the explanations used to explain a simulation are based on the explanations used to generate the simulator itself. The link between the numerical simulated behavior and the conceptual descriptions is maintained by tracking the corresponding qualitative distinctions as they change over time. For instance, when physical processes start or stop or when objects come into existence, disappear, or change in a very significant way (e.g., phase changes), such physical events are noted in a *history* (Hayes 1985) that provides a qualitative summary of the behavior. This history provides the bridge between the numerical behavior and the causal understanding of the system.

From an algorithmic perspective, we note that self-explanatory simulators can be compiled in polynomial time, as a function of the size of the system to be simulated (Forbus and Falkenhainer 1995). This is important for scaling up: Simulators involving thousands of parameters can be created quickly. It is equally important to note that the simulators produced are compact and efficient. All qualitative reasoning is done at compilation time, not run time. Thus the simulators produced run asymptotically close in speed to an equivalent numerical simulator for the same system. The only extra overhead is the maintenance of the history, and this requires only a few extra tests per time step and only requires space proportional to the qualitative complexity of the behavior (i.e., the number of significant physical events), rather than as a function of the time step chosen. This makes them practical in a wide variety of circumstances. For instance, we have run simple simulators on MS-DOS palmtops (8mhz, 640KB of RAM), and as Java applets on web pages.

Turning self-explanatory simulators into active illustrations involves two issues: Selecting the right levels of explanation, and providing the illusion of interacting with a physical system, rather than a complex piece of software. I discuss each in turn.

Providing appropriate levels of explanation: The structured explanation system internally contains the full range of representations used to create the simulation. Not all explanations are appropriate for all audiences: As noted above, middle-school students cannot be expected to understand differential equations. Our solution has been to put filters on the explanation system, to hide information that would be inappropriate for the intended audience. For middle-school students, for example, we focus on the kind of causal information that students are supposed to be learning. As the interaction earlier demonstrated, questions that students can ask include what can affect a parameter and what can it affect. The answers they receive are in terms of causal qualitative relationships (*influences*, in the terms of qualitative process theory (Forbus 1984a)), for example, "X can be affected by…" in the dialog above. While the explanation system knows the type and sign of the influence, this information is suppressed because it is something that the student should be learning, along with the relative magnitudes of various effects.[2]

Even within the level of causal explanations, it is sometimes useful to filter out information. For example, in the evaporation laboratory the concept of thermal conductivity is something that we, in the role of curriculum designers, want the student to discover, rather than telling them about it explicitly. (The inclusion of a diamond cup is intended to lead students in this direction. Few students can resist trying the diamond cup, and since diamond has a thermal conductivity that is orders of magnitude larger than most substances, they are faced with some dramatic behavior differences to explain.) We tackle this problem by a "can't say, don't tell" policy in the software. Each element in the structured explanation system has a natural language phrase associated with it.

These phrases are generated semi-automatically by the compilation process; they can be edited separately after the simulation is compiled to support localization. If an explanation element does not have an associated natural language phrase, the explanation system will not use it in any explanation it constructs. Editing tools are provided that enable curriculum designers to adjust the explanation system in this way.

Providing the illusion of interacting with a physical system: Initializing the parameters of even a simple simulation can be complicated, since the choice of parameters must be made with an eye towards physical consistency. Yet the expertise needed to evaluate physical plausibility is part of what we want students to learn from doing simulation experiments. This is a conceptual problem, not a standard HCI problem. Providing a large menu of numerical and logical parameters, even in the cleanest, well-organized GUI, can easily lead to bewilderment. Our solution is to simplify this process by using a metaphor from drama—the idea of a *prop*. A prop on a stage represents something in the imagined world being created on-stage. In our simulators, props represent a coherent subset of the simulator's parameters that naturally make sense to consider together. Each simulator has a set of *catalogs*, each catalog containing props that impose different constraints on a particular subset of the simulator's parameters. In the evaporation laboratory, for instance, there are two catalogs, cups and environments. The choice of cup constrains the shape and dimensions of the cup, as well as its thermal conductivity (e.g., the thermal conductivity of diamond is orders of magnitude higher than just about anything else). Figures 14 and 15 show the catalog contents currently used in the evaporation laboratory. The choice of environment constrains the temperature and pressure and vapor pressure of the atmosphere, as well as the limits over which these parameters can be varied. (While it is possible in theory for Las Vegas to get colder than the top of Mt. Everest, it would be very surprising, and providing constraints that prevent two props from being identical in the simulator helps maintain the suspension of disbelief.)

In addition to solving the technical problem of setting up a simulation, props also provide pedagogical benefits, by helping the student see relationships between physical objects and circumstances and their properties. Props also provide a simple path to customization: Adding props representing familiar objects and situations (e.g., a student's favorite cup or home town) also provides a simple form of customization that can make software more engaging.

How Active Illustrations Can Be Used

There are several settings in which active illustrations can be used. I discuss each in turn.

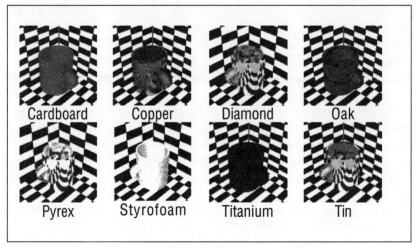

Figures 14. Catalog of cups for the evaporation laboratory.

Students can change the amount and temperature
of the water for whatever cup they choose.

Figure 15. Catalogs of environments used in the evaporation laboratory.

Simulation Laboratories

Student can use active illustrations as a laboratory for running experiments, such as the evaporation laboratory above. The evaporation laboratory and several other simulation laboratories have been publicly available from our web site for several years now, and the reasons given for downloading range from intended classroom use to science fair projects. We are also developing two new simulations, an ecosystem for a hypothetical Mars base and a solar house simulation, to be used in curricula we are developing in collaboration with teachers from the Chicago Public Schools[3] and as motivating phenomena in new research we are doing on helping middle-school students learn how to create models.

Hypermedia Component

Active illustrations can be a powerful new type of media in hypermedia systems. A student might start using an active illustration included to provide a concrete example of some phenomenon, and branch back out to the rest of the hypertext network based on the concepts in the active illustration's explanation system. For example, the on-line *Principles of Operation Manual* for a simulation based on NASA's *Deep Space One* autonomous spacecraft used several active illustrations to enable players to experiment with basic principles of rocketry and orbits.[4]

Virtual Artifacts in Shared Virtual Environments

Virtual environments are being explored by many groups as environments for students to interact with each other and instructors in an arena designed to support learning. Because interaction is computer-mediated, such spaces provide additional opportunities for software-based coaching and assessment of student progress. In collaboration with Ken Koedinger and Dan Suthers, we have explored the use of active illustrations in *Science Learning Spaces* that support reflection and coaching (Koedinger et al. 1999). In addition to providing preconstructed virtual artifacts, efforts are underway to develop a *construction kit* approach to enable students to significantly modify existing objects, and even create new designs (Erignac 2000).

With the exception of on-line construction kits, the research groundwork for these applications is already in place. Three things are needed for broadscale deployment.

First, significant investment in software engineering is needed. The software prototypes described above are exactly that: research prototypes. They are robust enough that they can be used in schools, but only by developers with strong expertise. Making it easy for curriculum developers, teachers, and students to create simulators will require making the runtime shells far more robust. Better tools for design, debugging, and tuning of domain theories and simulators are needed, combined in a supportive simulator development environment. Second, libraries of domain theories, created by experts, are needed. With off-the-shelf domain theory libraries and the automated modeling capabilities of self-explanatory simulation compilers, the burden of modeling will be greatly reduced for curriculum designers, enabling them to focus more on pedagogical issues. Third, we need to learn how to best exploit this new technology in curricula and activities that achieve educational goals.

Discussion

Advances in artificial intelligence, particularly in qualitative reasoning, provide the scientific foundation for new kinds of educational software. *Articulate soft-*

ware, this chapter has argued, has revolutionary potential for science and engineering education. I believe that software that embodies a conceptual understanding of its domain can help students learn better. As the CyclePad experience shows, articulate virtual laboratories can be valuable in engineering education. As the active illustrations we have built suggest, simulators that provide causal, qualitative explanations can help students explore complex physical phenomena.

The examples presented here are, I think, only the beginning. The architectures described here can be applied to a broad set of phenomena and systems to support science and engineering education. And other architectures for articulate software could also be valuable. Consider these:

Articulate training simulators. Combine self-explanatory simulators of a complex system that people operate (i.e., ships, aircraft, spacecraft, power plants) with a model of the goals and context of a system and the procedures for operating that system, to teach someone how to operate that system. By context, I mean what the system is used for and what social and economic, as well as physical, constraints govern its operation. Tankers should not produce oil slicks, for example. The context provides the background needed for the simulator to understand why the procedures are the way they are, and the potential consequences of mistakes. This understanding can be used to set up challenging problems for trainees, and provide better post-mortems than would otherwise be possible (cf. Wilkins and Bulitko 1999).

Articulate game engines. Computer games can provide a highly motivating setting for students, who happily learn complex ideas for the sake of successfully interacting with and in a simulated world. Often the simulated world underlying these games (e.g., SimCity, SimEarth, Civilization) operate by combining dynamical models with a spatial, map-like model of some sort (e.g., a cellular automata). Domain theories that describe the physics and economics of the simulated world could be used in compiling game engines that embody that conceptual understanding, as a new form of self-explanatory simulator. This conceptual understanding can then be used by in-game tutors, coaches, and opponents (Dobson and Forbus 1999).

In the long run, I believe software that understands in a humanlike way what is to be learned, and uses that understanding to help people learn, will be ubiquitous in education. Someday we will not give students educational software that does not contain such understanding, any more than we would today give them software without a graphical user interface. There are still many challenges—scientific, software engineering, and pedagogical design—to be met before that day will come, but even our first steps are providing enough benefits to convince us that the journey is worth it.

Acknowledgements

The work described here rests on basic research funded by the Office of Naval

Research: The qualitative reasoning ideas have been developed through the support of the Computer Science Division, and the analogical processing ideas have been developed through the support of the Cognitive Science Division. The research on articulate virtual laboratories was supported by the Applications of Advanced Technology program of the Education and Human Resources Directorate of the National Science Foundation. The research on active illustrations was supported by grants from NASA JSC and NASA Ames, and by DARPA through the Computer Aided Education and Training Initiative (CAETI). Paul Feltovich, Joyce Ma, and Karen Carney all provided valuable suggestions that improved this chapter.

Notes

1. The historical interest in perpetual motion machines and its manifestations today (the "free energy" inventors and those dabbling in "over unity technologies") suggests that this problem is not limited to students.

2. Several teachers have recommended adding a "nerd switch" so that interested students could see the equations. We have not alas had the resources to do this yet.

3. This is thanks to the National Science Foundations' Center for Learning Technologies in Urban Schools, a joint project of Northwestern University, University of Michigan, and the Chicago and Detroit public school systems.

4. http://www.qrg.nwu.edu/projects/vss/docs/index.html

Chapter Eight

Animated Pedagogical Agents in Knowledge-Based Learning Environments

*James C. Lester, Charles B. Callaway, Joël P. Grégoire,
Gary D. Stelling, Stuart G. Towns, & Luke S. Zettlemoyer*

Since their conception more than a quarter of a century ago, knowledge-based learning environments (Carbonell 1970, Hollan et al. 1987, Lesgold et al. 1992) have offered significant potential for fundamentally changing the educational process. It has long been believed that presenting knowledgeable feedback to students increases learning effectiveness. Despite this promise, few learning environments have made the difficult transition from the laboratory to the classroom, and the challenge of developing learning environments that are pedagogically sound and intrinsically motivating has played no small part in this impasse.

Lifelike computer characters offer great promise for knowledge-based learning environments. Because of the immediate and deep affinity that children seem to develop for these characters, the potential pedagogical benefits they provide are perhaps even exceeded by their motivational benefits. By creating the illusion of life, lifelike computer characters may significantly increase the time that children seek to spend with educational software, and recent advances in affordable graphics hardware are beginning to make the widespread distribution of realtime animation technology a reality. We have recently begun to see the emergence of believable agents with lifelike qualities (Blumberg and Galyean 1995, Cassell, in press, Granieri et al. 1995, Kurlander and Ling 1995, Loyall and Bates 1997). By building on developments involving these intriguing interactive characters, we can create a new generation of knowledge-based learning environments that are inhabited by animated *lifelike pedagogical agents*. Featured prominently in learning environments, they could couple key feedback functionalities with a strong visual presence by observing learners' progress and providing them with visually contextualized problem-solving advice. However, with the notable exceptions of the groundbreaking work of the STEVE project at the University of Southern California / Information Sciences Institute (Rickel and Johnson 1997, 1999) and the PPP project at the German Center for Artificial Intelligence Research (DFKI) (André and Rist 1996, André et al. 1998), lifelike agents for pedagogy have received little attention.

For the past five years, we have been engaged in a large-scale research program on lifelike pedagogical agents.[1] The long-term goal of these projects is to create pedagogically effective computational mechanisms that contribute to fundamental improvements in learning environments. We focus in particular on developing behavior sequencing engines for lifelike pedagogical agents that dynamically control their behaviors in response to the rapidly changing problem-solving contexts in learning environments. By designing and implementing behavior sequencing engines, introducing them into fully functioning learning environments, and evaluating them with target learner populations, we take a strongly empirical approach to this work.

This chapter explores the promise of lifelike pedagogical agents by describing three projects underway in our laboratory. First, we examine the role that lifelike pedagogical agents can play in design-centered constructivist learning environments. This is realized in the *coherence-based behavior space* framework and illustrated with the Herman the Bug agent of the DESIGN-A-PLANT learning environment (Lester, Stone, and Stelling 1999; Stone and Lester 1996). Second, we look at a critical feature that lifelike agents for learning environments should exhibit, namely, deictic believability, which is the ability to coordinate gesture, locomotion, and speech in realtime to refer to objects in the environment. This is realized in the *spatial deixis* framework and illustrated with the Cosmo agent of the INTERNET ADVISOR learning environment (Lester, Voerman et al. 1999; Towns et al. 1998). Third, we examine the role that lifelike agents can play in 3D learning environments. This is illustrated with the *explanatory lifelike avatar* framework, which is implemented in the WhizLow agent of the CPU CITY learning environment (Grégoire et al. 1999; Lester, Zettlemoyer et al. 1999). For each agent capability, we overview the techniques that have been developed to address the necessary communicative functionalities, and we conclude by discussing results that have begun to emerge from empirical studies with implemented agents.

Animated Pedagogical Agents

Although knowledge-based graphical simulations (Hollan et al. 1987) are virtually *de rigueur* in contemporary learning environments, it is only in recent years, as a result of rapid advances in multimedia technologies, that full-scale intelligent multimedia interfaces have become standard components through which tutoring systems can provide clear visual feedback to learners. A particularly promising line of work underway outside of the intelligent tutoring systems community is that of lifelike animated intelligent agents. Because of these agents' compelling visual presence and their high degree of interactivity, there has been a surge of interest in *believable* intelligent characters (Blumberg and Galyean 1995, Granieri et al. 1995, Kurlander and Ling 1995, Loyall and Bates 1997), including the runtime incorporation of gesture and facial expression in communication (Cassell, in press; Pelachaud et al. 1996).

As a result of these developments, the ITS community is now presented with opportunities for exploring new technologies for pedagogical agents and the roles they can play in communication. Work to date on pedagogical agents is still in its infancy, but progress is being made on two fronts. First, research has begun on a variety of pedagogical agents that can facilitate the construction of component-based tutoring system architectures and communication among their modules (Mengele et al. 1998, Ritter 1997, Wang and Chan 1997), provide multiple context-sensitive pedagogical strategies (Frasson et al. 1997), reason about multiple agents in learning environments (Eliot and Woolf 1996), provide assistance to trainers in virtual worlds (Marsella and Johnson 1998), and act as colearners (Dillenbourg et al. 1997). Second, projects have begun to investigate techniques by which animated pedagogical agents can behave in a lifelike manner to communicate effectively with learners both visually and verbally (André and Rist 1996, Paiva and Machado 1998, Rickel and Johnson 1999). It is this second category, lifelike animated pedagogical agents, that is the focus of the work described here.

Creating lifelike pedagogical agents that are endowed with facilities for exhibiting learner-appropriate emotive behaviors potentially provides four important educational benefits (Elliott et al. 1999). First, a pedagogical agent that appears to care about a learner's progress may convey to the learner that it and she are "in things together" and may encourage the learner to care more about her own progress. Second, an emotive pedagogical agent that is in some way sensitive to the learner's progress may intervene when she becomes frustrated and before she begins to lose interest. Third, an emotive pedagogical agent may convey enthusiasm for the subject matter at hand and may foster similar levels of enthusiasm in the learner. Finally, a pedagogical agent with a rich and interesting personality may simply make learning more fun. A learner that enjoys interacting with a pedagogical agent may have a more positive perception of the overall learning experience and may consequently opt to spend more time in the learning environment.

Lifelike pedagogical agents seem to hold much promise because they could play a central communicative role in learning environments. Through an engaging persona, a lifelike pedagogical agent could simultaneously provide students with contextualized problem-solving advice and create learning experiences that offer high visual appeal. Perhaps as a result of the inherent psychosocial nature of learner-agent interactions and of humans' tendency to anthropomorphize software (Reeves and Nass 1996), recent evidence suggests that learning environments with lifelike characters can be pedagogically effective (Lester, Converse, Stone, et al. 1997), while at the same time having a strong motivating effect on learners (Lester, Converse, Kahler, et al. 1997). For example, the latter study, which was conducted with one hundred middle school students, demonstrated that well-designed pedagogical agents are perceived as being very helpful, credible, and entertaining. It is even becoming apparent that particular features (e.g., personal characteristics) of lifelike agents can have an important impact on learners' acceptance of them (Hietala and Niemirepo 1998).

In the same manner that human-human communication is characterized by multi-modal interaction utilizing both the visual and aural channels, agent-human communication can be achieved in a similar fashion. As master animators have discovered repeatedly over the past century (Jones 1989), the quality, overall clarity, and dramatic impact of communication can be increased through the creation of lifelike movement that underscores the affective content of the message to be communicated. By carefully orchestrating facial expression, full-body behaviors, arm movements, and hand gestures, animated pedagogical agents could visually augment verbal problem-solving advice, give encouragement, convey empathy, and perhaps increase motivation. Below, we describe three projects that investigate various aspects of lifelike pedagogical agents.

Lifelike Pedagogical Agents in Design-Centered Learning Environments

Constructivist learning (Piaget 1954) has received increasing attention in the education community in recent years because of its emphasis on the active role played by learners as they acquire new concepts and procedures. A particularly intriguing form of the constructivist's learning-by-doing techniques is "learning-by-designing." In the process of designing an artifact, learners—by necessity—come to understand the rich interconnections among the artifacts they devise and the environmental constraints that determine whether a given design will meet with success. Because design tasks are inherently complex, design-centered problem solving provides an excellent testbed for studying mixed-initiative interactions between learners and lifelike pedagogical agents who provide advice and explanations.

For example, consider learning interactions in DESIGN-A-PLANT, a learning environment for the domain of botanical anatomy and physiology we are developing for middle school students. In DESIGN-A-PLANT, a learner's goal in each problem-solving episode is to design a plant that will thrive in a given natural environment with specified conditions such as the amount of available sun-

Figure 1. Herman the Bug in the DESIGN-A-PLANT Learning Environment.

light. To do so, learners graphically assemble plants from a library of plant structures such as roots and stems. DESIGN-A-PLANT is inhabited by a lifelike pedagogical agent, Herman the Bug (figure 1), who interactively provides learners with contextualized advice about botanical anatomy and physiology as they build their plants.

In design-centered learning environments, it seems particularly critical that an animated pedagogical agent's behaviors exhibit contextuality, continuity, and temporality. An agent's advisory behaviors must be rhetorically contextualized within problem-solving episodes, and its physical behaviors must be graphically contextualized within the learning environment. To exhibit continuity of action, all of its behaviors must be visually coherent. Moreover, because many domains and tasks are highly complex and learning time is limited, sequencing a pedagogical agent's explanatory behaviors must take into account temporal resources to provide the greatest coverage of the domain in the given time. To address these issues, we have been developing the *coherence-structured behavior space* framework for dynamically sequencing animated pedagogical agents' behaviors. We focus in particular on animated pedagogical agents whose purpose is to provide instruction about the structure and function of a particular device or organism. Applying this framework to create an agent entails constructing a behavior space, imposing a coherence structure on

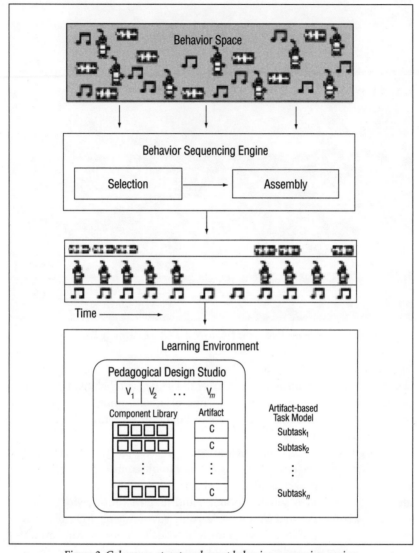

Figure 2. Coherence-structured agent behavior sequencing engine.

it, and developing a behavior sequencing engine that dynamically selects and assembles behaviors:

1. *Behavior space construction:* A behavior space contains animated segments portraying the agent performing a variety of actions, as well as audio clips of the agent's utterances. It is designed by a multidisciplinary team and rendered by a team of graphic artists and animators.

2. *Behavior space structuring:* The behavior space is structured by (a) a tripartite index of ontological, intentional, and rhetorical indices, and (b) a pedagogically appropriate prerequisite ordering. (These structuring features are discussed in detail below.)

3. *Dynamic behavior sequencing:* At runtime, the behavior sequencing engine creates global behaviors in response to the changing problem-solving context by exploiting the coherence structure of the behavior space. The sequencing engine selects the agent's actions by navigating coherent paths through the behavior space and assembling them dynamically (figure 2).

This framework supports the creation of seamless global behaviors in which the agent provides visually contextualized problem-solving advice. In addition, by attending to the amount of time available, it selects and composes explanatory behaviors so as to achieve the greatest coverage of the domain within the allotted time. It has been used to implement DESIGN-A-PLANT's pedagogical agent. In response to changing problem-solving contexts in DESIGN-A-PLANT, a behavior sequencing engine orchestrates Herman the Bug's actions by selecting and assembling behaviors from a behavior space of thirty animations and one hundred sixty audio clips (created by a team of twelve graphic artists and animators). It also employs a large library of runtime-mixable soundtrack elements to dynamically compose a score that complements the agent's activities.

Creating the agent's behavior repertoire entails setting forth precise visual and audio specifications that describe in great detail the agent's actions and utterances, rendering the actions, and creating the audio clips. The core of a behavior space is a highly interconnected web of animated segments depicting the agent performing a variety of explanatory behaviors. This is complemented by a set of audio clips of the agent's audio-primary utterances, as well as soundtrack elements (not discussed here) for the dynamically created score. To assist the sequencing engine in assembling behaviors that exhibit visual coherence, it is critical that the specifications for the animated segments take into account continuity. If an animated segment concludes with the agent in a position that were even slightly different than an animation that is selected for subsequent exhibition, the agent will appear to jump mysteriously from one position to another. Given that transitions between animations in practice occur very frequently (sometimes after as little as a second), the agent would seem to jump wildly between various orientations and positions on the screen. The effect would be unacceptably jarring. To combat this, we adopt the principle of *visual bookending* to create animated segments that can more easily be assembled into visually coherent global behaviors. Visually bookended animations begin and end with frames that are identical. Just as walk cycles and looped backgrounds can be seamlessly composed, visually bookended animated behaviors can be joined in any order and the global behavior will always be flawlessly continuous.

To construct a behavior space for an animated pedagogical agent, eight families of behaviors are specified collaboratively by the multi-disciplinary agent design team and then rendered by the graphic designers and animators. These behavior families are mentioned in the following paragraphs:

Conceptual explanatory animated segments: The agent explicates the structures and functions of the artifact under consideration. For example, the DE-SIGN-A-PLANT agent's behavior space contains an animated segment of the agent explaining how root hairs absorb water through osmosis.

Problem-solving advisory animated segments: The agent provides abstract, principle-based advice. Students must then operationalize this advice in their problem solving activities. For example, one animated segment of the DESIGN-A-PLANT agent depicts him pointing out the relation between leaf size and low sunlight (plants in limited sunlight sometimes have larger leaves) as he helps the student make a leaf design decision. In contrast to conceptual explanatory animated segments, problem-solving advisory animated segments focus not on knowledge in the abstract but on task recommendations for students'problem-solving actions.

Animated transition segments: These portray the agent moving from one *keyframe* (a frame initiating or terminating a segment in a bookended cluster) to another keyframe, or performing an action that will set the stage for several behaviors.

Audio-primary problem overviews: The agent introduces a student to a new problem. For example, the DESIGN-A-PLANT agent's behavior space contains audio clips of the agent describing environmental conditions (e.g., introducing the student to a desertlike environment with low rainfall). These utterances are played at the beginning of problem-solving episodes.

Audio-primary advisory reminders: The agent briefly reminds a student about principle-based advice that was presented earlier. For example, an audio clip in the DESIGN-A-PLANT agent's behavior space is a voiceover of the agent stating, "Remember that small leaves are struck by less sunlight."

Audio-primary direct suggestions: The advice presented by the agent is immediately operationalizable. For example, the DESIGN-A-PLANT agent's behavior space contains a voiceover of the agent stating, "Choose a long stem so the leaves can get plenty of sunlight in this dim environment." The agent makes these types of suggestions when a student is experiencing serious difficulties.

Audio-Primary Interjections: The agent remarks about the student's progress and makes off-the-cuff comments. For example, the DESIGN-A-PLANT agent's behavior space includes Audio-Primary Interjections in which the agent congratulates the student about the successful completion of a plant design. Because it appears that a large repertoire of interjections contributes significantly to an agent's believability, we believe that a behavior space should include a variety of Audio-Primary Interjections.

Audio-primary transitions: The agent makes meta-comments that signal an upcoming behavior. For example, the DESIGN-A-PLANT agent's audio-primary transitions include a clip of him stating, "it seems we're having some difficulty. let's see if this helps...."

Once the behavior space has been created, it must then be structured to assist the sequencing engine in selecting and assembling behaviors that are coherent. Charting the topology of a behavior space is accomplished by constructing a tripartite behavior index and imposing a prerequisite structure on the behaviors.

Tripartite behavior index: Just as the indexing of stories and advice is critical for case-based learning environments (Edelson 1993), indexing of behaviors is of paramount importance for animated pedagogical agents. To enable rapid access to appropriate behaviors so they can be efficiently sequenced at runtime, behaviors are indexed ontologically, intentionally, and rhetorically. First, an *ontological* index is imposed on conceptual explanatory behaviors. Each behavior is labeled with the structure and function of the aspects of the object that the agent discusses in that segment. For example, explanatory segments in the DESIGN-A-PLANT agent's behavior space are labeled by (1) the type of botanical structures discussed (e.g., anatomical structures such as roots, stems, and leaves), and by (2) the physiological functions they perform (e.g., photosynthesis). Second, an *intentional* index is imposed on advisory behaviors. Given a problem-solving goal, this structure enables the sequencing engine to identify the advisory behaviors that help the student achieve the goal. For example, one of the DESIGN-A-PLANT agent's behaviors indicates that it should be presented to a student who is experiencing difficulty with a "low water table" environment. Finally, a *rhetorical* index is imposed on audio-primary segments. This indicates the rhetorical role played by each clip (e.g., introductory remark or interjection).

Prerequisite Structure. The primary goal of an animated pedagogical agent is to guide students through a complex subject by clearly explaining difficult concepts and offering context-sensitive problem-solving advice. To assist the sequencing engine in making decisions about the selection of behaviors, we impose a prerequisite structure on the explanatory behaviors. Prerequisite relations impose a partial order on explanatory behaviors: a behavior can be performed only if all its (immediate and indirect) prerequisite behaviors have been performed. Prerequisites should be imposed conservatively; by imposing only those relations that are clearly mandated by the domain, greater flexibility is provided to the sequencing engine because the number of behaviors it may select at any given time will be greater.

The moment a student requests assistance, constructs an incorrect (complete or partial) solution, or fails to take action for an extended period of time, the sequencing engine (figure 2) is called into play to create the agent's next behavior. By exploiting the behavior space's coherence structure and noting different aspects of the current problem-solving context, the sequencing engine navigates through the space to weave the local behaviors into global behaviors.

It employs the following algorithm, which was tuned over the course of several informal studies with middle school students, to select and assemble local behaviors in realtime:

1. Compute n, the number of explanatory behaviors to exhibit. This quantity is computed by $\lfloor b/f \rfloor$. The quantity b is the number of explanatory behaviors that have not yet been exhibited. The function f, which is determined from empirical data, is the predicted number of future problem-solving situations in which explanatory behaviors can be exhibited. The floor is taken for noninteger results to be conservative (representing the number of conceptual explanatory animated segments that should be exhibited. Rather than clumping a large number of (relatively complex) explanations together in an indigestible form, employing n has the effect of evenly distributing these explanations over the course of the learning session.

2. Select all explanatory behaviors E^P that are pedagogically viable. First, apply the ontological index structure to index into behavior space and identify all conceptual explanatory animated segments that are currently relevant. By noting the current structures, functions, and problem-solving features that are active in the current problem, the sequencing engine can identify the animations that are pedagogically appropriate. Second, determine candidate behaviors whose prerequisite behaviors have already been exhibited by using the prerequisite structure to perform a topological sort of behaviors in the global behavior history.

3. Select explanatory behaviors $E^{P,V}$ that are both pedagogically and visually viable. Of the candidates in E^P chosen in step 2, select a subset $E^{P,V}$ such that $|E^{P,V}|$ is as close as possible to n without exceeding it.[2]

4. Select problem-solving advisory behaviors A that are pedagogically appropriate. Use the intentional and rhetorical indices to identify advisory behaviors that are germane to the topic of the current problem. A may include both animated and audio-primary behaviors.

5. Select the media with which to exhibit a subset A' of the behaviors in A. Inspect the behavior history to determine if advisory behaviors about the current topic have been exhibited. If no prior advisory behaviors on this topic have been presented, select an animated advisory behavior on this topic. If an animated advisory behavior on this topic has been previously exhibited, select an audio-primary verbal reminder on this topic. If an animated advisory behavior on this topic has been previously exhibited but a significant amount of time has elapsed, select it for repeat viewing. If both an animated advisory behavior and a verbal reminder on this topic have been exhibited recently, select an audio-primary direct behavior in which the agent will explicitly tell the student what problem-solving action to take.

6. Select animated and verbal transitions T. Use the indices and prerequisite structure to identify transition behaviors for $E^{P,V}$ and A'.

7. Assemble the final global behavior. Impose the following temporal ordering on the selected behaviors: (a) verbal transitions in T to introduce the up-

coming explanations; (b) animated explanatory behaviors in $E^{P,V}$ ordered by prerequisite structure; (c) animated advisory behaviors in A'; and (d) audio-primary reminders and direct advisory behaviors in A'.

The resulting global behavior is presented onscreen and the sequencing engine sleeps until the next invocation. While it is sleeping, it pseudo-randomly schedules audio-primary interjections. These interjections serve to maintain the agents presence. Early versions of the implemented system did not have this feature, and the resulting agent seemed to lack "liveness." With the pseudo-random audio-primary interjection feature, the agent seems to have a stronger onscreen presence and to be more connected to the student's activities. In addition to the audio-primary interjections, the agent's actions are complemented at all times by a continuous soundtrack whose voicing and tempo are dynamically updated to reflect changes in problem-solving contexts. Introductory measures are played as problems are introduced, and additional voicing is added as partial solutions are successfully constructed.

The coherence-based approach to behavior sequencing has been implemented in Herman the Bug, a talkative, quirky, somewhat churlish insect with a propensity to fly about the screen and dive into the plant's structures as it provides students with problem-solving advice. Throughout the learning session, he remains onscreen, standing on the plant assembly device when he is inactive (figure 1) and diving into the plant as he delivers advice visually. In the process of explaining concepts, he performs a broad range of activities including walking, flying, shrinking, expanding, swimming, fishing, bungee jumping, teleporting, and acrobatics. To illustrate the behavior of the sequencing engine that composes Herman the Bug's actions, consider the following situation in a DESIGN-A-PLANT learning session. A student has seen Herman the Bug present an overview of basic anatomy, watched him explain external anatomy in a prior problem-solving episode, and very quickly (relative to her peers using the system) reached the third level of problem complexity. As she assembles a plant that will thrive in the current environment, she selects a type of leaf that violates the environmental constraints. This action causes the problem-solving system to invoke the behavior sequencing engine, which has access to representations of: the student's partial (and incorrect) solution; the constraints and environmental settings in the current problem; a history of previous behaviors Herman the Bug has exhibited; and a history of the student's previous problem-solving episodes. First, the number of explanatory behaviors to exhibit is computed. Because the student reached the third complexity level quickly, and there are four total levels, the sequencing engine predicts that there will be only two opportunities (including the current one) for presenting explanations. Of the four explanatory behaviors not yet seen, it will show two of them. By using the ontological index structure to find the relevant candidate behaviors and then using the behavior history and the prerequisite structure of the behavior space to perform a topological sort, three explanatory behaviors are selected which are pedagogically viable. This produces explanatory behaviors of internal anatomy and transpiration.

Next, the sequencing engine exploits the intentional and rhetorical indices to identify advisory behaviors that are germane to the structure of interest (leaves) and the environmental attributes of interest (low rain and high temperature). The media with which to exhibit the behaviors is then selected. The sequencing engine notes that the student has been given no prior principle-based advice about leaves, so a behavior depicting Herman the Bug giving principle-based explanations of leaves—and which she will then have the opportunity to operationalize—is selected. (Alternatively, if the student had already seen the principle-based explanations of leaves, an audio-primary reminder would have been selected instead.) The principle-based explanations are introduced by an audio-primary transition in which Herman the Bug explains that, "The low rain and high temperature make some leaves unsuitable for this environment. Here's why…." Finally, the behavior sequencing engine orders the selected behaviors as follows: the animated segment of Herman the Bug explaining internal anatomy; the animated segment of Herman explaining transpiration; the verbal transition; the animated advisory segment about leaves in low-rain environments; and the animated advisory segment about leaves in high-temperature environments. Because of recency effects and the fact that the advisory explanations were communicated last, the student can more easily apply the advice to refine her plant design. She chooses an alternate type of leaf and continues to puzzle out the remaining structures. The net effect of the sequencing engine's activities is the students' perception that a lifelike character is carefully observing their problem-solving activities, moving in and out of the artifact they are designing, and providing advice just when it is needed.

Lifelike Pedagogical Agents with Deictic Believability

A second key problem posed by lifelike pedagogical agents is *deictic believability*. In the same manner that humans refer to objects in their environment through combinations of speech, locomotion, and gesture, animated pedagogical agents should be able to move through learning environments, point to objects, and refer to them appropriately as they provide problem-solving advice. Deictic believability in animated agents requires the design of an agent behavior planner that considers the physical properties of the world inhabited by the agent. The agent must exploit its knowledge of the positions of objects in the world, its relative location with respect to these objects, as well as its prior explanations to create deictic gestures, motions, and utterances that are both natural and unambiguous.

In the course of communicating with one another, humans constantly employ deictic techniques to create context-specific references. *Spatial deixis*, a much studied phenomenon in linguistics, is used to refer to specific locations and objects in the physical world (Jarvella and Klein 1982). Speakers use these techniques to narrow listeners' attention to particular entities. In one popular psycho-social framework for analyzing spatial deixis (the *figure-ground* model (Roberts 1993)), the world is categorized into *ground*, which is the common physical environment shared by the speaker and hearer, and the *referent*, which is the aspect of the ground to which the speaker wishes to refer. Through carefully constructed referring expressions and well-chosen gestures, the speaker assists the hearer in focusing on the particular referent of interest.

The ability to handle *spatial deixis* effectively is especially critical for animated pedagogical agents that inhabit virtual worlds. To provide problem-solving advice to students who are interacting with objects in the world, the agent must be able to refer to objects in the world to clearly explain their function and to assist students in performing their tasks. To effectively communicate advice and explanations to students, the agent must be able to create deictic references that are unambiguous. Avoiding ambiguity is critical for problem solving in virtual environments, where an ambiguous deictic reference can cause mistakes and foster misconceptions. Ambiguity is particularly challenging in virtual environments housing a multitude of objects, especially when many of the objects are similar.

To investigate lifelike animated agents for learning environments, we have developed a lifelike pedagogical agent, Cosmo, and the INTERNET ADVISOR, the testbed learning environment he inhabits.[3] The INTERNET ADVISOR consists of a virtual world with many routers and networks. Students interact with Cosmo, a helpful antenna-bearing creature with a hint of a British accent, as they learn about network routing mechanisms by navigating through a series of subnets. He has a head with movable antennae and expressive blinking eyes, arms with bendable elbows, hands with a large number of independent joints, and a body with an accordionlike torso. His speech was supplied by a voice actor. Given a packet to direct through from a specific source machine to a particular destination address, students are advised by Cosmo as they take the packet through the Internet one subnet at a time. At each subnet, they may send their packet to a specified router and view adjacent subnets. By making decisions about factors such as address resolution and traffic congestion, they learn the fundamentals of network topology and routing mechanisms. Helpful, encouraging, and with a bit of attitude, Cosmo explains how computers are connected, how routing is performed, what types of networks have particular physical characteristics, how address schemes work, and how traffic considerations come into play. Students' journeys are complete when they have successfully navigated the network and delivered their packet to the proper destination.

The environment and agent were designed to foster evaluation of mechanisms for animation behavior sequencing of lifelike characters, human-agent

Figure 3. Cosmo in the INTERNET ADVISOR *learning environment.*

conversational interaction, and realtime problem-solving assistance. For example, environmental features that force spatial deixis issues to the forefront are (1) a world populated by a multitude of objects, many of which are similar, (2) an agent that provides advice and explanations that must refer to these objects, and (3) a problem-solving task that requires students to make decisions based on factors present in the environment. The INTERNET ADVISOR (figure 3) provides such a "deictic laboratory." The INTERNET ADVISOR serves as an excellent testbed for exercising spatial deixis because each subnet has a variety of routers attached to it and the agent must refer unambiguously to them as it advises the students about their problem solving.

As students solve problems in the learning environment, the animated agent provides advice to assist them. In the course of observing a student attempt different solutions, the agent explains concepts and gives hints. It provides advice in two situations: (1) when a student pauses for an extended period of time, which may signal a problem-solving impasse, or (2) when a student commits an error. When the action interpreter detects a situation in which the agent should provide advice, it invokes the agent behavior planner (figure 4). The agent behavior planner consists of an explanation planner and a deictic planner. The explanation planner determines the content and structure of ex-

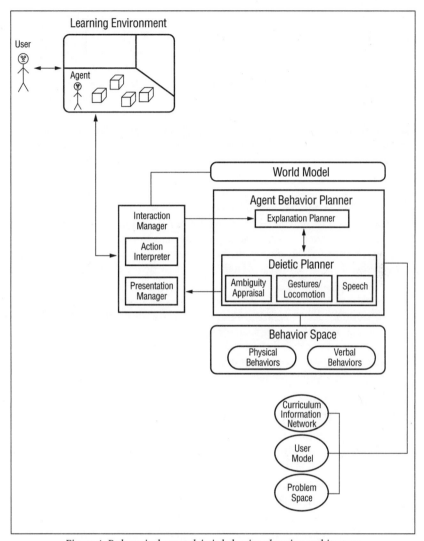

Figure 4. Pedagogical agent deictic behavior planning architecture.

planations by examining a curriculum information network, a user model, the current problem state, and the student's solution. It constructs a sequence of explanatory behaviors and explanations (typically six to ten utterances) which will collectively constitute the advice that will be delivered. In this way, problem-solving actions performed by the student are punctuated by customized explanations delivered by the agent.

Deictic planning comes into play when the behavior planner determines that an explanation must refer to an object in the environment. For each utterance that makes a reference to an environmental object, the explanation planner invokes the deictic system and supplies it with the intended referent R. The deictic system operates in the following three phases to plan the agent's gestures, locomotion, and speech:

1. *Ambiguity appraisal:* The deictic system first assesses the situation by determining whether a reference to R may be ambiguous. By examining the evolving *explanation plan*, which contains a record of the objects the agent has referred to in utterances spoken so far in the current explanation sequence, the deictic planner evaluates R's initial potential for ambiguity. This assessment will contribute to gesture, locomotion, and speech planning decisions.

2. *Gesture and Locomotion Planning:* To determine the agent's physical actions, the deictic system uses both a *world model*, representing the relative positions of the objects in the scene, as well as the previously made ambiguity assessment to plan the agent's pointing gestures and movement. By considering the proximity of objects in the world, the deictic system computes whether the agent should point to R, and if so, whether it should move to R.

3. *Utterance planning:* To determine what the agent should say to refer to R, the deictic system considers focus information, the ambiguity assessment, and the world model. Utterance planning pays particular attention to the relative locations of the referent and the agent, taking into account its planned locomotion from the previous phase. The result of utterance planning is a referring expression consisting of the appropriate proximal/nonproximal demonstratives and pronouns.

Ambiguity Appraisal

For each utterance in the evolving explanation plan that makes a reference to an object in the environment, the explanation planner invokes the deictic system. Deictic decisions depend critically on an accurate assessment of the discourse context in which the reference will be communicated. To correctly plan the agent's gestures, movements, and utterances, the deictic system determines whether the situation has the potential for ambiguity within the current explanation.[4] Because focus indicates the prominence of the referent at the current juncture in the explanation, the deictic system uses focus as the primary predictor of ambiguity: potentially ambiguous situations can be combated by combinations of gesture and locomotion. A referent R has the potential for ambiguity if it is currently not in focus or it is in focus but is one of multiple objects in focus. To determine if the referent is in focus, the deictic system examines the evolving explanation plan and inspects it for previous deictic references to R.

Gesture and Locomotion Planning

When potential ambiguities arise, endowing the agent with the ability to point and move to objects to which it will be referring enables it to improve its clarity of reference. The deictic system plans two types of physical behaviors: gestures and locomotion. In each case, it first determines whether a behavior of that type is warranted. If so, it then computes the behavior. To determine whether the agent should exhibit a pointing gesture to physically designate the referent within the environment, the behavior planner inspects the conclusion of the ambiguity computation in the previous phase. If the referent was deemed ambiguous or potentially ambiguous, the system will plan a pointing gesture for the agent. In addition to pointing, the agent can also move from one location to another to clarify a deictic reference which otherwise might be ambiguous. If the referent has been determined to be unambiguous (i.e., it is in a unique focus), the agent will remain stationary.[5] In contrast, if the referent is ambiguous (i.e., if it is a novel reference), the deictic system instructs the agent to move towards the object specified by the referent as the agent points at it. For example, if Cosmo is discussing a router which has not been previously mentioned in the last two utterances, he will move to that router as he points to it. If the referent is potentially ambiguous (i.e., it is a reference to one of the concurrently active foci), then the Deictic Planer must decide if locomotion is needed. If no locomotion is needed, the agent will point at R without moving towards it.

Deictic Referring Expression Planning

To effectively communicate the intended reference, the deictic system must combine gesture, locomotion, and speech. Having completed gesture and locomotion planning, the deictic planner turns to speech. To determine an appropriate referring expression for the agent to speak as it performs the deictic gestures and locomotion, the deictic system first examines the results of the ambiguity appraisal. If it was determined that R is in a unique focus, there is no potential for ambiguity because R has already been introduced and no other entities are competing for the student's attention. It is therefore introduced with a simple referring expression using techniques similar to outlined in (Dale 1992), for example, "the router" or "it" will be pronominalized. In contrast, if R is ambiguous or potentially ambiguous (i.e., R is a novel reference or is one of multiple foci), the deictic planner makes additional assessments, including categorizing the situation into one of two deictic families:

Proximal demonstratives: If the deictic planner determined that the agent must move to R or that it would have moved to R if it were not already near R, then employ a proximal demonstrative such as "this" or "these."

Nonproximal demonstratives: If the deictic planner determined that R was not nearby but that the agent did not need to move to R, then employ a nonproximal demonstrative such as "that" or "those."

The final referring expression, as well as the selected gestures and locomotive actions, are then passed to the behavior planner, which integrates them into the other speech and behaviors and passes them to the interaction manager's presentation engine in the order in which the agent should exhibit them.

To illustrate how the agent behavior planner produces deictic gestures, motion, and verbal advice as it provides problem-solving assistance in realtime, consider the following situation in an INTERNET ADVISOR[6] learning session. Suppose a student has just routed her packet to a fiber optic subnet with low traffic. She surveys the connected subnets and selects a router which she believes will advance it one step closer to the packet's intended destination. Although she has chosen a reasonable subnet, it is suboptimal because of nonmatching addresses, which will slow her packet's progress. She has made multiple mistakes on address resolution already, and so the explanation is somewhat detailed. The behavior planner selects behaviors with the following communicative acts:

1. *State-correct:* The explanation planner determines that the agent should interject advice and invokes the deictic planner. Since nothing is in focus because this is the first utterance to be planned for a new explanation and Cosmo currently occupies a position on the screen far from information about the subnet (i.e., the distance from his current location to the subnet information exceeds the proximity bound), he moves towards and points at the onscreen subnet information and says, "You chose the fastest subnet."

2. *State-correct:* Cosmo then tells the student that the choice of a low traffic subnet was also a good one. The focus history indicates that, while the type of subnet has already been the subject of a deictic reference, the traffic information has not. Cosmo therefore moves to the onscreen congestion information and points to it. However, the focus history indicates that he has mentioned the subnet in a recent utterance, he pronominalizes the subnet as "it" and says, "Also, it has low traffic."

3. *Congratulatory:* Responding to a congratulatory speech act, the sequencing engine selects an admiration emotive intent which is realized with an enthusiastic applauding behavior as Cosmo exclaims, "Fabulous!"

4. *Causal:* The sequencing engine's planner selects a causal speech act, which causes the interrogative emotive behavior family to be selected. These include actions such as head scratching and shrugging, for which the desired effects are to emphasize a questioning attitude. Hence, because Cosmo wants the student to rethink her choice, he scratches his head and poses the question, "But more importantly, if we sent the packet here, what will happen?"

5. *Deleterious-effect:* After the causal act, the sequencing engine's planner now selects a deleterious-effect speech act, which causes it to index into the disappointment behavior family. It includes behaviors that indicate sadness, which is intended to build empathy with the learner. Cosmo therefore informs the learner of the ill-effect of choosing that router as he takes on a sad facial expression, slumping body language, and dropping his hands, and says, "If that were the case, we see it doesn't arrive at the right place."

6. *Rationale:* To explain the reason why the packet won't arrive at the correct destination, Cosmo adds, "This computer has no parts of the address

matching." Because the computer that serves as the referent is currently not in the focus histories and Cosmo is far from that computer, the behavior planner sequences deictic locomotion and a gesture to accompany the utterance.

7. *Background:* The sequencing engine has selected a background speech act. Because all background and assistance speech acts cause the sequencing engine to index into the inquisitive behavior family, it obtains one of several "thoughtful" restrained manipulators such as hand waving. In this case, it selects a form of finger tapping which he performs as he explains, "Addresses are used by networked computers to tell each other apart."

8. *Assistance:* Finally, Cosmo assists the student by making a suggestion about the next course of action to take. Because the student has committed several mistakes on address resolution problems, Cosmo provides advice about correcting her decision by pointing to the location of the optimal computer—it has not been in focus—and stating, "This router has two parts of the address matching."

The agent's combined behaviors are then sequenced in realtime, providing a convincing illusion of a sentient being delivering advice that integrates lifelike locomotion, gesture, and speech.

Lifelike Pedagogical Agents in Three-Dimensional Learning Environments

A particularly intriguing development in learning environments is our newfound ability to introduce the third dimension. Like most learning environments of the past, both of the learning environments described above, DESIGN-A-PLANT and the INTERNET ADVISOR, exist in flat (or semiflat) worlds. However, we can now exploit rapidly evolving graphics capabilities to provide learners with engaging three-dimensional worlds. This development offers significant potential for fulfilling key educational desiderata which over the course of the past few decades have shifted from an emphasis on rote learning to constructivist learning (Mayer 1992). For example, to learn procedural tasks, a three-dimensional learning environment could enable students to perform the task directly in the environment. Hence, rather than memorizing an abstract procedure, students should be able to actively solve problems, perhaps by immersively interacting with rich three-dimensional models representing the subject matter.

Lifelike pedagogical agents can play a key role in a central problem posed by task-oriented three-dimensional learning environments: detecting and correcting misconceptions. From the classic work on student modeling (Brown and Burton 1978, Carr and Goldstein 1977), plan recognition (Chu-Carroll and Carberry 1994), and plan attribution (Hill and Johnson 1995), researchers have endeavored to unobtrusively track learners' problem-solving activities and dialogues and correct their misconceptions (McCoy 1989-90). Lifelike pedagogical agents can enable us to recast these problems into a solvable, restricted form. By designing task-oriented three-dimensional learning environments, representing detailed knowledge of their three-dimensional models and layout, and introducing lifelike avatars into these worlds, we can craft engaging educational software that effectively addresses learners' misconceptions. We have been investigating these issues by iteratively designing, implementing, and evaluating avatar-based three-dimensional learning environments that detect and correct *procedural misconceptions*. We define procedural misconceptions as erroneous problem-solving procedures that are either missing steps that are essential or contain steps that are incorrect. We have developed a three-phase avatar-based misconception correction framework:

1. *Misconception Detection:* As the learner solves a problem in a three-dimensional learning environment by directing her avatar to navigate through the world and to manipulate objects within it, a misconception detector tracks her problem-solving actions by inspecting a *task network*.

2. *Misconception Classification:* When she takes suboptimal actions, a *misconception classifier* examines a *misconception tree* to identify the most salient procedural misconception. The techniques for performing this classification procedure to identify the most specific applicable misconception are described in detail below.

3. *Misconception Correction:* Finally, a misconception corrector directs the avatar to address conceptual problems by examining a *curriculum information network* (Wescourt et al. 1981), intervening with verbal advice, and providing tailored responses to follow-up questions she poses.

By enabling the avatar to serve in the dual capacity of student representative and advice-giving agent, it tightly couples problem-solving to misconception correction. Avatar-based misconception detection and correction provide a critical link between task-oriented conceptual development and addressing learners' misconceptions directly in problem-solving contexts. The learner's avatar serves two key roles in addressing procedural misconceptions. First, she solves problems by manipulating a joystick to direct her avatar's behaviors. In response to these directives, the avatar performs actions such as picking up objects, carrying them, manipulating devices, and traveling from one location to another. Second, her avatar serves in an advisory capacity by providing explanations. When the student takes actions that indicate she harbors misconceptions about the domain—these are evidenced by her performing a procedure with erroneous steps, or perhaps performing steps that are correct but suboptimal—her avatar intervenes and corrects her misconceptions by providing appropriate advice. Hence, problem solving and advice both play out immersively in the three-dimensional world. This framework has been implemented in a lifelike avatar, WhizLow, who inhabits the CPU CITY three-dimensional learning environment testbed for the domain of computer architecture for

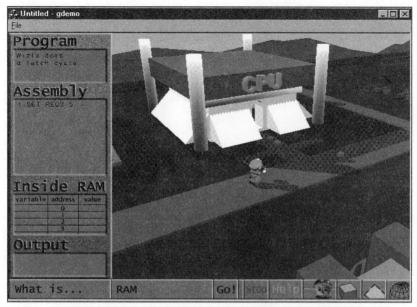

*Figure 5. The WhizLow explanatory lifelike avatar in the
CPU CITY three-dimensional learning environment environment.*

novices (figure 5). Given "programming assignments," learners direct WhizLow to pick up, transport, and insert data packets into registers to execute their programs. Below we describe each of the phases of the misconception correction framework and illustrate its operation with WhizLow.

In the avatar-based misconception correction framework, all of the avatar's misconception detection/correction functionalities are provided by the architecture shown in figure 6. To begin, the avatar verbally presents a problem for the student to solve. As the student begins to perform the task to solve the problem, her position and the changes she enacts to the objects she manipulates are reflected in continuous updates made to the *three-dimensional world model*, which represents the coordinates and state of all objects in the learning environment. All of her problem-solving activities are tracked by an *avatar misconception handler*, which observes and addresses the misconceptions she exhibits while interacting with the world.

Misconception Detection

Problem-solving begins when the avatar poses a problem for the learner to solve in the three-dimensional world. To take advantage of the immersive properties of three-dimensional worlds, the avatar-based framework described here focuses on procedural tasks in which learners acquire concepts relating sequences of steps in a coached-practice setting. For example, in the CPU CITY

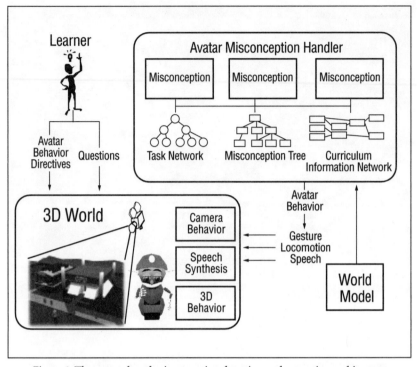

Figure 6. The avatar-based misconception detection and correction architecture.

learning environment testbed, students are posed problems about how to perform the fetch-execute cycle in the virtual computer and the avatar coaches
their problem-solving activities. Given a particular "programming assignment," their job is to manipulate the avatar through the world to transport data packets and manipulate hardware components such as the ALU, decoder,
and registers. After the avatar describes the problem, the misconception detector employs a goal-decomposition planner to create a hierarchical *task network*
representing the potentially correct problem-solving actions to be taken by the
learner. In contrast to more sophisticated (and labor-intensive) approaches to
task modeling such as task-action grammars (TAGs) (Payne and Green 1986)
or production systems (Newell 1990), task networks encode task knowledge in
graph structures that are reminiscent of early planning systems (Sacerdoti
1977). Their nodes represent actions at varying levels of detail, organized in a
hierarchy of time-ordered sequences. At the bottom of the hierarchy are primitive tasks whose actions require no further task decomposition. Each action
specification encodes information about the type of action, the actors involved, the objects affected, and potential subsequent actions.

As the student performs actions through the avatar in the environment, the misconception detector tracks her behaviors by traversing the leaves of the task network it generated. By inspecting the action types of active action specification nodes against student-driven actions performed by the avatar in the world, the misconception detector classifies each action she performs as either critical or noncritical. Actions are considered *critical* if they enact significant changes to the problem state. For example, in CPU CITY, critical actions include attempts to pick up and deposit objects (e.g., data packets), to pass through a portal from one architectural component to another, and to manipulate a device (e.g., pulling a lever of the ALU). Periods of latency that exceed a task-specific time limit are also considered critical actions. These are used to detect misconceptions in which the student does not know what course of action to follow next and "freezes." Example *noncritical actions* in CPU CITY include turning the avatar slightly to the left or walking forward (but not through a portal).

Efficiently managing classification of actions is essential to the intention monitoring enterprise. First, to combat the problem of enumerating the full set of noncritical actions, the misconception detector polls the world model for critical actions and considers all other actions to be noncritical. Second, in learning environments that provide instruction about tasks of any complexity, multiple solution paths are possible. The misconception detector must therefore exploit a representation that is sufficiently flexible to accommodate more than one solution. Hence, the misconception detector generates task networks that are lattices of branching, partially ordered task specifications. When the student embarks on a solution that consists of a particular order of atomic actions, the misconception detector tracks her activities by traversing the task network via the particular solution path she adopts. It produces one of three outcomes: (1) if the current action is deemed noncritical, intention monitoring continues; (2) if the current action is deemed critical and correct, the misconception detector advances the action task node specification to the appropriate successors; (3) if the current action is critical but incorrect, the misconception detector invokes the misconception classifier to classify a potential misconception. While student modeling, misconception detection, and plan recognition are notoriously difficult problems (Brown and Burton 1978, Carr and Goldstein 1977, Chu-Carroll and Carberry 1994), by making the twin simplifying assumptions that (a) the "concept" the student is attempting to learn is a skill that can be encoded in a task network, and (b) the student's actions in performing the task with the avatar closely mirror her mental model of the procedure, the avatar-based misconception framework addresses a restricted but important class of the classic student modeling problem.

Classifying Misconceptions

When the student performs a critical action that is suboptimal, the misconception classifier determines the type of misconception the student may have about the subject matter. Rather than invasively probing the student with questions, the misconception classifier exploits the knowledge about the student's problem-solving activities to make its diagnosis. To do so, it first inspects (1) the active task specification nodes[7] in the task network and (2) the specific action performed by the student. Next, it searches through a misconception tree to determine the most specific misconception that is relevant to the student's suboptimal actions. The *misconception tree* represents the most common misconceptions about procedural knowledge and the most common misconceptions about conceptual knowledge that may induce procedural missteps. It encodes a decision tree, where the children of each node represent specialized categories of misconceptions. At each level, the most salient problem-solving actions performed by the student and key environmental features of the three-dimensional world are used to distinguish different categories of misconceptions. Beginning at the root, the classifier traverses the tree as deep as it can to determine the most specific misconception class applicable to the current situation.

To illustrate, suppose a student interacting with the avatar of CPU CITY has been given a "programming exercise" in which she must retrieve the next microcode instruction. To do so, she must pull the load lever in the RAM. She directs the avatar to pull the lever but has neglected to put the address in the RAM input register. Because pulling a lever is a critical action but does not successfully advance the current goal to a legitimate subsequent goal in the task network, the misconception detector signals a misconception and invokes the misconception classifier. The classifier searches through a misconception tree (figure 7). The first decision in the tree is to determine whether the physical location of the avatar is correct with respect to the current goal. Since she is currently in the RAM, a misconception about location (*incorrect environment*) is ruled out and the classifier turns to potential inappropriate actions taken in the correct location (*rationale absent*). Because her actions have been tracked by the misconception detector, it is known that the offending behavior involved manipulating devices in the RAM, in this case, the load lever (*incorrect lever*). Finally, by inspecting the task tree, the classifier determines that a lever pull action is currently inappropriate but will be appropriate soon; the student has skipped over an intermediate prerequisite step, a common problem in learning procedural tasks (*step skip*). Because a leaf in the tree has now been reached, the most specific category has been identified.

Correcting Misconceptions

After the student's most likely misconception has been identified, the misconception classifier invokes the misconception corrector. Given the specific category of misconception and its contextually instantiated arguments, the corrector indexes into a curriculum information network (CIN) (Wescourt et al. 1981) that encodes misconception correction advisory topics and the prerequisite relations that hold between them. For example, given the step skip cate-

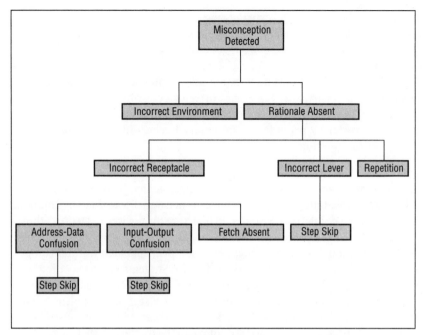

Figure 7. Example traversal of the misconception tree for CPU CITY.

gory identified above and the specific arguments (RAM-load-attempt), the corrector for the CPU CITY avatar indexes into the CIN and directs the avatar to provide verbal advice on a particular topic. A template associated with the selected topic is instantiated with lexicalizations of arguments from the current situation and the avatar is directed to provide verbal advice. In this case, the avatar informs the student, "You're skipping a step. You forgot to X," where X is instantiated here as, "put the address in the RAM input register." The strings are annotated with prosodic markups, passed to the speech synthesizer, and then spoken by the avatar.

Misconceptions are further corrected with two student-initiated question-asking techniques. If the student asks for further assistance by pressing a "help" button, the corrector executes the following three-step algorithm. (1) The corrector examines the students recent actions, the active task action specifications nodes in the task network, and the world model to index into the CIN. (2) It inspects an *overlay student model* (Carr and Goldstein 1977) associated with the CIN to assess the student's prior exposure to the concept(s) discussed in the selected CIN node. (3) If the prior exposure is limited, it directs the avatar to provide a general (abstract) explanation of the relevant concepts; if there has been some degree of prior exposure, the avatar will be instructed to provide more specific assistance; if the student has been exposed to the current material multiple times and is still experiencing difficulty, the avatar will offer to perform the task for the student and explain it using pedagogical agent demonstration techniques (André et al. 1998, Lester, Zettlemoyer et al. 1999, Rickel and Johnson 1999). Students may also request additional assistance by asking specific questions via a pop-up question-asking interface. If they request information about a particular topic, the corrector performs a topological sort of overlay CIN nodes to determine prerequisites of the selected concept. It then directs the avatar to provide the necessary background information and addresses the question.

An Implemented Lifelike Avatar for the CPU City Learning Environment

The misconception framework has been implemented in WhizLow, a lifelike avatar who inhabits the CPU CITY three-dimensional learning environment testbed for the domain of computer architecture for novices.[8] CPU CITY's three-dimensional world represents a motherboard housing nearly one hundred three-dimensional models that represent the principal architectural components including the RAM, CPU, and hard drive. Students are given "programming" tasks in which they direct through the virtual computer. The avatar's operators used to generate task networks to track students' problem-solving activities range from operators for picking up and depositing data, instruction, and address packets to operators for interacting with devices that cause arithmetic and comparison operations. Its misconception classifier handles a broad range of misconceptions including incorrect locations for operation attempts, procedural subtask repetitions and step skips, inappropriate device manipulations where pre-conditions have not been satisfied, and confusions between addresses and data and between input and output. The avatar's misconception corrector addresses these misconceptions by employing a CIN with more than 60 nodes. By (1) detecting students' misconceptions via tracking task networks, (2) classifying misconceptions via traversing misconception trees based on features of the task and physical characteristics of the three-dimensional learning environment, and (3) correcting misconceptions via directing the avatar to deliver topical advice based on prerequisites in a CIN, lifelike avatars like WhizLow can serve as effective tools for addressing misconceptions.

Emerging Empirical Results

While animated pedagogical agent technologies are still in their infancy, it has become apparent that they offer significant promise for learning in a variety of tasks and domains. Each of the agents and learning environments described above has been the subject of a number of empirical studies to gauge impact on learning effectiveness and motivation. To date most of these have been informal studies involving twenty to forty students. These studies typically focus on a particular characteristic of an agent's behavioral technology such as the deictic behavior planner or the misconception correction facility. In these studies, a functionality is ablated and then a comparison is made between a version of a learning environment with the functionality and one in which it is absent. These kinds of evaluations provide insight into the criticality of that particular functionality and suggest avenues for improving it.

More telling, however, are studies with full-scale learning environments involving rigorous pre-tests and post-tests. Some of the more mature technologies have been involved in these formal studies to carefully measure learning impact (Lester, Converse, Stone, et al. 1997). To date, the largest study involving animated pedagogical agents was conducted on-site at a middle school with one hundred students. We first developed five *clones* of the agent and introduced each one into a copy of the DESIGN-A-PLANT learning environment. These clones varied in their repertoires of explanatory behaviors, with differences in the type and amount of problem-solving assistance provided. The clones could provide three types of communicative behaviors. One type of behavior was a short animated segment which combined animations of an object in the domain (e.g., the plant) and spoken descriptions by the agent to convey principle-based advice about the object. Learners had to operationalize this advice in their problem-solving activities. The second type of communicative behavior was high-level advice spoken by the agent. This type of advice was similar to that provided by the advisory animations, but it was conveyed without the benefit of the accompanying animations. For example, Herman might say, "Remember that small leaves are struck by less sunlight." The final type of advisory behavior was a direct, task-specific suggestion spoken by the agent about what action the student should take. This advice was immediately operationalizable. For example, Herman might say, "Choose a long stem so the leaves can get plenty of sunlight in this dim environment." Each of the five clones differed from their siblings with respect to their modes of expression and in the level of advice they offered in response to students' problem-solving activities:

Fully expressive: This agent exhibits all of the three types of communicative behaviors. For example, it may give principle-based animated advice to challenge the student, or employ the task-specific audio advice if the student is having difficulty.

Principle-based animated/verbal: This agent is limited to providing only principle-based animated advice accompanied by the spoken descriptions. It may not employ either the abstract audio-only advice as a reminder of previously seen animations nor may it offer direct verbal-only advice.

Principle-based verbal: This agent can only provide principle-based verbal advice.

Task-specific verbal: This agent can only provide task-specific verbal advice.

Muted: This agent can provide no advice at all about the plant components that are affected by the environmental factors.

Twenty learners interacted with each clone, which was identical to the others in all respects except for those noted above (e.g., all were identical in appearance and in vocal qualities). Each learner was given a pre-test, a post-test, and a Likert scale instrument that measured affective impact.

The study (Lester, Converse, Kahler et al. 1997, Lester, Converse, Stone et al. 1997) established the following three findings:

1. *Baseline result:* Students interacting with learning environments with an animated pedagogical agent show statistically significant increases from pre-tests to post-tests. Some critics have suggested that animated agents could distract students and hence prevent learning. This finding establishes that a well-designed agent in a well-designed learning environment can create successful learning experiences.

2. *Multi-level advice, multi-modality effects:* Animated pedagogical agents that provide multiple levels of advice combining multiple modalities yield greater improvements in problem solving than less expressive agents. This finding indicates that there may be important learning benefits from introducing animated agents that employ both visual (animated) and auditory (verbal) modalities to give both "practical" and "theoretical" advice.

3. *Complexity benefits:* The benefits of animated pedagogical agents increase with problem-solving complexity. As students are faced with more complex problems, the positive effects of animated pedagogical agents on problem solving are more pronounced. This finding suggests that agents may be particularly effective in helping students solve complex technical problems (as opposed to simple "toy" problems).

The study also revealed the *persona effect* (Lester, Converse, Kahler et al. 1997): the very presence of a lifelike character in an interactive learning environment can have a strong positive effect on learners' perception of their learning experience. Together, these findings suggest that animated pedagogical agents can make important contributions to learning experiences.

As the technologies mature, we will formally assess learning effectiveness on motivation in onsite classroom studies to determine precisely the situations in which animated pedagogical agents can contribute to learning. For example, in collaboration with cognitive psychologists, we have begun to investigate the precise relationships among agent behavior, task complexity, and problem-solving transfer to other tasks. The long-term goal of this work is to provide a comprehensive account of the impact of animated pedagogical agents on learners' cognitive processes and the eventual outcomes they produce.

Conclusion

Because of their strong lifelike presence, animated pedagogical agents offer significant potential for capturing students' imaginations and playing a critical motivational role in keeping them deeply engaged in learning. While these technologies are new, they are beginning to mature, and we have already begun to see the emergence of techniques for real-time behavior sequencing in response to rapidly changing learning contexts. The first five years of work have yielded computational models for providing animated explanations and advice in design-centered learning environments, coordinating pedagogical agents' deictic gesture, locomotion, and speech, and detecting and correcting misconceptions in problem-solving activities playing out in three-dimensional learning environments. We have also begun to establish an empirical basis for how and when animated pedagogical agents can be most effective.

The projects described here represent a promising first step toward creating animated pedagogical agents that can play an important role in students' learning activities. Clearly, significant challenges remain, including endowing agents with the full complement of communicative capabilities that human teachers exploit so easily. By employing an iterative design process in which agents are constructed, introduced into rich learning environments, and rigorously evaluated, we can hasten the arrival of a learning technology that addresses the twin goals of learning effectiveness and motivation in the classrooms of tomorrow.

Acknowledgements

The authors wish to thank all of the members of the North Carolina State University IntelliMedia Initiative during the past five years for their contributions to the DESIGN-A-PLANT, INTERNET ADVISOR, and CPU CITY projects. Special thanks are extended to the following individuals and organizations: Patrick FitzGerald, Director of the School of Design's branch of the IntelliMedia Initiative, for leading the three-dimensional modeling and animation teams; the students and faculty of Martin Middle School and Ligon Middle School of Wake County, North Carolina, for their participation in the learning environment studies; and Bradford Mott, for comments on earlier drafts of this chapter. Support for this work was provided by the following organizations: the National Science Foundation under grants CDA-9720395 (Learning and Intelligent Systems Initiative), IRI-9701503 (CAREER Award Program), and REC-9973157 (Research on Education Policy and Practice Program); the North Carolina State University IntelliMedia Initiative; Novell, Inc.; and equipment donations from Apple and IBM.

Notes

1. This work is carried out by a multidisciplinary team of computer scientists, animators, three-dimensional modelers, graphic designers, curriculum and instruction specialists, and cognitive scientists at North Carolina State University's IntelliMedia Initiative: (http://multimedia.ncsu.edu/imedia).

2. Note that steps 2 and 3 must be interleaved when selecting multiple behaviors because prerequisites can be met dynamically in the process of exhibiting a global behavior.

3. In addition to the authors, the INTERNET ADVISOR was created by nine graphic artists (environment designers, three-dimensional modelers, and animators), as well as a musician, a voice actor, and several programmers.

4. This initial phase of ambiguity assessment considers only discourse issues; spatial considerations are handled in the following two phases.

5. More precisely, the agent will not perform a locomotive behavior. In fact, for purposes of believability, the agent is always in motion, performing actions such as an "antigravity" bobbing motion.

6. Cosmo and the INTERNET ADVISOR environment are implemented in C++ and employ the Microsoft Game Software Developer's Kit. Cosmo's behaviors run at 15 frames/second with 16 bits/pixel color on a PC. Cosmo, as well as the routers and subnets in the virtual Internet world, were modeled and rendered in three-dimensional on SGIs with Alias/Wavefront. The resulting bitmaps were subsequently post-edited with Photoshop and AfterEffects on Macintoshes and transferred to PCs where users interact with them in a two-dimensional environment. Cosmo can perform a variety of behaviors including locomotion, pointing, blinking, leaning, clapping, and raising and bending his antennae. His verbal behaviors include two hundred utterances ranging in duration from one to twenty seconds.

7. Multiple task specification nodes may be active because of multiple (alternate) paths through the task network to achieve a particular goal.

8. The current implementation runs on Pentium II 300 MHz machines, with 64 MB of memory and an 8MB SGRAM Permedia2 OpenGL accelerator at frame rates between approximately 10-15 FPS. WhizLow's speech is synthesized with the Microsoft Speech SDK 3.0. Generating speech for a typical sentence requires approximately 1/8 of a second, which includes the time to process prosodic directives. The misconception handler, avatar behavior generator, and the CPU CITY learning environment consists of approximately 60,000 lines of C++ and employs the OpenGL graphics library for real-time three-dimensional rendering.

Chapter Nine

Exploiting Model-Based Reasoning in Educational Systems

Illuminating the Learner Modeling Problem

Kees de Koning and Bert Bredeweg

We discuss the application of existing techniques and representations from the field of model-based reasoning (MBR) in building educational software systems. With MBR we refer to a range of techniques that have been used in mainly technical domains to support the construction, modification and maintenance of physical systems (cf. Weld and de Kleer 1990). An important feature of MBR is the notion of an explicit model of the physical system that is reasoned about. This model serves as a self-contained software component by means of which behavioral features of the physical system can be derived. We claim that the development of educational software can benefit substantially from the results that have been achieved in this field of artificial intelligence in terms of theoretical grounding of educational software research as well as in terms of reuse and generality. In particular the field of MBR has a lot to offer to support making the knowledge involved in education explicitly available and well-defined.

The variety in educational software systems, both with respect to instructional domains and with respect to the educational philosophy underlying their operation, is too big to justify any statements about how in general an educational system should be built. In this chapter, we confine ourselves to what we will call *knowledgeable educational software systems* that interact with a learner about a subject on which all relevant knowledge is explicitly available to the system. Usually, although not necessarily, this goes together with a particular instructional method; the system serves as a reactive knowledge base, and the learner interacts with this knowledge base via experimentation assignments and/or question-answer dialogues.

In order to support this interaction, a detailed and articulate representation of the subject matter is required. That is, a *subject matter model* should contain all relevant knowledge at the finest level of detail that still may be relevant in the educational process. In addition, the model must provide *handles* for interaction; the structure and indexing schemes of the model should facilitate effective communication of the individual model elements.

However, a major problem in developing educational software is that these models are very expensive to build, maintain, and reuse. Moreover, many reasoning techniques that have been developed are only applicable for one specific subject matter representation and cannot be easily adapted for new domains. Therefore, the development of educational software research would benefit greatly from establishing (a set of) standard representations and techniques to address common modeling and reasoning bottlenecks. In particular MBR can fulfill an important role in this process; it allows for explicit representation and indexing of knowledge in a well-defined model formalism, as well as for the reuse of existing techniques for generation, inspection and manipulation of these models to support the communication with the learner.

The content of this chapter is as follows. In the next three subsections we first discuss some general issues concerning education, interaction and the use of simulation models. In the second part of this chapter we discuss an architecture for model-based educational software. We describe the role of the main functional units within this architecture and briefly discuss ongoing research for some of these. We will then focus on a specific function from the architecture, namely interpretation of learner behavior, and we show how model-based diagnostic techniques developed for technical domains can be adapted and reused for educational purposes.

Individualized Interaction and Diagnosis

Knowledgeable educational software systems, as defined above, require some degree of individualization of the interaction with the learner. Despite all the merits that are ascribed to explorative learning, learners still need guidance in order not to get lost in the exploration environment (Elsom-Cook 1990, de Jong 1991, van der Hulst 1996). This guidance requires knowledge about the learner. We focus on teaching *structured problem solving* tasks, that is, problem solving according to some well-defined, although not necessarily fixed method, as opposed to, for instance, impasse-driven problem solving in unknown situations. Because problem solving is a complex cognitive task, we cannot expect the learner to report explicitly every individual part of the reasoning process; this would be too time-consuming and would probably reduce the motivation of the learner. Hence, acquiring the knowledge about the learner that is required for guidance calls for some form of interpretation of that part of the (cognitive) behavior of the learner that is not explicitly reported.

This can be done by matching the learner's behavior to some normative model in the educational software system. When the learner's behavior deviates (according to some metrics) from the norm, pedagogical action may be taken to help the learner. This pedagogical action is often based on some additional knowledge that is acquired about the learner's deviation. The process of acquiring this additional knowledge is called *diagnosis.*

In several artificial intelligence and education (AIED) projects, diagnosis played a central role, and was accomplished by explicitly representing faulty procedures (mental models) that learners may have about the domain (van Lehn 1990). The *bug catalogues* required for this approach were acquired by experimental research on how learners attack the problem domain. Although relatively successful, the costs of creating the bug catalogues were huge, and reuse in different domains was generally impossible.

We address the problem of development costs and lack of reusability by taking a *model-based* approach to educational diagnosis (de Koning 1997, de Koning et al. 2000). This way we can avoid the laborious specification of bug catalogues. We show that model-based diagnosis can be applied to tackle the problem of diagnosing the reasoning behavior of a learner, a problem that is often considered too difficult and expensive to be worth addressing. Moreover, the application of existing and well-defined techniques enforces a very precise definition of what constitutes a diagnosis or a model. The theoretical grounding facilitated by such precise definitions is considered one of the important contributions of AI to AIED research, as well as to education in general (Self 1998).

Behavior Analysis

The problem solving task we consider in this chapter is qualitative prediction of behavior (Forbus 1984a, Bredeweg 1992). The educational objective is to have the learner predict the possible behavior of some (usually, but not necessarily, physical) system in qualitative terms. This includes an understanding of the qualitative relationships that govern the behavior of the specific system as well as the more general reasoning techniques involved in structured prediction of behavior. A simple example system is shown in figure 1.

The piston system consists of a movable piston in a container. In the container, there is some gas, and under the container there is a heater which heats the gas. The student's task is to predict what will happen to the piston system. Most (but not all) of the quantities needed in predicting the behavior of the piston system are presented in figure 1. At the initial state of the system, the temperature of the gas T_g and that of the outside world T_w are given to be equal ($T_g = T_w$), and the heater is just started, expressed by the fact that its temperature (Ts) is higher than that of the gas ($T_s > T_g$). Furthermore, the temperature of the outside world is given not to change ($\dot{T}_w = 0$).

Given this boiler-piston assembly, we do not want the learner only to under-

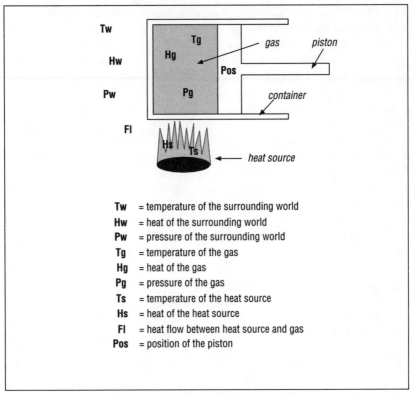

Figure 1. *A simple boiler-piston assembly.*

stand that "the piston will move." Instead, the system's behavior should be expressed in terms of the specific qualitative relations involved, such as the relationship between heat and temperature, the relevance of the heat path between the burner and the container for the heat flow, etc. Furthermore, we want the learner to be able to reason about all possible behaviors of this system, that is, about all possible sequences of consistent differing behavioral states.

The reasons for choosing the domain of behavior prediction as the teaching domain is twofold. First, qualitative analysis has long been recognized as an important prerequisite for expert problem solving in physics domains (e.g., Larkin et al. 1980, Chi et al. 1981, Elio and Sharf 1990). In fact, there is experimental evidence suggesting that starting out with qualitative models of physics helps learners in developing an understanding of physics concepts (Hartley 1998). A second reason for the choice of the teaching domain is that people have to deal with the behavior of a lot of systems, both in their daily lives and at work (cf. Bredeweg and Winkels 1998). Both the operation of a VCR and the control of a nuclear power plant can be, although for very different audiences, very difficult tasks that require reasoning about behavior at a qualitative level.

An accompanying advantage of the domain of qualitative reasoning is that existing simulators (such as GARP, Bredeweg 1992) can be employed to generate the required subject matter models, as will be explained in detail in the Representation section.

A Model-Based Approach

The requirements for individualized interaction in simulation-based educational systems, as laid out above, include detailed models of the subject matter to be communicated to the learner. In general, such models are expensive to develop and are usually specific for the exact subject matter that is considered: for every new domain, the modeling task has to be done anew. As a result, the whole idea of individualized instruction is sometimes considered infeasible.

To alleviate the problem of high costs, we propose to exploit existing techniques from the field of MBR. In particular, we adopt a particular model-based representation of the subject matter, the *component-connection* paradigm (e.g., Davis 1984), that facilitates the use of existing model-based techniques such as consistency-based diagnosis. The resulting model has two outstanding features. First of all, because the subject matter model representation allows for consistency-based diagnosis, we can analyze learner behavior without the necessity of explicit fault models (or bug catalogs). Secondly, the models of the correct subject matter can be *generated* by existing techniques in qualitative simulation. We will show that the output of the existing simulator GARP (Bredeweg 1992) can be automatically transformed into a component-connection representation of the subject matter model.

If these features are indeed implemented, we not only have available a way of dynamically generating subject matter models, but we can also apply model-based techniques to these models. However, to accomplish this, a number of research questions need to be answered, which will be done in the remainder of this chapter:

- What *exactly* is in the subject matter model? This question is answered below in the next section.
- What model-based techniques can be and/or should be applied to the model? This question is answered below in several subsections, discussing the various educational functions that we consider to be essential in supporting knowledgeable interactions with the learner.
- How can the subject matter model be generated automatically, and how are the resulting models employed in educational functions from a pragmatic point of view? This question is answered in the Representation and Reasoning sections below, where we present the STAR framework for MBR about learner behavior.

The work reported here concentrates on modeling the subject matter and on diagnosing the problem solving behavior of learners as being the subjects of our initial exploration. To this end, we first present a functional overview of simulation-based educational systems. Subsequently, we describe our specific implementation of this functionality in the STAR framework. The Representation section describes the models employed, and the Reasoning section describes the functionality that exploits these models.

Towards Model-Based Educational Systems

In our view, the model of the subject matter is of vital importance in the support of individualized, knowledgeable interactions. Based on this model, all educational functions can be defined. Figure 2 shows the different function groups that play a role in simulation-based educational systems and their interactions. Note that each function group may cover a broad range of actual functional parts of the educational system; for instance, discourse management incorporates all functions that have to do with natural language communication. The purpose of the figure is to show how the different parts of a simulation-based educational system can be functionally categorized. The remainder of this section further explains how we define each of these functional parts. It is by no means intended as an overview of the state on the art on educational systems, but it serves to highlight what we conjecture to be the "hot spots" of research in artificial intelligence and education.

Modeling

The two models, represented in figure 2 as the rectangular transparent boxes, serve very different roles. On the one hand, the subject matter model can be considered the core of the educational system, and as such determines the nature of all interactions between learner and system. The learner model, on the other hand, serves mainly as a means to improve and refine the educational planning and the interaction. The purpose of this section is to detail this difference.

Subject Matter Model

Any subject matter model should have a number of characteristics in order to be useful; it should be articulate enough that the educational system can communicate about its contents, and it should contain enough detail to satisfy all possible explanatory demands. In other words, it should contain sufficient structure and indexing. As long as subject matter models are created by hand, such characteristics could serve as guidelines, and fulfilling them constitutes the craftsmanship of building good models. However, when subject matter

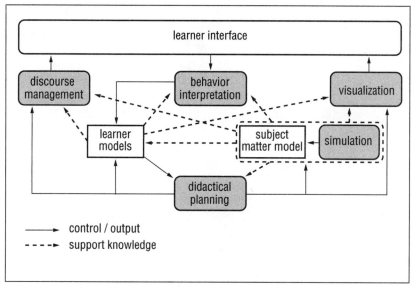

Figure 2. Functional parts of a simulation-based educational system.

models are to be generated dynamically, these requirements need to be opera-tionalized, and hence their definition needs to be much more precise.

For the interpretation of the learner's behavior, we want the subject matter model to represent all aspects of the reasoning process that the learner is sup-posed to go through that are still educationally relevant; the primitive parts of the reasoning task should be explicitly modeled and available for interaction. Furthermore, the individual *components* of the model (in terms of the compo-nent-connection paradigm) should adhere to the *no-function-in-structure* principle (de Kleer and Brown 1984); the behavior of components is described locally, independent of the context (function) in which they operate.

In accordance with the field of knowledge engineering, the primitive com-ponents of a reasoning task are often referred to as *(primitive) inferences* (Wielinga et al. 1992). When using primitive inferences as the building blocks of the subject matter model, we need to account for the difference that is made between two types of knowledge involved in reasoning: *generic (or static)* and *dynamic* domain knowledge.

To illustrate these ideas, let us consider the simple inference of calculating a *qualitative proportionality* (Forbus 1984), as shown in figure 3.

Here, the *quantity proportionality* component models the primitive inference that calculates the derivative of the pressure, P, at the bottom of a container from the derivative of the level, L, of the contained liquid, using the *proportion-ality relation* pos_prop(L, P)[1] the level is positively proportional to the pressure. We consider it important to separate the piece of domain knowledge that is in-

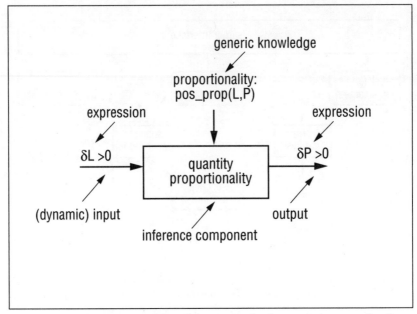

Figure 3. Component-connection model representation for a quantity proportionality.

volved in a certain inference (here, pos_prop(L, P)) from the actual inference it-self; this way, we can express the difference between a learner that does not un-derstand how a proportionality relation should be calculated from a learner who does not know the specific relation between the level and the pressure. In the next section we will discuss the model representation in more detail.

The Learner Model

The learner model (or student model) serves as a repository for all information that is known about an individual learner, i.e., everything that has to do with individualization of the educational process. The task of learner modeling is usually supportive; the information is used for guiding the educational pro-cess, rather than serving a purpose in itself (as is the case when a learner's scores are recorded for a human teacher). In research on intelligent tutoring systems (ITS), learner models are often conceived as mental models (Gentner and Stevens, 1983) of the cognitive state of the learner—in fact, Ohlsson's (1986) definition of cognitive diagnosis as being "the process of inferring a person's cognitive state from his or her performance" has been widely cited in AIED literature. However, the particular notion of a learner model as a (proba-bilistic) overlay (Carr and Goldstein 1977) of the correct subject matter is con-sidered too restricted: the mental model of a learner cannot be seen as only a subset of some correct domain model.

Although we subscribe to the statement that an overlay model can not in general be considered an adequate model of the learner's cognitive state, we draw a different conclusion: instead of trying to make the representation of the learner model more sophisticated, we adopt a more pragmatic and workable definition of a learner model. In this respect, we found the distinction between two different roles that learner modeling can play to be essential: learner modeling may be long-term (global) or short-term (local)—see Bredeweg and Breuker (1993). This difference is reflected in the difference between *learner model management* (i.e., the maintenance of the learner model over time) and *behavior diagnosis* (i.e., acquiring the information that is stored in the learner model). Global learner modeling is usually done by attaching measures to the elements of the subject matter model that indicate to what extent (the system believes that) the learner has mastered that element. It may involve numerous specific AI techniques, such as belief revision and reason maintenance (Huang et al. 1991, Paiva and Self 1994, Conati et al. 1997), and should deal with model inconsistencies (i.e., contradictory information about the learner is gathered) as well as learner inconsistencies (i.e., a learner may hold inconsistent beliefs) (Kono et al. 1994). Global learning modeling is not discussed further in this chapter, but instead we focus on behavior diagnosis (which is further discussed in the Behavior Interpretation subsection).

Simulation

Simulation can play different roles in an educational system. Hence, the class of educational systems that we would call "simulation-based" is rather diverse, ranging from systems in which simulation is used purely for the purpose of illustration, to highly interactive simulators that serve as the core of an educational environment. Thus, the two main uses of simulations are:

- *Exposition:* The main goal of simulation in most educational systems is to show the behavior of some system under certain conditions. In most cases, the learner is the observer of a simulation that is determined by the educational system.
- *Manipulation:* Viewing the simulation as an interaction component means that the learner is directly manipulating the simulated system, possibly during simulation. This way, the learner can change the system's parameters and immediately observe the effects on its behavior.

The main difficulty with truly interactive simulation and direct manipulation in an educational system is not creating the interactive simulation itself—this has already been shown to be feasible (e.g., Forbus, chapter 7). The major problem lies in the large amount of freedom in interaction that the learner has and the resulting issue of interpreting the learner's behavior (see below).

Behavior Interpretation

The interpretation of what the learner is doing can be separated in two parts: behavior assessment and behavior diagnosis.

Behavior Assessment

When a learner can interact with a running simulation, or can have a free-form interface to interact with the system, the task of determining what the learner is doing exactly is not trivial. Note that behavior assessment is not about interpreting the behavior, but only about identifying its "status." For instance, in the simple case of a learner answering a subtraction exercise as $34 - 19 = 25$, behavior assessment is only the identification of the number 25 as being a faulty answer. Determining the reason for the error (e.g., the learner does not know how to lend) is the task of behavior diagnosis.

Behavior Diagnosis

Behavior diagnosis, in the case of problem solving, amounts to the task of determining from the observable input of the learner (answers) what elements of this problem solving process account for an error. So, in contrast to identifying the erroneous behavior, as is done in the case of assessment, the goal of diagnosis is to identify the cause of this malfunctioning. Often, diagnosis is done by mapping explicitly represented "faulty" elements onto the observations, hence trying to explain the learner's behavior in terms of known bugs (Brown and Burton 1978). The nature of these elements can vary from "incorrect mental models" (Stevens and Collins 1980) to "procedural bugs" (Anderson and Lebière 1998). Notwithstanding the usefulness of an elaborate set of mental (fault) models or bug rules, the costs of constructing such models manually are practically prohibitive. To alleviate the cost problem and also the lack of flexibility of these enumerative approaches, there are also approaches that generate bugs dynamically, such as SIERRA (vanLehn 1990). A difficult research question for these generative approaches is to construct theories on how bugs or incorrect mental models come into being.

In contrast, consistency-based diagnostic techniques from the field of model-based reasoning do not require explicit fault models and can still be very helpful in supporting the learner. The definition of the subject matter model, shown above, in terms of individual primitive reasoning steps restates the model-based diagnosis task in the educational domain as follows:

> *Model-based diagnosis of learner behavior:*
> Given a set of observations about the learner's problem solving behavior, identify those sets of primitive reasoning steps whose correct behavior is inconsistent with the observations.

As a result, behavior diagnosis is not the same as cognitive diagnosis: we do not strive for building cognitive or mental models, but instead diagnose on the level of problem solving behavior. This greatly reduces the development costs of the diagnostic module, in particular, when the diagnostic model (i.e., the subject matter model) can be generated automatically (see next section).

Discourse Management

The term "discourse management" is used here as a general name for any function that is concerned with the interaction with the learner. One possible classification of interaction-related functions is into language-based interactions (e.g., textual questions, answers, explanations, as well as dialog and discourse management) and graphical interactions (e.g., pictorial explanations, animations, video).

Although this dichotomy may not do justice to certain mixed-media interactions, it suits our purposes because we present a "bottom-up view" on interaction here; the central question regarding interaction is: "What features should the subject matter model possess in order to facilitate knowledgeable interaction with the learner, and what techniques can be used to communicate the represented knowledge in such models to the learner?" The generation of discourse is an interesting and promising line of future research, and can build on a vast base of existing research on text generation (McKeown 1985, Mann and Thompson 1987), mixed-media explanation generation (Feiner and McKeown 1991, Wahlster et al. 1993, Pilkington 1996), or discourse planning (Hovy 1993). Especially relevant to the task of educational discourse is the work of Winkels (1992) in the course of the EUROHELP project (Breuker 1990), where discourse is planned using the notion of a *local need,* which is typically determined by diagnosing the learner's behavior. A first glance at the potential for Winkels's Didactic Discourse Planner in explaining qualitative models can be found in Salles et al. (1997).

In this chapter we concentrate on the articulate representation of the subject matter. To support communication with the learner, the model representation should facilitate sufficient *handles* to select the appropriate knowledge elements from the model. This issue was first reported when quantitative simulations were used as part of the educational software developed in the STEAMER project (Hollan et al. 1984) and was addressed in the SOPHIE projects (Brown et al. 1982) to lead to the genesis of qualitative reasoning as a new field of research. For instance, a quantitative simulation using Newton's law $F = ma$ cannot be used as is to explain the underlying causal relations between mass, force, and acceleration. To do so, we need an explicit representation of what F, m, and a are, and what (causal and noncausal) relations hold among them. This is exactly what qualitative models do; they specify, for instance, that a mass is a quantity that has possible values of zero or bigger than zero, and that the mass of an object is negatively proportional to its acceleration. This articulation is a very important prerequisite for any form of discourse generation.

Didactic Planning

Didactic planning amounts to the sequencing of subject matter in pursuit of some educational goal. Our framework is currently based on individual simulation models. Didactic planning can thus be seen as consisting of two parts, one concerned with selecting and generating an appropriate simulation model, and one with selecting the appropriate knowledge within this model for communication with the learner.

Choosing what simulation to use in an educational situation may depend on a number of factors—for instance, using an analogous system to explain a badly understood part, or throwing in a counter-example to reject a faulty hypothesis. This requires a computational theory of analogy and similarity that is applicable to qualitative models, such as SME (Falkenhainer et al. 1989).

We may also structure different simulations according to some cognitive theory on knowledge development or conceptual change. In this respect, theories like model progression (White and Frederiksen 1991) and cognitive flexibility theory (Spiro et al. 1988, Spiro and Jehng 1990) may be applicable to the STAR framework. However, the main problem with such theories is that they rely on static models that are usually built manually. In the case of model progression, there is no operational theory of how the sequence of models for a certain subject matter should be constructed—the implementation support of the theory merely consists of a number of guidelines that can be used by a model constructor. To apply model progression theory in a dynamic environment, we need to extend the techniques for automatic subject matter model generation to create a *sequence* of models of increasing cognitive complexity rather than one model. In de Koning et al. (1994) we present a way of doing so by employing a variant of Falkenhainer and Forbus's compositional modeling approach.

Representation: Subject Matter Modeling

The previous section described our view on how research on simulation-based educational systems could be focused by clearly defining the different parts of its functionality, and the role of the subject matter model in an educational interaction.

The sketched framework has been the coordinating principle of our research in the past years, and we have made important progress in developing several of the components. We started with experimental research on the necessary contents of the subject matter model (de Koning and Bredeweg 1998) and defined the representation of the subject matter model, which we usually refer to as the *base model*. As indicated in the previous section, the resulting model should contain all knowledge at the most detailed level still relevant to education. The two main problems with modeling the subject matter at this level of detail are the development costs involved in constructing the models; and the size of the resulting models, and hence the computational costs of using them. How we dealt with these problems is discussed below.

The Model Representation

As previously indicated, we build on the results of the knowledge engineering community, where a lot of work has been done on how to represent problem solving knowledge. In particular, we adopt the definition of *primitive inferences* from the CommonKADS approach (Schreiber et al. 1993, Schreiber et al. 1994) as being the smallest individual reasoning steps that are individually represented as the basis for our subject matter models. In CommonKADS, primitive inferences are organized in inference structures that represent the way in which tasks can be performed.

One important difference between the KADS inference structure and its implementation in the component-connection representation in the STAR framework is that inference components are *instantiated reasoning steps* representing one execution of that inference given a specific "location" in the reasoning process, whereas a KADS inference is a *generic* description of an inference type. As a result, one occurrence of a KADS inference can map on several different instantiations of that same inference in the subject matter model. For instance, it is not uncommon for a model about the prediction of one behavior state to contain several "compute correspondence" components for calculating different correspondences between various quantities. These components are all described by the same KADS primitive inference. Our approach thus facilitates individual representation of each educationally relevant reasoning step in the problem solving process as one specific instantiation of a primitive inference.

This approach addresses the issue of explicit representation, but it does not guarantee that the resulting models are practically usable. In fact, our first experiences with subject matter models that were generated for relatively small physical systems were that these models were too big to be feasible without the addition of extra structure. A network of hundreds of individual inferences alone is not suitable as a vehicle for guiding students through a reasoning task. The additional structure required for education can come from different sources, but an important issue is that it should be added *automatically*, because of the dynamic nature of the subject matter models. One way of doing so is by adding hierarchical structure to the model, according to certain principles that govern what set of components can be considered as "belonging to the same higher-level part of the reasoning process." How this is realized is discussed later.

To introduce the subject matter model representation, consider the following explanation fragment about the behavior of the container-piston assembly

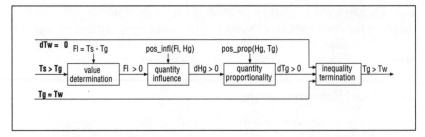

Figure 4. Fragment of the model for the piston-container assembly.

(figure 1): "Because the temperature of the heater is higher than the temperature of the gas, there will be a heat flow from the heater to the gas, which will increase the temperature of the gas. Therefore, the temperature of the gas will no longer be equal to the temperature in the outside world, but will become higher." The fragment of the subject matter model that is involved in making this derivation is represented in figure 4.

The four components in the model represent the four primitive inferences that are underlying the argumentation that was presented above. Note that the heat of the gas (whose derivative is inferred in the second inference component in the figure) is not explicitly mentioned in the explanation fragment. What exactly is modeled is determined by the modeling choices made by the constructor of the model: for a certain domain and a certain target audience, a selection has to be made about what is considered educationally relevant.

Four different types of inference are shown in figure 4: a *value determination* that derives the existence of a heat flow *Fl* from a temperature difference *Ts − Tg*, a *quantity influence* that derives that the heat of the gas *Hg* increases because of the positive heat flow, a *quantity proportionality* that derives the increase of gas temperature *Tg* from the increase of its heat, and finally an *inequality termination* that derives the inequality between the temperature of the gas and the temperature of the outside world *Tw* in the next state, given the equality in the current state together with the fact that the temperature of the gas increases.

The basic set of components consists of sixteen different inferences. This set was constructed by analyzing the interaction protocols of human teachers and learners discussing qualitative system behavior (de Koning and Bredeweg 1998), and it forms a bridge between qualitative simulation and human prediction of behavior: every inference has some (although not always primitive) counterpart in qualitative simulation models, and is at an educationally relevant level of detail (although not necessarily mentioned in every dialog). The 16 inference types are generic for qualitative behavior analysis. For a detailed description of the model components, see de Koning (1997).

Generating Subject Matter Models

We attack the problem of costs of subject matter model development by automatically generating the models by means of qualitative simulation. Of course, this still leaves the input of the simulator (i.e., a domain theory and a scenario) to be developed, but that task is not specific to the simulation-based educational environment that is being developed, and off-the-shelf models for various physical and nonphysical systems can be reused.

The most detailed subject matter model (the *base model*) is generated by qualitative simulation in a two-step process. First, the simulator GARP (Bredeweg 1992) is used to produce a simulation of the behavior of the system in question. Next, this output is transformed into a base model by mapping it on the set of 16 component types we defined.

An important aspect of this transformation is its "reverse-engineering" nature; to guarantee both correctness *and* cognitive adequacy, we start building the model by taking the correct *facts* that make up the individual states in the envisionment, guaranteeing that every state indeed contains the correct factual information.[2]

Next the *reasoning steps* needed to derive these facts are included from the cognitively relevant set that was experimentally determined. Figure 5 illustrates this process. Important to note is that we do not use the inference steps made by the simulator, but instead only use the bare *results* (facts) produced by the simulator. Then, we start from the set of 16 model component types and insert all components that make a valid (in terms of the component's behavioral rules) derivation. In other words, we start with the set of all facts that should be derived, and add all inference steps connecting them, where the set of possible inference steps (components) is not based on the simulator's reasoning, but on observed human reasoning.

Size Does Matter

The dynamic generation of the subject matter models does not solve the problem of the size of the models. The problem of computational complexity and size is not to be underestimated in this case. While all the knowledge contained in the model for the piston-container assembly from figure 1 is considered "educationally relevant" (i.e., no model element is too low-level to be ever used in communication), it contains over eight hundred components and eight hundred data elements for a behavior prediction consisting of nine states plus the transitions between them. Clearly, the dynamic generation process will not scale up to modeling really complex systems. But even for the given model of eight hundred components, there are a number of features of the base models that are disadvantageous with respect to model-based diagnosis; the connectivity between the components is relatively low, the number of observations,

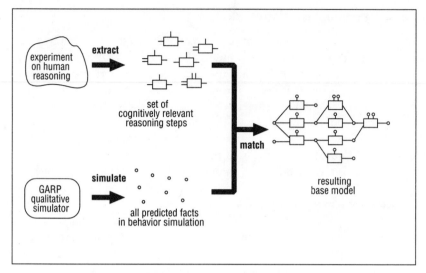

Figure 5. Base model generation.

and particularly observed outputs, is low, and because of the relatively weak qualitative calculi used, the behavior rules for backward propagation cannot be defined for all components. The combination of these characteristics, together with the large number of components, provides a "worst case scenario" for model-based diagnosis.

One common solution to this problem is to add hierarchical structure to the models (e.g., Mozetič 1991). The initial applications of hierarchical diagnosis were in the field of electronics, for which the choice of the higher-level, abstract components was mostly guided by the function of a set of components (e.g., a set of electronic components comprises an amplifier) and/or by the structural grouping on individual circuit boards (i.e., a display adapter in a PC). In the case of a reasoning network there is no such thing as a blue print or a physical device to guide the hierarchical organization. Hence, if we want to generate hierarchical models automatically, we need a set of operational criteria of which sets of components can be abstracted to a higher-level component. An important requirement is that these abstractions should result in models for which the points are still "measurable," that is, the remaining domain knowledge indeed facilitates a communication with the student at a higher abstraction level.

We propose three different principles for combining components.

Hiding irrelevant details means that some components and points of the model are discarded at a higher level because they are less important for the main prediction at hand. Hiding is used to abstract from fully-corresponding quantities, for example *volume* and *amount* of the gas in the piston example: if two quantities are completely interchangeable in the model, then one of them can be left out. At the higher level, one quantity remains.

A second form of hiding is in leaving out inference steps that do not strictly belong to the main track of the solution. For instance, if the container is heated for some time, a second heat flow from the gas to the outside world will emerge. When we are predicting a situation in which this effect is negligible, we can leave out the corresponding reasoning components in the model.

Chunking amounts to compiling subsequent transitive reasoning steps into one abstract inference. In natural language, this means that an inference like "the heat is increasing, therefore the temperature is increasing, and the pressure as well" can be replaced by "the heat is increasing, therefore the pressure increases as well." First, only chains of components of equal type are chunked. Second, different types are chunked. For instance, the chain formed by the *value determination, quantity influence,* and *quantity proportionality* in figure 4 can in principle be compiled to one inference component deriving $\delta T_g > 0$ from $T_s > T_g$ immediately (called a *combined influence*).

Grouping composes the different behavioral states and transitions between these states. Actually, grouping results in a top-level view on the state transition graph generated by the simulator. All components belonging to the specification of a state are grouped, as well as all components belonging to a transition between two states. In the boiler-piston assembly, grouping will, among others, result in one component for the initial state of the system (water temperature is still constant), and a component for the transition to the next state (water temperature is increasing).

These three principles form the basis of the abstraction algorithm. Figure 6 provides an overview of the model generation and abstraction process.

Reasoning: Behavior Diagnosis

The hierarchical models as discussed in the previous section were designed in such a way that they adhere to the representational constraints of model-based diagnosis. Hence, techniques such as the general diagnostic engine (GDE, de Kleer and Williams 1987), successfully used for diagnosing digital circuits, can in principle be applied without modification.

Retrieval Components

The model introduced so far represents the necessary reasoning steps that make up the problem solving task. The "contents" of these reasoning steps, that is, the support knowledge that is used to make the inference, is represented as an additional input to the reasoning component. For instance, the "quantity correspondence" component shown in figure 7, inferring the amount of pres-

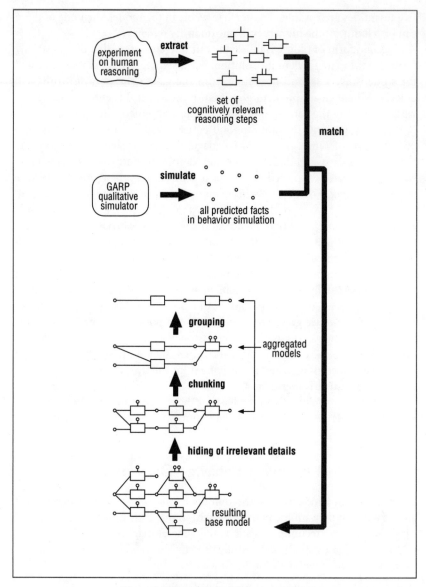

Figure 6. Hierarchical model construction.

sure P at the bottom of a container from the level L of a liquid column above it, has two inputs: the inequality $L > 0$ *and* the correspondence relation dir_corr(L, P). However, these inputs are of different nature: the first one is a given, something that the learner is supposed to see or read on the screen, and

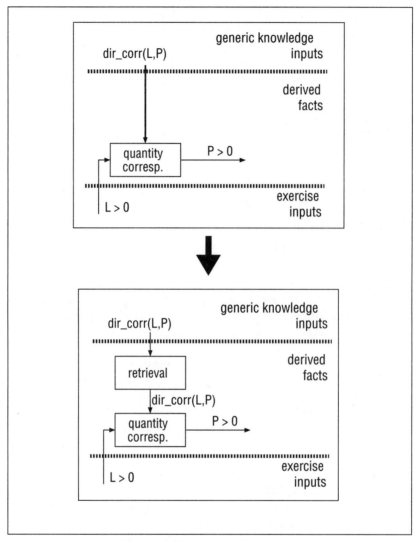

Figure 7. Adding a retrieval component.

hence it can be assumed to be known by the learner. The second input dir_corr(L, P) embodies knowledge that the learner may not (yet) master. From a diagnostic point of view, this difference is important; in model-based diagnosis, all inputs are assumed to be correct, and a diagnosis can only be in terms of deficient components. Hence, no diagnosis can be found that express-es the fact that the learner does not know the relation between level and pres-sure—that is, that the input dir_corr(L, P) is incorrect or missing. What we *can* express is that the learner does not know how to *apply* the relation in this situation by blaming the quantity correspondence component. Nevertheless, we want to be able to differentiate between not knowing domain knowledge and not being able to apply it in a certain inference.

We therefore introduce an additional component type called *retrieval*, as shown in figure 7. The retrieval component now models whether some fact is *known*, whereas the component it is linked to represents the *application* of the fact in an inference.

Retrieval components have one input and one output, and the output is equal to the input if the component is functioning correctly. Hence, "faulty" retrieval of a component represents the situation in which the learner does not know (cannot reproduce or "retrieve") an expression like dir_corr(L, P).

Consistency-Based Diagnosis

In GDE, the diagnostic process consists of three steps: conflict recognition, candidate generation, and candidate discrimination. Conflict recognition amounts to finding (minimal) sets of components that, if assumed to be working correctly, result in behavior that conflicts with the observations. From each of these sets (called *conflicts*), at least one component should be faulty for the overall behavior to be consistent with the observations. Candidate generation creates those sets of components (called *candidates*) that cover each conflict. Candidate discrimination is concerned with sequential diagnosis: given a set of observations, the set of possible diagnoses may not be satisfactory, and additional observations are then necessary to discriminate between the possible candidate diagnoses.

Within the STAR framework, the first two steps are applied without significant modification of the GDE approach. The third step however is different. The reason is that the nature of the components is significantly different in STAR subject matter models as compared to digital circuits. In a digital circuit, two components of the same type may behave according to the same rules, but are still physically distinct instances. In a subject matter model, this is not necessarily the case. One reasoning step applied correctly in one part of the model is very likely to behave correctly as well in another part: by their nature, different components of the same type are likely to fail collectively. A learner that does not know how to apply a *quantity correspondence* is likely to exhibit the same error (faulty *quantity correspondence*) at several places in the model. This different nature of knowledge models is exploited by the diagnostic algorithm: the failure probability of a set of instances of the same component type is defined to be equal to that of a single component. For example, a candidate diagnosis [IC_1, IC_2, IC_3, IC_4] consisting of four failing *quantity correspondence* components, has the same probability as a single component candidate [IC]. One way to view this is that we interpret a candidate at the level of *generic* inferences, instead of at the level of individual, *instantiated* reasoning steps (cf. The Model Representation section above): the first candidate can be interpreted as "unable to calculate quantity correspondence," which is at this level of interpretation a single fault. This interpretation does not hold for the single component candidate; this may well be an incidental instantiation error or slip.

The only exception is formed by components of the *retrieval* type: here, different instantiations are indeed independent operations because they refer to the retrieval of different knowledge facts. The error of not correctly "retrieving" the relation between level and pressure is usually not related to an incorrect retrieval of the negative influence of the flow rate on the volume. For retrieval components, it is possible to employ another heuristic in candidate discrimination: because most errors made in the experiment appeared to be caused by missing or confused domain knowledge, retrieval components can be assumed to have a higher a priori failure rate than inference components. Similarly, higher-level *decomposable* components have a higher a priori failure rate than individual base model components because these components incorporate a number of reasoning steps in the base model.

The STAR*light* Prototype

To exemplify the ideas presented in this chapter, we present a dialog between a learner and the prototype system we built to try out the ideas developed in the STAR framework. This prototype, called the STAR*light* system,[3] implements the subject matter model as discussed in the previous sections, the machinery for generating them and adding hierarchical structure, and a diagnostic reasoning component. To end up with a working educational system, we added "light" versions of functional components for learner modeling, discourse management, and didactical planning that were discussed earlier. The resulting system is capable of having simple dialogues with a learner who is answering multiple-choice questions. In the case of an answer provide by the learner that is inconsistent with the subject matter model, this dialog is directly based on the candidate diagnoses delivered by the diagnostic component; it dynamically structures the questions (i.e., probes) to be asked to arrive at a component it can explain (i.e., a satisfactory diagnosis). All explanations as well as questions are dynamically generated. In figure 8, a screen dump of the system is shown in which the learner is working on a so-called balance problem.

The subject matter problem here is to predict the behavior of a balance with containers on each balance arm. Both containers are assumed to be equal in weight. Depending on the difference in the mass of the liquid contained by the containers, one side of the balance may be heavier than the other. Therefore,

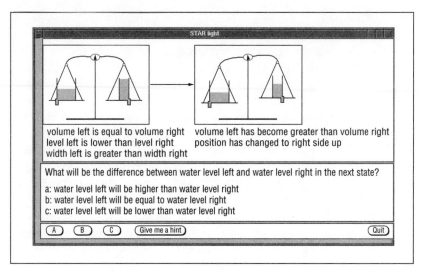

Figure 8. The STAR*light prototype system.*

after releasing it from the starting position the balance may change its position. Through outlets near the bottom of the containers the liquid gradually flows out of the containers. Depending on the pressure at the bottom, the flow rates from the two containers may be different. As a result, the balance may move to a different position because the difference in weight between the two balance arms changes. Eventually, when both containers are empty, the balance will reach an equilibrium.

We conducted a small set of test sessions with nine learners, four of them having some previous experience with structured behavior analysis, and five of them having little or no experience. To exemplify the diagnostic approach in the prototype system, we present a fragment of the interaction between one of the more advanced learners and the system. The indented phrases in italics are think-aloud remarks made by the learner. In this example, the initial behavior state of the balance (the leftmost situation depicted in figure 8) has just been presented to the learner. The dialogue starts when the learner is asked to predict the second state (the situation on the right in figure 8), which is at this moment not yet visible to the student.

1. What will be the difference between volume left and volume right in the next state?
2. *Hey, look, the volumes are equal. I didn't take notice of that.*
3. *Yes, I think they stay equal?*
4. **b: volume left will be equal to volume right.**
5. That's not correct.
6. Before we go on with the prediction, I would like to know what you think about the present situation.

7. Please answer the following question:
8. What do you know about the difference between the decrease in volume left and the decrease in volume right?
9. *Volume left decreasing slower than volume right?*
10. *No, at the same speed I would say.*
11. **b: volume left is decreasing at the same speed as volume right.**
12. That's not true.
13. Please answer the following question:
14. What do you know about the difference between outflow left and outflow right?
15. *Well I would say that the outflow is equal, but that is now when the pressure [incomprehensible].*
16. *Ah! Is that it? The outflow left is smaller.*
17. **c: outflow left is smaller than outflow right.**
18. That's right.
19. Please answer the following question:
20. Which quantity causes a change in volume?
21. *The outflow, or the pressure, yes the outflow.*
22. **c: outflow.**
23. That's right.
24. I think you don't fully understand the following:
25. The difference between outflow left and outflow right has a direct influence on the difference between the decrease in volume left and the decrease in volume right.
26. This means that because outflow left is smaller than outflow right volume left is decreasing slower than volume right.
27. Let's continue with the exercise where we left off.
28. *All right, interesting…*

The discussion displayed here starts out at a moment when the diagnostic component is not yet active. Because the learner answers the first question incorrectly (4), the diagnostic component is called with the observation "volume left is equal to volume right (instead of the correct "volume left is greater than volume right"). This observation indicates one data point in the model. The resulting diagnostic cycle yields a set of two candidate diagnoses, namely

1. "The learner does not understand the derivation of the inequality between the volume decrease left and right from the inequality between the levels"; a high level component in the hierarchical structure, representing a complex compound inference in one component.
2. "The learner does not know how to derive the change of the equality between the volumes into an inequality because the difference in their decrease rate"; this is actually an example of a primitive inference (a so-called *inequality termination*): an equality changes to an inequality in the next behavior state if the derivatives differ.

In order to distinguish between these two possible diagnoses, a *probe question* is asked (8). In this case, there is only one probe point that provides discriminating information for the two candidate diagnoses. The answer results in the first candidate diagnosis mentioned above being delivered as the "final" diagnosis. Because this diagnosis consists of a higher-level component, it is decomposed into a lower level model. Now the diagnostic engine is called again, delivering a new set of possible diagnoses, and determining a new probe point (14). This process is repeated one more time (20) until there is one unique diagnosis left to be explained (25-26).

Without going into detail about what exactly happens "under the hood,"[4] there is one thing that is immediately clear from this protocol excerpt: the dialog with the learner is directly and solely determined by the diagnostic component. One central assumption underlying the STAR framework is that diagnosis is not merely a tool that can be used in teaching, but that it is a requirement for educational systems to be effective in supporting the learner.

Impressions of the Test Sessions

Although the experimental setup and the number of subjects do not allow firm conclusions, the overall performance of the diagnostic component is satisfactory; with an average of three probe questions, the diagnostic component is capable of identifying one or more "faulty components" in the reasoning process of the learners. These faulty components represent those inferences that cannot have been performed correctly by the subject. An important observation made in the test sessions is the difference between novice learners and learners who do have some experience with behavior analysis. For the less experienced subjects, the explanations were not always understood or considered adequate. The model-based approach taken in the STAR framework seems to be best suited to support the "fine-tuning" of advanced learners' reasoning behavior, rather than to teach less experienced subjects the initial knowledge for a domain or task. This focus on fine-tuning is not motivated by educational benefits; it is obvious that in a full-fledged educational software system both functions are required. The explanation of individual reasoning steps may not be the optimal educational strategy for less experienced subjects because the context in which this explanation should be interpreted is not always sufficiently understood. Hence, clarification of the context and explanation at higher levels of abstraction is required.

The advanced subjects (four out of nine) were all positive about the questions asked, as well as the number of probes used. They also had the idea that the system did understand the errors they made, although they noticed that the system's last probes and/or final diagnosis were sometimes "outdated'; the diagnoses sometimes indicated a reasoning step that indeed was performed incorrectly given the observations, but that was already self-repaired by the subject.

...thought it was clear. Let's see, that was at a certain moment, these pressures I didn't take into account. What did he think again? That I didn't understand that *if* there is a pressure difference then the outflows are unequal as well. But *that* I did understand actually. I only didn't know that there was a difference in pressure. Or at least, I didn't realize that. Well, in fact it is right that I didn't think about this determining the difference.

Yes it was something I did already understand, but it's handy that it's confirmed then. So it's not like "Oh, I didn't know," but more like that I didn't think about it but that I had it in the back of my head that that may be the case.

In such cases, the final diagnosis served as a confirmation of this self-repair (see below). When no self-repair occurred, the advanced subjects considered the explanations mostly adequate; the explanations indeed indicated reasoning steps they did not yet understand.

Discussion

We have put forward our view on the important potential of using existing model-based reasoning techniques in educational systems. Here we will put this view in a broader perspective. First, we discuss the reasons why model-based reasoning has hardly been applied to educational systems to date. Second, we consider the educational philosophy underlying our approach. Finally, we present the roads ahead for further development of the framework.

The STAR Approach

One reason that to date these techniques have not been applied often is their computational complexity. The STAR framework applies hierarchical aggregation to help control this complexity. Self (1993), presents four additional reasons why a model-based approach may be problematic. Below, these problems are taken as a lead to set out the ideas underlying the STAR framework.

The Purpose of Diagnosis

For devices, the purpose of diagnosis is to enable faulty components to be mended or replaced. In education, the diagnostic engine should serve the educational goals, and hence its purpose is less evident than that of device diagnosis. We take a particular view on the role of diagnosis in educational systems. Instead of serving as a tool for the educational system, we consider the diagnostic component to play a central role in education. People learn from their errors, but often they are unable to exactly locate their errors, or fail to notice them at all. Therefore a detailed diagnosis of the learner's behavior is crucial for supporting learning. A major requirement for such diagnoses is that they are in terms of errors in the reasoning process, rather than in terms of the misconceptions that may cause these errors. Dillenbourg and Self (1992) make a good attempt at clarifying the distinction between errors in reasoning behavior and misconceptions. They reserve the term bug for errors at the behavior level, and misconceptions are situated at the conceptual level. As observed by Dillenbourg and Self, this distinction is usually not explicated in existing approaches to cognitive diagnosis and learner modeling. We employ the distinction to define the role of diagnosis in education: diagnosis should focus on identifying bugs at the behavioral level, in order to guide the learner in locating the errors they made. This view is supported by the results of the test sessions conducted with the STAR^{light} prototype. In a large number of the diagnostic sessions, the learners were not able to identify the error directly after it was made, while the sequence of probes following an observed error induced a self-repair. Consequently, the final diagnosis serves as a confirmation of this self-repair rather than as an indication of a necessary repair.

The Role of Diagnosis in Education

The comparison of educational diagnosis with model-based device diagnosis "unfortunately reinforces the outdated view that cognitive diagnosis should focus on knowledge deficiencies.... Current ideas about tutoring system design are moving away from knowledgeable systems remediating ignorant students towards environments which support students in managing their learning activities" (Self 1993). We choose to diagnose deficiencies in the learner's reasoning process. This approach is fully in line with the idea of supporting them in their learning activities. The educational system that we envisage does not aim at repairing knowledge deficiencies through remediation, but rather at pointing learners to problems in their reasoning behavior. Hence, the use of diagnosis is not restricted to knowledgeable systems remediating ignorant students. When defining diagnosis in terms of identifying a reasoning step that cannot have been applied correctly, this does not imply the type of one-way delivery teaching that is usually associated with focussing on knowledge deficiencies. This is demonstrated by the STAR framework, which is aimed at providing guidance in simulation-based interactive learning environments. Within a simulation environment, diagnosis can be used to guide the learning activities of the learner by stimulating self-repair and providing detailed feedback.

Defining "Device Models"

Given our view on the role of diagnosis in education, we need to answer the question of how the diagnostic models can be defined and constructed. A basic assumption underlying the model-based approach is that the diagnostic object, in our case the learner's reasoning behavior, can be represented in terms of context-independent inference components. This assumption is not commonly accepted. Moreover, even if this assumption is accepted, the problem is how to acquire the "device models" needed:

> We cannot assume that we, as diagnosticians, know what "circuits" are or should be in student's heads. ... In general, it is hard to see how this problem can be ad-

dressed without bringing in almost all the issues of knowledge representation in AI and cognitive science (Self 1993).

The STAR framework addresses this problem by defining the diagnostic models in terms of derivation graphs of problem solving behavior. In a derivation graph, each instantiated inference can be represented as a component. This way, the context-independence is guaranteed, because the behavior of each reasoning step is only determined by its inputs. The definition of diagnoses in terms of incorrect reasoning steps induces a specific view on the role of diagnosis in education.

Stability of the Diagnostic Model

According to Self, the occurrence of self-repair may hamper the transfer of model-based diagnostic techniques to educational systems. Because model-based diagnosis relies on the stability of the model and the observations during a diagnostic session, this complicates a formal treatment of model-based diagnosis in education. Indeed, we cannot guarantee the correctness of the diagnostic process to the same degree as this can be done in device diagnosis. On the other hand, the consequences of an incorrect diagnosis are not as problematic in education as they are in device diagnosis, especially when this incorrect diagnosis is the result of self-repair: we may sometimes explain an error that was just discovered by the learner. Two features of the STAR framework are particularly important with respect to instabilities in the learner's behavior. Firstly, the size of the diagnostic models is relatively small as a result of the hierarchical structuring mechanisms employed. This minimizes the impact of instabilities in the learner's problem solving behavior on the diagnostic performance. Secondly, the diagnostic component can be reset as soon as one explanation has been given; no effort has to be made to ensure that all errors made are dealt with. Although not dictated by the framework, this is a reasonable choice because only one thing can be explained at a time, and explanations are assumed to change the learner's behavior, if not already changed by self-repair.

The STAR Framework in an Educational Context

People can learn from their errors. The value of learning from errors has been recognized in influential educational philosophies such as Socratic tutoring (Stevens and Collins 1977, Collins and Stevens 1980) and LOGO (Papert 1980). The principle also plays an important role in contemporary discovery or explorative learning environments (cf. van der Hulst 1996). By means of exploration and experimentation, a learner can develop models of the subject matter knowledge involved. Errors can be a valuable aid in adjusting and refining the models developed by the learner. Knowledgeable support of the learner's trial-and-error behavior can help the learner to learn from his or her errors in an effective and efficient way.

An emphasis on learning from errors requires a view on education that is not commonly practiced by human teachers; they appear to rely mainly on pattern recognition on the basis of known misconceptions, rather than on detailed diagnostic search (cf. Breuker 1990, Kamsteeg 1994). On the one hand, this is influenced by traditional educational views on errors: "School teaches that errors are bad; the last thing one wants to do is to pore over them, dwell on them, or think about them" (Papert 1980). But more importantly, detailed structured diagnosis is often computationally infeasible for human teachers.

Compared to model-based diagnosis of reasoning behavior, diagnosis on the basis of bug catalogues is not merely another technique to arrive at the same result. Instead, the use of pre-stored bugs involves a significantly different approach to educational guidance: in this case, the diagnostic activity is aimed at matching known misconceptions that may explain the errors made. As a result, diagnosis is often heuristic and shallow, and does therefore not play a decisive role in the teaching process. A focus on learning from errors as supported by the STAR framework yields a different teaching style: instead of directly mapping errors on misconceptions to be remediated, zooming in on the specific incorrect reasoning step causing the error guides the learner in discovering this error and self-repairing it.

Summarizing, the way in which the STAR framework provides support is one that is generally difficult or even impossible for human teachers. In the STAR approach, every error in the learner's problem solving process can be traced back to a reasoning step that cannot have been applied correctly given the observations. The probing mechanism accounts for a structured sequence of questions that, as a side effect, will stimulate the learner's self-repair behavior. The educational methodology following from this approach is difficult if not impossible to realize with other means than knowledge-based educational systems. The diagnostic task as it is defined in the STAR framework is not easily performed by human teachers.

Extension of the STAR Framework: Where to Go Next

The presentation of the STAR framework in this chapter focused on subject matter modeling and behavior diagnosis. Recalling the conceptual architecture in figure 2, other functional components such as discourse management and didactic planning leave a lot of interesting possibilities for further development, some of which were touched upon previously.

The development of the STAR framework incorporated a number of design decisions. These decisions were mainly based on the aims of maximizing generality and reuse of existing model-based diagnosis techniques. As a result, the diagnostic engine is applicable to every model that can be expressed in terms of the component-connection representation. This generality is one of its main features, and hence every extension to the diagnostic engine should be judged as to whether it constrains this generality. We distinguish two main types of extensions: *domain-specific extensions* and *general design extensions*.

Domain-Specific Extensions

Possible extensions to the STAR framework are the use of a priori fault probabilities and domain-specific fault models. Both extensions require modification of the diagnostic engine, but these modifications are domain-independent. The determination of a priori fault probabilities and the definition of fault models are domain-specific, and hence sacrifice generality: the subject matter models can no longer be generated from a given simulation model alone. Nevertheless, the use of fault models or probabilities can increase the effectiveness of the diagnostic process. This is demonstrated by the results of the test sessions with the STAR^{light} prototype. In almost all probe sequences that included a question on the derivation of the pressure at the bottom from the level of the water column, there was also a probe question about the derivation of the flow rate from the pressure at the bottom. Invariably, the former derivation was the problematic one: the relation between level and pressure is often unknown. Hence, a higher a priori fault probability for this relation may in these cases avoid one probe question. Extending the STAR framework with the possibility for using fault models and probabilities seems a fruitful direction for further development.

General Design Extensions

The second type of extension refers to modifications to the design of the diagnostic engine that minimally affect its generality. One example of a general design extension is the enlargement of the scope of the reasoning covered by the base model. Besides quantity manipulation, another important subtask in prediction is the selection of the right knowledge given the description of the problem. From an educational point of view, the interpretation of some structural constellation in terms of physics concepts deserves particular attention: novice learners have great difficulties in mapping a real-world situation onto the relevant physics concepts (Jansweijer et al. 1986). For instance, conceiving a bicycle pump and a tire together as "one container closed by a piston" is not obvious. In qualitative reasoning terms, doing this amounts to the selection and combination of model fragments from the library to build a model for a given scenario. The reasoning involved in this modeling process may also be incorporated in the base model. In de Koning et al. (1994), an initial analysis is presented of the reasoning knowledge involved in the prediction task, including the modeling process. Additional (experimental) research will be needed to define the inferences involved in this modeling process in sufficient detail.

Another possible extension is to provide not only models and (hence) support for reasoning at the level of individual inferences, but also for *task-level* reasoning. The STAR framework models the domain knowledge and the reasoning steps as used in predicting the behavior of a system, but no meta level representation of this prediction process is provided yet. That is, it can be used to support an interaction about the actual prediction of behavior, but not about the "activity" of prediction. This can be accomplished by modeling the task-level knowledge of (qualitative) prediction, as laid out in Bredeweg (1992 and 1993), and transforming this to the component-connection representation in a similar way as was done for the inference level.

A third example of a design extension, related to the previous, is to enlarge the scope of the aggregation process by including aggregation over states. In the research reported, we focussed on aggregation within states to support behavior diagnosis and other educational functions. Extending the STAR framework with additional principles for aggregating over states may prove useful when the subject matter model is based on a simulation containing a very large number of states. The ideas about abstraction developed in qualitative reasoning may be exploited to realize such aggregations.

Finally, other strategies than aggregation can be employed to focus the educational process. One interesting extension is to allow the system to focus on one particular quantity of the device over the entire simulation. In qualitative reasoning, this is referred to as *histories* (Hayes 1979). Focussing on one quantity may be employed in explanation as well as diagnostic probing. In terms of the models defined in the STAR framework, the use of histories amounts to focussing on specific paths through the model.

Application

The STAR^{light} prototype system is clearly not intended to be a full-fledged educational environment. We envisage the application of the STAR framework in interactive learning environments based on (qualitative) simulations. The educational goals of such systems may vary from teaching elementary physics principles to high school students to supporting people in learning to design, monitor, or diagnose complex artifacts. The hierarchical subject matter models and the diagnostic engine can be employed to structure the educational support that the learner may need in reasoning about the simulated behavior. This support is not necessarily only in terms of questions and answers. For instance, when the simulation is graphically visualized, support can be given by highlighting certain objects or quantities that are considered to be important for the learner at that moment. By the same token, the diagnostic engine can use the learner's manipulations of the simulation as observations.

An important direction of further research that goes along with applying the STAR framework in real world educational systems is the generation of new scenarios for simulation. Switching to another simulation can serve different didactic goals, such as introducing a new subject or providing another view on a problematic concept. Especially the latter can benefit from existing theories on analogy reasoning, as for instance developed in the Structure Mapping Theory (Gentner 1983).

Conclusions

Model-based reasoning has a large potential for educational systems. We presented a framework for simulation-based educational systems that exploits existing representations and techniques from, in particular, qualitative reasoning and model-based diagnosis. The main contribution of this framework is that it addresses and alleviates the inevitable tension between individualization of the interaction on the one hand and domain specificity and development costs on the other. Furthermore, the (re)use of model-based reasoning techniques dictates a very careful and precise specification of the models and functional components in the educational system. The key insights resulting from this specification are the following:

1. The primitive reasoning steps as used by learners and human teachers when communicating about system behavior can be generated on the basis of qualitative simulation models.
2. The complexity problems attached to detailed subject matter modeling can be alleviated by automatically added hierarchical structure.
3. There is a significant difference between global/long term and local/short term learner modeling. The former is concerned with *learner model management,* the latter with *(problem solving) behavior diagnosis.*
4. Diagnosis of learner behavior is the core functionality underlying individualized interaction.
5. The aim of diagnosis of learner behavior, as we define it, is not to construct mental models of a learner, but to find those individual reasoning steps in the learner's problem solving process that cannot have been applied correctly given the observations.

We developed and implemented techniques for automatic subject matter modeling, hierarchical structuring, and behavior diagnosis. Existing qualitative simulators and diagnostic algorithms are employed in the framework with only minor adaptations. The STAR^{light} prototype system that was developed to test drive the diagnostic component is capable of maintaining a dialog based on the results of local diagnosis of the learner's problem solving behavior.

The STAR framework and the STAR^{light} prototype provide a test bed for developing other model-based functional components for educational systems. The articulate subject matter models and the diagnostic engine can and should be supplemented with educational functions such as model-based explanation and learner modeling. On the basis of our research so far, we are convinced that the STAR framework can serve as a solid basis for a large variety of educational systems.

Notes

1. In the original (Forbus 1984) paper, this same pos_prop(L, P) relation was defined as $P \mu Q + L$.

2. Assuming, obviously, that the simulator delivers a correct prediction of behavior.

3. The acronym STAR stands for "system for teaching about reasoning." The prototype implements hierarchical subject matter model generation and the diagnostic function of the STAR system in detail, and the other components necessary for its operation in a "light" version—hence the name STAR^{light}.

4. For an extensive discussion of the working of the prototype and the tryout sessions, see (de Koning and Bredeweg 1997, de Koning et al. 1997).

Chapter Ten

The Case for Considering Cultural Entailments and Genres of Attachment in the Design of Educational Technologies

Lisa M. Bouillion and Louis M. Gomez

This chapter is different from others in this book in that it does not focus directly on the use of smart technologies in education. Rather, it raises a set of considerations we believe are necessary if technological innovations are to be successful in the classroom. These hold for any innovative educational technologies, including those based on computers.

There has been widespread introduction of computers into the schools in recent years, with an increase in Internet access from thirty-five percent of schools in 1994 to eighty-nine percent of schools in 1998 (National Center for Education Statistics 1999). Such radical changes lead to new assumptions about possibilities for instructional practice, such as breaking down the wall between schools and the outside world. Science curricula, for example, can leverage new technologies to create opportunities for students to collect and compare data from peers across the country (e.g., Songer 1996), communicate with and receive guidance from scientist mentors (e.g., O'Neill and Gomez 1998), or collaborate with out-of-school communities in designing solutions to science-related problems (e.g., Bouillion, Gomez, and Williams 1999).

While the technology opens up new possibilities, we need to rethink how these new forms of collaboration fit with current practices. Here, we will rethink a range of questions relating to the ways in which new artifacts are used differently in different contexts. We argue that design, both of the artifacts themselves and of the implementation of technological artifacts, is not a neutral activity. As a function of design, artifacts come with a set of cultural entailments, that is, embodied characteristics that represent the goals, expectations, histories, values and practices associated with a particular community of practice (Lave and Wenger 1991). The tacit nature of cultural entailments has led designers and implementers often to overlook the ways in which these entailments shape design and innovation. Highlighting the role cultural entailments play in the design and implementation process leads us to address the fit of the cultural entailments of a technological innovation with the cultural entailments of a community of practice.

We argue that the possible areas of conflict between the cultural entailments of designed artifacts and communities of practice may be mediated if they are "made visible" to both designers and practitioners (Suchman 1995). Making cultural entailments visible may allow designers to strategically support implementation "fit" in targeted settings by bringing to awareness the ways history, goals, experiences, and practices of a particular community can be accommodated or altered through the enactment of the innovation. Our focus is on the study of enactment itself. We want to see how these factors, what we refer to as cultural entailments, become important in the "doing" or use of an innovation. Our overarching goal is to understand how to use enactment information of this sort as a feedback mechanism in design. The aim, ultimately, is that diversity in cultural entailments across communities of practice will not be a roadblock to the use of innovations.

We will explore the issue of cultural entailments through two case studies of enactment of a curricular innovation we call "mutual benefit partnerships" (MBPs) (Radinsky, Bouillion, Lento, and Gomez in press; Radinsky et al. 1998). This analysis will demonstrate the way in which processes of enactment and adaptation make visible the cultural entailments in both the innovation and context of implementation. We will follow this analysis with a consideration of how genres, as an example of what Brown and Duguid (1994) call "border resources," can help users of innovations determine what conventions are at play so that they can respond in ways that satisfy both internal (i.e., designer) and external (i.e., local context) demands. Together, these two lenses (cultural entailments and genres) provide both micro and more macro perspectives on understanding the role of context in artifact design and use. We claim that taken together, making visible cultural entailments and leveraging genres of socially shared conventions will make it easier to successfully situate innovations in diverse communities of practice.

Cultural Entailments in Designed Artifacts

Culture and context are increasingly viewed as critical to understanding learning processes. In particular, the framework of situated cognition (Brown, Collins, and Duguid 1989), grounded in cultural-historical research (e.g., Cole and Engestrom 1993; Engestrom 1987; Luria 1928, 1932; Vygotsky 1929, 1960; Wertsch 1985), advances the concept of tool mediation, wherein tools and artifacts are the media through which culture is both created and sustained. This line of research challenges the possibility of "neutral" innovations, arguing that cultural biases, goals, and practices are a necessary accompaniment to artifacts such as technology, curriculum, and instructional practice (e.g., Anyon 1981; Apple 1979). Designers of learning innovations, however, seldom consider how their own cultural entailments will be reflected in the designed artifact. This lack of awareness increases the possibility of a mismatch between the cultural entailments of an artifact and the community targeted for use of that innovation, which in turn may explain observations of learning "failure" and disengagement (e.g., Delpit 1995; Freire and Macedo 1987).

Several recent research projects consider the strategic use of these cultural entailments as resources for teaching and learning. For example, Lee's work in cultural modeling (1995) uses the cultural discourse pattern of "signifying" in African American communities to help students learn formal literary analysis, while Everyday Math (LoCicero, Fuson, and Allexaht-Snider 1999; Fuson, De La Cruz, Smith, Lo Cicero, Hudson, Ron, and Steeby 2000) and the Algebra Project (Moses, Kamii, Swap, and Howard 1989) leverage students' out-of-school experiences to support the learning of math. Pinkard (1998) and Hooper (1996) utilize cultural resources in the design of technology-supported learning environments. The Funds of Knowledge Project (Moll and Greenberg 1990; Moll, Tapia and Whitmore 1993) draws attention to the knowledge and skills found in predominately Mexican, working-class communities in Tucson, Arizona to improve classroom teaching, and Lee (1999) considers the role of students' cultural "world views" in the teaching and learning of science.

While necessary, these efforts to locate and leverage the cultural resources of diverse communities of practice is insufficient to come to grips with the cultural entailments involved in the design and implementation processes. We need to identify explicitly the cultural dimension of designed artifacts by making clear the assumptions, frames of reference, goals and conventions embedded in designed artifacts. Further, we need to make visible the process through which different communities of practice view and respond to those embedded aspects in relation to their local context. We will explore these issues through two case studies of enactment of a curricular innovation we call "mutual benefit partnerships" (MBP).

In one case study of an MBP project, Garfield Junion High School,[1] we will argue there was a close match between the cultural entailments of the design and those of the school, leaving the nature of those entailments implicit and unchallenged. In the other case study, Wheaton Elementary School, the teachers indicated they felt many of the assumptions embedded in the MBP design-did not fit with their own, and it was through the processes of negotiation and adaptation that the cultural entailments in the artifact were clarified. The direct consequence of this is that the data we report for Garfield is almost necessarily less rich in making visible cultural entailments than in the Wheaton case. However, we do not believe this needs to be the case. We will argue that a sensitivity to and understanding of the expression of cultural entailments in enactment make it possible to study their impact in a more planful way from the beginning of an innovation's introduction into a community of practice. We will return to this idea when we make suggestions for future research in the spirit of arguments made here.

Through an analysis of cultural entailments in these two cases, we differentiate between those features of MBP that constitute the "center," those that are considered essential and expected to be common across contexts, and those at the "periphery," which represent variations in use (Brown and Duguid 1994). We follow this analysis with a discussion of how Brown and Duguid's notion of "genres" can be used to invoke socially shared practices that bridge the center-periphery divide.

Two Case Studies:
An Analysis of Cultural Entailments Made Visible

Mutual benefit partnerships (MBPs) bring together classroom and out-of-school communities to investigate and solve real world problems.[2] The MBP consortium includes nine school districts across Illinois, Northwestern University, Western Illinois University, Argonne National Laboratories and the Illinois State Board of Education. The diverse participating school districts are in rural, urban, and suburban contexts, spanning grade levels K-12, and represent Mexican-American, African-American, and European-American classrooms and communities. All of the schools were selected because they serve majority numbers of students labeled as "disadvantaged" according to numbers of students receiving free lunches.

The MBP design has evolved and continues to evolve through an iterative process of collaboration among the consortium participants. While most of the nine school districts have now enacted four iterations of the design, the two case studies we present here are from the first year of implementation. At the beginning of that first year, mutual benefit partnerships were broadly defined by four design elements:

   1. Open-ended, real-world problems: Projects are organized around existing

problems that are of interest to the partnering communities and serve as anchors around which curricular activity is organized;

2. School-business-community partnerships: Partnerships are founded on the principles of mutual benefit and enlightened self-interest. These projects help businesses conduct work related to their needs, help schools meet their curricular goals, and help students understand not only what skills are required in nonschool communities, but why certain academic skills are meaningful and relevant in those contexts;

3. Problem-based learning: Problems are investigated by classroom communities in collaboration with the partner organizations. These investigations include a research stage (e.g., understanding the problem) as well as a solution development stage;

4. Final product or presentation: All projects include a culminating activity in which students share their recommendations, findings, and/or product solutions with the partner organization.

Together, these four elements represented the idealized "center" of the MBP design. We analyze how the details of these features were interpreted and enacted differently in two schools, making visible the cultural entailments in the design and in the targeted community of use. We will then discuss how these case studies of enactment helped us to reconsider the borders of the innovation and think about how to support enactment in diverse contexts. We chose these two cases to contrast how one MBP project confirmed many of our early design assumptions while the other case challenged these same assumptions. This case contrast serves to provide a sharper focus on the cultural entailments of the design process.

The first case study was conducted at Garfield Junior High, a 6–8 school in a predominately European-American neighborhood in a Chicago suburb. Garfield developed an MBP project, which was coplanned and facilitated by an interdisciplinary team of seventh-grade teachers and the school's media center specialist. These five teachers (representing science, math, English, social studies and reading specialties) teach the same group of 150 students and integrated the project activity across all their subject areas. The second case study was conducted at Wheaton Elementary a K–6 school in a predominately Mexican-American neighborhood near downtown Chicago. This study took place during the 1996–97 academic year, and involved an MBP project that was coplanned and facilitated by two fifth-grade classroom teachers (responsible for teaching all subjects except science, gym and music), their students, the school's science teacher, and an English-as-a-second-language (ESL) instructor who split her time between the two participating classrooms.

Both case studies use a "design experiment" research methodology (Brown 1992) in which the first author played the role of coparticipant and codesigner of the MBP projects. A variety of data was collected as a part of these case studies. Regularly scheduled teacher planning meetings were attended, audio taped, and transcribed. Classroom activity was observed 2-3 times per week over the course of the MBP projects, during which field notes were taken and transcribed. Pre- and postinterviews were conducted with teachers and students, and a variety of artifacts were collected including, e-mail correspondence, teacher-designed instructional tools and examples of student work.

Cultural Entailments of Real-World Problems

A major premise of the mutual benefit partnership design is that students are capable of contributing products of value to nonschool communities and that the associated experiences provide valuable learning opportunities. The language used in the original proposal for MBP, and by the designers[3] in their support of first-year implementation efforts, implied a model in which students would participate in the "reality of work beyond the classroom" as consultants to out-of-school organizations.

> Much too often, classroom learning is *disconnected from the problems faced by professionals in the world beyond school.* Students feel the disconnection. They often ask questions like "Why are we learning this?" We envision classrooms where the tasks and projects that teachers and students are engaged in *are tightly coupled to the reality of work beyond the classroom.* This project, Reality Based Learning, envisions a network of schools in which students use their knowledge and technology skills to address real world problems, generated through an active collaboration of business, government, community, higher education, elementary and secondary schools and parents. (Technology Challenge Grant Proposal, 1996)[4]

The definition of *real world problem* in this vision is implied as those which are "faced by professionals in the world beyond school." In this scenario, it was assumed that the "client" organizations would bring their real world problem to students for consulting services. During their 1997–1998 MBP project, the Garfield teachers went out in search of organizations within their own community who would be interested in partnering with them and their students around a real world problem. Through this informal networking, one of the teachers was referred to the local chapter of United Way. United Way board members and the team of Garfield teachers agreed to construct a project around United Way's problem, which was that the local community had little awareness of the services provided by their organization. United Way board members stressed two messages in their presentation to Garfield students: first, that this is "serious business" because United Way really needs a solution to this problem; and second, that while United Way board members would be available to help out and lend their expertise, the students were the ones expected to do the work. The United Way board president said:

> The problem is awareness. We have problems in our community that we can't turn away from and United Way has all these agencies that can help. ... So *this is serious business.* (...)It's important that when you encounter a problem that you

try to work through it, but when you're banging your head against the wall, we'll be ready to jump in and make some suggestions.... We've got probably hundreds of years of experience on the board of directors.... *So we intend to be very actively involved, because this is important to us and we want to make sure it goes right. [But] you're going to do the work.* (kick-off meeting, 10-2-97)

Both members of the United Way board and Garfield teachers emphasized the theme of "serious business" throughout the project. The Garfield teachers indicated a belief that students would be motivated by high expectations, an opportunity to participate in the "adult world," and a chance to impress and perform well for adults other than their teachers.

I think the energy comes from that the kids, in a very real sense, become very connected with what they're doing because *they have to impress someone,* and it's not just the teacher who's always grading whatever they hand in. So, after a while, they really don't feel the need to impress me anymore, you know, and so when it's an outside source, then that gives them energy (preinterview, 9-30-97).

The kids were able to see these people and that *there were people out there that they were working for.* It wasn't just what we were saying. It gives the kids the ownership of it (DK Postinterview, 2-5-98).

The project called on Garfield students to design and administer a survey of community awareness about United Way. Students were then to brainstorm different awareness building strategies. Based on these ideas, ten development teams were organized to design products including, a web page, a flyer, a logo/mascot, a magnet, a restaurant tray liner, a celebrity night, a drama performance, a song/commercial, and a service event. In addition, a student management team was formed to facilitate the collaboration across these teams and with the United Way partner representatives. Once each of the teams had developed and delivered its product, the awareness survey was re-administered within the community as a post measure. In conclusion, a group of students representing all the teams prepared and gave an electronic slide presentation on their findings at a United Way board meeting.

Garfield students reported in postinterviews that they were indeed motivated to work on this project. They felt like this was the real world and that they were doing something that mattered. In talking about their sense of the purpose regarding this kind of project, students' comments provide insight to their perspective on and understanding of the "real world." For these predominately white middle class seventh graders growing up in a suburban community, there was talk of this project experience preparing them for futures that included college, professional jobs and the expectations and responsibilities that go along with those new adult roles.

The purpose that they told us was to inform people about United Way. But the purpose of RBL was um to get us involved in real world problems and *what it's like in the real world, but also kind a what its going to be like in college* because you have less dependency, the teachers don't like guide you.

RBL was I think a different way of teaching us *how its going to be ... like when we're grown up.*

To prepare us for when we're adults.

I thought it was like *preparing you for a job*, and working with other people to get something done in a certain time limit or you're fired.

(Excerpts from student postproject focus group, 2-13-98.)

These data suggest cultural entailments in their appeal to standard corporate organizations of work and related experiences in the Garfield community. That is, the adults in this community predominately work in professional (versus service) jobs and represent sources of expertise and knowledge related to those fields. The history and experience of Garfield members support enculturation and training as legitimate forms of preparation to participate in those workplace communities. Shaped by these cultural entailments, the Garfield vision for real world is focused on socialization and exposure to prepare students to be successful participants in the adult professional workplace.

A Contrasting Case

The Wheaton teachers shared the aspirations of the Garfield teachers to connect students to the world beyond school and to have students see that their actions have consequences beyond the classroom. However, these teachers differed in how they thought about the "real world" and the structures for connecting to that world that would support the learning goals and needs of their students. These differences were negotiated through the collaborative design process and challenged us to reconsider our assumptions about the mutual benefit partnership design. An analysis of that process helps to make visible the way in which cultural entailments of the Wheaton context played a role in how the teachers made sense of the MBP design and implemented a project that would be successful and meaningful for their students.

Early in the first year, the Wheaton teachers asked questions and expressed concerns that challenged the definition of "real world" described in the original proposal and represented in the MBP project designed with the Grissom teachers. This prompted us to consider more explicitly the assumptions behind our design rationale. For example, they asked:

Who creates/cocreates the problem-based curriculum?

What role will children have in the creations of the PBL?

Children ownership?

Will the professionals talk down to or work at the level of the children?

What will the children get out it? (E-mail, 1-16-97.)

Wheaton teachers were particularly concerned that their students would be exploited by the outside business organization. There was a clear sense from the Wheaton teachers that they were working in a context in which the children they teach face challenges that are intimately connected with the experience of growing up in an urban setting, being poor and speaking English as a second language.

> When we thought of [reality based learning], our concern was that some company was going to come in and exploit our children and then we were going to have to do this project that was very top-down. And that doesn't work within our classrooms because we have to include much of what they're interested in. *We work with a community that's oppressed....* Our kids deal with gangs and violence, I don't want to say daily but it's on fairly regular basis. (RBL videotape, 1997.)

> Our audience is our community, an inner city neighborhood facing the hurdles of poverty, gangs, second language acquisition and racism. (Wheaton School website.)[5]

In this community the adults predominately work in labor and service jobs and represent sources of expertise and knowledge related to those fields. Many of the families also come from agricultural traditions in rural Mexico. The history and experience of Wheaton community members is that racism, poverty and language isolation are barriers to successful participation in professional workplace communities. Shaped by these cultural entailments, the Wheaton vision for real world and the goal for its students is to empower and "give voice" to students so that they can overcome oppression and participate in society.

Toward this goal, the Wheaton teachers decided that the real world problem should come from the students rather than an outside organization, thus broadening the realm of real world problems to include those not only faced by professionals in the worlds of work, but also those of students and their families in the world of their community. The problem identified by the Wheaton students was the pollution of and illegal trash dumping on a portion of the banks of the Chicago River located near their school. Outside organizations (described as partners), such as the Friends of the Chicago River, were brought in to teach students about the river and about the environment. The students then engaged in a number of activities, which evolved from classroom discussions and brainstorming sessions. Students wrote letters to the landowner asking for removal of the debris, they created and performed a play for the community to educate them about the environment, and they collected data on the river's water quality and the point source of pollution, which was presented at a local hearing on restoration of the river. These, as well as a number of other activities, eventually led to the landowner bringing in bulldozers to remove the trash from that portion of the riverbank, and agreeing to lease the property for development as a neighborhood "green space."

The teachers described the audience for this project as the students and the neighborhood community at large, rather than a particular business or community organization. The teachers emphasized that this process was "student driven," that it emerged from the students' discoveries and discussions in a way that might have been constrained if forced to fit under the needs of a particular "client" organization.

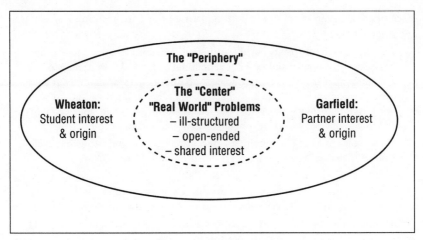

Figure 1. The center periphery divide.

...this *organic process* of students brainstorming solutions, identifying the problem and searching for a client comes from the students. This is [a] *student driven [project]* with plenty of room to negotiate with our students.... The river project has extended its [project] boundaries (in a number of directions). Though I know these things cannot all be directly connected back to "the client" I truly believe the theme, river, along with the problem provides so many teachable opportunities. *Trying to make it all fit under the needs of the client seems confining*...this is a multipurpose activity which the client may or may not of had us explore. (E-mail, 3-24-97.)

Prior to the Wheaton case, we had assumed real world problems were at the core of the mutual benefit partnership design without explicitly considering how our own biases and perspectives (i.e., cultural entailments) on what real world meant got represented in the design (e.g., client/consultant language). The Wheaton teachers' adaptation of MBP to fit their own cultural entailments (i.e., goals and practices) challenged us to redefine the border between the core and periphery of this design feature. This redefinition has taken place over the three years since this case and has involved the participants from all nine school districts implementing the MBP design. Together we have asked and discussed: What counts as a real world problem?, What variations are possible and still recognizable as MBP? Our experience with these and similar MBP implementations has led us to decide that what defines an MBP problem at the core is that it be open-ended (unsolved), ill-structured (multiple solutions), and of interest to all participants. At the periphery, the origin of the problem and what constitutes "interest" in the problem are defined at the local level (see figure 1).[6]

Cultural Entailments of Other Aspects of MBPs

Just as in the case of "real world" problems, the Garfield and Wheaton teachers differed in their adaptation of the other three MBP design features (partnerships, problem based learning, and products of mutual benefit) as mediated by the cultural entailments of each of their local contexts. In the case of partnering with an out-of-school community, the Garfield the teachers adopted the language in the original MBP proposal, referring to their partner organization as the "client" and their students as the "consultants." The focus was on the outside organization being a "mentor" and source of information so that the students could better develop a solution that would meet the partner's needs.

> They [the outside organization] should be a mentor—be assessable so the students can talk to them and get information from them. They're presenting a problem and they're a source for the students and it's an audience that the students are going to be presenting to (preproject teacher focus group, 9-30-97).

As described earlier, the Garfield teachers felt that giving students an opportunity to work on a task that was associated with an outside agency gave more legitimacy, and thus student ownership, to the project. This is in line with the cultural entailment of expecting professional workplace communities to be the ones to set the standard for workplace preparation.

> The kids were able to see these people and that there were *people out there that they were working for*. It wasn't just what we [the teachers] were saying. It gives the kids the ownership of it. (D. N. postinterview, 2-5-98.)
>
> I think the energy comes from that the kids, in a very real sense, become very connected with what they're doing because *they have to impress someone*, and it's not just the teacher who's always grading whatever they hand in. So, after a while, they really don't feel the need to impress me anymore, you know, and so when it's an outside source, then that gives them energy (preproject teacher focus group, 9-30-97).

In contrast, the Wheaton teachers described the role of their partners being to "uplift" their students, to help them to become "agents of change," and to help them find a "power place within this society."

> Our partners are the agencies, educational establishments and businesses that will *uplift and empower our students* so that they, the children are able to work as *agents of change* within the community. (Wheaton School website.)
>
> Our goals [were]...to have them do something that would create a sense of community and a sense of empowerment...to *show them that small voices can be heard* (postinterview, 6-17-97).
>
> *It's about empowerment.* It's about providing our kids with skills that will not only help them academically [but it also] motivates our kids and gives them a reason to learn. (RBL videotape, 1997.)
>
> Students will establish a *positive sense of themselves, a power place within this society*, and sense of citizenship by providing community service. (Wheaton School website.)

In line with the different cultural entailments of these two contexts, the teachers at Garfield and Wheaton focused on different classroom structures and instructional strategies to support students' problem-based learning activity. At both schools, teachers used their MBP activities to help students learn targeted curricular material. For example, Garfield students learned key math concepts as they analyzed the results of their survey and Wheaton students learned key science concepts as they explored the sources of pollution along the riverbank. At Garfield, however, the path of investigation, questions considered, and resources used were predominately structured by partner relevant concerns, as the emphasis was on solving the outside partner's problem. The focus at Garfield was on the development of workplace valued expertise (i.e., marketing, research), in line with a school-to-work orientation.

At Wheaton, the path of investigation stemmed from and was shaped by student questions and interests. Although workplace expertise was leveraged in this case also (i.e., environmental science, governmental lobbying), the teachers' primary goal was to affirm and build on the experiences and prior knowledge that students brought to school from their families and community. These teachers pointed out that many of their students come from families in which the parents from Mexico "have extensive knowledge of the earth." And although there are few "green spaces" in this Chicago neighborhood where students might themselves have personal knowledge of the earth, most families have a variety of plants in their homes that are used for cooking or medicinal purposes. The Wheaton teachers structured the problem based learning activity of their MBP project to build on these kinds of student knowledge and experience. The Garfield teachers did not talk about explicitly leveraging students' "home" knowledge, except in terms of everyday experience. That everyday experience in the Garfield context represents what Delpit (1995) calls the "culture of power," including the tacit rules and conventions set as the standard by the dominant culture in society.

In both the Wheaton and Garfield cases there is strong evidence to suggest the outcomes of the projects were of mutual benefit to all participants. This is essential as an underlying assumption to the mutual benefit partnership design in that distributed expertise is most effectively leveraged in a context in which all parties feel a significant investment in the process, and further, that this investment is in part influenced by the sense that all parties will get something of value out of the process. What constitutes "benefit," however, is largely defined by local conditions. Students at Garfield appeared motivated to work for an outside professional community that would take them seriously and help prepare them for future careers. Students at Wheaton appeared motivated to work on a problem that would directly affect and improve the conditions in their lives and those of their neighbors.

The teachers in both cases felt these projects helped them to meet curricular objectives in a more applied and meaningful context. Additionally, both the

Garfield and Wheaton partner organizations indicated a perceived value in the product of students' work. Garfield's partner, United Way, felt students succeeded in raising awareness about their organization in the local community in ways that they might not have been able to do themselves, particularly by representing a "youth" perspective. United Way subsequently invited the Garfield team of students and teachers to present their project at the National United Way Conference and created a new "student" position on their board of directors to ensure a youth perspective on future efforts.

According to the scientists at Friends of the Chicago River, one of the key things that the Wheaton students brought to the process was a knowledge of and connection to the community members. Restoration activities are in large part about building awareness, creating consensus, and motivating action. In the community surrounding the targeted riverbank, the scientists from this organization were likely to face tremendous barriers in their restoration efforts as a product of both language barriers and a lack of legitimacy or trust within the community. The Wheaton students used their Spanish and English language skills to bring together and create a bridge between the partner organization and the community helping to create a "green space" in their neighborhood.

Genres of Attachment: Bridging the Center-Periphery Divide

These two cases exemplify a negotiation of artifact and context, differentiating what Brown and Duguid (1994) identify as the center and periphery of artifacts. Faced with differential interpretation and use of innovations at the periphery, designers must identify which features of the design constitute the center, and are expected to be common and continuous across contexts. Variations in implementation may make the goals of continuity and commonality seem illusive. Brown and Duguid argue that what is central to one practice at one time may be peripheral at another, and wherever a line is drawn, some users may claim important features have been left out, while others may claim that peripheral features have been brought in.

To help deal with this problematic periphery, Brown and Duguid propose the use of resources at the center-periphery border, such as genres, which represent socially shared and constructed interpretive conventions. The argument is that if a feature of an artifact is recognized in association with a larger genre, the socially shared conventions of that genre can be used by the user to anticipate, make sense of, and enact the artifact writ large. These genre then become tools for attaching aspects of the local context to those in the designed artifact. In the case of mutual benefit partnerships, we can imagine several genres that may be invoked as interpretive tools to make sense of real world problem solv-

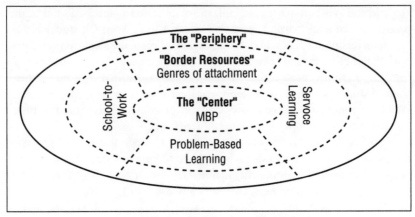

Figure 2. Genres of attachment to MBP.

ing, including school-to-work (e.g., Rosenbaum 1992), service learning or community action (e.g., Youniss and Yates 1997), and problem-based learning (e.g., Hmelo, Gotterer, and Bransford 1997) (see figure 2).

The genre of school-to-work, for instance, may be especially useful to high school communities of practice, invoking familiar practices such as the use of workplace problems as curricular anchors, a focus on the development of skills associated with professional work domains, and use of an apprenticeship model of teaching and learning. Through an analysis of how the Garfield and Wheaton schools implemented the mutual benefit partnership design, we came to realize that many of the conventions (e.g., cultural entailments) associated with the school-to-work genre were embedded in the original curricular artifact. Our conjecture is that because these entailments matched well with those in the Garfield context, the genre of school-to-work was recognizable and useful in supporting the Garfield teachers' enactment of the MBP design (see table 1.)[7]

It is uncertain whether the genre of school-to-work was explicitly invoked for the teachers at Wheaton as well, but it was clear that the cultural entailments of the original design as interpreted by the teachers did not match well with the Wheaton context. These teachers demonstrated what we would consider an unusually reflective and dedicated effort to make this artifact fit, searching for an alternate genre of attachment that was aligned with the cultural entailments of their specific context. In hindsight, we recognize this genre as community action (see table 2). We can imagine many scenarios in which faced with such a mismatch, the target users would simply decide not to participate or to create a cover story of surface implementation to appease external expectations (i.e., designers, administrators).

The lesson learned is that genres, as border resources, are invoked to assist

The "Center"	Genre of Attachment	The "Periphery"	
Mutual Benefit Partnerships[1]	School-to-Work	Enactment Decisions	Cultural Entailments
1. Real world problem	Relevant to professional workplace community	Partner defined problem, negotiated with teachers to fit seventh grade curriculum	Adults in community predominately employed in professional jobs Enculturation and training as legitimate ways to prepare for workplace participation Students home culture is the dominant culture in workplace settings – related conventions and rules Middle school model of teacher collaboration across subject areas
2. School/Out-of-School partnership	Partner roles include expert, mentor, client	Teacher chose business partner linterested in collaborating with schools	
3. Problem-based learning	Focus on leveraging workplace resources & practices	Path of investigation predominately structured by partner concerns and timelines Opportunities for participation in partner community Use of business tools and practices (e.g. agendas, progress reports)	
4. Final product	Targeted outcomes meet workplace needs and standards	Multiple products developed to allow all 150 students to be meaningfully involved Final product of primary value to partner organization Student benefit in form of "doing something real" (e.g. related to workplace)	

Table 1. Garfield MBP enactment.

interpretation whether explicitly or implicitly represented in the artifact. The implication, we argue, is that case study analyses of enactment can help to make visible the cultural entailments of a design that arise through designers' often tacit assumptions of shared practices and conventions. The danger of these entailments, left unquestioned, is the risk of inadvertently invoking a genre of conventions that conflict with or are irrelevant to a particular community of practice. The design opportunity is to identify the range of possible genres available as interpretive tools and to strategically use those resources as

The "Center"	Genre of Attachment	The "Periphery "	
Mutual Benefit Partnerships	Community Action	Enactment Decisions	Cultural Entailments
1. Real world problem	Relevant to community betterment	Students identified problem through teacher-facilited inquiry	Adults predominately employed in labor and service jobs Poverty, racism, and language isolation are barriers to participation in professional workplace communities and other sectors of society Agrarian traditions & knowledge in students home communities from rural Mexico Self contained classrooms, grade level teams
2. School/Out-of-School partnership	Partner roles include collaborator, uplifter, audience, expert	Students problem shopped to various interested parties	
3. Problem-based learning	Focus on leveraging home cultural resources Student activism	Path of investigation predominately student-driven— "organic process" Opportunities for participation in home community Focus on leveraging home cultural resources	
4. Final product	Targeted outcomes improve community conditions	Final product (i.e. green space for community) of primary benefit to students and their families Intermediary products (e.g. data on pollution levels in the river) important to different audiences at different times	

Table 2. Wheaton MBP enactment.

enactment hooks to support implementation in diverse contexts. In this analysis we observed that the "border resource," seeing the world through the lens of school-to-work in the one case and community action in the other, can help to understand two distinct patterns of enactment. We conjecture that even in cases of common genres of attachment, what we interpret as cultural entailments will cause those genres to be seen differently in different communities. The border resource itself is a valuable, unifying concept. But we believe it can lose some of its value if its assumed connections to the core of the innovation are not mitigated by clear and visible connections to the problematic periphery. For example, all of our experience with Wheaton and Garfield suggests to us that if school-to-work were a common genre of attachment, it too would have been articulated differently given differences in cultural entailments.

Summary and Design Implications

We have argued that as a function of design, artifacts come with a set of cultural entailments, representing the goals, expectations, histories, values, and practices associated with a particular community of practice. Left unquestioned, these entailments may inadvertently clash with the entailments of a community targeted for use of the innovation. The design challenge is to "make visible" those entailments and understand the process through which different communities of practice view and respond to those embedded aspects in relation to their local context. In the cases of enactment presented here, cultural entailments were made visible through a contrasting or "challenge" case. We do not believe that this needs be the case. Work circles (Shrader, Williams, Lachance-Whitcomb, Finn, and Gomez 1999), for example, are a method of bringing together researchers and educators to collaboratively design and enact curriculum. Studying the talk and artifacts that are products of this design experience represents an alternate method of making visible the cultural entailments of these two communities in ways that can be strategically used to account for diversity and support enactment (Reiser, Spillane, Steinmuller, Sorsa, Carney, and Kyza 2000). Experiences like these should make it less necessary for a community of practice like Wheaton to challenge and to force re-negotiation in order to successfully implement an innovation.

Further, we use Brown and Duguid's (1994) model to differentiate features at the idealized center of the artifact, the variations in implementation at the periphery, and the "border resources," such as genres of attachment, which represent socially shared conventions that help mediate the center-periphery divide. The cases presented here suggest the powerful role that genres of attachment can play in helping users interpret, make sense of, and adapt an innovation to their local context. The design task here is two-fold. First, we need to identify the range of genres that attach or bridge different contexts to an innovation. Second, we need to make these border resources and patterns of variation more explicit to the potential users of an innovation so that they can more easily see how that artifact can be made to work in their context in ways that also maintain the core "essence" of the design. Our hope is that the concepts outlined in this chapter will spark a conversation within the community and contribute to future research by ourselves and others in efforts to strategically respond to issues of context and culture in design.

Acknowledgements

This research was funded by the Reality Based Learning Project, U.S. Department of Education Grant #R303A60162, the SBILE Project, National Science Foundation Grant #REC-9720377, and the National Science Foundation Grant #REC-9720383 to the Center for Learning Technologies in Urban Schools. The authors would like to give a special thanks to all the educators, administrators, students, families, and partner organizations that are a part of the Reality Based Learning community. This work builds on the concept of mutual benefit partnerships developed in collaboration with Josh Radinsky, Dan Vermeer, Kirsten Hanson, Barry Fishman, and Eileen Lento. A special thanks to Rich Halverson for his thoughtful critique of and editing suggestions for this manuscript.

Notes

1. Pseudonyms are used to protect the anonymity of project participants.

2. MBPs are developed and implemented through a five-year grant called "Reality Based Learning," and funded by a 1996 U.S. Department of Education Technology Challenge Grant.

3. Designers in this case are the university and school partners who helped to write the original proposal and in the first year of funding helped to communicate these ideas to teachers implementing the MBP design for the first time.

4. Italics indicates emphasis added during analysis.

5. This website was constructed by the Wheaton teachers to share their project experience with others and represents their views.

6. We recognize Brown and Duguid's (1994) admonition against graphic representation of cultural negotiation. Their admonition noted, we attempt to display the process of cultural negotiation graphically while maintaining the spirit of their argument that the cultural categories are not rigid and separate, but permeable and interrelated.

7. The center is represented in its "idealized" form, acknowledging that cultural entailments are also represented in the designed artifact. We argue that by making visible those entailments, the designer can strategically design the artifact to signal the possible use of multiple genres of attachment to support implementation in diverse settings.

Chapter Eleven

Learners' (Mis) Understanding of Important and Difficult Concepts

A Challenge to Smart Machines in Education

Paul J. Feltovich, Richard L. Coulson, and Rand J. Spiro

Of subject matters we try to learn and understand, some are more difficult to master than others (e.g., Feltovich, Spiro, and Coulson 1989). In addition, when misunderstandings develop in learning, these can be of fundamentally different forms, some of which can be more difficult to correct than others (e.g., Chi 1992; Chi, Slotta, and de Leeuw 1994). We have argued in other places that, unfortunately, the kinds of concepts that are both difficult to learn and resistant to correction when misunderstood, are just the kind that are increasingly pertinent in our complex and changing world (Feltovich, Spiro, and Coulson 1997). If a certain sort of learning material is at once difficult to learn and prone to error, highly germane to functioning in our modern society, and highly resistant to ordinary forms of instruction, then improved education for such material can be posed as a special challenge for smart machines in education. Can smart technology help with learning of the really hard material, difficult material that, nonetheless, needs to be learned?

Such a challenge is cast in this chapter. After presenting some background, we present an analytic scheme which can be applied to subject matter to help determine how hard this material will be for students to learn and understand. It also yields some direction about the manner in which the material will be misunderstood when it is misunderstood. Following that, we give a detailed analysis of one learner's misunderstanding of a set of difficult concepts, and relate this back to the scheme for determining difficulty. Finally, we present a set of mental operations, "knowledge shields," that learners employ to rationalize misunderstanding and avoid changing their beliefs. The picture painted is one of considerable error in understanding of subject matter that has particular characteristics. Unfortunately, the kind of difficult learning material that is misunderstood is very important in our current world. Hence, any help that can be provided by smart machines will be most pertinent and beneficial.

Misunderstanding and Conceptual Stability

Research in the cognition of science and in science education has revealed that lay people, students, and even those who have undergone the "appropriate" instruction, often maintain fundamental misconceptions about important scientific concepts. This has been shown in fields such as physics (McCloskey 1983, Clement 1982), climatology (Collins and Gentner 1983), mathematics (Brown and Burton 1978) and biology (Buckley 1992; Myers, Feltovich, Coulson, Adami, and Spiro 1990; Patel, Kaufman, and Magder 1991; Richardson, Rovick et al. 1999). Much of our own research has involved identifying misconceptions held by medical students and professional practitioners about biology and biomedicine (Coulson, Feltovich, and Spiro 1989; Feltovich, Spiro, and Coulson 1989), identifying maladaptive ways of thinking (what we have called "reductive biases") that contribute to the development of these misconceptions (Feltovich et al. 1989; Feltovich, Spiro, Coulson, and Myers-Kelson 1995; Spiro, Feltovich, Coulson, and Anderson 1989; Spiro, Vispoel, Schmitz, Samarapungavan, and Boerger 1987; Wimsatt 1980) and developing methods of instruction that may help to overcome these deficiencies and limitations (Feltovich, Spiro, Coulson, and Feltovich 1996; Spiro, Coulson, Feltovich, and Anderson 1988; Spiro, Feltovich, Jacobson, and Coulson 1991a, 1991b; Spiro and Jehng 1990). In addition to being widely held across diverse disciplines, misconceptions can also be quite difficult to change; that is, they can be strongly held and intransigent to correction by typical classroom instruction (e.g., Champagne, Gunstone, and Klopfer 1985).

It seems clear that conceptual beliefs, and misconceptions that are associated with them, can differ in their robustness and in their difficulty for changing (cf. Elio and Pelletier 1997). For instance, some propositions seem obviously to differ in their inherent verifiability, in the amount and nature of data that would bear on their truth or falsity, their interrelationship with other concepts, and on other dimensions that might affect conceptual resiliency. Consider in this regard, for example, the difference between the two propositions "There are twenty-seven windows in that house" versus "My mother is a good woman."

General theories of human belief have been advanced that may shed light on differences in resistance to change among conceptual beliefs (e.g., Pollock

1979; Sosa 1980). According to *foundation* theories, belief in a composite of propositions (making up a complex concept) is thought to rest on, and to build in a more or less linear fashion from, one or a small number of critical, "keystone" propositions. Undermining one of these keystone "props" will cause belief quickly and easily to crumble. In contrast, according to *coherence* theories of belief, belief depends on an intricate system of interlocking, interdependent propositions, no one of which is of sufficient power to undermine (or uphold) the others, and all of which conspire to bolster each other. (There has been some suggestion from empirical studies of explanation that coherence in explanation by a belief holder contributes to belief in the truth of the thing being explained and to the strength of this belief, for example, Patel and Groen 1992). According to coherence theory, changing belief is a much more complex and difficult matter, since, for instance, the undermining of any component of belief may be overridden by the intermeshed effects of others (cf. Coulson et al. 1989; Feltovich et al. 1989; Sloman, Love, and Woo-Kyoung 1998).

One can imagine different scientific (or other areas of subject matter) conceptual structures as conforming more or less well to those espoused by these two theories, with differing implications for their ease of change. Furthermore, *empirical*, as well as theoretical, studies of conceptual understanding and misconception have differed in their resulting characterizations of conceptual belief and structure. Some studies have claimed these to be constituted of fragmented and labile (unstable, fleeting) components (e.g., diSessa 1988) and others, including our own, have claimed considerably more entrenchment and interwoven, network-like structure (Coulson et al. 1989, Feltovich et al. 1989).

What at first might appear to be controversy can be reconciled by proposing that conceptual beliefs can *vary* in their nature and degree of entrenchment, from those that are relatively simply structured and easily changeable, to those that are complexity structured and highly intransigent. In particular, not all misconceptions are hard to change, *but some are* (including many we have studied, because we have focused in advance on concepts that are supposed to be the most difficult, widely held, and difficult to remedy in a knowledge domain—see Dawson-Saunders, Feltovich, Coulson, and Steward 1990).

We have in other places argued that such a distinction has important implications for instruction. Misconceptions that are likely to be intransigent, of concepts that are themselves particularly important in a body of subject matter (because, for instance, they are especially critical to a wide range of knowledge applications or to the successful understanding of a large number of satellite concepts), are likely to be high payoff targets for special, albeit time and resource consuming, focus in instruction (Feltovich et al. 1992, 1993). For this reason, it would be highly beneficial to be able to predict in advance of the design of instruction for a curriculum (and fluidly as the curriculum is being developed and implemented), the important concepts and conceptual areas that are likely to be the most difficult to understand correctly, and that are likely to lead to misconceptions that are especially hard to emend.

We have adopted the term "stability" to refer to three aspects of conceptual understanding (including misconceptions) that are pertinent to difficulty of conceptual change; that is, to the *stability* of a set of concepts: (1) *pervasiveness* is the extent to which a conceptual belief is held across individuals, (2) *robustness* is the degree of resistance to change of a conceptual belief by challenges posed to it by instruction, and (3) *constancy* refers the presence, unchanged in an individual, of the conceptual belief over time.

Our research group has been working on a scheme for analysis of concepts (and of their related misconceptions) that can potentially help to predict which concepts in a body of subject matter will be hard to change. It should be stated that the building of this scheme, the "conceptual stability scheme" (css) (Feltovich et al. 1993, gives an overview of css), has been iterative, with incarnations of the scheme interspersed with studies from our laboratories to test implications, followed by adjustments to the scheme, followed by further laboratory investigation, and so forth.

A major goal for this chapter is to present the css in some detail. This will be done by showing its instantiation in detail to a complex biological (and biomedical) concept, *opposition to blood flow in the human cardiovascular system (cardiovascular impedance)*, and the salient related misconceptions that students acquire in learning about this concept.

An overview of css is presented next. It should be noted that the scheme cannot be applied to concepts in isolation. This is because the understanding and stability of any particular concept may be highly dependent on numerous other associated concepts, and misconceptions can also be highly intertwined and networklike (e.g., Coulson et al. 1989; Feltovich et al. 1989). After the overview, we give an example application of the scheme. That is, in order to give a sense of how the scheme is applied to a concept and its set of highly related concepts, selected parts of the scheme are applied to a group of concepts pertaining to the cardiovascular system, all associated with opposition to the flow of blood (the concept of cardiovascular impedance). These are ideas about why some misconceptions are widely and strongly held among learners.

Overview of the Scheme for Predicting Conceptual Difficulty and Stability

The scheme for predicting the stability of a concept and the stability of misconceptions associated with it has three major parts. The *first* involves the nature of the correct concept to be learned and its set of related concepts. Included, for example, are the difficulty of the individual concepts that are involved in the network of concepts that define the target concept, and how strongly and in what ways members of this group are related to each other. The *second* pertains to characteristics of the network of component misconceptions that make up the overall misconception: that is, to the network of incorrect or faulty interpretations of the correct ideas. Important in this regard is the degree of reciprocation among the members of the network of misconceptions, the degree to which believing one makes it easier to believe others, and vice versa. In general, the higher the overall reciprocation, the greater would be the expected stability (although one can envision exceptions to this—for *extremely* high degrees of reciprocation, for example, the network may come to resemble so much a unity that it does not behave much like a network at all but, rather, more like a single concept, with robustness against change perhaps reduced). Characteristics of the relationship *between* the correct ideas and the faulty interpretations of them (misconceptions) are also important. For example, because our research has suggested an inclination in many people (Spiro, Feltovich, and Coulson 1996; Schommer 1993; Schommer and Walker 1995) toward preference and adoption of simple interpretations (Coulson et al. 1989; Feltovich et al. 1989; Spiro et al. 1989), we would predict that misconceptions that are simple, of concepts that are actually complex and difficult, would be especially stable (cf. Dember 1991; Zook and DeVesta 1991). The *third* major factor bearing on stability of a misconception is the way the misconception is typically treated by authorities—by "experts"—teachers, textbooks, popular media, and the like. The more that valued sources such as these promote the misconception, the more widely and strongly it will be held.

In sum, according to CSS, the stability of a concept (and its related concepts) depends broadly on characteristics of the misconception itself, characteristics of the appropriate understanding to be achieved, differences between them, and various kinds of external sources of support.

One source of *internal* support has to do with the complexity of cognitive processing required for understanding a concept appropriately, in comparison to the processing involved in "understanding" the misconception. It is predicted that the less complex and taxing the processing for the misconception, in comparison to the more correct understanding, the more readily adopted and stable the misconception will be. For example, the concept as misunderstood might involve interpreting as linear, relationships that are actually nonlinear. When learners interpret the more complex dimensions as though they were the simpler ones, we say they are engaging in the "reductive bias" (e.g., Feltovich, Spiro, and Coulson 1989). Relevant dimensions of difficulty and complexity are listed below, with the less complex processing requirements listed first in each pair (taken from Feltovich et al. 1993, pp. 193-94):

- *Concreteness/Abstractness:* Are processes concrete and visualizable versus abstract?

- *Discreteness/Continuity*: Are attributes and processes discrete or continuous?
- *Sequentiality/Simultaneity*: Do processes occur in a sequential, step-wise fashion, or are there aspects of simultaneity?
- *Mechanism/Organicism:* Are effects tractably traceable to the actions of external agents (mechanistic), or are they the product of more holistic, organic functions (see Pepper 1942, for further explication of the pertinent distinctions)?
- *Separability/Interactiveness:* Do different processes run independently of each other (or with only weak interaction), or are processes strongly interactive and multidimensional?
- *Universality/Conditionality:* Are there principles of function or relationships among entities that are universal in their application or validity, or are regularities much more local and context-dependent?
- *Linearity/Nonlinearity:* Are functional relationships among processes linear or nonlinear?

There are three other notable sources of internal support. These involve the nature of an individual's existing or prior knowledge as it relates to the correct and incorrect ideas. One we call "p-prim congruence" because it pertains to the construct of a p-prim proposed by diSessa (1983). According to diSessa, a *p-prim* is a fundamental belief about how the world works. This is similar to what we, ourselves, have called a "prefigurative" scheme or "world view" (Feltovich et al. 1989). The more that components of a misconception are congruent with p-prims, and components associated with the correct interpretation are not, the more widespread and strongly held the misconception will be. The misconception will seem intuitive, and the correct conception will not. Another source of internal support involves available examples or analogies that seem to be in agreement with the misconception. Availability and salience in memory of phenomena that conform to the misconception (or to its components) increase pervasiveness and stability of the misconception. A third knowledge-related source of support has already been mentioned and involves internal consistency or congruence among the components of the misconception. Particularly important in this regard is the extent to which components of a misconception bolster each other, reciprocate and make each other easier to believe.

Besides internal sources of support, there are other sources that are *external* to the individual. These involve credence offered by authorities. Misconceptions may be taught or suggested in textbooks or taught by professors in classes. For example, one of the factors that contributes to the wide-spread and strongly held belief in a misconception about heart failure that has been the focus of other papers (Coulson et al. 1989; Feltovich et al. 1989) is that it is commonly proffered by medical textbooks and in clinical teaching.

Example Application of the Scheme to a Set of Concepts

In this section CSS is applied to a cluster of concepts in order to give a better sense of the nature of the scheme and its use. The set of ideas to be discussed are all related to the concept of opposition to blood flow in the cardiovascular system: to what is usually termed "cardiovascular impedance." A short discussion of impedance is therefore necessary as background.

The Concept of Cardiovascular Impedance

Cardiovascular impedance refers to the net effect of all factors that oppose the flow of blood in the cardiovascular system. There are three major sources of this opposition. One is *resistance*, which depends upon the length and diameter of blood vessels but also importantly upon the viscosity of the blood. Resistance exists in all liquid flow systems (even, for instance, standard household plumbing) because for resistance to exist it does not matter whether the driving force (pressure) that moves the liquid is constant or changing. However, because the pressure produced by the beating heart is pulsatile, constantly changing, two other sources of opposition are germane. These other two embody the flow-related concepts of *compliance* and *inertance*.

The contributions inertance and compliance make to opposition, akin to resistance, are dependent upon the length and diameter of the blood vessels. However, unlike resistance, neither compliance nor inertance depends upon the viscosity of the blood. Furthermore, the former, compliance, is highly dependent upon the physical stiffness of the materials from which the vessels are made. The latter, inertance, depends greatly upon the density of the blood moving in the vessels and represents the constant acceleration and deceleration of the mass of blood being moved in the vessels by the pulsatile pressure. Unlike resistance, the contributions that compliance and inertance ultimately make to the opposition to blood flow are totally dependent on the frequency with which the heart beats (the number of cycles of pressure and flow change the system undergoes per unit time).

In a complex manner, when compliance and inertance are considered in the context of the rate with which the heart beats, their contributions to the total opposition to the flow of blood can be determined in the form of two additional constructs—*compliant reactance and inertial reactance*. These factors contribute to opposition to blood flow in as real a manner as resistance does, but, for the most part, as functions of different sources. Three main factors, then, contribute to the opposition to blood flow in the cardiovascular system: resistance, compliant reactance, and inertial reactance. However, the three do not combine in a straightforward manner to determine the total opposition to blood flow in the cardiovascular system. The total opposition is a vectorial, and not a scalar, additive function of the three basic components. *Hence, it is impossible to assess the total opposition without knowledge of all three factors, and the interaction of the three factors is complicated.* In addition, it is not possible to judge the contribution of any one factor without consideration of the others. It is not possible to assess what effect a change in, say, vascular compliance will have on total opposition without knowing the status of the other factors. In particular, making the blood vessels more compliant (stretchy) can, under particular circumstances, lead to a decrease, increase, or no change at all in total opposition to blood flow, depending upon the status of the other major contributors.

The main misconception used as an example in this section is this: that vascular compliance contributes to opposition to blood flow solely through the relative ability of more or less stretchy vessels to change their vascular radii. (Compliance, again, is related to the ease with which a vessel can be stretched, by blood volume or pressure.) The misconception is that with greater compliance a vessel is more easily able to expand to incoming blood, thus assuming a greater radius and, in this way, offering less opposition to blood flow (through resistance factors affected by radius). Hence we will call this misconception the "Compliance Acts Like Resistance" (CALR) misconception.

In this misconception, the role of compliance in opposition is treated in a resistance-like way, and this way of thinking contributes largely to a widely held view of the entire cardiovascular system that is also highly resistance-based. That is, real factors of opposition that are not resistance-based are ignored or made to conform to a resistance kind of interpretation (as we will discuss regarding the role of compliance), a view of opposition that is more in conformance with systems that have constant driving pressure (e.g., a city water supply and household plumbing) than it is with the pulsatile cardiovascular system.

The description just given of CALR and its role in learners' misconceptions about cardiovascular impedance is actually an oversimplification of a complex misconception, involving several components (which will be elaborated below). However, the basic idea behind CALR is that it is easier to push something into a vessel that has "flabby" walls than to push it into a vessel that has stiff walls. In reality, while a more compliant vessel will expand more to a given pressure, this expansion will be compensated by a greater recoil, as pressure falls (pressure in the cardiovascular system is cyclic), so that two vessels with otherwise similar characteristics, but different compliances, will have the same mean radii over the pulsation cycle. Hence, the contribution of compliance to opposition to blood flow cannot be through the misconstrued mechanism. In addition, even though greater compliance will make it easier to expand a vessel, it will also make it more difficult to *change* the pressure in the vessel (pressure is always changing in a cyclic pressure system), and, in a complex manner, it is this property that ultimately accounts for the role of compliance in opposition to blood flow. But, understanding the real role of compliance is extremely difficult, requiring understanding of the cardiovascular system as a cyclic (alternating, or AC "current"—using an electrical analogy to fluid flow) pressure and flow system, and requiring understanding of interacting factors that are a function of continuous change of pressure and flow, rather than of the simple magnitude of either.

Although cardiovascular impedance and the contribution to it of vascular compliance is ultimately complicated, an admitted simplification here may help the reader get a better sense of the relevant concepts and of the ways students misunderstand: All the energy (in the form of pressure) available to move blood is produced by the pumping action of the heart. Overcoming resistance, that is, overcoming internal bonding (viscous) forces within the blood so that the blood will move, depletes some of this total energy. Resistance would deplete some of the energy of the "pump" whether the pump were a constant pressure pump (like a vacuum cleaner, or roughly like the water tank on the edge of town) or an oscillating one like the heart. Because the heart *does* produce pulsatile pressure, two other sources of opposition come into play. Because of pulsatile pressure, some energy must be used to constantly accelerate and decelerate the blood—so, some energy is depleted in this inertance-related way in addition to that lost in overcoming resistance. Furthermore, because the heart produces pulsatile pressure and because the vessels are "stretchy" (compliant), some of the energy produced by the heart gets used in producing an actual, *real flow* into and out of the expanding and recoiling vessel walls, in addition to the flow that moves downstream through the circulation. Like the blood flow that moves "downstream," this compliance-related flow has a resistance, compliance, and inertance. Hence, this compliance-related flow also costs energy—that is, contributes to opposition of flow.

One of the reasons many students have trouble understanding the compliance-related flow as a legitimate flow is that they cannot believe it has a resistance. This is partly because they also wrongly believe that resistance is the result of some kind of frictional interaction between the blood and the blood vessel wall. How could the compliance-related flow be a flow, and therefore have a resistance, if there is no wall to scrape against? We have observed this "Resistance Results from Friction on the Walls" misconception so often that we have come to consider it a sixth (in addition to the five to be discussed in the next section) component of CALR. Some example statements from subjects:

"(If) the blood is more viscous and more thick, then it's going to be flowing less fast, it is going to be flowing, than it would if it were nice and fluidy and more like water. This is because the more viscous it is, the more friction it is going to have against the vessels it is running through."

"The first thing I think about (with regard to opposition to blood flow) is friction on the inside of vessels...friction is just something that will, can't be changed. I would say that that's a constant, friction within the blood vessel itself. And that will, that will occur throughout the entire system."

What is wrong here is that when fluid passes through or over solids, the two interfaces do not scrape each other (as is more the case with two solids). The first layer of liquid in touch with the solid is stationary at the wall, and resistance results from the remainder of the liquid, not in touch with the wall, having to deform itself in moving forward.

Hence, even though students usually have a reasonable general understanding of resistance, as it is related to vessel width, vessel length, and blood viscosity, even on this concept there are fundamental flaws. Learners retain a purely "obstructional" (also, see DiSessa 1983, "Ohm's p-prim") view, that of something blocking the passage of blood through a vessel, rather than one of depletion of energy in the flow system. Understanding cardiovascular impedance requires a change in point of view with regard to "opposition," from one of opposition as something "blocking" or "fighting back" at some agent, to one something more like "sapping the agent's strength."

Appropriate understanding of cardiovascular impedance is important. This concept is directly related to cardiovascular hypertension (high blood pressure) which is, in turn, related to heart failure and myocardial infarction ("heart attack"). These are major causes of death throughout the world. It is our contention that if impedance were understood better, that is, in ways more commensurate with its true complexity, and not oversimplistically as it often is, the diagnosis and treatment of hypertension could be improved (Coulson, Feltovich, and Spiro 1997).

The Scheme Applied to Cardiovascular Impedance and Its Related Conceptual Components

Application of CSS requires identification of the component and associated misconceptions that make up a particular misconception, so that the scheme can be applied to these and so that the interaction (e.g., reciprocation) among them can be studied. To convey some of the nature of this endeavor, the scheme is now applied to the misconception described above, compliance as having its effect through radius change, and to its allied misconceptions. This will be done using the following format:

Component misconception: A synopsis of a component misconception is given.

Test item: A "test item" statement involving each misconception is presented. These statements are from one of our studies in which medical student subjects were presented a large set (the full set of items used can be found in Feltovich, Coulson, Spiro, and Adami 1994) of such statements and were required to express their extent of agreement with each statement (on a four point scale ranging from strongly disagree through disagree, agree, and strongly agree) and to explain the reasons for their choices. The test items are short-form devices for assessing the existence of a target misconception in students that were only possible to build after extensive laboratory work, involving more elaborate investigation, was conducted with regard to a set of misconceptions.

Response: The subject's response to the test item is given, including the subject's reasons for why she agreed or disagreed. All quotes presented below are from the same subject *in order to convey the sense in which component misconceptions can cohere by supporting each other in an individual system of belief.* However, the number of students (of nine total) who answered the item correctly is also given; these are subjects from the same study from which the example subject portrayed here was chosen (see Feltovich et al. 1994, for more details).

The correct idea: A description of correct understanding of the conceptual component is presented.

Conceptual stability scheme: An analysis of the correct idea and the misconception, with regard to elements of CSS, is presented.

Components of the misconception, involving the role of compliance in cardiovascular impedance, are now presented according to the format just described, including selected instantiations of CSS for these components:

Component Misconception 1—Compliance Acts through Radius

According to this misconception, the contribution of compliance (or lack thereof) to the opposition to blood flow is through the ability of a vessel to expand its radius. This misconception treats the role of compliance in opposition to blood flow as being a form of resistance (resistance being the oppositional factor that actually is largely dependent on radius): a more compliant vessel offers less opposition because it can "open up" to blood, forming a wider vessel with less resistance.

Test item: The more compliant (stretchy) a vessel is, the less opposition to blood flow it will provide because the more compliant vessel can more easily expand its radius to let blood pass through.

Response: "I strongly agree. The more stretchy a vessel is, or compliant, the fact that its radius, like it says here, its radius can get larger. And the fact that its radius can get larger decreases the resistance to the flow of blood through it, so that the blood can move faster with the less resistance that's provided."

One of nine, eleven percent of students, answered this item correctly.

The correct idea: The root of this faulty understanding lies in the idea that opposition to blood flow is only the product of how easy it is for a "bolus" of blood to get to the next place in the vascular circulation. What is not understood is that the cardiovascular circulation is a circuit with various circuit elements that affect flow. The compliance is a circuit element that operates in parallel with the resistance. Blood that flows into the compliance (into the stretching of the vessel) does not continue directly on through the compliance and pass into or through the resistance (related to the mean radius of a pulsatile system). It must flow back out (AC or alternating flow) of the compliance while continuing on through the resistance.

When oppositional elements are in parallel, the flow that results is greater through the lesser oppositional elements. The AC components of flow in the cardiovascular system, therefore, divide flow between the compliance and the resistance, with the majority going to the compliance (stretching the wall) which is a smaller oppositional factor than the resistance. It is easy for the blood flow (AC component) to move into the compliance compared with into the resistance, so most of it goes there (into the compliance). The non-alternating (the "DC," or "direct current" component of the flow—again, using an electrical analogy to fluid flow) component of flow does not go into the compliance (into the stretching of the vessels) at all, in any instantaneous sense. It just sets the mean (average) of vessel size about which the AC component of flow oscillates.

In pulsatile (AC) flow, the size of a vessel oscillates equally above and below a mean size set by the direct (DC) component of flow (see above). While a more compliant vessel will have wider "swings" of size than a less compliant vessel, with greater decreases below the mean compensating for greater expansions above the mean, the mean size will be the same as for a less compliant vessel, as long as its other dimensions are the same; hence, the resistance aspects will be the same. The real role of compliance in opposition to blood flow is complicated and abstract, involving the property of compliance as an opposition to change-of-pressure (more compliance in a vessel makes it harder to change pressure, which must be done continuously in a pulsatile pressure system) and the interaction of this property with numerous other cardiovascular circuit properties (including the component oscillatory frequencies of pressure/flow pulsation).

Conceptual stability scheme: The misconception is concrete; one can easily envision blood pushing into and expanding a vessel, making its diameter wider. There is no way to envision the real role of compliance. It is difficult to reify opposition to change of pressure, let alone *instantaneous* opposition to change of pressure, and the ways that this could ever ultimately result in an opposition to the flow of blood. Causally, the misconception is mechanistic; the agent (blood) pushes open the object (the vessel) locally. In the correct interpretation, no such single agent can be identified as causing the contribution of compliance to opposition to blood flow, since this opposition is ultimately the emergent result of a number of simultaneously operative factors. In addition, under the misconception, the contribution of compliance is linear, or at least monotonic—the more compliant the vessel, the greater the radius, the less the "resistance," the less the opposition. As has been noted earlier, the real contribution of various degrees of compliance to degrees of opposition to blood flow is nonlinear (that is, it contributes to a construct, compliant *reactance*, which itself combines in a *vectorial* way with other factors to determine the degree of *impedance*) and not easily describable at all.

Component Misconception 2—Greater Compliance Implies Larger Mean Radius

According to this misconception, for a given mean pressure (within a pulsatile pressure system), a more compliant vessel expands faster and closes down more slowly—hence, it operates at a higher mean radius. The idea that a vessel might close down during pulsation to something less than the mean radius is not in the picture—the vessel just oscillates above and down to something like the "real" radius, which is a structural property of the vessel itself. This component misconception is particularly important: it is, perhaps, the key to reconciling the basically DC view that students have of many of the components of the cardiovascular system (interpretations that would be consistent with a heart that produces steady pressure/flow) with the fact that they know that the heart pulses and that vessels actually expand and rebound.

Test item 2a: In the pulsing cardiovascular system, two vessel segments which would have the same diameter at constant pressure (not pulsing) will both have the same average diameter in the pulsing system, even though one is highly compliant (stretchy) and the other is very stiff.

Response 2a: "I strongly disagree because if, if you have a constant pressure, if you have a constant pressure and both diameters are the same, so the radius of both vessels is the same, but if the cardiovascular system pulses so there is an increase in pressure at certain points in time, then the more compliant vessel is going to increase its radius with each pulse or with each minute increase in pressure, whereas the one that is very stiff isn't going to be able to increase its radius so its going to have a smaller radius and it's going to have more resistance to the flow. So, I would strongly disagree with the statement."

Zero of nine, zero percent of students, answered this item correctly.

Test item 2b: In the pulsing cardiovascular system, of two vessels which would have the same diameter at constant pressure (not pulsing), the more compliant (stretchy) one will open up faster and close down more slowly during pulsation than the stiffer one, resulting in a greater average radius for the more compliant vessel.

Response 2b: "I agree. I'm going to strongly agree because of the fact that the more compliant one will open up faster and will close down more slowly during pulsation than the stiffer one—because the stiffer one doesn't have the compliance and it can't open up as far and it's going to snap back real quick. So, therefore, there's a much greater average radius for the more compliant vessel and by having a greater radius, then it's going to have decreased resistance to blood flow. So the blood is going to go through faster than the stiffer one."

Zero of nine, zero percent of students, answered this item correctly. Because this component is so central to the misconception, we will take the liberty here of presenting a particularly revealing response from a different subject:

"This is exactly true! I strongly agree. That's what I was trying to say before when they asked me whether ah, whether ah, it would have an average ah, whether the average radius would be the same or not. What I meant to say was that it would open up faster and close down more slowly because it's more, more compliant, um (pause) okay? Um, um, if they had a constant pressure, a constant diameter would not be pulsing. When it does pulse, the blood does rush in there and the, that's ah, more compliance is gonna expand faster and it will close down more slowly later because, ah, there'll be less push against the blood to, to, push it out. So, it'll have a greater average radius. My confidence rating on that is very high, 80 percent."

The correct idea: (Note, these two items and responses—2A and 2B—are targeted at the same misconception, but the second expresses the item in a way that will elicit the opposite response from a subject who is consistently misunderstanding the concept: the subject can express the same misunderstanding in both a positive and negative fashion. There were similar matched pairs for all misconceptions addressed in the study, as well as other statements that bear on each misconception from slightly different angles.)

The operative mean size of a vessel, through cycles of pulsation, is a function both of structural properties of the vessel and of the magnitude of the DC component of flow (the AC component is always superimposed on the DC component). The DC component, or mean, sets the base degree of stretch in the vessel, which is always greater than the stretch that would exist if the circulation were empty. In general, the rate of stretch during the rising phase of the pulse is faster than the rebounding phase, but the distance traveled (by a point on the vessel wall) is the same out as in, and equal above and below the mean for every component frequency of the pulse. This is because each of the component frequencies of the pressure wave is a sinusoid, symmetrical about the mean. Because the component frequencies of the pulse are out of phase, the result of all of them together can look like an asymmetrical event, with a rising part which is faster (in velocity) than the falling part, but the distance traveled out and in must be the same—and the mean radii of two vessels differing in compliance but with otherwise identical properties would be the same.

Conceptual stability scheme: A "real" radius for a vessel is easy to imagine, as when a vessel (tube) is sitting on a table. A different, dynamic base width of a vessel, that only exists as an emergent property resulting from an embedded component (the "DC" part) of the total blood flow is more abstract. Oscillation above, and perhaps especially below, this dynamic base-level radius is also difficult to imagine. From early years of a student's schooling, oscillation is depicted as cycling around a zero value, assuming in the process both positive and negative values. Pendular movement in physics and alternating current electricity are likewise portrayed. Hence, there are likely numerous experienced examples that serve to define oscillation by swings around zero and by the presence of negative values. There are no negative values of pressure or flow in the cardiovascular system (which would amount to backwards flow) and no points where there is zero flow. This is because a constant level of flow (the DC component) is superimposed upon the oscillatory component (the AC component); oscillation is about some positive value rather than about zero. The wealth of examples of oscillation about a zero value leads students to believe that the cardiovascular system is not an alternating circuit because, as students in our studies have claimed, "there is no backward flow." This may explain the failure, within the misconception just described, to account for the relatively (about the base state) negative radius changes that negate any expansion differences in vessels due to differences in their stretchability (i.e., their relative compliances).

Component Misconception 3—Opposition Is Monotonic with Stiffness

Only "stiffness" (lack of compliance) could ever provide opposition to blood flow. Greater compliance could never lead to greater opposition to blood flow. The contribution of stiffness to opposition to blood flow is a direct relationship—at least a monotonic (nondecreasing) relationship. Greater stiffness leads to greater opposition.

Test item: Increasing the compliance (stretchiness) of the walls of the vessels of the cardiovascular system can increase the opposition to blood flow provided by the vascular system.

Response: "I strongly disagree because as you increase the compliance of the walls of the vessels, you're going to decrease the opposition to flow provided by the system. I mean, it's when you decrease the compliance that you increase the opposition to blood flow. So, if you're going to go ahead and make the walls more stretchy, the resistance to blood flow will decrease because the radius will become larger."

Zero of nine, zero percent of students, answered this item correctly.

The correct idea: Greater "stretchiness" or compliance in a vessel can even contribute to *greater* opposition to blood flow. The ultimate contribution of the degree of compliance to the total opposition to blood flow is a complex relationship, involving interactions among compliant reactance, inertial reactance, and resistance, as these interact with factors such as heart rate (more accurately, component frequencies of the pressure pulse). There can be situations in which an increase (or decrease) in compliance would lead to either an increase, decrease, or no change in opposition to blood flow.

Conceptual stability scheme: A primary difference within CSS between the misconception and the correct notion is the p-prim congruence of the misconception relative to the correct idea. The idea that something that "complies," "gives way," or "accommodates" to blood (as a more compliant vessel is interpreted by students to do) could ever provide greater opposition to blood flow is highly counter-intuitive (in fact, it appears to clash with the

"Ohm's p-prim" described by diSessa), in comparison to the direct relationship of greater opposition with greater stiffness embodied in the misconception. In addition, the correct relationship is nonlinear (vectorial) and conditional (no universal statement of the impact of an increase/decrease in compliance on opposition to blood flow can be made) versus linear and universal in the misconception.

Component Misconception 4—Compliance's Contribution to Opposition Is Independent of Heart Rate

The contribution of lack of compliance (stiffness) to opposition to blood flow will be independent of frequencies of pulsation—for example, heart rate—since the contribution of compliance is a kind of resistance (which is independent of such frequencies).

Test item: The opposition to blood flow provided by the vessels of the cardiovascular system does not depend on heart rate.

Response: "I strongly agree. Because it's not the—the resistance doesn't depend on the heart rate, it depends on the size of the vessels and the diameter of the walls. It doesn't have anything to do with heart rate, I hope."

Unlike this subject, seven of nine, seventy-seven percent of students, answered this item correctly. However, when they did, they usually answered correctly for wrong reasons, reasons consistent with CALR.

The correct idea: The contribution to opposition from compliance (and from inertance, the other factor besides resistance ultimately contributing to opposition to blood flow) is different from that of resistance. While the contribution from resistance is not dependent on the component frequencies of the pressure wave (as exemplified to a large extent by the heart rate), the contribution from compliance, as well as the overall opposition to blood flow, is dependent on such frequencies in a major way.

Conceptual stability scheme: This misconception relies heavily on the notion that compliance acts like resistance, dependent mainly on vessel width or radius, a concrete and easily envisioned phenomenon. The real factors that affect the contribution of compliance are highly abstract. The component frequencies of the pressure wave, upon which the contribution of compliance to opposition to blood flow is dependent, do not even have any clear physical embodiments (although heart rate is an approximation); they are mathematical abstractions that, nonetheless, have demonstrable implications for opposition to blood flow, through the effects of compliant and inertial reactance. Furthermore, the dependence of these reactances on components of the pressure wave is not linear. The component frequencies can affect compliant and inertial reactance, two sources of opposition to blood flow, differently—so that the two sources might in different circumstances augment each other, diminish each other, or cancel out the effects of each other.

Component Misconception 5—Opposition is Entirely Obstructional

The contribution of lack of compliance (stiffness) to opposition to blood flow is a kind of resistance, with the same kind of properties as resistance. Compliance is not a fundamentally different kind of factor from resistance in its contribution to impedance. The only thing that opposes the flow of blood is physical obstruction (as exemplified by a wider or slimmer vessel).

Test Item: The role that vessel stiffness plays in opposing the flow of blood is basically the same as the role that vessel radius plays in opposing the flow of blood.

Response: "Well, I'm going to strongly agree because it's the stiffness that, if, if, the less stiff a vessel is, the more ability it has to increase its radius so they're somewhat related to each other because of the fact that the stiffness is, you know, if the vessel is more stiff, then its radius is going to be smaller than if it is less stiff, when it can, you know, more compliance and it can open up more and decrease its opposition to flow."

Zero of nine, zero percent of students, answered this item correctly.

The Correct Idea: See the correct idea section of Component Misconception 1 above.

Conceptual stability scheme: One problem in the student's interpretation involves not recognizing that the compliance and the resistance are different elements in the circuit sense. Because the same conduit, the blood vessel, is the physical location of both the compliance and the resistance (not to mention the inertance, the opposition to change of motion of blood) in the cardiovascular system, there is no salient cue to lead an individual to distinguish among the different functions served by the same vessel. This is in contrast to other analogous systems where such distinct functions are served by physically different components. In electrical systems, for example, "resistors" and "capacitors," the analogs of resistance and compliance respectively (not to mention "chokes," the analog of inertance), are clearly discrete elements. Even if students' think about mechanical systems, the distinctness of "dash pots" and "springs" (not to mention "masses") is clear also. Hence, numerous examples and analogies (e.g., from electricity) are available to reinforce the notion that importantly different functions must be performed by different physical structures in a system. In fluid systems, such as the cardiovascular system, the discreteness of different oppositional elements is just not overtly apparent. In our studies, the idea that a single physical structure (in this instance, the same blood vessel) can have different functional properties has persistently been difficult for our subjects to understand. This is exemplified, for example, in assertions that the small blood vessels are "resistance" vessels and the larger vessels are "storage" vessels (when, in fact, both kinds of vessels have both kinds of functions). In addition to having support from examples and analogies, the incorrect idea, that is, that different functions must be served by different physical structures, is more concrete. It also involves separability of structure/function, compared with the more correct view in which the same physical structure serves different functions, as a result of different interactions of the structure with some ongoing process (in this case, pulsatile flow).

This analysis of a misconception of the role compliance plays in the opposition to blood flow, in particular that it functions through the relative ability of vessels to expand their radii in response to the inflow of blood (or pressure) in a very resistance-like way, has illustrated that on many dimensions of comparison, components of the target misconception are simpler than the appropriate idea which is misunderstood. In addition, a set of misconceptions appear to be related to the target misconception, and to cohere in such a way that they provide mutual support. The misconception is also more concrete, carries with it more salient examples and analogies, and is more congruent with intuition (p-prim congruent). In such a situation we would expect the misconception to be widely held and to be difficult to change. This misconception of compliance (and the related resistance-based misconception of the cardiovascular system) is, in fact, one of the more widely held misconceptions we have observed in our studies.

The CSS has implications for education and educational research when focus on difficult subject matter is a concern. Even when procedures are followed to isolate significant concepts for special handling within a curriculum or within, say, a text (e.g., by polling of teachers/practitioners, Dawson-Saunders et al. 1990; by analyzing results of old tests; or by some other means), it would be helpful to have some means to distinguish further among these concepts the ones that are likely to require the most extensive and particularly tailored attention in instruction—because they will be the more difficult to understand and/or the more difficult to emend when they are misunderstood. The proposed scheme is potentially useful for this purpose. In addition, in our own laboratories, the scheme has been useful in directing us to candidate concepts (and components) toward which to direct basic research about students' conceptual understanding and in suggesting particular aspects of these concepts that are likely to be troublesome for learners.

An important and perhaps novel characteristic of CSS is that is takes into consideration specified contrasts between the appropriate understanding of a concept to be learned and what are liable to be the misconceptions that develop. Hence, employing the scheme requires at least expert advice/intuition about appropriate understanding and also some input about likely misconceptions. Initially, these can come from the insights of teachers or from directed research. Iterations of instruction in the class or of laboratory work, and related adjustments of the scheme for a concept, can help to refine initial analyses of a concept.

The CSS will be useful for purposes such as these to the extent it is valid in predicting conceptual (and [mis]conceptual) stability in the sense we have defined—involving *pervasiveness, robustness, and constancy.* We have conducted research on students' learning and understanding of cardiovascular impedance (and the related concepts about the role of compliance), the topic analyzed in this chapter. This can provide at least a preliminary assessment of the worth of the scheme in predicting results of learning and understanding for this set of concepts. The analysis of cardiovascular impedance and related misconceptions presented in this chapter would suggest that the misconceptions about impedance and compliance should be stable, since the appropriate understanding and the misconceptions differ with regard to CSS in many ways that would lead to the prediction that these misconceptions, once acquired, should be stable.

Pertinent research from our laboratory suggests that indeed both the general misconception, that opposition to blood flow is just a matter of resistance, and the more particular one that casts compliance as operating in opposition through the ability of a vessel to expand and increase its radius, are stable in all three senses of stability we have proposed. The misconceptions are pervasive, in that many students hold them, robust, in that they are resistant to change by instructional challenges, and they are persistent, with students exhibiting the same errors over periods of months. The details of this experimentation are beyond the scope of the present chapter (but are presented in Feltovich, Coulson, Spiro, and Adami 1994). We will, however, discuss briefly here some of the mental operations that we found learners to engage that helped them to avoid changing their misunderstandings.

Knowledge Shields for Fending off Conceptual Change

We conducted a study (Feltovich et al. 1994) in which 24 "Agree-Disagree" items of the sort that have been presented in this chapter were assigned randomly in equal numbers to create a pre- and post-test about opposition to blood flow. In between taking the pre- and post-tests, twenty medical student subjects were led through a set of propositions that were instructional in the sense that they were correct statements regarding each of the major component misconceptions and were in direct contrast to faulty beliefs held by most subjects. Two examples of these proposition sets are given as figures 1 and 2. (It should be noted that the last item in figure 2 is longer than others we have used and presented in this chapter. This was the last item seen by subjects in this instructional "challenge" sequence and was meant to be a sort of comprehensive "capstone.")

On average, the "instructional" propositions had little or no effect on changing subjects' faulty beliefs (although a few subjects seemed to improve substantially). Scores on the pre- and post-tests were not significantly different: 41.1 percent correct, approximately. 5/12 items on pre-test; 50 percent,

1. As a vessel expands during the ascending phase of a pulse, this does not mean that all of the blood in the expanded vessel simply flows downstream through a now larger vessel, since some of it, for instance, flows into the expansion of the vessel itself.

2. In the pulsing cardiovascular system the ability of the more compliant (stretchy) vessel to expand its radius during the pulse does not affect the resistance of the vessel (which affects the flow downstream) because the resistance depends upon the average radius of the vessel which can be the same whether the vessel is stiff or stretchy.

3. In the cardiovascular system, vessel radius contributes to how difficult it is for blood to flow downstream through the circulation. Vessel stiffness helps determine the compliance of a blood vessel, which contributes to how difficult it is for blood to flow into and out of the bulging of the vessel wall during a pulse.

4. In the pulsing cardiovascular system, blood flows:
    a. into and back out of the expanding and contracting vessel; and
    b. downstream through the vessel.

The more compliant (stretchy) the vessel is, the easier it is for the blood to flow into stretching it rather than flowing downstream. The stiffer the vessel is, the more difficult it is for blood to flow into stretching it, allowing more of it to flow downstream.

5. In the pulsing cardiovascular system, some of the energy produced by the heart is used up in making blood flow into and out of the expansion of vessel walls. Hence, factors associated with flow into and out of the vessel walls such as wall stiffness and heart rate contribute to opposition to blood flow.

Figure 1. Challenge propositions to component misconception #1, that "opposition to blood flow acts solely through the radius of the vessel."

6/12 items on post-test (Feltovich *et al.* 1994). (It should be noted that for a subject to be counted "correct," he/she only had to mark on the appropriate *side* of the four agree/disagree items of our scale; that is, Agree and Strongly Agree were treated the same, as was their opposites). This exercise did, however, provide a distinct opportunity to investigate what subjects' would do when they were confronted with information (the instructional propositions—see figures 1 and 2) contrary to what they already believed. In fact, when subjects were confronted with the correct propositions, they engaged a wide variety of mental maneuvers to help them avoid having to change their minds. We have chosen to call these "knowledge shields" (Feltovich et al. 1994). The knowledge shields can be seen to resemble mental operations for handling information anomalous with belief proposed by Chinn and Brewer (1993), but the knowledge shields are more extensive, differentiated, and detailed. Particular knowledge shields subjects employed in the instructional study are listed in figure 3.

1. In the cardiovascular system not all of the energy generated by the heart is used up in making blood flow downstream through the resistance of the circulation. Other factors involving heart rate, stretchiness of the vessels, and the density of the blood compete for the energy generated by the heart and thus contribute to opposition to blood flow.

2. Pressure generated by the heart provides the energy to circulate the blood in the cardio-vascular system. Any factor that detracts from this pressure energy and hence makes less of it available to propel blood through the circulation is a source of opposition to blood flow.

3. In the pulsing cardiovascular system some of the energy produced by the heart is used up in making blood flow into and out of the expansion of vessel walls. Hence, factors asso-ciated with flow into and out of the vessel walls such as wall stiffness and heart rate con-tribute to opposition to blood flow.

4. In the cardiovascular system some of the energy produced by the heart is used up in accelerating and decelerating blood with every beat of the heart. Hence, factors associated with accelerating and decelerating blood such as blood density and heart rate contribute opposition to blood flow.

5. The energy provided by the pumping action of the heart that drives blood in the circula-tion has the form of pressure. This pressure is not constant in the cardiovascular system but changes rhythmically with the pulse. As blood moves through oppositional elements in the circulation, the pressure drops as energy is converted into movement of blood. Some of the pressure energy is converted into downstream movement of the blood by dropping across the resistance of the blood vessels. All pressure drops across resistance whether it is pulsing or not. Another portion of the pressure energy is converted into back and forth movement of blood as the vessels bulge out and recoil back in during the pulse. This pres-sure is said to drop across the compliant reactance. Still another portion of the pressure energy is converted into acceleration and deceleration of the blood in response to the pulse and is said to drop across the inertial reactance. Only pulsing pressure drops across the elements of compliance and inertance. Energy is consumed (i.e., the pressure drops) by blood moving across all three of these elements (resistance, compliant reactance, and inertial reactance) and thus all are factors which contribute to the opposition to the flow of blood. Since the pressure energy in the pulse is fixed at the time it leaves the heart, any element that drops pressure, besides the resistance, will reduce the energy available to drive blood through the resistance and in this way opposes the flow of blood downstream. Since resistance, compliant reactance, and inertial reactance combine in a complex (vecto-rial) way, it is not a simple matter to specify exactly how a change in any one of these will affect the total opposition to blood flow (the cardiovascular impedance). However, it is clear that there is more to opposition to the flow of blood in the cardiovascular system than just vascular resistance.

Figure 2. Challenge propositions to component misconception #5, that "opposition to blood flow is purely obstructional."

For example, a subject employing the demean effect shield acknowledges that what is being proposed might be correct, but dismisses its import by claiming that the implications of its being true are negligible—"That may be true, but it is no big deal." The exchange below depicts a subject's response to a true proposition that demonstrates demean effect. The proposition presented

1. (IS) ILLEGITIMATE SUBSUMPTION

Subject makes new material a special case of old; the learner has a way to account for new material with a bad model. For example, subject argues that compliance, something he does not understand well, acts just like resistance, something he does know more about.

1a. (PLS) PARTLY LEGITIMATE SUBSUMPTION

Old knowledge accounts in part for correct information. E.g., the learner knows that resistance and compliance might play different roles, but lacks ideas of how—hence can't, doesn't change mind.

2. (AU) ARGUMENT FROM AUTHORITY

The new (correct) material is judged wrong because Dr. X told the subject something different.

3. (DEM) DEMEAN EFFECT

Subject judges that some statement might be right, but dismisses its effect as insignificant.

4. (AA) ADD APPENDAGE

Subject judges that some information might be right, but it's just an add-on to what he/she already believes (when it actually controverts it).

5. (ANAL) RESORT TO BAD ANALOGY

For example, subject judges that something about the heart can't be right because of something he knows (but doesn't know correctly) about the lungs

6. (DE) DECOUPLING OF EFFECTS

Causally related processes/things are treated as separate. For example, compliance affects how difficult it is for blood to flow into buldging of a vessel, but not how difficult it is for the blood to flow out.

6a. (CC) CORRELATION AS CAUSATION

For example, blood slipping over itself doesn't cause resistance because radius, viscosity, and length do.

6b. (ACR) ARGUMENT FROM FAULTY CAUSAL REASONING

Subject agrees/disagrees because of some cooked up causal argument that is flawed

7. (ISE) IGNORING OF SECONDARY EFFECTS

For example, rebound of vessel doesn't require energy, only expansion does.

8. (AE) ARGUMENT FROM EXTREMES

The phenomenon does not exist between the extremes, as in the example: Yes, increasing compliance can increase opposition, but only when the vessel gets so flacid that blood just stagnates there.

8a. (ASC) ARGUMENT FROM SPECIAL CASE

Something could be true if special boundary conditions held. (Like AE, above, but just applies to specified conditions rather than extreme ones. E.g., compliant and stiff vessel could have the same average radius if they were different sizes to start with.

9. (CI) COUNTERINTUITION

It just seems like that CAN'T be right!

Figure 3a. "Knowledge shields" reactions to true, but discrepant information.

10. (RADD) (false) REDUCTIO AD ABSURDUM

This new thing implies a consequence that conflicts with this other thing that I KNOW is right, where it either doesn't really imply that or the thing subjects think is right is actually wrong, etc. (e.g., if the last layer of blood were actually stationary, some blood cells would be there for life)

11. (TR) THEORETICAL-REALITY DICHOTOMY

That may be true in theory, but it isn't like that in reality (e.g., that blood is stationary at the blood—vessel-wall interface).

12. (EXT) EXTIRPATION OF EFFECTS

Effect is isolated or removed from its larger context. For example, increasing heart rate will keep the vessel relatively more expanded because the vessel doesn't have time to close down between beats. The more compliant the vessel, the more the radius gain from rate will be). (If this were true, it would lead to explosion!)

13. (FA) FALLACIOUS ALTERNATIVE

Subject disagrees because he has a fallacious alternative explanation. E.g., a stiff vessel sets a lower bound on how far compliant vessel could recoil. Compliant vessel could never recoil to a smaller diameter than the stiffer one.

14. (OKC) PRIOR KNOWLEDGE CLASH

That is simply incongruent with what I know to be true. (like others, but has simple notion of "I know better")

15. (IC) IMPERTINENT COMPLEXIFICATION

"Yeh, but there's more to it than that."

16. (AEQ) ARGUMENT FROM EQUATION/FORMALISM

That's not right because of this equation I know (inappropriate equation, erroneous application, etc.) Pressure equals heart rate x resistance, etc.

17. (ARD) ARGUMENT FROM REDUCED DIMENSIONS

Subject argues using only one or a few of the pertinent dimensions of a situation. For example, that's not right because $P = R \times F$.

18. (RAP) RESTRICTED APPLICABILITY OF PRINCIPLE

That might be right, but it only applies in special circumstances. For example, increased stiffness will only cause increased opposition in veins..

19. (ASR) ARGUMENT FROM STATIC REPRESENTATION OF THE DYNAMIC

For example, argument that assumes that rate equals volume.

20. (ASE) ARGUMENT FROM SALIENT EXAMPLE

That can't be true because of this example I know. Not used so much as analogy, but as an example of the issue under contention (but misplaced). Decreasing compliance always leads to greater opposition, because of atherosclerosis etc.

21. (AUA) ARGUMENT FROM UNRELATED ALTERNATIVE

That's not right because this other thing I know is. For example, heart rate can't be related to the contribution to opposition made by stiffness because the sympathetics determine stiffness. . .

Figure 3b. "Knowledge shields" reactions to true, but discrepant information.

to the subject asserts correctly that during the ascending phase of a pressure pulse some blood must flow into the expansion of the vessel itself and is not flowing downstream through a then wider vessel. This is a challenge to one of the components of CALR. The subject asserts that such flow may happen, but then wrongly asserts that "it's not a big part of it":

(Presented item) As a vessel expands during the ascending phase of a pulse, this does not mean that all of the blood in the expanded vessel simply flows downstream through a now larger vessel, since some of it, for instance, flows into expansion of the vessel itself.

(long pause) "Um, I'm going to agree. It sounds, it makes sense, that some of it would flow into the expansion of the vessel, but I'm sure it's not a big part of it. My confidence is 50 percent.

Other shields are demonstrated below. In the first, a subject dismisses a fact about vessels in the cardiovascular system by importing a (false) analogy about the pulmonary vascular system—argument from faulty analogy (figure 3). In the next, a subject agrees with a proposition we would have expected him to disagree with—that opposition to blood flow is affected by heart rate. However the subject manages to agree only by employing two knowledge shields that protect the subject from the need for an actual change of mind—argument from (faulty) causal reasoning and extirpation (excision of something from its context—ignoring effects of context). Blood does not flow backward during a beat (faulty causal reasoning), and one could only believe that it could by viewing phenomena locally and ignoring the full, system-wide environment of any vessel: that the pressure gradient necessary for any forward or backward flow (as opposed to flow into the walls) is always in the direction of the atria of the heart; that is, flow is always downstream whether the vessel is expanding or contracting (there is actually a brief exception to this in the region of the aorta, but this is irrelevant to what this subject is portraying).

(Presented item) (a) In the pulsing cardiovascular system, two vessel segments which would have the same diameter at constant pressure (not pulsing) will both have the same average pressure in the pulsing system, even though one is highly compliant (stretchy) and the other is very stiff.

Um. Well, I would disagree because it's kind of like the pulmonic valve and the aorta. The pulmonary system is more compliant so the diameter's bigger when it's bulging. If that makes sense. My confidence rating is 70 percent.

(Presented item) (b) In the pulsing cardiovascular system, some of the energy produced by the heart is used up in making blood flow into and out of the expansion of the vessel walls. Hence, factors associated with flow into and out of the vessel walls, such as wall stiffness and heart rate, contribute to opposition to blood flow.

And, I agree with that, um, because when blood flows into an expanded vessel, and then that expanded area contracts, the blood's going to go both backwards and forwards, and this is going to create opposition to the blood flow coming in, and I would say I'm (inaudible) confident.

As a final example of the use of knowledge shields, consider the subject's statement included next. Again, this subject agrees with a proposition we would not expect him to agree with, but he does so because he engages shields that avoid the need for any change to his fundamental misunderstanding. The presented proposition is an appropriate description of the causal basis for resistance in blood flow, involving static liquid (blood) at the interface with the vessel walls and the need to overcome molecular bonds within the remaining blood itself. This is in conflict with component misconception #6 of CALR (discussed earlier), a component in which it is assumed that resistive forces to blood result from some kind of frictional interaction between the moving blood and the vessel wall surface. First, in the faulty analysis, the subject leaves some room open for some frictional effect by viewing the outer layer of blood as *relatively* stationary, not stationary (demean effect), and then further bolsters the need for some motion there by engaging a false reductio ad absurdum—that if the outer layer did not move some blood cells "would stay in the body forever." The latter is a kind of static representation of the dynamic life of a cell; that is, that a cell is created and survives in the same form forever.

> (Presented item) The resistance to the flow of blood in a vessel ultimately results, in large part, from the blood in contact with the vessel being stationary and the blood not in contact with the wall being in motion and having to slip over itself.

> Yes, I agree. In fact, I strongly agree. The blood that actually contacts the vessel wall is relatively stationary. Of course, nothing is totally stationary although, as you (would) find that ah, some red blood cells would be in your body forever. But, it's relatively stationary and the, the center level or layer flows much faster than the outer level and slips over itself and glides. So, I strongly agree, my confidence rating is 80 percent.

Summary and Conclusions

In this section, a summary of what has been presented in the chapter is given first. This is followed by some conclusions and implications.

Background regarding our research was presented first. This included, most importantly, a discussion of the focus of the research on important and difficult concepts of a subject matter; the description of a "calculus" for capturing the nature and structure of the many misconceptions that students acquire about these concepts; and presentation and discussion of some prevalent ways of thinking, reductive biases, that contribute to the acquisition of the faulty understandings.

A scheme—CSS—was presented for analyzing a concept and its related concepts for potential stability. Such analysis can be used to indicate how prone a cluster of concepts is to be misunderstood in learning and for predicting how stable the ensuing misconceptions are likely to be once they are acquired. The scheme was instantiated for a misconception (CALR—and a related "resistance-only" model of overall opposition to blood flow) about the cardiovascular system, and in this analysis the misconception was predicted to be highly stable: *pervasive* among learners, *robust* in the face of challenge, and *constant* over time. Some results from studies were presented that suggest that the misconception that was predicted to be highly stable according to CSS was, in fact, highly stable.

Knowing, in advance, how subjects would think, and think incorrectly, about a set of important concepts provided a fine opportunity to examine how the subjects would handle correct information at odds with their erroneous beliefs. These challenges were provided by the challenge propositions of the "instructional" study. It was discovered that the students routinely engaged mental maneuvers to rationalize the discrepancies between their own beliefs and the correct information, in ways that enabled them to keep from changing their own faulty models—from "changing their minds" (cf. Edwards 1968; Einhorn and Hogarth 1978; Festinger 1957; Ross and Lepper 1980). Numerous knowledge shields were identified, and some examples of their use by subjects were presented in the chapter.

Our studies, taken as a whole, verify that misconceptions can be held pervasively, with a high degree of internal consistency and coherence, and *tenaciously* (see below). For example, the results of the instructional/challenge study indicated that for many subjects the instructional part might as well not have even been there; it had so little effect on improving students' understanding. Furthermore many, and *many different kinds*, of knowledge shields were engaged by students to protect their prior knowledge, and the challenges to their knowledge often upset them. For example, the statement below gives the reaction of a subject during a part of the procedure in which the appropriate role of compliance in opposition was explained, along with the fact that increases in compliance in a vessel need not always decrease opposition, and that increases need not always increase it. As the subject himself said, "I *don't want* to think this way!"

> This is dangerous thinking. No, to my mind, I don't want to think this way. No, because I could say, I'd then have to think backwards. I'd have to think, unless I still haven't gotten your point, I would then have to conclude that it's good to have non-compliant vessels... Furthermore, I mean, the whole structure of cardiovascular physiology, the whole framework I use to understand it, is based on, you know, some key points. And this isn't one of them!

Our results also indicate that resistance to change of belief is opportunistic. As has been noted, many different kinds of shields were used, and in many different places and kinds of circumstances. It is as though the subjects would muster whatever means they could to ward off the potential effects of discrepant information, any time they encountered it. In this sense, the fending off of conceptual change among students seemed more unprincipled and timely than it did calculated and systematic.

This suggests one reason why the emending of misconceptions about complex concepts and subject matter may be especially difficult. In other papers we have proposed a complex and intricate structure for groups of related complex concepts (Coulson et al. 1989, Feltovich et al. 1989). This structure is network-like, with many interlinked components that can bolster each other in diverse and complicated ways, so that, for instance, the effects of a change in one component can be overridden by the conjoint effects of many others. If the application of knowledge shields is catch-as-catch can, as our results suggest, then conceptual change should be especially difficult for concepts of the kind we have examined. This is because in this kind of structure *there are so many places to hide* the effects of discrepant information. For example, there can be no such thing as a critical challenge to some key part of the network because of the multiplicity of influences on belief. This kind of conceptual network provides so many sources of resiliency, that some way can be found by the learner to accommodate the implications of a challenge to credibility. Changing belief probably requires a multi-faceted, systematic affront, a process of dismantling and reconstructing a large part of a belief *system.*

In other articles (e.g., Feltovich, Spiro, and Coulson 1997) we have argued that the kinds of subject matter and concepts that our research has shown to be so difficult for learners to understand—the continuous, the simultaneous, the interactive, the conditional (see "dimensions of difficulty" earlier in this chapter)—are just the kinds that are increasingly important for understanding our progressively complex, dynamic, and interconnected world. As we inspect the chapters of this book on "Smart Machines in Education," it seems that not much of current instructional work is being directed toward such subject matter. An exception is the educational work based on Qualitative Process Theory (e.g., de Koning and Bredeweg, chapter 9; Forbus, chapter 7) that addresses students learning and understanding of continuous, dynamic processes of the sort we have found to be so difficult for students to learn. It is hoped that when the next such volume is published, more attention will have been addressed to aiding the learning and understanding of this kind of important and complex learning material.

Chapter Twelve

Building the Right Stuff

Some Reflections on the CAETI Program

and the Challenge of Educational Technology

Kirstie L Bellman

The computer-aided education and training initiative (CAETI) was one of the largest research and development programs ever sponsored by the United States in computer-based education. CAETI, to a large number of researchers and developers, was a major source of research and development funding for three years. For dozens of teachers it was an opportunity for training and for entree into a new world of educational techniques. For hundreds of researchers and teachers, it was a call to arms, a passion to show how we could "do it right." To me, a DARPA program manager at the time, it was a program that I helped develop, managed and at midnight, worried about. The purpose of this chapter is to give the reader a retrospective of the CAETI research and development program directed towards K-12, its technology insertion experiments into the Department of Defense schools for dependents stationed overseas, and to discuss frankly the continuing difficulties and challenges to both building high quality educational technology and having it be the "right stuff" in the classroom.

CAETI had without question some of the top researchers and developers in the country, chosen for both research capability and a track record in fielded applications in schools. CAETI also tried out many enlightened policies for technology insertions into the schools: The teachers were paid for their extra time and trained. They helped us develop content and evaluation criteria and were brought early into the tool development cycle. The projects purposely spanned K-12 and cut across fields (the usual math and science emphasis, but also the social sciences and humanities were included) in order to develop a more consistent set of experiences with the technology for the learners over their school careers.

Did CAETI succeed? Yes, in many ways, but we want to examine why it was so hard, so expensive and more limited than our vision. As a research and development program, it has impacted a generation of researchers. It has brought many new researchers in top organizations (both academic and commercial) into the field of education and training. It has supported dozens of new scientific and technical developments in computer-based tools for education and in critically needed evaluation techniques and underlying infrastructure that will contribute to long-term use and development of educational systems. Two years after CAETI, a quick search of CAETI-related websites brought up over *five hundred* websites, many documenting the history or results of a particular project under CAETI, demonstrating an educational capability, or discussing continuing user experiences. Unfortunately the scope of this chapter does not allow description of more than a few representative projects and citation of a few representative technical papers and websites. It also precludes discussion of any of the projects having to do with adult education and training, of which there were many.

But the CAETI vision encompassed much more than even a vibrant research program. We wanted to explore new ways in which the scientific and technical community could reach out to school systems, teachers and students and work with them to develop "the right stuff" and help thereby to transform education. Although we had some successes here, we fell far short of our dream. One major goal of this chapter is to discuss our experience and, perhaps by doing so, help forewarn and better develop the next generation of technology insertion programs. We also wanted to explore new ways of organizing this type of transforming development—among communities of necessarily disparate technical fields and among diverse and competing academic and commercial partners. Hence CAETI was full of many types of experiments; some obvious to the casual observer, such as the creation of new technologies and insertions of technologies into the schools. Other organizational and managerial goals were behind the scenes and dealt with how to organize such a large project and induce people to work together. The reason for discussing such organizational experiments in a chapter on a technology program is that both the successes and the failures in this area greatly impact how schools and technology work together. Later in this chapter, I give my opinions on what worked and what did not. Hopefully this open discussion will lead to better successes in future programs. This is because one thing is clear: the needs that CAETI identified are still there and new programs sponsored by the government—large, encompassing, multi-disciplinary—are as necessary as ever.

Up front I want to apologize to all my CAETI researchers and developers— they did so much more than what could be recorded in a single book, much less a chapter. I have given short shrift to their efforts, skimmed and omitted some of my favorite parts, projects, findings and even people. The purpose is to give readers a sense of the spectrum of work occurring in CAETI. Hopefully I have retained just enough to make others curious enough to contact individuals and go to websites and references for much more.

The chapter is organized into roughly three parts as follows. First I briefly give an overview of the history of the CAETI program in order to help the reader understand some of the reasons for both the choices in what technologies were emphasized and the structure of the program. Then I describe the major goals of the program and in broad terms the results of both the technology development and insertions into K-12 classrooms. Finally, I give my opinion as to what worked well and what needs to be done better in future technology insertion programs.

The Start of the CAETI Program

The history of the CAETI program may strike the reader as a digression that has little to do with the development of educational technology and a lot to do with politics. In fact, many researchers would be the first to agree that their applications have been undermined by the terribly difficult politics surrounding most attempts to insert technology—or indeed, most curriculum innovations into the schools. Many of these researchers would characterize these failures of their programs as "political" and "social" however and certainly not "scientific" or "technical." I disagree. We have seen the development of some stunning beginnings in educational technology, but it's not yet the "right stuff." Educational technology needs to be able to support different teaching and learning styles, gracefully specialize to individual differences, handle diverse theories of pedagogy and learning, evaluate performance within a variety of media, support group as well as individual learning, and incorporate rich and deep content resources. When the technology does all of this well, we will find that while many current "political" and "organizational" issues will not disappear magically, we will have a technology and scientific base capable of addressing some of these politically charged issues directly *by* supporting diverse requirements, viewpoints, and specializations (cf. Bouillion and Gomez's work presented in chapter 10.)

In order to develop such an ambitiously flexible technology, one must start by listening to all the different goals, dreams, and needs of those who will use it. Out of this will come the functional specification for the technology. One must then listen to all the diverse contributors to the design of the technology; this includes much more than the researchers who investigate the computer-based tools and techniques. The design of educational technology is difficult precisely because it sits at the intersection of so many fields. It requires expertise in the content (meaning every discipline and skill we have defined), expertise in the cognitive sciences (for theories of pedagogy, learning, evaluation, user models, and appropriate sensory interfaces), expertise in cultural, social and small group processes, and expertise in engineering and product development. These are some of the voices needed to design educational technology. From its inception, one of the primary goals of CAETI was to develop research and applications that reflected such a complex and diverse set of participants.

The computer-aided education and training initiative had an inauspicious beginning in 1994 that included: a funding earmark pushed through by the Senate Appropriations Committee, the resigned approval of the Department of Defense (DoD) to use some of its limited research dollars in this fashion, the Defense Advanced Research Projects Agency (DARPA) as the reluctant receiver of the direction to make a research and development program out of these dollars, and the Department of Defense Dependent Schools (DoDDS) system that wanted to control these funds and initially resented being partnered with a research program. The funding came with an unusually liberal directive: "do something right" with computer-based technology for education, and make the DoDDS school system the recipient of the benefits. The DoDDS are schools for the children of US servicemen and women stationed overseas, with (in 1997) eighty-five thousand pre-kindergarten to grade twelve students and one hundred and sixty-seven schools located in fourteen countries. The program needed some vision of what the technology could do and to quickly bring together and manage a top-notch technology research and development team who could build the computer-based systems and help insert them into the selected schools. Not surprisingly, DoD turned to DARPA.

DARPA is the premier research and development sponsoring organization in DoD, and arguably one of the premier and unique research sponsoring organizations in government. One of its special capabilities is to bring together often-competing organizations drawn from leading industry and academic groups under a common umbrella program. It has had a leadership role for many years in the information sciences and other technological areas. Because it is not bound by some of the same review and contracting strictures of other organizations, it can often work in novel ways to form programs and to move rapidly out in areas of interest. Tice DeYoung, a colleague from NASA, while we were at DARPA once called DARPA the "green berets of technology." Indeed, DARPA's role in technology development has often been to get everyone's attention, organize a critical mass of researchers to address some especially abstruse research problem, go in and "hit the beach hard," clearing the way for a longer term, more sustained effort by other organizations to obtain the goals.

Having DARPA develop the technology and insertion program would in fact shape the program in a number of ways: first, the hard technical challenges of building the right new type of technology would be emphasized over the equally hard and valid challenges of managing the organizations and sociology of changing school systems and the training of existing personnel. The latter concerns would perhaps have pushed the program to de-emphasize creating new technology and would have instead studied more about the use of some of the gems that already existed in educational technology. Secondly, DARPA as a DoD organization would be looking for educational applications that furthered the development of training applications or were generalizable to other domains of military interest (such as new technical developments in underlying infrastructure and evaluation.) This meant that the program, for example, would only marginally address some of the needed cognitive studies in children's and adult learning, but would address more fully some of the issues of building large scale, networked and interoperable software architectures.

Training and related domains have always been of interest to some extent within DARPA because these domains often drive the needs for the development of certain types of technologies such as advanced simulation, interface technologies, mobile devices, and so forth. It is also true that DoD spends an enormous amount of money each year on education and training, and hence there is ripe opportunity for demonstrating the utility and the savings stemming from new technologies. Even though the Pentagon was justifiably leery about the politics of "peace dividends" drawing away badly needed research dollars, the military community, nonetheless, was keenly aware of the needs for advancements in educational and training technologies. Hence, on July 9, 1994, Under Secretary of Defense John Deutch hosted an interagency federal seminar on learning productivity. He stressed that the development and use of advanced education and training technologies is of significant importance to the readiness of our forces in order to ensure that our military is capable of performing the high technology jobs required by the armed services. During this same seminar, Anita Jones, then Director, Defense Research and Engineering (DDR&E), emphasized that there is a range of applications for learning technology needed by defense, from the individual pilot, technician, etc. to teams such as tank crews, fire fighters, special operations forces, and decision makers such as commanders and battle staffs. All of the armed services have recognized the increasing importance of education and training because of the advancements in sophisticated weapons and support technology, the increased reliance on part-time personnel, and the decrease of experienced personnel, hours and real estate available for real world training.

At that time, I was a program manager at DARPA, heading programs in software engineering, architectures, formal methods for computer science, and beginning a modest DARPA program in computer-based education and training. I was far below the level for participating in the political dramas swirling around the funding that would become the CAETI program. I became involved after attending some early sessions at the Pentagon where a small group was brainstorming how one might best use the original funding. I had already participated in several brainstorming sessions, sponsored by the White House Office of Science and Technology Policy, on how to best use computer-based technology to further educational and training goals. Anita Jones gave me the charge to develop the program, and CAETI was born.

Developing CAETI Attitudes and Themes

As a DARPA program, CAETI sought to identify opportunities to hit hard at bottlenecks in the current technology and gain some immediate payoffs that would add substance to the hyperbole underlying the promotion of educational technology. The good part of having DARPA in charge of the program would be that it would use its unique organizational capabilities to bring in some of the best and the brightest and make some technical breakthroughs. It would not be interested in just deploying some reasonably good commercial work or networking the schools, but would lay the foundations for needed technical development. This would also serve DARPA's requirements for acting as a driver for research and development that could then be useful to other domains. These domains would include training and adult education applications for DoD.

Hence from the beginning CAETI had the very difficult job of juggling both K-12 and DoD adult training and education needs. CAETI was carefully designed to provide education and training software and an integration architecture that has the flexibility to serve both DoDDS and the Services' education and training programs. However, although there were technical advantages to serving both learner populations (in terms of designing more robust and flexible technology and the additional support and feedback we received from the teachers and trainers for adults), it was nonetheless a further complication in the lives of many of the CAETI researchers who were already feeling stretched by the demands of live teachers and classrooms. We did allow researchers to focus on different populations according to their interests, but the coordination of their efforts was more difficult. Although not described in this chapter, there was wonderful work accomplished in cooperation with many different military organizations, on language training applications, adult tutoring, medical training, in field evaluation and after action review, web-based courses, and so forth (See Landauer and Bellman 1999 and 1998 for some references). Many of the CAETI K-12 participants did not realize that every year there was an equally large set of CAETI meetings on such things as training applications and scenario generation.

The Tedious Conversation

We noted above that the design of educational technology is difficult precisely because it sits at the intersection of many fields and is desired by many different users who impose different and often competing requirements on such systems. From its inception, one of the primary goals of the CAETI was to develop research and applications that reflected such a complex and diverse set of participants. "The tedious conversation," as I often termed it in CAETI meetings, is the difficult but necessary conversations (and eventual agreements) among all the different participants in a successful application of educational computer-based technology. This diverse but necessary group includes, of course, students and teachers, but also curriculum developers (in the school system and in the textbook publishing houses) and the psychologists and educational experts at the universities working on pedagogy, standards, and theory. It also includes the researchers who invent novel technology, the other researchers who evaluate and critique the theoretical and the practical applications of this technology, and the engineers and businesses that turn these prototypes into reliable products. This group also includes a few research and development sponsoring organizations, such as NSF, NASA, NIST, and the Naval Research Laboratory. Each has its legitimate interests and needs for education programs—some as users, some as inventors and evaluators of technology, and most often, as both. Finally, little recognized by all these factions in the often-fractious conversations are the parents. There are a few exceptional programs that have in fact made an effort to bring in the parents (NSF has several examples, and a few school systems have done outstanding jobs in bringing in active parents), but by and large, the parents are supposed to sign the permission slips for our experiments and then cluck approvingly at our science fairs and open houses. This is unfortunate because educational policies reflect our deepest cultural and ethical values: What is important to impart from our culture? Who should have what knowledge? (Often seen as who should be allowed in to what disciplines or have what opportunities.) Who should teach whom? What kinds of skills—intellectual, emotional, and social—are necessary? Ignoring these implications often results in the surprise that educational reformers or researchers experience when their straightforward (to them) new ideas are so vehemently rejected. In fact, the different participants in the "tedious conversation" rarely recognized the need for the other participants until deep into the process of developing and using the technology.

In CAETI, we worked from the outset to involve all the needed participants in early and continuous conversations about the development of the technology and—most importantly—about the proposed insertions of this technology. In contrast to the usual "throw it over the wall" method of introducing a computer program, we incorporated or developed a series of techniques and processes. These carefully elicited and then mapped the goals of the school system, the teachers' personal goals, and the curriculum standards to the proposed technologies. We, like most other creators of educational technology applications, involved students too little in this initial planning stage, although their reactions and, of course, performance is a key part of all the evaluations (we will critique our use of students later). We attempted to involve from the outset all grades and content areas, and to develop experiments that would directly address how school systems could provide staff and students with continual technology experience and use. We also involved all (several hundred) researchers and users under CAETI in the development of the evaluation criteria and metrics (both for the human performance and for the software engineering aspects of the technology). In CAETI, as program manager, I spent a lot of time trying to be sure all the voices were heard, and further, that no voices overpowered the others. One of the ways that I supported this conversation was to incorporate a lesson I learned from Erik Mettala, a talented DARPA program manager who created many well-known software and manufacturing programs. Basically he set up several of his technology insertion programs with contracts that teamed domain experts, researchers, businesses and customers organizations. As he so correctly understood, the customers pulled for useable results, the businesses provided an economic base for emerging new tools, and the researchers and the domain experts together provided a better specification for the correct capabilities. We also knew from experience that technology transfer is still most effectively done by putting people together. Hence early in the program, I solicited and encouraged teaming arrangements. Many productive teams of universities and industry partners resulted, and these, in turn were coupled with either DoDDS as the customer or in programs across the military services.

The Core Architecture Team

Encouraging the different parties to talk is just one type of coordination activity required in a large program. It is often the first step in a number of integration processes that need to be set up in a large technology insertion program. While DARPA and many sponsoring organizations have always supported interdisciplinary programs, they often have made the mistake of not paying for it. In not doing so they are essentially saying to the researchers, "You are now funded to do the following work, but, by the way, make sure you collaborate with all these other superb people that we've brought together in this community." That approach does not work. One of the things that has worked in CAETI is to take essentially one-fourth of the funding and devote it explicitly to having people and methods who are charged with management and coordination among the different technologies and user requirements. This included the architecture and the evaluation efforts, as well as an investment in new research about how to integrate and manage interdisciplinary work.

Part of the reason for elaborating the context as I have just done is that the different stakeholders, the different goals for the programs and the requirements on it all impacted the scientific and technical development of the program. It encouraged us from the beginning to treat the development and insertion of the technology as a system problem. Educational systems have many formidable challenges, but some of them are similar to the problems of any large complex system. Many of the CAETI researchers and developers had worked with other large system development programs, such as space systems, military systems, health systems, commercial networks and so forth. Some of the common risks associated with technology insertions in such programs are: Immature technology, lack of appropriate new "concepts of operations" (i.e., suggested practices for using the system) and outdated policies, failure to integrate the new with older system capabilities (we never get a clean slate), good answers for the wrong problems, and the cost of always rebuilding capabilities partly due to not reusing prior experience, technology, or results. Furthermore, new technology insertions are frequently associated with an increased likelihood of schedule and cost overruns. Hence I purposely pulled into the program some of the more experienced and creative system architects I could find from other large programs. One of the interesting and exciting problems of both applying previous methods and developing new system engineering and architectural approaches was that education (like health care) is a service industry that is beginning to require technological components. Hence, these new architectures would bring to the fore the need to represent and reason about human activities and requirements immersed in a man-made and engineered environment. (Bellman and Landauer 2000a.)

It became clear very early in the program that if it was to succeed we needed to conduct some sophisticated organizational experiments. One such experiment was the organization of this very large program into a core architecture team (CAT) and "clusters." CAT was responsible for developing the organizational and architectural frameworks that would help integrate different efforts, conduct experiments, organize technology insertions, monitor progress and problems, and help evaluate the "health and status" of the program. The clusters were groups of related technologies (according to the CAETI themes described below) led by a cluster leader. The cluster leader had no fiscal or managerial authority over the members of the clusters (an initial concern of many CAETI developers). However, the cluster leaders did represent and advocate the needs of their cluster members to the CAT, to the independent evaluation team, and often to me. They helped set up opportunities for demonstrations, including the important selection of projects for DoDDS, and promoted their members' technologies for inclusion in various adult DoD programs. They kept an eye out for integration opportunities and other opportunities for their members, helped organize their cluster responses to developing evaluation metrics and architectural standards for that sub-discipline, and generally fought quite hard for additional resources for their clusters (I can attest to that!) Although at first the other CAETI participants were worried about a two-tier system in CAETI, where the cluster leaders would be part of a privileged elite, I believe that the majority eventually felt that they were receiving a valuable integration service. I had gotten what I had hoped for—a core of individuals dedicated to looking across the program for all of our sakes in order to help integrate and develop the capabilities of all participants to the fullest extent.

Forming CAT was an experiment in distributed decision-making; I did not believe that any single group could architect the entire CAETI program with its diverse stakeholders and goals. I was enormously fortunate in CAT. They were amazingly dedicated, determined, brilliant and articulate. CAT itself—what it was trying to do and its own internal dynamics—was always difficult. We argued a great deal and sometimes it was difficult to make progress. However, on the whole it did create a suitable arena for the expression of the diverse voices of CAETI, and it remains a fascinating case study on new ways of organizing and managing large systems and on the types of computer technology *we needed* to do that type of group design and development.

Eventually the core architecture team contained me, the cluster leaders, a DoDEA liaison member, my own support personnel for program management, and two new roles that were identified (thanks to the ISX Corporation) during the early days of the program: the site coordination and site integration leads. These latter two individuals coordinated the handling of the crucial chores of coordinating all visits and interactions among researchers and developers and the schools. They dealt with the local architectural and technology insertions issues. An integration laboratory was mocked up with exactly the same systems as a DoDDS school, and software was tested and integrated there prior to releasing it to the schools. It was also common to have other CAETI participants at the frequent CAT meetings to discuss particular issues.

Lastly, education is full of fads, movements, and passionate advocates. Although we had great interest in CAETI in supporting many of the new educational paradigms, such as collaborative and project-based curricula, I also felt strongly that the most revolutionary thing one could do was to support a diversity of styles and modes of interaction for both students and teachers. Education fundamentally involves individuals—both the individuals who teach with different predilections and talents and the individuals who learn with different preferences and styles. One of the great promises of educational technology is the ability to scale up by customizing the presentation and feedback to any number of different kinds of individuals. This should also include the ability to support lots of individual teaching styles—even for the same teacher.

The Four CAETI Clusters

Projects were focused on innovative approaches and techniques that would enable significant advances in learning performance through the effective use of advanced computer and networking technologies. They were selected to provide the program with a mixed portfolio of near-term and longer-term research and development products, each with a technology insertion and/or transfer plan. The products were clustered according to three technology themes: Smart navigators to access and integrate resources (SNAIR), collaborative applications for project-based educational resources (CAPER), and expert associates to guide individualized learning (EAGIL). In addition, there was a fourth cluster that comprised enabling or integration tools that were used to develop a CAETI open systems architecture and evaluation framework, as well as system engineering and evaluation capabilities (called the enabling technology cluster or "ETC.").

Smart Navigators to Access and Integrate Resources (SNAIR)

One of the first promises of computer resources for teachers and students was access to quality material—no matter where it was located. The current limitation is to find good quality material in the form one wants, out of the enormous amount of both good but not relevant material and what I have called "cybertrash." Even fabulous material—pictures, text, and processes—doesn't automatically turn into valuable material for education, industry or any other kind of endeavor. Hence SNAIR emphasized not only the problem of identifying the material but also turning it into useable material for one's purposes. Making it useable includes integrating it with other types of processes, such as new types of educational tutors and agents, other educationally helpful tools, additional content, and suitable presentation and evaluation environments. The original thrust of this cluster was to create intelligent computational resources for students and instructors that access, mediate, tailor, and integrate networked data and computational resources. SNAIR techniques for customizing digital material would allow much better representation of the users and the type of information they needed for a given task. This "user model" would then be utilized by other tools and techniques to automatically screen digital information (from such sources as the internet, world wide web, or digital libraries) and present it to the user in the form required—a lesson plan, a text document, a room in a virtual environment, as part of the knowledge of a "tutor," or as the input into numerous other types of simulation and processing programs. We drew not only from technologies already being explored for education such as web technologies, but also from the software engineering disciplines, including especially the idea of higher-level specification languages to help describe the user and the user's tasks in more analyzable forms. SNAIR projects were loosely coordinated with current NSF/ARPA digital library projects and drew upon advances in navigators, browsers, mediators, (Maluf, Wiederhold, Linden, and Panchapagesan 1997) advanced and customizable user interfaces, user and domain modeling, human language technology, and Associates technology.

Don McKay (then at Lockheed Martin), the cluster leader for SNAIR, had to contend with a wide range of technologies in a time of enormous development in and use of web technologies for education (McKay 1997). We needed to handle new types of resources and diverse commercial standards and architectures. To these we wanted to add new capabilities in resource discovery, resource composition and resource repositories. Several of the projects dealt with providing web-based resources to teachers and students: On Line Learning Academy (OLLA), developed by Lockheed Martin, Educational Technologies and the Franklin Institute Science Museum, provided a simple to use but powerful set of websites with educational hands-on resources and was one of the most popular CAETI products in DoDDS. Shepherd (University of Texas, Arlington team under the much missed leadership of the late Karan Harbison) was also a web-based environment for storing, organizing and sharing information about Internet resources, extending the idea of just "bookmarking" internet resources in a number of ways and making them so that they could be collaboratively developed, shared, and searched in rich ways. The purpose of the Texas A&M's Walden's Paths "path authoring tool and server" was to let teachers (and students) collect, organize, and present Web information and to focus their web searches. It was one of the projects explored by art and music courses. One of the nice results was that students created paths for other students.

Several of the other projects were geared towards more fundamental underlying capabilities that would lead to more powerful uses of existing digital resources. The purpose of the Princeton University Media Center project was to let teachers and students search in a nonlinear fashion, view, annotate, and use digital video so that the digital video would become as useable in a classroom as traditional text sources. This would allow widespread access to video as primary and secondary sources, e.g., current events, historic video, lectures, design. The purpose of the CMU "TOM" infrastructure project was to relieve the teachers, students and school systems from the burden of manually adapting material and some of the problems with installing software and hardware upgrades. It provided an infrastructure for handling and adapting information, e.g., file conversion, mail messages, and deframing with the use of expert services distributed across the Net. Gateways provide web services and then TOM provides type brokers that translate between types of documents.

The Latent Sematic Analyzer (Tom Landauer, University of Colorado) project provided concept-based search, automatic essay-based assessment and diagnosis, matching students to learning materials, and domain and student knowledge modeling. In their preliminary results, students benefited from the improvements in choosing appropriate texts for them based on these methods. The company, Intelligent Automation Inc. worked on a project that included developing a formal representation language for courseware and student description, a "soft" infrastructure using computed web links (CooL Links) and agents for optimization of resource selection. The University of Colorado's (Dennis Heimbigner) SERL software dock project (part of both the SNAIR and ETC clusters) purpose was to provide a rapid configuration and deployment of software and data in a scalable fashion at a distance over the Internet. Their research addressed managing many multiple, autonomous producers and consumers, complex inter-artifact dependencies, and the use of agents. In 1997 they demonstrated the successful simulated deployment of the OLLA system over the Internet, using an automated, recursive install and update of major subsystems. Many of the capabilities of SNAIR were integrated with the other clusters. One of the interesting cultural changes in CAETI was watching the gradual rapprochement between those working on the web-based notion of collaboration and shared spaces, and the virtual worlds and multi-user virtual environments (MUVE) notions of collaboration and shared spaces which is described next.

Collaborative Applications for Project-Based Educational Resources (CAPER)

A key resource we want to access in the new information age is ourselves. The original goal of CAPER was to produce authentic, multimedia, and synthetic environments that supported involvement, experimentation, exploration, and collaboration in cross-disciplinary projects. CAPER leveraged off advancements in distributed simulation, visualization and multimedia environments, a spectrum of virtual reality and virtual worlds (including immersive techniques as well as text-based collaborative games) and developments in project-based curricula. We wanted not only to work on and share material artifacts but also to facilitate human interactions. Surprisingly, some of the best ideas for creating interesting places with realistic human interactions come from the efforts of Internet barnstormers inventing text-based multi-user role-playing games. I first became acquainted with multi-user dungeons, (MUDs)—later called multi-user virtual environments (MUVEs)— when looking for collaborative environments for space system design (one of my colleagues, Mike O'Brien, dragged me out of my office in 1992 and set me down in front of his machine, and I was hooked from then on). Later, I in turn made use of the technology in my DARPA programs. One of the interesting cultural experiences I had was conducting some of the first "MUDs and education" workshops, which included, among others, diehard virtual reality military researchers and Internet cyberpunks. To everyone's credit, they dived in and developed many productive collaborations. Because the reasons for being interested in MUDs in education are not well known, I will take the opportunity to discuss them in a little more depth before summarizing the CAPER applications. Developed originally in 1979, MUDs are one of the most interesting new developments in computing to come along in many years (Riner and Clodius 1995) (Leong 1999). Just in the last few years, they have moved out of the "game" arena into educational and corporate environments for distance learning, collaborative learning, literacy support (at all grade levels, including adult), corporate meeting support, professional organizations, and even technical conferences (Landauer and Bellman 1999, 1998; Bellman 1997b).

Imagine reading a story set in some time and place. If the story is well written, it can feel like one is actually experiencing that situation or even becoming that character, regardless of whether the story is fiction or nonfiction. Stories can present information about a situation that is usually only learned through experience; they are particularly good at descriptions of complex settings that are very hard to construct (Dautenhahn 1998). If a multi-user virtual environment is designed well, it is like a well-written story in its power to transport the user to a different situation, but it has three other important features. First, for already created stories (often called "quests"), it is interactive, which means that the reader can affect the behavior and outcome of the story, so, in particular, the reader can explore the story in many different ways. Based on the reader's experiences in that world so far, they will also be exposed to certain characters, actions, and parts of the story. Second, it is also multi-user, so that the reader can work with, play against, or interact with other readers. All users within the same room can see each other's actions, character descriptions, and conversation with others (except when others "whisper," which is a private point-to-point communication not broadcast to the rest of the room). Third, and most important of all, there is plenty of "room" (and much encouragement within this subculture) for users to create their own "stories," characters, and places. Both humans and computer programs enter these worlds and act within them as distinct characters with names, descriptions, and behaviors.

These MUVE stories are stored as databases on servers (that provide other services for managing the multi-user world), accessed by the users (both human and computer-based processes) with client programs. A simple command language is provided by all the server programs for MUVEs that allows users to move around, act and talk within the virtual world. There is also a simple construction language in many MUVEs that makes it easy for a player to immediately become a builder (a creator) in that world. A MUVE implements a notion of *places* that *we* create, in which *we* interact with each other, and *we use* our computing tools, together, instead of having all tool use and collaborative interactions *mediated through* tools used individually. Like other Virtual Reality environments, MUVEs employ an underlying spatial metaphor. Humans use spatial maps for many things. We are able to organize an enormous amount of data and information if we can place it in a spatial context. MUVEs elicit a surprisingly powerful sense of space using only text. Characters may gather in the same location for conversations and other group activities, where their interactions are not restricted (or interpreted) by the servers, and because the servers do not get in the way, it is as if they have become almost transparent. The sense of "being there" can be quite strong, and in fact, the emotional "reality" of human users comes across surprisingly well, and this in turn greatly enhances the sense of being there, making MUVE experiences very compelling. This is why MUVEs are VR programs: the human interactions are real; only the physical ones are not (Clodius 1994; Riner Clodius 1995; Clodius 1995). One reason for being interested in multi-user domains is because there may be hundreds of people in the MUVE at any given time, moving around separately and independently, creating objects in real-time, and interacting with each other. From just a social science viewpoint, MUVEs are clearly an important new phenomenon. There are hundreds of internationally populated MUVEs, some with as many as ten thousand active players. These players are not simply visitors as to a website, but rather users who spend often several hours a day within that world. Many of them describe their MUVEs as some of the places they live. Some of these virtual communities have now been in existence as long as ten years. They have elected town officials in some places; they walk around their towns, have their own places which they build, and describe themselves as "living" there. They have imbued these virtual places with meanings. They have roles and functions that they play within those communities. As scientists, we want to understand more about why some of these virtual communities flourish over years and why others vanish within a month. Certainly for anyone interested in collaborative technologies, we need to know what MUVE participants are doing right that they are able to live, work and build together in these virtual communities.

In CAETI, we added to the basic MUVE capabilities in several ways. We developed more advanced MUVE architectures, especially ones with the ability to keep a text, two-dimensional, and three-dimensional version of the world in sync (as in the CENTRE project described below). This was important in a number of ways, not the least of which was that it always allowed users very simple ways of sharing in the world, even in a limited way. The advanced architectures also allowed us to distribute the functionality underlying these worlds in more powerful ways. A good example of this was in better-distributed database management. We also made it possible to have many more types of heterogeneous tools available from within the environment. Some of these tools were new types of embodied intelligent utilities and agents that helped individual users (librarians, guides, and tutors) or conducted support activities across the world (evaluation agents.) Some of these new tools also helped tailor resources to an individual user. V. J. Saraswat (who contributed to CAPER while at Xerox PARC and is now at ATT) points out, in "Education in the Post-Modern Era" a number of educationally interesting MUVEs and features of them. "Among other points, one stands out: these spaces help make concrete and explicit the actual practice of teaching in the form of a log already symbolically registered and accessible for future reflection and analysis. Because the participants are working through a server, it is possible to log their ongoing fine-grained interactions in powerful ways that reflects the multiplicity of the participants' contributions ... makes the actual practice concrete and accessible. In this way they open the door to powerful support for the development of tools both formal and informal (intelligent evaluation and assessment agents, tutors, intelligent access, learning assistants) and to social practices but in a fundamentally social context." One of my CAETI dreams is that eventually learners will have wonderfully rich places where they can have both the advantages of one-on-one tutoring, via intelligent companion tutors, and the benefits of the collaborative and social interactions within these places.

Like those heading the other clusters, Mark Pullen (George Mason University) as cluster leader was faced with the daunting task of coordinating a wide variety of projects in CAPER and the further one of taking the very new types of capabilities offered in the ideas of "learning spaces" and somehow dovetailing them with the needs of traditionally taught curricula in DoDDS. Although project-based and collaborative technologies were of deep interest to the teachers in the testbeds, there was little curriculum material developed to support it. Hence most of the educational MUVEs were used to support literary skills. This is still true, although hopefully, with the development of more and more environments with significant simulation capabilities, this will change and become a learning space where children can not only show their understanding in the descriptions of the worlds they create, but also in the behaviors that occur within those worlds. Some of the projects for collaborative "learning spaces" included a team (Intermetrics, Yale, University of Illinois at Chicago) developing a multimedia math/science world called "Wyndhaven." Another team (Xerox PARC, Phoenix College) created several impressive virtual communities (including ones that combined schoolchildren with senior citizens) and focused on inserting into these environments better simulation, construction, experimentation, and reflection capabilities for the learners. The SUMMIT program at Stanford (Parvati Dev) created a number of distributed multimedia MUVEs geared towards both medical education and support groups related to health. SUMMIT also had methods for authoring multimedia content that passed one of the more difficult tests, e.g., the doctors actually used them to create materials for their courses. The ExploreNet project (University of Central Florida) used older children to help create the educational worlds for younger children, thereby benefiting both age groups. Their projects emphasized both social science and literary curricula. GMU taught programming courses in a C++ MUVE. Peg Syverson and John Slatin at UT Austin have been conducting very successful undergraduate English classes on CheshireMOOn, a "delightfully literate place" (Saraswat 1997) set in the story of Alice in Wonderland. The SAIC corporation and University of California, San Diego worked on developing intelligent agents for virtual worlds, including a "librarian" that interacts with students to help them find information. During the course of the program, gradually more and more EAGIL (see below) tutors and agents were introduced also into the MUVEs, one of the successful examples of cross-program integration.

CAPER projects also included a number of educational simulations. These efforts are particularly important in deepening the level of content in educational technology. Examples include GMU and Shodor that provided several impressive simulations on a number of topics, including galaxy formation and the mathematics of fractals, AMPHION, developed by the University of Wyoming and NASA-Ames to visualize space objects for collaborative use, and "Function machines," a graphic programming language for math/science by BBN. Similarly, several of the projects developed impressive multimedia content with associated analysis tools. A good example of this is the Intelligent Multimedia/Thinking Skills project (GMU) that built instructional modules for social studies, with an online coach/tutor and tools, that support higher-order thinking skills, and excellent source materials for a module on slavery in the U.S. Other collaborative projects deserve, like all these projects, a chapter in themselves. Hands on Universe (Lawrence Berkeley Laboratories) in collaboration with the Lawrence Hall of Science, TERC Inc, Adler Planetarium, and Yerkes Observatory, as well as an international network of educators and astronomers, allowed high school students to conduct real science in an apprentice role and to direct the use of large telescopes accessed over the Internet. Other projects, such as UNC's collaborative web applications and Guzdial and Kolodner's important work at Georgia Tech on learning through design and complex problem solving, were developing both fundamental new methods (including formal methods) for supporting collaboration and new theory for understanding the collaboration of small groups of learners.

Expert Associates to Guide Individualized Learning (EAGIL) for Students and Instructors.

One of the first potentials recognized for computers in education was the promise that computer-based solutions would allow individualized education and training by appropriate presentation, customization of material, and feedback in the hope of gaining some of the advantages of human one on one tutoring (Bloom 1984.) The original goal of EAGIL was to produce intelligent guides, tutors or associates that adapt to student learning styles, respond to student progress, and support individualized learning. They were to incorporate expertise in domain knowledge, user models, training methods, evaluation techniques and draw from advances in artificial intelligence, cognitive sciences, and software engineering. For example, such advances include the ability of users to author and adapt tutors, the incorporation of distributed intelligent agents, enhancement of multimedia and visualization technology, and new work in associates (a class of intelligent agents focused on supporting an individual's performance as opposed to instruction (see below). Also, EAGIL emphasized customized intelligent support for instructors' curriculum development, lesson plans, administrative tasks, and professional development. EAGIL leveraged off the last thirty years of development of computer-based "tutors" and "trainers." The problem with many of the earlier tutors was that most had been written as one large monolithic computer program that included all of its content, associated analyses and interfaces, pedagogy, and user models. This made it difficult to add new content or to make use of the excellent capabilities of different tutors or learning aids. Many tutors, especially commercial products, had not made use of the available academic work in student modeling, coaching, inquiry skills and critical thinking. EAGIL was to develop architectures, standards, and tools to open up the different tutoring systems and also develop new ways of utilizing tutoring agents in very different ways within virtual environments or in conjunction with other processing tools.

The phrase I used was "blowing out the back-end" of the tutor, and I wanted not only to open up tutoring systems because it would be important for sharing their resources, but also because we could then make tutors essentially a front-end to a potentially enormous number of new resources, including of course the world wide web. I also wanted to open up the tutor so that it could absorb the information from a common environment with the learner. The hope was that by essentially "co-experiencing" the simulations or virtual world or tool environment along with its learner, the tutor could observe and guide the learner while situated in an appropriate setting. In this idea of course I drew from the excellent ongoing work of Forbus, Koedinger, Gomez, Suthers and many others in the program (see the bibliography and related chapters in this book). To make the tutor a front-end for new resources or to make them coexperience an environment, clearly posed fundamentally new types of capabilities for tutors. Whereas before they had been written rather like an oracle, with complete knowledge (at least of the knowledge they had), now they would have to change the kind of knowledge and intelligence they had. They would have to know a lot about recognizing an instance of their own type of knowledge. For example, if I'm an astronomy tutor, I would have to be smart enough first to recognize that a particular astronomy site on the web is my kind of knowledge and then to organize it and transform it suitably to my target population and my form of pedagogy.

The goal of the EAGIL tutors and associates was never to replace teachers or parents but rather to help with more routine tasks so that they could focus on the critical tasks with the learners. I was recently asked at a UCLA talk why any teacher would want tutors at all. The answer is simple, economy of scale. We have too much new information to ever be an expert in the old-fashioned sense of knowing everything that humans know about a subject. Teachers certainly will no longer be able to be the local "expert" as they were a hundred years ago in nearly any topic – maybe even for the younger elementary ages. Public school teachers also have too many people, with too many individual needs and differences, to give them the highest quality of personal attention and time. This does not mean just the kids who need more help to conquer a subject, but the brightest kids who need just as much attention to reach their potential. If we can have an automated way of providing meaningful and well-organized content that a learner can absorb at his or her own pace (and eventually in the best style for them) for even half of the required material, the teacher could have the joy of teaching again – that is the joy of watching an individual learner "get it" because that teacher was able to help, guide, suggest, coax, and inspire.

Neil Jacobstein (Teknowledge, Inc.) was the talented and able leader of the EAGIL cluster, and together that cluster accomplished a great deal in CAETI. They built several open tutors and subcomponents and developed several associates with open components, some of which could work through Internet browsers. They also developed "tutors not found in the COTS world that are focusing on higher order skills such as inquiry, investigation, simulation and model building, and construction of logical advice." (Jacobstein 1997). They also developed several experimental architectures. Neil Jacobstein and the EAGIL cluster made the following distinctions between tutors and associates, "A tutor provides *individualized instruction* to a student in a specific domain. An associate does not attempt instruction; its purpose is *performance support* to a teacher, a parent, a student, or a person performing some other role. Associates can provide knowledge-based, peer-to-peer, *coaching and guidance*. Associates will accept and perform delegated tasks, with increasing sophistication. Associates may be thought of as multifaceted agents that have a broad and growing repertoire of performance support behavior." (Jacobstein 1997.)

Again, the diversity of the projects in EAGIL was impressive. The tools ranged from relatively mature tutoring systems like PUMP Algebra, Advise, BELVEDERE, and Multimedia Tutor to research on associate systems like the CENTRE Associate, and Bayesian nets for student modeling. Some program products participated in the DoDEA Schools—Teacher's Associate, PUMP, BELVEDERE, Advise, and Diagnosis and Repair. Other program products were used in cross cluster integration experiments like Active Illustrations, CENTRE Associate, Teacher's Associate, and BELVEDERE (one such integration experiment is described below in more depth). Other associate programs were used in commercial and training applications; I do not describe them here (see the bibliography for some citations and the last section in this chapter for a list of websites).

The tutor projects included the popular and impressive PUMP algebra tutors (Ken Koedinger) and University of Massachusetts Intelligent Multimedia Tutors (Beverly Woolf). Northwestern contributed several impressive tutoring projects: The Advise multimedia problem solver (Kass), Active Illustrations simulation construction kit with explanations (Ken Forbus), and SIBLE inquiry based learning notebook (Louis Gomez). Many of the projects also included the development of general core resources for tutors, especially on assessment methods, as did the University of Georgia, Diagnosis and Repair for testing (Bruce Britton) and a supportive project from Princeton (George Miller) on Wordnet, a lexicon for reading and vocabulary training. The University of

Pittsburgh BELVEDERE constructivist problem-solving project will be described in more depth in an example of a CAETI integration experiment. Working on "Associates" or Associate related technologies were Teknowledge (Sams) User Associate, a productivity aid and guide for users (CAETI CENTRE, Desktop); ISX (Bewley) Teacher's Associate, a productivity aid for teachers; Search's (Duncan) Personal Digital Associate (PDA), and Teacher's Associate, a Teknowledge (Williams) Parent's Associate for coaching parents. Several other projects were developing not only Associates, but core capabilities for other Associates such as University of Pittsburgh (Van Lehn) Bayesian Student Models and Barbara Hayes-Roth's Virtual Theatre "puppets."

The Enabling Technology Cluster or "ETC"

ETC was dedicated to providing new tools and techniques that would allow many of these new technologies to work together and to be used across many different computing environments. One of the most important promises of the new computer technology was that it was all supposed to work together. Computer scientists and software engineers have too often claimed such interoperability, but we are often confronted with the bleak, frustrating reality of how fragile this interoperability is in our everyday work life. CAETI also developed evaluation techniques for assessing the outcomes at many different levels for new types of technologies. Because educational technology cuts across all the diverse fields and participants noted above, it is very difficult to create the suitable integration and evaluation frameworks. Hence, we didn't do it alone, and we didn't try to impose our ideas of architecture and evaluation on either users or developers. Instead everyone in CAETI was required, contractually, to coordinate his or her efforts with our architectural and evaluation teams. This in practice meant that all were part of a community of interest attempting to develop suitable standards, integration strategies, architectures and metrics for their particular content or technology. The evaluation and architecture teams provided hours of free consultation and "free" (paid for by CAETI not the individual project) expertise on the appropriate strategies that a given project could employ given its goals, cost limitations etc. We also hoped to do experiments actually comparing different evaluation approaches, but that turned out to be infeasible given the difficulties described below in just conducting any long-term studies in the schools.

Minimal Architectural Requirements

I cannot include in this chapter all the excellent work done on software engineering, language development, formal methods, and especially architectures for CAETI. Some of the most important outcomes of CAETI were the architectural efforts, such as the opening up and agreements among different tutoring tools and environments and the concept of "minimal architectural requirements." As discussed in the introduction, I came into the program having experience in information architectures, and one of the first things I did was cajole some of the best teams and individuals from other software architecture programs and formal methods to become interested in education and work on CAETI. We were beginning to have sophisticated and helpful methods for representing and reasoning about complex systems, for designing these systems and for maintaining them, and there was no reason why educational systems should not have (at last) the benefits of such techniques and technology. CAETI had too many stakeholders— companies, organizations, and universities—to try to come in heavy-handedly and require compliance to one set of requirements, standards or ways of interacting. The participants differed in the money and time they could commit to such a process and in their willingness to do so for any number of social and technical reasons. One of the keys to the minimal architecture notion (worked on in depth by the technical members of the core architecture team, which included in this instance, me, all the cluster leaders (Lynne Gilfillan, Karan Harbison, Don McKay, Neil Jacobstein, and Mark Pullen) and a few special others, including Bob Balzer of USC/ISI and Bruce Bullock of ISX) was that architecture here is not seen as a fixed structure but rather as a set of relationships and agreements, and just like a relationship, they can be found to be useful and strengthen and grow over time with trust and mutual benefits. Hence the idea was to set a very low entry bar and then have individual organizations decide at what level they wanted to place themselves, based on their interests, motivations, needs, requirements, finances, etc. Key to this was to have a minimal set of compliance requirements and then to have a very clear table that laid out the benefits accrued with each additional level of compliance. This is very different from the way that the government has pursued a number of architectural schemes, where the individuals are forced to comply fully with no clear benefits (sort of a "trust me" attitude).

One point of disagreement was how low I set that entry bar. All I required from participants was that each of the tools "grow ears and a nervous system"—that is, becomes a callable process. They didn't even have to in fact make their tools available to others. I then depended upon human nature to be curious. My reasoning was that once they had gotten over the hurdle of doing whatever it took to make their programs more open, they couldn't resist taking a look at what others were doing and also having others take a look at their capabilities and make use of them. I did not try to prescribe who would work with whom; I allowed individuals to become interested in each other and then in meetings rewarded those who had teamed with others with recognition, and even additional resources. One of the successes of CAETI was that many new teaming relationships started in CAETI and have not only continued but also strengthened and grown since the close of the program. An example of some of the fruitful interactions in CAETI stemming from this approach is seen in the following snippet from Dan Suthers final CAETI report (1998, section 2.3.2)

> Under CAETI funding, participants David Luckham and Frank Belz developed and promoted an abstraction hierarchy for describing and modeling CAETI architectures, in particular a MOO architecture (Luckham et al. 1997). Dan Suthers (the author of this report) recognized the value of this abstraction hierarchy in clarifying our own work on architectures, and brought it to the attention of the P1484 Working Groups on Standards for Learning Technology. This led to a collaboration between Frank Belz, Dan Suthers, and Tom Wheeler of Army CECOM (one of the founders of P1484) towards a refined abstraction hierarchy. Our collaboration resulted in addition of the Application Model layer, and refinement of the conception of Luckham, Vera, and Beltz's "User-Interface" and "Concepts of Operations" into the "Interaction Model" and "Conceptual Model." All other aspects of the following are to be credited to David Luckham and Frank Belz, not the present project.

As noted in the previous section, we conducted many organizational and system wide experiments in CAETI. These included projects that helped to develop sophisticated models of the CAETI program (and not just for the architectural framework for the technology products), just as one would for the design of a large space system, military system or any other complex system. Some were architectural models in formal languages to experiment with creating a more analyzable structure for evaluating CAETI progress. There were many important technical issues raised during CAETI in terms of how to model and manage organizationally this type of system design, engineering and maintenance. There were also technical issues on how to take the activities of groups, such as the CAT that were designing very large systems, and capture their joint efforts in a shareable and analyzable form. Eventually we ended up using CAETI technology for investigations into exactly these types of issues. Hence towards the end of the program, we started to develop a virtual environment, called the Cyberlab for Education and Technology Research (CENTRE). Its goal was to act as a repository for all CAETI results and tools and a place for continuing CAETI collaborations among the researchers, developers, potential users and sponsors. It would house all the CAETI tools, the documentation about the CAETI tools, the evaluation reports, and would also include services such as robots that showed one around the environment, based on one's interests or demonstrated products. At the time I left DARPA, CENTRE had been implemented to a modest extent, with a multi-user Virtual World accessible by a text-based, two-dimensional or three-dimensional rendered interface. It had two robots, a guide agent and a limited "demobot," examples of CAETI tools accessible through the CENTRE world and virtual offices for the developers. Unfortunately a lack of future funding left the valuable beginnings of building a sustained community and repository floundering, and CENTRE is now a vacant world.

Clearly there were many other infrastructure projects that we have not been able to discuss here. These included projects such as the internet-based distance education project at George Mason University that supported CAETI needs for network assistance and for teacher professional development. Many other similar activities attempted to provide new types of support functions, especially ones that could be provided by experts over the Internet to the test schools. Many of these projects utilized the same new technologies that were being developed for the educational applications.

Evaluation—Always One of the Hardest Issues

We cannot go forward in a scientific and technical sense until we have ways of evaluating the results of what we have done. This feedback is essential to the development of better scientific and engineering results. And we need better science and engineering to make better educational technology. It is also essential for resolving political and organizational issues, although many involved in evaluations may feel like it just causes more political problems than it solves. It does this by providing eventually a more objective and neutral basis for the discussion of the current state of some given system and the system requirements, laying the groundwork for the always-difficult discussion and interpretation of policies and objectives.

Evaluation in education is tough. First, these evaluations often reflect or are dominated by one set of participants and their values and viewpoint. Hence teachers may well wonder about the relevancy of web site "hits" to the effectiveness of an educational tool. Or researchers may be frustrated by the lack of more methodical and revealing experiments on the use of their tools in the classroom. Second, as taught in any elementary statistics course, many "results" are not important, relevant, or "significant" in terms of what they mean to the people attempting to live by them. It is very hard to map our current evaluation efforts into the diverse and often conflicting, hopes and educational values held by the teachers, students, parents, and society at large. CAETI didn't solve this problem, but it made some significant contributions to placing such debates on a firmer foundation for review and discussion. Regardless of the difficulties, CAETI was committed to developing some type of evaluation criteria for all of its new technologies and for all of its technology insertions programs. As Peg Syverson, who is developing new methods for evaluating students and for the use of educational technology, especially virtual worlds, said, "It is no longer adequate simply to assert that because students are using computers, they are achieving meaningful academic goals. Increasingly we are responsible for demonstrating that the commitment of resources, staff, and class time produces measurable gains in students' achievement. Although conventional models of large-scale assessment cannot yet address the new forms of learning enabled by computer-enhanced environments, students are often expected to show gains by these measures." She goes on to describe how their computer-supported "learning record system" provides another model of assessment based on interviews, samples of students' work, observations, and interpretations of this evidence (Syverson 1999).

The Technology Insertion Program

One of the important approaches in the CAETI program as we have discussed was to have the participants work with us to develop suitable architectural standards, evaluation criteria and metrics. That way the standards and metrics reflected the values and the objectives of the different parties in the program. In the last few sections we spoke about objectives very much from the point of view of researchers and developers. The technology insertion plan (TIP) was one of our methods for getting the same type of input and involvement from the teachers in the CAETI program. In earlier studies, John Cradler found that teachers would only "find telecommunications relevant if they had an opportunity to conceptualize and implement a classroom level project or plan for telecommunications use." Their approach helped "teachers to define their curriculum objectives, instructional strategies, and assessment strategies for incorporating new technologies" (see Cradler website) This method was called the Classroom Telecommunications Intervention Plan (C-TIP). Over 100 C-TIPs have been developed, implemented and were updated and shared with other teachers on line. (Cradler 1999 Website) Cradler helped the CAETI project adapt this classroom planning model into a technology insertion plans (TIP), focusing on CAETI technologies that the teacher was interested in, DoDDS curriculum, and local equipment and budget constraints. At the website, Cradler gives a good example of a TIP for one of the CAETI tools, the teachers associate technology (TA). TA is a tool to help the teacher manage and make instructional decisions. TA links teachers on demand to curriculum lessons, technology-based resources aligned with their curriculum, student information, schedules, and Internet resources. In the example TIP, one sees a wide range of information including what types of students are being targeted, what the subjects are, specific examples and expectations for use of the tools, equipment, support, and training needs. TIP finishes with how the teacher intends to evaluate, in this case, special education fifth grade students. Cradler found in evaluations that TIP helped to increase teacher commitment, with a concomitant increased use of the technology, and improved the planning of the technology insertions, selections of insertions, and coordination with curriculum and classroom practice. It also helped communication among teachers about their use of the technology.

Enterprise Evaluation

One of the ideas that Lynne Gilfillan, Karan Harbison and I started developing under CAETI was something that we called "enterprise evaluation." This approach is essentially a systems view of the evaluation process, recognizing that complex systems have many different levels and kinds of concerns. Particularly, we were concerned with "who needs what information to make what decisions?" This includes the enterprise level. Although many researchers have been working, appropriately, on developing measures for teacher-student performance and for technology evaluation, we have found that not many people have been thinking about the kinds of information that a school system needs to collect in order to make its decisions about whether to incorporate a given technology for a given student population. That is, the overall organization makes decisions that are different from both developers and users. For example, even if a given technology works beautifully and students indeed perform superbly with it, the school must still decide the target populations and curriculum to use with the technology. This must be traded off against existing methods, costs, equity issues, and so forth. Some of these concerns and evaluation requirements will not be compatible, and one sets up the evaluation studies so that they can provide the organization with information to use with such trade-offs in mind. If one looks at evaluation from a systems point of view, then one can reduce needless expenses and especially avoid "going through the motions" but not getting the information one needs. As with any systematic endeavor, one starts with a clear task analysis and a staged plan with priorities (a systems view allows us to set the priorities). During the evaluation process, one starts to identify factors, focuses in as needed on differences, and tries to do just enough evaluation and no more. In my own work, I have continued to develop some of these ideas and apply them to military programs.

Independent Evaluators and Technology Insertion Studies

Lynne Gilfillan was the cluster leader for the CAETI evaluation team, a team consisting of a number of different researchers and evaluators. As in the architectural and integration activities, the rest of CAETI became very appreciative of this hardworking team's efforts. A lot of extra time was spent on each project, helping to evaluate its readiness for various demonstrations or technology insertion projects, and helping to develop metrics that would best reflect both the capabilities of the new technology and the desired outcomes for users of that technology. Gilfillan and her group traveled constantly to the DoDDS experimental testbeds. It was very difficult trying to organize reasonable studies with new technology in working school systems. One of the commitments of the CAETI program was to conduct long term evaluation experiments, analyzing the impact of different technologies in the classrooms, from the viewpoint of many different communities. Further, we were going to compare across evaluation methodologies. As in all real life projects, we didn't do it all. We didn't have enough time, money, or people, but at least we started some new types of evaluation concepts, and we accomplished a great deal.

We spent considerable time setting up a careful process for experimentation that dovetailed with the schedules, time commitments, and realities of our population and setting. In the evaluation process, we first set up communities of interest, where teachers could become interested in different CAETI projects and receive materials and start to talk with the developers involved. One of the important requirements of our experiments was that no teachers were required to participate in CAETI, nor to use a tool that they had not requested. Indeed, in order to use any of the CAETI tools, they had to develop a TIP with help from our CAETI team. I also worked with the teachers' union and the school system to make sure that no teacher was penalized for participating in the program, especially since many of them were just beginning to use computers and may never have tried to develop suitable computer-based curricula for their courses before. On its side, DoDDS was working actively with CAETI to help set up the appropriate computer architectures that integrated their current technology base and personnel with the demands of CAETI. They also worked with us to develop suitable criteria for use of the technology, curriculum, content, and metrics.

After the community of interest stage, described above, interested teachers could then become involved with "in-situ casual experimentation." In other words, they started to invest some serious time into learning about the technology of interest, played with it, and spoke with the developers. A great deal of useful feedback was given at just this point to the researchers, who often with the use of modern software techniques could rapidly modify the presentation of the material, the use of the tools, the kinds of tools available and so forth. This was a fruitful stage for many tools, but it wasn't easy on either side. It very much involved that "tedious conversation." Also, teachers live by a rather rigid timetable in their classrooms, compared to the time requirements of the researchers. Teachers needed to know exactly when they could expect different type of services in order to plan out their school year that was already packed with requirements of many kinds. The researchers certainly had their own time requirements (including how long their funding for the research lasted) and it was often difficult to synchronize their timing with the school year.

The CAT worked very hard to mitigate the inevitable tensions between researchers and developers, with their motivations, requirements, and enthusiasm for seeing their technologies and methods used in real classrooms and the teachers, with their motivations, requirements, and expectations for the new technologies. One of the places where the CAETI program ended up being rather rigid was in its rule that all interactions between developers and teachers had to be mediated by the CAT. This arose in the early days of the program because there were a few incidents in which teachers were dropped in on (disrupting local school schedules) by overly-eager researchers or where teacher expectations were wildly out of sync with the reality of a given research product. We eventually developed a careful process with DoDEA (the organization in charge of DoDDS) headquarters for selecting participating teachers, for visits by CAETI personnel to any schools, and for the insertion of a given technology. Although still experimental, the technologies that were tried in DoDDS classrooms had already gone through a rigorous set of hurdles. These included "integration and test" with the same computer systems as in the target school, evaluation of its applicability to the DoDEA curriculum, and the scrutiny by the interested teachers and the schools for capabilities, content, requirements, and so forth. The last stage in the CAETI technology insertion was the pilot experiments that included extensive teacher training and support by CAETI personnel.

Overall we had CAETI tools in ninety-nine classrooms, of which thirty-two were on a single computer and the rest were on five or more computers in the classroom. We had experimental programs set up in four of the DoDDS school systems: Aviano, Italy, and Kaiserslautern, Wuerzburg, and Hanau in Germany. Choosing which schools could participate was very difficult. This was done after a combination of site visits, interviews and then in a subsequent review by DoDEA Headquarters and me, with input from the rest of CAT. In these schools hundreds of children were exposed to CAETI technologies. The experiments were distributed fairly evenly across the four school districts. Within school districts, we attempted to spread the projects across elementary, middle and high school classes, but in the end, Gilfillan reported a modest edge to the number of high school projects (1997).

Not unexpectedly and certainly as is the case in other real world educational and medical programs, we were never able to develop the type of control groups that we wanted. Part of the original plan for the evaluation studies was that there would be control groups with access to general computer technology and new practices, therefore differing from the experimental groups only in the actual use of the specific computer technologies under study. Such a control group would be the best test of whether or not a given computer-based technology was making the difference in the performance of the learners or whether or not it was just the presence of any computers or the presence of new types of teaching methods and content that could be used by the teachers regardless of computer technology. However, we did not have the time and money to support the development of such control groups since they would have had to be provided with the same computers and similar training in the pedagogy and content as the experimental group.

An example of how well the evaluation process worked from the point of view of the developer is seen in Suthers' report on CAETI (1998):

> BELVEDERE was used in the first semester of 1997 by five teacher participants in 4 Department of Defense Dependents' Schools (DoDDS) in Germany and Italy. The classes included ninth grade science, and ninth to twelfth grade physics, chemistry, and science and technology. During this time, evaluation of the BELVEDERE classroom implementation was conducted by a third party evaluator,

Lynne Gilfillan, who was under contract with the CAETI program to perform this evaluation in the DoDDS testbed. Gilfillan used classroom observation forms focused on CAETI program objectives and the use of CAETI infrastructure. She also videotaped selected classroom sessions. We provided her with additional observation forms to record the activities of teachers and students, and their use of components of our software and methodology. The location of schools prevented extended observations on our part, but analysis of these forms, along with analysis of student generated artifacts (such as inquiry diagrams, Excel graphs, and student reports) for learning gains, is ongoing.

The important point of this example is that the evaluations were not a test against any of the technologies but rather, in the spirit of rapid prototyping, a way of learning how to do the next stage better (i.e., formative rather than summative evaluation.) The researchers received a great deal of information from the independent evaluator, such as observations on the student activity, reactions, ways of using, how teachers and students interacted about the tools and before and after reflections. To continue the example on BELVEDERE from Suthers' report (Suthers 1998):

> The independent evaluator also reported a striking difference in classroom organization before and after the introduction of the BELVEDERE approach. The classroom changed from a traditional format, with students doing work at their desks in rows, to a group-centered organization, in which students were gathered around computers or hands-on activities "like campfires" and engaged in active discussion. One of the greatest challenges for realizing the potential of technology and of active inquiry-based learning is implementation in the real world class. Such a class has many students, few computers, limited time, and in some cases, a teacher who is not experienced in the use of technology or in alternative approaches to organizing class activity (Schofield 1996).

As difficult as the evaluation studies were to conduct, they were invaluable for helping us to define both better technology and better strategies to help support the use of technology in classrooms with the limitations cited above.

In all, twenty-two tools made it through the stringent review process described above for pilot insertion into the schools (although since the completion of the DARPA program, DoDEA did continue to insert a few more CAETI tools.) These were the on line learning academy, Shepherd, Walden's Paths, and Hypervideo Media Center from the SNAIR cluster. The Pump Algebra tutor, Teacher's Associate, BELVEDERE, Explanation based Advisor, and the Diagnosis and Repair project were part of the technology insertion experiments from EAGIL. And from CAPER, a large number of tools were evaluated in DoDDS: Cobweb, Explorenet, Pueblo, Hands on Universe, Master Galaxy, C++ Muve and Taming the Internet MUD, Master Fractals, Function Machines, Human Anatomy, and Intelligent Multimedia Thinking Skills. Some of the tools not used in CAETI classrooms were in fact used in other classrooms around the United States under the initiative of the researchers and developers.

Gilfillan characterized the successful technologies in these classrooms as

having the following organizational qualities: staff development that supported the classroom integration, consistent and timely support to the users, reliability, and ease of use, e.g., an "intuitive user model, with a relatively low learning curve" (Gilfillan 1997.) She further reported that the most successful
technologies were ones that supported individualized instruction, provided
flexibility with respect to instructional styles, supported teacher input into
content, enhanced classroom permeability, demonstrated "substantial added
value—quickly ," and were "at least as capable as the software students and
teachers have access to at home." One of the measures gathered by the evaluation team was how many teachers chose to continue to use a tool once it was
introduced. Although most of the tools were found to be useful by at least
some of the experimental classrooms (at least from the teacher's point of
view), two of the tools OLLA and Teacher's Associate were at least in our first
round of assessments the most popular. By the time teachers were part of the
formal experiments, we had a group of highly talented, committed, and motivated teachers. Hence, the comments back from the teachers did what we
hoped they would do and helped the developers identify troublesome issues
and correct those issues. Some of the most common concerns mentioned were
speed, reliability, and integration with other classroom systems. Most of the
times when a given teacher dropped tools, it was because the relevancy to their
classroom material and practice was unclear.

Overall the Gilfillan evaluation team found that the educational technology
insertions, "increased student and teacher motivation," increased technology
skills for students and teachers, and changed attitudes and the style of interaction between students and teachers. An interesting side effect of the lack of
computers was noted. The limit of having only five computers in some classrooms caused many tools that were originally to be used in single-user mode
to be used in a small group mode, apparently in a highly successful fashion. In
addition, Gilfillan reported that teachers frequently reported, working harder
and more efficiently, working differently, and learning more techniques and
subject matter. The teachers also reported that students were more engaged as
seen in voluntary after hours use, learning new skills and new domains, and
more confident and self-reliant. Gilfillan contributed the evaluation studies
and reports on each of the projects tested to the building of the CENTRE virtual
world described earlier. Of special interest to the evaluation teams were what
Gilfillan called "exceptional teachers." In her words, these teachers, "effectively
used the CAETI technologies, developed successful classroom management
strategies, used the technology to support project-centered, authentic activities, used the technology, in most cases, to support cooperative learning, have
exciting and engaging classrooms and were absent less frequently." She found
teachers in exceptional CAETI classrooms were "flexible and adaptive, took an
experimental approach to teaching, learn continuously and autonomously,
were willing to take reasonable risks in the classroom, were comfortable in a

multi-tasking classroom environment, embrace the cooperative learning paradigm, and welcome the role of teachers and students as co-learners." (Gilfillan 1997, p.17) Clearly this was a very brief overview of the evaluation results, and as we can see there were many encouraging signs. However, as in every other technology insertion program, we found much that was discouraging. Below I discuss my view of what went well in CAETI and what remained a difficult, problematic part of the program.

CAETI: The Good, The Bad, and The Hard

Aside from the general platitudes of "keep up the good work" and "do more," I wanted to use this chapter as an opportunity to express openly some of the good and some of the bad choices I made in the CAETI program. These are now my own opinions—not my technical colleagues or the evaluation team, and certainly not the government's official viewpoint. My reason for discussing these issues is that I am hoping we can start a franker dialogue in the country on the strengths and weaknesses of the programs we have sponsored so far. Some of my good and bad choices were much like those in other programs I have seen, and if we are going to develop even better programs then we need the discussion. Much in the spirit of unilateral disarmament, I'll go first.

Things We Did Right

In a sense this highlights many of the points of this chapter up to now, as I think I have made it quite clear what I am proud of. We emphasized many of the right things in the program: supporting the necessary interdisciplinary "tedious conversation," emphasizing evaluation and using TIP and other techniques to get the teacher into the evaluation and technical process early, emphasizing integration across the program and managing the program as technology insertion into a complex system. We correctly focused on defining the functional requirements for the different educational technologies and for the educational architectures in the different schools overall. This remains, as we discuss later, a very difficult problem for the same reasons that the social sciences are harder than the physical sciences—we know less! (And because this was a DoD program there was not as much emphasis on the cognitive studies of children that are so badly needed if we are to continue to develop better educational systems.) Although we correctly emphasized long-term evaluation studies and more interesting evaluation studies (such as comparing evaluation methodologies), as we describe below, what we accomplished fell far short of our evaluation vision for many reasons.

One of the strengths of CAETI was its emphasis on developing an architectural framework that many different kinds of companies and universities could live with and become increasingly committed to. Although the architectural results did not complete the full vision, there were many successes along the way, including the fact that many groups that started integrating their work under CAETI are still working in that direction. For example, Suthers (1998) describes one of the integration experiments in depth in his CAETI report:

> In collaboration with CAETI contractors Ken Forbus (Northwestern) and Ken Koedinger (Carnegie Mellon), and assisted by Danny Bobrow (Xerox), Mark Shirley, and Bob Balzer (USC/ISI), we participated in the third integrated feasiblilty demonstration we called the "Science Learning Space Demonstration." We demonstrated the feasibility of composing three different existing, independently developed components into a "science learning environment" with integration at the semantic level. Two of the components were complete intelligent learning environments in their own right: Active illustrations (Forbus 1997) enables learners to experiment with simulations (in the demonstration, global climate), and to receive explanations concerning the causal influences behind.... Forbus had already made use of the MOO for communication between the active illustration simulation engine and a simulation user interface.... This use of an open communication "bus"—the MOO— made it easy to add a tutor agent to monitor student performance as the basis for providing context-sensitive assistance. Koedinger employed the plug-in tutor agent architecture described in Ritter and Koedinger (1997), which recommends the use of a simple translator component to manage the communication between the tools and tutor agents. The translator watched for messages between the Simulation Interface and the active illustration server, extracted messages indicating relevant student actions, and translated these student actions into a form suitable for the tutor agent's rule-based model tracing engine.... Subsequently, we added the BELVEDERE system and Argumentation Coach.... Integration of the BELVEDERE subsystem into the MOO required the addition of one translator component...no modification to BELVEDERE itself was required. The translator watched the MOO for hypothesis and simulation run objects sent by the simulation interface. When seen, these were converted to BELVEDERE hypothesis and data objects and placed in the user's "in-box" for consideration. (Section 2.3.5.2.)

Like many of the other integration experiments, these partnerships were not predefined before the program or required at any point by me during the program. They arose out of the efforts to open tools up and to create common frameworks, out of the enthusiastic and passionate desire to make real progress in educational technology and out of the personal vision of the CAETI participants. In addition to this, there were substantial and new kinds of efforts in formalizing and representing educational architectures and standards, new partnerships, new openness among traditional university laboratories, exciting demonstrations of integrated products, and much more. Whether officially under its aegis or because of the interactions of CAETI participants with other government groups, CAETI helped bring the critical need for software architectures in education and training to national attention.

One of my original goals and successes in CAETI was to attract the attention of and recruit some of the best and brightest in universities and industry to work on the critical needs of education and training in our culture. On many campuses, after the polite mouthing of how important education is, it is still considered a weak subject compared to the sciences. Under CAETI, many new researchers and developers—in a wide range of disciplines—became interested in education and training and have continued to contribute after the close of the program. Good people were kept going in an under-funded field (educational research receives enormous attention, but not nearly enough funding), new graduate students started, new top institutions and businesses were interested, friendships were started, and new ideas were introduced and promoted. Also, CAETI did good science. There were dozens of associated conferences and workshops. High quality papers and reports are still being generated from research and development started or sustained under CAETI. There was lively and enjoyable technical interchange under the CAETI umbrella that allowed some traditional competitors to work together and cooperate. The scientific and technical legacy of CAETI will continue for years.

In the CAETI program, we learned a great deal from the experiments in technology insertion. Many of our decisions were sound: don't throw the technology over the wall, use methods like TIP, sponsor a diversity of subjects and grades, and use the technology to support a variety of learner and teacher styles. We also made a number of good decisions in regards to teacher training and involvement. We worked with the unions to make sure that the teachers foray into technology was a safe experiment. We tried to develop in each school a critical mass, build up mentoring relationships and advocates (although it was really the NSF complementary program in the DoDDS after CAETI started that helped us considerably there.) We also made the decision to try to pay the teachers in at least some fashion for their extra time and costs to train. We also made the good decision to start with the teachers who were interested and enthusiastic. The idea was not to work on the problem of getting teachers to adopt new technology first. Rather, since the focus of the program was to develop new types of capabilities and to test whether these capabilities work or not, we wanted to have no hurdles in terms of attitude problems with the teachers. This of course did not work perfectly; some teachers joined the program just to receive the computers and were not interested in adopting new technologies (beyond the use of the computer) or methods. Happily, many of the teachers were wonderfully supportive of the goals of CAETI and they greatly added to CAETI with their own creativity in using the technology to good purposes in the classroom.

The Things I Would Do Differently

However, there were some choices that were not as effective as I had hoped.

I Didn't Utilize Kid Power As Much As Possible

I over-emphasized the teachers and under-emphasized the students in the early planning stages of CAETI, and unfortunately the program remained dominated by teacher issues. I didn't utilize "kid power" enough. Some of the individual teachers were smarter than we were and did utilize kid power, as seen in Gilfillan's characterization of exceptional CAETI classrooms described earlier. One of my reasons for initially emphasizing the teachers was based on my conversations thirty years ago with researchers who were trying to cajole doctors and nurses to accept the use of computer-based tools for patient monitoring and drug interactions in hospitals. They found that if they first created tools that the doctor found personally useful for his or her own less desirable tasks—like bookkeeping or analyzing lab results—it apparently increased the likelihood that they would accept computer-based tools for use with their patients. Using similar reasoning, I thought that if I brought in the teachers first, made them feel confident and the most knowledgeable about the technology, then it would help their acceptance of the technology into the classroom and avoid some of the problems of culture shock. Another reason for the emphasis on teacher tools first was the hope that such tools would free up the teachers' time to do more valuable parts of their job—like teaching. These notions had some merit, and certainly our tools for the teachers did support some current and new activities and helped them generate new ideas on the use of technology for their students. But it also placed the emphasis on the teachers—their needs, their preferences, and their concerns—rather than on the learners. This had a number of consequences.

First, CAETI, DoDDS, and every other educational technology program I've heard about has been promoting some variant of "learner-centric education" with the student increasingly in charge of their own educational experience. Along with that there is usually some slogan that promotes a new role for the teacher from "sage on the stage to guide by the side." But many of the initial conversations about the technology—what to choose and how to choose it—were conducted by DoDEA headquarters, CAETI participants, school administrators and teachers speaking for the children. That does not automatically mean that many excellent choices were not made on behalf of the children. But it did mean that valuable time and money was being spent on dealing with the teachers' issues first, essentially adult education, and not the K–12 learners. An interesting possibility for new programs is to think about how to bring the children in much earlier.

Second, there was a lot of "kid power"—knowledge and computer savvy—that I didn't utilize in the program. I didn't push the use of the students in setting up some of the computing systems, maintaining them, helping teachers with problems, and interacting with the developers. I allowed myself to be overruled by DoDEA in terms of not using kid power to install some of the computing infrastructure and software and maintain the equipment. True, there were some difficult legal and ethical issues surrounding privacy of school records and installation and labor requirements in Europe. But I also spent a tremendous amount of the budget on providing some types of site support—troubleshooting minor problems and some of the day-to-day training of teachers—which might have been handled superbly by knowledgeable high school students. There are a number of schools that have anecdotally reported the use of students to help program, develop content, install software and hardware, and so forth. We should have tried some experiments and worked directly on providing technical solutions to some of the DoDEA concerns in using students. For example, perhaps certain types of security measures might have worked to protect necessarily private files from junior assistants or to help circumscribe what helpful activities they were able to perform.

The last, and by far the most serious, issue is that if a technology insertion program is geared towards teacher acceptance first, there could be real risks of "dumbing" down contents and new technological approaches, not because of the children involved but because of the discomfort and insecurities of the teachers. One only has to stand inside a K-MART or a Sears store and watch very young children fearlessly approach VCRs and computers to become aware of how profound this generation gap is. Not only are many children fearless about the new technology, but in their lives they are going to have to compete in a profoundly different culture. It may not be as pictured in our mythological films of Cyberspace, but it will involve a set of very different skills. Computing will be very competitive. If we do not use it to the greatest extent, other countries will and their educational policies reflect that!

I Should Have Emphasized Mobility:
Wearable Devices, Mobile Devices, and Wireless Technologies

Carl Hewitt (MIT) was one of the few CAETI performers who continually challenged us to think about the impact on education of wireless and mobile devices. We certainly knew the developing trends and there was even great interest within the program about the potentials of these technologies. We were using some relatively mobile devices (the handheld PDAs) but largely for the teachers' benefits. Many of us wanted children out from behind boxes and into the real world, manipulating objects and not mouses and exercising their bodies along with their minds. Furthermore, we speculated on the use of wireless networks in the DoDDS school systems when we were faced with enormous costs to rewire old buildings. However, unfortunately there were a number of reasons why we were not able to use wireless in those particular cases. We should have invested more research into the use of these technologies. Within a small number of years, many students will be walking into classrooms with palm pilots, certainly the increasingly sophisticated calculators that are quickly turning into personal digital assistants (PDAs), and other small but powerful computational devices. The implications of this is that, potentially, students will walk in and contribute computational power to a mobile network, configured dynamically (there are many active network and mobile networks being developed currently). How will this/could this become used in classrooms? How would the capabilities of one student's platform be useful to others? How does this change collaborative activities at both the user and the software levels?

The Hard Parts—Challenges for the Next Programs

While we made substantial progress in CAETI, the "tedious conversation" is not over. It needs to be continued, deepened, and extended to more of the system issues in education.

Continuity and Momentum

Educational technology programs produce many products. There are the tangible ones, like software and reports. There are the intangible ones, like the lessons that were learned, the enthusiasm and the energy of teams that have finally broken through the tedious conversation, and the momentum of accumulating results and understandings that build on top of the previous efforts. How do we retain the value that came from our investments as a culture in research and development? A concrete example of this problem showed up at the end of the CAETI program. I tried to invent an idea, the CENTRE that would provide to the research community and interested users openly available repositories for all of CAETI's products and a place for developers to continue to meet and collaborate. DARPA, NSF, and many organizations spend an enormous amount of money to build research communities. The community building takes time—often years. Then at the end of the program, often three years, the organizations leave it to the individuals to continue those relationships or those efforts in a catch as catch can fashion. What a waste of our efforts! Many times the findings are collecting dust inside the offices of program managers (I know I had many dusty volumes inherited from previous occupants of those offices). The internet is improving the retention and availability of materials as the references in this chapter attest. Nonetheless a lot more could be done to retain the investment of time and effort it took to establish collaborations among diverse groups by providing more support for such places as the CENTRE. The CENTRE made an interesting demonstration, but it died when the funding stopped and no other organizations picked it up. Hence there are many valuable CAETI assets, such as Gilfillan's evaluation reports and other documentation, clippings, and user manuals for many CAETI tools that are currently not available for the research community to study and analyze.

Different Worlds: Teachers and Researchers

There are serious cultural differences between researchers and teachers, and these impacted the evaluation studies and the continual development of new technologies. For example, even though medicine is part art, it has two advantages over education in the acceptance of technology: (1) there are some relatively well defined and widely agreed upon outcomes; (2) it has a culture that has long-accepted a style of scientific observations and experimentation. As to the first point, there is of course still a great deal of discussion on what defines health and illness, especially across different subgroups and individuals. However, unlike education many of the outcomes are more immediately observable. In fact, it is interesting to note that the arguments are often exactly on those outcomes that are less immediately observable, such as those associated with smoking, exercise regimes, eating habits, chronic conditions and health practices. The second point is key to many of the cultural difficulties in education technology insertions. Doctors and nurses have a long history of conducting medical experiments. They are used to making careful observations and notes on what works and doesn't work on their patients, participating in studies, introducing new devices, methods, drugs, and practices. In fact, one of the reasons that they have better defined outcomes is because of this scientific background and practice. This scientific and technical training is a core part of all their training—from specialist to generalist, from orderly to nurse to doctor.

Education on the other hand has emphasized other skills. Some of these are as seriously required and important as any grounding in the scientific culture. Solid understanding of subject material and the ability to organize and communicate it—especially to young people or to new learners—are very difficult and challenging intellectually. However, this different set of skills does have an impact on how readily the average teacher was ready to participate in the type of prototyping, tool development, and evaluation experiments that were a key part of the CAETI program. Although, there are certainly teachers who take careful notes on how their individual students respond to different teaching methods and use their notes to discuss these students with others, teachers do not usually produce their notes in order to combine them with others into methodical studies of practices and techniques. Certainly there are also many observable measures that are used for determining whether or not some student has mastered the desired material. However, teachers are more independent in their practice than medical practitioners, who must all record certain types of information in very similar fashions.

The result of this cultural mismatch is cost and time in the development of appropriate educational technology. It is expensive and time-consuming to build special isolated laboratory classrooms, and there are still the difficulties of evaluating that technology in and transferring it to "real" classrooms. On

Bruce Brittons CAETI Project
www.ai.uga.edu/~bbritton/eagil.html
CAETI Evaluation of Shepherd with sixth grade students
www.csdl.tamu.edu/~marshall/caeti/observations.html
Computational Logic, Inc.: Formal work with Real-time Evaluation Agents
www.cli.com/software/caeti/statebot/index.html
Architecture on Collaborative Tools Community
www.npac.syr.edu/users/gcf/cilt/ciltframeprop.html
University of Colorado: SERL Project www.cs.colorado.edu/users/serl/main.html
Educational Object Economyimportant new business concepts for education www.eoe.org/
ExploreNet Experiments in CAETI. Charles E. Hughes, J. Michael Moshell, Mark C. Kilby, and
Joel Rosenthal. University of Central Florida www.cs.ucf.edu/~moshell/STS1.html
Gambles work on Verifying Integrated Heterogeneous Systems
euler.mcs.utulsa.edu/gamble/rfg_darpa.html
Hands on Universe (HOU)
pennypacker@lbl.gov
Hyperlearning Meter
www.cne.gmu.edu/cne/publications/index.html
One CAETI integration experiment June 1997
advlearn.lrdc.pitt.edu/advlearn/examples/caeti97demo.html
Intelligent Automation, Inc.
www.i-a-i.com/projects/cool/demo/coolwelcome.html
Learning and Intelligent Systems Symposium Proceedings, June 1, 1996
www.nsf.gov
Lockheed Martin/Educational Technologies/Franklin Institute Science Museum
nac.odeDoDEA.edu/olla
An Architecture for Intelligent Resource Agents. Jon A. Pastor, Suzanne Liebowitz Taylor, Donald
P. McKay, and Robin McEntire. Lockheed Martin
www.navpoint.com/~pastor/jon/Papers/COOPIS/coopis10.html
NASA site with some references to CAETI work and other educational material
www.earth.nasa.gov/education/edreports/mtpeedjan22.html
A Prototyping System for Parallel and Distributed Applications
wwwx.cs.unc.edu/Research/proteus/onr-fy95.html
Pueblo Home Page Global Learning Collaboratory
pcacad.pc.maricopa.edu/Pueblo/index_frame.html
Rapide and CAETI: Formal architectural work
pavg.stanford.edu/rapide/whats-new.html
SAIC VWs
galactic.saic.com/Projects/IT/infotechcontracts.html
VJ Saraswat and the next step after MUDs
sunset.usc.edu/groupware/ and matrix.research.att.com/vj/desiderata.html and
www.pc.maricopa.edu/community/pueblo/writings/aaaPaper.html

*Figure 1. A sample of cognitive structure diagnosis and repair
research and development project web sites.*

the other hand, it is also expensive and time-consuming to conduct experiments in working school systems and to find those "exceptional" teachers who work so effectively and creatively with their researcher and developer counterparts. We know that when we do find those exceptional teachers, the tool development soars and the difficulties of matching tools to appropriate curriculum and classroom practice is greatly reduced. For some, this cultural mismatch is so severe that they advocate abandoning traditional school systems and instead concentrate on setting up alternative educational resources and marketing those alternatives directly to students (and their parents.) Some of this is already occurring as we can see in commercial educational software. However, I believe that although such resources can complement our educational systems, they provide only patchy solutions since they are not coordinated into a program covering the child's development over many years and across many disciplines. Furthermore, school systems provide a market that is large enough to encourage these commercial products towards developing more substantial content and skills. It may be that these cultural problems are temporary—a sign of a transitional generation. Certainly, both teachers and students are changing rapidly in their familiarity with computers and technology. In another decade, schools in fact may become more like the medical community, incorporating a style of continual small experiments as new results and tools become known. Perhaps eventually we will have "research schools" associated with education schools in much the same way as we now have "teaching hospitals" associated with medical schools. Meanwhile, however, this cultural mismatch is a formidable issue for any technology development and insertion program.

Little Agreement on Desired Outcomes

Teachers, reflecting their multi-faceted culture, disagree about what constitutes good or excellent performance and knowledge. The desired outcome for many educational activities is controversial. In fact, the impact of technology has been partially to heat up many of these controversies and to make them now widely discussed throughout the culture. Not only are the arguments about controversial topics touching religious beliefs, such as those about evolution, but even about the most fundamental skills and attitudes of students. Should children be seen but not heard? Should they be obedient? Docile? Creative? Bold? Should they be outside? Walking around the classroom? Sitting at their desk? Should we get back to basics? Do we still need arithmetic—after all, there are calculators? Do we still need writing—after all, there are speech recognition devices that may make that obsolete? One of the things I learned in numerous conversations with teachers and parents was that it doesn't take long before people will let down their hair and express very different beliefs about the nature of education, children, and culture. The average teacher may give lip service to whatever current standards or educational theory is in vogue, but I have found very few who don't smile a little when they close the classroom door and go back to doing things their way. That is not because they are indifferent to doing the right thing. Au contraire, it is because they are often such highly dedicated and experienced individuals that they quietly wait out the next fad and try ardently to sift the possible benefits of some new theory or toolset from the great enthusiasm with which each next "revolution" is invariably announced.

Gio Wiederhold Mediators
    www-db.stanford.edu/LIC/MIFT.html
University of Hawaii
    www.ee.eng.hawaii.edu/~alex/Research/Projects/CAETI/Overview/problem.html
USC/ISI
    www.isi.edu/software-sciences/dssa.html
SENTAR evaluation and agents work
    www.advicom.net/~sentar/caeti_cust.htm
Roger Schank and Chris Riesbeck, ILS, Evidence-Based Reasoning and Reporting
    www.ils.nwu.edu/
Dan Suthers, Brant Cheikes, Neil Jacobstein, and Tom Murray organized a workshop at ITS 96,
    entitled Architectures and Methods for Designing Cost-Effective and Reusable ITSs. There were
    over 40 international participants. advlearn.lrdc.pitt.edu/
Peg Syverson, Problems in Evaluating Learning in MOOs and MUDs
    www.cwrl.utexas.edu/~syverson/caeti
ISX - Teacher's Associate
    isx.com/isxcorp/programs/ta.html
TEKNOWLEDGE and CENTRE Associates
    www.teknowledge.com/desktop_associate/agents.htm
Texas A&Ms Walden's Paths
    www.csdl.tamu.edu/walden
Tinkerteach
    Educational Infrastructure
    David Garlan, Mary Shaw, and Jeannette Wing. School of Computer Science, Carnegie Mellon
    University, Pittsburgh
    www.cs.cmu.edu/afs/cs/project/tinker/www/sow.txt

Figure 2. A sample of scenario generation project web sites.

I found education to be full of passionate advocates. Unfortunately the slogans often are superficial and provide little of the necessary detail for selecting
better approaches and technologies. At the early CAETI meetings, we spent a
great deal of time trying to elicit from teachers and education experts what they
really wanted, expected from the technology and how they would live with the
technology. Did they for example expect students to watch a teacher standing
before a large video wall? Or would they walk with their students amid mead-
ows with mobile devices? Would they cluster around computers in small groups
or would each student have his or her own computer? Would students interact
with experts or teachers at a distance, or would the teacher walk around the
room, helpfully looking over their shoulder? Were curricula now to be reconfig-
ured into project-based cross sections? Did we imagine students freely wander-
ing around the school into different pockets of activity or laboratories? What
were the newer higher-level cognitive skills that we need to teach? How would
we instrument this technology in order to measure impacts? What became clear
in these discussions is that many educational endeavors have very local goals,
and yet the slogans address very broad outcomes. Hence, teachers and school
systems are evaluated based upon the standards for that subject matter and

grade and are limited in their use of texts and other materials by their local environments. Meanwhile a national debate rages over our notions of the critical knowledge and skills we will need in future work environments and what we need to teach in order to retain our cultural heritage.

To further complicate matters, education is always a moving target because its job is to impart the knowledge and skills valued by the culture. In a time of great change, like now, it is a formidable challenge indeed to equip the new generation with the intellectual skills they will need. There is much more information than ever before and that alters what it means to be "educated" or "expert" in anything. Expertise will certainly no longer mean knowing everything that humans have learned about a given topic. It will mean that we will become more like the expert who has the ability to discern what to pay attention to, where to go for the information, and whom to ask. People may be tempted to think that this computer culture will enable a lot of ignorant or untrained people to function better because there is so much support. I believe it is just the opposite. Minimal intellectual skills will now be done by the computer so we won't need people to do them or value them particularly. Certain intellectual skills may even go the way of ditch digging, such that now people manage the equipment that does that hard labor. That means that the competition between cultures will be on the most challenging of cognitive skills (e.g., asking the right question, noticing and recognizing the interesting or novel feature of a problem, prioritizing correctly, demonstrating discernment, and the creative integration of information). Our educational technology must prepare our students to be intellectually sophisticated and adaptive. Philosophical and social issues aside, the problem with these culturally moving targets is that it greatly impacts one's ability to build the "right stuff." Our engineering is based on building and evaluating systems based on desired outcomes. Without at least moderately agreed upon outcomes, it is very difficult to build good educational technology. At the moment, we're overly dependent on teacher/parent/student acceptance, and have only limited performance measures. Many of these performance measures are not necessarily fully compatible. For example, we want to have both high scores on existing tests and yet have students become increasingly self-paced, independent, and creative. And it will take many more experiments to tease apart the relationships of the features of the technology to the performance measures we want.

Other Hard Issues: Individual
Differences, Content, and Scalable Systems

We know that each human being is a bundle of his or her own combination of skills and talents, and that individuals differ in how and when and why they learn different things. Yet at the same time, cultures require that we all deal in some common medium with each other. It is how we communicate and share knowledge with each other, share endeavors with each other, and so forth. So education always is a tension between the body of knowledge and skills which we want to standardize across individuals and yet at the same time, the allowance for differing skills and capabilities. Of course the next step beyond tolerance is to nurture these individual skills because it is these differences whereby cultures continue to grow and thrive. In other words, the role of education is not to just impart its set knowledge to the individual but to nurture the individual—out of such differences will come all the advances in the sciences and the arts. When we evaluate current computer- based education we can say that it is scoring reasonably well in imparting known knowledge (and even doing it in a way that is tailored to an individual's pace and presentation preferences) and quite poorly in the latter case, of nurturing creativity. Our ability to handle individual differences will impact greatly our ability to handle the scalability of systems. Although it is common for people to think of scalability as a matter of numbers (and certainly any e-commerce or website will tell you that numbers do matter to the technology), scalability also has to do with handling different *kinds*. One can think of this difference as the difference between amounts and coverage. The ability to rapidly specialize for different users, processes, or purposes will depend upon some of the same capabilities that will allow us to represent, reason about and respond to individual differences.

One type of scalability is having sufficient depth of content. The Office of Science and Technology Policy has been emphasizing the critical need to push for major efforts in educational content for over four years. They're right. Many of our current systems are at best like a textbook as compared to journal articles. To help individuals reach their full potential they must have substantially more content than is offered in many of the current educational tools. Although it is improving there is still much work to be done in terms of providing a student the opportunity to fly as high as they want and to go as far as they can. Apprenticeship, utilizing the Internet, will help since it will provide a range of opportunities allowing many different kinds of children to participate in authentic and meaningful work and research efforts. We need a repertoire of clever strategies to help deepen the content we have available for students. For example, one could imagine each student in a classroom having a hand-held device (much like the current calculators that are becoming increasingly more sophisticated or the next generation of palm computers). The device would be carried by the student everywhere, used to quickly consume any gems that are developed or found by other sources and helpfully supported by a core editing, storage, and processing capability. Meanwhile one would continue to develop deeper content for existing tools; that is, develop the "journal" version of content for these tools and supply the material for a year's worth of work. Also, we should call upon many groups to start developing content for students as a public service on their websites or in their Virtual Worlds.

There are other hard problems that we unfortunately do not have the space to discuss here such as the type of maintenance and support services needed by teachers, teacher mentorship, the role of educational activities outside of school systems, and the need for new commercial models to support education and educational technology in interesting ways. There are some additional CAETI lessons learned on these topics to be covered in a future report.

Closing Thoughts

Whether one attributes the problem to the overblown language and hyperbole of technology developers or the hopeful, but overly optimistic expectations of potential users, there is a huge gap between the promises of educational technology and the reality of the current implementations. The gap still exists and is seen in the limited content of educational tools, the limited ability to integrate across different computer-based capabilities, and the limited time working with tools for most school children across the country. The reasons for this gap are complex and far-reaching, spanning social, economic, and technical challenges. Some of the social barriers are equity (what populations to target and how much) and the willingness of teachers and students. There is the collision of values, as local cultures struggle for control and the right to impose their values against the globally available culture, widely available through the media, but now even more so through the world wide web. Some of the economic issues are also clear and hard (e.g., how to provide basic resources to poorer school districts or to widely dispersed schools in rural areas, the training of teachers, and the need for increasing the commercial viability of R&D educational technology prototypes.)

The economic and social issues are being much discussed. This is appropriate but sometimes misleading because it promotes the notion that the only issues now are ones of overcoming the social and economic barriers. One frequently sees articles in the media on educational technology that imply that the only unresolved issues are ones of how to equitably deploy existing educational technology. However, within the research and development community, we know in fact that although there are gems (good computer-based technology supporting sufficient content to support many current classroom activities,) most educational technology falls far short of our R&D desires and user expectations. One of the contentions of the CAETI program was that in fact the right stuff to fulfill the promises had not been invented. This is why the National Science Foundation and other basic research organizations need to continue to lead in deep educational and cognitive research. There is great need for new theory about complex information systems so that we can begin to address the implications of cyberspace as a collaborative and cognitively supportive learning space. The same is true if we start talking about other kinds of hard, interesting issues such as: What does it mean to have distributed intelligence that is somehow coordinated into common activity? How do we blend real and virtual worlds? We do not even have the vocabulary for speaking about some of things that we are trying to deal with. And we're not going to develop large, advanced educational systems without such deeper knowledge.

All technology insertions are hard because people underestimate how profoundly they will be changed by them in their everyday work. They often think of the technology insertions as there to do better the jobs they currently are doing, but they rarely realize how much the insertion will change not only their current work but what else they do and how they do it. Also, all technology insertions have similar problems to those we discussed above—of defining outcomes, cultural clashes and the tedious conversation, scalability, evaluation and so forth. Technology will not produce utopia. Yet, it will change our culture profoundly. Can we design for only good outcomes? *No,* there are always side effects and trade-offs. There are conflicting goals that we must recognize and make decisions about, and construct delicate balances between. How we do that is to instrument, measure, improve and tune. In other words, appropriate changes and compromises will occur through incremental insertions and not grand edicts.

Technology is a mixed blessing. We need to start stating explicitly desired outcomes and work towards these outcomes with technology and other solutions too. Children do not need to be in front of even perfect computer boxes all day. Children are always going to need other people; social interactions are as critical for this culture's survival as anything else is. The caring adults around children are much more than a source of information—they are a model for how to live and be in this world. Teachers, because of their educational skills, their personal skills and their humanity will always be necessary in the lives of children. Technology may open up the possibility of having many new types of teachers available to a child, but it will not change the child's need for them. As V. J. Saraswat stated:

> The myth is that through the promise of distance education, knowledge can be delivered from the experts to the person needing it, anytime anywhere. Recorded thought patterns—video, web pages—can, but the construction and communication of knowledge is much more than the transmission of disembodied, decontextualized information (however multi-media it might be). Who will help raise the provocative questions, guide group discussion, help the group of learners make sense together? Even though the videotapes and web pages may come from the world's best educators on that topic, the need for a group of students to understand that material in their own terms, to translate it into their own context of usage and meaning, adapted to their own current views of the world will not be diminished. And hence the need for "live" teachers—who understand the educational process, the material and the students at hand, and who have access to (and are adaptive to) the actual context of learning—will not be diminished, only transformed somewhat (1997, p. 1).

This chapter has spanned practical programmatic remarks through the theoretical and philosophical. But then so did CAETI! Because, in fact, if we are to really live up to the potentials in computer-based education we will need to integrate across all these disciplines. This can be a sometimes tedious conversation, but maybe in the end one of the most exciting we have ever had.

From this Revolution to the Next

Kenneth D. Forbus and Paul J. Feltovich

In this book we have shown you a snapshot, a sample of the efforts that are moving advanced artificial intelligence technology out of the laboratory and into everyday classroom use. The new capabilities for educational technologies that they provide will, we believe, have a revolutionary impact on education. One can imagine a world where there are capable teachers and assistants at every learner's elbow, with time and attention for each and every student, whenever they are ready to learn and for however long that takes. We will never achieve such a world with only human teachers and assistants; it is neither economically feasible nor realistic to impose such extreme demands on people. (Even the most dedicated teachers have to sleep. Being on call twenty-four hours a day, seven days a week may be a necessary for some jobs, but few would be willing to impose it on teachers.) Software that provides new and engaging environments for students to work in, that helps students articulate their ideas, that synthesizes explanations on demand, and that uses cognitive models of students to help them interactively, all provide assistance that is similar in kind to what teachers provide. As many of the projects in this book have noted, such software provides teachers with new tools for helping their students learn, as well as better scaffolding for learners working on their own.

Revolutions in education are slow. There are many reasons for this, some good and some not so good. Educating the next generation has always been one of the most important tasks of a culture, so conservatism in this endeavor is fairly natural. It takes time for ideas and techniques to be adapted, adopted, and evolved to work with the local constraints of teachers and students in their environments. Computing infrastructure is still expensive, relative to the financial setups of most schools even in technologically advanced nations, let alone less wealthy nations. But the percolation of computing technology through societies is continuing rapidly, and new generations of students and teachers are growing more comfortable with it. Tremendous investment is required to bridge the gap between laboratory work and successful educational technologies. However, the problems of education are serious and important, and the new needs for lifelong learning will place novel burdens on our educational systems. Enlisting smart machines in service of education will be one of the key ways we will meet these challenges.

It may seem premature to consider what might be the next revolution, given that the current one is only starting. However, despite the hype about "internet time," scientific and technological progress still take a long time. The projects described in this book rest on decades of basic scientific research in artificial intelligence and cognitive science. The time to plant the seeds of the next revolution is now, so that in ten or twenty years there will be a new crop of technologies to harvest. Consequently, we identify some research areas and trends that, if encouraged now, could end up heading in directions that would lead to even larger benefits for education and training.

The first broad area of research is increasing the communication bandwidth between people and machines. In communications, bandwidth is (roughly) the amount of information that can be transferred in some unit of time. Today's graphical user interfaces are better than yesterday's command line interfaces, but are nowhere close to the kind of fluent, flexible interactions that occur between people. In our communications we use overtly linguistic channels (i.e., the contents of our writing or speaking) but also other channels, such as prosody, gesture, and other signals to help establish attention and flow in conversations. Conversations are collaborations, and making computers into conversational partners will require endowing them with more human-like visual and auditory capabilities. For example, students' gestures, facial expressions, and tone of voice, are often critical clues in figuring out how to help them.

Tackling these problems suggests some different directions, even for the component technologies that would eventually go into such systems. In speech understanding, for example, it suggests moving away from tuning dictation-oriented models still further and towards a robust theory of auditory understanding. In natural language processing, it suggests renewed emphasis on understanding dialogue and discourse. In vision, it suggests looking at understanding diagrams and sketches and how visual representations convey conceptual content, in addition to traditional computer vision topics. And research on combining such techniques to exploit their synergies is needed. One example is research into multimodal interfaces, interfaces that combine modalities such as speech, gesture, and drawing to enable machines to participate fluently in communication. The eventual payoffs of such research will include software that is far more natural to use than today's systems. This should for example enable learners to focus more on content issues than learning how to drive a computer program. It should also lead to more engaging characters in virtual environments, when combined with richer endowments of knowledge, as described next.

The second broad area of research is increasing the shared understanding between people and machines. Educational software, even the systems described in this book, are specialists, aimed at teaching some specific subject area within some assumed range of expertise. Human experts are of course far more flexible: They have a range of expertise, and a broad base of knowledge gleaned from culture and experience with the world to back it up. These cultural reference points and experiences provide additional shared context that can be exploited by participants in learning interactions. A teacher can, for instance, suggest a relevant everyday example the student should be familiar with to illustrate a point. Similarly, a student could raise an example from his or her own experience to support an argument.

The chasm between human experience and what can be provided as knowledge to a program is obviously enormous. Even so, using richer knowledge bases in educational software could enable it to help students learn even better. There are several promising starts, projects already underway to encode broad-based representations of common sense knowledge. However, much research lies ahead, both in formalizing the many areas of knowledge that common sense involves, and in discovering techniques to use it efficiently and effectively to support education. Endowing software with enough knowledge of our cultures so that it can understand and use cultural reference points is a daunting, but important, problem. Developing techniques that let domain experts, teachers, and students extend the knowledge bases used in educational software will be a key milestone, since the work can be distributed among many stakeholders instead of the (relatively small) AI research community.

In addition to the significant payoff of richer interactions, systems whose knowledge can be extended via everyday interactions can provide companions, assistants, tutors, and colearners that relate to learners over extended periods, months and years instead of hours and weeks. For instance, a good way to learn something is to teach it, although as teachers know, it can sometimes be hazardous for the learner. Imagine if all students had a program that they taught based on what they were learning, so that the program would learn along with them. Such software could become valuable aids to reflection, and subtly nudged back into line (via network connections) if its misconceptions started drifting too far.

In another vein, a key problem for students is learning how to tell when they don't really understand something. It is easy to absorb "facts" without analysis and inspection. It is harder to learn to fit them carefully into a comprehensive world view, only after careful scrutiny and testing. It is even harder to be able to adopt different perspectives, seeing the same phenomena from multiple points of view instead of one's typical ways of handling it. And it is hardest of all to discover that a sizable chunk of the world view that you have created needs major adjustment, or even has to be abandoned. Helping students learn to do these things is one of the hardest things teachers do. Software with wide-ranging knowledge could help in these processes. Imagine a simulated person from another culture, willing to spend arbitrary amounts of time helping you understand the way they view the world, to help students see things from different perspectives. Imagine a software debate partner who, when a student makes an argument, pokes holes in the argument and provides examples that undercut it. Some students can get many such experiences through interactions with other people, via travel or networked communications, given enough time and financial resources. But to make such experiences universally available will require even smarter machines, so that all students can have more extensive and intense experiences than they could otherwise have.

The third broad area of research is deeper understanding of human cognition and learning. Cognitive science has made tremendous strides, but if our goal is a computational account of human cognition, it is safe to bet that more research lies ahead than behind. While there have been various models of learning, modeling the range of conceptual learning that people exhibit remains a grand challenge. We do not yet know how to build a system that can read a book's worth of new material and figure out how to apply it, or accurately predict the set of misconceptions a population of learners will glean from a course of instruction, or even improve its world model by accumulating knowledge over long spans of time from a variety of sources. Understanding how people do such things will have two kinds of benefits. First, by understanding the nature of human learning better, we can better design educational systems of all kinds, not just software. Second, we can build many kinds of new educational software: simulated students, for rapid evaluation of educational materials, better cognitive diagnosis systems, higher-fidelity nonplayer characters in virtual environments, and better tutors.

Although it might seem paradoxical, advances in neuroscience will almost certainly continue to be irrelevant to these efforts. Neuroscience research is interesting in its own right, but its applications to education have been, and remain, dubious[1]. There are simply too many levels of abstraction between the operations of human cognition and the level of phenomena that modern neuroscience can address. Reducing cognitive science to neuroscience makes about as much sense as reducing neuroscience to quantum mechanics, or studying the structure of a modern computer operating system by studying electronics. One relies on the other, in an implementation sense, but the emergent phenomena at different levels are best explained in their own terms. The advances in cognitive science that are critical for education lie in psychology (especially, but not exclusively, cognitive psychology), artificial intelligence, linguistics, and cultural anthropology.

These new directions may seem truly radical, or even impossible. However, it should be noted that twenty years ago it would have seemed equally impossible to many that there could be software that helped children learn to read, or do algebra, or understand complex domains—all of which have been accomplished to some degree, as this book has illustrated. Certainly significant scientific progress will be necessary to lay the foundations. And the technological infrastructure required might seem extreme by today's standards. But if we assume that Moore's[2] law-style improvements continue, the necessary computing and network infrastructures will be in place and at a price affordable to everyone. Such visions thus appear in the realm of the possible.

Our species has thrived by learning about the world and by using tools. Building even smarter machines to help us learn more and learn better is simply the next step in this process.

Notes

1. Understanding the deficits incurred with brain damage is an exception.

2. Moore's law originally referred to a predicted doubling of transistors on memory chips, at half the price, every 18 months, based on empirical data. It is now common to project similar improvements in other computer system properties, i.e., increased CPU speed, network bandwidth, etc. With silicon it appears that Moore's law improvements can continue until around 2010, at which point continued progress will rely on other computing substrates, such as optical computing, biological computing, quantum computing, or nanotechnology. Physics may not be the ultimate limiter; fabrication of smaller devices has typically required more investment, and as the perceived gap between available computing power and computing needs for various tasks drops, investment gets harder. Business concerns may end the progression long before technology does.

Bibliography

Aist, G. S. 1997a. A General Architecture for a Real-Time Discourse Agent and a Case Study in Oral Reading Tutoring. Master's thesis, Robotics Institute and Computer Science Department, Carnegie Mellon University.

Aist, G. S. 1997b. Challenges for a Mixed-Initiative Spoken Dialogue System for Oral Reading Tutoring. Paper presented at the Computational Models for Mixed Initiative Interaction AAAI Spring Symposium, 24–25 March, Stanford, Calif.

Aist, G. S. 1998. Expanding a Time-Sensitive Conversational Architecture for Turn Taking to Handle Content-Driven Interruption. Paper presented at the Fifth International Conference on Speech and Language Processing, December, Sydney, Australia.

Aist, G. S., and Mostow, J. 1997a. Adapting Human Tutorial Interventions for a Reading Tutor That Listens: Using Continuous Speech Recognition in Interactive Educational Multimedia. Paper presented at the Conference on Computer Assisted Language Learning, 21–23 September, Exeter, England.

Aist, G. S., and Mostow, J. 1997b. A Time to Be Silent and a Time to Speak: Time-Sensitive Communicative Actions in a Reading Tutor That Listens. Paper presented at the AAAI Fall Symposium on Communicative Actions in Humans and Machines, 8–10 Nov., Cambridge, Massachusetts.

Aist, G. S., and Mostow, J. 1998. Estimating the Effectiveness of Conversational Behaviors in a Reading Tutor That Listens. In Applying Machine Learning to Discourse Processing, ed. J. Chu-Carroll and N. Green. Technical Report SS-98-01, American Association for Artificial Intelligence, Menlo Park, Calif.

Aist, G. S., and Mostow, J. 1999. Measuring the Effects of Backchanneling in Computerized Oral Reading Tutoring. Paper presented at the European Speech Communication Association Workshop on Prosody and Dialogue, 1–3 September, Eindhoven, Netherlands.

Aist, G. S., and Mostow, J. 2000. Balancing Learner and Tutor Control by Taking Turns: Efficiency and Effectiveness of Mixed-Initiative Task Choice in a Reading Tutor That Listens. Paper presented at the Fifth International Conference on Intelligent Tutoring Systems, Montreal, Canada, June.

Aist, G. S.; Chan, P.; Huang, X. D.; Jiang, L.; Kennedy, R.; Latimer, D.; Mostow, J.; and Yeung, C. 1998. How Effective Is Unsupervised Data Collection for Children's Speech Recognition? Paper presented at the Fifth International Conference on Speech and Language Processing, 30 Nov. – 4 Dec., Sydney, Australia.

Aleven, V.; Koedinger, K. R.; and Cross, K. 1999. Tutoring Answer-Explanation Fosters Learning with Understanding. In *Artificial Intelligence in Education, Open Learning Environments: New Computational Technologies to Support Learning, Exploration, and Collaboration, Proceedings of AIED-99*, eds. S.P. Lajoie and M. Vivet, 199–206. Amsterdam: IOS Press.

Amador, F.; Finkelstein, A.; and Weld, D. 1993. Real-Time Self-Explanatory Simulation. In Proceedings of the Eleventh National Conference on Artificial Intelligence, 562–567. Menlo Park, Calif.: American Association for Artificial Intelligence.

Amarel, S. 1968. On Representations of Problems of Reasoning about Actions. In *Machine Intelligence 3*, 131–171, ed. D. Michie. Edinburgh, Scotland: Edinburgh University Press.

American Heart Association. 1987. Textbook of Advanced Cardiac Life Support. Second ed. American Heart Association, Dallas, Texas.

Anderson, J. R. 1990. Analysis of Student Performance with the Lisp Tutor. In *Diagnostic Monitoring of Skill and Knowledge Acquisition*, eds. N. Frederiksen, R. Glaser, A. Lesgold, and M. G. Shafto, 27–50. Hillsdale, N.J.: Lawrence Erlbaum.

Anderson, J. R., and Lebière, C. 1998. *The Atomic Components of Thought*. Hillsdale, N.J.: Lawrence Erlbaum.

Anderson, J. R., and Reiser, B. 1985. The Lisp Tutor. *Byte* 10(4): 159–175.

Anderson, J. R.; Boyle, C.; and Yost, G. 1985. The Geometry Tutor. In Proceedings of the Ninth International Joint Conference on Artifical Intelligence (IJCAI-85), 1–7. Menlo Park, Calif.: International Joint Conferences on Artificial Intelligence.

Anderson, J. R.; Conrad, F. G.; and Corbett, A. T. 1989. Skill Acquisition and the Lisp Tutor. *Cognitive Science* 13(4): 467–505.

Anderson, J. R.; Corbettt, A. T.; Koedinger, K. R.; and Pelletier, R. 1995. Cognitive Tutors: Lessons Learned. *The Journal of Learning Science* 4(2): 167–207.

André, E., and Rist, T. 1996. Coping with Temporal Constraints in Multimedia Presentation Planning. In Proceedings of the Thirteenth National Conference on Artificial Intelligence, 142–147. Menlo Park, Calif.: American Association for Artificial Intelligence.

André, E.; Rist, T.; and Müller, J. 1998. Integrating Reactive and Scripted Behaviors in a Life-Like Presentation Agent. In Proceedings of the Second International Conference on Autonomous Agents, 261–268. New York: Association for Computing Machinery.

Anyon, J. 1981. Social Class and School Knowledge. *Curriculum Inquiry* 11(1):3–41.

Apple, M. W. 1979. *Ideology and Curriculum*. Boston: Routledge and Kegan Paul.

Arroyo, I.; Beck, J. E.; Schultz, K.; Woolf, B. 1999. Piagetian Psychology in Intelligent Tutoring Systems. Paper presented at the Ninth International Conference on Artificial Intelligence in Education, LeMans, France 19–23 July.

Arroyo, I.; Beck, J. E.; Woolf, B.; Beal, C.; and Schultz, K. 2000. Gender and Cognitive Differences in Learning with Respect to Hint Interactivity and Symbolism. Paper presented at the Third International Conference on Intelligent Tutoring Systems, Montreal, Quebec, Canada, 19–23 June.

Baher, J. 1998. How Articulate Virtual Labs Can Help in Thermodynamics Education: A Multiple Case Study. Paper presented at the Twenty-Seventh Annual Frontiers in Education Conference, 4–7 November, Tempe, Arizona.

Balac, N.; Katzlberger, T.; and Leelawong, K. 1998. *Agent-Enhanced Intelligent Learning Environments*, Technical Report CS-TR-05, Department of Computer Science, Vanderbilt University.

Bareiss, R., and Osgood, R. 1993. Applying AI Models to the Design of Exploratory Hypermedia Systems. Paper presented at the Hypertext Conference, Seattle Wash., 14–18 November.

Bargh, J. A., and Schul, Y. 1980. On the Cognitive Benefits of Teaching. *Journal of Educational Psychology* 72(5): 593–604.

Barron, B.; Vye, N. J.; Zech, L.; Schwartz, D.; Bransford, J. D.; Goldman, S. R.; Pellegrino, J. W.; Morris, J.; Garrison, S.; and Kantor, R. 1995. Creating Contexts for Community-Based Problem Solving: The Jasper Challenge Series. In *Thinking and Literacy: The Mind at Work*, 47–71, eds. C. Hedley, P. Antonacci, and M. Rabinowitz. Hillsdale, N.J.: Lawrence Erlbaum.

Barsalou, L. W. 1991. Deriving Categories to Achieve Goals. In *The Psychology of Learning and Motivation*, (Volume 27), 1–64, ed. G. H. Bower. San Diego, Calif.: Academic Press.

Bartle, R. 1990. Early MUD History. E-Mail Concerning Interactive Multi-User Computer Games, 15 November. MUSE, Ltd. URLs: ftp://ftp.lambda.moo.mud/pub/MOO/papers/mudreport and http://www.apocalypse.org/pub/u/lpb/muddex/bartle.txt

Bates, R., and MacGregor, R. 1987. The LOOM Knowledge Representation Language. Report, ADA 183415 RS-87-188, Information Sciences Institute, University of Southern California.

Beal, C. R.; Beck, J. E.; and Woolf, B. P. 1998. Impact of Intelligent Computer Instruction on Girls' Math Self-Concept and Beliefs in the Value of Math. Paper presented at the Annual Meeting of the American Educational Research Association, 13–17 April, San Diego, Calif.

Beal, C. R.; Beck, J. E.; Woolf, B. P.; and Rae-Ramirez, M. A. 1998. WHALEWATCH: An Intelligent Model-Based Mathematics Tutoring System. In Proceedings of the Fifteenth IFIP World Computer Congress, ed. J. Cuena, 472–483 Vienna, Austria: Austrian Computer Society.

Beal, C. R.; Woolf, B. P.; Beck, J. E.; Arroyo, I.; Schultz, K.; and Hart, D. 2000. Gaining Confidence in Mathematics. Paper presented at the International Conference on Mathematics/Science Education and Technology (M/SET-00), 3–6 March, San Diego, California.

Beck, J. E., and Woolf, B. P. 2000. High-Level Student Modeling with Machine Learning. In *Proceedings of the Fifth International Conference on Intelligent Tutoring Systems*, eds. G. Gauthier, C. Frasson, and K. VanLehn, 584–593. New York: Springer-Verlag.

Beck, J. E.; Arroyo, I.; Woolf, B. P.; and Beal, C. R. 1999. An Ablative Evaluation. Paper presented at the Ninth International Conference on Artificial Intelligence in Education, LeMans, France, 19–23 July.

Beck, J. E.; Stern, M.; and Woolf, B. P. 1997. Cooperative Student Models. Paper presented at the Eighth World Conference on Artificial Intelligence in Education, 18–22 August, Kobe, Japan.

Beck, J. E.; Woolf, B. P.; and Beal, C. R. 2000. Learning to Teach: A Machine-Learning Architecture for Intelligent Tutor Construction. Paper presented at the Seventeenth National Conference on Artificial Intelligence, Austin, Texas, 30 July – 3 August.

Bédard, J., and Chi, M. T. H. 1992. Expertise. *Psychological Science* 1(4): 135–139.

Bell, B.; Bareiss, R.; and Beckwith, R. 1993. Sickle Cell Counselor: A Prototype Goal-Based Scenario for Instruction in a Museum Environment. *The Journal of the Learning Sciences* 3(4): 347–386.

Bell, D. G.; Bobrow, D. G.; Raiman, O.; and Shirley, M. H. 1996. Dynamic Documents and Situated Processes: Building on Local Knowledge in Field Service. Paper presented at the International Working Conference on Integration of Enterprise Information and Processes, Rethinking Documents. 14–15 November, Cambridge, Massachusetts.

Bellman, K. L. 1997. Sharing Work, Experience, Interpretation, and Maybe Even Meanings between Natural and Artificial Agents. In Proceedings of the IEEE International Conference on Systems, Man, and Cybernetics, 4127–4132. Washington, D.C.: IEEE Computer Society.

Bellman, K. L. 1999. Toward a Theory of Virtual Worlds. In Proceedings of the Virtual Worlds and Simulation Conference, eds. C. Landauer and K. L. Bellman, 17–21. San Diego, Calif.: The Society for Computer Simulation.

Bellman, K. L., and Landauer, C. 1999. Playing in the MUD: Virtual Worlds Are Real Places. In Proceedings of the European Conference on Artificial Intelligence, Workshop W14 on Intelligent Virtual Environments, 25 August 1998, Brighton, United Kingdom.

Bellman, K. L., and Landauer, C. 2000a. Integration Science Is More Than Putting Pieces Together. In Proceedings of the 2000 IEEE Aerospace Conference, 18–25. Washington, D.C.: IEEE Computer Society.

Bellman, K. L., and Landauer, C. 2000b. Virtual Worlds as Meeting Places for Formal Systems. Paper presented at the Seventh Bellman Continuum, International Workshop on Computation, Optimization and Control, 24–25 May, Santa Fe, New Mexico.

Berry, D. C., and Dienes, Z. 1993. *Implicit Learning: Theoretical and Empirical Issues.* Hillsdale, N.J.: Lawrence Erlbaum.

Beyer, H. and Holtzblatt, K. 1998. *Contextual Design: Defining Customer-Centered Systems.* San Francisco, Calif.: Morgan Kaufmann.

Bloom, B. S. 1984. The 2-Sigma Problem: The Search for Methods of Group Instruction as Effective as One-to-One Tutoring. *Educational Researcher* 13(3) (June–July): 4–16.

Bloom, C. P. 1996. Promoting the Transfer of Advanced Training Technologies. In *Proceedings of the Third International Conference on Intelligent Tutoring Systems,* eds. C. Frasson, G. Gauthier, and A. Lesgold, 1–10. New York: Springer-Verlag.

Blumberg, B., and Galyean, T. 1995. Multi-Level Direction of Autonomous Creatures for Real-Time Virtual Environments. In Proceedings of SIGGRAPH 95, 47–54. New York: Association of Computing Machinery.

Bobrow, D. G.; O'Day, V. L.; Shirley, M. H.; and Walters, J. 1998. Learning from Simulations in Virtual Worlds: Generalizing Reciprocal Teaching. In Proceedings of Virtual Worlds and Simulations (VWSIM 98), eds. C. Landauer and K. Bellman, 167–171. San Diego, Calif.: The Society for Computer Simulation.

Bouillion, L.; Gomez, L.; and Williams, K. 1999. Building Community Intellectual Capital: Mutual Benefit Partnerships between Schools and Non-Profit Organizations. Paper presented at the Annual Conference of the Association for Research on Nonprofit Organizations and Voluntary Action, 4–6 Nov., Arlington, Virginia.

Bowers, P. G. 1993. Text Reading and Rereading: Determinants of Fluency beyond Word Recognition. *Journal of Reading Behavior* 25(2): 133–153.

Boyle, C., and Encarnacion, A. 1994. METADOC: An Adaptive Hypertext Reading System. *User Models and User Adapted Interaction* 4(1): 1–19.

Bransford, J. D., and Schwartz, D. L. 1999. Rethinking Transfer: A Simple Proposal with Multiple Implications. In Review of Research in Education 24, eds. A. Iran-Nejad and P.D. Pearson, 61–101. Washington D.C.: American Educational Research Association.

Bransford, J. D., and Stein, B. S. 1993. *The Ideal Problem Solver.* 2d ed. New York: Freeman.

Bransford, J. D.; Brophy, S.; and Williams, S. 2000. When Computer Technologies Meet the Learning Sciences: Issues and Opportunities. *Journal of Applied Developmental Psychology.* 21(1): 59–84.

Bransford, J. D.; Brown, A. L.; and Cocking, R. R. 1999. *How People Learn: Brain, Mind, Experience, and School.* Committee on Developments in the Science of Learning Commission on Behavioral and Social Sciences and Education. National Research Council. Washington, D.C.: National Academy Press.

Bransford, J. D.; Franks, J.; Vye, N.; and Sherwood, R. 1989. New Approaches to Instruction: Because Wisdom Can't Be Told. In *Similarity and Analogical Reasoning,* 470–497, eds. S. Vosniadou and A. Ortony. New York: Cambridge University Press.

Bransford, J. D., Sherwood, R. S.; Hasselbring, T. S.; Kinzer, C. K.; and Williams, S. M. 1990. Anchored Instruction: Why We Need It and How Technology Can Help. In *Cognition, Education and Multimedia,* eds. D. Nix and R. Spiro. Hillsdale, N.J: Erlbaum.

Bransford, J. D.; Zech, L. K.; Schwartz, D. L; Barron, B.; Vye, N.; and Vanderbilt Cognition and Technology Group. 2000. Designs for Environments that Invite and Sustain Mathematical Thinking. In *Symbolizing and Communicating in Mathematics Classrooms: Perspectives on Discourse, Tools and Instructional Design,* eds. P. Cobb, E. Yackel, and K. McClain, 275–324. Mahwah, N. J.: Lawrence Erlbaum.

Bredeweg, B. 1992. Expertise in Qualitative Prediction of Behaviour. Ph.D. dissertation, Dept. of Social Science Informations, University of Amsterdam.

Bredeweg, B. 1993. Qualitative Prediction of Behavior. In *KADS: A Principled Approach to Knowledge Engineering,* 337–358, eds. A. T. Schreiber, B. J. Wielinga, and J. A. Breuker. San Diego, Calif.: Academic Press.

Bredeweg, B., and Breuker, J. A. 1993. Device Models for Model-Based Diagnosis of Student Behavior. In Proceedings of the World Conference on Artificial Intelligence in Education, eds. P. Brna, S. Ohlsson, and H. Pain, 441–448. Charlottesville, Va.: Association for the Advancement of Computing in Education.

Bredeweg, B., and Winkels, R. 1998. Qualitative Models in Interactive Learning Environments: An Introduction. *Interactive Learning Environments* 5(1–2): 1–19.

Breuker, J. A., ed. 1990. EUROHELP: Developing Intelligent Help Systems. Technical Report, Kopenhagen, Amsterdam/Manchester, Leeds, European Community.

Broverman, C. 1991. Constructive Interpretation of Human-Generated Exceptions during Plan Executions. Ph.D. dissertation, Technical Report, 91-9, Computer Science Department, University of Massachusetts.

Brown, A. L. 1992. Design Experiments: Theoretical and Methodological Challenges in Creating Complex Interventions in Classroom Settings. *The Journal of the Learning Sciences* 2(2):141–178.

Brown, J. S., and Burton, R. R. 1978. Diagnostic Models of Procedural Bugs in Basic Mathematical Skills. *Cognitive Science* 2(2): 155–192.

Brown, A. L., and Campione, J. C. 1994. Guided Discovery in a Community of Learners. In *Classroom Lessons: Integrating Cognitive Theory and Practice,* ed. K. McGilly, 229–270. Cambridge, Mass.: MIT Press.

Brown, J. S., and Duguid, J. 1994. Borderline Issues: Social and Material Aspects of Design. *Human-Computer Interaction* 9(1): 3–36.

Brown, J. S.; Burton, R. R.; and de Kleer, J. 1982. Pedagogical, Natural Language and Knowledge Engineering Techniques in SOPHIE I, II, and III. In *Intelligent Tutoring Systems,* eds. D. Seeman and J. S. Brown, 227–282. San Diego, Calif.: Academic Press.

Brown, J. S.; Collins, A.; and Duguid, P. 1989. Situated Cognition and the Culture of Learning. *Educational Researcher* 18(1)(Jan.–Feb.): 32–42.

Bruer, J. 1993. *Schools for Thought: A Science of Learning in the Classroom.* Cambridge, Mass.: MIT Press.

Brusilovsky, P., and Pesin, L. 1994. ISIS-TUTOR: An Intelligent Learning Environment for CDS/ISIS Users. Paper Presented at the Complex Learning in Computer Environments Workshop, University of Joensuu, Joensuu, Finland, 16–19 May.

Brusilovsky, P., and Schwarz, E. 1997. User as Student: Toward an Adaptive Interface for Advanced Web-Based Applications. In *Proceedings of the Sixth International Conference on User Modeling,* eds. A. Jameson, C. Paris, and C. Tasso, 177–188. New York: Springer-Verlag.

Brusilovsky, P.; Schwarz, E.; and Weber, G. 1996. ELM-ART: An Intelligent Tutoring System on World Wide Web. In *Proceedings of Third International Conference on Intelligent Tutoring Systems,* eds. C. Frasson, G. Gauthier, and A. Lesgold, 261–269. New York: Springer-Verlag.

Buckley, B. C. 1992. Multimedia, Misconceptions, and Working Models of Biological Phenomena: Learning about the Cardiovascular System. Ph.D. dissertation, School of Education, Stanford University, Stanford, Calif.

Bulitko, V. V., and Wilkins, D. C. 1999. Automated Instructor Assistant for Ship Damage Control. In Proceedings of the Eleventh Conference on Innovative Applications of Artificial Intelligence, 778–785. Menlo Park, Calif.: American Association for Artificial Intelligence.

Burka, L. P. 1999. The MUDdex: A Hypertext History of Multi-User Dimensions. (www.apocalypse.org/pub/u/lpb/muddex/

Burton, R. R., and Brown, J. S. 1979. An Investigation of Computer Coaching for Informal Learning Activities. *International Journal of Man-Machine Studies* 11(1): 5–24.

Campbell, R. 1988. *Hearing Children Read.* London and New York: Routledge and Kegan Paul.

Carbonell, J. R. 1970. AI in CAI: An Artificial Intelligence Approach to Computer-Assisted Instruction. *IEEE Transactions on Man-Machine Systems* 11(4): 190–202.

Carr, B., and Goldstein, I. 1977. Overlays: A Theory of Modeling for Computer-Aided Instruction, AI Memo, 406, Artificial Intelligence Laboratory, Massachusetts Institute of Technology.

Cassell, J. 2001. Embodied Conversation: Integrating Face and Gesture into Automatic Spoken Dialogue Systems. In *Automatic Spoken Dialogue Systems,* ed. S. Luperfoy. Cambridge, Mass.: MIT Press. Forthcoming.

Champagne, A. B.; Gunstone, R. F.; and Klopfer, L. E. 1985. Effecting Changes in Cognitive Structures among Physics Students. In *Cognitive Structure and Conceptual Change*, eds. L. H. T. West and A. L. Pines, 163–187. San Diego, Calif.: Academic Press.

Chan, T. W., and Baskin, A. B. 1988. Studying with the Prince: The Computer as a Learning Companion. In Proceedings of the International Conference on Intelligent Tutoring Systems, 194–200. New York: Association for Computing Machinery.

Cheng, P. W., and Holyoak, K. J. 1985. Pragmatic Reasoning Schemas. *Cognitive Psychology* 17(3): 391–416.

Chi, M. T. H. 1992. Conceptual Change within and across Ontological Categories: Examples from Learning and Discovery in Science. In *Cognitive Models of Science: Minnesota Studies in the Philosophy of Science*, ed. R. Giere, 129–186. Minneapolis, Minn.: University of Minnesota Press.

Chi, M. T. H.; Bassok, M.; Lewis, M.; Reimann, P.; and Glaser, R. 1989. Self-Explanations: How Students Study and Use Examples in Learning to Solve Problems. *Cognitive Science* 13(2): 145–182.

Chi, M. T. H.; Feltovich, P. J.; and Glaser, R. 1981. Categorization and Representation of Physics Problems by Experts and Novices. *Cognitive Sciencs* 5(2): 121–152.

Chi, M. T. H; de Leeuw, N.; Chiu, M.; and LaVancher, C. 1994. Eliciting Self-Explanations Improves Understanding. *Cognitive Science* 18(3): 439–477.

Chi, M. T. H.; Slotta, J. D.; and de Leeuw, N. 1994. From Things to Processes: A Theory of Conceptual Change for Science Learning. *Learning and Instruction* 4(1): 27–43.

Chinn, C. A., and Brewer, W. F. 1993. The Role of Anomalous Data in Knowledge Acquisition: A Theoretical Framework and Implications for Science Instruction. *Review of Educational Research* 63(1): 1–49.

Chu-Carroll, J., and Carberry, S. 1994. A Plan-Based Model for Response Generation in Collaborative Task-Oriented Dialogues. In Proceedings of the Twelfth National Conference on Artificial Intelligence, 799–805. Menlo Park, Calif.: American Association for Artificial Intelligence.

Clancey, W. J. 1983. The Epistemology of a Rule-Based Expert System: A Framework for Explanation. *Artificial Intelligence* 20(3): 215–252.

Clancey, W. J. 1986. From GUIDON to NEOMYCIN and HERACLES in Twenty Short Lessons. *AI Magazine* 7(3): 40–60.

Clancey, W. J., and Letsinger, R. 1984. NEOMYCIN: Reconfiguring a Rule-Based Expert System for Application to Teaching. In *Readings in Artificial Intelligence*, eds. W. J. Clancey and E. H. Shortliffe, 361–381. Reading, Mass.: Addison Wesley.

Clark, H. H., and Brennan, S. E. 1991. Grounding in Communication. In *Perspectives on Socially Shared Cognition*, eds. L. B. Resnick, J. M. Levine, and S. D. Teasley, 127–149. Washington, D. C.: American Psychological Association.

Clay, M. 1993. *Reading Recovery: A Guidebook for Teachers in Training*. Portsmouth, N.H.: Heinemann.

Clement, J. 1982. Students' Preconceptions in Introductory Mechanics. *American Journal of Physics* 50(1): 66–71.

Clodius, J. 1994. Concepts of Space and Place in a Virtual Community. (www.dragon-mud.org/people/jen/space.html)

Clodius, J. 1995. Computer-Mediated Interactions: Human Factors. Paper presented at the DARPA MUDshop II, 6–8 September, San Diego, Calif.

Coglianese, L. H. 1998. Toward a Visual Integration Architecture Baseline. In Proceedings of VWSIM 98, 58–63, eds. C. Landauer and K. Bellman. San Diego, Calif.: The Society for Computer Simulation.

Cohen, P.; Kulik, J. A.; and Kulik, C. C. 1982. Educational Outcomes of Tutoring: A Meta-Analysis of Findings. *American Educational Research Journal* 19(2): 237-248.

Cole, M., and Engestrom, Y. 1993. A Cultural-Historical Approach to Distributed Cognition. In *Distributed Cognition: Psychological and Educational Considerations*, ed. G. Salomon, 1–46. Cambridge, U.K.: Cambridge University Press.

Collins, A. M. 1992. Toward a Design Science of Education. In *New Directions in Educational Technology*, eds. E. Scanlon and T. O'Shea, 15–22. Springer-Verlag: Berlin.

Collins, A. M., and Gentner, D. 1983. Multiple Models of Evaporation Processes. Paper presented at the Fifth Annual Meeting of the Cognitive Science Society, 18–20 May, Rochester, New York.

Collins, A. M.; Brown, J. S.; and Newman, S. E. 1989. Cognitive Apprenticeship: Teaching the Crafts of Reading, Writing, and Mathematics. In *Knowing, Learning, and Instruction: Essays in Honor of Robert Glaser*, 453–494, ed. L. B. Resnick. Hillsdale, N.J.: Lawrence Erlbaum.

Conati, C., and Van Lehn, K. 1999a. A Student Model to Assess Self-Explanation while Learning from Examples. Paper presented at the Seventh International Conference on User Modeling, Banff, Canada.

Conati, C., and Van Lehn, K. 1999b. Teaching Meta-Cognitive Skills: Implementation and Evaluation of a Tutoring System to Guide Self-Explanation while Learning from Examples. Paper presented at the Ninth World Conference of Artificial Intelligence and Education, 19–22 July, Le Mans, France.

Conati, C.; Gertner, A.; VanLehn, K.; and Druzdzel, M. 1997. On-Line Student Modeling for Coached Problem Solving Using Bayesian Networks. Paper presented at the Sixth International Conference on User Modeling, 2–5 June, Chia Laguna, Sardinia, Italy.

Corbett, A. T., and Anderson, J. R. 1990. The Effect of Feedback Control on Learning to Program with the Lisp Tutor. In *Proceedings of the Twelfth Annual Conference of the Cognitive Science Society*, 796–803. Hillsdale, N.J.: Lawrence Erlbaum.

Corbett, A. T., and Anderson, J. R. 1991. Feedback Control and Learrning to Program with the CMU Lisp Tutor. Paper presented at the Annual Meeting of the American Educational Research Association, Chicago, Illinois, April 10–14.

Corbett, A. T., and Anderson, J. R. 1994. Knowledge Tracing: Modeling the Acquisition of Procedural Knowledge. *User Modeling and User-Adapted Interaction* 4(4): 253–278.

Corbett, A. T.; Anderson, J. R.; and O'Brien, A. T. 1995. Student Modeling in the ACT Programming Tutor. In *Cognitively Diagnostic Assessment*, eds. P. Nichols, S. Chipman, and R. Brennan, 19–41. Hillsdale, N.J.: Lawrence Erlbaum.

Corbett, A. T.; Koedinger, K. R.; and Anderson, J. R. 1999. Intelligent Computer Tutors: Out of the Research Lab and into the Classroom. Paper presented at the Annual Meeting of the American Educational Research Association, Montreal, Canada, April 19–23.

Corbett, A. T.; McLaughlin, M.; and Scarpinatto, K. C. 2000. Modeling Student Knowledge: Cognitive Tutors in High School and College. *User Modeling and User-Adapted Interaction* 10(2–3): 81–108.

Coulson, R. L.; Feltovich P. J.; and Spiro R. J. 1989. Foundations of a Misunderstanding of the Ultrastructural Basis of Myocardial Failure: A Reciprocation Network of Oversimplifications. *Journal of Medicine and Philosophy* 14(2): 109–146.

Coulson, R. L.; Feltovich P. J.; and Spiro R. J. 1997. Cognitive Flexibility in Medicine: An Application to the Recognition and Understanding of Hypertension. *Advances in Health Sciences Education* 2(2): 141–166.

Cradler, J. 1999. Implementing Technology in Education: Recent Findings from Research and Evaluation Studies. San Francisco: WesEd, Inc. (www.wested.org/techpolicy/recapproach.html)

Cradler, J., and Bridgforth, E. 1994. Comparison of Educational Technology and Telecommunications Plans. Byting Back: Policies to Support the Use of Technology in Education. Oak Brook, Ill.: North Central Regional Educational Laboratory.

Cradler, J., and Yrchik, J. 1994. The National Information Infrastructure: Requirements for Education and Training. Washington, D.C.: National Coordinating Committee on Technology in Education and Training (NCC-TET).

Craik, F. I. M., and Lockhart, R. S. 1972. Levels of Processing: A Framework for Memory Research. *Journal of Verbal Learning and Verbal Behavior* 11(6): 671–684.

Crews, T. R.; Biswas, G.; Goldman, S. R.; and Bransford, J. D. 1997. Anchored Interactive Learning Environments. *International Journal of Artificial Intelligence in Education* 8(2): 142–178.

Curtis, M. E. 1980. Development of Components of Reading Skill. *Journal of Educational Psychology* 72(5): 656–669.

Dale, R. 1992. *Generating Referring Expressions.* Cambridge, Mass.: MIT Press.

Dautenhahn, K. 1998. Story-Telling in Virtual Environments. In Proceedings of the European Conference on Artificial Intelligence, Workshop W14 on Intelligent Virtual Environments, 25 Aug., Brighton, United Kingdom.

Davis, R. 1984. Diagnostic Reasoning Based on Structure and Behavior. *Artificial Intelligence* 24(1–3): 347–410.

Dawson-Saunders, B.; Feltovich, P. J.; Coulson, R. L.; and Steward, D. E. 1990. A Survey of Medical School Teachers to Identify Basic Biomedical Concepts Medical Students Should Understand. *Academic Medicine* 65(7): 448–454.

de Jong, T. 1991. Learning and Instruction with Computer Simulations. *Education and Computing* 6(3–4): 217–230.

de Kleer, J., and Brown, J. S. 1984. A Qualitative Physics Based on Confluences. *Artificial Intelligence* 24(1–3): 7–83.

de Kleer, J., and Williams, B. C. 1987. Diagnosing Multiple Faults. *Artificial Intelligence* 32(1): 97–130.

de Koning, K. 1997. *Model-Based Reasoning about Learner Behaviour.* Amsterdam: IOS Press.

de Koning, K., and Bredeweg, B. 1998. Qualitative Reasoning in Tutoring Interactions. *Interactive Learning Environments* 5: 65–80.

de Koning, K., Bredeweg, B., and Breuker, J. A. 1997. Automatic Aggregation of Qualitative Reasoning Networks. In *Proceedings of the Eleventh International Workshop on Qualitative Reasoning, QR97,* 77–88. Pavia, Italy: Istituto di Analisi Numerica C.N.R.

de Koning, K.; Bredeweg, B.; Breuker, B.; and Wielinga, B. 2000. Model-Based Reasoning about Learner Behaviour. *Artificial Intelligence* 117(2): 173–229.

de Koning, K.; Bredeweg, B.; Schut, C.; and Breuker, J. A. 1994. Dynamic Model Progression. In Proceedings of the East-West Conference on Computer Technologies in Education, 136–141. Moscow, Russia: International Center for Scientific and Technical Information.

de Koning, K.; Breuker, B.; and Bredeweg, B. 1997. Constructing Aggregated Reasoning Networks for Coaching Qualitative Prediction of Behaviour. In *Artificial Intelligence in Education: Knowledge and Media in Learning Systems*, eds. B. du Bouley and R. Mizoguchi, 442–449. Amsterdam: IOS Press.

Delpit, L. 1995. *Other People's Children: Cultural Conflict in the Classroom*. New York: New Press.

Dember, W. N. 1991. Cognition, Motivation, and Emotion: Ideology Revisited. In *Cognition and the Symbolic Processes*, eds. R. R. Hoffman and D. Palermo, 153–162. Hillsdale, N.J.: Lawrence Erlbaum.

Deno, S. L. 1985. Curriculum-Based Measurement: The Emerging Alternative. *Exceptional Children* 52(3): 219–232.

Detterman, D. K. 1993. The Case for the Prosecution: Transfer as an Epiphenomenon. In *Transfer on Trial: Intelligence, Cognition, and Instruction*, eds. D. K. Detterman and R. J. Sternberg, 1–24. Norwood, N.J.: Ablex.

Dev, P., Engberg, D.; Mather, R.; Hodge, D.; and Dutta, M. 1998. The Collaborative Curriculum Web for Medicine: A Virtual Representation of Medical School Resources. In Proceedings of the 1998 Conference on Virtual Worlds and Simulation, 29–30, eds. C. Landauer and K. Bellman. San Diego, Calif.: The Society for Computer Simulation.

Dewey, J. 1916. *Democracy and Education*. New York: Macmillan.

Dienes, Z., and Perner, J. 1999. A Theory of Implicit and Explicit Knowledge. *Behavioral and Brain Sciences* 22(5): 778–779.

Dillenbourg, P., and Self, J. A. 1992. A Framework for Learner Modeling. *Interactive Learning Environments* 2(2): 111–137.

Dillenbourg, P.; Jermann, P.; Schneider, D.; Traum, D.; and Buiu, C. 1997. The Design of MOO Agents: Implications from an Empirical CSCW Study. In *Proceedings of the Eighth World Conference on Artificial Intelligence in Education*, 15–22. Amsterdam: IOS Press.

diSessa, A. A. 1983. Phenomenology and the Evolution of Intuition. In *Mental Models*, eds. D. Gentner and A. L. Stevens, 15–34. Hillsdale, N.J.: Lawrence Erlbaum.

diSessa, A. A. 1988. Knowledge in Pieces. In *Constructivism in the Computer Age*, eds. G. Forman and P. Pufall, 49–70. Hillsdale, N.J.: Lawrence Erlbaum.

Dobson, D., and Forbus, K. D. 1999. Toward Articulate Game Engines. In AI and Computer Games, ed. Daniel Dobson and K. Forbus, 32. Technical Report SS-99-02, American Association for Artificial Intelligence, Menlo Park, California.

Donahue, P. L.; Voelkl, K. E.; Campbell, J. R.; and Mazzeo, J. 1999. The NAEP 1998 Reading Report Card for the Nation & the States. In *Education Statistics Quarterly* 1(2) (Summer) (nces.ed.gov/nationsreportcard/pubs/main1998/1999500.shtml). Washington, D. C.: National Center for Education Statistics.

Doyle, P., and Hayes-Roth, B. 1998. Annotating Virtual Worlds. In Proceedings of the Conference on Virtual Worlds and Simulation (VWSIM 98), eds. C. Landauer and K. Bellman, 195–200. San Diego, Calif.: The Society for Computer Simulation.

Drury, J.; Fanderclai, T.; and Linton, F. 1999. CHI 99 SIG: Automated Data Collection for Evaluating Collaborative Systems. *SIGCHI Bulletin* 31(4): 49–51.

Dunbar, K., and Klahr, D. 1989. Developmental Differences in Scientific Discovery Processes. In *Complex Information Processing: The Impact of Herbert Simon,* eds. D. Klahr and K. Kotovsky, 109–143. Hillsdale, N.J.: Lawrence Erlbaum.

Eccles, J. S.; Wigfield, A.; Harold, R. D.; and Blumenfeld, P. 1993. Age and Gender Differences in Children's Self and Task Perceptions during Elementary School. *Child Development* 64(3): 830–847.

Edelson, D. 1993. Learning from Stories: Indexing and Reminding in a Socratic Case-Based Teaching System for Elementary School Biology, Technical Report, 43, The Institute for the Learning Sciences, Northwestern University.

Edelson, D. C. 1992. When Should a Cheetah Remind You of a Bat? Reminding in Case-Based Teaching. In Proceedings of the Tenth National Conference on Artificial Intelligence, 667–672. Menlo Park, Calif.: American Association for Artificial Intelligence.

Edwards, W. 1968. Conservatism in Human Information Processing. In *Formal Representation in Human Judgment,* ed. B. Kleinmuntz. New York: Holt Rinehart and Winston.

Einhorn, H., and Hogarth, R. 1978. Confidence in Judgment: Persistence in the Illusion of Validity. *Psychological Review* 85(5): 395–416.

Elio, R., and Pelletier, F. J. 1997. Belief Change as Prepositional Update. *Cognitive Science* 21(4): 419–460.

Elio, R., and Sharf, P. B. 1990. Modeling Novice-to-Expert Shifts in Problem-Solving Strategy and Knowledge Organization. *Cognitive Science* 14(4): 579–639.

Eliot, C. R., and Woolf, B. P. 1994. Reasoning about the User within a Simulation-Based Real-Time Training System. Paper presented at the Fourth International Conference on User Modeling, 15–19 August, Hyannis, Cape Cod, Mass.

Eliot, C. R., and Woolf, B. P. 1995. An Adaptive Student-Centered Curriculum for an Intelligent Training System. *User Modeling and User-Adapted Interaction* 5(1): 67–86.

Eliot, C. R., and Woolf, B. P. 1996a. A Simulation-Based Tutor that Reasons about Multiple Agents. In Proceedings of the Thirteenth National Conference on Artificial Intelligence (AAAI-96), 409–415. Menlo Park, Calif.: American Association for Artificial Intelligence.

Eliot, C. R., and Woolf, B. P. 1996b. Iterative Development and Validation of a Simulation-Based Medical Tutor. In *Proceedings of the Third International Conference on Intelligent Tutoring Systems,* 540–549. New York: Springer-Verlag.

Elliot, C. R.; Rickel, J.; and Lester, J. 1999. Lifelike Pedagogical Agents and Affective Computing: An Exploratory Synthesis. In *Artificial Intelligence Today,* eds. M. Wooldridge and M. Veloso, 195–212. Berlin: Springer-Verlag.

Eliot, C. R.; Williams, K.A.; and Woolf, B. P. 1996. An Intelligent Learning Environment for Advanced Cardiac Life Support. In *Proceedings of the 1996 American Medical Informatics Association (AMIA) Fall Symposium,* ed. J. J. Cimino, 7–11. Philadelphia, Pa.: Hanley and Belfus.

Elsom-Cook, M., ed. 1990. *Guided Discovery Tutoring: A Framework for ICAI Research.* London: Paul Chapman.

Engestrom, Y. 1987. Learning by Expanding: An Activity-Theoretical Approach to Developmental Research. Helsinki: Orienta-Konsultit.

Erignac, C. 2000. Interactive Semi-Qualitative Simulation. Paper presented at the Fourteenth International Workshop on Qualitative Reasoning, Morelia, Mexico 6–8 June.

Eskenazi, M. 1996. KIDS: A Database of Children's Speech. *Journal of the Acoustical Society of America* 100(4): 27–59.

Eskenazi, M., and Mostow, J. 1997. The CMU KIDS Speech Corpus. Philadelphia, Penn.: Linguistic Data Consortium (University of Pennsylvania).

Everett, J. O. 1999. Topological Inference of Teleology: Deriving Function from Structure via Evidential Reasoning. *Artificial Intelligence* 113 (1-2): 149–202.

Everett, J. O., and Forbus, K. D. 1996. A Garbage-Collecting Truth Maintenance System. In Proceedings of the Thirteenth National Conference on Artificial Intelligence, 614–620. Menlo Park, Calif.: American Association for Artificial Intelligence.

Falkenhainer, B., and Forbus, K. D. 1991. Compositional Modeling: Finding the Right Model for the Job. *Artificial Intelligence* 51(1–3): 95–143.

Falkenhainer, B.; Forbus, K. D.; and Gentner, D. 1989. The Structure-Mapping Engine: Algorithm and Examples. *Artificial Intelligence* 41(1): 1–63.

Feiner, S., and McKeown, K. 1991. Automating the Generation of Coordinated Multimedia Explanations. *IEEE Computer* 24(10): 33–41.

Feltovich, P. J.; Coulson, R. L.; and Spiro, R. J. 1997. Issues of Expert Flexibility in Contexts Characterized by Complexity and Change. In *Expertise in Context: Human and Machine,* eds. P. J. Feltovich, K. M. Ford, and R. R. Hoffman, 125–126. Menlo Park, Calif.: AAAI Press.

Feltovich, P. J.; Coulson, R. L.; Spiro, R. J.; and Adami, J. F. 1994. Conceptual Understanding and Stability, and Knowledge Shields for Fending Off Conceptual Change. Final Report, Contract N00014-88-K-0077, Cognitive Science Division, Office of Naval Research. Also CKRP Technical Report #7, School of Medicine, Southern Illinois University, Springfield, Ill.

Feltovich, P. J.; Coulson, R. L.; Spiro, R. J.; and Dawson-Saunders, B. K. 1992. Knowledge Application and Transfer for Complex Tasks in Ill-Structured Domains: Implications for Instruction and Testing in Biomedicine. In *Advanced Models of Cognition for Medical Training and Practice,* eds. D. Evans and V. Patel, 212–244. Berlin: Springer-Verlag.

Feltovich, P. J.; Spiro, R. J.; and Coulson, R. L. 1989. The Nature of Conceptual Understanding in Biomedicine: The Deep Structure of Complex Ideas and the Development of Misconceptions. In *Cognitive Science in Medicine: Biomedical Modeling,* eds. D. A. Evans and V. L. Patel, 111–172. Cambridge, Mass.: MIT Press.

Feltovich, P. J.; Spiro, R. J.; Coulson, R. L.; and Feltovich, J. 1996. Collaboration within and among Minds: Mastering Complexity Individually and in Groups. In *CSCL: Theory and Practice of an Emerging Paradigm,* ed. T. Koschmann, 25–44. Hillsdale, N.J.: Lawrence Erlbaum.

Feltovich, P. J; Spiro, R. J.; and Coulson, R. L. 1993. Learning, Teaching, and Testing for Complex Conceptual Understanding. In *Test Theory for a New Generation of Tests,* eds. N. Frederiksen and I. Bejar, 181–217. Hillsdale, N.J.: Lawrence Erlbaum.

Feltovich, P. J; Spiro, R. J.; Coulson, R. L.; and Myers-Kelson, A. 1995. The Reductive Bias and the Crisis of Text (in the Law). *Journal of Contemporary Legal Issues* 6(1): 187–212.

Firth, I. 1972. Components of Reading Disability. Ph.D. dissertation. School of Education Studies, University of New South Wales.

Fletcher, J. D. 1988. Intelligent Training Systems in the Military. In *Defense Applications of Artificial Intelligence: Progress and Prospects*, eds. S. J. Andriole and G. W. Hopple. Lexington, Mass.: Lexington Books.

Fletcher, J. D. 1995. What Have We Learned about Computer-Based Instruction in Military Training? Research Study Group, RSG 16, Workshop on Lessons Learned, North Atlantic Treaty Organization, Brussels, Belgium

Fletcher, J. D. 1996. Does This Stuff Work? Some Findings from Applications of Technology to Education and Training. In Proceedings of Conference on Teacher Education and the Use of Technology-Based Learning Systems. Warrenton, Va.: Society for Applied Learning Technology.

Fletcher, J. D., and Orlansky, J. 1986. Recent Studies on the Cost-Effectiveness of Military training in TTCP Countries, IDA Paper P-1896, Institute for Defense Analyses, Alexandria, Virginia.

Fletcher, J. D., and Rockway, M. R. 1986. Computer-Based Training in the Military. In *Military Contributions to Instructional Technology*, ed. J. A. Ellis. New York: Praeger.

Fletcher, J. D.; Hawley, D. E.; and Piele, P. K. 1990. Costs, Effects, and Utility of Microcomputer-Assisted Instruction in the Classroom. *American Educational Research Journal* 27(4): 783–806.

Forbus, K. D. 1984a. An Interactive Laboratory for Teaching Control System Concepts. Technical Report 5511. Cambridge, Mass., Bolt Beranek and Newman.

Forbus, K. D. 1984b. Qualitative Process Theory. *Artificial Intelligence* 24(1): 85-168.

Forbus, K. D. 1994. Self-Explanatory Simulators: Making Computers Partners in the Modeling Process. *Mathematics and Computers in Simulation* 36(2): 91–101.

Forbus, K. D. 1996. Qualitative Reasoning. In *CRC Handbook of Computer Science and Engineering*. Grand Rapids, Mich.: CRC Press.

Forbus, K. D. 1997. Using Qualitative Physics to Create Articulate Educational Software. *IEEE Expert* 12(3): 32–41.

Forbus, K. D., and de Kleer, J. 1993. *Building Problem Solvers*. Cambridge, Mass.: MIT Press.

Forbus, K. D., and Falkenhainer, B. 1990. Self-Explanatory Simulations: An Integration of Qualitative and Quantitative Knowledge. In Proceedings of the Eighth National Conference on Artificial Intelligence, 380–387. Menlo Park, Calif.: American Association for Artificial Intelligence.

Forbus, K. D., and Falkenhainer, B. 1995. Scaling Up Self-Explanatory Simulators: Polynomial-Time Compilation. In Proceedings of the Fourteenth International Joint Conference on Artificial Intelligence, 1798–1805. Menlo Park, Calif.: International Joint Conferences on Artificial Intelligence.

Forbus, K. D. and Kuehne, S. E. 1998. ROBoTA: An Agent Colony Architecture for Supporting Education. In Proceedings of the Second International Conference on Autonomous Agents, 455–456. New York: Association of Computing Machinery.

Forbus, K. D., and Stevens, A. 1981. Using Qualitative Simulation to Generate Explanations. In Proceedings of the Third Annual Meeting of the Cognitive Science Society. Mahwah, N.J.: Lawrence Erlbaun Associates, Inc.

Forbus, K. D., and Whalley, P. B. 1994. Using Qualitative Physics to Build Articulate Software for Thermodynamics Education. In Proceedings of the Twelfth National Conference on Artificial Intelligence, 1175–1182. Menlo Park, Calif.: American Association for Artificial Intelligence.

Forbus, K. D., and Whalley, P. B. 1998. Using Qualitative Physics to Build Articulate Software for Thermodynamics Education: A Preliminary Report. *Journal of Interactive Learning Environments* 1(1): 19–32.

Forbus, K. D.; Everett, J.; Ureel, L.; Brokowski, M.; Baher, J.; and Kuehne, S. E. 1998. Distributed Coaching for an Intelligent Learning Environment. Paper presented at the Twelfth International Workshop on Qualitative Reasoning, 26–29 May, Cape Cod, Massachusetts.

Forbus, K. D.; Ferguson, R.; and Gentner, D. 1994. Incremental Structure-Mapping. In *Proceedings of the Sixteenth Annual Meeting of the Cognitive Science Society.* Mahwah, N.J.: Lawrence Erlbaun Associates, Inc.

Forbus, K. D.; Gentner, D.; and Law, K. 1995. MAC/FAC: A Model of Similarity-Based Retrieval. *Cognitive Science* 19(2): 141–205.

Forbus, K. D.; Whalley, P.; Everett, J.; Ureel, L.; Brokowski, M.; Baher, J.; and Kuehne, S. 1999. CYCLEPAD: An Articulate Virtual Laboratory for Engineering Thermodynamics. *Artificial Intelligence* 114(1–2): 297–347.

Forester, P. A. 1984. *Algebra I: Expressions, Equations, and Applications.* Reading, Mass.: Addison-Wesley.

Foss, C. 1987. Learning from Errors in ALGEBRALAND, Technical Report, IRL-87-0003, Institute for Research on Learning, Palo Alto, California.

Frasson, C.; Mengelle, T.; and Aimeur, E. 1997. Using Pedagogical Agents in a Multi-Strategic Intelligent Tutoring System. Paper presented at the AI-ED 97 Workshop on Pedagogical Agents, 19 August, Kobe, Japan.

Freedman, R., and Evens, M. W. 1996. Generating and Revising Hierarical Multi-Turn Text Plans in an ITS. In *Proceedings of the Third International Conference on Intelligent Tutoring Systems,* eds. C. Frasson, G. Gauthier, and A. Lesgold, 632–640. New York: Springer-Verlag.

Freedman, R.; Rose, C.; Ringenberg, M.; and VanLehn, K. 2000. ITS Tools for Natural Language Dialogue: A Domain-Independent Parser and Planner. In *Proceedings of the Fifth International Conference on Intelligent Tutoring Systems,* eds. G. Gauthier, C. Frasson, and K. VanLehn, 433–442. New York: Springer-Verlag.

Freire, P., and Macedo, D. 1987. The Illiteracy of Literacy in the United States. In *Literacy: Reading the World and the World,* eds. P. Freire & D. Macedo, 120–140. South Hadley, Mass.: Bergom and Garvey.

Fuson, K., De La Cruz, Y.; Smith, S.; Lo Cicero, A.; Hudson, K.; Ron, P.; and Steeby, R. 2000. Blending the Best of the Twentieth Century to Achieve a Mathematics Equity Pedagogy in the Twenty-First Century. In *Learning Mathematics for a New Century,* ed M. J. Burke and F. R. Curcio, 197–212. Reston, Va.: National Council of Teachers of Mathematics.

Gaskins, E.; Downer, M.; Anderson, R.; Cunningham, P.; Gaskins, R.; and Schommer, M. 1988. A Metacognitive Approach to Phonics: Using What You Know to Decode What You Don't Know. *Remedial and Special Education* 9(1): 36–41.

Gentner, D. 1983. Structure-Mapping: A Theoretical Framework for Analogy. *Cognitive Science* 7(2): 155–170.

Gentner, D., and Stevens, A. L., eds. 1983. *Mental Models.* Hillsdale, N.J.: LEA Associates.

Gick, M. L., and Holyoak, K. J. 1980. Analogical Problem Solving. *Cognitive Psychology* 12(3): 306–355.

Gick, M. L., and Holyoak, K. J. 1983. Schema Induction and Analogical Transfer. *Cognitive Psychology* 15(1): 1–38.

Gick, M. L., and McGarry, S. J. 1992. Learning from Mistakes: Inducing Analogous Solution Failures to a Source Problem Produces Later Successes in Analogical Transfer. *Journal of Experimental Pscyhology: Learning, Memory and Cognition* 18(3): 623–639.

Gilfillan, L. 1997. CAETI Evaluation Results … First Look. Paper presented at the CAETI Community Meeting, 3–5 June, George Mason University, Arlington, Virginia.

Gluck, K. 1999. Eye Movements and Algebra Tutoring. Ph.D. dissertation, Psychology Department, Carnegie Mellon University.

Godden, D. R., and Baddeley, A. D. 1975. Context-Dependent Memory in Two Natural Environments: On Land and Underwater. *British Journal of Psychology* 66(3): 325–331.

Gordon, E. E., and Gordon, E. H. 1990. *Centuries of Tutoring.* New York: University Press of America.

Gordon, E. E.; Ponticell, Judith A.; and Morgan, Ronald R. 1991. Closing the Literacy Gap in American Business: A Guide for Trainers and Human Resource Specialists. New York: Quorum Books.

Goswami, U. 1988. Orthographic Analogies and Reading Development. *Quarterly Journal of Experimental Psychology* 40A(2): 239–268.

Gough, P. B., and Hillinger, M. L. 1980. Learning to Read: An Unnatural Act. *Bulletin of the Orton Society* 30: 179–196.

Gough, P. B.; Juel, C.; and Griffith, P. L. 1992. Reading, Spelling, and the Orthographic Cipher. In *Reading Acquisition,* eds. P. Gough, L. Ehri, and R. Treiman. Hillsdale, N.J.: Lawrence Erlbaum.

Graesser, A. C., and Person, N. K. 1994. Question Asking during Tutoring. *American Educational Research Journal* 31(1): 104–137.

Graesser, A. C.; Person, N. K.; and Magliano, J. P. 1995. Collaborative Dialogue Patterns in Naturalistic One-on-One Tutoring. *Applied Cognitive Psychology* 9(6): 495–522.

Granieri, J. P.; Becket, W.; Reich, B.; Crabtree, J.; and Badler, N. 1995. Behavioral Control for Real-Time Simulated Human Agents. Paper presented at the1995 Symposium on Interactive 3D Graphics, 9–12 April, Monterey, Calif.

Greeno, J. G.; Collins, A. M.; Resnick, L. B. 1996. Cognition and Learning. In *Handbook of Educational Psychology,* eds. D. C. Berliner and R. C. Calfee, 15–46. New York: Macmillan.

Grégoire, J.; Zettlemoyer, L.; and Lester, J. 1999. Detecting and Correcting Misconceptions with Lifelike Avatars in 3D Learning Environments. In *AI-ED '99: Proceedings of the Ninth International Conference on Artificial Intelligence in Education,* 586–593. Amsterdam: IOS Press.

Guzdial, M.; Carlson, D.; and Turns, J. 1995. Facilitating Learning Design with Software-Realized Scaffolding for Collaboration. Paper presented at the Twenty-Fifth Annual Frontiers in Education Conference. Atlanta, Ga. 1–5 November.

Guzdial, M.; Hmelo, C.; Hubscher, R.; Nagel, K.; Newstetter, W.; Puntambekar, S.; Shabo, A.; Turns, J.; and Kolodner, J. L. 1997. Integrating and Guiding Collaboration: Lessons Learned in Computer-Supported Collaborative Learning Research at Georgia Tech. Paper presented at the Computer Support for Collaborative Learning Conference, 10–14 December, Toronto, Canada.

Guzdial, M.; Kolodner, J. L.; Hmelo, C.; Narayanan, H.; Carlson, D.; Rapping, N.; Hubscher, R.; Turns, J.; and Newstetter, W. 1996. Computer Support for Learning through Complex Problem-Solving. *Communications of the ACM* 40(1): 39–42.

Guzdial, M.; Rappin, N.; and Carlson, D. 1995. Collaborative and Multimedia Interactive Learning Environment for Engineering Education. In Proceedings of the ACM Symposium on Applied Computing Nashville, 5–9. New York: Association of Computing Machinery.

Halgren, S. L.; Fernandes, T.; and Thomas D. 1995. Amazing Animation™: Movie Making for Kids. In Proceedings of CHI 95 Conference on Computer-Human Interaction, 519–524. Reading, Mass.: Addison-Wesley.

Hall, R.; Kibler, D.; Wenger, E.; and Truxaw, C. 1989. Exploring the Episodic Structure of Algebra Story Problem Solving. *Cognition and Instruction* 6(3): 223–283.

Hart, D. M.; Arroyo, I.; Beck, J.; Woolf, B. P.; and Beal, C. R. 1999. WHALEWATCH: An Intelligent Multimedia Math Tutor. Paper presented at the International Conference on Mathematics/Science Education and Technology (M/SET-99), 4 March, San Antonio, Texas.

Hartley, J. R. 1998. Qualitative Reasoning and Conceptual Change: Computer-Based Support in Understanding Science. *Interactive Learning Environments* 5(1–2): 53–64.

Hauptmann, A. G.; Chase, L. L.; and Mostow, J. 1993. Speech Recognition Applied to Reading Assistance for Children: A Baseline Language Model. In Proceedings of the Third European Conference on Speech Communication and Technology, 2255–2258. Berlin: European Speech Communication Association.

Hauptmann, A. G.; Mostow, J.; Roth, S. F.; Kane, M.; and Swift, A. 1994. A Prototype Reading Coach That Listens: Summary of Project LISTEN. In *Proceedings of the ARPA Workshop on Human Language Technology,* ed. C. Weinstein, 237. San Francisco, Calif.: Morgan Kaufmann.

Hayes, J. R. 1989. *The Complete Problem Solver.* Hillsdale, N.J.: Lawrence Erlbaum.

Hayes, P. J. 1985. Naïve Physics 1: Ontology for Liquids. In *Formal Theories of the Commonsense World,* eds. R. Hobbs and R. Moore. Norwood, N.J.: Ablex.

Hayes, P. J. 1979. The Naïve Physics Manifesto. In *Expert Systems in the Micro-Electronic Age,* ed. D. Michie, 42–270. Edinburgh: Edinburgh University Press.

Hayes-Roth, B., and van Gent, R. 1996. Improvisational Puppets, Actors, and Avatars. Paper presented at the Computer Game Developers Conference, 30 March–2 April, Santa Clara, California.

Haywood, R. W. 1985. *Analysis of Engineering Cycles: Power, Refrigerating and Gas Liquefaction Plant.* Oxford, U.K.: Pergamon.

Hebb, D. O. 1949. *The Organization of Behavior.* New York: Wiley.

Heffernan, N., and Koedinger, K. R. 1997. The Composition Effect in Symbolizing: The Role of Symbol Production versus Text Comprehension. In *Proceedings of the Nineteenth Annual Conference of the Cognitive Science Society,* 307–312. Hillsdale, N.J.: Lawrence Erlbaum.

Heffernan, N., and Koedinger, K. R. 1998. A Developmental Model for Algebra Symbolization: The Results of a Difficulty Factors Assessment. In *Proceedings of the Twentieth Annual Conference of the Cognitive Science Society*, 484–489. Hillsdale, N.J.: Lawrence Erlbaum.

Herrick, E. 1990. Literacy Questions and Answers. Contact Center, Lincoln, Nebraska.

Hietala, P., and Niemirepo, T. 1998. The Competence of Learning Companion Agents. *International Journal of Artificial Intelligence in Education* 9(3–4): 178–192.

Hill, R., and Johnson, W. L. 1995. Situated Plan Attribution. *Journal of Artificial Intelligence in Education* 6(1): 35–66.

Hirschfeld, L., and Gelman, S., eds. 1994. *Mapping the Mind: Domain Specificity in Cognition and Culture.* New York: Cambridge University Press.

Hmelo, C. E.; Gotterer, G. S.; and Bransford, J. D. 1997. A Theory-Driven Approach to Assessing the Cognitive Effects of PBL. *Instructional Science* 25(6): 387–408.

Hollan, J. D.; Hutchins, E. L.; and Weitzman, L. M. 1984. STEAMER: An Interactive Inspectable Simulation-Based Training System. *AI Magazine* 5(2): 15–27.

Hollan, J. D.; Hutchins, E. L.; and Weitzman, L. M. 1987. STEAMER: An Interactive, Inspectable, Simulation-Based Training System. In *Artificial Intelligence and Instruction: Applications and Methods,* ed. G. Kearsley, 113–134. Reading, Mass.: Addison-Wesley.

Hooper, P. K. 1996. They Have Their Own Thoughts: A Story of Constructionist Learning in an Alternative African Centered Community School. In *Constructionism in Practice: Designing, Thinking and Learning in a Digital World,* eds. Y. Kafai & M. Resnick, 241–254. Hillsdale, N.J.: Lawrence Erlbaum.

Hovy, E. H. 1993. Automated Discourse Generation Using Discourse Structure Relations. *Artificial Intelligence* 63(1–2): 341–385.

Huang, S. X.; McCalla, G. I.; Greer, J. E.; and Neufeld, E. 1991. Revising Deductive Knowledge and Stereotypical Knowledge in a Student Model. *User Modeling and User-Adapted Interaction* 1(1): 87–115.

Huang, X. D.: Alleva, F.: Hon, H. W.: Hwang, M. Y.; Lee, K. F.; and Rosenfeld, R. 1993. The SPHINX-II Speech Recognition System: An Overview. *Computer, Speech, and Language* 7(2): 137–148.

Iwasaki, Y., and Low, C. 1993. Model Generation and Simulation of Device Behavior with Continuous and Discrete Changes. *Intelligent Systems Engineering* 1(2).

Jacobstein, N. 1997. EAGIL Cluster Overview. Paper presented at CAETI Community Meeting, 3–5 June, George Mason University, Arlington, Virginia.

Jacobstein, N., Murray, W.; Sams, M.; and Sincoff, E. 1998. A Multi-Agent Associate System Guide for a Virtual Collaboration CENTRE. In Proceedings of the Virtual Worlds and Simulation Conference (VWSIM 98), 215-220, eds. C. Landauer and K. Bellman. San Diego, Calif.: The Society for Computer Simulation.

Jansweijer, W. N. H.; Elshout, J. J.; and Wielinga, B. J. 1986. The Expertise of Novice Problem Solvers. Paper presented at the European Conference on Artificial Intelligence, Brighton, United Kingdom, 20–25 July.

Janvier, C. 1987. *Problems of Representation in the Teaching and Learning of Mathematics.* Hillsdale, N. J.: Lawrence Erlbaum.

Jarvella, R., and Klein, W. 1982. *Speech, Place, and Action: Studies in Deixes and Related Topics.* New York: Wiley.

Johnson, L., and Soloway, E. M. 1984. Intention-Based Diagnosis of Programming Errors. In Proceeding of the Second National Conference on Artificial Intelligence, 162–168. Menlo Park, Calif.: American Association for Artificial Intelligence.

Johnson, W. L.; Marsella, S.; and Rickel, J. 1998. Pedagogical Agents in Virtual World Training. In Proceedings of Virtual Worlds and Simulation Conference (VWSIM 98), 72–77, eds. C. Landauer and K. Bellman. San Diego, Calif.: The Society for Computer Simulation.

Johnston, B. R., and Fletcher, J. D. 1995. Effectiveness of Computer-Based Instruction in Military Training. Institute for Defense Analyses, Alexandria, Virginia.

Jones, C. 1989. Chuck Amuck: The Life and Times of an Animated Cartoonist. New York: Avon.

Just, M., and Carpenter, P. 1987. The Psychology of Reading and Language Comprehension. Newton, Mass.: Allyn and Bacon.

Kafai, Y. B.; Franke, M.; Ching, C.; and Shih, J. 1998. Games Design as Interactive Learning Environments for Fostering Teachers and Students Mathematical Thinking. International Journal of Computers for Mathematical Learning 3(2): 149–193.

Kamsteeg, P. 1994. Teaching Problem Solving by Computer. Ph.D. dissertation, Department of Social Science Informatics, University of Amsterdam, Amsterdam, The Netherlands.

Kaput, J. 1995. Creating Cybernetic and Psychological Ramps from the Concrete to the Abstract: Examples from Multiplicative Structures. In Software Goes to School: Teaching for Understanding with New Technologies, eds. D. Perkins, J. Schwartz, M. West, and M. Wiske, 130–154. New York: Oxford University Press.

Katz, S., and Suthers, D. 1998. Guiding the Development of Critical Inquiry Skills: Lessons Learned by Observing Students Interacting with Subject-Matter Experts and a Simulated Inquiry Coach. Paper presented at the American Educational Research Association 1998 Annual Meeting, San Diego, California, April 13–17.

Katzlberger, T. 1998. An Object-Oriented Implementation of the Adventure Player System in JAVA, Technical Report CS-TR-04, Department of Computer Science, Vanderbilt University.

King, A. 1998. Transactive Peer Tutoring: Distributing Cognition and Metacognition. Educational Psychology Review 10(1): 57–74.

Klahr, D., and Carver, S. M. 1988. Cognitive Objectives in a LOGO Debugging Curriculum: Instruction, Learning, and Transfer. Cognitive Psychology 20(3): 362–404.

Klahr, D., and Robinson, M. 1981. Formal Assessment of Problem-Solving and Planning Processing in School Children. Cognitive Psychology 13(1): 113–148.

Klahr, D., and Varver, S. M. 1988. Cognitive Objectives in a LOGO Debuggging Curriculum: Instruction, Learning, and Transfer. Cognitive Psychology 20(3): 362–404.

Klein, G., and Calderwood, R. 1988. How Do People Use Analogues to Make Decisions? In Proceedings: Workshop on Case-Based Reasoning (DARPA), 209–218, ed. J. Kolodner. San Francisco, Calif.: Morgan Kaufmann.

Koedinger, K. R. 1991. On the Design of Novel Notations and Actions to Facilitate Thinking and Learning. In Proceedings of the International Conference on the Learning Sciences, 266–273. Charlottesville, Va.: Association for the Advancement of Computing in Education.

Koedinger, K. R. 1998. Conjecturing and Argumentation in High School Geometry Students. In *New Directions in the Teaching and Learning of Geometry,* eds. R. Lehrer and D. Chazan, 319–348. Hillsdale, N.J.: Lawrence Erlbaum.

Koedinger, K. R., and Alibali, M. W. 1999. A Developmental Model of Algebra Problem Solving: Trade-Offs between Grounded and Abstract Representations. Paper presented at the Annual Meeting of the American Educational Research Association, Montreal, Canada, April 19–23.

Koedinger, K. R., and Anderson, J. R. 1990. Abstract Planning and Perceptual Chunks: Elements of Expertise in Geometry. *Cognitive Science* 14(4): 511–550.

Koedinger, K. R., and Anderson, J. R. 1993. Effective Use of Intelligent Software in High School Math Classrooms. In Proceedings of the World Conference on Artificial Intelligence in Education, 241–248. Charlottesville, Va.: Association for the Advancement of Computing in Education.

Koedinger, K. R., and Anderson, J. R. 1998. Illustrating Principled Design: The Early Evolution of a Cognitive Tutor for Algebra Symbolization. *Interactive Learning Environments* 5(2): 161–180.

Koedinger, K. R., and MacLaren, B. A. 1997. Implicit Strategies and Errors in an Improved Model of Early Algebra Problem Solving. In *Proceedings of the Nineteenth Annual Conference of the Cognitive Science Society,* 382–387. Hillsdale, N.J.: Lawrence Erlbaum.

Koedinger, K. R., and Sueker, E. L. 1996. PAT Goes to College: Evaluating a Cognitive Tutor for Developmental Mathematics. In Proceedings of the Second International Conference on the Learning Sciences, 180–187. Charlottesville, Va.: Association for the Advancement of Computing in Education.

Koedinger, K. R., and Tabachneck, H. J. 1994. Two Strategies Are Better Than One: Multiple-Strategy Use in Word Problem Solving. Paper presented at the Annual Meeting of the American Educational Research Association, New Orleans, Louisiana, April 8–12.

Koedinger, K. R.; Anderson, J. R.; Hadley, W. H.; and Mark, M. A. 1997. Intelligent Tutoring Goes to School in the Big City. *International Journal of Artificial Intelligence in Education* 8(1): 30–43.

Koedinger, K. R.; Suthers, D. D.; and Forbus, K. D. 1999. Component-Based Construction of a Science Learning Space. *International Journal of Artificial Intelligence in Education* 10(3–4): 292–313.

Koedinger, K. R.; Suthers, D.; and Forbus, K. 1998. Component-Based Construction of a Science Learning Space. Paper presented at the Fourth International Conference on Intelligent Tutoring Systems, August, San Antonio, Texas.

Kolodner, J. 1993. *Case-Based Reasoning.* San Francisco, Calif.: Morgan Kaufmann.

Kominek, J.; Aist, G. S.; and Mostow, J. 1998. When Listening Is Not Enough: Potential Uses of Vision for a Reading Tutor That Listens. In Intelligent Environments, ed. M. Coen. Technical Report SS-98-02. American Association for Artificial Intelligence, Menlo Park, Calif.

Kono, Y.; Ikeda, M.; and Mizoguchi, R. 1994. THEMIS: A Non-Monotonic Inductive Student Modeling System. *International Journal of Artificial Intelligence in Education* 5(3): 371–413.

Kopeikina, L.; Brandau, R.; and Lemmon, A. 1988. Case-Based Reasoning for Continuous Control. In *Proceedings: Workshop on Case-Based Reasoning* (DARPA), 233–249, ed. J. Kolodner. San Francisco, Calif.: Morgan Kaufmann.

Kopisch, M, and Gunter, A. 1992. Configuration of a Passenger Aircraft Cabin Based on Conceptual Hierarchy, Constraints, and Flexible Control. In *Industrial and Engineering Applications of AI,* Germany, eds. F. Belli and F. J. Radermacher, 423–430. Lecture Notes in Artificial Intelligence. Berlin: Springer-Verlag.

Koschmann, T. 1996. *CSCL: Theory and Practice of an Emerging Paradigm.* Hillsdale, N.J.: Lawrence Erlbaum.

Kotovsky, K., Simon, H. A. 1990. What Makes Some Problems Really Hard: Explorations in the Problem Space of Difficulty. *Cognitive Psychology* 22(2): 143–183.

Kuipers, B. J. 1986. Qualitative Simulation. *Artificial Intelligence* 29(3): 289–338.

Kulik, C. C., and Kulik, J. A. 1991. Effectiveness of Computer-Based Instruction: An Updated Analysis. In *Computers in Human Behavior.* 7(1–2): 75–95.

Kurlander, D., and Ling, D. T. 1995. Planning-Based Control of Interface Animation. In Proceedings of the Conference on Human Factors in Computing Systems (SIGCHI), 472–479. New York: ACM Press

La Cicero, A.; Fuson, K. C.; Allexaht-Snider, M. 1999. Making a Difference in Latino Children's Math Learning: Listening to Children, Mathematizing their Stories, and Supporting Parents to Help Children. In *Changing the Faces of Mathematics: Perspectives on Latinos,* ed. L. Ortiz-Franco, N. G. Hernendez, and Y. De La Cruz, 59–70. Reston, Va.: National Council of Teachers of Mathematics.

Lajoie, S. P., and Derry, S. J., eds. 1993. *Computers as Cognitive Tools.* Hillsdale, N.J.: Lawrence Erlbaum.

Lancaster, J., and Kolodner, J. 1987. Varieties of Learning from Problem-Solving Experience. In *Proceedings of the Ninth Annual Conference of the Cognitive Science Society,* 447–453. Hillsdale, N.J.: Lawrence Erlbaum.

Landauer, C., and Bellman, K. L. 1998. MUDs, Integration Spaces, and Learning Environments. Paper presented at Thirty-First Hawaii Conference on System Sciences, 6–9 January, Kona, Hawaii.

Landauer, C., and Bellman, K. L., eds. 1998. Proceedings of the Virtual Worlds and Simulation Conference, Simulation Series 30(2). San Diego, Calif.: The Society for Computer Simulation.

Landauer, C., and Bellman, K. L., eds. 1999. Proceedings of the Virtual Worlds and Simulation Conference, Simulation Series 31(2). San Diego, Calif.: The Society for Computer Simulation.

Langer, E. 1989. *Mindfulness.* Reading, Mass.: Perseus.

Larkin, J. H., and Simon, H. A. 1987. Why a Diagram Is (Sometimes) Worth Ten Thousand Words. *Cognitive Science* 11(1): 65–99.

Larkin, J. H.; McDermott, J.; Simon, D. P.; and Simon, H. A. 1980. Expert and Novice Performance in Solving Physics Problems. *Science* 208: 1335–1342.

Lave, J., and Wenger, E. 1991. *Situated Learning: Legitimate Peripheral Participation.* New York: Cambridge University Press.

Lee, C. 1995. Signifying as a Scaffold for Literary Interpretation. *Journal of Black Psychology* 21(4): 357–381.

Lee, O. 1999. Science Knowledge, World Views, and Information Sources in Social and Cultural Contexts: Making Sense after a Natural Disaster. *American Educational Research Journal* 36(2): 187–219.

Leelawong, K. Wang, Y. Biswas, G. Vye, N. Bransford, J. and Schwartz, D. L. 2001. Qualitative Reasoning Techniques to Support Learning by Teaching: The Teachable Agents Project. Paper presented at the Fifteenth International Workshop on Qualitative Reasoning, St. Mary's University, San Antonio, Tx., 17–19 May.

Lehrer, R., and Erickson, J. 1998. The Evolution of Critical Standards as Students Design Hypermedia. *Journal of the Learning Sciences* 7(3–4): 351–386.

Lehrer, R.; Randle, L.; and Sancilio, L. 1989. Learning Pre-Proof Geometry with LOGO. *Cognition and Instruction.* 6(2):159–184.

Leong, Lydia. 1999. The MUD Resources Collection. (www.godlike.com/muds/)

Lesgold, A.; Chipman, S.; Brown, J. S.; and Soloway, E. 1990. Intelligent Training Systems. In *Annual Review of Computer Science, Volume 4,* 383–394. Palo Alto, Calif.: Annual Reviews.

Lesgold, A.; Lajoie, S.; Bunzo, M.; and Eggan, G. 1992. SHERLOCK: A Coached Practice Environment for an Electronics Trouble-Shooting Job. In *Computer-Assisted Instruction and Intelligent Tutoring Systems: Shared Goals and Complementary Approaches,* eds. J. Larkin R. Chabay, and C. Sheftic, 201–238. Hillsdale, N.J.: Lawrence Erlbaum.

Lester, J., and Porter, B. 1996. Scaling Up Explanantion Generation: Large-Scale Knowledge Bases and Empirical Studies. In Proceeding of the Fourteenth National Conference on Artificial Intelligence, 416–423. Menlo Park, Calif.: American Association for Artificial Intelligence

Lester, J.; Converse, S.; Kahler, S.; Barlow, T.; Stone, B.; and Bhogal, R. 1997. The Persona Effect: Affective Impact of Animated Pedagogical Agents. In Proceedings of CHI '97 (Human Factors in Computing Systems), 359–366. New York: Association for Computing Machinery.

Lester, J.; Converse, S.; Stone, B.; Kahler, S.; and Barlow, T. 1997. Animated Pedagogical Agents and Problem-Solving Effectiveness: A Large-Scale Empirical Evaluation. In Proceedings of the Eighth World Conference on Artificial Intelligence in Education, 23–30. Amsterdam, The Netherlands: IOS Press.

Lester, J.; Stone, B.; and Stelling, G. 1999. Lifelike Pedagogical Agents for Mixed-Initiative Problem Solving in Constructivist Learning Environments. *User Modeling and User-Adapted Interaction* 9(1–2): 1–44.

Lester, J.; Voerman, J.; Towns, S.; and Callaway, C. 1999. Deictic Believability: Coordinating Gesture, Locomotion, and Speech in Lifelike Pedagogical Agents. *Applied Artificial Intelligence* 13(4–5): 383–414.

Lester, J.; Zettlemoyer, L.; Grégoire, J.; and Bares, W. 1999. Explanatory Lifelike Avatars: Performing User-Designed Tasks in 3D Learning Environments. In Proceedings of the Third International Conference on Autonomous Agents, 24–31. New York: Association for Computing Machinery.

Levy, A.; Iwasaki, Y.; and Fikes, R. 1995. Automated Model Selection Based on Relevance Reasoning, Technical Report, KSL-95-76, Knowledge Systems Laboratory, Stanford University.

Littlefield, J.; Delclos, V.; Lever, S.; Clayton, K.; Bransford, J.; and Franks, J. 1988. Learning LOGO: Method of Teaching, Transfer of General Skills, and Attitudes toward School and Computers. In *Teaching and Learning Computer Programming*, ed. R. E. Mayer, 111–135. Hillsdale, N.J.: Lawrence Erlbaum.

Lombard, M., and Ditton, T. 1997. At the Heart of It All: The Concept of Presence. *Journal of Computer-Mediated Communication* 3(2).

Loyall, B., and Bates, J. 1997. Personality-Rich Believable Agents That Use Language. In Proceedings of the First International Conference on Autonomous Agents, 106–113. New York: Association of Computing Machinery.

Luckham, D. C.; Vera, J.; and Belz, F. 1997. Toward an Abstraction Hierarchy for CAETI Architectures, and Possible Applications. Technical Report, CSL-TR-97-727, Computer Systems Lab, Stanford University.

Luria, A. R. 1928. The Problem of the Cultural Development of the Child. *Journal of Genetic Psychology* 35: 493–506.

Luria, A. R. 1932. *The Nature of Human Conflict*. New York: Liveright.

Ma, J. 1998. A Computer-Based Learning Environment for Teaching High School Students Feedback Control through Design. Paper presented at the Twenty-Seventh Annual Frontiers in Education Conference, 4–7 November, Tempe, Arizona.

Ma, J. 1999. A Case Study of Student Reasoning about Feedback Control in a Computer-Based Learning Environment. Paper presented at the Twenty-Ninth Annual Frontiers in Education Conference, 10–13 Nov., San Juan, Puerto Rico.

Major, N. P; Ainsworth, S.; and Wood, D. 1997. REDEEM: Exploiting Symbiosis between Psychology and Authoring Environments. *International Journal of Artificial Intelligence in Education* 8(3–4): 317–340.

Malone, T. W. 1981. What Makes Computer Games Fun? *BYTE Magazine,* 6(12): 258–277.

Maluf, D. A.; Wiederhold, G.; Linden, T.; and Panchapagesan, P. 1997. Mediation to Implement Feedback in Training. *CrossTalk: Journal of Defense Software Engineering*. Washington, D.C.: Software Technology Support Center, U. S. Department of Defense.

Mann, W. C., and Thompson, S. A. 1987. Rhetorical Structure Theory: A Theory of Text Organisation. Technical Report ISI/RS-87-190, Information Sciences Institute, University of Southern California, Marina del Rey, Calif.

Marsella, S., and Johnson, W. L. 1998. An Instructor's Assistant for Team-Training in Dynamic Multi-Agent Virtual Worlds. In *Proceedings of the Fourth International Conference on Intelligent Tutoring Systems,* 464–473. Berlin: Springer-Verlag.

Marshall, C. C., and Rogers, R. A. 1992. Two Years before the Mist: Experiences with Aquanet. In Proceedings of the Fourth ACM Conference on Hypertext, 53–62. New York: Association for Computing Machinery.

Mathematics Council. 1989. Curriculum and Evaluation Standards for School Mathematics. Reston, Va.: The National Council of Teachers of Mathematics.

Matz, M. 1982. Toward a Process Model for High School Algebra Errors. In *Intelligent Tutoring Systems,* eds. D. Sleeman and J. S. Brown. San Diego, Calif.: Academic Press.

Mayer, R. 1992. Cognition and Instruction: On Their Historic Meeting within Educational Psychology. *Journal of Educational Psychology* 84(4): 405–412.

Mayer, R. E., ed. 1988. *Teaching and Learning Computer Programming: Multiple Research Perspective*. Hillsdale, N.J.: Lawrence Erlbaum.

McCloskey, M. 1983. Naïve Theories of Motion. In *Mental Models*, eds. D. Gentner and A. L. Stevens, 299–324. Hillsdale, N.J.: Lawrence Erlbaum.

McCoy, K. (1989–1990). Generating Context-Sensitive Responses to Object-Related Misconceptions. *Artificial Intelligence* 41(2): 157–195.

McDonald, D.; Pepe, C. O.; Bowers, H.; and Dombroski, E. 1997. Desktop Underwriter: Fannie Mae's Automated Mortgage Underwriting Expert System. In Proceedings of the Fifteenth National Conference on Artificial Intelligence and Innovations in Artificial Intelligence, 875–882. Menlo Park, Calif.: American Association for Artificial Intelligence.

McGuiness, C. 1986. Problem Representation: The Effects of Spatial Arrays. *Memory and Cognition* 14(3): 270–280.

McGuinness, D. 1997. *Why Our Children Can't Read and What We Can Do about It: A Scientific Revolution in Reading.* New York: Free Press.

McKay, D. 1997. SNAIR Cluster Overview. Paper presented at the CAETI Community Meeting, 3–5 June, George Mason University, Arlington, Virginia.

McKendree, J. 1990. Effective Feedback Content for Tutoring Complex Skills. *Human-Computer Interaction* 5(4): 381–413.

McKeown, K. 1985. Discourse Strategies for Generating Natural Language Text. *Artificial Intelligence* 27(1): 1–41.

Mengelle, T.; De Léan, C.; and Frasson, C. 1998. Teaching and Learning with Intelligent Agents: Actors. In *Proceedings of the Fourth International Conference on Intelligent Tutoring Systems*, 284–293. Berlin: Springer-Verlag.

Miller, C. S.; Lehman, J. F.; and Koedinger, K. R. 1999. Goals and Learning in Microworlds. *Cognitive Science* 23(3): 305–336.

Moll, L. C., and Greenberg, J. 1990. Creating Zones of Possibilities: Combining Social Contexts for Instruction. In *Vygotsky and Education: Instructional Implications and Applications of Sociohistorical Psychology*, ed. L. Moll, 319–348. Cambridge, Mass.: Cambridge University Press.

Moll, L. C.; Tapia, J.; and Whitmore, K. F. 1993. Living Knowledge: The Social Distribution of Cultural Resources for Thinking. In *Distributed Cognitions: Psychological and Educational Considerations*, ed. G. Salomon, 139–163. Cambridge, Mass.: Cambridge University Press.

Moore, J. 1995. Discourse Generation for Instructional Applications: Making Computer Tutors More Like Humans. Paper presented at the Seventh World Conference on Artificial Intelligence in Education, Washington, D.C.

Moses, R. P.; Kamii, M.; Swap, S. M.; and Howard, J. 1989. The Algebra Project: Organizing in the Spirit of Ella. *Harvard Educational Review* 59(4): 423–443.

Mostow, J. 1995. A Reading Coach That Listens: Project LISTEN (4-minute video). In Video Proceedings of the Eighth Annual Symposium on User Interface Software and Technology. New York: Association of Computing Machinery.

Mostow, J. 1996. A Reading Tutor That Listens. Video presented at the DARPA CAETI Community Conference, 19–22 November, Berkeley, California.

Mostow, J. 1997a. Collaborative Research on Learning Technologies: An Automated Reading Assistant That Listens. In Proceedings of the NSF Interactive Systems Program Grantees Workshop. Arlington, Va.: National Science Foundation.

Mostow, J. 1997b. Guiding Spoken Dialogue with Computers by Responding to Prosodic Cues. In Proceedings of the NSF Interactive Systems Program Grantees Workshop. Arlington, Va.: National Science Foundation.

Mostow, J. 1997c. Pilot Evaluation of a Reading Tutor That Listens. Video presented at the Fourteenth National Conference on Artificial Intelligence and at the Ninth National Conference on Innovative Applications of Artificial Intelligence. 27–31 Aug., Providence, R. I.

Mostow, J. 1998. *Project LISTENs Reading Tutor Is Helping Me Learn to Read.* 10-minute video. Pittsburgh, Penn.: Robotics Institute, Carnegie Mellon University.

Mostow, J., Aist, G. S., Burkhead, P., Corbett, A., Cuneo, A., Eitelman, S., Huang, C., Junker, B., Platz, C., Sklar, M. B., and Tobin, B. 2001. A Controlled Evaluation of Computer Versus Human-Assisted Oral Reading. Paper presented at the Tenth Artificial Intelligence in Education (AI-ED) Conference, San Antonio, Texas, 19–23 May.

Mostow, J.; Aist, G. S.; Huang, C.; Junker, B.; Kennedy, R.; Lan, H.; Latimer, D.; O'Connor, R.; Tassone, R.; Tobin, B.; and Wierman, A. Forthcoming. Four-Month Evaluation of a Learner-Controlled Reading Tutor that Listens. In *Speech Technology for Language Learning,* ed. P. DeCloque and M. Holland. Amsterdam: Swets and Zeitlinger.

Mostow, J., and Aist, G. S. 1997a. Project LISTEN: A Reading Tutor That Listens. Live demonstration presented at the World Conference on Educational Multimedia and Hypermedia, 14–19 June, Calgary, Canada.

Mostow, J., and Aist, G. S. 1997b. The Sounds of Silence: Toward Automated Evaluation of Student Learning in a Reading Tutor That Listens. In Proceedings of the 1997 National Conference on Artificial Intelligence, 355–361. Menlo Park, Calif.: American Association for Artificial Intelligence.

Mostow, J., and Aist, G. S. 1997c. When Speech Input Is Not an Afterthought: A Reading Tutor That Listens. In Proceedings of the Workshop on Perceptual User Interfaces, 20–21 Oct., Banff, Canada.

Mostow, J., and Aist, G. S. 1999a. Authoring New Material in a Reading Tutor That Listens. In Proceedings of the Sixteenth National Conference on Artificial Intelligence, 918–919. Menlo Park, Calif.: American Association for Artificial Intelligence.

Mostow, J., and Aist, G. S. 1999b. Giving Help and Praise in a Reading Tutor with Imperfect Listening Because Automated Speech Recognition Means Never Being Able to Say You're Certain. *CALICO Journal* (Special issue [ed. M. Holland], Tutors That Listen: Speech Recognition for Language Learning)16(3): 407–424.

Mostow, J., and Aist, G. S. 1999c. Reading and Pronunciation Tutor. United States Patent No. 5,920,838. Filed June 2, 1997; issued July 6, 1999. Washington, D.C.: United States Patent and Trademark Office. (www.uspto.gov).

Mostow, J., and Eskenazi, M. 1995. Guiding Spoken Dialogue with Computers by Responding to Prosodic Cues. In Proceedings of the NSF Interactive Systems Program Grantees Workshop, ed. R. Jacobs. Arlington, Va.: National Science Foundation.

Mostow, J., and Eskenazi, M. 1997. A Database of Children's Speech. In Proceedings of the NSF Interactive Systems Program Grantees Workshop. Arlington, Va.: National Science Foundation.

Mostow, J.; Hauptmann, A. G.; and Roth, S. 1995. Demonstration of a Reading Coach That Listens. In Proceedings of the Eighth Annual Symposium on User Interface Software and Technology, 77–78. New York: Association of Computing Machinery.

Mostow, J.; Hauptmann, A. G.; Chase, L. L.; and Roth, S. 1993. Toward a Reading Coach That Listens: Automated Detection of Oral Reading Errors. In Proceedings of the Eleventh National Conference on Artificial Intelligence, 392–398. Menlo Park, Calif.: American Association for Artificial Intelligence.

Mostow, J.; Roth, S.; Hauptmann, A. G.; and Kane, M. 1994. A Prototype Reading Coach That Listens. In Proceedings of the Twelfth National Conference on Artificial Intelligence, 785–792. Menlo Park, Calif.: American Association for Artificial Intelligence.

Mostow, J.; Roth, S.; Hauptmann, A. G.; Kane, M.; Swift, A.; Chase, L.; and Weide, B. 1993. Getting Computers to Listen to Children Read: A New Way to Combat Illiteracy (7-minute video). Produced by Jim Kocher. Pittsburgh, Penn.: Carnegie Mellon Robotics Institute, Carnegie Mellon Univ.

Mostow, J.; Roth, S.; Hauptmann, A. G.; Kane, M.; Swift, A.; Chase, L.; and Weide, B. 1994a. A Reading Coach That Listens. Video presented at the Twelfth National Conference on Artificial Intelligence. Menlo Park, Calif.: American Association for Artificial Intelligence.

Mostow, J.; Roth, S.; Hauptmann, A. G.; Kane, M.; Swift, A.; Chase, L.; and Weide, B. 1994b. A Reading Coach That Listens: Edited Video Transcript. In Proceedings of the Twelfth National Conference on Artificial Intelligence, 1507. Menlo Park, Calif.: American Association for Artificial Intelligence.

Mozeti, I. 1991. Hierarchical Model-Based Diagnosis. International Journal of Man-Machine Studies 35(30): 329–362.

Murphy, M.; Ralston, E.; Friedlander, D.; Swab, R.; and Steege, P. 1997. The Scheduling of Rail at Union Pacific Railroad. In Proceeding of the Fifteenth National Conference of Innovative Applications of Artificial Intelligence, 903–912. Menlo Park, Calif.: American Association for Artificial Intelligence.

Murray, T. 1998. Authoring Knowledge-Based Tutors: Tools for Content, Instructional Strategy, Student Model, and Interface Design. Journal of the Learning Sciences (Special Issue on Authoring Tools for Interactive Learning Environments) 7: 5–64.

Myers, A. C.; Feltovich, P. J.; Coulson, R. L.; Adami, J. F.; and Spiro, R. J. 1990. Reductive Biases in the Reasoning of Medical Students: An Investigation in the Domain of Acid-Base Balance. In Teaching and Assessing Clinical Competence, eds. B. Bender, R. J. Hiemstra, A .J .J. A. Scherbier, and R. P. Zwierstra, 155–160. Groningen, The Netherlands: BoekWerk.

Nathan, M. J. 1998. Knowledge and Situational Feedback in a Learning Environment for Algebra Story Problem Solving. Interactive Learning Environments 5(1): 135–159.

Nathan, M. J.; Koedinger, K. R.; and Tabachneck, H. J. M. 2000. Teachers and Researchers Beliefs of Early Algebra Development. In Proceedings of the Nineteenth Annual Conference of the Cognitive Science Society, 554–559. Hillsdale, NJ: Erlbaum.

National Center for Education Statistics. 1993a. Adult Literacy in America, Technical Report GPO 065-000-00588-3. Washington, D.C.: U.S. Department of Education.

National Center for Education Statistics. 1993b. NAEP 1992 Reading Report Card for the Nation and the States: Data from the National and Trial State Assessments, Technical Report 23-ST06. Washington, D.C.: U.S. Department of Education.

National Center for Education Statistics 1998. The Condition of Education, 1998. T. Snyder & J. Wirt (Eds.), NCES Report Number 98013. Washington, D. C.: Government Printing Office (nces.ed.gov/pubs98/condition98/index.html).

National Center for Education Statistics. 1999. Digest of Education Statistics, May. Washington, D. C.: National Center for Education Statistics.

National Research Council. 1996. National Science Education Standards. Washington, D.C.: National Research Council.

Newell, A. 1990. *Unified Theories of Cognition.* Cambridge, Mass.: Harvard University Press.

Nhouyvanisong, A. 1999. Enhancing Mathematical Competence and Understanding: Using Open-Ended Problems and Informal Strategies. Ph.D. dissertation, Psychology Department, Carnegie Mellon University.

Nhouyvanisvong, A., and Koedinger, K. R. 1998. Goal Specificity and Learning: Reinterpretation of the Data and Cognitive Theory. In *Proceedings of the Twentieth Annual Conference of the Cognitive Science Society,* 764–769. Hillsdale, N.J.: Lawrence Erlbaum.

Nilsson, N. J. 1980. *Principles of Artificial Intelligence.* San Francisco, Calif.: Morgan Kaufmann.

Novak, J. 1990. Concept Mapping: A Useful Tool for Science Education. *Journal of Research in Science Teaching* 27(10): 937–949.

Novak, J. D. 1998. *Learning, Creating, and Using Knowledge: Concept Maps as Facilitative Tools in Schools and Corporations.* Hillsdale, N.J.: Lawrence Erlbaum.

O'Connor, R., and Jenkins, J. 1994. Interventions in Phonological Awareness: New Procedures for Early Identification and Treatment of Children Who Will Have Difficulty Learning to Read. Paper presented at the Annual Meeting of the Pacific Coast Research Conference, 9–11 April, La Jolla, California.

O'Day, V. L.; Bobrow, D. G.; and Shirley, M. 1996. The Social-Technical Design Circle. In Proceedings of the ACM Conference on Computer-Supported Cooperative Work, ed. M. S. Ackerman, 160–169. New York: Association of Computing Machinery.

O'Day, V. L.; Bobrow, D. G.; Bobrow, K.; Shirley, M.; Hughes, B.; and Walters, J. 1998. Moving Practice: From Classrooms to MOO Rooms. Computer-Supported Cooperative Work. *The Journal of Collaborative Computing* 7(1): 9–45.

O'Day, V. L.; Bobrow, D. G.; Hughes, B.; Bobrow, K. B.; Saraswat, V. A.; Talazus, J.; Walters, J.; and Welbes, C. 1996. Community Designers. In Proceedings of the Participatory Design Conference, 3–13. Palo Alto, Calif.: Computer Professionals for Social Responsibility.

O'Neil, H. F., and Klein, C. D. 1997. Feasibility of Machine Scoring of Concept Maps. CSE Technical Report, 460, National Center for Research on Evaluation, Standards, and Student Testing. Los Angeles, Calif.: University of California, Los Angeles.

O'Neill, D. K., and Gomez, L. M. 1994. The Collaboratory Notebook: A Distributed Knowledge-Building Environment for Project-Enhanced Learning. In *Educational Multimedia and Hypermedia: Proceedings of Ed-Media 94,* ed. T. Ottmann and I. Tomek, 416–423. Charlottesville, Virginia: Association for the Advancement of Computing in Education.

O'Neill, D. K., and Gomez, L. M. 1998. Sustaining Mentoring Relationships On-Line. Paper presented at the Annual Conference of Computer-Supported Collaborative Work, 14–18 Nov., Washington, D.C.

Ohlsson, S. 1986. Some Principles of Intelligent Tutoring. *Instructional Science* 14(3): 293–326.

Okada, T., and Simon, H. A. 1997. Collaborative Discovery in a Scientific Domain. *Cognitive Science* 21(2): 109–146.

Olson, R. K., and Wise, B. W. 1992. Reading on the Computer with Orthographic and Speech Feedback: An Overview of the Colorado Remedial Reading Project. *Reading and Writing: An Interdisciplinary Journal* 4(2): 107–144.

Paiva, A. M., and Machado, I. 1998. VINCENT, an Autonomous Pedagogical Agent for On-the-Job Training. In *Proceedings of the Fourth International Conference on Intelligent Tutoring Systems*, 584–593. Berlin: Springer-Verlag.

Paiva, A. M., and Self, J. A. 1994. TAGUSA User and Learner Modeling Workbench. *User Modeling and User-Adapted Interaction* 4(3): 197–226.

Palinscar, A. S., and Brown, A. L. 1984. Reciprocal Teaching of Comprehension-Fostering and Monitoring Activities. *Cognition and Instruction* 1(2): 117–175.

Pane, J. F.; Corbett, A. T.; and John, B. E. 1996. Assessing Dynamics in Computer-Based Instruction. In Proceedings of ACM CHI'96 Conference on Human Factors in Computing Systems, 197–204. New York: Association of Computing Machinery.

Paolucci, M.; Suthers, D.; and Weiner, A. 1996. Automated Advice-Giving Strategies for Scientific Inquiry. In *Proceedings of the Intelligent Tutoring Systems Third International Conference*, eds. C. Frasson, G. Gauthier, and A. Lesgold, 372–381. New York: Springer.

Papert, S. 1980. *Mindstorms: Children, Computers and Powerful Ideas*. New York: Basic Books.

Patel, V. L., and Groen, G. J. 1992. The Representation of Medical Information in Novices, Intermediates, and Experts. In *MEDINFO 92*, eds. K. D. Lun, P. Degoulet, T. E. Piemme, and O. Rienoff, 1344–1349. North Holland: Elsevier Science.

Patel, V. L.; Kaufman, D. R.; and Magder, S. 1991. Causal Explanation of Complex Physiological Concepts by Medical Students. *International Journal of Science Education* 13(2): 171–185.

Payne, S., and Green, T. 1986. Task-Action Grammars—A Model of the Mental Representation of Task Languages. *Human-Computer Interaction* 2(2): 99–133.

Pelachaud, C.; Badler, N.; and Steedman, M. 1996. Generating Facial Expressions for Speech. *Cognitive Science* 20(1): 1–46.

Pepper, S. 1942. *World Hypotheses*. Berkeley, Calif.: University of California Press.

Perkins, D. N. 1993. Person-Plus: A Distributed View of Thinking and Learning. In *Distributed Cognitions: Psychological and Educational Considerations*, ed. G. Salomon, 88–111. Cambridge, U.K.: Cambridge University Press.

Perkins, D. N.; Crismond, D.; Simmons, R.; and Unger, C. 1995. Inside Understanding. In *Software Goes to School: Teaching for Understanding with New Technologies*, eds. D. Perkins, J. Schwartz, M. West, and M. Wiske, 70–87. New York: Oxford University Press.

Perlin, K. 1995. Real-Time Responsive Animation with Personality. *IEEE Transactions on Visualization and Computer Graphics* 1(1): 5–15.

Perlin, K., and Goldberg, A. 1999. Improvisational Animation. In Proceedings of the Conference on Virtual Worlds and Simulation (VWSIM 98), 9–14, eds. C. Landauer and K. Bellman. San Diego, Calif.: The Society for Computer Simulation.

Piaget, J. 1954. *The Construction of Reality in the Child*. New York: Ballentine.

Pichumani, R., Walker, D.; Heinrichs, L.; Karadi, C.; Lorie, W. A.; Der, P. 1998. The Design of Frog Island: A VRML World for Biology. In Proceedings of the Conference on Virtual Worlds and Simulation (VWSIM 98), 31–36, eds. C. Landauer and K. Bellman. San Diego, Calif.: The Society for Computer Simulation.

Pilkington, R., and Grierson, A. 1996. Generating Explanations in a Simulation-Based Learning Environment. *International Journal of Human-Computer Studies* 45(5): 527–551.

Pinkard, N. N. 1998. Leveraging Background Knowledge: Using Popular Music to Build Children's Beginning Reading Skills. Ph.D. Dissertation, Learning Sciences, School of Education and Social Policy, Northwestern University, Evanston, Ill.

Plato. 1922. *Laches, Protagora, Meno, and Euthydemus,* trans. E. R. M. Lamb. Cambridge, Mass.: Harvard Press.

Plaut, D. C.; McClelland, J. L.; Seidenberg, M. S.; and Patterson, K. 1996. Understanding Normal and Impaired Word Reading: Computational Principles in Quasi-Regular Domains. *Psychological Review* 103(2): 56–115.

Ploetzner, R.; Dillenbourg, P.; Preier, M.; and Traum, D. 1999. Learning by Explaining to Oneself and to Others. In *Collaborative Learning: Cognitive and Computational Approaches,* ed. P. Dillenbourg, 103–121. Amsterdam: Pergamon.

Poli, C.; Grosse, I.; and Woolf, B. P. 1999. Multimedia-Based Active Tutors—A New Approach to Teaching Design for Manufacturing. Paper presented at the ASME Design for Manufacturing Conference, 12–15 Sept., Las Vegas, Nevada.

Pollock, J. 1979. A Plethora of Epistemological Theories. In *Justification and Knowledge,* ed. G. Pappas, 93–114. Dordrecht, The Netherlands: Reidel.

Pullen, J. M. 1997. CAPER: Collaborative Applications for Project-Based Learning Resources. Paper presented at CAETI Community Conference, 3–5 June, George Mason University, Arlington, Virginia.

Pullen, J. M., and Nah, M. 1999. A Multi-User Virtual Environment with Extensible User-Friendly Web-Based Interfaces. In Proceedings of the Conference on Virtual Worlds and Simulation (VWSIM 98), 78–83, eds. C. Landauer and K. Bellman. San Diego, Calif.: The Society for Computer Simulation.

Quafafou, M.; Mekaouche, A.; and Nwana, H. S. 1995. Multi-Views Learning and Intelligent Tutoring Systems. Paper presented at the Seventh World Conference on Artificial Intelligence in Education. Washington, D. C., 16–19 August.

Radinsky, J.; Bouillion, L.; Hanson, K.; Gomez, L.; Vermeer, D.; and Fishman, B. 1998. A Framework for Authenticity: Mutual Benefit Partnerships. Paper presented at the American Educational Research Association, San Diego, California, April 13–17.

Radinsky, J.; Bouillion, L.; Lento, E.; and Gomez, L. In press. Mutual Benefit Partnership: A Curricular Design for Authenticity. *Journal of Curriculum Studies.*

Reeves, B., and Nass, C. 1996. *The Media Equation: How People Treat Computers, Television, and New Media Like Real People and Places.* Cambridge, U.K.: Cambridge University Press.

Regian, J. W. 1997. Functional Area Analysis of Intelligent Computer-Assisted Instruction. Report, TAPSTEM ICAI-FAA Committee, Brooks Air Force Base, Texas.

Regian, J. W., and Shute, V. J. 1992. *Cognitive Approaches to Automated Instruction.* Hillsdale, N.J.: Lawrence Erlbaum.

Regian, J. W., and Shute, V. J. 1993. Basic Research on the Pedagogy of Automated Instruction. In *Simulation-Based Experiential Learning,* eds. D. M. Towne, T. de Jong, and H. Spada, 121–132. Berlin: Springer-Verlag.

Regian, J. W., and Shute, V. J. 1994. Evaluating Intelligent Tutoring Systems. In *Technology Assessment in Education and Training,* eds. E. L. Baker and H. F. O'Neil, Jr., 79–96. Hillsdale, N.J.: Lawrence Erlbaum.

Reimann, P., and Chi, M. T. H. 1989. Human Expertise. In *Human and Machine Problem Solving,* ed. K. J. Gilhooly, 161–191. New York: Plenum.

Reiser, B. J.; Anderson, J. R.; and Farrell, R. G. 1985. Dynamic Student Modeling in an Intelligent Tutor for Lisp Programming. In Proceedings of the Ninth International Joint Conference on Artificial Intelligence, 8–14. San Francisco: Morgan Kaufmann.

Reiser, B. J.; Spillane, J. P.; Steinmuller, F.; Sorsa, D.; Carney, K.; and Kyza, E. 2000. Investigating the Mutual Adaptation Process in Teachers' Design of Technology-Infused Curricula. Paper presented at the International Conference of the Learning Sciences, 14–17 June, Ann Arbor, Michigan.

Reiter, E., and Mellish, C. 1993. Optimizing the Costs and Benefits of Natural Language Generation. In Proceedings of the Thirteenth International Joint Conference on Artificial Intelligence. Menlo Park, Calif.: International Joint Conferences on Artificial Intelligence.

Resnick, L., and Chi, M. T. H. 1988. Cognitive Psychology and Science Learning. In *Science for the Fun of It: A Guide to Informal Science Education,* ed. M. Druger, 24–31. Arlington, Virginia: National Science Teachers Association.

Reusser, K. 1993. Tutoring Systems and Pedagogical Theory: Representational Tools for Understanding, Planning, and Reflection in Problem Solving. In *Computers as Cognitive Tools,* eds. S. P. Lajoie and S. J. Derry, 143–177. Hillsdale, N.J.: Lawrence Erlbaum.

Richardson, J. A.; Richardson, D.; Rovick, A.; Modell, H.; Bruce, D.; Horwitz, B.; Hudson, M.; Silverthorn, D.; Whitescarver, S. and Williams, S. 1999. Undergraduate Students Misconceptions about Respiratory Physiology. *Advances in Physiology Education* 22(1): S127–S135.

Rickel, J., and Johnson, W. L. 1997. Intelligent Tutoring in Virtual Reality: A Preliminary Report. In *Proceedings of the Eighth World Conference on AI in Education,* 294–301. Amsterdam: IOS Press.

Rickel, J., and Johnson, W. L. 1999. Animated Agents for Procedural Training in Virtual Reality: Perception, Cognition, and Motor Control. *Applied Artificial Intelligence* 13(4–5): 343–382.

Rickel, J., and Porter, B. 1994. Automated Modeling for Answering Prediction Questions: Selecting the Time Scale and System Boundary. In Proceedings of the Twelfth National Conference on Artificial Intelligence, 1191–1198. Menlo Park, Calif.: American Association for Artificial Intelligence.

Riner, R., and Clodius, J. 1995. Simulating Future Histories. *Anthropology and Education Quarterly* 26(1): 95–104.

Ritter, S. 1997. Communication, Cooperation, and Competition among Multiple Tutor Agents. In *Proceedings of the Eighth World Conference on AI in Education,* 31–38. Amsterdam: IOS Press.

Ritter, S., and Koedinger, K. R. 1995. Toward Lightweight Tutoring Agents. In Proceedings of the World Conference on Artificial Intelligence in Education, 161–166. Charlottesville, Va.: Association for the Advancement of Computing in Education.

Ritter, S., and Koedinger, K. R. 1996. Toward Lightweight Tutor Agents. Paper presented at the Workshop on Architectures and Methods for Designing Cost-Effective and Reusable ITSs, 10–14 June, Montreal, Canada.

Ritter, S., and Koedinger, K. R. 1997. An Architecture for Plug-In Tutoring Agents. *Journal of Artificial Intelligence in Education* 7(3–4): 315–347.

Ritter, S.; Anderson, J. R.; Cytrynowitz, M.; and Medvedeva, O. 1998. Authoring Content in the PAT Algebra Tutor. *Journal of Interactive Media in Education.* 98(9).

Roberts, L. 1993. *How Reference Works: Explanatory Models for Indexicals, Descriptions, and Opacity.* New York: State University of New York Press.

Roschelle, J. 1994. Designing for Cognitive Communication: Epistemic Fidelity or Mediating Collaborative Inquiry? *Arachnet Electronic Journal on Virtual Culture* 2(2).

Rosenbaum, J. E., ed. 1992. Youth Apprenticeship in America. Washington, D.C.: American Youth Policy Forum.

Ross, B. H. 1996. Category Learning as Problem Solving. In *The Psychology of Learning and Motivation 35,* 165–192, ed. D. L. Medin. New York: Academic Press.

Ross, L., and Lepper, M. 1980. The Perseverance of Beliefs: Empirical and Normative Considerations, 17–36. In *Fallible Judgment in Behavioral Research,* ed. R. Shweder. San Francisco, Calif.: Jossey-Bass.

Rowley, M., and Carlson, W. 1998. WYNDHAVEN: A Multimedia Virtual World for Learning. In Proceedings of the Conference on Virtual Worlds and Simulation (VWSIM 98), 161–166, eds. C. Landauer and K. Bellman. San Diego, Calif.: The Society for Computer Simulation.

Ruiz-Primo, M. A.; Shavelson, R. J.; and Schultz, S. E. 1997. On the Validity of Concept Map-Base Assessment Interpretations: An Experiment Testing the Assumption of Hierarchical Concept Maps in Science CSE Technical Report, 455, University of California at Los Angeles.

Russell, M.; Brown, C.; Skilling, A.; Series, R.; Wallace, J.; Bohnam, B.; and Barker, P. 1996. Applications of Automatic Speech Recognition to Speech and Language Development in Young Children. Paper presented at the Fourth International Conference on Spoken Language Processing, 3–6 Oct., Philadelphia, Pennsylvania.

Rutherford, F., and Ahlgren, A. 1990. *Science for All Americans.* Oxford, U.K.: Oxford University Press.

Sacerdoti, E. 1977. *A Structure for Plans and Behavior.* New York: Elsevier.

Salles, P.; Bredeweg, B.; and Winkels, R. 1997. Deriving Explanations from Qualitative Models. In *Proceedings of the European Conference on Artificial Intelligence,* 106–112. London: Pitman.

Salomon, G. 1993. No Distribution without Individuals Cognition: A Dynamic Interactional View. In *Distributed Cognitions: Psychological and Educational Considerations,* ed. G. Salomon, 111–138. Cambridge, U.K.: Cambridge University Press.

Scardamalia, M., and Bereiter, C. 1994. Computer Support for Knowledge-Building Communities. *The Journal of the Learning Sciences* 3(3): 265–283.

Schank, R. 1982. *Dynamic Memory.* New York: Cambridge University Press.

Schank, R. 1990. *Tell Me A Story.* New York: Scribners.

Schank, R. 1999. *Dynamic Memory Revisited.* New York: Cambridge University Press.

Schank, R. C., and Cleary, C. 1995. *Engines for Education*. Hillsdale, N.J.: Lawrence Erlbaum.

Schoen, D. 1992. Designing as Reflective Conversation with the Materials of a Design Situation. *Knowledge-Based Systems Journal* (Special Issue on AI and Design) 5(1): 3–14.

Schoenfeld, A. 1989. Explorations of Students Mathematical Beliefs and Behavior. *Journal for Research in Mathematics Education* 20(1): 338–355.

Schofield, J. 1996. *Computers and Classroom Culture*. New York: Cambridge University Press.

Schofield, J. W.; Evans-Rhodes, D.; and Huber, B. R. 1990. Artificial Intelligence in the Classroom: The Impact of a Computer-Based Tutor on Teachers and Students. *Social Science Computer Review* 8(1): 24–41.

Schommer, M. 1993. Epistemological Development and Academic Performance among Secondary Students. *Journal of Educational Psychology* 85(3): 406–411.

Schommer, M., and Walker, K. 1995. Are Epistemological Beliefs Similar across Domains? *Journal of Educational Psychology* 87(3): 424–432.

Schön, D. 1983. *The Reflective Practitioner: How Professionals Think in Action*. New York: Basic.

Schooler, I., and Anderson, J. 1990. The Disruptive Potential of Immediate Feedback. In *Proceedings of the Twelfth Annual Conference of the Cognitive Science Society*, 702–708. Hillsdale, N.J.: Lawrence Erlbaum.

Schreiber, A. T.; Wielinga, B. J.; and Breuker, J. A., eds. 1993. *KADS: A Principled Approach to Knowledge Engineering*. San Diego, Calif.: Academic Press.

Schreiber, A. T.; Wielinga, B. J.; de Hoog, R.; Akkermans, J. M.; and van de Velde, W. 1994. COMMONKADS: A Comprehensive Methodology for KBS Development. *IEEE Expert* 9(6): 28–37.

Schwartz, D. L.; Lin, X.; Brophy, S.; and Bransford, J. D. 1999. Toward the Development of Flexibly Adaptive Instructional Design. In *Instructional-Design Theories and Models: A New Paradigm of Instructional Theory, Volume 2*, ed. C. M. Reigeluth, 183–213. Hillsdale, N.J.: Lawrence Erlbaum.

Scrase, R. 1997. Using Scanners Linked to Talking Computers as Tools for Teaching Children to Read. *British Journal of Educational Technology* 28(4): 308–310.

Seidel, R. J., and Perez, R. S. 1994. An Evaluation Model for Investigating the Impact of Innovative Educational Technology. In Technology Assessment in Software Applications, eds. H. F. O'Neil, Jr., and E. L. Baker, 177–208. Los Angeles, Calif.: Graduate School of Education and Information Studies, University of California, Los Angeles.

Seidel, R. J.; Park, O.; and Perez, R. S. 1988. Expertise of ICAI: Developmental Requirements. *Computers in Human Behaviors* 4(3): 235–256.

Seifert, C.; Abelson, R.; and McKoon, G. 1986. The Role of Thematic Knowledge Structures in Reminding. In *Knowledge Structures*, 185–210, eds. J. Galambos, R. Abelson, and J. Black. Hillsdale, N.J.: Lawrence Erlbaum.

Self, J. 1988. Bypassing the Intractable Problem of Student Modeling. In Proceedings of the First International Conference on Intelligent Tutoring Systems, 18–24. Montreal: University of Montreal.

Self, J. 1993. Model-Based Cognitive Diagnosis. *User Modeling and User-Adapted Interaction* 3(1): 86–106.

Self, J. 1998. Hanging by Two Threads: The Evolution of Intelligent Tutoring Systems Research. Invited talk presented at the Fourth International Conference on Intelligent Tutoring Systems (ITS98), August, San Antonio, Texas.

Self, J., ed. 1988. *Artificial Intelligence and Human Learning.* London: Chapman and Hall.

Shipman, F. M., and McCall, R. 1994. Supporting Knowledge Base Evolution with Incremental Formalization Design Evaluation. In Proceedings of ACM CHI94 Conference on Human Factors in Computing Systems, 285–291. New York: Association for Computing Machinery.

Shrader, G.; Williams, K.; Lachance-Whitcomb, J.; Finn, L. E.; and Gomez, L. 1999. Work in the Work Circle: Collaborative Design to Improve Teaching Practice. Paper presented at the Spencer Conference on Collaborative Research for Practice, 11–12 March, New Orleans, Louisiana.

Shulman, L. 1987. Knowledge and Teaching: Foundations of the New Reform. *Harvard Educational Review* 57(1): 1–22.

Shute, V. 1995. SMART Evaluation: Cognitive Diagnosis, Mastery Learning, and Remediation. In Proceedings of Artificial Intelligence in Education, 123–130. Charlottesville, Va.: AACE, Inc.

Shute, V. J., and Psotka, J. 1995. Intelligent Tutoring Systems: Past, Present, and Future. In *Handbook of Research on Educational Communications and Technology,* 570–600, ed. D. Jonassen. New York: Scholastic.

Shute, V. J., and Regian, J. W. 1993. Principles for Evaluating Intelligent Tutoring Systems. *Journal of Artificial Intelligence in Education* 4(3): 245–272.

Sibun, P. 1992. Generating Text without Trees. *Computational Intelligence* 8(1): 102–122.

Siegler, R. S. 1995. How Does Change Occur: A Microgenetic Study of Number Conservation. *Cognitive Psychology* 28(3): 225–273.

Singh, S.; Kearns, M. S.; Litman, D. J.; and Walker, M. A. 1999. Reinforcement Learning for Spoken Dialogue Systems. In Advances in Neural Information Processing Systems 12 (NIPS*99), ed. S. A. Solla, T. K. Leen. Cambridge, Mass.: The MIT Press.

Singley, M. K., and Anderson, J. R. 1989. *Transfer of Cognitive Skill.* Hillsdale, N.J.: Lawrence Erlbaum.

Sloman, S. A.; Love, B. C.; and Woo-Kyoung, A. 1998. Feature Centrality and Conceptual Coherence. *Cognitive Science* 22(2): 189–228.

Smolensky, P.; Fox, B.; King, R.; and Lewis, C. 1987. Computer-Aided Reasoned Discourse, or, How to Argue with a Computer. In *Cognitive Science and Its Applications for Human-Computer Interaction,* ed. R. Guindon, 109–162. Hillsdale, N.J.: Lawrence Erlbaum.

Snow, C. E.; Burns, M. S.; and Griffin, P., eds. 1998. *Preventing Reading Difficulties in Young Children.* Washington, D.C.: National Academy.

Songer, N. B. 1996. Exploring Learning Opportunities in Coordinated Network-Enhanced Classrooms: A Case of Kids as Global Scientists. *Journal of the Learning Sciences* 5(4): 297–327.

Sosa, E. 1980. The Raft and the Pyramid: Coherence versus Foundations in the Theory of Knowledge. *Midwest Studies in Philosophy* 5(1): 3–25.

Sowa, J. F. 1984. *Conceptual Structures.* Reading, Mass.: Addison-Wesley.

Spache, G. D. 1981. Diagnostic Reading Scales. Del Monte Research Park, Monterey, California.

Speech-Recognition System: An Overview. *Computer Speech and Language* 7(2): 137–148.

Spiro, R. J., and Jehng, J. C. 1990. Cognitive Flexibility and Hypertext: Theory and Technology for the Nonlinear and Multi-Dimensional Traversal of Complex Subject Matter. In *Cognition, Education and Multi-Media: Exploring Ideas in High Technology*, eds. D. Nix and R. J. Spiro, 163–205. Hillsdale, N.J.: Lawrence Erlbaum.

Spiro, R. J.; Coulson, R. L.; Feltovich, P. J.; and Anderson, D. K. 1988. Cognitive Flexibility Theory: Advanced Knowledge Acquisition in Ill-Structured Domains. In *Proceedings of the Tenth Annual Conference of the Cognitive Science Society*, 375–383. Hillsdale, N.J.: Lawrence Erlbaum.

Spiro, R. J.; Feltovich, P. J.; and Coulson, R. L. 1996. Two Epistemic Worldviews: Prefigurative Schemas and Learning in Complex Domains. *Applied Cognitive Psychology* 10(Special Issue):S51–S61.

Spiro, R. J.; Feltovich, P. J.; Coulson, R. L.; and Anderson, D. K. 1989. Multiple Analogies for Complex Concepts: Antidotes for Analogy-Induced Misconception in Advanced Knowledge Acquisition. In *Similarity and Analogical Reasoning*, eds. S. Vosniadou and A. Ortony, 498–531. Cambridge, Mass.: Cambridge University Press.

Spiro, R. J.; Vispoel, W. L.; Schmitz, J.; Samarapungavan, A.; and Boerger, A. 1987. Knowledge Acquisition for Application: Cognitive Flexibility and Transfer in Complex Content Domains. In *Executive Control Processes*, ed. B.C. Britton, 177–199. Hillsdale, N.J.: Lawrence Erlbaum.

Spiro, R. L.; Feltovich, P. J.; Jacobson, M.; and Coulson, R. L. 1991a. Cognitive Flexibility, Constructivism, and Hypertext: Advanced Knowledge Acquisition in Ill-Structured Domains. *Educational Technology* 31(5): 24–33.

Spiro, R. L.; Feltovich, P. J.; Jacobson, M.; and Coulson, R. L. 1991b. Knowledge Representation, Content Specification, and the Development of Skill in Situation-Specific Knowledge Assembly: Some Constructivist Issues as They Relate to Cognitive Flexibility Theory and Hypertext. *Educational Technology* 31(9): 22–25.

Spohrer, J. 1998. Authoring Tools, Communities, and Contexts. In Proceedings of the Conference on Virtual Worlds and Simulation (VWSIM 98), 87–88, eds. C. Landauer and K. Bellman. San Diego, Calif.: The Society for Computer Simulation.

Stallman, R. M., and Sussman, G. J. 1977. Forward Reasoning and Dependency-Directed Backtracking in a System for Computer-Aided Circuit Analysis. *Artificial Intelligence* 9(2): 135–196.

Steg, D. R.; Fox, C.; Lazar, I.; and Swinton, S. 1998. CAETI Handbook. Stanford, Calif.: Stanford University.

Steg, D. R.; Lazar, I.; and Boyce, C. 1994. A Cybernetic Approach to Early Education (Using the Talking Typewriter in the Self-Controlled Interactive Learning Systems Program). *Journal of Educational Computing Research* 10(1): 1–27.

Steg, D. R.; Vaidya, S.; and Hamdan, P. F. 1982. Long-Term Gains from Early Intervention through Technology: An Eleven-Year Report. *Journal of Educational Technology Systems* 11(3): 203–214.

Stenning, K., and Oberlander, J. 1995. A Cognitive Theory of Graphical and Linguistic Reasoning: Logic and Implementation. *Cognitive Science* 19(1) 97–140.

Stern, M.; Beck, J. E.; and Woolf, B. P. 1996. Adaptation of Problem Presentation and Feedback in an Intelligent Mathematics Tutor. In *Proceedings of the Third International Conference on Intelligent Tutoring Systems*, eds. C. Frasson, G. Gauthier, and A. Lesgold, 605–613. New York: Springer-Verlag.

Stern, M.; Steinberg, J.; Lee, H. I.; Padhye, J.; and Kurose, J. 1997. MANIC: Multimedia Asynchronous Networked Individualized Courseware. Educational Media and Hypermedia. Technical Report. Dept. of Computer Science, Univ. of Massachusetts, Amherst, Mass.

Stern, M.; Woolf, B. P.; and Kurose, J. F. 1997. Intelligence on the Web? *Journal of Artificial Intelligence in Education*, 8(2): 490–497.

Stevens, A. L., and Collins, A. 1977. The Goal Structure of a Socratic Tutor. In Proceedings of the Association for Computing Machinery (ACM), 256–263. New York: Association of Computing Machinery.

Stevens, A. L., and Collins, A. 1980. Multiple Models of a Complex System. In *Aptitude, Learning, and Instruction*, Volume 2, eds. R. Snow, P. Frederico, and W. Motague, 177–197. Hillsdale, N.J.: Lawrence Erlbaum.

Stone, B., and Lester, J. 1996. Dynamically Sequencing an Animated Pedagogical Agent. In Proceedings of the Thirteenth National Conference on Artificial Intelligence, 424–431. Menlo Park, Calif.: American Association for Artificial Intelligence.

Strauss, S., and Shilony, T. 1994. Teachers Models of Childrens Mind. In *Mapping the Mind: Domain Specificity in Cognition and Culture*, 455–473, eds. S. Gelman and L. Hirschfeld. New York: Cambridge University Press.

Streitz, N. A.; Hannemann, J.; and Thuring, M. 1989. From Ideas and Arguments to Hyperdocuments: Traveling through Activity Spaces. Paper presented at Hypertext 89, Pittsburgh, Pennsylvania, Nov. 5–8.

Suchman, L. 1995. Making Work Visible. *Communications of the ACM* 38(9): 56–63.

Suthers, D. 1993. Preferences for Model Selection in Explanation. In Proceedings of the Thirteenth International Joint Conference on Artificial Intelligence (IJCAI-93), 1208–1213. Menlo Park, Calif.: International Joint Conferences on Artificial Intelligence.

Suthers, D. 1995. Designing for Internal versus External Discourse in Groupware for Developing Critical Discussion Skills. Paper presented at the CHI95 Research Symposium, Denver, Colorado, May 7–11.

Suthers, D. 1998. Computer Aided Education and Training Initiative Tech. Report. Learning Research and Development Center, Univ. of Pittsburgh, Pittsburgh, Penn. (advlearn.lrdc.pitt.edu/advlearn/papers/FINALREP.html)

Suthers, D. 1999. Representational Support for Collaborative Inquiry. In Proceedings of the Thirty-Second Annual Hawaii International Conference on System Sciences (CD ROM). Washington, D.C. IEEE Computer Society.

Suthers, D. 2001. Towards a Systematic Study of Representational Guidance for Collaborative Learning Discourse. *Journal of Universal Computer Science* 7(3) (www.jucs.org/jucs_7_3/towards_a_systematic_study).

Suthers, D., and Jones, D. 1997. An Architecture for Intelligent Collaborative Educational Systems. In *Proceedings of AI-Ed 97, the Eighth World Conference on Artificial Intelligence in Education*, 19–22 August, Kobe, Japan, eds. B. Boulay and R. Mizoguchi, 55–62. Amsterdam: IOS Press.

Suthers, D., and Weiner, A. 1995. Groupware for Developing Critical Discussion Skills. Paper presented at the First International Conference on Computer Support for Cooperative Learning.Bloomington, Indiana, 17–20 October.

Suthers, D.; Toth, E.; and Weiner, A. 1997. An Integrated Approach to Implementing Collaborative Inquiry in the Classroom. In *Proceedings of the Second International Conference on Computer Supported Collaborative Learning 97*, 272–279, ed. R. Hall, N. Miyake, and N. Enyedy. Toronto: University of Toronto Press.

Suthers, D.; Weiner, A.; Connelly, J.; and Paolucci, M. 1995. BELVEDERE: Engaging Students in Critical Discussion of Science and Public Policy Issues. In Proceedings of AI-Ed 95, the Seventh World Conference on Artificial Intelligence in Education, 16–19 August, Washington D.C., ed. J. Greer, 266–273. Charlottesville, Va.: Association for the Advancement of Computing in Education.

Suthers, D.; Woolf, B. P.; Cornell, M. 1992. Steps from Explanation Planning to Model Construction Dialogues. In Proceedings of the Tenth National Conference on Artificial Intelligence (AAAI-92), 24–30. Menlo Park, Calif.: American Association for Artificial Intelligence.

Syverson, M. A. 1999. Beyond Portfolios: The Learning Record Online. University of Texas at Austin: Computer Writing and Research Laboratory (www.cwrl.utexas.edu/ ~syverson/olr/)

Tabachneck, H. J. M.; Koedinger, K. R.; and Nathan, M. J. 1994. Toward a Theoretical Account of Strategy Use and Sense-Making in Mathematics Problem Solving. In *Proceedings of the Sixteenth Annual Conference of the Cognitive Science Society*, 836–841. Hillsdale, N.J.: Lawrence Erlbaum.

Taylor, R., ed. 1980. *The Computer in the School: Tutor, Tool, Tutee*. New York: Teachers College Press.

Tecuci, G., and Hieb, M. H. 1996. Teaching Intelligent Agents: The Disciple Approach. *International Journal of Human-Computer Interaction* 8(3): 259–285.

Tecuci, G., and Kodratoff, Y., eds. 1995. *Machine Learning and Knowledge Acquisition: Integrated Approaches*. San Diego, Calif.: Academic Press.

Toth, J.; Suthers, D.; and Weiner, A. 1997. Providing Expert Advice in the Domain of Collaborative Scientific Inquiry. In *Proceedings of the Eighth World Conference on Artificial Intelligence in Education (AIED97)*, 19–22 August, Kobe, Japan, eds. B. Boulay and R. Mizoguchi, 55–62. Amsterdam: IOS Press.

Toulmin, S.; Rieke, R.; and Janik, A. 1984. *An Introduction to Reasoning*. 2d ed. New York: Macmillan.

Towne, D.; Munro, A.; Pizzini, Q.; Surmon, D.; Coller, L.; and Wogulis, J. L. 1990. Model-Building Tools for Simulation-Based Training. *Interactive Learning Environments* 1(1): 33–50.

Towns, S.; Callaway, C.; Voerman, J.; and Lester, J. 1998. Coherent Gestures, Locomotion, and Speech in Life-Like Pedagogical Agents. Paper presented at the Fourth International Conference on Intelligent User Interfaces, San Antonio, Texas, 16–19 Aug.

Trzebinski, J., and Richards, K. 1986. The Role of Goal Categories in Person Impression. *Journal of Experimental Social Psychology* 22(3): 216–227.

Tulving, E., and Thompson, D. M. 1973. Encoding Specificity and Retrieval Processes in Episodic Memory. *Psychological Review* 80(5): 352–373.

U.S. Office of Technology Assessment. 1993. Adult Literacy and New Technologies: Tools for a Lifetime. Technical Report OTA-SET-550. Washington, D.C.: U.S. Congress.

Utgoff, P. 1986. Shift of Bias for Inductive Concept Learning. In *Machine Learning: An Artificial Intelligence Approach, Volume 2*, eds. R. Michalski, J. Carbonell, and T. Mitchell, 107–148. San Francisco, Calif.: Morgan Kaufmann.

Van Haneghan, J. P.; Barron, L.; Young, M. F.; Williams, S. M.; Vye, N. J.; and Bransford, J. D. 1992. The Jasper Series: An Experiment with New Ways to Enhance Mathematical Thinking. In *Enhancing Thinking Skills in the Sciences and Mathematics*, ed. D. F. Halpern, 15–38. Hillsdale, N.J.: Lawrence Erlbaum.

Van Lehn, K. 1988a. Student Modeling. In *Foundations of Intelligent Tutoring Systems*, eds. M. C. Polson and J. J. Richardson, 55–78. Hillsdale, N.J.: Lawrence Erlbaum.

Van Lehn, K. 1988b. Toward a Theory of Impass Driven Learning. In *Learning Issues for Intelligent Tutoring Systems*, 19–41, eds. H. Mandl and A. Lesgold. New York: Springer-Verlag.

Van Lehn, K. 1989. Rule Acquisition Events in the Discovery of Problem-Solving Strategies. *Cognitive Science* 15(1): 1–48.

Van Lehn, K. 1990. *Mind Bugs: The Origins of Procedural Misconceptions*. Cambridge, Mass.: MIT Press.

Van Lehn, K. 1996. Conceptual and Meta-Learning during Coached Problem Solving. Paper presented at the Third International Conference on Intelligent Tutoring Systems (ITS-96), 12–14 June, Montreal, Quebec, Canada.

Van Marcke, K. 1998. GTE: An Epistemological Approach to Instructional Modeling. *Instructional Science* 26(2): 147–191.

van der Hulst, A. 1996. Cognitive Tools. Ph.D. dissertation, Department of Social Science Informatics, University of Amsterdam, Amsterdam, The Netherlands.

van Joolingen, W. R.; King, S.; and de Jong, T. 1997. The SimQuest Authoring System for Simulation-Base Discovery Environments. In *Knowledge and Media in Learning Systems*, eds. B. du Boulay and R. Mizoguchi, 79–87. Amsterdam: IOS Press.

Vanderbilt University Cognition and Technology Group. 1990. Anchored Instruction and Its Relationship to Situated Cognition. *Educational Researcher* 19(6): 2–10.

Vanderbilt University Cognition and Technology Group. 1992. The Jasper Series: A Generative Approach to Improving Mathematical Thinking. In *This Year in School Science 1991*, 109–140, ed. S. M. Malcom, L. Roberts, and K. Sheingold. Washington, D. C.: American Association for the Advancement of Science.

Vanderbilt University Cognition and Technology Group. 1997. *The Jasper Project: Lessons in Curriculum, Instruction, Assessment, and Professional Development*. Hillsdale, N.J.: Lawrence Erlbaum.

Vanderbilt University. Cognition and Technology Group. 1998. Designing Environments to Reveal, Support, and Expand Our Children's Potentials. In *Perspectives on Fundamental Processes in Intellectual Functioning: A Survey of Research Approaches, Volume 1*, ed. S. Soraci, 313–350. Stamford, Conn.: Ablex.

Vanderbilt University. Cognition and Technology Group. 2001. Adventures in Anchored Instruction: Lessons from Beyond the Ivory Tower. In *Advances in Instructional Psychology 5*, 35–99, ed. R. Glaser. Machwah, N.J.: Lawrence Erlbaum Publishers.

Vye, N. J.; Schwartz, D. L.; Bransford, J. D.; Barron, B. J.; Zech, L.; and Vanderbilt Cognition and Technology Group. 1998. SMART Environments That Support Monitoring, Reflection, and Revision. In *Metacognition in Educational Theory and Practice*, eds. D. Hacker, J. Dunlosky, and A. C. Graesser, 305–346. Hillsdale, N.J.: Lawrence Erlbaum.

Vygotsky, L. S. 1929. The Problem of the Cultural Development of the Child. *Journal of Genetic Psychology* 36: 414–434.

Vygotsky, L. S. 1960. The Development of Higher Psychological Functions (in Russian). Moscow: Izdeal'stov Akademii Pedagogicheskikh Nauk.

Vygotsky, L. S. 1978. *Mind in Society*. Cambridge, Mass.: Harvard University Press.

Wahlster, W.; André, E.; Finkler, W.; Profitlich, H.-J.;and Rist, T. 1993. Plan-Based Integration of Natural Language and Graphics Generation. *Artificial Intelligence* 63(1–2): 387–427.

Walker, M. A. 1993. Informational Redundancy and Resource Bounds in Dialogue. Ph.D. dissertation, Department of Computer and Information Science, University of Pennsylvania, Philadelphia, Penn.

Walters, J., and Hughes, B. 1999. PUEBLO: Value and Values that Sustain Community through Transition. In Proceedings of the Conference on Virtual Worlds and Simulation (VWSIM 99), 125–130, eds. C. Landauer and K. Bellman. San Diego, Calif.: The Society for Computer Simulation.

Wang, W., and Chan, T. 1997. Experience of Designing an Agent-Oriented Programming Language for Developing Social Learning Systems. In *Proceedings of the Eighth World Conference on AI in Education*, 7–14. Amsterdam: IOS Press.

Ward, N. 1996. Using Prosodic Clues to Decide When to Produce Back-Channel Utterances. Paper presented at the 1996 International Symposium on Spoken Dialogue, 2–3 October, Philadelphia, Pennsylvania.

Wasik, B. A. 1998. Volunteer Tutoring Programs in Reading: A Review. *Reading Research Quarterly* 33(3): 266–292.

Wasik, B. A., and Slavin, R. E. 1993. Preventing Early Reading Failure with One-to-One Tutoring: A Review of Five Programs. *Reading Research Quarterly* 28(2): 178–200.

Weaver, F., ed. 1989. *Promoting Inquiry in Undergraduate Learning, Volume 38*. New Directions in Teaching and Learning Series. San Francisco, Calif.: Jossey-Bass.

Webb, N. M. 1983. Predicting Learning from Student Interaction: Defining the Interaction Variables. *Educational Psychologist* 18(1): 33–41.

Webb, N., and Palincsar, A. 1996. Group Processes in the Classroom. In *Handbook of Educational Psychology*, eds. D. Berlmer and R. Calfee, 841–873. New York: Macmillan.

Weld, D., and de Kleer, J., eds. 1990. *Readings in Qualitative Reasoning about the Physical World*. San Francisco, Calif.: Morgan Kaufmann.

Wenger, E. 1987. *Artificial Intelligence and Tutoring Systems*. San Francisco, Calif.: Morgan Kaufmann.

Wertheimer, R. 1990. The Geometry Proof Tutor: An Intelligent Computer-Based Tutor in the Classroom. *Mathematics Teacher*. 83(4)(April): 308–317.

Wertsch, J. 1985. *Vygotsky and the Social Formation of Mind*. Cambridge, Mass.: Harvard University Press.

Wescourt, K.; Beard, M.; and Barr, A. 1981. Curriculum Information Networks for CAI: Research on Testing and Evaluation by Simulation. In *University-Level Computer-Assisted Instruction at Stanford: 1968-1980,* ed. P. Suppes, 817–839. Stanford, Calif.: Stanford University Press.

Whalley, P. 1992. *Basic Engineering Thermodynamics.* Oxford, U.K.: Oxford University Press.

White, B. Y., and Frederiksen, J. R. 1990. Causal Model Progressions as a Foundation for Intelligent Learning Environments. *Artificial Intelligence* 42(1): 99–157.

Wielinga, B. J.; Schreiber, A. T.; and Breuker, J. A. 1992. KADS: A Modeling Approach to Knowledge Engineering. *Knowledge Acquisition Journal* 4(1): 5–53.

Wiggs, C. L., and Seidel, R. J. 1987. An Overview of Computer-Based Instruction in Military Environments. In *Computer-Based Instruction in Military Environments,* eds. R. J. Seidel and P. D. Weddle. New York: Plenum.

Wiley, J., and Voss, J. 1996. The Effects of Playing Historian on Learning History. *Applied Cognitive Psychology* 10(Special Issue): S63–S72.

Willis, J., and Crowder, J. 1974. Does Tutoring Enhance the Tutor's Academic Learning? *Psychology in the Schools* 11(1): 68–70.

Wilson, B.G.; Jonassen, D.H.; and Cole, P. 1993. Cognitive Approaches to Instructional Design. In *The ASTD Handbook of Instructional Technology,* ed. G.M. Piskurich, 21.1–21.22. New York: McGraw-Hill.

Wimsatt, W. C. 1980. Reductionistic Research Strategies and Their Biases in the Units of Selection Controversy. In *Scientific Discovery: Case Studies,* ed. T. Nickles, 213–259. Dordrecht, The Netherlands: D. Reidel.

Winkels, R. G. F. 1992. *Explorations in Intelligent Tutoring and Help.* Amsterdam: IOS Press.

Wolf, W. 1995. On the Road to Symmetric Multimedia Services. Paper presented at the Convention Industry Council (CIC) Forum, Bethesda, Md., July.

Wolf, W. 1996. Key Frame Selection by Motion Analysis. Paper presented at the International Conference on Acoustics, Speech, and Signal Processing (ICASSP '96), 7–10 May, Atlanta, Ga.

Wolf, W.; Liang, Y.; Kozuch, M.; Yu, H-H.; Phillips, M.; Weekes, M.; and Debruyne, A. 1996. A Digital Video Library on the World Wide Web. In Proceedings of ACM Multimedia '96, 433–434. New York: Association of Computing Machinery.

Wolf, W.; Liu, B.; Wolfe, A.; Yeung, M.; Yeo, B.-L.; and Markham, D. 1995. Video as Scholarly Material in the Digital Library. In *Advances in Digital Libraries '95.* New York: Springer-Verlag.

Woolf, B.P. 1992. AI in Education. In *Encyclopedia of Artificial Intelligence,* ed. S. Shapiro, 434–444. 2d ed. New York: Wiley.

Woolf, B. P., and Hall, W. 1995. Multimedia Pedagogues: Interactive Systems for Teaching and Learning. *IEEE Computer* (Special Issue on Multimedia) 28(5): 74–80.

Woolf, B. P.; Blegen, D.; Verloop A.; and Jensen, J. 1986. Tutoring a Complex Industrial Process. In Proceedings of the Fourth National Conference on Artificial Intelligence, 722-728. Menlo Park, Calif.: American Association for Artificial Intelligence.

Woolf, B. P.; Poli, C.; and Grosse, I. 1997. Multimedia Systems and Intelligent Tutors for Teaching Design for Manufacturing. Paper presented at the Twenty-Seventh Annual Frontiers in Education Conference, Pittsburgh, Penn., 5–8 November.

Woolf, B. P.; Poli, C.; Grosse, I.; Haugsjaa, E.; and Riggs, B. 1996. Multimedia Tutors for Design for Manufacturing. Paper presented at the Twenty-Sixth Annual Frontiers in Education Conference, 6–9 November, Salt Lake City, Utah.

Wu, C., and Burke, T. J. 1998. Intelligent Computer-Aided Optimization on Specific Power of an OTEC Rankine Power Plant. *Applied Thermal Engineering* 18(5): 295–300.

Wu, C., and Dieguez, M. 1998. Intelligent Computer-Aided Design on Optimization of Specific Power of Finite-Time Rankine Cycle Using CYCLEPAD. *Journal of Computer Application in Engineering Education* 16(1): 9–13.

Yang, C.-S., and Moore, D. M. 1995. Designing Hypermedia Systems for Instruction. *Journal of Educational Technology Systems* 24(1): 3–30.

Youniss, J., and Yates, M. 1997. *Community Service and Social Responsibility in Youth.* Chicago: University of Chicago Press.

Yu, H.-H., and Wolf, W. 1997a. A Visual Search System for Video and Image Databases. In Proceedings of IEEE Multimedia '97, 517–524. Washington, D.C.: IEEE Computer Society.

Yu, H.-H., and Wolf, W. 1997b. Hierarchical, Multi-Resolution Algorithms for Dictionary-Driven Content-Based Image Retrieval. Paper presented at the International Conference on Image Processing (ICIP '97), 26–29 October, Washington, D. C.

Zhang, J. 1997. The Nature of External Representations in Problem Solving. *Cognitive Science* 21(2): 179–217.

Zook, K. B., and DeVesta, F. J. 1991. Instructional Analogies and Conceptual Misrepresentations. *Journal of Educational Psychology* 83(2): 246–252.

Name and Subject Index

Names

Subjects